To Be Continued .... The
...........................Alcoholics Anonymous
....World
....Bibliography
....1935-1994

Gratefully,
Charlie Bishop, Jr.

Charles Bishop, Jr.
&
Bill Pittman

The Bishop of Books
Wheeling, West Virginia

1994

This is the Second Edition, First Printing

This is copy No. 288 of 1,500 copies.

Published by: The Bishop of Books
46 Eureka Ave., Wheeling, WV 26003
[304] 242-2937

ISBN 1-877686-07-7

Dedication

to

Ernest Kurtz, Ph.D.
who opened the door

&

All the new AA historians & archivists
[you know who you are!]

CONTENTS

Acknowledgements

Our heartfelt, spiritual thanks to the following authors, Fellowship members, institutions, and individuals for their advice, suggestions, and information.

= to Alcoholics Anonymous Archives and the many AA Archivists and historians around the country, especially Doug B., Wally P., and Andrea M.

= to Steve Berg and Richard Koehn, the former Executive Director of Guest House, where much of the work on Berg's bibliographies on spirituality was done.

= to Mark Keller, General Editor of The International Bibliography of Studies on Alcohol, the landmark 3-volume Rutgers set, 1966-80.

= to the late Barry Leach and the late John L. Norris, authors of "Factors in the Development of Alcoholics Anonymous" in Kissin & Begleiter, editors, Treatment and Rehabilitation of the Chronic Alcoholic. Vol. 5, Plenum Press, NY, 1977. Their early bibliographical research was an historic landmark in the literature of AA.

= to Julianne Phillips, author of the 1974 Alcoholics Anonymous. An Annotated Bibliography 1935-1972.

User's Manual

The reader is advised this bibliography is the successor of the first edition which appeared in 1989 and is now out of print. Since then we have doubled the number of citations and added six new chapters on Grapevine Publications, Foreign Publications, Ephemera, Tapes, TV & Films, and Works in Progress.

The index has been completely revised. It is still a broad indexing based on AA's spiritual inclusiveness and openmindedness. We aimed at suggestiveness and AA's open doors, not scientific terminology. We have leaned heavily toward Fellowship language. For example, "hitting bottom" and "surrender" have been used rather than technical terms. For many short works which only briefly describe or comment on AA, the terms "basics" or "mention" are used to indicate repetition of brief, commonly-known facts about AA.

How AA members are listed alphabetically as authors has changed. In this edition, we have listed AA members by their first name, then last initial. So an article written by AA member John S. will be found under "J" for John and not under "S." The exceptions are Bill Wilson, AA's Co-Founder, who will be found in most instances under "W" for Wilson [since that is how most AA members commonly refer to him]; for Robert H. Smith, M.D., AA's other Co-Founder, he again is listed under "D" for his common AA name of "Dr. Bob." Also Marty Mann and others who used their full names and did not hide their membership in the years before the Traditions were accepted. AA members who have broken their anonymity are listed under the initial of their last name.

We have dropped several indexing terms, including "doctors" and "clergy" to indicate authorship by members of those two groups. When the two terms now appear in the index, they indicate works in which the content concerns doctors or clergy as a group.

If the reader cannot find an author or article in the chapter on Popular Magazine Articles, it may be listed in another chapter, maybe the one on Chapters About AA in Books if it has been anthologized or perhaps the chapter on Books and Pamphlets About AA if it has been reprinted separately.

Please note that reprints of the Big Book will not be found in the chapter on A.A. Approved Publications but rather in the chapter Books & Pamphlets about AA since these reprints were not published by AAWS.

If you can't find a work under author or title in one chapter, try other appropriate chapters.

Obvious as it is, we stress that neither approval nor disapproval is implied by the inclusion of any author or work here and any evaluations of them are, of course, the authors.

Abbreviations

A.A. or AA = Alcoholics Anonymous
A.A.W.S. = Alcoholics Anonymous World Services
A.B.A. = American Bar Association
Al-Anon = Al-Anon Family Groups
ALMACA = Association of Labor-Management
Administrators & Counselors on Alcoholism
A.M.A. = American Medical Association
Big Book = the book Alcoholics Anonymous
dj = dust jacket for a book
EAP = employee assistance program
GSO = General Service Office of AA
GV = AA Grapevine
ICYPAA = Int'l Confernce of Young People in AA
IDAA = Int'l Doctors in AA
ILAA = Int'l Lawyers in AA
MMPI = Minnesota Multiphasic Personality Inventory
NALGAP = Nat'l Assn. of Lesbian & Gay Alcoholism Professionals
NCA = Nat'l Council on Alcoholism [also NCEA]
NCADI = Nat'l Clearinghouse for Alcohol & Drug Information
NCCA = Nat'l Clergy Conference on Alcoholism
NIAAA = Nat'l Institute on Alcohol Abuse & Alcoholism
pb = paperback
QJSA = Quarterly Journal of Studies on Alcohol, Rutgers
UMI = University Microfilms Int'l., 300 Zeeb Road, POBox 1346,
Ann Arbor, MI 48106, publisher Dissertation Abstracts Int'l.
[ordering dissertation copies or scholarly journal articles,
call 1-800-521-3042]

Pre-1939 Books Early AAs Read

Nell Wing's List of "Books Early AAs Read"

Allen, James. As a Man Thinketh
Browne, Lewis. This Believing World
Browne, Lewis. The Conversion Experience
Clark, Glenn. I Will Life Up Mine Eyes
Fox, Emmet. The Sermon on the Mount
James, William. The Varieties of Religious Experience
Peabody, Richard. The Common Sense of Drinking
Russell, A. J. For Sinners Only
Troward, Thomas. The Edinburgh Lectures on Mental Science.

Dr. Bob's Required Reading List

The Holy Bible. King James Version
The Sermon on the Mount
The Lord's Prayer
The Book of James
The 13th Chapter of Corinthians

The Upper Room. Methodist periodical

Drummond, Henry. The Greatest Thing in the World

James, William. The Varieties of Religious Experience

Russell, A. J. For Sinners Only

[the above books were uncovered through the research of Bill Pittman and are reprinted by permission from his book, AA The Way It Began, Glen Abbey Books, Seattle, WA, 1988]

To Be Continued . . .

by
Charles Bishop, Jr.

Our title for this second edition of the Bibliography of Alcoholics Anonymous captures, we hope, the spirit of this book. The doors of AA are very wide. The Fellowship in its literature has always emphasized suggestiveness, openmindedness, spiritual serendipity, and progress not perfection. "To Be Continued" leaves plenty of room for the grace of God and human imperfection together; allows ample space for growth while assuming the experience, strength, and hope of the past.

Since the first edition in 1989, this work has grown immensely. Thus, we were bold enough to call this book a "World" bibliography. New chapters on foreign publications, ephemera, electronic mediums and works in progress plus over 2,900 citations, double the number in the first edition, remind one of that wonderful phrase from the first edition [2nd thru 16th printings, p. 394] of the Big Book, "the warp and woof of A.A. everywhere."

Looking at the thousands of works here, one is immediately impressed by the sheer quantity of what's here and, even more, one stands in awe of what's not here. The new chapter on Tapes about AA only selects some 200 tapes from the hundreds of thousands of tapes recorded around the world for the past 50 plus years. Our new chapters on Foreign Publications, Ephemera, and TV-Films are nothing more than a hint of a whisper. They only suggest beginnings. Perhaps others will reve up their computers and launch safaris into these virgin lands. Right now, this author is drained.

Overall, this edition holds over 2,900 citations, double the first edition listings but while publications from non-AA sources reflects that, the literature from AA itself, Conference-approved and Grapevine material, has not grow massively. It is obvious that the foundations of AA remain unchanged since the 1939 publication of Alcoholics Anonymous, the "Big Book." Clearly, the history, ideology, spirituality, principles, philosophy, and fellowship of AA remain rock-solid. There have been no changes in the Three Legacies of Recovery, Unity, and Service: the Twelve Steps, Traditions and Concepts. The basic texts of AA, the Big Book, The Service Manual, The Twelve Steps & Twelve Traditions, Alcoholics Anonymous Comes of Age: A Brief History of A.A., etc., have not been revised. They have withstood the test of time and the anvil of experience from new generations of Fellowship members and not been found wanting. New publications from AA include the Daily Reflections meditation book, the Grapevine Index, and others, but these hold no new primary principles. Work on the projected History of AA book has been put on the back burner for two years, this after three different sets of authors brought it through various drafts. The difficulty of getting this full-scale history of the Fellowship into a final draft and published certainly has concerned the General Service Conference of A.A. for several years. One wonders what the practical and spiritual holdups on this book are, and, at the same time, anxiously awaits its appearance.

Well, if no new historical works have come from A.A., this is certainly not the case with an exciting, dynamic, spiritual group of authors who are expanding and deepening and preserving AA's history, both inside and outside the A.A. service structure.

It all started with Ernest Kurtz, Ph.D. who was given full access to the A.A. Archives. In 1979 his book, NOT-GOD: A History of Alcoholics Anonymous, was published. Although other studies of AA history and its development preceded his, none had the explosive impact his did. NOT-GOD now stands as the definitive history of AA to date, although Kurtz would be the first to reject the "definitive" adjective. NOT-GOD has become the inspiration for all the "new archivists of the Fellowship." The floodgates were opened and a river of books has flowed forth! Original research, interpretations of AA ideology, past experiences from AA oldtimers, biographies of founding members, histories of AA in local areas...the list is long. We now live in the most exciting times for AA history since the founding years!

Books about Sister Ignatia, Fellowship slogans and prayers, the Washingtonians, the Oxford Group, Sam Shoemaker, early AA history, AA oldtimers, histories of AA in Washington, Oregon, West Virginia, Arizona, etc., interpretations of AA's Twelve Steps, reprints of the Big Book and its early stories, bibliographies, concordances, etc. ... these are all documented in this bibliography along with a new chapter on forthcoming Works in Progress.

One is immediately impressed with the authorship almost universally [with exceptions, of course] characterized by respect for AA's Traditions, especially anonymity. The authors of all these new volumes have left out their last names if they are AA members or not revealed their Fellowship membership if they have used their full names. They have again almost all been motivated by a deep loving passion for their spiritual roots. This author has maintained contact professionally with the vast majority of them. One is impressed that the temptations of money, power and prestige have not seduced them. Many have been AA area archivists within the service structure and labored long without pay or pride or power to preserve and pass on local AA history.

This new river of books is in no way a criticism of AA itself since the General Service Office, the Archives, or the Grapevine would not be able to publish these books without breaking Traditions or stepping into "opinions on outside issues" to mention but two reasons. And one can also note that none of these new books have challenged any of the Fellowship's Three Legacies. To the contrary, they have deepened their appreciation and strengthened the historical documentation of them.

Turning to another area worthy of comment, this bibliography documents a long-standing friction between the language of AA and the language outsiders use to describe and discuss the Fellowship. An explosive example: an AA oldtimer told this author he didn't attend AA meetings any more because of all the "psychobabble" and talk about "drugs and dually-addicted everything under the sun but alcoholism." He was voicing in traditional oldtimers blunt language the unwelcome intrusion into AA of outside influences and definitions of the Fellowship.

One of the difficulties we faced in the index to this bibliography was choice of index terms. While we leaned heavily toward Fellowship language, often we were confronted by scientific terms from the scholarly community and the chemical dependency treatment industry which really fail to respect AA's definition of itself as a "Fellowship" and a "Society." When a scholar in a Ph.D. dissertation labels or defines AA a "therapy" or a "treatment," a great injustice is done both to AA and to the exactitudes the academic community espouses. When a client in a chemical dependency treatment facility is labeled "dually-addicted," is it any wonder that the client-AA newcomer attending his first Fellowship meetings introduces himself that way and actually believes AA's membership is open to not only alcoholics but also drug addicts, overeaters, and persons with any other addiction. Although the term "referral" is commonly used in the Fellowship, one questions whether, as many oldtimers in AA have, it has replaced AA's Twelfth Step. When a gay member of AA writes about the "religious nature" of AA's Twelve Steps, he obviously does not understand the distinction between religion and spirituality. Numerous misunderstandings between AA and the courts, treatment facilities, the academic community, the ministry, and other professionals have hurt both groups.

These influences from the outside world do enter the Fellowship and cause basic disunity. Clearly, AA does not exist in a vacuum. A long-standing tradition of "Being Friendly with Our Friends" as well as Traditions Six, Ten and others reveals that AA knows this. This volume points out some of these misdefinitions and friction points in numerous citations. What is clearly needed is for the professional community-at-large to accept AA for what it is and not to redefine it. More importantly, it should be obvious that AA needs to Twelfth-Step the professional community with its own message of what it is and is not.

We have tried to respect the spirit of anonymity in this book. "After all, it's half our name!" as AA members say. When an AA member breaks the Eleventh Tradition, we have not hidden that anonymity break. However, we faced a sort of a dilemma concerning listings from the NCCA's Blue Books. These annual anthologies from the National Clergy Conference on Alcoholism contained many fine articles written usually by Catholic clergy in AA who used their full names in print. The Blue Books were never published for public sale and had very limited press runs for NCCA members and heads of mostly Catholic religious orders and seminaries only. Almost everyone was an AA member. But they might be of service to researchers in the academic and religious fields. We felt that listing the authors' full names would be breaking their anonymity on our part so we dropped the last names and listed them under their first name and last initial.

The Tradition of Anonymity has been hammered out on the anvil of experience and there are numerous citations before the Traditions were accepted of authorship by Bill Wilson, Marty Mann, and others. After the tradition was established, anonymity breaks in citations are noted. Today anonymity breaks seem more prevalent among public figures from the entertainment industry, sports, politics, and the gay community. One of the latest gurus, a prominent speaker, has suggested it might be time for AA to shed its old-fashioned anonymity tradition because most of the past stigma about alcoholism has been eradicated. A front-page article from a gay newspaper printed during the A.A. Int'l Convention in Seattle in 1990 suggested there was nothing to be ashamed of and it was time for AA to "come out of the closet." This bibliography documents the opposite: overwhelmingly, AA members who write about AA do not break their anonymity.

Today, membership in AA is about two million worldwide. AA conducts triannual surveys of its own membership. Although the hard data from the surveys is but a sampling, our interpretation of it suggests AA in the United States may be declining for the first time in its history. Literature sales and Grapevine subscriptions have definitely dropped. Group contributions to GSO are down. Worldwide, AA's growth continues to be astounding, especially in Latin and South America. And for the first time in its history, there are probably more AA members outside the U.S. than inside. One survey question revealed that out of 100 newcomers, only 4 to 6 were able to maintain their newfound sobriety for a year. The vast majority slipped! This was not the case in AA's early years.

One needs to remember that counting heads, demographics, the "numbers game," etc., is not a science in AA. The Fellowship does not have membership lists, not all AA groups are registered, not all members belong to a home group. Quantifying AA is like counting the straws in a haystack; at best you'll get a guestimate. That's because the Fellowship itself is spiritual and not measurable by scientific, material means. Once one realizes that, one can see the folly of some scientific, scholarly works in this bibliography which base a Ph.D. thesis on a sampling of 28 or even 200 AA members.

Research on AA should be approached gingerly. The underlying difficulties of applying the scientific method to spirituality should give every scholar great pause. If a scientist were to ask an AA oldtimer how AA works, the answer "Just fine!" could be expected. We don't know if the academic community has yet fully accepted the great scientific fact that "AA works." This is not to suggest scholarly research on AA is a non-productive effort.

AA has always had its critics. We document a new wave of books which promote their "alternatives to A.A." by riding on AA's coattails. Looking at the citations on the new rational recovery books, one questions the need for them to promote themselves by tearing down AA. Historically, AA has never felt the need to defend itself in the public arena and has always viewed such critics with Tenth Tradition tolerance.

A can of worms was opened in 1985 when the the loss of the copyright on the first edition of the Big Book was discovered. Later, the second edition was also discovered to be in the public domain. Subsequently AA engaged a legal firm and began reviewing all its copyrights. The circle-and-triangle symbol used on all A.A. Conference-approved Literature was trademarked. Some private firms producing medallions and other gift items refused to stop using the circle-and-triangle and AA sued them. Clearly, AA filing legal actions in a public court of law brought about discussion immediately of the Tenth Tradition. The recent General Service Conference of A.A. has corrected the situation by ordering the cessation of those legal actions.

The incident is important here for two reasons. First, it illustrates AA's ability to correct itself through the group conscience. Second, one questions whether all the private reprints of AA literature [listed in this bibliography] no longer "owned" by AA have really done AA any harm. Recently, a private firm brought out an abridged Big Book, the first 164 pages, and it sold like wildfire. AA followed suit with its own short edition, perhaps more in response to this outside publishing than it might like to admit. Certainly these events involving AA literature have provoked much discussion of the Traditions and of Steps Four through Nine.

The birth and growth of other anonymous groups using the Twelve Steps modified to their particular problem is evident in the catalogs of recovery publishers and on the shelves of recovery sections in many nationally-franchised or chain bookstores. Much of that material is not appropriate here but some has been listed where comparisons are made with AA.

We hope this bibliography is of service. This author would like to thank his co-author, Bill Pittman, for his contributions, some of which did not make the first edition but are now present. We welcome your comments, compliments and criticisms. Servus, Thank you !

Chapter I = A.A.-Approved Publications

1. A A. NY: The Alcoholic Foundation (A.A.); April 1940.
The second pamphlet published by A.A. contained an editorial on A.A. from The Houston Press (TX), then a series of 6 articles "By a Member of Alcoholics Anonymous" and reprinted from that newspaper, an article by W. D. Silkworth, M.D., New York, entitled "A New Approach to Psychotherapy in Chronic Alcoholism" (reprinted from the journal Lancet, July, 1939, Vol. LIX, No. 7) which same title was used in the 1943 revision but now includes stories from the Big Book, and a review of the Big Book, Alcoholics Anonymous, by Dr. Harry Emerson Fosdick. This rare pamphlet is 33 pages of text and 5 1/2 x 8 1/2" in format. The member of A.A. who wrote the series sobered up in Cleveland, Ohio. The foreword to a later printing notes that A.A.'s membership was about 5,000 in 1941, while an April, 1943, printing lists the membership at "about 8,000." Discontinued in 1945 (?).

2. (The 10th) Tenth General Service Conference of Alcoholics Anonymous. 1960 Final Report. New York: AAWS, Inc.; 1960.
Note: Confidential.
This 35-page large booklet states "The Sense of The Conference" and the "Dominant Theme" was the "Need for Improved Internal and External Communication." Bill wrote two articles for this report and for the conference: "A.A. in an 'Era of Change': Steps, Traditions Unlikely to Change; Service Functions May" and "Group Conscience Does Work at World Service Level: Bill Describes Approach To Definition of Twelve Concepts of World Service.".

3. (The 11th) Eleventh General Service Conference of Alcoholics Anonymous. 1961 Final Report. New York: AAWS, Inc.; 1961.
Note: Confidential.
The report states the sense of the meeting was "Determination to Work and Grow Together, And With Others" as the theme. Bill wrote in this report "A True and A High and A Constant Purpose: Bill Calls on A.A. to 'Look Out Upon Its Destiny' as A Society." In it, he emphasized the importance of the "Conference Structure to assure sound growth of the Fellowship.".

4. (The 12th) Twelfth General Service Conference of Alcoholics Anonymous. 1962 Final Report. New York: AAWS, Inc.; 1962.
Note: Confidential.
This 36-page large booklet listed "The Sense of the Conference" as "One Primary Purpose' and deep Devotion to Concept of Unity." Bill's article, "The Future Belongs to You," points out that this meeting "opens a somewhat new era in our affairs. Since all my main service tasks are now complete, it seems right that my primary and long-held responsibility for our world operation ought to end with this session. This should be the final step in placing A.A. wholly on its own." "Bill recalled that his and Dr. Bob's actual first steps away from 'active parenthood' of A.A.'s old-timers had been taken in 1946, with publication of the

Twelve Traditions. The second step, he said, was taken in 1951 with the experimental formation of the General Service Conference. The third and last step, 'though of a lesser venture,' is bound to be a turning point of considerable importance, Bill wrote. It means that I should now finally and fully transfer the remainder of my primary world service leadership to A.A.'s Trustess.".

5. 13th through 15th Meetings of the General Service Conference(s) of Alcoholics Anonymous. Final Report(s). 1963-1965. New York.: AAWS, Inc.; 1963-1965.
   Note: Confidential.

6. The 16th Meeting of the General Service Conference of Alcoholics Anonymous. Final Report. 1966. New York: AAWS, Inc.; 1966.
   Note: Confidential.
   The theme was "Principles Before Personalities.".

7. (The 19th) Nineteenth Meeting of the General Service Conference of Alcoholics Anonymous. 1969 Final Report. New York: AAWS, Inc.; 1969.
   Note: Confidential.
   The theme was "Our Group Conscience: Voice of A.A." This 57-page booklet also contains Bill's comments at the closing session: "It is my conviction that the men and women of A.A. will continue to help themselves and others over the coming years. This, despite the fact that we are living in the most perilous of times - perils imminent and perils potential. Furthermore, I do not think that the men and women of A.A. are afraid...".

8. The 20th Meeting of the General Service Conference of Alcoholics Anonymous. Final Report. 1970. New York: AAWS, Inc.; 1970.
   Note: Confidential.
   The theme was "Service - The Heart of A.A.".

9. The 21st Annual Meeting of the General Service Conference of Alcoholics Anonymous. 1971 Final Report. New York: AAWS, Inc.; 1971.
   Note: Confidential.
   The theme of this conference was "Communication: Key to A.A. Growth.".

10. The 22nd Annual Meeting of the General Service Conference of Alcoholics Anonymous. 1972 Final Report. New York: AAWS, Inc.; 1972.
    Note: Confidential.
    The theme was "Our Primary Purpose.".

11. The 23rd Annual Meeting of the General Service Conference of Alcoholics Anonymous. 1973 Final Report. New York: AAWS, Inc.; 1973.
    Note: Confidential.
    The theme was "Responsibility - Our Expression of Gratitude.".

12. The 24th Annual Meeting of the General Service Conference of Alcoholics Anonymous. 1974 Final Report. New York: AAWS, Inc.; 1974.
Note: Confidential.
The theme was "Understanding and Cooperation - Inside and Outside A.A.".

13. The 25th Annual Meeting of the General Service Conference of Alcoholics Anonymous. 1975 Final Report. New York: AAWS, Inc.; 1975.
Note: Confidential.
The theme was "Unity: Through Love and Service.".

14. The 26th Annual Meeting of the General Service Conference of Alcoholics Anonymous. 1976 Final Report. New York: AAWS, Inc.; 1976.
Note: Confidential.
The theme was "Sponsorship - Our Privilege and Responsibility.".

15. The 27th Annual Meeting of the General Service Conference of Alcoholics Anonymous. 1977 Final Report. New York: AAWS, Inc.; 1977.
Note: Confidential.
The theme was "The A.A. Group - Where It Begins.".

16. The 28th Annual Meeting of the General Service Conference of Alcoholics Anonymous. 1978 Final Report. New York: AAWS, Inc.; 1978.
Note: Confidential.
The theme was "The Member and the Group - Recovery Through Service.".

17. The 29th Annual Meeting of the General Service Conference of Alcoholics Anonymous. 1979 Final Report. New York: AAWS, Inc.; 1979.
Note: Confidential.
The theme was "The Legacies: OurHeritage and My Responsibility.".

18. The 30th Annual Meeting of the General Service Conference of Alcoholics Anonymous. 1980 Final Report. New York: AAWS, Inc.; 1980.
Note: Confidential.
The theme was "Participation: The Key to Recovery.".

19. The 31st Annual Meeting of the General Service Conference of Alcoholics Anonymous. 1981 Final Report. New York: AAWS, Inc.; 1981.
Note: Confidential.
The theme was "A.A. Takes Its Inventory.".

20. The 32nd Annual Meeting of the General Service Conference of Alcoholics Anonymous. 1982 Final Report. New York: AAWS, Inc.; 1982.
Note: Confidential.
The theme was "The Traditions - Our Way of Unity.".

21. _The 33rd Annual Meeting of the General Service Conference of Alcoholics Anonymous. 1983 Final Report_. New York: AAWS, Inc.; 1983.
Note: Confidential.
The theme was "Anonymity - Our Spiritual Foundation.".

22. _The 34th Annual Meeting of the General Service Conference of Alcoholics Anonymous. 1984 Final Report_. New York: AAWS, Inc.; 1984.
Note: Confidential.
The theme was "Gratitude - The Language of the Heart.".

23. _The 35th Annual Meeting of the General Service Conference of Alcoholics Anonymous. 1985 Final Report_. New York: AAWS, Inc.; 1985.
Note: Confidential.
The theme was "Golden Moments of Reflection.

24. _The 36th Annual Meeting of the General Service Conference of Alcoholics Anonymous. 1986 Final Report_. New York: AAWS, Inc.; 1986.
Note: Confidential. 60pp.
The theme of this conference was "A.A.'s Future - Our Responsibility." This report includes a wrap-up on the 1985 Montreal Int'l Convention, A.A.'s 50th anniversary.

25. _The 37th Annual Meeting of the General Service Conference of Alcoholics Anonymous. 1987 Final Report_. New York: AAWS, Inc.; 1987.
Note: Confidential.
The theme of this conference was "The Seventh Tradition - A Turning Point.".

26. _The 38th Annual Meeting of the General Service Conference of Alcoholics Anonymous. 1988 Final Report_. New York: AAWS, Inc.; 1988.
Note: "Confidential.".
The theme of this year's conference was "Our Singleness of Purpose - Key to Unity." This 70-page booklet contains reports on all phases of A.A. service, finances, conference advisory actions, and demographics.

27. "44 Questions". New York: AAWS; 1952.
This 37-page pamphlet "answers the questions most frequently asked about A.A. by alcoholics seeking help, as well as by their families and friends.".

28. _The 8th General Service Conference of A.A. Final Report. 1958_. New York, NY: GSO of A.A.; 1958.
Note: Confidential. 28pp.
"Promise and Progress" were the keynotes of this conference. "The most-widely discussed session was the closed meeting stage by the Area Delegates...(with) vigorous and fociferous debate." Bill W. said "fine!" to that because "friction of opposing viewpoints is part of the very modus operandi on which (democracy) proceeds." This was the first report to be printed by letterpress.

29. (The 9th) Ninth General Service Conference of Alcoholics Anonymous. 1959 Final Report. New York: Alcoholics Anonymous Publishing, Inc.; 1959.
Note: Confidential.
The 32-page large booklet states that "Confidence, Absence of Fear of Future, Were Main Themes." On the opposite page, Bill W.'s talk at the opening dinner revolves around the theme that "The Society of Alcoholics Anonymous cannot operate except in an atmosphere of trust of its 'servants' at all levels of the movement.".

30. A.A. - 44 Questions. NY: AAWS, Inc.; 1952.
This pamphlet "answers the questions most commonly asked about A.A. by alcoholics seeking help as well as by their families and friends.".

31. A.A. 30. A Book about A.A.'s 30th Anniversary Year and International Convention. Toronto, Ontario, Canada, July 2-4, 1965. First ed. New York: AAWS; 1965; 47pp.
Note: photos.
This memento of the AA Int'l Convention in Toronto, Canada, 1965, contains messages from Bill & Lois, the Prime Minister of Canada, Dr. Jack; AA in Canada and Around the World; Guest Speakers for the convention; sketches of the first 3 Int'l Conventions in Cleveland, St. Louis, and Long Beach; and an update on the AA Story. Photos throughout include the non-alcoholic and non-anonymous members of the General Service Board of A.A., historic places, AA literature, non-alcoholic speakers, GSO scenes as endpapers, AA pioneers, etc.

32. A.A. A Unique American Phenomenon. NY: AAWS, Inc.; 1952.
Note: Reprint of the Fortune magazine article of Feb. 1951. Discontinued in 1971 (?).
(see separate listing in popular magazines chapter.).

33. A.A. and the Armed Services. NY: AAWS, Inc.; Jan. 1974.
In this pamphlet, "ten personal stories tell how a man or a woman in the military - any rank, any age - can beat a drinking problem through A.A.".

34. "A.A. and the Gay-Lesbian Alcoholic". New York: AAWS; 1989.
In this 23-page pamphlet, "excerpts from the experience, strength and hope of sober gay and lesbian alcoholics point out that the tie that binds us all together is freedom from alcohol.".

35. "The A.A. Anniversary Fund". New York: General Service Office of A.A.; 1958-1966.
This small 4-page pamphlet suggests personal contributions to AA on an annual basis consistent with "their years of sobriety" with a limit of $100. per member. It was set up in 1958 to meet the financial needs of a larger Fellowship. Discontinued.

36. _A.A. as a Resource for the Medical Profession_. NY: AAWS, Inc.; 1982.
This "leaflet provides information about the Fellowship and describes some approaches that doctors use in referring problem drinkers to A.A.".

37. "A.A. as a Resource for the Health Care Professional". New York: AAWS; 1989?
This is a revision of "A.A. as a Resource for the Medical Profession" [see separate listing].

38. _A.A. at a Glance_. NY: AAWS, Inc.; 1977.
"Public information flyer condensing facts on the Fellowship. no charge.".

39. _A.A. Conference-Approved Literature and Other Service Materials_. New York: AAWS, Inc.; 1968.
As A.A. has grown, its literature has progressed and this 8 1/2 x 11" literature order form has expanded from 4 pages to the current 12-page catalog.

40. _A.A. Directories: International, Canadian, Western U.S., Eastern U.S., & A.A. Groups in Correctional Facilities_. NY: AAWS, Inc.; 1988.
All 5 directories above are CONFIDENTIAL and are available to A.A. members only. Ordering through A.A. groups. Each directory lists hundreds and thousands of "home" groups throughout the area covered, a contact person and phone number, along with name of the group/meeting and time and date of meeting. Directories are not to be used for non-A.A. purposes (such as outside mailings, requests for contributions to non-A.A. agencies or foundations, etc.).

41. _A.A. Fact File_. NY: AAWS, Inc.; 1956.
"For writers and editors. Ready-to-file folder provides detailed public information on A.A., its program, and its Traditions.".

42. "A.A. for the Native North American". New York: AAWS; 1989.
This 45-page pamphlet is "addressed to and contains stories by Native American A.A. members.".

43. _A.A. for the Woman_. NY: AAWS, Inc.; 1968.
Note: pamphlet.
Completely revised text and updated stories relate the experiences of alcoholic women - all ages and from all walks of life. It was revised in 1971 and again in June, 1986.

44. _The A.A. Group_. NY: AAWS, Inc.; 1963.
"Informal guide tells how a group works most effectively, how a new group can be started, how each group can be linked to A.A. as a whole." This pamphlet was originally titled _Partners in A.A._

45. _A.A. Guidelines_. NY: AAWS, Inc.; 1988.
"There are 14 A.A. Guidelines from G.S.O., sharing experience on many topics of concern to members, groups, or committees. They are titled: Armed Services; Central or Intergroup Offices; Clubs; Conferences and Conventions; Cooperating with Court, A.S.A.P., and Similar Programs; Correctional Facilities Committees; Public Information; Relationship between A.A. and Al-Anon; On Current Usage of the A.A. Directories (U.S. and Canada); For A.A. Members Employed in the Alcoholism Field; Forming Local Committees on Cooperation with the Professional Community; A.A. Answering Services; Carrying the A.A. Message to the Hearing-Impaired Alcoholic; and Treatment Facilities Committees." Many of these guidelines are based on past experience and on the Traditions and, as such, these suggestions keep A.A.s from repeating the mistakes of the past and benefiting from the positive groundwork laid down by earlier A.A.s.

46. "A.A. in Correctional Facilities".
Note: [see listing under "A.A. in Prisons"].

47. _A.A. in Prison: Inmate to Inmate_. First ed. New York: AAWS; 1991; 127pp; ISBN: 0-916856-41-0.
Note: pb.
This is a collection of 32 stories of AA members, male and female, who have recovered through the Program. They are in prison or out on parole. All the stories of recovery appeared originally in the Grapevine from the 1940s through 1980s.

48. _A.A. in Prisons_. NY: AAWS, Inc.; 1964.
This pamphlet presents "experience based on the functioning of A.A. groups in prisons, with institutional opinions recommending A.A. as a helpful ally.".

49. _A.A. in Treatment Facilities_. NY: AAWS, Inc.; 1961.
Note: Originally published in 1961 as "A.A. in Hospitals"; then in 1979 as "A.A. in Treatment Centers." It was revised in May, 1987.
This pamphlet "shares the experience of treatment facility administrators and of A.A.s who have carried the message into these facilities.".

50. _A.A. in Your Community_. NY: AAWS, Inc.; 1966.
This "six-page folder explains how A.A. is geared to work in any community to help alcoholics. Prepared especially to help groups, central offices, and P.I. committees interpret A.A. to the community.".

51. _A.A. Meeting Sign_. NY: AAWS, Inc.; 1988.
This sign is "offered as a service to groups, to be displayed outside meeting rooms. 8 1/2" diameter.".

52. The A.A. Member. NY: AAWS, Inc.; 1975.
Note: Originally published in 1975 under the title, "Alcoholics Anonymous: A Community Resource For Coping With a National Health Problem" with highlights of the earlier survey.
This pamphlet "summarizes the latest survey of membership in the U.S. and Canada: who A.A.s are (age, sex, occupation), and who helped them find A.A.".

53. The A.A. Member. NY: AAWS, Inc.; 1988.
This display (29" x 40" wide) poster on a double easel "pictures a typical A.A. meeting through survey-based statistics on age, sex, occupation, length of sobriety.".

54. The A.A. Member - Medications and Other Drugs. NY: AAWS, Inc.; 1948.
Note: Published earlier under many titles including:
"Sedatives," Works Pub. Co., 1948, subtitled "Are They an A.A. Problem?" which was a reprint of 5 Grapevine articles by A.A. members: 1. Evidence of the Sleeping Pill Menance; 2. Pills and 12th Step Work; 3. Those "Goof Balls"; 4. Sedatives Easy, And Deadly, Too; & 5. Does a Pill Jag Count as a Slip?
"Sedatives and the Alcoholic" 1952 to 1956(?), advice to A.A. members on the unsupervised use of sedatives.
"Tranquilizers, Sedatives and the Alcoholic" Dec. 1962 to 1964, six A.A. case histories.
"Sedatives, Stimulants and the Alcoholic" July 1964 to 1973. A Report from a group of doctors in A.A.
"The A.A. Member and Drug Abuse" 1974 to 1984.
The last 4 pamphlets above were all published by AAWS, Inc., NY.
This pamphlet report summarizes findings from a "group of doctors in Alcoholics Anonymous. A.A. members share their experience concerning medications and other drugs.".

55. "The A.A. Member and Drug Abuse". New York: AAWS; 1974 to 1984.

56. "A.A. Membership Survey". New York: AAWS; 1975.
Note: Updated every three years based on the latest triannual AA survey.
This 29 x 40" wide poster pictures "a typical A.A. meeting through survey-based statistics on age, sex, occupation, length of sobriety.".

57. "A.A. Quarterly Report from G.S.O."; 1980s-1993; quarterly: 6pp.
Note: CONFIDENTIAL.
This reports activities of the General Service Board including A.A.W.S., Inc., and the A.A. Grapevine, Inc. Literature, finances, archives, correctional facilities, etc., updates are in this "confidential bulletin for use only within A.A.".

58. A.A. Surveys Its Membership: A Demographic Report and a Preliminary Draft of the Analysis of the Survey. New York: AAWS, Inc.; 1984.
Note: 6pp.

59. A.A. Surveys its Membership: A Demographic Report. New York: AAWS, Inc.; Fall, 1987.
Note: This 2 page report was prepared by General Service Office.

60. A.A. Tradition - How It Developed. New York: Works Publishing Co.; 1947.
This 47-page booklet discusses the Twelve Traditions of AA. Reprinted from the 1946-47 Grapevine articles by Bill W.

61. "AA Membership Survey[s]". New York: AAWS; 1968-1992.
Every three years since 1968, the General Service Office conducts a random survey of AA's membership "to keep A.A. members informed on currents trends in membership characteristics and to provide information about A.A. to the professional community and to the general public as part of the effort to reach those who still suffer from alcoholism." The nine triannual surveys to date query AA members in a dozen areas: length of sobriety, sex, meeting attendance, how they were introduced to AA, age, occupation, sponsorship, home group membership, etc. The questions have changed over the years: recently a question about dual addiction was dropped because AA has no opinion on drugs other than alcohol. From 1977 through the 1989 survey, an analysis or commentary of up to 24 pages was done by the GSO staff but that has been discontinued.

62. About AA; 1980s-1993.
This 2-page quarterly "newsletter for professional men and women" gives them information about a wide range of AA activities.

63. About the Alcoholic Husband. NY: The Alcoholic Foundation (A.A.); early 1940s.
This pamphlet is a reprint of Chap. 8, "To Wives," from the Big Book, pp117-134.

64. Advisory Actions of the General Service Conference of Alcoholics Anonymous. NY: AAWS, Inc.; 1988.
Note: Annual booklet.
This annual booklet gives a summary of Conference recommendations from 1951 to 1986, as well as the current year's actions.

65. The Alcoholic Employee. NY: AAWS, Inc.; 1952.
This pamphlet contains "A Word for Employers," "Alcoholism as a Management Problem," and "Helping the Alcoholic Employee." The title was changed in 1976 (?) to A.A. and the Alcoholic Employee. The pamphlet was discontinued in April, 1980.

66. The Alcoholic Husband. NY: AAWS, Inc.; Jan. 1954.
This pamphlet contained A.A.'s message of hope to the wives of problem drinkers. In 1976, the title was changed to Do You Think You're Different?(?).

67. The Alcoholic Wife. NY: AAWS, Inc.; Jan. 1954.
This pamphlet was a message to husbands about A.A. from an active alcoholic spouse. The pamphlet was discontinued in 1975.

68. Alcoholics Anonymous. New York: The Alcoholic Foundation [AA]; March, 1939 [possibly as early as Jan. or Feb.].
Note: Excessively scarce, this 16-page 5.5 x 7.5" pamphlet was reprinted by The Bishop of Books, Wheeling, WV, in a limited edition of 1,000 copies in March, 1991.
This is probably the FIRST AA PAMPHLET! It was a prospectus asking AA members to buy a $25. share of stock in "The One Hundred Men Corporation" which was to publish the book - "One Hundred Men," which, of course, became the AA Big Book. The budget, market potential, profits, and operation of the corporation were discussed. Investors were asked to mail their check to Henry "Hank" G. Parkhurst, Inc., 17 William St., Newark, New Jersey, or William J. Ruddell, 108 Harvey St., Hackettstown, New Jersey. Hank P. and Bill Wilson were the "promoters" of this prospectus and corporation.

69. Alcoholics Anonymous. Freed Slaves of Drink, Now They Free Others. NY: Works Publishing, Inc.; 1941.
This pamphlet reprints the Jack Alexander article in the Saturday Evening Post, 1941.

70. Alcoholics Anonymous and the Medical Profession. NY: AAWS, Inc.; 1945.
This 1955 pamphlet reprints papers presented to the Medical Society of the State of New York and to the American Psychiatric Assn. It is a revision of the earlier 1944 pamphlet, Medicine Looks at A.A.

71. "Alcoholics Anonymous Tradition Anonymity - Part One & Part Two". New York: The Alcoholic Foundation; 1946.
Note: 7pp.
This 7.5 x 5.5" pamphlet reprints the January & March 1946 Grapevine articles on Traditions.

72. Alcoholics Anonymous in Your Community. NY: AAWS, Inc.; June 1966.
This pamphlet contains a brief description of "how the Fellowship of A.A. is geared to work in your community to help alcoholics.".

73. Alcoholics Anonymous and Occupational Alcoholism Programs. NY: AAWS, Inc.; 1981.
"Of interest especially to management and union officials, this leaflet gives a concise description of the help A.A. can offer to the alcoholic employee.".

74. Alcoholics Anonymous Eighth World Service Meeting Manual. New York City: AAWS, Inc.; October 21-25, 1984; 100+ pp.
Large looseleaf folder with numerous reports from countries around the world on the status of their A.A. Service. Includes also 6 workshops; committee agendas; and 10 miscellaneous reports including keynote address by John H. The 1983 estimated world membership of A.A. is over one million members. The 1984 International A.A. Directory, a 56-page pamphlet for CONFIDENTIAL USE of A.A. members only, is included. Of historical interest is a 17-page "History of World Service Meeting," the first of which was held in 1969 in New York City. A summary of "Recommendations from the World Service Meetings 1969-1982", a 27-page report, is also included in the folder.

75. "Alcoholics Anonymous and Employee Assistance Programs". New York: AAWS.
"Of interest to management and union officials, this leaflet gives a concise description of the help A.A. can offer to the alcoholic employee.".

76. Alcoholism is a Management Problem. NY: AAWS, Inc.; 1970.
This pamphlet advises that the solution to industries' employee alcoholism problems is in working with A.A. It was discontinued in Jan. 1980.

77. Analysis of the 1980 Survey of the Membership of A.A. New York: AAWS, Inc.; 1980.
This mimeographed six page report with tables was prepared by the General Service Office. GSO no longer prepares these.

78. Analysis of the 1983 Survey of the Membership of A.A. New York: AAWS, Inc.; 1984.
This mimeographed five page reports with charts was prepared by the General Service Office.

79. Anonymity Wallet Card. NY: AAWS, Inc.; 1988.
This card "provides a clear statement on Traditions Eleven and Twelve.".

80. Archives Scrapbook. NY: AAWS, Inc.; 1988.
"Offset reproduction of newspaper clippings about A.A. 1939-1942." Folio, 17" X 18 1/2". Spiral bound, clear plastic covers. Excellent early history of A.A. from newspaper clippings scrapbooks in the A.A. Archives in New York.

81. Background Editorial Material. NY: AAWS, Inc.; 1988.
This packet "includes 13 sample news features that P. I. committees can adapt for local news use.".

82. Background Radio-TV Material. NY: AAWS, Inc.; 1988.
This packet contains "sample announcements for local stations and channels; formats, suggestions, and a script for radio programs.".

83. Bauer, W. W./Tiebout, Harry M., Dr. "Medicine Looks at Alcoholics Anonymous". in: [Wilson, Bill]. Alcoholics Anonymous Comes of Age. A Brief History of A.A. NY: AAWS, Inc.; 1957: pp235-251; 333pp.
This section of the book is a reprint of the proceedings of the Twentieth Anniversary Convention's Medical Panel. Dr. Bauer of the AMA and Dr. Tiebout, A.A.'s first friend in the field of psychiatry, give their views of A.A., how they cooperated with A.A., and how A.A. influenced their own thinking and practice.

84. Bill W. "A.A.'s Legacy of Service". New York: AAWS; 1951. Note: pp5-18.
"In this foreword to The A.A. Service Manual, Bill W. describes the beginnings of group and general services, the origin of the Traditions and the birth of the General Service Conference.".

85. Bill W. A.A.'s Legacy of Service. NY: AAWS, Inc.; 1969 & many reprints.
In this 16-page pamphlet "reprint of the foreword and historical background to The A.A. Service Manual," Bill W. answers the question "What is the basic A.A. service?" and describes the Fellowship's responsibility, the pioneers' battle for the Big Book, news stories and sudden A.A. growth, the beginnings of group and general services, the origin of theTraditions, and the birth of the Conference.".

86. "Bill's Last Message". New York: AAWS; 1970.
Bill's last message was read by Lois at the N.Y. Intergroup Assn. 1970 dinner. It "stressed the spiritual and practical side of anonymity." On 13 x 17" parchment, suitable for framing.

87. Box 4-5-9. NY: AAWS, Inc.; 1956-1993.
This newsletter of the Fellowship carries A.A. news from around the world, with special departments on Public Information, Cooperation with Professional Community, Treatment Facilities and Correctional Facilities. Prepared and edited at the G.S.O., it is mailed to all groups six times a year. Spanish and French editions also available. Individual subscriptions cost $1.50 per year.

88. "Bridging the Gap - Between Treatment and A.A. Through Temporary Contact Programs". New York: AAWS.
This 8-page pamphlet is "for A.A.s who carry the message into treatment facilities.".

89. A Brief Guide to Alcoholics Anonymous. NY: AAWS, Inc.; 1971.
"Originally designed for use in schools, this folder also lends itself to other P.I. purposes." In simple language, this public information pamphlet "describes our program and offers general information about A.A." The pamphlet was introduced in 1971 as a Student's Guide to Alcoholics Anonymous.

90. By one of the Originators. [Wilson, Bill]. "Basic Concepts of Alcoholics Anonymous". in: Medicine Looks at Alcoholics Anonymous. New York: Works Publishing, Inc.; 1949-50?: pp3-11; 21 pp.
Note: A note at the beginning of the pamphlet states "the author's name has been omitted in this reprint to conform with the AA principle of anonymity.".
Bill W. in this pamphlet, a reprint of his address to the Medical Society of the State of New York, May, 1944, outlines the A.A. program. He compares what medicine and religion have to say to the alcoholic, states the 12 Steps, discusses the spirituality of the A.A. approach, and acknowledges A.A.'s debt to the medical field. Three doctors, Foster Kennedy, G. Kirby Collier, and Harry M. Tiebout, gave responses to his address.

91. Came To Believe...The spiritual adventure of A.A. as experienced by individual members. First ed. New York: Alcoholics Anonymous World Services, Inc.; 1973; 120pp; ISBN: 0-916856-05-4.
Note: pb.
Individual A.A. members from all over the world share their spiritual insights in print on prayer, release from obsession, spiritual awakening, the search, coincidence?, a Higher Power, spiritual progress, and "in all our affairs.".

92. Carrying the Message Inside the Walls. NY: AAWS, Inc.; Dec. 1978.
This one page flyer answers questions often asked by A.A.'s about speaking in correctional facilities, prisons, etc.

93. "Chapter Five. How It Works". Akron, OH: Inter-Group Office; 1980s.
This is a reproduction of the "Final Draft of Chapter Five [of the book Alcoholics Anonymous] as It Appeared in 1938." It is 8.5 x 11" and seven pages.

94. Circles of Love and Service. NY: AAWS, Inc.; 1978.
"Based on the G.S.O. filmstrip of that title, this leaflet outlines A.A.'s service structure clearly in full-color designs, as well as in words.".

95. The Clergy Ask about Alcoholics Anonymous. NY: AAWS, Inc.; 1979.
This 18-page pamphlet contains an "introduction to A.A. for members of the clergy unfamiliar with the Fellowship; further discussion for those seeking greater understanding of A.A.'s program of recovery." It was originally titled A Clergyman Asks About A.A. [21pp] in 1961. It was revised in 1979.

96. The Co-Founders of Alcoholics Anonymous. NY: AAWS, Inc.; 1972.
Note: In this one page flyer, the co-founders full names are given: William Griffith Wilson (1895-1971) and Robert Holbrook Smith, M.D., (1879-1950). Their photos were also published.
This pamphlet gives "brief biographical sketches of Bill W. and Dr. Bob, together with their last major talks.".

97. Conference Digest. New York: General Service Office of Alcoholics Anonymous; 1962.
Note: One example only is included here.
This is usually an 8-page newsletter(s) distributed to delegates and area committeemen before and during each annual General Service Conference and contains conference news, highlights, agendas, articles on various services, financial data, and conference sidelights. It is not A.A.-approved as to content but rather is a service to delegates, etc.

98. Cooperation But Not Affiliation. New York: Gen. Service Office of A.A.; circa 1960.
This 14-page large pamphlet outlines with 20 questions and answers "How A.A. cooperates with outside organizations within the Framework of A.A. Traditions.".

99. Cooperation With the Professional Community Workbook. NY: AAWS, Inc.; 1988.
A loose-leaf workbook on how to do C.P.C. It contains appropriate Guidelines, bulletins, pamphlets and other material.

100. Correctional Facilities Workbook. NY: AAWS, Inc.; 1988.
"A loose-leaf workbook that is helpful to A.A.s carrying the message into correctional falcilities, (it) contains assorted pamphlets, guidelines, sample letters and other useful information.".

101. "The D.C.M.". New York: AAWS; 1988.
"A flyer outlining the responsibilites of the district committee member.".

102. Daily Reflections. A Book of reflections by A.A. members for A.A. members. First ed. New York: AAWS; 1990; 382pp; ISBN: 0-916856-37-2.
Note: Index, pb.
This volume began in an Advisory Action of the 1987 General Service Conference and "fulfills a long-felt need in the Fellowship for a collection of reflections that moves through the calendar year - one day at a time." The membership was asked for help and over 1,300 submissions came in. The book focuses on AA's three Legacies of Recovery, Unity and Service. Each day begins with a quote from A.A. Approved Literature followed by a comment by a member. The foreword states it hopes the book will be "an aid to individual meditation and a stimulant to group discussion and ... lead to a still wider reading of all our literature." For years before this book, AA members used Twenty-Four Hours A Day, a

daily meditation book that emphasized Oxford Group principles and was the number 2 best-seller among the Fellowship. That book was not A.A. Conference-Approved Literature. This book "fulfills a long-felt need" for the Fellowship to have its own daily meditation book. Reflections immediately went through several printings of 50,000 copies.

103. Digest of Proceedings at (the) Dinner given by Mr. John D. Rockefeller, Jr., in the interest of Alcoholics Anonymous at (the) Union Club, New York City, Feb. 8, 1940. NY: AA; 1941. Note: This 14-page pamphlet was first printed under the title "The Alcoholic Foundation" in 1941, then revised in 1949.

104. Directory of A.A. Groups in Correctional Facilities. NY: AAWS, Inc.; 1988.
This directory "gives location, contact, and other information about A.A. groups in prisons throughout the world." (CONFIDENTIAL; for A.A. Members only.).

105. Do You Think You're Different? NY: AAWS, Inc.; 1976.
This pamphlet speaks to newcomers who may wonder how A.A. can work for someone 'different' --- Black or Jewish, teenaged or nearing 80, plus nine other people, including a gay man and lesbian woman, who tell how the A.A. program has worked for them.

106. Dowling, Edward, S.J./Shoemaker, Samuel, Rev. "Religion Looks at Alcoholics Anonymous". in: [Wilson, Bill]. Alcoholics Anonymous Comes of Age. A Brief History of A.A. NY: AAWS, Inc.; 1957: pp253-271; 333pp.
This section of the book presents the St. Louis addresses of Father Dowling of the Jesuit order and of Dr. Shoemaker, the Episcopal clergyman, early friends of A.A. Both comment in depth on the spirituality of A.A., God, agnostics, prayer and other religious/spiritual topics.

107. Dr. Bob and Bill. The General Service Conference of Alcoholics Anonymous. Your Third Legacy. Will You Accept It? First ed. New York: The Alcoholic Foundation [AA]; November, 1950; 28pp.
Note: 3.5 x 8.5" pamphlet. photocopy of original.
"This is a proposal to form 'The General Service Conference of Alcoholics Anonymous' - a small body of State and Provincial A.A. Delegates meeting yearly, who could assume direct responsibility for the guidance of the A.A. General Service Headquarters at New York City." The historic document begins "We who are the older members of A.A. bequeath to you who are younger these three legacies - the '12 Steps of Recovery,' the '12 Traditions' and now the General Services of Alcoholics Anonymous. Two of these legacies have long been in your keeping. By the 12 Steps we have recovered; by the 12 Traditions we are achieving a fine unity." The Co-Founders of AA, Dr. Bob Smith and Bill Wilson, outline their proposal for the formation of the GSC, its charter, election of delegates, its financing, and equitable representation and then lists questions and answers concerning it. This proposal, in effect, hands over the

guidance of the AA Fellowship from the co-founders to the Fellowship at large through elected delegates. It was accepted at the First International Convention of AA in Cleveland, Ohio, in 1950.

108. *Dr. Bob and the Good Oldtimers. A biography, with recollections of early A.A. in the Midwest*. First ed. New York, N.Y.: Alcoholics Anonymous World Services, Inc.; 1980; 373pp; ISBN: 0-916856-07-0.
Note: dj.
Robert Holbrook Smith, M.D., affectionately know as "Dr. Bob" to A.A. members, died in 1950, when A.A. was only 15 years old. With Bill W., Dr. Bob founded A.A. and they are its Co-Founders. This book details Dr. Bob's early life and drunken career until 1935 when he met Bill W. Historic developments in early A.A. are described: the trial-and-error methods of early A.A.; uneasy connections with the Oxford Group; dissension over the writing of the Big Book, finances, participation by members' wives and minorities in A.A. "Through it all, Dr. Bob was a steadying central figure," the jacket notes. Much history on Akron, the birthplace of A.A., and Cleveland and other Ohio history. Illustrated with historic photographs. index. The definitive biography of Dr. Bob to date.

109. *Dr. Bob's Farewell Talk*. NY: AAWS, Inc.; 1988.
Companion piece to "Bill's Last Message", it shows a sketch of the co-founder above last talk. Dr. Bob's remarks on simplicity, love and service were made at the First International Convention, 1950. Parchment. Suitable for framing, 13" x 17 1/4".

110. *Fifty Years with Gratitude. A Family Album and Souvenir of the International A.A. Convention, Montreal, Quebec, Canada, July 4-7, 1985*. First ed. New York, N.Y.: AAWS, Inc.; 1985; 71pp; ISBN: 0-916856-14-3.
Well-illustrated with photographs, the book contains chapters on A.A.'s beginnings, Service: the Third Legacy, the Big Book, the Grapevine, A.A. around the world and in Canada, Lone members & Internationalists, A.A. Behind the Walls, in Hospitals & Treatment Centers, in Business and Industry, in the Armed Services, its Growth on Record, and capsule portraits of the past 5 year conventions from Cleveland in 1950 to Montreal in 1985.

111. "Flow Chart of a Conference Advisory Action". New York: AAWS.
This 24 x 37" poster clearly explains how advisory actions of the General Service Conference begin, go through the committee process, and are either adopted, rejected, or tabled for further time, consideration and study.

112. "For Seamen Who Drink! Here is What We Alcoholic Seamen Are Doing to get More out of Life.". New York: Alcoholic Anonymous Seamen's Club, Inc.; 1940s (?).
Note: pamphlet.
The AA Seamen's Club was at 334 1/2 West 24th St., New York 11, New York.

113. G.S.R. May Be the Most Important Job in A.A. NY: AAWS, Inc.; 1988.
"For a new General Service Representative, this leaflet outlines responsibilities and useful sources of information; for a group, what to keep in mind when electing a G.S.R.".

114. The Group Handbook. NY: AAWS, Inc.; 1988.
This "looseleaf book contains key pamphlets and other information for group use. Particularly valuable for G.S.R.s and other group officers. Recommended for U.S./Canada groups only.".

115. Guide for Leading Beginners Meetings. NY: AAWS, Inc.; 1987.
This packet "includes an 8-page service pamphlet of suggestions - plus ten Conference-approved pamphlets.".

116. Handbook for Setting Up an Alcoholics Anonymous Archival Repository. New York: AAWS; 1986.
This 40-page handbook "contains plans for archival center, statements of policy, calendar of holdings and classifications in G.S.O. Archives, Oral History Guidelines and Forms, and reference information for A.A. archivists.".

117. "Happy AA Birthday". New York: AAWS; 1980s.
This one page flyer suggests members make an "individual A.A. Birthday" contribution during their birthday month. They will receive a "Happy Birthday" card from GSO.

118. How A.A. Members Cooperate With Other Community Efforts to Help Alcoholics. NY: AAWS, Inc.; 1974.
This public information pamphlet answers specific queries on working within A.A. Traditions. This was revised in 1980 and 1988.

119. How It Works. NY: AAWS, Inc.; 1939, 1955, 1976.
Printed as a one page flyer, this is an excerpt in large type from beginning of Chapter 5, the Big Book, which includes the Twelve Steps. It is often read at the start of A.A. meetings.

120. "How to order the book...`Alcoholics Anonymous". New York: The Alcoholic Foundation; 1939-40.
This one page flyer states you can order the AA book by check, money order or C.O.D. and you have a seven-day examination period with guaranteed refund of $3.50.

121. <u>If You Are a Professional, A.A. Wants To Work With You</u>. NY: AAWS, Inc.; 1972.
"Directed at professionals of all types who deal with alcoholics, this folder explains how A.A.s and non-A.A.s can work together. Revised.".

122. <u>Information for Delegates</u>. <u>Tenth General Service Conference of Alcoholics Anonymous</u>. <u>1960</u>. New York: G.S.O., A.A.; 1960.
Note: Confidential.
This spiral-bound booklet, 70pp+, contains advance information for delegates to the conference. Included are sections on General Data & Agenda, Background Information, G.S.O. Reports, Financial Data, 1960 Convention, Rosters & Miscellaneous. Generally, one of this background booklets is prepared in advance of the conference for the delegates.

123. <u>Information on Alcoholics Anonymous</u>. NY: AAWS, Inc.; 1980.
"Public information sheet for P.I. & C.P.C. use." It was revised in 1986.

124. <u>Inside A.A.</u> NY: AAWS, Inc.; 1966.
Note: Also available in a modern two-color, 54 x 35" poster version of the pamphlet.
This pamphlet "explains the A.A. service structure in the U.S. and Canada, describing all elements linking member and group with the General Service Conference." It was copyrighted in 1974.

125. "Is A.A. for Me?". New York: AAWS; 1989.
"Based on the 12 questions in 'Is A.A. for You?', this 32-page pamphlet is an illustrated easy-to-read version.".

126. <u>Is A.A. For You</u>? NY: AAWS, Inc.; 1956.
In this pamphlet, "symptoms of alcoholism are summed up in 12 questions most A.A.s had to answer to identify themselves as alcoholics.".

127. <u>Is There an Alcoholic in Your Life</u>? NY: AAWS, Inc.; 1976.
This pamphlet "explains the A.A. program as it affects anyone close to an alcoholic - spouse, other family member, friend.".

128. <u>It Happened to Alice</u>. NY: AAWS, Inc.; 1968.
Note: [produced by Archie Enterprises, Inc., Mamaroneck, NY, 1985].
This is an "easy-to-read 'comic book' style pamphlet for women alcoholics (with) new color illustrations for the latest printing.".

129. <u>It Sure Beats Sitting in a Cell</u>. NY: AAWS, Inc.; 1979.
This illustrated pamphlet "presents the experience of seven inmates who found A.A. while in prison. It also offers suggested do's and dont's for staying sober after release.".

130. The Jack Alexander Article About A.A. NY: AAWS, Inc.; 1952. "Published in 1941 (in the Saturday Evening Post), this marks a highlight in A.A. history. It sparked the first great surge of interest in A.A."and was responsible in large part for A.A.'s growth from about 2,000 to almost 8,000 members in one brief year. It was originally reprinted as an A.A. pamphlet in 1952 titled Alcoholics Anonymous.

131. The 17th Meeting of the General Service Conference of Alcoholics Anonymous. Final Report. 1967. New York: AAWS, Inc.; 1967.
Note: Confidential.
The theme was "Sponsorship: The Hand of A.A.".

132. The 18th Meeting of the General Service Conference of Alcoholics Anonymous. Final Report. 1968. New York: AAWS, Inc.; 1968.
Note: Confidential.
The theme was "Personal Recovery Depends on A.A. Unity.".

133. Letter to a Woman Alcoholic. NY: AAWS, Inc.; 1954.
This pamphlet "describes with sensitive understanding the problem of the alcoholic woman. It is addressed to the woman who is still drinking and who suspects she may be an alcoholic.".

134. Living Sober. Some methods A.A. members have used for not drinking. First Printing ed. New York: Alcoholics Anonymous World Services, Inc.; 1975; 87pp; ISBN: 0-916856-04-6.
Note: paperback.
Thirty-one brief essays demonstrate through simple example how A.A. members live and stay sober one day at a time. Staying away from the first drink, using the 24-hour plan, avoiding all chemical mood-changers, telephone therapy, and other proven insights from individual A.A.'s all focus on the fact that not drinking is the beginning of staying sober and working the program of recovery contained in Alcoholics Anonymous and Twelve Steps and Twelve Traditions.

135. Lois Burnham W. "The Story of Alcoholics Anonymous". New York: AAWS; 1950.
This 4-page pamphlet is Lois's perspective on Bill and AA.

136. 1st through 8th General Service Conference(s) of A.A. Final Reports. 1951 through 1958. New York: G.S.O. of A.A./ Alcoholics Anonymous Publishing, Inc.; 1951-1958.
Note: Confidential.
"Traditionally, all members have the right of access to information about all phases of A.A.'s General Services. This (these) report is designated as 'Confidential' only because certain members are necessarily identified by name. The 'confidential' designation is designed to assure the personal anonymity of such members.".

137. Markings. Your Archives Interchange; Feb. 1981-1993; Vol. 1-13: 4-8pp.
This twice-a-year newsletter for AA archivists includes news of historic items of AA interest, articles on archival preservation and restoration, and events and projects of other area archives in the U.S., Canada, and around the world. It is published by GSO Archives, NY.

138. Medicine Looks at Alcoholics Anonymous. NY: Works Publishing, Inc.; 1944.
Note: (see also "Alcoholics Anonymous and the Medical Profession" pamphlet.).
This pamphlet contains papers presented to the Medical Society of the State of New York and to the American Psychiatric Association, also Bill W.'s speech of May, 1944. It was reprinted in 1949 and 1953.

139. A Member's-Eye View of Alcoholics Anonymous. NY: AAWS, Inc.; 1970.
This pamphlet "explains the A.A. program to social workers, counselors, physicians, and others in the alcoholism field. It also provides fresh insight into A.A. for all members.".

140. "Members of the Clergy Ask About Alcoholics Anonymous". New York: AAWS.
"Introduction to A.A. for member of the clergy unfamiliar with the Fellowship; further discussion for those seeking greater understanding of its program.".

141. Memo to an Inmate Who May Be an Alcoholic. NY: AAWS, Inc.; 1961.
This recovery pamphlet "is a message from A.A.s who have themselves been inmates. Their personal stories offer a new outlook to inmate alcoholics who want to know how A.A. can help.".

142. "A Message to Correctional Facilities Administrators". New York: AAWS; 1988.
This one-page flyer contains "information about what A.A. is and can do, and how groups function in a correctional facility.".

143. A Message to Teenagers. NY: AAWS, Inc.; 1980.
This flyer was "adapted from the pamphlet "Too Young?" for public information in schools." It contains a simple 12-question quiz designed to help you decide if you are alcoholic or having a drinking problem. It was revised in 1988.

144. A Newcomer Asks. NY: AAWS, Inc.; 1979.
This pamphlet "gives straightforward, brief answers on 15 points that once puzzled many of us.".

145. One of the Originators. <u>Basic Concepts of Alcoholics Anonymous</u>. New York: The Alcoholic Foundation; [1944].
Note: Apparently this early pamphlet exists, although the compilers have not seen it. It was referred to in Oscar W. Richie's "A Sociohistorical Survey of Alcoholics Anonymous," [QJSA, Vol. 9, Issue 1, 1948, pp119-156.].

146. <u>'Pass It On' The Story of Bill Wilson and how the A.A. message reached the world</u>. First ed. New York: Alcoholics Anonymous World Services, Inc.; 1984; 429pp; ISBN: 0-916856-12-7.
Note: dj.
This is the definitive biography to date of Bill Wilson, (1895-1971) Co-Founder of A.A. One of the most significant figures of the twentieth century, Wilson was A.A.'s primary writer and thinker. The dust jacket declares that "every word is documented, every source checked" in the five-year preparation of this biography. Illustrated with historic photographs. Twenty pages of sources & index.

147. <u>Patterns of A.A. Cooperation with Hospitals</u>. New York: GSO of A.A.; 1966.
This 8-page large pamphlet discusses the Sixth Tradition and gives seven plans for sponsoring A.A. groups in hospitals, clinics, mental health facilities, etc.

148. "Press Release from The Trustees of The Alcoholic Foundation". New York: The Alcoholic Foundation; Sept. 12, 1946.
Because of the activities of persons in and out of AA, the Trustees issued this press release stating AA does not endorse any fund-raising efforts.

149. "Primary Purpose Card". New York: AAWS; 1989.
This blue card [front & back] "states A.A.'s primary purpose for both open and closed meetings for those groups who wish to read it at meetings.".

150. "Problems Other Than Alcohol".
Note: [see listing under "Wilson, Bill"].
Excerpts from the pamphlet.

151. Public Information Committee, General Service Office, A.A. "For Those Who Wear Two Hats". in: Staub, George E., & Kent, Leona M., Editors. <u>The Para-Professional in the Treatment of Alcoholism (A New Profession)</u>. Springfield, Illinois: Charles C. Thomas, Publisher; 1973: Chap. XI, pp115-129; 165+ pp.

152. <u>Public Information Literature Display Container</u>. NY: AAWS, Inc.; 1988.
This "easel-design cardboard container for doctors' offices, health fairs, etc., comes with 100 flyers 'A.A. at a Glance.".

153. Public Information Workbook. NY: AAWS, Inc.; 1988.
This "loose-leaf workbook contains sections on how to do P.I., Guidelines, TV and radio scripts, print media article ideas, and literature order forms. The A.A. Fact File and a selection of 15 pamphlets and leaflets are included.".

154. Questions and Answers on Sponsorship. NY: AAWS, Inc.; 1953.
This pamphlet "uses shared A.A. experience to answer 34 questions likely to be asked by persons seeking sponsors, persons wanting to be sponsors, and groups planning sponsorship activity." The pamphlet was first issued in 1953 as Sponsorship.

155. "Report of June 30, 1940". New York: Works Publishing, Inc.; 1940.
This report of 8 pages is on the finances of early AA.

156. Responsibility Wallet Card. NY: AAWS, Inc.; 1988.
Note: This is also published in a large 19" x 29" placard format.
This has the "I Am Responsible' declaration on one side, the reverse side blank (except for circle & triangle) to allow you to stamp or imprint your group meeting place and time - or area conference or convention dates.".

157. Sedatives. New York: Works Publishing Co.; 1948.
Subtitled "Are they an A.A. problem?" this 16-page pamphlet reprints five Grapevine articles on pills and other non-alcohol drugs. With the modern advent of poly-addicted alcoholics, it is worth noting that very early in AA the Fellowship dealt with the "drug" problem forthrightly.

158. "Sedatives and the Alcoholic". New York: AAWS; 1952 to 1956(?).
Advice to AA members on unsupervised use of sedatives.

159. "Sedatives, Stimulants and The Alcoholic". New York: AAWS; 1964-1973.
Note: This Conference-approved pamphlet was discontinued in 1973 and replaced in 1974 through 1984 with "The A.A. Member and Drug Abuse.".
This 16-page pamphlet is a report from "a Group of Doctors in A.A." showing how certain drugs may hurt as well as help the alcoholic. At this time, the "pill problem" was common in AA with members misusing drugs, often as a substitute for alcohol, and threatening their sobriety. This report at the beginning notes "AA is a program for alcoholics who seek freedom from alcohol. It is not a program against drugs.".

160. "Self-Supporting Through our own Contributions". New York: AAWS; 1990.
Note: see also "Supporting the A.A. Support System".
This 6-page foldout pamphlet contains suggested plan for group contributions toward all A.A. services.

161. The Serenity Prayer. NY: AAWS, Inc.; 1988.
Note: Available in parchment 12 x 17" for framing.
Usually read at the beginning of a meeting, the full text is: "God grant me the serenity to accept the things I cannot change, courage to change the things I can, and wisdom to know the difference.".

162. Silkworth, W. D., M.D. "The Doctor's Opinion". in: [Wilson, Bill]. ALCOHOLICS ANONYMOUS. The Story of How Many Thousands of Men and Women Have Recovered from Alcoholism. First, Second & Third ed. New York City: AAWS, Inc., & Works Publishing Company; 1939-1955-1976-1989: pp xxiii-xiv; 400pp; ISBN: 0-916856-00-3.
Dr. Silkworth introduces the reader to the "Big Book" of A.A. by first painting a gloomy picture of his experiences in trying to help alcoholics. Then he relates the story of Bill W. whom he treated and his recovery. He endorses A.A. fully and "advises every alcoholic to read this book through, and though he came to scoff, he may remain to pray.".

163. Smith, Bernard B. "A Friend Looks at Alcoholics Anonymous". in: [Wilson, Bill]. Alcoholics Anonymous Comes of Age: A Brief History of A.A. New York: AAWS, Inc.; 1957: pp273-283.
Smith, a New York attorney, was a Trustee and Chairman of A.A.'s General Service Board. Subtitled "The Individual, A.A., and Society," this article was based on talks Smith gave at the first six General Service Conferences. A non-alcoholic, Smith discusses meeting Bill W., his service over the years to A.A., the three Legacies, the Conference, materialism, happiness in A.A., and A.A. as the "outstanding spiritual phenomenon of our century.".

164. Speaking at Non-A.A. Meetings. NY: AAWS, Inc.; 1962.
This pamphlet is "for A.A.s asked to speak to organizations outside the Fellowship about A.A., alcoholism, and the alcoholic, (and) it suggests what to say and how to say it." It was revised in 1974 and in May, 1981.

165. "Statement Regarding Use of Circle-Triangle Symbol". New York: AAWS; April 29, 1993.
This one page announcement mailed to all AA groups in the U.S. and Canada states "AAWS will no longer oppose use of the circle/triangle symbol on medallions, jewelry or other items." Prior to this, AAWS had trademarked the symbol and entered into lawsuits against firms marketing items with the symbol. The 1993 General Service Conference recommended this action to remove AA from an obvious conflict with Tradition Ten.

166. Steps and Traditions Window-Shade Displays. NY: AAWS, Inc.; 1988.
These three by six feet displays are also published individually and in a smaller 13 x 17" parchment format as a set and individually.

167. Supporting the A.A. Support System. NY: AAWS, Inc.; 1988. This pamphlet has a long history, including: "The 60/30/10 Plan" 1979; was: "a penny a day for Sobriety" 1975; was: "How Far Can $3.00 Go Today Towards Helping Drunks ALL Over the World?" 1973; was: "You, Your Group and A.A. Worldwide!" 1964; was: "What Happens When You Put $3.00 in the Hat for your General Service Office." 1961-63. Also: "I Am Responsible," 1967-68, How members and groups can help extend the hand of A.A. All these pamphlets concern finances, donations, and A.A. Service. The current pamphlet is a "full-color folder that uses diagrams to explain ways of apportioning group contributions to suit varying service needs and it describes services that contributions help provide.".

168. "This is a Closed [Open] Meeting of Alcoholics Anonymous" card. New York: General Service Office of A.A.; March, 1989. This 4 x 6" card describes an Open meeting of A.A., "our singleness of purpose and our Third Tradition" and asks all to confine their discussion to problems with alcohol. The back describes a Closed meeting of A.A. which is "limited to persons who have a desire to stop drinking." It is often read at the beginning of AA meetings, closed or open.

169. This is A.A. NY: Works Publishing Inc./AAWS,Inc.; 1953. "Introductory pamphlet describing the kind of people A.A.s are and what A.A.s have learned about alcoholism. For anyone who thinks he or she may have a problem with alcohol.".

170. Tiebout, Harry M., M.D. "Therapeutic Mechanism of Alcoholics Anonymous". in: Medicine Looks at Alcoholics Anonymous. New York: Works Publishing, Inc.; 1949-50?: pp12-19; 21pp. This "A.A. Publication," a pamphlet, is a reprint from the article in The American Journal of Psychiatry, January 1944. Dr. Tiebout, an early friend of A.A., relates his experiences with early A.A. and discusses, at length, the spirituality of the program and the changes which occur in newcomers to A.A.

171. Time to Start Living. NY: AAWS, Inc.; 1979. This pamphlet "addresses the older alcoholic, with nine stories of men and women who came to A.A. after the age of 60." It is also published in a large-print edition.

172. Too Young? NY: AAWS, Inc.; 1977. "With a full-color cover, this cartoon pamphlet speaks to teenagers in their own language, telling the varied drinking stories of six young people (ages 13 to 18) and showing their welcome to A.A." It was revised in Aug. 1979 and Nov. 1987.

173. "Tranquilizers, Sedatives and the Alcoholic". New York: AAWS; Dec. 1962 to 1964. This pamphlet shares six A.A. case histories.

174. Treatment Facilities Workbook. NY: AAWS, Inc.; 1988. A loose-leaf workbook that will be helpful to A.A.s carrying the message into treatment facilities, it contains pamphlets, guidelines and sample letters.

175. *The Twelve Concepts Illustrated*. NY: AAWS, Inc.; 1986.
This pamphlet has a "brief, easy to read text and clever illustrations (which) make the Twelve Concepts for World Service clear and understandable.".

176. "Twelve Steps and Twelve Traditions Tabletop Display". New York: AAWS.
The Steps and Traditions are on this 29 x 40" wide double easel.

177. "The Twelve Steps Parchment". New York: AAWS.
The steps on 13 x 17.25" parchment, suitable for framing.

178. "Twelve Steps Window-Shade Display". New York: AAWS.
The 12 Steps are on this 3 x 6 foot display for meeting rooms. It rolls up like a window shade.

179. "Twelve Traditions Flyer". New York: AAWS.
8.5 x 11" flyer with Traditions in large type face.

180. *The Twelve Traditions Illustrated*. NY: AAWS, Inc.; 1971.
This pamphlet has "all 12 Traditions transposed to lively sketches with brief explanations in words, presenting both the spirit and the practical application of our Traditions. Based on a Grapevine series." It was revised in May, 1979.

181. "The Twelve Traditions Parchment". New York: AAWS.
The Traditions on 13 x 17.25" parchment, suitable for framing.

182. *Twelve Traditions Posters*. NY: AAWS, Inc.; 1988.
This is a set of 8 1/2 x 11" black and white posters based on the drawings from the pamphlet *Twelve Traditions Illustrated*.

183. "Twelve Traditions Window-Shade Display". New York: AAWS.
The 12 Traditions are on this 3 x 6 foot display for meeting rooms. It rolls up like a window shade.

184. *Understanding Anonymity*. NY: AAWS, Inc.; 1972.
This pamphlet "explains clearly what anonymity means both within and outside A.A." It was revised in Oct., 1978 and 1981.

185. "Unity Placard". New York: AAWS.
The Declaration of Unity is displayed on this two color, 19 x 29" cardboard poster.

186. *Wallet card*. NY: AAWS, Inc.; current.
A plastic card containing the Preamble, 12 Steps, 12 Traditions, and Serenity Prayer.

187. What Happened to Joe. NY: AAWS, Inc.; 1967.
Note: [produced by Archie Enterprises, Inc., Mamaroneck, NY, 1985].
This pamphlet contains the "dramatic story of a young construction worker and his drinking problem, told in brightly colored `comic book'style (with) new illustrations in latest printing.".

188. Where Do I Go From Here? NY: AAWS, Inc.; 1978.
"For people leaving treatment facilities, this single-sheet flyer tells of continuing help offered by `outside' A.A." It was discontinued in 1980.

189. [Wilson, Bill]. The A.A. Service Manual - combined with - Twelve Concepts for World Service by Bill W. First ed. NY: AAWS, Inc.; 1951 & 1962; 123pp + 76pp.
The Service Manual is an outgrowth of the Third Legacy Manual, drafted first by Bill W. in 1951. In its 123 pages are included the following articles identified in the contents as written by Bill: A.A.'s Legacy of Service, foreword and historical background; What makes an A.A. "leader"?; and Can the Conference act for A.A. as a whole?. Basically, the Service Manual "explains the whole Conference structure and its year-round importance and includes the Conference Charter and General Service Board Bylaws. The Concepts - principles of service that have emerged from A.A.'s service accomplishments and mistakes from its beginning - are set forth by Bill W. The Twelve Concepts were adopted by the 12th Annual General Serice Conference of A.A. on April 26, 1962, and published in 1962. This book emobodies A.A.'s Legacy of Service and sets forth the structure and methods by which the Fellowship executes its basic service - the Twelfth Step - carrying the message to other suffering alcoholics. The service manual is indexed. The manual/concepts book was copyrighted in 1969.
The Concepts are "an interpretation of A.A.'s world service structure...(and) aim to record the `why' of our service structure in such a fashion that the highly valuable experience of the past, and the lessons we have drawn from that experience, can never be forgotten or lost." Among the principles that Bill Wilson describes are the "Right(s) of Decision, of Participation, of Appeal, and of Petition." The Concepts "try to design a structure in which all may labor to good effect, with a minimum of friction.".

190. [Wilson, Bill]. A.A. Tradition - How It Developed. NY: AAWS, Inc.; 1947.
Note: This pamphlet was first published in pamphlet form by Works Publishing, Inc., in 1947; it was revised in 1955 and 1983. (See the "GrapevineArticles Written by Bill W." section for separate Grapevine articles on each of the Traditions.).
"Bill W.'s 1946-47 Grapevine articles on the Traditions trace the evolution of the principles for A.A. unity and growth.".

191. [Wilson, Bill]. The A.A. Way of Life - a reader by Bill - Selected Writings of A.A.'s Co-Founder. First Edition, First Printing ed. New York: Alcoholics Anonymous World Services, Inc.; 1967; 332 pp; ISBN: 0-916856-03-8.
Note: Later retitled: As Bill Sees It - The A. A. Way of Life... - selected writings of A.A.'s Co-Founder. (see separate listing under that title).
Includes several hundred excerpts from A.A. literature. Many of these were written by Bill Wilson and published in the A.A. Grapevine. Another major source of this material was Wilson's large personal correspondence. "The Discussion and Reading Guide" at the front lists these among many topics, usually one page being devoted to each subject: acceptance, courage, gratitude, Higher Power, Sex, Twelfth-Stepping, Unity, Surrender, etc. Bill identifies himself as the author of Alcoholics Anonymous (the Big Book), Twelve Steps and Twelve Traditions, Alcoholics Anonymous Comes of Age, and "Twelve Concepts for World Service," the latter becoming part of the Third Legacy Manual. 4 1/2 x 6". Original dust jacket was orange with white and black lettering.

192. [Wilson, Bill]. ALCOHOLIC'S ANONYMOUS. Photocopy of "Multilith" pre-publication manuscript ed. New York City: AAWS, Inc.; modern reproduction of 1939 original manuscript (NOT the published First Edition, First Printing).; 156pp.
Note: 8 1/2 x 11". At least two different formats for this facsimile have been found: one blue wrappers bound with five metal screw-type holders at the spine; another plain white wrappers with black plastic spiral binding. Reproduced often.
The content of these facsimiles of the 1939 manuscript for the first edition preserves all the original wording, some of which was changed for the first edition of the book. For example, in Chapter Five, How It Works, Step 12 reads: "Having had a spiritual experience as the result of this course of action, we tried to carry this message to others, especially alcoholics, and to practice these principles in all our affairs." These and other differences between the manuscript and the final published first edition are noteworthy subjects of study.

193. [Wilson, Bill]. Alcoholics Anonymous. Multilith facsimile ed. 17 William St., Newark, NJ: Works Publishing Co.; 1939; 160pp.
Note: Actual multilith copes are extremely rare.
This is a facsimile of the "multilith" Big Book, of which 400 copies were printed as advance review copies prior to the actual publication of the Big Book in April, 1939. This facsimile was owned by Clarence S., the early A.A. member from Cleveland, Ohio. The pagination is as follows: title page, index, foreword, Part I comprising 76 pages, The Alcoholic Foundation (appendix, one page); Part II Index to Personal Stories, 79 pages.

194. [Wilson, Bill]. ALCOHOLICS ANONYMOUS. The Story of How One Hundred Men Have Recovered from Alcoholism. First Edition, First Printing ed. New York City: Works Publishing Company, Church Street Annex Post Box 657, New York City; April, 1939; 400 pp.
Note: Red cloth, the only edition or printing so published, all the rest being in blue cloth with the exception of the first edition, third printing, which was in green cloth. 400 pages. The dust jacket is commonly referred to as the "circus" dust jacket because of its wild colors of black, red, white and yellow. The printing is always noted on the dust jacket at the top of the inside front flap. The first edition had 16 printings, all of which had the "circus" dj. Later a plain blue and white dust jacket was adopted for the second and third edition printings. The copyright page notes that the book was printed in the United States of America by the Cornwall Press, Inc., Cornwall, N.Y. The first printing had a press run of slightly less than 5,000 copies. Before the first edition, a small edition of several hundred copies was printed in a multilith or multigraph format and sent out to doctors and others as a sort of advance review copy for comments before publication. (also see: [Wilson, Bill] Alcoholics Anonymous The Story etc., 1985, a facsimile reprint issued for the 50th anniversary of A.A., by Carry the Message, Akron, Ohio, in the section "Books and pamphlets about A.A.).
This is the most important book on alcoholism in human history! The book is divided roughly into two parts: the first 164 pages give the program of recovery, embodied in the Twelve Steps. The table of contents lists a Foreword, The Doctor's Opinion, written by William D. Silkworth, M.D., and then Chap. I, Bill's (the Co-founder) Story, followed by ten more chapters which explain and illustrate the disease of alcoholism (allergy) and the program of recovery, the Twelve Steps. The second half of the book, from page 165 to the end is comprised of 29 "Personal Stories" written by the first 100 members of Alcoholics Anonymous. These stories authenticate the successful application of the Twelve Steps and provide the reader with examples he or she can identify with. This second section of the book opens with "The Doctor's Nightmare," the personal story of Dr. Bob, the other Co-founder of A.A. The book concludes with a two-page appendix on The Alcoholic Foundation, a Trust to handle the book publishing and administrative and financial matters for A.A., and on how to order the book, Alcoholics Anonymous. It originally cost $3.50. This book remains the basic "text" of A.A. and has remained substantially unchanged in all subsequent printings, excepting the second part where the personal stories have been expanded and changed to reflect better the general membership of A.A. The book is affectionately called "the Big Book" by A.A. members. It details the founding of A.A. and its purpose is "To show other alcoholics precisely how we have recovered." It was written by Bill Wilson.

195. [Wilson, Bill]. ALCOHOLICS ANONYMOUS The Story of How Many Thousands of Men and Women Have Recovered from Alcoholism. New & Revised Second ed. New York City: Alcoholics Anonymous Publishing, Inc. (Works Publishing Inc. is now known as Alcoholics Anonymous Publishing, Inc., Grand Central Annex Post Box 459 New York (17), N. Y., the copyright page notes).; 1955; 575pp.
This new and revised edition of "The Big Book" has 33 new stories in the Personal History Section, totaling 110,398 words, the first printing of this second edition dust jacket tells us. Pages 1 through 164 remain unchanged. This edition has the reversible dust jacket, which, when turned inside out, is a solid blue color, thus protecting the anonymity of the reader. A preface and a foreword to the second edition are new, as are some of the appendixes at the back. This edition has 37 "case histories" which reflect the expanding membership of A.A. at large. The second edition went through sixteen printings.

196. [Wilson, Bill]. Alcoholics Anonymous Comes of Age. A Brief History of A.A. First ed. New York: Alcoholics Anonymous Publishing, Inc.; 1957; 335pp; ISBN: LC 57-10949.
Note: A pre-publication copy was produced in 1957. It was 8 1/2 x 11 inches, blue softcover, 168 pages. The front cover was marked "Confidential - A.A. Comes of Age - Pre-publication copy - 1957." The title page has the following note: "This manuscript is the property of Alcoholics Anonymous Publishing, Inc. Not for publication in any part, this is a loan copy only, intended for the assistance of the editors." Probably only two or three hundred copies were made and the vast majority turned back in after review and comments. It is thus very scarce; the editor having seen only one copy in 15 years.
Bill W. set down the basic history of A.A. The first part of the book presents a panoramic sketch of the historic Twentieth Anniversary St. Louis Convention in 1955 at which the Fellowship of A.A. came of age and assumed full responsibility for all its affairs. The second part includes three talks, edited and enlarged, on the history of A.A. Recovery, Unity and Service, the Three Legacies, which were given by Co-founder Bill W. at the St. Louis gathering. The third part contains addresses by A.A.'s friends. Included are Dr. Harry Tiebout, psychiatrist; Dr. W. W. Bauer of the American Medical Association; Father Edward Dowling of the Society of Jesus, a Jesuit priest; Dr. Samuel Shoemaker, Episcopal clergyman; and Mr. Bernard B. Smith, New York attorney and recent Chairman of the General Service Board of A.A. Six appendixes and an index conclude the book. The volume is nicely illustrated with historic photos of A.A.

197. [Wilson, Bill]. ALCOHOLICS ANONYMOUS The Story of How Many Thousands of Men and Women Have Recovered from Alcoholism. Third ed. New York City: Alcoholics Anonymous World Services, Inc.; 1976; 575pp; ISBN: 0-916856-00-3.
Note: While the first and second editions of the Big Book had 16 printings each, this third edition is now over 20 printings as of 1988.
The basic text of Alcoholics Anonymous. The number of personal stories in this edition has been increased to 44 in order to represent more accurately the wide variety of individuals now finding recovery from alcoholism in A.A. The basic text from pages 1 to 164 remains unchanged, just as it was in 1939 when first published. This edition contains 13 new stories not in the previous two editions. Forewords to the First and Second Editions are reprinted here. By 1993, the combined total of all three editions printed was over 10 million.

198. [Wilson, Bill]. ALCOHOLICS ANONYMOUS The Story of How Many Thousands of Men and Women Have Recovered from Alcoholism. First printing [Third Ed., 24th printing] of the First Paperback ed. New York City: Alcoholics Anonymous World Services, Inc.; November 1986; 575pp; ISBN: 0-916856-18-6.
Note: Referred to as the "Portable" Big Book. 4 1/2 x 7". soft-cover.
Historic first paperback edition. The content remains exactly the same as other printings of the third edition. The blue covers are completely blank except for the ISBN in small gold letters on the back cover and the words "Alcoholics Anonymous" in blind stamping on the front cover, making them very difficult to see, and thus protecting the anonymity of the reader.

199. [Wilson, Bill]. Alcoholics Anonymous (Braille Big Book). NY: AAWS, Inc.; 1988.
The Big Book for the blind in seven large volumes.

200. [Wilson, Bill]. ALCOHOLICS ANONYMOUS The Story of How Many Thousands of Men and Women Have Recovered from Alcoholism. Third Edition, (36th Printing?) Large-print ed. New York City: AAWS, Inc.; 1990; 575pp; ISBN: 0-916856-33-X. LC 76-4029.
This is the large print edition of the Big Book. This Third Edition printing is 7 x 9 3/16" softbound.

201. [Wilson, Bill]. Alcoholics Anonymous. First abridged paperback ed. New York: AAWS; July, 1993; 189pp; ISBN: 0-916856-59-3.
Note: 3.5 x 5.5" blue pb.
This is the first paperback printing of the abridged version of the third edition of Alcoholics Anonymous. It contains the original first 164 pages of the Big Book, Dr. Bob's Nightmare, and the 6 Appendixes.

202. [Wilson, Bill]. As Bill Sees It. The A.A. Way of Life...selected writings of A.A.'s Co-Founder. First ed. New York: Alcoholics Anonymous World Services, Inc.; 1967; 332 pp.
Note: Originally titled The A.A. Way of Life, the above title was substituted to more accurately reflect Bill's comment in the preface of the first printing: "Of course, all this material reflects my personal viewpoint on A.A.'s way of life. As such it is bound to have its limitations and imperfections. Nevertheless, one may hope that this new publication will meet a genuine need," April, 1967. The dust jacket color has been changed from the original orange to red and the title "As Bill Sees It" occupies the most prominent place on the front cover of the dust jacket.
Contains the same material as The A.A. Way of Life / a reader by Bill / Selected writings of A.A.'s Co-Founder.

203. [Wilson, Bill]. Bill's Recommenations on the Structure of the General Service Board and the Trustees' Comments and Recommendations. New York: General Service Office of Alcoholics Anonymous; 1962.
Note: "The 1962 General Service Conference asked that this pamphlet (of 42 pages) be prepared and distributed to Conference Delegates and Area Committeemen." It includes letters from trustees and Bill Wilson, as well as his "minority report.".

204. [Wilson, Bill]. Let's Be Friendly With Our Friends. NY: AAWS, Inc.; 1988.
In this pamphlet, a Grapevine reprint, "Bill W. explains the importance of cooperating with doctors, social workers, etc.".

205. [Wilson, Bill]. Problems Other Than Alcohol. NY: AAWS, Inc.; 1968.
Note: Put in pamphlet form first in 1968, this reprints the Feb. 1958 Grapevine article Bill wrote on the subject. "Bill's thoughts on the status of drug addicts within A.A. are as timely as when they appeared in a 1958 Grapevine article.".

206. [Wilson, Bill]. The Third Legacy Manual of A.A. World Service. New York: Alcoholics Anonymous General Service Headquarters, Inc.; 1951.
For abstract, see: [Wilson, Bill] A.A. Service Manual/ etc. It was written by Bill W.

207. [Wilson, Bill]. Three Talks to Medical Societies by Bill W., Co-founder of A.A. NY: AAWS, Inc.; 1950.
Note: First published in 1950 as "The Society of Alcoholics Anonymous" (one paper); then in 1955 as two talks titled "Alcoholism the Illness"; then in 1972 called "Bill on Alcoholism." The present title was adopted in 1973.
This pamphlet "contains Bill's ideas of how how A.A. works, principles borrowed from medicine and religion, and a summary of A.A.'s first 23 years.".

208. [Wilson, Bill]. Twelve Steps and Twelve Traditions. First Edition. ed. New York: Alcoholics Anonymous World Services, Inc.; April, 1953; 192 pp; ISBN: L.C. 53-5454.
Note: The book was also published in a "Pocket" or "Gift" Edition in 1965 which is exactly the same in content but is a smaller hardback, 4x6".
"This present volume proposes to broaden and deepen the understanding of the Twelve Steps as first written in the earlier work (Alcoholics Anonymous, 1939)," the foreword states. When this book was published, 18 years after A.A.'s founding, the society had grown to more than 100,000 alcoholic men and women. The pioneering period of A.A. history had ended and a "prodigious chain reaction" had set in with tens of thousands of new members coming into A.A. The book sets forth an "explicit view of the principles by which A.A. members recover (the Steps) and by which their society functions (the Traditions).".

209. [Wilson, Bill]. Twelve Concepts for World Service By Bill W. First ed. New York, New York: Alcoholics Anonymous World Services, Inc.; 1962; 76pp.
Note: (For abstract, see: [Wilson, Bill] The A.A. Service Manual/combined with/Twelve Concepts for World Service by Bill W.).
First published separately, then combined with the A.A. Service Manual.

210. [Wilson, Bill]. Twelve Concepts for World Service. By Bill W. Draft Edition for Delegates ed. New York, NY: A.A.; 1962 (?); a-m, 121pp.
Note: 8 1/2 x 11".
This was the working draft submitted to delegates. The main difference between this and the present 12 Concepts is an introduction of 13 pages which includes the Charter for the General Service Conference of Alcoholics Anonymous (North American Section).

211. [Wilson, Bill]. Twelve Steps and Twelve Traditions. First large print ed. New York: AAWS; Feb., 1991; 192pp; ISBN: 0-916856-34-3. LC 91-076726.
Note: pb.
[see the first edition listing].

212. [Wilson, Bill]. "Why Alcoholics Anonymous Is Anonymous". in: Alcoholics Anonymous Comes of Age. A Brief History of A.A. NY: AAWS, Inc.; 1957: Appendix B: pp286-294; 333 pp.
Written "by Bill" [Wilson, William G.].

213. [Wilson, Lois]. The Story of Alcoholics Anonymous. NY: AAWS, Inc.; 1950.
Note: Lois Burnham W. was the way Lois signed her name to this article.
This four-page pamphlet give Lois's perspective on Bill Wilson and A.A.

214. Young People and A.A. NY: AAWS, Inc.; 1953.
Note: This pamphlet was first printed in 1953, then revised in 1969 & May 1979.
"Ten young A.A.s - ages 16 to 27 - tell how the program works for them.".

215. Your A.A. General Service Office. NY: AAWS, Inc.; 1975.
This "illustrated folder describes the services provided by your G.S.O.".

Chapter II = Grapevine Articles

216. The AA Grapevine, Inc., Box 1980.; June, 1944-March 1994; Vol. 1, No. 1, to Vol. 50, No. 10-(present); ISSN: 0362-2584. Note: [cirulation peaked at 136,000 in 1991; in 1994, it was 122,000.].

This is "The International Journal of Alcoholics Anonymous. The Grapevine presents the experiences and opinions of AA members and others interested in the AA program. Opinions expressed herein are not to be attributed to Alcoholics Anonymous as a whole, nor does publication of any article imply any endorsement by either AA or the AA Grapevine." It is "Our meeting in print." Published monthly, usually 48 pages, each issue reproduces the 12 Steps and 12 Traditions, one or more pages of order/ subscription forms, a centerfold photo of two pages with a thought-provoking saying or quote, table of contents usually on the back cover, usually about 10 articles by members of AA and others about the entire range of AA subjects. For the first years, the size was 10 x 12 inches; later color covers were added and the size dropped down to 5 1/2 x 7 1/2 inches. Each issue also includes a POBox 1980, letters to the editor column; calendar of coming AA events; & About Alcoholism, notes, quotes and reviews of alcoholism information, treatment and research some of which is contrary to AA philosophy. The About Alcoholism section was dropped recently and fragments of AA history and reprints of earlier stories in the Big Book substituted. Special issues devoted to one topic are issued irregularly; e.g., Dr. Bob Memorial Issue, etc. Address: The Grapevine, Inc., Grand Central Station, P.O. Box 1980, New York, NY 10163.

217. Aharan, Charles H., Ph.D. "Problems of Cooperation Between AA and Other Treatment Programs". Grapevine; April 1971; 27(11): pp17-23.
Aharan, Director, Alcoholism and Drug Addiction Research Foundation, Lake Erie Region, London, Ontario, Canada, gave this speech at the 35th AA Anniversary Convention, Miami Beach, Florida. He discusses the attitudes necessary for cooperation between AA and non-AA treatment services. He describes individual attitudes and practices observed in AA members that he believes stifle useful cooperation between the two groups. Recommendations for the improved functioning of AA by itself and in its mutual endeavors with other treatment programs are also made.

218. Alexander, Jack. "The Faith that Moves Drunks Can Move the World". Grapevine; April 1951; 7(11): pp3-4.
Alexander, Associate Editor of The Saturday Evening Post, talks about "Feel-Gud" pills people all around the world are in need of and how AA members once tried alcohol and failed but now use faith. The author of the famous 1941 SEP article about AA remarks about the "drunken" conduct of American foreign relations and human suffering during the Korean War.

219. Alexander, Jack. "Jack Alexander of Saturday Evening Post Fame Thought AA's Were Pulling His Leg". Grapevine; May 1945; 1(12): pp1 & 8.
Note: The writer relates details of researching his famous Saturday Evening Post March 1, 1941, article about AA.

220. Alexander, Michael. "Is AA's Future Guaranteed?". Grapevine; April 1981; 37(11): pp26-29.
Alexander discusses the creation of the Twelve Traditions and the initial unwillingness of AA members to accept them. He describes Bill W's early efforts to win approval of the Traditions and offers his own support of them as the unifying force that assures the ongoing survival of the Fellowship.

221. Anderson, Dwight (Director of Public Relations, Medical Society of State of New York). "Committee for Education on Alcoholism Historic Event, Says Dwight Anderson.". Grapevine; Oct. 1944; 1(5): p1.
This Grapevine issue is the first public announcement of the birth of the National Committee for Education on Alcoholism (later the National Council on Alcoholism (NCA). Marty Mann (one of the first women in AA) was named executive director. Anderson said "AA made possible such an institution as this by first laying the groundwork in its thoroughly-proved and tested rationale for group therapy, which convinced people that the alcoholic can be helped."
NCEA's mission was to inform the public that the alcoholic is sick, can be helped, is worth helping and the responsibility for the problem rests with the healing professions, health authorities and the general public.

222. Aring, Charles D., M.D. "The Jekyll-And-Hyde in All of Us". Grapevine; Oct. 1962; 19(5): pp10-15.
Note: Reprint from The American Scholar.
"Would AA's Fourth Step have changed the ending of the famous old horror story?" a famous doctor thinks it might have!

223. B. L. "You Mean, Just Let Anybody In?". Grapevine; Sept. 1976; pp26-29.
B.L. describes the 1945 incident of a man who showed up at AA in order to discuss the AA's Third Tradition: "The only requirement for AA membership is a desire to stop drinking." The man described himself as "a jailbird, mental case, narcotics addict, homosexual, and alcoholic." (NALGAP 341).

224. Baker, Russell. "Bad News for the Old Booze School". Grapevine; May 1966; 22(12): pp17-19.
Note: Reprint.
New York Times columnist Baker envisions the American Family 20 years in the future when children are required to learn social drinking techniques, "boozology," in school.

225. Baker, Russell. "The Drugcase Is Getting Heavier". Grapevine; Sept. 1966; 23(4): pp12-14.
Note: Reprinted from NYT.
New York Times columnist Baker takes a satirical look at a couple as they pack all the pills that they think they will need for a long trip.

226. Bauer, William W., Dr. "AA + GP = Progress". in: AA Today. First ed. New York: Grapevine; 1960: pp 20-22.
Director of Health Education for the American Medical Assocation, Dr. Bauer describes the physical illness due to drinking that general practioneers must be prepared to treat and the critical role that they can play in motivating alcoholic patients to seek AA assistance. He urges doctors to maintain regular contact with alcoholic patients so they can continue to reinforce the suggestion of an AA affiliation. He endorses the cooperative efforts of the clergy, medical profession and AA in treating alcoholism.

227. Bell, R. G., M.D. "Alcohol and Your Brain". Grapevine; March 1963; 19(10): pp11-16.
Physical and psychological effects of alcohol on the brain reviewed.

228. Bisher, M.D., William. "A Doctor's 12 Observations". Grapevine; Nov. 1970; 27(6): pp12-13.
Twelve insights about alcoholism from a doctor who worked with AA and alcoholics for 20 years.

229. Bisher, William, M.D. "Alcohol and Pills". Grapevine; May 1970; 26(12): pp7-8.
Note: Reprint from AMA's American Medical News.
"This is an appeal for discontinuing the common practice of prescribing or dispensing addictive medications to known alcoholics.".

230. Blaine, Howard T., Ph.D. "The Alcoholic Personality". Grapevine; June 1963; 20(1): pp32-37.
Psychologist discusses personality traits which are commonly observed among alcoholics.

231. Blanton, Smiley, M.D. "The Secret of 'Easy Does it". Grapevine; July 1963; 20(2).
Psychiatrist offers advice on using the unconscious and divine powers to help solve problems.

232. Block, Marwin A., M.D. "Alcoholism and Alcoholics Anonymous". Grapevine; Feb. 1974; 30(9): pp12-14.
Block discusses AA activities and makes recommendations for strengthening the Fellowship. He suggests a program that maintains the interest of successfully-recovered alcoholics so that they will remain active in AA and provide incentive for newcomers.

233. Block, Marvin A., M.D. "The Doctor's View". Grapevine; June 1953; 10(2): pp19-21.
The noted medical authority on alcoholism gives his views on the use of sedatives and the alcoholic.

234. Block, Marwin A., M.D. "Don't Place Alcohol on a Pedestal". Grapevine; Oct. 1976; 33(5): pp15-17.
Block, Chairman of the AMA's Committee on Alcoholism (1956), criticizes the goal of teaching alcoholics to become social drinkers. He denounces all research that is based on the premise that alcohol is a social necessity that even its known addicts should learn to accomodate and opposes public financing of any research of this kind.

235. Bloom, Herbert, Rabbi. "Non-Alcoholics Need To Listen". Grapevine; July 1958; 15(2): pp26-28.
The non-alcoholic may be limited in helping alcoholics if a few simple rules are not followed. "The value of communication is to produce the common area of meaning between two human beings. To me, it seems that communication between the alcoholic and the non-alcoholic should engender in the minds of both the mutual enterprise of building a better life with each respecting, if not always understanding the other," the Rabbi writes.

236. Bloom, Herbert, Rabbi. "A Rabbi Speaks". Grapevine; May 1954; 10(10): pp38-40.
Rabbi Bloom discusses the attitudes developed by AA members and their usefulness for people who are addicted not to alcohol, but to materialism, selfishness and arrogance. He recommends that non-alcoholics try to live by the program so that they can better understand themselves and the recovering alcoholic.

237. Bloom, Herbert I., Rabbi, Ph.D. "Twelfth Step". Grapevine; October 1951; 8(5): pp24-25.
Rabbi Bloom, of Kingston, New York, interprets the AA program in a poem which begins: "I should turn my life to God, and teach others the way.".

238. Brisolara, Ashton, M.Ed. "Self-Help Groups". Grapevine; Aug. 1975; 32(1): pp26-31.
Brisolara, Executive Director, Committee on Alcoholism and Drug Abuse for Greater New Orleans, Inc., discusses the common objectives of self-help groups and the general mechanisms by which these groups operate. Specific attention is paid to these mechanisms as they are applied by AA. Frequent criticisms and misinterpretations of the program are evaluated and cooperative efforts of AA and nonalcoholic professionals are endorsed.

239. Brodie, Donald W., M.D. "Alcoholism - A Medical Bombshell". Grapevine; Feb. 1963; 19(9): pp26-30.
AA is part of a 29-year-old revolution in our thinking about alcoholism.

240. Cassels, Louis. "As Our Friends See Us". Grapevine; Jan. 1975; 31(8): pp22-23.
Note: Reprint.
Cassels, UPI religion correspondent, applauds the rapid growth and progress made by AA and describes the supportive behavior of its members that has contributed to its great success.

241. Churan, Charles A. "Cure". Grapevine; March 1965; 21(10): pp38-40.
Churan criticized the use of the word "cure" when applied to sober alcoholics because it implies that the "cured" patient is no longer powerless over alcohol and can return to social drinking. He also rejects this term because it presupposes correct diagnosis, which is seldom achieved when alcoholism is involved.

242. Collins, James P., Rev. "Arranging That First Contact". Grapevine; Oct. 1967; 24(5): pp10-11.
Collins discusses the need to help released convicts establish contact with AA groups outside of prison.

243. Cooppan, S., Dr. "Appreciation of AA from South Africa". Grapevine; Oct. 1960; 17(5): pp40-42.
AA's work in Durban, South Africa, cited.

244. Cunningham, Bill. "Bill Cunningham, Top-Flight Columnist, Likes Being An AA 'Side-Room Rooter". Grapevine; January 1945; 1(8): p1.
This writer for The Boston Herald tells of AA saving a drunken baseball star and gratitude from individuals who read about AA in Cunningham's column years before. Cunningham was referring to Rollie, the baseball catcher who broke his anonymity and later slipped.

245. D'Alonzo, C. Anthony, M.D. "The Problem of Alcoholism in Industry". Grapevine; Nov. 1960; 17(6): pp16-21.
Note: Speech delivered at 25th Anniversary Convention of AA, Long Beach, California, by the Medical Director of E. I. duPont Co., Wilmington, Delaware.
Alcoholism as disease discussed.

246. Dancey, M.D., T. E. untitled. Grapevine; Oct. 1968; 24(5): Oct. 1968.
Dancey was a non-alcoholic Trustee, AA General Service Board; Chief of Service/Psychiatry at Queen Mary Veterans Hospital, Montreal, Canada; and Senior Psychiatrist at Montreal General Hospital. He discusses the advantages and disadvantages of psychotherapy for alcoholics. He concludes that treatment can be valuable for sober AA members who use it to cope with problems other than drinking. He stresses the dangers of trying to substitute psychotherapy for the AA program. He also notes similarities between group psychotherapy and AA meetings.

247. Dancey, T. E., M.D. "Do AA's Need Psychiatry?". Grapevine; Nov. 1966; 23(6): pp6-10.
Dancey, a psychiatrist, questions the compatability of psychotherapy and the Twelve Step program of AA. He feels that individual psychotherapy fails completely when applied to alcoholism because this treatment method produces high levels of anxiety that frequently prompt alcoholics to drink. He recommends psychotherapy only for those alcoholics who rigidly adhere to the Twelve Step program but need help for problems other than drinking.

248. de Kruif, Paul (1890-1971). "God Is Not Yourself". Grapevine; July 1951; 8(11): pp3-11.
This American bacteriologist and Reader's Digest Editor believes "AA's aren't ordinary human beings because they've all been so near dead it seems spooky that they're still alive and healthy. Every AA has first nearly died of the disease which later he becomes the master physician." A case study of "Earl's" life as an AA and the dangers of scientific explanations of alcoholism are discussed.

249. Deering, G. E., M.D. "Doctor, Why Can't I Stop Drinking?". Grapevine; Aug. 1970; 27(3): pp7-10.
A psychiatric perspective of the usefulness of AA membership for those suffering from drinking problems is the theme of this article. "AA substitutes a worthwhile experience for guilt and remorse.".

250. Delahanty, Edward J., M.D. (doctors and AA) untitled. Grapevine; Feb. 1969; 24(9): pp 26-31.
Delahanty, Chairman, Colorado Commission on Alcoholism, and Advisor, Alcoholism Div. of the Colorado State Health Dept., explains how physicians can use AA to maximize their success in treating alcoholic patients. He suggests that doctors become intimately acquainted with AA whenever possible so they can act as allies in treating alcoholism. He describes three phases of alcoholic recovery that doctors should be aware of and urges caution when prescribing medicine to alcoholics.

251. Demeret, William, Dr. "Dreaming is Good for You". Grapevine; July 1962; 19(2): pp37-40.
Note: Reprint from Science magazine.
Dreams, even "drunk dreams," are necessary to health.

252. Dojc, Josip, Dr. untitled. Grapevine; Oct. 1959; 16(5): pp27-29.
This Yugoslavian psychiatrist discusses alcoholism treatment at Zgreb Institute in Yugoslavia.

253. Dole, V. P., M.D. "AA, Drug Addiction and Pills". Grapevine; Oct. 1972; 29(5): pp2-4.
Dr. Dole, Nonalcoholic Trustee, AA General Service Board, discusses AA's capacity to treat people with dual addictions and with addictions to substances other than alcohol. He maintains that AA must remain faithful to its specific mission to help sick alcoholics by allowing other agencies to treat other addictions. He also urges AA to help alcoholic drug addicts cope with their alcoholism and to accept their need for medication to control narcotics addiction as they would any other medical problem.

254. Dowd, Alfred E. "A Twentieth Century Miracle". Grapevine; Nov. 1960; 17(6): pp22-28.
This speech by the Warden of Indiana State Prison was delivered at the 25th Anniversary Convention of AA, in Long Beach, California. In it, Dowd reviews A.A.'s work in prisons.

255. Dowling, Edward J., S.J. "A.A. Steps for the Underprivileged Non-A.A.". In: AA Today. First ed. New York: Grapevine; 1960: pp 64-65.
Note: This Jesuit priest, longtime friend of A.A., shows how the Twelve Steps of A.A. can be effectively applied to any problem in life and proves it with his own recovery from 240-pound gluttony to 180-pound abstinence from starch, butter, salt and sugar, his own "alcoholic gluttony." Fr. Dowling died shortly before this was published.

256. Dowling, Edward, S.J. "Three Dimensions of AA". Grapevine; July 1955; 12(2): pp26-28.
This Jesuit priest from St. Louis believes the Twelfth Step indicates three jobs that outline the three dimensions of AA. They are: Breadth - "Carry this message to other alcoholics." Depth - "Having had a spiritual awakening as the result of these steps." and Length - "Practiced these principles in all our affairs." These areas are discussed by Father Dowling with the deepest dimension of AA being - God's love and His grace.

257. "Dr. Bob's Last Major Talk". Grapevine; 1973; 30(1): p2.
Note: [The Cleveland, Ohio, AA central office has published for many years a 19-pamphlet of the full text of his last talk.].
Robert H. Smith, M.D., (August 8, 1879 - November 16, 1950), A.A.'s beloved co-founder, gave this, his last major talk, at the First International Convention of Alcoholics Anonymous in Cleveland, Ohio, on July 30, 1950. Perhaps the most famous and often quoted part of his talk is the following: "But there are two or three things that flashed into my mind on which it would be fitting to lay a little emphasis; one is the SIMPLICITY of our program. Let's not louse it all up with Freudian complexes and things that are interesting to the scientific mind but have very little to do with our actual AA work. Our Twelve Steps when simmered dow to the last, resolve themselves into the words LOVE and SERVICE. We understand what love is and we understand what service is.

So let's bear those two things in mind."
Bill Wilson's writings, organization skills, longer life, and inquisitive explorations into many areas perhaps seem to overshadow his co-founder but for the immense counterweight of this, Dr. Bob's last talk.

258. Duffy, Clinton. "I didn't want to want to...". in: AA Today. First ed. New York: Grapevine; 1960: pp 58-60.
Duffy, the former warden of San Quentin Prison, tells how Prison Groups offer alcoholic inmates a means for recovery from the disease that very often is directly responsible for their criminal records. San Quentin, under Warden Duffy, pioneered the first AA Prison Group in 1941. He cites the "hundreds who have been helped" by the AA program in prisons over the past 18 years.

259. Durfee, Charles H., Ph.D. "To Drink or Not to Drink". Grapevine; June 1952; 9(1): pp40-44.
Note: (see separate book listing under Durfee).
Exerpts from the 1942 book by Durfee are discussed.

260. Edwards, G., M.D. "The Puzzle of A.A.". Grapevine; April 1965; 21(11): pp26-31.
Edwards discusses the success of AA by comparing it to group psycho-therapy. He emphasizes the ways that AA differs from ordinary group psychotherapy, particularly in its ability to function with no visible leaders.

261. Elkins, Harry K., M.D. "Our Mutual Sins". Grapevine; April 1966; 22(11): pp28-33.
Dr. Elkins, Director of the Santa Clara County Alcoholic Rehabilitation Clinic in San Jose, California, lists seven sins, or errors, that are committed by non-alcoholic professionals who treat alcoholics or by sober AA members. These errors drive the two groups apart in their efforts to help alcoholics. Elkins expresses dismay at the extremist attitude that you must be an alcoholic to help an alcoholic. He calls upon alcoholics to educate non-alcoholics so the boundaries between the two groups will be erased.

262. Ford, John C., S.J. "Gratitude and Serenity: Two Sides of the Coin of Sobriety". Grapevine; Nov. 1957; 14(6): pp2-6.
Professor of Moral Theology at Weston College, Weston, Mass., Fr. Ford discusses the spiritual aspects of the AA program, including the Serenity Prayer. "It calls for serenity to accept, but courage to act - passivity in activity. Easy does it. But do it!".

263. Ford, John C., S.J. untitled. Grapevine; Nov. 1956; 13(6): pp3-5.
Four reasons are given why alcoholism is a disease.

264. Fosdick, Harry Emerson, Dr. "Those Marvelous 12 Steps". in: AA Today. First ed. New York: Grapevine; 1960: pp69-70. "No words can adequately express the gratitude which many of us feel who have watched with admiration the amazing progress of Alcoholics Anonymous," Dr. Fosdick, Minister Emeritus of Riverside Church, Manhattan, writes in this laudatory article. He praises the Twelve Steps, especially for the avoidance of self-pity, "God as we understand Him" in the AA program, and the basic spirituality of AA principles.

265. Fox, Ruth, M.D. "Al-Anon's Role in the Alcoholic's Home". in: AA Today. First ed. New York: Grapevine; 1960: pp80-83. The Medical Director of the National Council on Alcoholism discusses the plight of the family of an alcoholic and its twin rays of hope, AA and Al-Anon. Dr. Fox was a psychiatrist practicing in the field of alcoholism.

266. Fox, Ruth. "Antabuse". Grapevine; May 1950; 6(12): pp10-11. Note: Dr. Harry M. Tiebout is quoted in this article. Antabuse in the treatment of alcoholism is discussed by this New York psychiatrist.

267. Fox, Ruth, M.D. "Imagine Such a Disease...". Grapevine; Feb. 1967; 23(9): p23.
Note: Reprinted from "Roundabout.".
Fox describes, in a few short paragraphs, the epidemic proportions that alcoholism has reached in this country and the widespread impact that this disease has on various aspects of society. Fox was the Medical Advisor to the National Council on Alcoholism.

268. Fox, Ruth, M.D. "What a Doctor Learned From AA". Grapevine; Jan. 1973; 29(8): pp26-28.
Dr. Fox, Founder and First President, American Medical Society on Alcoholism, endorses AA as the best treatment for alcoholism available. She discusses other methods she has tried with patients who are not responsive to AA and addresses several questions that are frequently asked about these alternative methods.

269. Fox, V., M.D. "Escape". Grapevine; Dec. 1966; 23(7): p14. Fox outlines the differences between constructive and destructive escapes. Most of his recovering alcoholic patients reach a decision that all forms of escape are destructive. Fox describes the constructive use of escape to take time to assess the purpose of one's life and to find reality, not hide from it. He uses the story of Jesus' forty-day stay in the desert to illustrate this.

270. Frost, Earl W. (untitled article). Grapevine; April 1950; 6(11): pp14-15.
Frost, Municipal Court Judge, Kansas City, Missouri, has used referral to AA for public drunkenness cases since 1941. "The judges of the Kansas City Municipal Court heartily support and endorse AA and its most worthwhile objectives.".

271. Gehrmann, G. H., M.D. (untitled). Grapevine; Dec., 1947; 4(7): p3.
The Medical Director of duPont Company reports on progress of AA work in his company.

272. Gitlow, Stanley E., M.D. "A Pharmacological Approach to Alcoholism". Grapevine; Oct. 1968; 24(5): pp12-27.
Associate Clinical Professor of Medicine, Mt. Sinai Medical School, New York, NY, Gitlow describes the biochemical effects of alcohol on the body. He discusses the nature of addiction, the differences between alcohol addiction and alcoholism, and the possibility of a biochemical predisposition to alcoholism. The use of Antabuse and the problems associated with using certain drugs to treat alcoholism are also covered.

273. Golin, Milton. "Pills for the Year 2000". Grapevine; Aug. 1962; 19(3): pp36-37.
Note: Reprint from Medicine at Work.
"AA's have other sources of hope than pills and gadgets - but the medics are working on some weird ones".

274. Greenleaf, Robert K. "Choosing To Be Aware". Grapevine; June 1966; 23(1): pp26-28.
Note: Second of six articles.
The author pinpoints the choice to be aware and foresee. People who live productively can foresee emergencies and plan their actions in advance so they do not act out of panic and stress when urgent situations arise. Greenleaf describes saving a man's life on the train because he was aware of the location of the emergency cord while others had paid no attention to it.

275. Greenleaf, Robert K. "Choosing To Grow". Grapevine; July 1966; 23(2): pp11-13.
Note: Third of six articles.
Discussing the choice to grow, Greenleaf recommends that people continue to pursue goals and create new challenges for themselves even after they have reached a comfortable level of achievement. He urges people to regard all of the circumstances in their lives, good and bad, as opportunities to grow.

276. Greenleaf, Robert K. "Choosing Greatness". Grapevine; Sept. 1966; 23(4): pp26-30.
Note: Fifth in series of six articles.
About the choice to attain greatness within one's sphere of influence, Greenleaf emphasizes that personal greatness is available to anyone who chooses to pursue it and urges people to aim high in their endeavors.

277. Greenleaf, Robert K. "Choosing the Nobler Belief". Grapevine; Oct. 1966; 23(5): pp27-31.
Note: The final article in a series of six.
In his final article, Greenleaf discusses an over-arching choice that every person makes regarding a faith to live by. Every person chooses a central belief that governs all other choices. Greenleaf discusses his over-arching choice to believe in a universal level of consciousness. He periodically withdraws to this level to evaluate his choices from a new perspective.

278. Greenleaf, Robert K. "Seven Choices for Mature Living". Grapevine; May 1966; 22(12): pp2-5.
Note: The first article in a series of six.
Greenleaf discusses one of six definite choices a person can make about his or her life. The first is the choice to be responsible. He describes the acceptance of responsibility as both a necessary condition for a full life and a frequent road to recovery from illness. For alcoholics, recovery begins when one assumes responsbility for oneself and fellow alcoholics. Greenleaf also relates the story of a former student who salvaged her marriage by accepting responsibility for its success.

279. Greenleaf, Robert K. "Two More Choices". Grapevine; August 1966; 23(3): p22.
Note: Fourth in series of six articles.
The author discusses the choice to be human and to be ourselves. To be human, an individual must strive to make the lives of others more rewarding no matter how intolerable his or her own life seems to be. To be ourselves, each person must choose to find a unique mission in life rather than conform to popular stereotypes or to the expectations of others.

280. Grimmer, B., M.D. "The Essential Ingredient in Recovery". Grapevine; Sept. 1974; 31(4): pp18-20.
Grimmer discusses the inability of doctors to work with alcoholic patients on a spiritual level. He discusses AA's unique ability to meet the spiritual needs of its members and attributes the success of the Fellowship to its emphasis on "a loving God.".

281. Grutchfield, Lee A., M.Ed. "What AA Meetings Taught a Non-AA Counselor". Grapevine; Dec. 1977; 34(7): pp14-18.
Grutchfield describes the positive effects that participation in AA through open meetings and Al-Anon meetings has had on her personal life and her career as a counselor. She encourages others in the field of alcoholism education or treatment to develop close ties with AA.

282. Haggard, H. W./Jellinek, E. M. "Two Yale Savants Stress Alcoholism as a True Disease". Grapevine; June 1944; 1(1): p1.
Note: First Article, First Page, First Issue of the Grapevine. The founders of the Yale Center of Alcohol Studies (now Rutgers) report on the first two months of Yale Plan Clinics in New Haven and Hartford, Connecticut, and treatment of 70 alcoholics who are brought into contact with local AA groups. The article ends with "the problem of the alcoholic is too great to be solved by any one person or even by any one organization. The cooperation of all individuals and all organizations, based on mutual respect and understanding, is needed to bring success to the efforts of all those who are interested in bringing back the alcoholic into the life of the community.".

283. Heard, Gerald. "The Search for Ecstasy". Grapevine; May 1958; 14(12): pp15-17.
"This, then, is what I believe to be the comprehensive meaning of AA. First, it has proved itself to be salvation for those caught by the gravest symptom of our general distress - alcoholism. Next, it has been seen that its twelve step method can be applied to succor those stricken by other distresses for which our educational training give no adequate preparation. Third, since it indicates that because man is made for growth in consciousness as well as conduct and character and so must tire of everything but ecstasy - we must all of us learn how to train ourselves with the exercises that teach us to meet life's accidents as ordeals which, when thus taken, lead to initiation. Only thus can we keep the initiative toward experience. Only thus can all events come to be regarded as opportunities for an embryonic growth, here and now, which prepares us for a maturity yet to come.".

284. Heilig, Henry Max. "What Good Does AA Do In Prison?". Grapevine; March 1962; 18(10): pp22-26.
A noted prison official from Avon Park, Florida, tells why AA members' visits to penal institutions are important work.

285. Hoffer, Abram, M.D./Osmond, Humphry, M.D. "Alcoholism and the Researcher". Grapevine; Jan. 1960; 16(8): pp19-23.
"Therefore, we in research hope that many more AA's will presently appear on the scene, wearing not only the shield of sobriety but carrying also the sword of research in the battle against alcoholism.".

286. Hopkins, Arthur. "Alcoholics Give Famous Producer Moving Experience". Grapevine; Aug. 1944; 1(3).
Hopkins reflects on attending an AA meeting at Webster Hall, an "unforgettable experience" in which he felt the presence of God nearer than he had known before.

287. Huxley, Aldous. "The History of Tension". Grapevine; Nov. 1957; 14(6): pp17-23.
Note: Excerpt from the Annals of the New York Academy of Sciences, May, 1957.
Huxley discusses William James and his book, Varieties of Religious Experience, and alcoholism.

288. Huxley, Aldous. "Man and Reality". in: AA Today. First ed. New York: Grapevine; 1960: pp90-92.
The world famous novelist contributes a philosophical essay around the idea "that we cannot see the moon and the stars so long as we choose to remain within the aura of street lamps and whiskey advertisements." Recommends the "necessity of seeking first the kingdom of God and waiting for all the rest to be added,"which for him lies more in the "divine East" than the decadent West.

289. J. N. "I Want To Belong". Grapevine; Oct. 1977: pp9-11.
J.N. discusses the harmful effects of anti-homosexual humor found in some AA meetings. (NALGAP 433).

290. J. P. "Acceptance is a Two-Way Street". Grapevine; April 1985: pp29-31.
J.P. discusses the lack of understanding that sometimes exists between homosexual members of AA and non-homosexual members. The thesis of the article is that homosexuals need to practice acceptance, too. (NALGAP 304).

291. Jackson, Joan K., Ph.D. "Portrait of An Alcoholic's Family". Grapevine; Oct., 1955; 12(5): pp26-31.
This is the story of a family's progressive decline through alcoholism and its progressive recovery through AA and is a condensation of an article appearing originally in the QJSA published by Yale.

292. Jellinek, E. M. "Letters to Grapevine...". Grapevine; April 1945; 1(11): p2.
Jellinek quotes an 1820 comment on drunkenness.

293. Jellinek, E. M. "Scientist Discusses 2 Points Raised by Wylie's Article". Grapevine; Sept. 1944; 1(4): p3.
The Director of Alcohol Studies, Yale University, discusses the connection between epilepsy and alcoholism, cultural patterns of alcoholism and the role of tension as a factor in drunkenness.

294. Jellinek, E. M., Dr. "A Thought from an Old Friend". in: AA Today. First ed. New York: Grapevine; 1960: p 41.
Jellinek, Co-founder and former Director of the Center of Alcohol Studies, Yale University, discusses his first encounter with AA and the elements of the Fellowship that will assure its survival over time. He also cautions against the dangerous development of excessive pride within groups.

295. Jones, Thomas T., M.D. "A Doctor Takes Inventory". Grapevine; Oct. 1957; 14(5): pp34-36.
This physician discusses alcoholism.

296. K. S. "Exclusive---or More Inclusive?". Grapevine; Oct. 1977.
In this discussion of the role of special purpose groups in AA, the author cites homosexual groups as one example. (NALGAP 531).

297. Keith-Lucas, Alan, Ph.D. "Helping People is a Ticklish Business". Grapevine; June 1962; 19(1).
The author tells how to deal with discouragement when trying to help an alcoholic.

298. Keith-Lucas, Alan, M.D. "Helping People is a Ticklish Business". Grapevine; Dec. 1970; 27(7): pp8-14.
Note: Reprint of paper from The Christian Scholar by Keith-Lucas, Professor of Social Work at the University of North Carolina.
The pitfalls on the road of good intentions are outlined. "To give help really means to offer someone an opportunity to change." Humility is the basis of all helping.

299. Kel L. "Here I Am". Grapevine; Jan. 1980: pp13-14.
Kel, a lesbian, discusses her higher power whom she calls Herhim. But her thesis is that straights in AA can help homosexual alcoholics. (NALGAP 343).

300. Kellermann, Joseph. "A Family Affair". Grapevine; Oct. 1974; 31(5): pp10-12.
Note: Excerpt from the article "AA-A Family Affair" in Addictions, Spring 1974, Vol. 21, No. 1.
Kellermann, Executive Director of the Charlotte, North Carolina, Council on Alcoholism, advises AA to address alcoholism as a family illness and a social disorder. He discusses the enabling effect that families have on alcoholic members when they accept or excuse their drinking problem. He also discusses four steps in the recovery process that the late psychiatrist Dr. Harry M. Tiebout learned from Bill W.

301. Kolodner, George, M.D. "Voyage of Discovery". Grapevine; June 1975; 32(1): pp11-12.
Kolodner discusses the series of events that led him to alter his conception of alcoholism and develop an improved understanding of the illness.

302. Krouse, William, M.D. "Doctor's Report". Grapevine; August 1965; 22(3): pp25-28.
Krouse describes how poorly his training as a general practioneer prepared him for the treatment of alcoholism. He attributes his understanding of the disease to his assocation with AA. He urges other physicians to be more receptive to treating alcoholics and to call upon AA to help them do so.

303. Larrabee, C. B. "Alcohol - A Management Problem". Grapevine; July 1947; 4(2): p6.
Note: Reprint of Printer's Ink, May 9, 1947, editorial.
The problem of executive alcoholism is reviewed by the President of Printer's Ink.

304. Lincoln, Abraham, American President. "Address to the Washington Temperance Society, 1842". Grapevine; Feb. 1964; 20(9): pp6-8.
Note: reprint.
In his address, Lincoln discusses the dilemna of the habitual drunkard as the victim of a disease. Lincoln suggests that alcoholics be treated with compassion and supported in their efforts to abstain. He criticizes reformers who are uncharitable in their definition of alcoholics as immoral, corrupt and a threat to temperate society.

305. Logan, Albert B. "Can We Permit Justice to Remain Blind?". Grapevine; March 1961; 17(10): pp26-29.
Before a Joint Session of the Law Society of England and the American Bar Association, an attorney stresses "the need for the legal profession to recognize alcoholism as a disease.".

306. London, Jack. "Review of John Barleycorn". Grapevine; Nov., 1947; 4(6): p8.
Jack London talks about his novel about alcoholism.

307. MacCormick, Austin H. "Keep AA Alive in Our Jails!". Grapevine; April 1963; 20(11): pp21-23.
MacCormick praises the Fellowship for existing AA growth in jails and institutions and calls for more growth.

308. MacLeod, Alastair, M.D. "Can Psychiatry Help?". Grapevine; May 1962; 18(12): pp35-38.
Is alcoholism a psychiatric disorder or is psychiatry powerless to help the alcoholic who does not wish to be helped? Dr. MacLeod's views on the role of psychiatry in the treatment of alcoholism.

309. Magnum, Eugene K. "Court Class on Alcoholism". Grapevine; May 1965; 21(12): pp33-34.
Magnum, Chief Magistrate, Phoenix City Court, Arizona, describes the weekly Phoenix Court Class on Alcoholism. The class is attended by drunks who are jailed that day or a few days prior to it so they can be released for the meeting. Members of their families and several AA members also attend. Court class is conducted like a regular AA meeting. AA members present encourage the drunk to join the program. Another Phoenix City Court program suspends the sentences of some drunks and gives them the opportunity to join AA.

310. Maher, Richard. "How It Goes with AA in Calcutta". Grapevine; Nov. 1967; 24(6): pp13-16.
A non-alcoholic newspaperman, Maher describes his experience with AA in Calcutta and the difficulties associated with establishing the Fellowship in that city in India.

311. Malcolm, Andrew. "As Others See Us". Grapevine; June 1976; 33(1): pp37-38.
Note: Excerpted from "What's in Store for the Chemophilic Society," Addiction, Winter, 1975, issue.
Malcolm advises AA to continue to operate under the fundamental principle that members must simply stop drinking without necessarily discovering why they were compelled to become alcoholics. He suggests that rehabilitation clinics adopt the AA concept of sponsorship. He also explains his opposition to the suggestion that alcoholics might reasonably seek to become social drinkers.

312. Manning, Ernest C. "Thoughts of a Premier". in: AA Today. First ed. New York: Grapevine; 1960: pp 52-53.
The Premier of Alberta, Canada, reflects that the misconceptions, stigma, and concealment of alcoholism are being swept away through a rapidly-growing awareness of the problem and its time-tested treatment, namely AA. Cites the progress AA has made in his Province of Alberta.

313. Martin, Robert A., Fr. "In Praise". Grapevine; October 1949; 6(5): pp20-22.
Father Martin predicts AA will help in the definite solution of other social ills if AA doesn't fall prey to the temptations which have caused disunity in the church.

314. Maxwell, Milton A. "Changing Patterns of Sponsorship". Grapevine; Sept. 1975; 32(4): pp12-15.
Maxwell, a Class A Trustee of the AA General Service Board, discusses the growing tendency of new AA members to have non-AA professional contact before coming to AA. He suggests that AA sponsors respond to this trend by recognizing the point in recovery that newcomers are at when they arrive at AA and by assisting in the transition from a treatment center program to the AA program. He cautions against criticizing non-AA professional help for which AA newcomers may feel grateful.

315. McQueen, Spencer D., Rev. "AA Is the Chaplain's Ally". Grapevine; June 1960; 17(1): pp14-18.
The author, Senior Protestant Chaplain at Wheelus Air Force Base in Libya, relates his working with an AA group at an Air Force base in Florida.

316. Melville, Iadbelle. "Canada's New Kind of Prison". Grapevine; March 1963; 19(10): pp36-38.
A reporter views AA's work in Canadian prisons.

317. Menninger, Karl, Dr. "An A.A. Appraisal". in: AA Today. First ed. New York: Grapevine; 1960: pp14-15.
Menninger, Chief of Staff, Menninger Foundation, Topeka, Kansas, discusses the difficulties and rewards of medical professionals who treat alcoholics. He endorses AA as a non-medical approach to treating alcoholism that is more successful than any other known treatment. He also discusses the effects of defining alcoholism as a sickness in the treatment process.

318. Menninger, Karl A., M.D. "The Vital Balance". Grapevine; July 1965; 22(2): pp13-16.
Menninger discusses the univeral need to maintain a balance of tension. When tensions accumulate, the threat of disorganization develops. This causes the active alcoholic to drink. The recovering one learns to cope with imbalance without drinking. Menninger also discusses the role of AA in persuading alcoholics to direct their self-love and self-indulgence toward others like themselves who need help.

319. Miller, J. P. "The Private Life of Curly Baines". in: AA Today. First ed. New York: Grapevine; 1960: pp88-89.
Miller, author of The Days of Wine and Roses and other major TV and film productions, contributes a fictional bar scene to AA Today. The rationalizations an alcoholic deludes himself with are portrayed, amid many martinis.

320. Moore, M.D. "The Treatment of Alcoholism". Grapevine; Feb., 1954; 10(9): pp26-32.
Dr. Moore discusses the physical and psychological approaches to the treatment of alcoholism. He defines alcoholics as sick people and describes the roles that general practioneers, psychiatrists, family members and AA play in their recovery. He urges the development of an enlightened public attitude toward alcoholism as a disease and cooperation between the medical profession and AA in its treatment.

321. Mortenson, Clemens. (untitled article). Grapevine; April 1945; 1(11): p2.
Note: Mortenson is also cited on page 10 of the March, 1946, Grapevine.
The personnel manager of the American Hardware Corp. said: "As we in industry turn to technical experts for advice in any given field, so we can now turn with confidence to AA for help in dealing with our alcoholics.".

322. Mowrer, O. Hobart, M.D. "How `White' Is a `White Lie?". Grapevine; Sept. 1962; 19(4): pp10-15.
A psychiatrist comments on the "honesty part.".

323. Mowrer, O. Hobart, Ph.D. "Make Friends With Your Conscience". Grapevine; Feb. 1963; 19(9): pp13-17.
Psychologist reviews his opinions on alcohol use, misconceptions held by the public, and his work with AA. "In fact, one of secrets of the success of Alcoholics Anonymous is that it helps individuals achieve a real experience of community instead of the illusory one that intoxication produces.".

324. Mowrer, O. Hobart, Ph.D. "Sponsor, Be Yourself". Grapevine; May 1963; 19(12): pp2-5.
"It is not enough for the `sponsor' to be willing to hear another person's admission of wrongdoing, he must also be willing and able to share in the confession of sin.".

325. Naylor, Kenneth, Archdeacon, D.D. "A.A. and the Archdeacon". in: AA Today. First ed. New York: Grapevine; 1960: pp 93. The Montreal, Canada, minister notes the cheerfulness, thankfulness, mutual support and un-self-consciousness of AA members. He expresses his gratitude that a "big tough like Dave" can do a better job of helping a fellow alcoholic than he, a man of the cloth, could do.

326. Niebuhr, Reinhold. "Letter to AA from...". in: AA Today. First ed. New York: Grapevine; 1960: p 65. "I have always told the people in the Church that AA was a great witness to the power of grace...(AA) prevents self-righteousness which so frequently mars the life of Christians...these (AA) achievements are tremendous in the history of religion and in the history of therapeutic medicine.".

327. Niebuhr, Reinhold, Dr. "The Serenity Prayer...its origins traced...". Grapevine; Jan., 1950; 6(8): pp6-7. Niebuhr, of the Union Theological Seminary, New York City, remarks on his writing of the Serenity Prayer in 1932.

328. Norris, J. L. "Doctors and A.A.". Grapevine; 1968; 24(5): p4.

329. Norris, Jack, Dr. "Guest Editorial". Grapevine; April 1959; 15(11): p46. Norris comments on the 2nd Tradition.

330. Norris, John L., M.D. "1967-1977: The Challenge to AA". Grapevine; Nov. 1967; 24(6): pp5-8. Norris, Chairman of the AA General Service Board, identifies the primary AA challenge to spread the program to suffering alcoholics. He suggests several ways to meet this challenge. Particular emphasis is placed on the value of befriending professionals who may refer alcoholics to the program.

331. Norris, John L., M.D. "Acting within the Traditions". Grapevine; Feb. 1972; 20(9): pp15-16. Norris, Nonalcoholic Chairman, AA General Service Board, urges AA members to stimulate public acceptance of alcoholism as a treatable illness. He argues that public interest in alcoholism will pressure the medical profession to give it greater priority as a disease and to treat alcohol-related medical emergencies more seriously. He also urges individual AA members to cooperate with agencies that help alcoholics in areas beyond the scope of AA.

332. Norris, John L., M.D. "Alcoholism in Industry". Grapevine; March 1951; 7(10): pp14-18.
Note: This article is a reprint of a paper presented at the Massachusetts Public Health Association, meeting at Amherst, Mass., June 16, 1950.
Norris, Medical Director, Eastman Kodak Company, discusses the effect of alcoholism on industry, how AA can help employees in industry, and the work of AA at Eastman Kodak. Norris states, although adequate, treatment of alcoholics must be improved: "Preventing must be the goal of Public Health. Public education is, in this field also, our own most effective tool. Here is our challenge and our duty.".

333. Norris, John L., M.D. "Changing Attitudes and New Hope". Grapevine; Jan. 1974; 30(8): pp30-31.
The Nonalcoholic Chairman of the AA General Service Board reports on the progress that AA is making in the military based on observations made during a visit to four U.S. Air Force bases in Europe. He also discusses certain problems that a military career creates for recovering alcoholics.

334. Norris, John L., M.D. "The General Service Board Proposals & Recommendations, 1965". Grapevine; Jan. 1966; 22(8): pp3-7.
Norris, Chairman of the AA General Service Board, presents the Board's proposals to the General Service Conference for changes in the Board's structure. The recommendations concern the Class A/Class B ratio of Trustees and the term of office served by those who are Class A. An increase in the number of Regional Trusteeships in the U.S. and Canada is also advised. The proposed recommendations were subject to the approval of the 1966 Conference.

335. Norris, John L., M.D. "The Hazards of AA's Counseling for Pay". Grapevine; Oct. 1970; 27(5): pp2-3.
Norris, the Nonalcoholic Chairman, AA General Service Board, recommends to AA members interested in paid counseling of alcoholics receive competent educational training and have at least two to three years sobriety. "AAs are needed in these jobs. No one can do them as well if the AAs who go into them are prepared.".

336. Norris, John L., M.D. "A Look at A.A.". Grapevine; Nov. 1965; 22(6): pp17-23.
Norris, the Chairman of the AA General Service Board, reviews the vast expansion of the AA movement during its first 30 years. He applauds its success in reaching isolated alcoholics in prisons and remote areas around the world. He also discusses the skeptical attitude of many AA members toward the medical profession and urges them to be more flexible in these attitudes. He recommends AA to professionals as an essential component of the treatment of alcoholism.

337. Norris, John L., M.D. "Our Primary Purpose and the Special-Purpose Group". Grapevine; 34(5): pp6-9.
Norris, Chairman of the AA General Service Board, addresses the issue of special-purpose AA groups for people who have common interests in addition to alcoholism. He distinguishes between special purpose groups and special purpose meetings and discourages the formation of groups that are not open to every alcoholic with a desire to stop drinking. He encourages special-purpose meetings devoted to the interests of a specific group of alcoholics as long as all alcoholics are welcome.

338. Norris, John L., M.D. "Sharing Recovery". Grapevine; April 1964; 20(1): pp13-14.
Norris, Chairman of AA's General Service Board since 1961 and non-alcoholic Trustee of AA since 1951, discusses the attempts of industrial physicians to understand alcoholism and to recognize its early symptoms so they çan try to prevent workers from becoming alcoholics. He urges recovering alcoholics in AA to invite non-alcoholic professionals to meetings so that they can develop an understanding of how AA works. He also discussed personal successes and failures he has witnessed.

339. Norris, John L., M.D. "Sponsor Your Doctor". Grapevine; Jan. 1976; 32(8): pp8-9.
Norris, Nonalcoholic Chairman of the AA General Service Board, urges AA members to share their experience of coping successfully with alcoholism with the clergymen, nonalcoholic professionals, and others who have tried to help them so that these people can develop a better understanding of the disease.

340. Norris, John L., M.D. "Three Doctors Speak". Grapevine; Dec., 1953; 10(7): p6.
Norris advises AA members on how to help their doctors understand alcoholism.

341. North, John W. (untitled). Grapevine; Feb. 1975; 31(9): pp12-13.
North, Director, Nebraska Division on Alcoholism, comments on the multiplicity of definitions of "the AA way" that have resulted in stereotypes and misinterpretations of this concept. He broadly defines the AA way as a plan that has its origin in surrender and calls for living each day under the guidance of the Twelve Steps.

342. Olivere, Peter J., M.D. "An Aid to Emotional Sobriety". Grapevine; Dec. 1964; 21(7): pp26-30.
Dr. Olivere describes a method of avoiding anxiety and tension that can cause worry-related illnesses such as ulcers, insomnia and alcoholism. The "Decisive Thinking" method teaches individuals to learn to control abnormal tensions by using worry-avoidance techniques. The most important principles of the method are listed in the article.

343. "One Size Fits All". Grapevine; March 1981: p35.
We can infer that the anonymous author of this letter is a Black lesbian. She argues that the AA program works because alcoholics' similarities are greater than their differences. She concludes: "I am not a gay alcoholic or a black alcoholic or a female alcoholic. I am just an alcoholic." (NALGAP 463).

344. "The Only Requirement...". Grapevine; May 1975: p17.
The author, a lesbian, focuses her remarks on AA's Third Tradition: "The only requirement for AA membership is a desire to stop drinking." (NALGAP 464).

345. Oursler, Fulton. "Charming is the Word for Alcoholics". Grapevine; July, 1944; 1(2): p1.
The Senior Editor of Reader's Digest says AA's are charming due to their sense of humor, of universal truth, sensitivity, and imagination which is relected in their service to God.

346. Panjwani, Harry K., M.D. "Treating the Total Person". Grapevine; Dec. 1974; 31(7): pp22-23.
Dr. Panjwani, a psychiatrist, discusses the importance of caring for the needs of the alcoholic beyond that of attaining sobriety. He emphasizes certain emotional needs that must be fulfilled if recovery is to be complete.

347. Parker, Sam, M.D. "Dr. Sam Parker of Kings County Suggests 'Criteria For AA Work in Hopitals". Grapevine; March 1945; 1(10): pp 1 & 8.
Parker, Chief of Psychiatric Division of Kings County Hospital, Brooklyn, NY, states "all hospitals should be encouraged to develop wider cooperation with AA in planned programs of handling alcoholics.".

348. Paton, Alan. (untitled). Grapevine; Oct. 1959; 16(5): pp9-11.
The author of "Cry the Beloved Country" relates his experiences of AA in South Africa.

349. Peale, Norman Vincent. "Do You Yearn for Fellowship?". Grapevine; October 1947; 4(5): p15.
This is a reprint of September Guideposts magazine article about alcoholics and AA members longing for fellowship.

350. Peale, Norman Vincent. "Speech". Grapevine; Dec., 1947; 4(7): p.14.
The pastor of the Marble Collegiate Reformed Church, New York City, speaks at the 13th Annual AA banquet in New York City, Nov. 6, 1947. "Alcoholics Anonymous is not an organization. It is a movement. Moreover, it is one of the greatest movements for good of our generation.".

351. Perelman, S. J. "The Meditations of Old Mr. Perelman on 'Dynamic Drunks". Grapevine; Nov., 1944; 1(6): p1.
The famous American humorist, writer of Marx Brothers film scripts, and New Yorker magazine contributor, reflects on his negative encounters over the years with writers who drank too much alcohol.

352. Perrier, Hector. "Across the Border". in: AA Today. First ed. New York: Grapevine; 1960: p 30.
The Judge of Superior Court, Montreal, Quebec, Canada, congratulates AA on its many accomplishments achieved during its first 25 years.

353. Potter, Milton G., M.D. "Alcoholism - A Challenge to the Medical Profession". Grapevine; April 1949; 5(11): pp5-7.
Note: Reprinted from the New York State Journal of Medicine, Vol. 48, No. 24, Dec.15, 1948.
Potter, Chairman, Committee on Problems of Alcoholism, Medical Soceity of State of New York, reviewed the New York State plan on Alcoholism and writes that "credit must be given to the Alcoholics Anonymous movement for spark-plugging the medical profession into action.".

354. Powdermaker, Florence, M.D. "Dr. Powerdermaker Discusses the Role of a Psychiatrist in Alcoholics Anonymous". Grapevine; Feb., 1945; 1(9): pp 1 & 8.
The doctor is supportive of AA's 12 Steps to help the alcoholic with his personality but psychiatric help may be necessary for AA's in dealing with life problems during childhood and adolesence that were not resolved.

355. Pryka, Mary. "Textbooks Are Not Enough". Grapevine; May 1972; 28(12): pp35-36.
A nonalcoholic college student speaks of her experiences working in an alcoholism rehabilitation center and expresses her hope that recovering alcoholic and nonalcoholic professionals will take united actions against alcoholism.

356. Roth, Robert S., S.J. "William James and Alcoholics Anonymous". Grapevine; Aug. 1967; 24(3): pp26-31.
Note: Fr. Roth was Associate Professor of Philosophy at Fordham University in New York and author of "The Religious Philosophy of William James" (Thought, June, 1966).
Roth, a Jesuit priest, discusses the Jamesian philosophy of pragmatism and its impact on the thought of Bill W. He also describes the role of a Higher Power in AA and the influence that James had on the formation of that concept in AA.

357. Rotman, D. B., M.D. "Alcoholism as a Social Disease". Grapevine; June 1945; 2(1): p6.
Note: Partial reprint of Rotman's A.M.A.Journal March 10, 1945, article of same title.
He lists reasons for the phenomenal growth of AA, predicts no limit to AA's expansion. Adolph Meyer's, M.D., 1932 statement of an AA-type movement starting is also quoted (AA was founded in 1935).

358. Ruark, Robert C. "A Hangover for Every Type". Grapevine; April 1946; 2(11): p8.
Note: The Scripps-Howard staff writer tells about different varieties of hangovers. "A hangover is the unpaid balance on easy credit ectasy.".

359. Sa'adah, Mounoir, Rev. "Encounter with Old Age". Grapevine; Nov. 1962; 19(6): pp20-23.
Remarks on depression and old age.

360. Sa'adah, Mounir R., Rev. "Man is greater ... than anything that can happen to him". Grapevine; 18(11): p2.
An Easter message from a New England minister.

361. Sa'Adah, Mounir, Rev. "Survival". Grapevine; Jan. 1960; 16(8): pp3-5.
The minister of the Universalist Church of Woodstock, Vermont, relates his concept of the spiritual way to serenity.

362. Schwenk, Emerson S. "The New Year's Present". Grapevine; Jan. 1963; 19(8): p15.
Unitarian minister tells of an AA member painting the church meeting room free as a way of rebuilding his life.

363. Seale, Ervin, M.D. "Alcoholic Ills and A.A. Compared to Mankind". Grapevine; January 1947; 3(8): p1.
The president of the International New Thought Alliance relates attending an AA meeting.

364. Seixas, Frank A., M.D. "My First Alcoholic Patient". Grapevine; Sept. 1974; 31(4): pp2-5.
The Medical Director of the National Council on Alcoholism shares the trials and rewards of his relationship with an alcoholic patient who died of cancer after six years of sobriety.

365. Seltzer, Louis B. "I Must Try - Somehow". Grapevine; Feb., 1949; 5(9): pp1-2.
The Editor of The Cleveland Press has seen chronic alcoholism over the years and views it as an illness. He advises those who deal with alcoholic relatives and friends to "stay with them" until they find God.

366. Sessions, P. M. "Self-Indulgence vs. Self-Destruction". Grapevine; March 1966; 22(10): pp30-33.
Sessions responds to an earlier article by Dr. Karl Menninger ("The Vital Balance," July, 1965) that describes alcoholics as people who indulge and love themselves excessively because they are unloved by others. Sessions offers the opinion that alcoholics do not love themselves too much, but, rather, hate themselves and drink to create their own suffering. He defines alcoholism as a symptom of an illness due to the inability to accept and have esteem for the self.

367. "Shattered". Grapevine; April 1986; 42(11): pp29-30.
The author tells about how his life and sobriety were affected when he learned he had AIDS. (NALGAP 566).

368. Sheahen, Allen N. "Definite Economic Service". Grapevine; March 1950; 6(10).
Sheahen, personnel manager of Thompson Products, Cleveland, Ohio, states that "the attitude of our company is one of deepest sympathy with the aims and purpose of AA." The firm has an AA group in its plant which has rescued "20 confirmed drunkards who had become a serious drag on the economic life of our company." Procedures for assisting an employee with a drinking problem are outlined.

369. Shedd, Charlie, Dr. "The Big Hump". Grapevine; Jan., 1955; 11(8): pp38-42.
The minister of the First Presbyterian Church of Ponca City, Oklahoma, writes on his experience hearing Fifth Steps by AA members. Dr. Shedd believes there are three basic ingredients to a good Fifth Step and offers them as a possible guide for those seeking suggestions as to how to go about taking the Fifth Step: 1. belief in a forgiving God. 2. One must want to take it. & 3. a thorough Fourth Step.

370. Sherley, Jack M., Rev. "A Chaplain Looks at AA". Grapevine; April 1960; 16(11): pp7-10.
Note: Reprint from The Key, a publication of the U. S. Public Health Service Hospital, Lexington, Kentucky, where the author is Protestant Chaplain.
"AA, then, is a transforming group experience and set of ideas concrete enough to help, but not constricting and enslaving. I am profoundly grateful for the life-saving power that I have experienced as I have been privileged to share closely in the lives of AA members, especially during the past six years at this hospital.".

371. Shoemaker, Samuel M., Rev. "The Spiritual Angle of AA". Grapevine; Oct., 1955; 12(5): pp2-7.
Note: Reprint of Shoemaker's talk at AA's 20th Anniversary Convention at St. Louis.
The Episcopolian minister outlines the four factors necessary in all genuine spiritual awakenings: conversion, prayer, fellowship and witness and how AA's Twelve Steps facilitate this awakening.

372. Shoemaker, Sam, Rev. "The Spiritual Part of A.A.". Grapevine; Nov. 1960; 17(6): pp9-15.
Minister's speech at the 25th Anniversary Convention of A.A., Long Beach, California. The historical development of A.A. at Shoemaker's Calvary Church is cited. Shoemaker's views on the spiritual meaning of the Twelve Steps are reviewed.

373. Shoemaker, Samuel M., Rev. Canon, D.D. "Those Twelve Steps as I Understand Them". Grapevine; Jan. 1964; 20(8): pp26-34. Rev. Shoemaker discusses the Twelve Steps as universally revelant not only for alcoholics but also for everyone who must cope with problems in their lives. He describes the Steps as great spiritual truths and explains how each one can apply to the life of every individual.

374. Shofstall, W. T. "Alcohol". Grapevine; March 1966; 22(10): pp12-15.
The Dean of Students at Arizona State University lists several basic facts about alcoholism that he feels are crucial to the education of college students. He suggests a program to provide students with information about alcohol and alcoholism that will ultimately discourage them from drinking. A change in the intellectual and spiritual climate is necessary for such a program to work effectively.

375. Silkworth, William Duncan, M.D. "Doctor Calls 'Slip' More Normal than Alcoholic". Grapevine; January 1947; 3(8): pp 1 & 4-5.
"The alcoholic slip" is not a symptom of a psychotic condition. There's nothing "screwy" about it at all. The patient simply didn't follow directions and that's human nature! It's life! It's happening all the time, not merely among alcoholics but among all kinds of people," the doctor writes. Silkworth compares tubercular and cardiac cases with alcoholics who do not follow directions during remission.

376. Silkworth, William D., M.D. "A Prescription for Sobriety". Grapevine; June 1945; 2(1): pp 1 & 8.
An interview with Silkworth, of Towns and Knickerbocker Hospitals in New York, on prevention of "slips.".

377. Simcox, Carrol E., Dr. "An Example of Redemption". Grapevine; April 1951; 7(11): pp11-14.
Reprint of a sermon delivered by rector Simcox at Zion Episcopal Church, Manchester, Vermont. He relates his thoughts about AA after attending AA meetings. The average church member's idea about God's Power of Redemption differs from his AA counterpart. AA members believe "I am redeemed by the power of God from alcoholism and if I am to stay redeemed, I must give it away.".

378. Simpson, Thomas, Rev. "What Does 'Walk Humbly' Mean?". Grapevine; Feb. 1963; 19(9): pp40-41.
The Serenity Prayer is discussed. "When a man has come to recognize God as God, then he also comes to recognize his own limitations.".

379. Sinclair, Upton. "Some Writers I Have Known". Grapevine; May 1963; 19(12): pp26-32.
Excerpt from The Cup of Fury, on alcoholism and writers.

380. Smith, B. "The Lost Commandment, the Dictionary and AA". Grapevine; June 1954; 11(1).
Note: Opening address by the non-alcoholic Chairman of the Board of Trustees of The Alcoholic Foundation to the Fourth Annual General Service Conference of AA.
Smith discusses the difficulties in obeying the Ten Commandments in a leisure-time society that idealizes materialism and personal gains. He describes the Twelve Steps as spiritually-conceived to meet this challenge and explains how the AA Fellowship downplays the materialism that infuses modern society.

381. Smith, Bernard B. "The Conference, AA and Society". Grapevine; August 1953; 10(3): pp3-7.
The non-alcoholic Chairman's of the Board of Trustees of The Alcoholic Foundation speech at the Third General Service Conference April 1953 reprinted. Smith discusses the underlying responsibility and opportunity that the growing maturity of AA brings with it.

382. Smith, Bernard B. "The 'Happiness Part". Grapevine; Nov. 1962; 19(6): pp8-10.
Note: An excerpt from a talk by Bernard B. Smith, the chairman of AA's Board of Trustees, at the Fourth General Service Conference.
"We owe an obligation to society to insure that this ideal Fellowship which we possess survives, that this flame of faith, this beacon light of hope for the world, must never be extinguished.".

383. Smith, Delos. "Alcoholics Can't Forget". Grapevine; June 1962; 19(1): p40.
Research indicates alcoholics may have difficulty in "accentuating the positive.".

384. Smith, Margaret Chase, U.S. Senator. "A Senator Evaluates The Steps and Traditions". in: AA Today. First ed. New York: Grapevine; 1960; pp86-87.
The Maine Republican Senator points out the value of the 12 Steps and Traditions to alcoholics and non-alcoholics alike. "Clearly, AA is a program for a new way of life without alcohol...(and) is working successfully for many tens of thousands of men and women..." she writes.

385. Smith, Robert H., Mrs. "Great Expectations: A New Year's Greeting". Grapevine; Jan. 1948; 4(8): p1.
Greeting from Bill W. & Dr. Bob.

386. Smith, William J., S.J. "A Jesuit Applauds AA". Grapevine; Feb., 1954; 10(9): pp17-19.
Note: Second in a series of religious views of AA by non-alcoholics of various faiths.
Father Smith, a Catholic priest, praises the spiritual nature of the AA program. He refers to AA Twelfth Steppers as apostles to other alcoholics.

387. Stratton, Ray, Chaplain. "The Truth in the Myth". Grapevine; Aug. 1969; 26(3): pp12-14.
Stratton, Director of the Rehabilitation Program for Alcoholics of Western State Hospital, Fort Supply, Oklahoma, explains the meaning of the myth, "only an alcoholic can help an alcoholic." He describes it as being literally false, but spiritually true in suggesting that only one who can identify with or become an alcoholic in spirit can help an alcoholic.

388. Strecken, Edward A., M.D. "Fundamentals of Psychiatry". Grapevine; August 1947; 4(3): p15.
Reprint of part of Strecker's Fundamentals of Psychiatry, pp81-88.

389. Streeseman, Adele E., M.D. "A Psychiatrist's Appreciation of Alcoholics Anonymous". in: AA Today. First. ed. New York: Grapevine; 1960: pp42-44.
Streeseman, President, New York City Medical Society on Alcoholism, discusses the great advantage that AA has over psychoanalysis in its ability to gain the trust of alcoholics and to establish lasting human relations. She attributes AA's success to its insistence on the spiritual growth of its members and discusses the crucial role that spiritual belief plays in recovery. She also discusses AA's role in defining alcoholism as an addiction.

390. Strong, Leonard V., Jr., M.D. "On Anonymity". Grapevine; Dec., 1950; 7(7): pp10-12.
Bill W.'s brother-in-law and Trustee of AA shares his thoughts on anonymity. He believes the Grapevine serves to reflect current thought and activities in AA and can serve to keep principles and policies alive by reiteration.

391. Strunk, H. J. "Potentiation: New Top Killer?". Grapevine; June 1966; 23(1): pp9-17.
Strunk, Editor of Pennsylvania Dept. of Health Journal, reviews existing medical research in the field of potentiation, the combined use of alcohol and drugs. He discusses several reports concerning the increased use of socially-acceptable tranquilizers such as valium in conjunction with alcohol. These reports concur in the finding that women are more likely than men to combine drugs and alcohol.

392. Suck, Richard L. "Alcoholics Make Good Workers". Grapevine; Jan., 1954; 10(8): pp36-36.
The assistant manager of a Pennsylvania hospital discusses the great success of a joint program with the local AA chapter to employ AA members at the hospital in nonprofessional positions.

393. Taylor, G. Aiken, Ph.D. "God and AA". Grapevine; Nov., 1953; 10(6): pp3-4.
Taylor, Pastor of the Northside Presbyterian Church, Burlington, North Carolina, places AA members in two categories: first, those who are very active in AA and apparently try to lose themselves in it, and, second, others who try and find themselves in AA with the help of God.

394. Thurber, James. "The Bear Who Let It Alone". Grapevine; 1971; 28(1): p24.
This modern fable was written by the famous Columbus, Ohio, humorist.

395. Tiebout, Harry M., M.D. "AA is Bridge to Happy Living". Grapevine; May 1948; 4(12): p1.
"The Alcoholics Anonymous Program is a bridge from the negative or egocentric personality of the sick alcoholic to the more desirable affirmative personality of the sober man," comments Dr. Tiebout at open meetings of the Manhattan Inter-Group.

396. Tiebout, Harry M., M.D. "The Act of Surrender in the Therapeutic Process". Grapevine; June 1974; 31(1): pp10-19.
Note: Reprinted from a pamphlet distributed by the National Council on Alcoholism.
Tiebout defines surrender as an act wherein the patient's unconscious feelings of defiance and grandiosity are rendered powerless. He explains how these two qualities function in alcoholics and discusses the nature of the positive emotional phase that follows the act of surrender. He also relates surrender to the therapeutic process and provides observations of patients' behavior during and after surrrender.

397. Tiebout, Harry M., M.D. "Conversion as a Psychological Phenomenon: In the Treatment of the Alcoholic". Grapevine; March 1954; 10(10): pp3-5.
Note: Part I of II, concluded in next issue.
Dr. Tiebout describes the conversion in personality by recovering alcoholics. He lists the characteristic traits of alcoholics prior to conversion and emphasizes the loss of feelings of isolation and loneliness as the most crucial element of the conversion process.

398. Tiebout, Harry M., M.D. "Conversion as a Psychological Phenomenon in the Treatment of An Alcoholic: What Takes Place in an Alcoholic's `Spiritual Awakening?". Grapevine; April 1954; 10(11): pp30-35.
Note: Part II of II.
Tiebout presents and discusses excerpts from several interviews with an institutionalized patient. The excerpts illustrate the gradual personality conversion process explained in Part I of this article. He also lists speculative questions about the concept of conversion that remain to be addressed.

399. Tiebout, Harry M., M.D. "The Pink Cloud and After". Grapevine; Sept., 1955; 12(4): pp2-7.
Note: Psychiatrist's speech at St. Louis 20th AA Anniversary Convention Session: "AA and the Medical Profession.".
The need for alcoholics to reduce their ego and surrender as part of their recovery in the AA program is discussed.

400. Tiebout, Harry M., M.D. "Surrender versus Compliance in Therapy". Grapevine; Sept., 1953; 10(4): pp3-8.
This is an abridgement of the often quoted and reprinted, famous Quarterly Journal of Studies on Alcohol article in Vol. 14, No. 1. Tiebout explains how comnpliance acts as an obstacle to the genuine surrender to alcoholism needed for continued sobriety. He defines compliance as a divided sentiment that expresses agreement without implying great enthusiasm or approval. He describes personality traits that complicate the process of total surrender and lead many alcoholics to a temporary compliance with their drinking problem that produces only short-term sobriety.

401. Tiebout, Harry M., M.D. "Treating the Causes of Alcoholism". Grapevine; Nov. 1963; 20(6): pp9-11.
Dr. Tiebout comments on the AA approach to treating alcoholism. "AA is not to be considered merely a symptomatic remedy, through its emphasis on the spiritual, it really digs much deeper." The spiritual elements of A.A. neutralize the negative feelings and attitudes that foster alcoholism.

402. Tiebout, Harry M., M.D. "What Does 'Surrender' Mean?". Grapevine; April 1963; 20(11): pp30-34.
Tiebout updates his 1955 talk on surrender.

403. Tiebout, Harry M., M.D. "When the Big 'I' Becomes Nobody". Grapevine; ?
Tiebout, Nonalcoholic Trustee of the General Service Board, discusses the importance of A.A. anonymity for the maintenance of sobriety. He hypothesizes that anonymity contributes to the state of humility that recovering alcoholics must possess to remain sober.

404. Tiebout, Harry M., M.D. "Why Psychiatrists Fail with Alcoholics". Grapevine; Sept., 1956; 13(4): pp5-10.
Note: Excerpt from a talk at the National States Conference on Alcoholism in Miami, Florida.
Dr. Tiebout stresses the need for more knowledge for M.D.'s on the disease nature of alcoholism and for more serious study of the illness of alcoholism.

405. Tiebout, Harry M., M.D. "The Wiley Ego". Grapevine; Dec. 1962; 19(7): p17.
This is an excerpt from Tiebout's "The Ego Factors in Surrender in Alcoholism.".

406. Trice, Harrison M., Ph.D. "Why Don't They Join A.A.?". Grapevine; Jan. 1963; 19(8): pp36-39.
Why do so many sick alcoholics avoid the therapy that might help them? What can be done to make them more receptive? These questions are answered by Trice, Professor at Cornell University and an AA Trustee, in this reprint from QJSA. Trice also offers tips to AA's on how to keep newcomers in the AA program.

407. Tunko, Walter F., Rev., D.D. (sermon). Grapevine; July 1948; 5(2).
This excerpt of a sermon was delivered in Akron, Ohio, at St. Paul's Episcopal Church. "We can't swing up a rope attached to our own belt straps. All our human efforts fail until they are anchored in the rock that is higher than I.".

408. Tunks, Walter F., Dr. "Eulogy of Dr. Bob". Grapevine; Jan., 1951; 7(8): pp45-46.
This Episcopal minister in Akron, Ohio, helped Bill W. meet Dr. Bob in 1934 and 16 years later the Reverend who conducted Dr. Bob's funeral writes an eulogy in this special issue of the Grapevine dedicated to Dr. Bob. "No man need stay the way he is. With God's help he can throw off the chains of any enslaving habit and be free again. His monument is not the money he left in the bank, but the gratitude in the hearts of so many men and women who own more than they can ever repay to his example.".

409. Twerski, Abraham J., M.D. "The Quality of Surrender". Grapevine; June 1980; 37(1): pp11-12.
Twerski, a psychiatrist involved in treatment of alcoholics, states "I have come to the conclusion that the essence of sobriety - the essence of the AA program - is the First Step: accepting one's powerlessness over alcohol. It is important, however, that we understand what acceptance of powerless means." He stresses continued participation in AA, the quality of surrender will change as self-esteem increases, and working the AA program is a circular affair, never ending, except, that is, in greater happiness.

410. Twerski, Abraham J., M.D. "Something's Wrong With Elaine". Grapevine; Dec. 1978; 35(7): pp14-16.
Rabbi Twerski relates the story of patient whose inability to surrender and accept powerlessness was due to her initial inability to understand that alcoholics are not fundamentally bad people simply because drinking is bad for them. He discusses the necessity of self-esteem and a positive image of alcoholics if surrender and Twelfth Step work are to be sincere.

411. Twerski, Abraham J., M.D. "The Story of Annabelle". Grapevine; Jan. 1975; 31(8): pp5-8.
Twerski, Clinical Director, Dept. of Psychiatry, St. Francis General Hospital, Pittsburgh, Pa., relates the story of the patient who gave him his first understanding of alcoholism and AA when she sought his help after four years of sobriety. He considers possible explanations for her decision to become sober at age fifty-seven with more than thirty years of drinking behind her. He also discusses the failure of his psychiatric training to prepare him to treat alcoholics.

412. Twerski, Abraham J., M.D. "To Be Always Teachable". Grapevine; Dec. 1975; 32(7): pp26-30.
Twerski discusses the ability of the AA program to inspire the continual personal growth of its members. He addresses the specific issue of re-entry into the program among members who relapse after many years of sobriety. He suggests that AA attempt to bring these members into contact with each other so they can share their common personal experiences.

413. Underwood, Ivan. "Problems with the Alcoholic Executive". in: AA Today. First ed. New York: Grapevine; 1960: pp 26-28.
Underwood, Nonalcoholic Trustee on the AA General Service Board, discusses the circumstances that encourage heavy drinking among high level executives while allowing them to hide this behavior from others. He also discusses the waste and inefficiency caused by alcoholism at the executive level and the grave consequences of drunken decision making.

414. W. B. "The Support We All Need". Grapevine; Jan. 1980: pp15-17.
The author comments on the all too common jokes about homosexuals and other minorities around AA. W.B.'s argument is that "if we are interested in attracting 'all' alcoholics, we need to show them through our words and other behavior that our talk about love and acceptance is something more than talk." (NALGAP 046).

415. Waldron, D.D. "AA and the Drug Addict". Grapevine; October 1965; 22(5): p38.
Waldron addresses the problem of narcotic addicts who seek help from AA. While he feels that AA is for alcoholics, he asks its members to welcome lone drug addicts who are unable to attend Narcotics Anonymous meetings. Where three or four drug addicts can gather together, he suggests that they form an NA group.

416. Warfield, Rebecca. "How Will You Behave Tomorrow?". Grapevine; Sept. 1962; 19(4): pp20-23.
Cycles of behavior are discussed in this reprint from Vogue.

417. Wetherill, Richard W. (untitled). Grapevine; Feb. 1961; 17(9): pp34-37.
This method was discovered by the author for alcoholics in recovery to turn dishonest thinking into honest thinking; called "Humanetics.".

418. Whitmeyer, G. Randell. "Help for the Revolving Door Drunk". _Grapevine_; Sept. 1964; 21(4): pp36-38.
Whitmeyer, City Judge of Shreveport, Louisiana, describes the "Honor Class," a program he devised to assist alcoholics that repeatedly appeared in his court. Alcoholic offenders sentenced to the class attend weekly meetings in the city courtroom that follow the AA format. The class is escorted to an AA meeting once a week. The Honor Class is designed to persuade its members to work closely with AA (when their sentence is completed).

419. Whittenore, Richard H. "An Indian Named `Tall Man". _Grapevine_; Nov. 1962; 19(6): pp14-17.
Whittenore, of the State of Maine Division of Alcoholic Rehabilitation, relates how AA helped a desperate situation between the Canadian Mounted Police in New Brunswick, Canada, and the Indian Malaseet Tribe.

420. [Wilson, Bill/Wilson, Lois]. "Anonymity". _Grapevine_; 28(7): pp8-9.
A message from Bill, delivered by Lois at the New York Intergroup Dinner in celebration of his 36th anniversary. Lois relays Bill's thoughts about the spiritual and practical aspects of anonymity that are essential to the individual and collective survival of AA.

421. [Wilson, Bill]. _A Report on the Grapevine: Its Situation and Prospects_. _By Bill_.; September 1960: 15 mimeographed pages.
Bill addresses topics "to help _The Grapevine_ to achieve a more permanent footing - in its operation and its structure." The paid staff, circulation and promotion enigma, financial status and outlook, _AA Today_, and other subjects are discussed.

422. Wilson, Lois. "Bill's Wife Remembers When He and She and the First AA's Were Very Young". _Grapevine_; Dec., 1944; 1(7): pi.
This article presents Lois' thoughts on Bill's drinking days and his early sobriety. Lois, the wife of AA Co-founder Bill Wilson, became angry with his constant activity with drunks until she realized that "I had been wallowing in self-pity; that Bill's change was simply miraculous; that his feverish activity with alcoholics was absolutely necessary to his sobriety; and that if I did not want to be left way behind, I had better jump on the bandwagon, too!".

423. Wilson, Lois. "Convention News: Families of Alcoholics at the AA Convention in St. Louis.". _Grapevine_; May 1955; 11(12): pp20-21.
Al-Anon Family Group participation at the convention announced.

424. [Wilson], Lois. "How One AA Wife Lives the 12 Steps". _Grapevine_; August 1953; 10(3): pp40-42.
Lois W., AA's "First Lady," as the wife of Bill, Co-founder of Alcoholics Anonymous, tells the story of her own adventure in growth applying the AA principles to her own life." She comments on each of the 12 Steps.

425. Wilson, Lois. "In AA's First Five Years". Grapevine; Jan. 1967; 23(8): pp2-5.
Founder of Al-Anon and wife of Bill W., Lois describes the first five years of Alcoholics Anonymous, before the Fellowship had a name or the Big Book was written. She discusses the events that led to the emergence of Al-Anon, the organization that she founded.

426. [Wilson], Lois. "...it might have been the time...I too needed spiritual devleopment.". Grapevine; Feb., 1950; 6(9) pp11-13.
The Co-founder's wife believes the AA program is also helpf to non-alcoholics as well as "thousands of alcoholics' relatives and friends now (in) their own lives." Lois realized she needed spiritual growth along with Bill's so s jumped on the AA bandwagon, too.

427. Wing, Nell. (history). Grapevine; Sept. 1977; 34(4): pp 26 31.
Wing, former secretary of Bill W. and AA's first archivist, reviews the progress of AA and the General Service Board during the 1940s, 1950s, and 1960s. She describes the archives project she designed to provide a complete historical account of AA's beginnings and development.

428. Wittner, John J., M.D. "Alcoholism - A Legitimate Basis fo Disability Retirement". Grapevine; July 1949; 6(2): p15.
Wittner, Assistant Vice President, Industrial Relations, Consolidated Edison Company of New York, Inc., describes Co Ed's activities to help alcoholic employees. He states "we recommend affiliation with AA.".

429. Wylie, Philip. "Philip Wylie Jabs A Little Needle into Complacency". Grapevine; September 1944; 1(4): p1.
Note: Bill Wilson and E. M. Jellinek both comment on this article in the same issue.
The author of Generation of Vipers (a critical survey of American institutions, 1942) relates his alcoholism and sobriety pre-AA with help from Jungian "transcendant symbol or religious experience. Wylie believed AA "represents to the first really effective effort to deal in kind and scale and in the right category, with alcoholism.".

Chapter III = Grapevine Articles by Bill Wilson

430. [Wilson, Bill]. "A.A. is not Big Business". Grapevine; Nov. 1950; 7(6): pp24-26.
"In gratitude," Bill explains, "a plan to preserve A.A....but not to rule it!" He discusses plans for more financial support from AA groups and a proposal for the General Service Conference of A.A. to begin meeting on a yearly basis.

431. [Wilson, Bill]. "AA Communication Can Cross All Barriers". Grapevine; Oct. 1959; 16(5): pp2-5.
Bill discusses low and high bottoms' ability to identify with each other as AA has broadened and deepened channels of communication.

432. [Wilson, Bill]. (AA membership) untitled. Grapevine; Aug. 1946; 3(3): pp 3 & 7.
An alcoholic is a member of AA as long as they say they are. AA does not wish to deny anyone their chance to recover from alcoholism.

433. [Wilson, Bill]. "AA's Tradition of Self-Support". Grapevine; Oct. 1967; 24(5): pp8-9.
Bill, AA's Co-founder, discusses the reasons why AA groups do not seek charity and why they support AA central services.

434. [Wilson, Bill]. "Adequate Hospitalization ... One Great Need". Grapevine; May 1947; 3(12): pp3-5.
The atmosphere of most hospitals is extremely conducive to a good first presentation of A.A. The idea of "sponsorship" is growing. Bill W. stresses cooperation by AA with hospital and other associations.

435. [Wilson, Bill]. "After Twenty-Five Years". Grapevine; March 1960; 16(10): pp20-22 & 27-29.
"For the many groups throughout the AA world who plan to hold 25th anniversary gatherings this year, our co-founder Bill W. has written this glimpse of the panorama of AA today.".

436. [Wilson, Bill]. "Again at the Crossroads". Grapevine; Nov. 1961; 18(6): pp3-6.
The substance of Bill's remarks at the closing session of AA's 1961 General Service Conference.

437. [Wilson, Bill]. "Anne S.". Grapevine; July 1949; 6(2): p6.
Memorial on the death of AA Co-founder Dr. Bob Smith's wife Anne.

438. [Wilson, Bill]. "An Anniversary Letter". Grapevine; June 1959; 16(1): p2.
Comments by Bill W. mark the AA Grapevine's 15th year of publication: "May God prosper the Grapevine always.".

439. [Wilson, Bill]. "Another Fragment of History". Grapevine; Feb. 1954; 10(9): pp2-5.
The work of Dr. Bob and Sr. Ignatia is cited.

440. [Wilson, Bill]. "The Antidote for Fear: Prudence, Trust, and Faith". Grapevine; Nov. 1959; 16(6): pp2-5.
This is Bill W.'s closing speech to the 1960 General Service Conference.

441. [Wilson, Bill]. (The Beginning of AA) (untitled). Grapevine; June 1965; 22(1): pp2-9.
Bill tells how AA began.

442. [Wilson, Bill]. "The Bill W. - Carl Jung Letters". Grapevine; Jan. 1963; 19(8): pp2-7.

443. [Wilson, Bill]. "Bill's Comments on Wylie Ideas & Hunches". Grapevine; 1; 4(pp1 & 3).
Bill praises Philip Wylie's article (Vol. 1, No. 4) on his alcoholism and opinions about alcoholism, which should not upset AA's as "the roads to recovery are many." The article includes Dr. Harry Tiebout's conclusion of his "Basic Techniques of AA.".

444. [Wilson, Bill]. "The Book is Born". Grapevine; Oct. 1945; 2(5): pp 2 & 6.
The Big Book, Alcoholics Anonymous, written partially as a means to reach still suffering alcoholics, as other plans for publicity were abandoned during the first three years (1935-1938) of AA, is discussed by Bill.

445. [Wilson, Bill]. "Book Publication Proved Discouraging Venture". Grapevine; July 1947; 4(2): p3.
Bill gives the history of the writing and the publishing of Alcoholics Anonymous, the Big Book.

446. [Wilson, Bill]. "Carrying the Message in `Fifty-Five". Grapevine; July 1980; 27(2): pp2-6.
Note: Part I of Two Parts.
This contains excerpts from a talk at a New York A.A. meeting dealing with history of A.A.'s first 21 years. Aspects of A.A. history reviewed were the Oxford Groups' contributions to A.A.; Twelfth-Stepping and early meetings at the Clinton St. home of Bill W.; and writing of the Big Book.

447. [Wilson, Bill]. "Carrying the Message in `Fifty-Five". Grapevine; August 1980; 27(3): pp4-10.
Note: Part II of Two Parts.
Bill W. talks at an AA New York City meeting in 1955, reviews A.A. history from 1939 to 1955, the Manhattan A.A. Groups' growth, 6,000 inquiries written to A.A. headquarters after Jack Alexander's Saturday Evening Post article, March 1, 1941, and evolution of the Twelve Traditions.

448. [Wilson, Bill]. "Central Office Notes: A Date With Destiny? ". Grapevine; 1; 5(p4).
Bill W. comments on Marty Mann's involvement as Director of the National Committee for Education on Alcoholism. He says Marty Mann's new career was not to be considered as "professional AA.".

449. [Wilson, Bill]. "Central Office Notes" column. Grapevine; June 1944; 1(1): p4.
Bill W. announces the central office move to Lexington Ave. and new mailing address (P.O.Box 459, Grand Central Station, New York, NY. Still used in 1985). Review of monthly activities in office; i.e., letters answered, literature sold, etc. Staff of four are overworked and Bill hopes no "good piece of publicity" is released as the understaffed office would be thrown weeks behind on answering vital first inquiries. Bill also disclaims any involvement in endorsement of AA pins being sold to the membership.

450. [Wilson, Bill]. "A Christmas Message from Bill". Grapevine; Dec. 1953; 10(7): p1.

451. [Wilson, Bill]. "A Christmas Message from Lois and Bill". Grapevine; Dec. 1954; 11(7): p3.

452. [Wilson, Bill]. "Christmas Greetings: From Lois and Bill". Grapevine; Dec. 1956; 13(7): p23.

453. [Wilson, Bill]. "Christmas Editorial". Grapevine; Dec. 1958; 15(7): p3.
"Surely we of AA have more reason to be merry than any person on earth. So, dear friends, a Merry Christmas to you all!".

454. [Wilson, Bill]. "Christmas Message". Grapevine; Dec. 1960; 17(7): p2.

455. [Wilson, Bill]. "A Christmas Message". Grapevine; Dec. 1961; 18(7): p2.

456. [Wilson, Bill]. "Christmas Greetings from Lois & Bill". Grapevine; Dec. 1962; 19(7): inside front cover.

457. [Wilson, Bill]. "A Christmas Message from Lois & Bill". Grapevine; Dec. 1963; 20(7): p24.

458. [Wilson, Bill]. "Christmas Message from Lois & Bill". Grapevine; Dec. 1964; 21(7): front cover.

459. [Wilson, Bill]. "Christmas Message from Bill". Grapevine; Dec. 1965; 22(7): pp24-25.

460. [Wilson, Bill]. "A Christmas Message". Grapevine; Dec. 1967; 24(7): p2.

461. [Wilson, Bill]. "A Christmas Message". Grapevine; Dec. 1968; 25(7): pp23-24.

462. [Wilson, Bill]. "Christmas Greetings from Lois & Bill". Grapevine; Dec. 1969; 26(7): pp24-25.

463. [Wilson, Bill]. "Christmas Message". Grapevine; Dec. 1970; 27(7): p15.
"Gratitude is just about the finest attribute we can have, and how deeply we of AA realize this at Christmastime.".

464. [Wilson, Bill]. "Clubs in A.A.: Are They With Us to Stay?". Grapevine; April 1947; 3(11): pp3-4.
History of the First AA club in New York City, "The 24th Street Club," reviewed. Principles for AA clubs outlined.

465. [Wilson, Bill]. "Dangers In Linking A.A. to Other Projects". Grapevine; March 1947; 3(10): pp 3 & 5.
Bill, briefly summarizing: "I'm rather sure our policy with respect to `outside' projects will turn out to be this: A.A. does not sponsor projects in other fields. But, if these projects are constructive and non-controversial in character, A.A. members are free to engage in them without criticism if they act as individuals only, and are careful of the A.A. name. Perhaps that's it. Shall we try it?".

466. [Wilson, Bill]. "Dr. Bob: A Tribute from Bill". Grapevine; Jan. 1951; 7(8): pp3-9.
Note: This issue is dedicated to Dr. Bob and all articles are about his life and service to A.A. (available in reprint, 1985).
The death on Nov. 19, 1950, of his fellow co-founder of A.A. is noted by Bill W., along with the history of their 1935 meeting and their 15 years work together. Bill W. states: "With no other person have I ever experienced quite the same relationship: the finest thing I know how to say is that in all the strenuous time of our association, he and I never had an uncomfortable difference of opinion. His capacity for brotherhood and love was often beyond my ken.".

467. [Wilson, Bill]. "Dr. Jung, Dr. Silkworth and A.A.". Grapevine; Jan. 1968; 24(8): pp10-15.
"Excerpt of what Dr. Jung told Rowland and what Dr. Silkworth told Lois, there might never have been any A.A. Bill got the verdict: He was doomed. Unless...".

468. [Wilson, Bill]. "Editorial: The Shape of Things To Come". Grapevine; June 1944; 1(1): p2.
Bill quotes Alcoholics Anonymous, Chapter 11: "A Vision for You" and says in the Grapevine's first issue that he hopes the Grapevine will help bring the AA message and its rays of hope and experience ever fall upon the current of our AA life and one day illumine every dark corner of the alcoholic world.".

469. [Wilson, Bill]. "Editorial on The First Tradition". Grapevine; Dec. 1947; 4(7): p2.
"We gladly aset aside personal ambitions whenever these might harm AA. We humbly confess that we are but a `small part of a great whole." Announcement of 48-page pamphlet available on 12 Points of Traditions.

470. [Wilson, Bill]. "Editorial: On the Second Tradition". Grapevine; Jan. 1948; 4(8): p2.
"The striking and almost unbelievable fact about AA is that the group conscience will, in the end, prove a far more infallible guide for group affairs than the decision of any individual member, however good or wise he may be.".

471. [Wilson, Bill]. "Editorial: on the Third Tradition". Grapevine; Feb. 1948; 4(9): p2.
"Let us of A.A. therefore resolve that we shall always be inclusive, and never exclusive, offering all we have to all men save our title. May all barriers be thus leveled, may our unity thus be preserved. And may God grant us a long life - and a useful one!".

472. [Wilson, Bill]. "Editorial: On the Fourth Tradition". Grapevine; March 1948; 4(10): p2.
"Obviously, if any individual, group or regional committee could take an action which might seriously affect the welfare of Alcoholics Anonymous as a whole, or seriously disturb surrounding groups, that would not be liberty at all. It would be sheer license; it would be anarchy, not democracy.".

473. [Wilson, Bill]. "Editorial: On the Fifth Tradition". Grapevine; April 1948; 4(11): p2.
"And may we reflect with ever deepening conviction, that we shall never be at our best except when we hew only to the primary spiritual aim of A.A. - That of carrying its message to the alcoholic who still suffers alcoholism.".

474. [Wilson, Bill]. "Editorial: On the Sixth Tradition". Grapevine; May 1948; 4(12): p2.
"Nowadays, the A.A. group answers its well wishers saying, 'Our expenses are trifling. As good earners, we can easily pay them. As we neither need nor want money, why risk its hazards? We'd rather stay poor. Thanks just the same!".

475. [Wilson, Bill]. "Editorial: On the Seventh Tradition". Grapevine; June 1948; 5(1): p8.
"When reflecting on these things, why should each of us tell himself, 'Yes, we AA's were once a burden on everybody. We were "takers." Now that we are sober, and by the Grace of God have become responsible citizens of the world, why shouldn't we now about face and become 'thankful givers'! Yes, it is high time we did!".

476. [Wilson, Bill]. "Editorial: On the 8th Tradition". Grapevine; July 1948; 5(2): p8.
"So, where needed, let's revise our attitude toward those who labor at our special services. Let us treat them as A.A. associates, and not as hired help; let's recompense them fairly and, above all, let's absolve them from the label of professionalism.".

477. [Wilson, Bill]. "Editorial: On the 9th Tradition". Grapevine; Aug. 1948; 5(3): p8.
"With such assurances, we shall without doubt continue to improve and extend our vital lifelines of special service; to better carry out our AA message to others; to make for ourselves a finer greater society, and, God willing, to assure Alcoholics Anonymous a long life and perfect unity.".

478. [Wilson, Bill]. "Editorial: On the 10th Tradition". Grapevine; Sept. 1948; 5(4): pp6-7.
"Our AA Traditions are those attitudes and practices by which we may deserve, as a movement, a long life and a useful one. To this end, none could be more vital than our 10th Tradition, for it deals with the subject of controversy - serious controversy.".

479. [Wilson, Bill]. "Editorial: On the 11th Tradition". Grapevine; Oct. 1948; 5(5): pp4-5.
The AA name, used by individuals in public, could easily be transferred into the midst of controversy, "So, it is becoming our code that there are things that no AA ever does, lest he divert AA from its sole purpose and injure our public relations. And thereby the chances of those sick ones yet to come. To the million alcoholics who have not yet heard our AA story we should ever say, 'Greetings and welcome. Be assured that we shall never weaken the lifelines which we float out to you. In our public relations, we shall, God willing, keep the faith.".

480. [Wilson, Bill]. "Editorial: On the Twelfth Tradition". Grapevine; Nov. 1948; 5(6): pp4-5.
"One may say that anonymity is the spiritual base, the sure key to all the rest of our Traditions!" The 12 Traditions are briefly reviewed.

481. [Wilson, Bill]. "Editorial: A Request and An Apology". Grapevine; Dec. 1948; 5(7): p8.
Bill W. discusses recent anonymity breaks carrying his full name.

482. [Wilson, Bill]. "Editorial by Bill". Grapevine; Nov. 1958; 15(6): p3.
Gratitude and service are important during Thanksgiving.

483. [Wilson, Bill]. "Editorial: The Grapevine's 25th Anniversary". Grapevine; June 1969; 26(1): p3.
"As we visualize that early time against the world scene of AA today, let us remember to give thanks for those twenty-five years in which the Grapevine and its people did so much to make AA what is now is. A 'true voice' indeed!".

484. [Wilson, Bill]. "Every Day is Christmas". Grapevine; Dec. 1952; 9(7): pp3-5.
AA encompasses all religious faiths throughout the world, Bill states, "So by whatever name we call it, the spirit of Christmas is in us all. How best to give and how to receive is our common aim." The Prayer of St. Francis is reprinted and Bill says St. Francis was able to practice the spirit of Christmas every day of the year.

485. [Wilson, Bill]. "The Finest Gift of All". Grapevine; Dec. 1955; 12(7).
Christmas message from Bill W. & first printing of the "Came to Believe" picture.

486. [Wilson, Bill]. "For Sister Ignatia: Our Everlasting Gratitude". Grapevine; Aug. 1966; 23(3): pp2-9.
Bill pays tribute to Sister Ignatia on her death.

487. [Wilson, Bill]. "A Fragment of History". Grapevine; June 1953; 10(2): pp3-9.
Bill answers the often-asked question: "Where did the Twelve Steps come from?".

488. [Wilson, Bill]. "A Fragment of History and a Tribute". Grapevine; May 1957; 13(12): pp24-25.
The passing of Dr. A. Wiese Hammer is cited by Bill. "The simple account of the passing of one of America's finest surgeons stirs memories that will always be bright in the annals of A.A. Dr. A. Wiese Hammer was one of the best friends AA will ever have.".

489. [Wilson, Bill]. "Freedom Under God: the choice is ours". Grapevine; Nov. 1960; 17(6): pp3-8.
Bill W's reflections on the Twelve Traditions delivered at AA's 25th Anniversary Convention in Long Beach, California.

490. [Wilson, Bill]. "God as We Understand Him: the Dilemma of No Faith". Grapevine; April 1961; 17(11): pp3-7.
First in 12-part series on the working of A.A. principles "...in all our affairs." Bill W. concludes the article with "Therefore, faith is more than our greatest gift; its sharing with others is our greatest responsibility. So may we of AA continually seek the wisdom and the willingness by which we may well fulfill that immense trust which the Giver of all perfect gifts has placed in our hands.".

491. [Wilson, Bill]. "The Grapevine: Past, Present, and Future". Grapevine; July 1945; 2(2): pp2 & 8.
Bill W. accepts the GV editorial position. "Always wishing to reflect AA, and nothing but AA, it will be the ideal of The Grapevine always to serve, never to dictate or command. Please help us make it a true voice.".

492. [Wilson, Bill]. "The Grapevine and you and me". Grapevine; June 1957; 14(1): pp24-25.
Bill W. writes a letter to AA members on efforts of the Grapevine to be true mirror of up-to-date AA thought, feeling, and activity.

493. [Wilson, Bill, & Dr. Bob]. "Great Expectations: A New Year's Greeting". Grapevine; Jan. 1948; 4(8): p1.
Greeting from Bill W. and Dr. Bob.

494. [Wilson, Bill]. "The Greatest Gift of All". Grapevine; Dec. 1957; 14(7): p2.
Bill discusses aspects of a spiritual awakening.

495. [Wilson, Bill]. "Guardian of A.A.: Our General Service Conference". Grapevine; April 1958; 14(11): pp2-6.
Bill discusses how the future of AA will be insured by the General Service Conference and the reasons why the Conference is important. "For all these compelling reasons, my friends, the future belongs to you. Embrace these new responsibilities eagerly, fear naught, and the Grace of God will surely be yours.".

496. [Wilson, Bill]. "He Kept the Faith". Grapevine; Nov. 1954; 11(6).
Memorial comment from Bill on the death of AA No. 3, Bill D.

497. [Wilson, Bill]. "How A.A.'s World Service Grew" (Part I). Grapevine; May 1955; 11(12): pp2-9.
Part I of a Manual on the Third Legacy which Bill was then writing. "For the purpose of this Manual, we can only supply a brief historical run-down, a simple timetable of the events that have brought our world services and AA Traditions into being, plus a condensed report of the total accomplishment." Bill W. reviews AA's founding, Rockefeller connections, writing of the "Big Book," and response to the March 1st, 1941, Saturday Evening Post article.

498. [Wilson, Bill]. "How AA's World Services Grew". Grapevine; June 1955; 12(1): pp38-44.
Part 2 of 3 installments from the Third Legacy Manual in which Bill W. tells "How We Learned to Recover - To Stay Together - and To Serve." The period from 1941 to 1950 reviewed.

499. [Wilson, Bill]. "How the Twelve Steps Were Born". Grapevine; Sept. 1962; 19(4): pp2-4.
Excerpt from AA Comes of Age.

500. [Wilson, Bill]. "Humility for Today". Grapevine; June 1961; 18(1): pp2-7.
Note: Second in a series.
Bill directs his comments to "Just what do we mean by 'humility for today?' and how do we know when we have found it?".

501. [Wilson, Bill]. "I Stand by the Door". Grapevine; Feb. 1967; 23(9): pp12-13.
Bill's recollections of Rev. Sam Shoemaker and comments on Helen Shoemaker's biography of her husband, Sam.

502. [Wilson, Bill]. "In AA's 30th Year Responsibility is Our Theme". Grapevine; July 1965; 22(2): pp2-10.
The International Convention in Toronto, Canada, is discussed.

503. [Wilson, Bill]. "In Memory of Harry". Grapevine; July 1966; 23(2): pp2-3.
Tribute to Dr. Harry M. Tiebout on his death.

504. [Wilson, Bill]. "In Remembrance of 'Ebby' 1896-1966". Grapevine; June 1966; 23(1): pp22-23.
Tribute by Bill to the man who brought him the message in 1934.

505. [Wilson, Bill]. "Incorporation. Their Use and Misuse.". Grapevine; Nov. 1947; 4(6): pp 2-3 & 12.
Traditions Six & Seven and questions and answers used to clarify problems of AA groups incorporating clubs are discussed. "This article has been written to help alleviate the many complications that have arisen throughout AA touching clubs, hospitals, and 'outside ventures.".

506. [Wilson, Bill]. "The Individual In Relation to A.A. As A Group". Grapevine; July 1946; 3(2): pp 2 & 6.
Traditions One and Three are compared.

507. [Wilson, Bill]. "Lack of Money Proved an A.A. Boon". Grapevine; June 1947; 4(1): pp 3 & 13.
Bill reviews AA history, the role John D. Rockefeller played, and formation of The Alcoholic Foundation.

508. [Wilson, Bill]. "Last Seven Years Have Made A.A. Self-Supporting". Grapevine; Aug. 1947; 4(3): pp 3 & 8.
The Rockefeller dinner, Liberty and Saturday Evening Post articles, and early money problems are reviewed by Bill W.

509. [Wilson, Bill]. "Leadership In A.A.: Ever a Vital Need". Grapevine; April 1959; 15(11): pp2-7.
Qualities necessary for good A.A. leadership are outlined.

510. [Wilson, Bill]. "Let Us Read - and Thank God". Grapevine; Oct. 1958; 15(5): p3.
Bill, in this "Across the Editor's Desk" column, comments on the Grapevine's first International Issue and the Grapevine as AA's "Magic Carpet" transporting members to "countless cities and hamlets.".

511. [Wilson, Bill]. "Let's Be Friendly with our Friends ... The Psychiatrists". Grapevine; July 1957; 14(2): pp2-4.
In this first in a series of 4 articles by Bill W., the growth of cooperation between AA and psychiatrists is discussed.

512. [Wilson, Bill]. "Let's Be Friendly with our Friends ... The Physicians". Grapevine; Aug. 1957; 14(3): pp2-4.
In this second in a series by Bill W., Dr. William Duncan Silkworth's contributions to AA are cited.

513. [Wilson, Bill]. "Let's Be Friendly with our Friends ... The Clergymen". Grapevine; Sept. 1957; 14(4): pp2-5.
This is the third in a series by Bill W. "Every River has a Wellspring at its source. AA is like that, too. In the beginning there was a spring which poured out of a clergyman, Dr. Samuel Shoemaker." "Therefore it is with the deepest feeling that I here cast up AA's debt to the clergymen: without their works for us, AA could never have been born; nearly every principle that we use came from them.".

514. [Wilson, Bill]. "Let's Be Friendly with our Friends ... Press, Radio & Television". Grapevine; Oct. 1957; 14(5): pp2-6.
In this fourth & final article by Bill W. in this series, the media's role in AA's growth is cited. "For all such couriers of good will, let us be everlastingly grateful. And let us always be worthy of their friendship.".

515. [Wilson, Bill]. "Let's Be Friendly with Our Friends: Friends on the Alcoholism Front". Grapevine; March 1958; 14(10): pp2-9.
This is an outline of U.S. efforts to help the alcoholic and history of the Research Council on Problems of Alcohol, Haggard, Jellinek, Marty Mann, and Yale University's education program. "So let us work alongside all these projects of promise to hasten the recovery of those millions who have not yet found their way out. These varied labors do not need our special endorsement; they need only a helping hand when, as individuals, we can possibly give it.".

516. [Wilson, Bill]. "Let's Back Them To The Limit!". Grapevine; Oct. 1960; 17(5).
Bill outlines AA's growth in foreign countries.

517. [Wilson, Bill]. "Let's Keep it Simple ... But How?". Grapevine; July 1960; 17(2): pp2-6.
Bill W. reflects on the first 25 years of AA and how "simplicity for today" has changed over the years for the improvement of A.A.

518. [Wilson, Bill]. "Let's Make Practical and Spiritual Sense". Grapevine; Aug. 1958; 15(3): pp14-17.
Letter written by Bill W. on his ideas on AA publishing a paperback "Big Book.".

519. [Wilson, Bill]. "A Letter to the Groups from Bill". Grapevine; July 1954; 11(2): pp22-23.
Bill discusses the General Service Conference decision to discontinue discounts on AA literature.

520. [Wilson, Bill]. "Meet the Non-Alcoholic Trustees". Grapevine; Nov. 1951; 8(6): pp38-41.
Brief biographies of trustees: Jack Alexander, Frank Amos, A. LeRoy Chipman, Frank Gulden, Dr. John Norris, Fulton Oursler, Bernard Smith, Dr. Leonard V. Strong, Willard S. Richardson, and Leonard V. Harrison.

521. [Wilson, Bill]. "A memo from Bill: The First World Service meeting". Grapevine; Oct. 1969; 26(5): pp12-13.

522. [Wilson, Bill]. "A Merry Christmas". Grapevine; Dec. 1951; 8(7): p20.
Season Wishes from Bill and Lois: "Once again we listen to our Lord's command: Freely ye have received, freely give.".

523. [Wilson, Bill]. "Merry Christmas Message from Bill & Lois". Grapevine; 1959; 16(7): p46.

524. [Wilson, Bill]. "A Message from Bill". Grapevine; May 1964; 20(12): pp2-5.
Bill emphasizes understanding the operation and needs of AA World Services.

525. [Wilson, Bill]. "Modesty One Plank for Good Public Relations". Grapevine; Aug. 1945; 2(3): pp 1 & 4.
Bill discusses how publicity has helped AA's growth - but cautions AA's on possible dangers of publicity. He cites the Washingtonian Movement (see July, 1945, GV) as an example of how publicity may destroy AA.

526. [Wilson, Bill]. "The Next Frontier - Emotional Sobriety". Grapevine; Jan. 1958; 14(8): pp3-5.
Bill discusses those troublesome depressions often encountered in sobriety and his own ideas on his failure to "grow up" emotionally and spiritually.

527. [Wilson, Bill]. "Of Interest to You". Grapevine; April 1950; 6(11): p2.
Announcement of The First International Conference of A.A. to be held at Cleveland, Ohio, July 28-30, 1950.

528. [Wilson, Bill]. "Our Anonymity Is Both Inspiration and Safety". Grapevine; March 1946; 2(10): pp 1 & 5.
The spiritual significance of anonymity and adoption of a national policy of anonymity suggested. "Great modesty and humility are needed by every AA for his own permanent recovery. If those virtues are such vital needs to the individual, so must they be to AA as a whole. This principle of Anonymity before the general public can, if we take it seriously enough, guarantee the Alcoholics Anonymous movement these sterling attributes forever. Our public relations policy should mainly rest upon the principle of attraction and seldom, if ever, upon promotion," Bill writes.

529. [Wilson, Bill]. "Our Critics Can Be Our Benefactors". Grapevine; April 1963; 20(11): pp2-4.
This article relates Bill W's views on AA's relationship to medicine, to religion, and to the world at large in the light of a recent magazine article that criticized certain aspects of A.A.

530. [Wilson, Bill]. "Our Final Great Decision: AA's Third Legacy". Grapevine; June 1954; 11(1): pp10-11.

531. [Wilson, Bill]. "Our Great Responsibility: the Guidance of AA's World Affairs". Grapevine; Jan. 1966; 22(8): pp8-15.
Bill W. endorses the Trustees' Program for reshaping of the General Service Board, AA's chief agency for World Services.

532. [Wilson, Bill]. "Point of View" column. Grapevine; Dec. 1944; 1(7): p2.
Note: The book, Alcohol Explored, 1942, by E. M. Jellinek and H. W. Haggard, is quoted in this article by Bill.
Bill responds to a letter, "How It Feels to be the Mother of an Alcoholic." And Bill lists his personality defects (great emotional sensitivity, childishness, and inferiority) that underlied his obsession to drink.

533. [Wilson, Bill]. "Problems Other than Alcohol: What Can Be Done About Them?". Grapevine; Feb. 1958; 14(9): pp6-10.
How the problems of drug addiction can be handled within the AA Fellowship and out are discussed by Bill W.

534. [Wilson, Bill]. "Respecting Money by Bill". Grapevine; Nov. 1957; 14(6): pp7-11.
The 7th & 8th Traditions relating to AA and money discussed.

535. [Wilson, Bill]. "Rules' Dangerous but Unity on Public Policies Vital to Future of AA". Grapevine; Sept. 1945; 2(4): pp2-3.
The importance of establishing a sound public relations policy is discussed.

536. [Wilson, Bill]. "Salute to Canada". Grapevine; May 1951; 7(12): p1.
"We are immeasurably grateful for fast friends from Halifax to Vancouver, they are always the same: devoted workers upon that great fabric which is AA of today - and of tomorrow!".

537. [Wilson, Bill]. "Seeking Guidance for Safe Use of Money". Grapevine; May 1946; 2(12): pp3-4.
Bill W. sheds light on the question: "What shall be our attitude toward voluntary contributions, paid workers, professionalism, and outside donations?".

538. [Wilson, Bill]. "Services Make AA Tick". Grapevine; Nov. 1951; 8(6): pp9-13.
This is an overview of services AA provides from 12th Step calls to General Headquarters broadcasts spanning the Seven Seas which all symbolize AA in action. "By our Twelve Steps we have recovered, by our Twelve Traditions we have unified and through our Third Legacy - Service -we shall carry the AA message down through all the corridors of time to come. Of this, I am happily confident," Bill writes.

539. [Wilson, Bill]. "The Shape of Things To Come". Grapevine; Fab. 1961; 17(9): pp24-25.
"While we need not alter our truths (the 12 Steps & 12 Traditions), we can surely improve their applications to ourselves, to AA as a whole, and to our relations with the world around us.".

540. [Wilson, Bill]. "The Significance of St. Louis: A.A. Comes of Age". Grapevine; April 1955; 11(11): pp6-7.
AA's 20th Anniversary Convention in St. Louis July 1-2-3, 1955, to be an occasion "to take full possession and full responsibility for our inheritance coming from the early years of AA - those vital legacies of Recovery, Unity and Service. No longer will the unity and functioning of our society depend upon its parents, elders or its founders. That will be the unique significance of St. Louis.".

541. [Wilson, Bill/Timmins, James P., Rev. Fr.]. Speeches. Grapevine; Dec. 1945; 2(7): p3.
Bill W's and Rev. Father James P. Timmins' talks at the 11th annual New York Metropolitan AA Dinner at the Commodore Hotel are quoted.

542. [Wilson, Bill]. "Spiritual Experiences". Grapevine; July 1962; 19(2): pp2-3.
Bill W's comments on Spiritual Experiences: "This is why I think we should question no one's transformation - whether it be sudden or gradual. Nor should we demand anyone's special type for ourselves, because our own experience suggests that we are apt to receive whatever may be the most useful for our needs.".

543. [Wilson, Bill]. "A Suggestion for Thanksgiving". Grapevine; Nov. 1949; 6(6): pp1-2.
Bill suggests the idea that Thanksgiving week be used by AA members and groups to reflect on the newly-adopted "short form" of the Traditions.

544. [Wilson, Bill]. "Take Step Eleven". Grapevine; June 1958; 15(1): pp2-5.
Bill W. relates his experience working the 12 Steps during 23 years of sobriety, with emphasis on the 11th Step.

545. [Wilson, Bill]. "A Thanksgiving Message from Bill". Grapevine; Nov. 1954; 11(6): p3.

546. [Wilson, Bill]. "Thanksgiving Time". Grapevine; Nov. 1955; 12(6).
"This is a season for counting our blessings and for giving our thanks.".

547. [Wilson, Bill]. "There Wasn't Time for A Stitch in Nine". Grapevine; June 1950; 7(1): p11.
Because the First International Conference of AA in Cleveland was announced so late Bill hopes regional AA conventions scheduled at that time don't lose attendance. There will be one year's notice next time an "International" convention is held, probably every 5 or 10 years.

548. [Wilson, Bill]. "This Matter of Honesty". Grapevine; Aug. 1961; 18(2): pp7-12.
"Let us therefore continue our several searches for self-deception, great or small. Let us painstakingly temper honesty with prudence and love. And let us never flinch from entire forthrightness whenever this is the requirement," Bill writes in this third article in a series.

549. [Wilson, Bill]. "This Matter of Fear". Grapevine; Jan. 1962; 18(8): pp6-10.
The Twelve Steps of AA enable members to try for all the freedom from fear that is possible for them to attain and a means to find both courage and grace to deal constructively with whatever fears remain.".

550. [Wilson, Bill]. "Those `Goof Balls". Grapevine; Nov. 1945; 2(6): pp 2 & 8.
This is a warning on use of barbituates by alcoholics. Bill W. relates his misuse of chloral hydrate .

551. [Wilson, Bill]. "Through the A.A. Looking Glass". Grapevine; Nov. 1950; 7(6): pp7-9.
"This is a plug for the Grapeviners and all their works. May they live long and prosper," begins Bill in this look behind the scenes of the Grapevine office and workers. "The A.A. Grapevine (is) our mirror of A.A. life and principal forum of written expression.".

552. [Wilson, Bill]. "To Father Ed (Dowling) - Godspeed!". Grapevine; June 1960; 17(1): pp8-11.
Tribute to Fr. Ed Dowling, S.J., on occasion of his passing away April 3, 1960, and his contributions to A.A.

553. [Wilson, Bill]. "To Serve Is To Live". Grapevine; June 1951; 8(1): pp3-5.
This is a review of the First General Service Conference of Alcoholics Anonymous in New York City, April, 1951. "To serve AA is to live. We gladly accept our Third Legacy and may we guard it well and use it wisely. God grant that the Legacy of Service remain safe in our keeping.".

554. [Wilson, Bill]. "A Tradition Born of Our Anonymity". Grapevine; Jan. 1946; 2(8): pp 2 & 10.
"In the years that lie ahead, the principle of Anonymity will undoubtedly become a part of our vital tradition." A four part outline is suggested for a tradition of anonymity.

555. [Wilson, Bill]. "Traditions Stressed by Bill in Memphis Talk". Grapevine; Oct. 1947; 4(5): pp 1 & 8.
Bill W's speech at Southeastern AA Regional Convention in Memphis, Tennessee, Sept., 1947. "12 Points to Assure Our Future, an Alcoholics Anonymous Tradition of Relations" is cited.

556. [Wilson, Bill]. "Tradition One". Grapevine; April 1952; 8(11): pp3-4.
Bill W. begins a new series of articles explaining the Twelve Traditions.. "By faith and by works we have been able to build upon the lessons of an incredible experience. These live today in the Twelve Traditions of Alcoholics Anonymous, which - God willing - shall sustain us in unity for so long as he may need us.".

557. [Wilson, Bill]. "Tradition Two". Grapevine; May 1952; 8(11): pp26-30.
Bill W. answers the questions "Where does AA get its direction? and Who runs it? Bill's experience of refusing a paid therapist position at Towns Hospital is reviewed.

558. [Wilson, Bill]. "Tradition Three". Grapevine; July 1952; 9(2): pp9-12.
For AA is really saying to every serious drinker "You are an AA member if you say so. You can declare yourself in; nobody can keep you out. No matter who you are, no matter how long you've gone, no matter how low you've gone, no matter how grave your emotional complications ... even your crimes ... we still can't deny you AA. We don't want to keep you out. We aren't a bit afraid you'll harm us, never mind how twisted or violent you may be. We just want to be sure that you get the same great chance for sobriety that we've had. So you're an AA member the minute you declare yourself!".

559. [Wilson, Bill]. "Tradition Four". Grapevine; Aug. 1952; 9(3): pp8-10.
The process of trial and error is illustrated which produced this tradition. Here is the story of the AA group that had 61 rules and regulations and how these 61 were abandoned in favor of Rule 62: "Don't take yourself too damn seriously.".

560. [Wilson, Bill]. "Tradition Five". Grapevine; Sept. 1952; 9(4): pp4-7.
"There is another reason for this singleness of purpose. We know that we can seldom keep the precious gift of sobriety unless we give it away.".

561. [Wilson, Bill]. "Tradition Six". Grapevine; Oct. 1952; 9(5): pp9-11.
Problems caused by not following Tradition Six are reviewed.

562. [Wilson, Bill]. "Tradition Eight". Grapevine; Dec. 1952; 9(7): pp30-33.
"Everytime we have tried to professionalize our Twelfth Step, the result has been exactly the same: our single purpose has always been defeated," Bill believes. "At last, however, a plain line of clevage could be seen between professionalism and non-professionalism. We cannot declare AA such a closed corporation that we keep our knowledge and experience top secret. If an AA member acting as a citizen can become a better researcher, educator, personnel officer, then why not? Everybody gains, and we have lost nothing.".

563. [Wilson, Bill]. "Tradition Nine". Grapevine; Jan. 1953; 9(8): pp12-14.
Bill W. comments on this tradition and answers the question: "How, then, can we have an unorganized movement which can and does create a service organization for itself?".

564. [Wilson, Bill]. "Tradition Ten". Grapevine; Feb. 1953; 9(9): pp34-36.
Lessons from the past helped shape AA traditon of non-involvement in outside issues and public controversy.

565. [Wilson, Bill]. "Tradition Eleven". Grapevine; March 1953; 9(10): pp18-20.
This tradition was constructed through trial and error. "To us, however, it represents far more than a sound public relations policy. It is more than a denial of self-seeking. This tradition is a constant and practical reminder that personal ambition has no place in AA. In it each member becomes an active guardian of our fellowship," writes Bill.

566. [Wilson, Bill]. "Tradition Twelve". Grapevine; April 1953; 9(11): pp28-30.
"The spiritual substance of anonymity is sacrifice." "We are sure that humility, expressed by anonymity, is the greatest safeguard that AA can ever have," Bill writes.

567. [Wilson, Bill]. "Tribute to Bernard B. Smith 1901-1970". Grapevine; Oct. 1970; 27(5): p9.
Eulogy to the attorney who served as nonalcoholic chairman and trustee of the AA General Service Board from 1944 to 1970.

568. [Wilson, Bill]. "Trustee Vote Fixes Policy on Gift Funds". Grapevine; June 1946; 3(1): pp 2 & 8.
Trustees of The Alcoholic Foundation pass a resolution on policy of accepting outside donations. Also, AA's as professionals in the alcoholism treatment field is discussed.

569. [Wilson, Bill]. "Twelve Suggested Points for A.A. Traditions". Grapevine; April 1946; 2(11): pp 2-3.
Bill W. "ventures to place in words these suggestions for an Alcoholics Anonymous Tradition of Relations - Twelve Points to assure our Future.".

570. [Wilson, Bill]. "The Twelve Traditions: Our Keys to Survival and Growth". Grapevine; Nov. 1956; 13(6): p21.
Bill W's introductory remarks to several articles on the Traditions.

571. [Wilson, Bill]. "The Vision of Tomorrow". Grapevine; Jan. 1952; 8(8): pp3-4.
"Clear vision for tomorrow comes only after a real look at yesterday." Bill W. reviews happenings of 1951 and AA's assumption of its Third Legacy of Service. Public interest in AA grows, professionals and agencies give approval to A.A. Bill W. concludes "For so long as we shall humbly meditate in this spirit upon our great yesterdays, just so long will God grant us our vision of tomorrow.".

572. [Wilson, Bill]. "We Approach Maturity". Grapevine; Oct. 1949; 6(5): pp4-5.
AA is 14 years old and approaching maturity, not adolescence. As AA grows it needs to remember its Fifth Tradition of "primary purpose," Bill writes.

573. [Wilson, Bill]. "We Come of Age". Grapevine; Sept. 1950; 7(4): pp3-10.
This is a lengthy report on activities at the First International Conference held at Cleveland, Ohio, July 28-30, 1950. The Twelve Traditions are adopted.

574. [Wilson, Bill]. "What is Our A.A. Grapevine?". Grapevine; Dec. 1946; 3(7): pp2 & 6-7.
The history of AA's beginning and how the Grapevine developed, its purpose and future, are traced. Bill hoped that "the AA Grapevine would take its place in the minds of all AA's as one of the essential central services, close alongside The (Alcoholic) Foundation, the A.A. book, and the Central Office.".

575. [Wilson, Bill]. "What Is the Third Legacy? World Service - Its Heart". Grapevine; July 1955; 12(2): pp5-11.
Part 3 of 3. "Our Twelfth Step - carrying the message - is the basic service that AA's Fellowship gives; this is our principal aim and the main reason for our existence. Hence, an AA service is anything whatever that helps us to reach a fellow sufferer - ranging all the way from the Twelfth Step itself to a ten-cent phone call and a cup of coffee, and to AA's General Service Headquarters for national and international action. The sum total of all these services is our Third Legacy.".

576. [Wilson, Bill]. "What is Freedom in A.A.?'. Grapevine; May 1960; 16(12): pp2-4.
Bill writes of the dimension of "choice" available to AA members, because AA adopts no governmental structure or measures.

577. [Wilson, Bill]. "What is Acceptance?". Grapevine; March 1962; 17(10): pp2-5.
"One way to get at the meaning of the principle of acceptance is to meditate upon it in the context of the Serenity Prayer.".

578. [Wilson, Bill]. "Where Will Power Comes In". Grapevine; May 1962; 18(12): pp4-5.
This is Bill's response to a letter asking about the role of will power in staying sober.

579. [Wilson, Bill]. "Why Alcoholics Anonymous is Anonymous". Grapevine; Jan. 1955; 11(8): pp2-11.
Traditions Eleven and Twelve are reviewed as they developed during the early days of AA. "We now fully recognize that 100 per cent personal anonymity before the public is just as vital to the life of AA as 100 per cent sobriety is to the life of each and every member." Bill W. writes of Dr. Bob's burial stone which carries no mention of AA. "I think that this great and final example of self-effacement will prove of more permanent worth to AA than could any spectacular public notoriety or fine mausoleum. We don't have to go to Akron, Ohio, to see Dr. Bob's memorial. Dr. Bob's real monument is visible throughout the length and breadth of AA. Let us look again at its true inscription...one word only, which AAs have written. That word is sacrifice.".

580. [Wilson, Bill]. "Why Can't We Join A.A., Too?". Grapevine; Oct. 1947; 4(5): pp 3 & 7.
The burden of Dr. Bob & Bill being founders of AA is discussed. Bill discusses his plans for New York's General Service Center and his writing more literature. Bill W. & Dr. Bob confess a deep yearning: "As private citizens of A.A., we shall often wish to come and go among you like other people, without special attention. And while we would like always to keep the wonderful satisfaction of having been among the originators, we hope you will begin to think of us as early AAs only, not as 'founders'. So, can't we join AA, too?".

581. [Wilson, Bill]. "Will A.A. Ever Have a Personal Government? ". Grapevine; Jan. 1947; 3(8): p3.
Reasons AA's would have difficulty with dictator-type organization are listed. "Shall we not do well, if instead, we can cling in some part to the brotherly ideals of the early Franciscans? Let all of us A.A.'s, whether we be trustees, editors, secretaries, janitors or cooks - or just members ever recall the unimportance of wealth and authority as compared with the vast import of our brotherhood, love and service.".

582. [Wilson, Bill, & Dr. Bob]. "Your Third Legacy". Grapevine; Dec. 1950; 7(8): pp6-9.
The Co-Founders proposal to form "The General Service Conference of A.A." - a small body of State and Provincial A.A. Delegates meeting yearly who could assume direct responsibility for the guidance of the A.A. General Service Headquarters in New York City.

Chapter IV = Grapevine Special Publications

583. "AA Grapevine History". New York: AA Grapevine, Inc.
This 8-page pamphlet gives a brief history of the AA Grapevine from 1944 to the present. An earlier 4-page version was probably printed in 1978.

584. AA Grapevine Workbook. First ed. New York: AA Grapevine, Inc.; 1985; 120pp.
Note: Red plastic looseleaf 10 x 11.5" binder.
The 1985 General Service Conference Advisory Action recommended a workbook be produced for GV committees. It contains material on the GV, special items published by the GV, the role of the GV Rep, workshops and presentations, "Most Frequently Asked Questions about the Grapevine" and other GV flyers, order forms, etc., totaling 17 items plus text.

585. "THE AA GRAPEVINE" Display Banner. New York: AA Grapevine, Inc.; current.
This long 7.5 x 29" yellow banner, "The AA Grapevine," is often used in GV displays of literature for sale.

586. "The AA Grapevine: Questions and Answers". New York: AA Grapevine, Inc.; [after 1977].
This 4-page pamphlet asks and answers eight common questions about the AA Grapevine.

587. "AA is not... AA does not...". New York: AA Grapevine, Inc.; ca1970s?
This 8.5 x 11" poster includes two 19th century prints of old women in an ale shop and a soap box reformer addressing a crowd. Below, the text states: "AA is not... a religious movment...a temperance movement...a cure...[etc.] [and] AA does not... solicit or accept funds from outside sources...run hospitals...prescribe or pay for treatment for alcoholics..." At the bottom: "The sole purpose of AA is to help the alcoholic who wants to stop drinking.".

588. AA Today. First ed. New York: AA Grapevine, Inc./Cornwall Press; 1960: 111pp.
Note: Reprinted four times in an illus. softbound format.
Originally published in hardcover to commemorate AA's 25th anniversary, it sold as the Grapevine item at the Long Beach, CA, Int'l Convention. It was also used as a premium with Christmas gift subscriptions in 1960 and reprinted in Sept., 1960. In 1964, the Board decided not to reprint it and the plates were scapped in 1965. Out of print for many years, it was reprinted in 1979, in response to many requests, in softcover. The contents include: articles by Dr. Karl Menninger, Dr. William W. Bauer, Ivan Underwood, Judge Hector Perrier of Montreal, Dr. E. M. Jellinek, Adele E. Streeseman, M.D., Ernest C. Manning, Premier of Alberta, Canada, Warden Clinton Duffy, Edward J. Dowling, S.J., Sen. Margaret Chase Smith, J. P. Miller, Aldous Huxley, Rev. Kenneth Naylor of Montreal, anonymous writers in various fields, and articles

by Co-Founder Bill W. on The Language of the Heart, AA Tomorrow, and Dr. Bob [see individual author listings for a discussion of each article]. The 40 articles by AA members and non-alcoholic friends of the Fellowship are accompanied by a foreword, Serenity Prayer, The Twelve Steps, The Twelve Traditions, and a quiz. The anonymous articles cover AA and alcoholism in the fields of movies, the stage, the Fourth Estate, a woman pioneer in AA, acting, writing, youth, music, diplomacy, and how AA grew around the world. The Grapevine today remains what it has always been: "An AA meeting in print." Back in 1944, Bill W. okayed a woman AA member's "crazy idea" of a newsletter for AA. The first issue was eight pages and cost 15 cents. It caught on and in 1945, it was recognized as the national AA magazine. In 1948, the format was reduced from the large newspaper size to its present pocket-size. In 1945, the GV discussed the "sleeping pill menace" and carried articles by spouses and children of alcoholics, long before the formation of Al-Anon and Alateen. And in 1945, the magazine printed Jellinek's questionnaire and much of that data mailed back by hundreds of AAs became the basis of his famed chart, "Phases of Alcohol Addiction." "To let the public know what we are and are not," the GV June, 1947, issue carried our Preamble, written by the first editor of the GV, using portions of the Foreword to the Big Book. Today, the Preamble is read at the opening of most AA meetings, a four-page GV History pamphlet states. Co-Founder Bill W. wrote extensively for the GV and the Twelve Traditions were born and grew into their present form as a series in the Grapevine by Bill.

589. Best Cartoons from the Grapevine. First ed. New York: AA Grapevine, Inc.,/Cornwall Press; 1970: 60pp.
Note: First edition was hardcover.
The Corporate GV Board approved this in July, 1969, to be presented at the 1970 Int'l Convention. It was also used as a premium with subscriptions purchased at the 1975 Int'l Convention. Since 1989, it has bee reprinted in softcover as the hardcover cost has become prohibitive. "In AA, laughter isn't just fun, it is a necessity," the foreword states. "This book is a distillation (oops!) of the best cartoons that have appeared in the past quarter-century in the GV. Included are examples of the Oliver Slipp and Victor E. running series of cartoons. Humor heals. Powerful medicine!".

590. The Best of Bill. New York: AA Grapevine, Inc.; 1965. "Published in the fall of 1965 in the form of five leaflets. Introduced at the Toronoto Int'l Convention. The hope at the time was to add other Bill W. articles to the packet, though this was never done. In 1982, when the cost of publishing five single leaflets had become prohibitive, it was reprinted as a single small 3.5 x 5.5" booklet." Included are Bill's thoughts on Fear, Faith, Honesty, Humility, and Love.

591. Best of the Grapevine. First ed. New York: AA Grapevine, Inc.; 1985: 288pp; ISBN: 0-933685-00-9.
Note: Vol. I, index, dj.
The Corporate Board authorized the "Best of the Grapevine" project in July, 1978. Lack of funds shelved it temporarily but it was revived in 1984 and published in 1985. This is an anthology of personal insights, spiritual sustenance, historical facts, etc., about the AA principles and a new way of life by members of the Fellowship. The 76 articles from 1944 to 1985 are a mirror of the AA Fellowship, a forum for debate, a meeting in print. Both Co-Founders, Bill W. and Dr. Bob, have selections here and Bill's first article introducing the Twelve Traditions is reprinted. Humorous small cartoons enhance the text throughout. Vol. I sold as the Grapevine item at the 1985 Int'l Convention at Montreal.

592. Best of the Grapevine. Volume II. First ed. New York: AA Grapevine, Inc.; 1986; 287pp; ISBN: 0-933685-12-2.
Note: index, dj.
This anthology contains another 70 of the best articles reprinted from the AA Grapevine from 1944 to 1986. Illustrated with small humorous cartoons from the GV, this volume contains articles by Bill W. and Dr. Bob, Jack Alexander, William James, Nell Wing, Lois W., and other AAs. The topics range from sex to the Sermon on the Mount, from marijuana to The Days of Wine and Roses, from prayer to anonymity.

593. Binders. New York: AA Grapevine, Inc.; 1966.
These green binders first produced in 1966 and introduced in the Jan., 1967, issue hold 12 issues of the GV for readers who want to save their GVs for rereading or preservation in archives.

594. "Co-Founders' Memorial Issues" packet. New York: AA Grapevine, Inc.; 1980.
The GV issues [Jan. 1951 for Dr. Bob and March 1971 for Bill] commemorating the co-founders, which were out of print, were approved for reprinting and distribution in a packet by the GV Corporate Board at its Feb. 1980 meeting. A packet was given free to every person who bought a GV subscription at the 1980 Int'l Convention in New Orleans.

595. Facsimile of First Issue of Grapevine. The Grapevine; June, 1944; 1(1): 8pp.
Note: 10 x 12".
The GV Corporate Board in Oct., 1978, approved reproducing this historical issue. The lead article is on alcoholism as a "true disease" by Howard W. Haggard and E. M. Jellinek, "Yale Savants." Also included were AA in the Armed Forces, AA Goes to Sea, Purpose of The Alcoholic Foundation [AA's first name], letters from AAs, book reviews, news from the Central Office and metropolitan groups, etc.

596. "The Grapevine Representative Handbook". New York: AA Grapevine, Inc.
This 12-page pamphlet provides GV reps with their suggested duties, resources, information on subscriptions, and answers to frequently-asked questions about the GV.

597. "Guidelines for Writing Grapevine Articles". New York: AA Grapevine, Inc.; 1980s?
This one page flyer sets out guidelines for writing GV articles.

598. GvR News; Summer 1986-1994: 4pp each.
This quarterly newsletter reviews GvR activities around the world, reprints historical GV articles, announces new GV special items, and reports on what's new in the AA Grapevine. It is mailed to all GvR's and others interested in the GV.

599. The Home Group: Heartbeat of AA. First ed. New York: AA Grapevine, Inc.; 1993; 128pp; ISBN: 0-933685-24-6. LC 93-71034.
Note: pb.
The AA Home Group is the focus in this collection of articles reprinted from the Grapevine. Where Recovery Begins, the Joys of Service, the Lessons of Experience, and the Traditions at Work are the four sections under which the home group is discussed.

600. "How can the Grapevine keep in touch with your group if you don't have a GvR?". New York: AA Grapevine, Inc.; 1993.
This 15 x 20" yellow poster has Victor E. shedding tears and asking this question.

601. Index The AA Grapevine June 1944 - December 1990 . First ed. New York: The AA Grapevine, Inc.; 1992; 330pp; ISBN: 0-933685-21-1.
Note: 8.5 x 11" softbound.
Although not A.A. Conference-approved literature, this is the first index to AA literature ever published for use by the AA membership. Every issue of the monthly AA Grapevine from the first in June, 1944, through Dec., 1990, has been indexed and each listing is identified as an article, editorial, letter, news item, reprint, quotation, or review as well as year, month, and pages. Probably over 20,000 listings in double columns cover the widest possible range of topics by or about AA, its history, development, ideas, members, problems, experience, spirituality, Steps, Traditions, Concepts, principles, slogans, etc. etc. etc. The General Service Conference recommended the Grapevine publish one special item for the general AA membership each year and this index is what Bill W. would have called "a ten strike.!" It should prove very helpful especially to AA archivists writing their local AA histories.

602. "It's a Good Policy to Insure Sobriety". New York: AA Grapevine; 1944-50s?
This foldout 7 x 17" pamphlet is designed to look like an insurance policy. The front and back covers contain information about the GV and the inside foldout has "Twelve Ways You Can Use the AA Grapevine to Strengthen and Insure Your Sobriety" which later became that separate pamphlet. A form at the bottom offers a GV one-year subscription for $2.50 and a GV mailing address of P.O.Box 85, Knickerbocker Station, New York 2, N.Y. The editorial office was then at room 206, 141 East 44th St., NY 17, NY.

603. "Let's Not Keep the Grapevine a Secret!". New York: AA Grapevine, Inc.; current.
This 8.5 x 11" poster features a cover from the GV with the world viewed from outer space, the three Legacies around it, and the GV address.

604. "Let's Not Keep The Grapevine a Secret!". New York: AA Grapevine, Inc.; 1993.
This 8.5 x 11" yellow poster has a smiling Victor E. with a sign "Our Meeting in Print - The AA Grapevine" and additional text.

605. <u>Man on the Bed</u> print [color painting]. in: <u>AA Grapevine</u>. New York: AA Grapevine, Inc.; Dec., 1955; about 8 x 11".
"This four-color reproduction of a painting given to Bill W. by one of the volunteer illustrators for the Grapevine was approved as a special item in Oct., 1955, and intended for use as a new-or-renewal subscription premium. It appeared as the centerfold of the Dec., 1955, GV. Originally titled "Came to Believe," when the booklet <u>Came to Believe</u> was published by AAWS, the name was changed to "The Man on the Bed." The color print shows two AA's twelfth-stepping a sick alcoholic, the man on the bed.

606. "Miniature Grapevine". New York: AA Grapevine, Inc.; pre-1952.
This 16-page small [3x4"] booklet is probably one of the oldest GV special items. "Originally conceived as a form of 'mild promotion,' it was distributed free. In Feb., 1953, the GV Board acted to discontinue distribution of the mini-GV after the supply was exhausted. In July 1959, the GV Board set a selling price and revived them." Contents include: 12 Steps, 12 Traditions, photos of AA Co-Founders Bill W. and Dr. Bob, Serenity Prayer, preamble, Declaration of Unity, history of AA and of the GV.

607. One Day at a Time [Grapevine wall calendar]. New York: AA Grapevine, Inc.; 1968-1994.
Note: 7.5 x 10", 26pp each.
"The first calendar [for 1968] was introduced in the Oct., 1967, GV issue. It was conceived because the then-existing custom of running photo-plus-quote center spreads several times a year in the GV." Each month has an inspirational photo, chosen from the annual photo contest open to all AAs. In recent years, the calendar was criticized because it did not contain any AA information and therefore didn't "carry the message." In 1990, quotes from the GV and Bill's writings were added to each month. At present, the General Service Conference has taken no action one way or another and the calendar will continue to be printed through 1995. About 30,000 are sold annually.

608. "Order Forms". New York: AA Grapevine, Inc.; 1953-93.
From one page 5 x 7" flyers to the current 6-page 8.5 x 11" catalog, numerous order forms for every Grapevine special item and publication over the years were printed. Prepublication forms, GV subscription pads, offers of premiums with renewals and gift orders, the wealth of order forms provides a living history of the Grapevine's efforts to "carry the message" from 1944 to the present. The current catalog of 6 pages offers 40 items. Many of the forms also are flyers containing full descriptions of the material: e.g., The Language of the Heart. The GV issues themselves often have tear-out order forms for the latest items.

609. Pocket Planner. New York: AA Grapevine, Inc.; 1981-93.
Note: 6.25 x 3.75"& 36pp.
The annual pocket planner was approved by the GV Corporate Board in Feb., 1980, and the first was printed in 1981. ["Interestingly, in Jan., 1969, the same idea had come before the Board and was rejected because it was felt it would compete with the Wall Calender - as indeed, it has."] Addresses, phone numbers, time zones, monthly quotes from the GV, and order forms are included.

610. "Portable AA Meeting: The Grapevine". New York: AA Grapevine, Inc.; 1981.
This 4-page leaflet was originally given as a presentation at the 31st General Service Conference of AA in 1981 by the Idaho delegate who views the GV as a valuable tool in Twelfth Step work, sponsorship, and one's own sobriety.

611. Preamble. New York: AA Grapevine, Inc.; May, 1956.
Note: 7.5 x 5.5" card.
"The old wording of the Preamble [with 'honest desire to stop drinking'] was published in a 'dressed-up' version in the center spread of the May 1956 issue of the GV and 10.5 x 15.5" large reprints were sent to each group as a gift from the GV. The Preamble was written by the first editor of the GV, and the GV holds the copyright. Extensive background [information] appears in Best of the Grapevine, Vol. I, and in the Grapevine Workbook." The Preamble is a basic

statement of what AA is and is not and is usually read at the beginning of most AA meetings.

612. "Serenity Prayer" card. New York: AA Grapevine, Inc.; pre-1961.
This 5.5 x 7.5" Serenity Prayer card was used in 1961 as a subscription premium with Christmas gift orders. It has long been used as the cover of the April GV and probably was made a special item as readers cut off the cover and framed it.

613. "Slogans". New York: AA Grapevine, Inc.; 1956-57.
This set of five slogans from early AA includes "Live and Let Live," "Easy Does It," "But for the Grace of God...," "Think, Think, Think," and "First Things First." Some members put them in that order and then read the first word of each: "Live Easy But Think First!" The slogans, in the hand-lettered version currently sold, originally appeared on the inside back cover of five issues of the GV [Sept.-Dec., 1956, and Feb. 1957]. The July 1956 GV Corporate Board decided that in order to make "the five AA slogans" available to the membership. Later they were offered for sale and also as a premium with an order of four GVsubscriptions. A packet of mini-slogans was offered in the Dec. 1965 GV as a subscription premium for Christmas gift subscriptions.

614. "Traditions Checklist". New York: AA Grapevine, Inc.; 1969-71.
This 4-page flyer contains 95 questions about the 12 Traditions which many groups use as a basis for wider discussion about them. The questions were originally published in the AA GV in conjunction with a series on the Twelve Traditions that began in Nov. 1969 and ran through Sept. 1971.

615. "Twelve Ways You Can Use The AA Grapevine To Strengthen and Insure Your Sobriety". New York: AA Grapevine, Inc.; current.
Twelve ways the GV helps individual AA members and AA groups are outlined.

616. "Victor E." name tag. New York: AA Grapevine, Inc.; 1977.
This 2.5 x 3.5" name tag shows GV cartoon character Victor E. saying "Hi!" It was produced at the request of the 1977 General Service Conference.

617. "What does a GvR (Grapevine Representative) do?". New York: AA Grapevine, Inc.
This one-page flyer suggests eight duties for GvR's and includes a form at the bottom for registering new GvR's with New York.

618. "Who Writes the Grapevine? YOU DO!". New York: AA Grapevine, Inc.; current.
This 8.5 x 11" illustrated flyer gives AA members information on writing for the GV and how manuscripts are selected for publication.

619. [Wilson, Bill]. Language of the Heart. Bill W.'s Grapevine Writings. First ed. New York: AA Grapevine, Inc.; Oct., 1988: 410pp; ISBN: 0-933685-16-5. LC 88-71930.
Note: The dust jacket was modified for the third printing, "55 Years - One Day at a Time, Seattle, Washington, July 5-8, 1990," being added as a commemorative for the A.A. Int'l Convention held there.
"In October 1972, the Grapevine Board approved publication of a volume of Bill W.'s collected writings, to commemorate the 40th Anniversary of A.A. The minutes do not state why the project did not come to fruition until Feb., 1986, when a volunteer committee renewed the idea. Several draft manuscripts were reviewed and turned down. Then the GV decided the more appropriate path would be to publish all of Bill's writings with a brief background text. Such a volume was published in Oct., 1988." The book is divided into three parts: 1944-50 - Hammering Out the Traditions; 1950-58 - The Service Structure; Relations with non-AA Friends; and 1958-70: Practicing Spiritual Principles "in all our affairs;" AA Spreads Around the World. A foreword by Bill's widow, Lois W., and a topical index are included along with memorial articles and reflections on the Grapevine itself. More than 150 articles written by Co-Founder Bill detail the growth of A.A. over 1944-1970 and this is the first time these articles have been published together.

Chapter V = Books & Pamphlets about AA

620. "A. A. You May be Asking These Questions about Alcoholics Anonymous". Birmingham, AL: Street Printing Co.; 1950-60s?
This four-page pamphlet asks and answers 20 questions newcomers to AA may have about affiliation and the Fellowship.

621. "A.A. A Simple Program Simply Explained". Chicago: Hygea magazine/Chicago Area A.A. Service Ofc.; July, 1948.
This 12-page 1975 reprint from the A.M.A. 1948 magazine is a brief exposition of what AA is.

622. "A.A. Bulletin 1". New York: The Alcoholic Foundation, National Headquarters - Alcoholics Anonymous; Nov. 14, 1940. Note: facsimile.
This single 8.5 x 11" sheet is the first A.A. Bulletin. Written and signed by Ruth Hock, AA's first nonalcoholic employee, it is "an effort to develop a mutual idea exchange sheet to establish a clear feeling of friendship between A.A. groups from the east coast to the west, and we hope it will prevent the secession from the A.A. ranks of our San Francisco group who threatened to call themselves 'Dipsomaniacs Incognito' unless they heard from us more frequently." It was mailed from Box 658, Church St. Annex, New York City. It listed 43 AA groups established or in growning pains around the U.S.

623. "A.A. is a Tender Trap". Chicago: Chicago Area A.A. Service Ofc.
This 21-page pamphlet focuses on one AA's interpretation of the program as a "tender, not terrible, trap" with many benefits, including faith and self-respect, "which the Almighty seems to reserve for some of His favorite children, the ex-drunkards.".

624. "A.A. Ocean Round-Up Keepsake Program". Miami, FL: Eastern Steamship Lines, Inc.; Oct. 8-11, 1976.
This 16-page program announces the first AA ocean "Cruise without Booze, "the most exciting event since Bill met Dr. Bob!" AA's took over the entire Emerald Seas ship for 4 days of fellowship that included AA and Alanon meetings, AA's Own Talent Show, shuffleboard contests, a stop in Nassau, etc. An 8-page song book includes songs like "After the Binge Was Over" and "Down by the Old Gin Mill.".

625. "Act Like A Winner. Unofficial 'Etiquette' for Attending A.A. or Al-Anon Meetings.". First ed. Center City, MN: Hazelden; March 1983; 21pp; ISBN: 0-89486-162-X.
After some basic information about A.A., this pamphlet sets down some norms to cover such topics as smoking, bad language, Antabuse, Valium and other drugs, types of meetings, etc. The author states the purpose of this pamphlet "is to tell the alcoholic precisely how to become a winner" (an alcoholic who obviously enjoys their sobriety). The anonymous author joined AA in 1967 and is a doctor.

626. Akron Inter-Group News; 1954-1993: each issue is usually 12pp.
Note: [The first issue of Nov., 1954, was reprinted in the June, 1993, issue.].
Published monthly for almost 40 years, this 8.5 x 11" AA newsletter contains cartoons, stories of recovery, opinions of controversial topics [profanity at meetings, drugs, etc.], news of AA events in the Akron area, especially the annual Founders Day weekend, held around June 10, to celebrate the birth of AA in Akron, June 10, 1935.

627. "Alcoholics Anonymous: An Interpretation of the Twelve Steps". Pontiac, MI: AA of Oakland County; nd.
This booklet divides the steps into four phases: the admission, the spiritual phase, the inventory and restitution, and the active work. Appropriate steps are explained in each section and discussion questions are suggested.

628. "Alcoholics Anonymous: An Interpretation of the Twelve Steps". Ferndale, MI: Alcoholics Anonymous of Greater Detroit; nd.
This pamphlet, in part, describes the spirituality of the AA program. Steps 2,3,5,6,7 and 11 are explained. In the discussion of Step 5, the pamphlet explains that Catholics can use confession to do this step and non-Catholics can use their ministers.

629. "Alcoholics Anonymous: An Interpretation of our Twelve Steps". Washington, DC: The "Paragon" Creative Printers; Oct. 1944.
This 20-page booklet "contains material for the discussion meetings [on the steps] for alcoholics only." "Experience" is still in Step Twelve. Four discussions with questions tackle Step One and Step Twelve separately and Steps 2, 3, 5, 6, 7, and 11 constitute the "spiritual phase" with Steps 4, 8, 9, and 10 the "inventory and restitution.".

630. "Alcoholics Anonymous". Indianapolis, IN: Indianapolis Group of AA; January 1949.
Note: 3.25 x 6.25".
This small 6-page foldout pamphlet contains basic information about AA and the Twelve Steps.

631. "Alcoholics Anonymous Birthplace Akron, Ohio". Akron, OH: ?; June, 1975.
This 24-page pamphlet includes historic photos and text on many of the early Akron, Ohio, meeting places of A.A. and its founders and other early sober alcoholics and non-alcoholic friends of the Fellowship.

632. Alcoholics Anonymous. Piscataway, NJ: Center of Alcohol Studies, Rutgers University; 1988; 57pp.
This bibliography of A.A. is a compilation of all listings from Rutgers' massive three volume reference work, International Bibliography of Studies on Alcohol, Mark Keller, General Editor. It includes annual updates up to 1988. This is volume B-310 in Rutgers' Alcohol Bibliography Series and includes over 500+ listings of literature by or about A.A.

633. Alcoholics Anonymous Online Newsletter; June 10, 1989; 1(1): 1p.
Note: [for more info, write: AAO, P.O. Box 19008, Akron, OH 44319].
This flyer from Akron, Ohio, announces "AA Joins the World of Computers" with a bulletin board meeting available to anyone in AA with a computer and modem or telephone hookup. AAO is available 24 hours a day, seven days a week, and any AA can leave messages for AAs anywhere else in the world. Meetings are conducted via the computer and AAO is "actually one large Home Group" composed of any AA who hooks up to the computer bulletin board. The meetings can be international or any locality depending on who's online. One AA said this AAO computer network is great for shut-ins, handicapped persons, and those living in remote regions where the nearest meeting may be 50 miles away. Anonymity is protected. One bulletin board is listed as "HHGH," Home Hobby Group Help. It doesn't attract much attention but AA's know it's the bulletin board meeting.

634. Alcoholics Anonymous Big Book Stories from the First & Second Editions. First ed. Oklahoma City, OK: anonymous; June, 1992; 246pp total.
Note: 5.5 x 8.5" spiral bound.
"This is a collection of 32 original stories, 7 from the Second Edition and 25 from the First Edition of the Big Book of Alcoholics Anonymous. These stories are NOT in the Third Edition," is stated on the first page. The volume has color cover reproductions of the front and back of the original "circus" dust jacket. Not A.A. Conference-Approved Literature. Members of the A.A. General Service Conference have discussed printing a fourth edition of the Big Book with all the stories from the three previous editions but have never acted on this. This facsimile edition of the 32 original stories dropped from the first and second editions in the third edition fills this void for those interested in reading all the original stories of recovery in all editions of the Big Book.

635. Alcoholism: A Source Book for the Priest. Pfau, Ralph, Fr./ et al, editors. First ed. Indianapolis, IN: National Clergy Council on Alcoholism [NCCA]; 1960; 685pp. (NCCA "Blue Books"); ISBN: LC 60-11243.
Note: The Blue Books were printed in very small numbers and were available only to members of the NCCA, most of whom were members of AA. Not being for sale to the general public, many of the authors' full names and theirmembership in AA were used. Obviously the potential for anonymity breaks existed but was extremely limited because of restricted availability. Since the authors' intentions were not to break their anonymity, we have deleted their membership in AA from the articles. [for individual authors and topics, check the sections on journals and chapters in books in this bibliography. Over 50 NCCA articles are listed.].
This collection of essays for priests, a selection from the previous ten NCCA annual Blue Books, was edited by Fr. Ralph Pfau, the founder and executive secretary of the NCCA. The articles focus on AA and priests and other religious, Christianity and Catholicism, recovery, and related topics. Some of the articles are: Rev. John C. Ford's "Alcohol Education for the Seminary" and "Moral Rearmament and AA," Dr. William D. Silkworth's "A History of Alcoholics Anonymous," Rev. Edward Dowling's "Catholic Asceticism and the Twelve Steps," Rt. Rev. Msgr. John A. McNulty's "The Spiritual and Medical Aspects of AA in New Jersey," Austin Ripley's "The Guest House Concept" and "Helping the Alcoholic Priest," Rt. Rev. Msgr. Raymond F. Harkin's "Alcoholism, AA, and the Alcoholic Priest," a panel chaired by Fr. Pfau on "Active Participation of Alcoholic Priests in AA," Theresa M. Rohan's "Therapy at the Knickerbocker Hospital," Mr. Lynn C.'s "Recovery at Hazelden," and Fr. John Doe's "A Factual Case History.".

636. Allen, Charles L. 12 Way To Solve Your Problem. Atlanta, GA: Charles L. Allen/Grace Methodist Church; 1964?; 31pp.
Allen, a Methodist minister, applies A.A.'s 12 Steps to a multitude of problems in any individual's life. "I have learned that the basic solution to all personal problems are pretty much the same. Bill and Dr. Bob worked out a twelve point Program of Recovery for the alcoholic. These same twelve steps work equally well, no matter what the trouble is. These are really basic principles of the Christian faith.".

637. Allen, James. As A Man Thinketh. reprint ed. New York: Grosset & Dunlap; 1930s; 72pp.
Note: dj.
This was one of the books early A.A. members read for spiritual guidance and inspiration before the publication of Alcoholics Anonymous.

638. Anderson, D. J. "Psychopathology of Denial". Center City, MN: Hazelden Foundation; 1981.
This 44-page pamphlet discusses defense mechanisms for alcoholism denial and breaking them down. The role of AA in health maintenance after successful treatment is examined.

639. Anne W. Take What Works. First ed. Center City, MN: Hazelden; Dec. 1989: throughout; 67pp; ISBN: 0-89486-636-2.
Note: paperback.
Subtitled "How I Made the Most of My Recovery Program," the author discusses the Steps of AA, the "Myths of the Fellowship," and other truths she feels are commonly-accepted but in need of questioning.

640. Anonym, Kenneth. Understanding the Recovering Alcoholic. Canfield, Ohio: Alba House Communications; 1974.
The author examines the human meaningfulness of the alcoholic's disease and the interpersonal recovery life-style of the A.A. program.

641. Anonymous. Big Book Study Guide. First ed. Little Rock, AR: Kelly Foundation, Inc.; 1985; c1987; 103pp.
Note: Alcoholics Anonymous has long resisted and rejected publication by A.A. itself of a book such as this on the grounds it would be viewed as too authoritive and definitive concerning individual topics. However, non-A.A. groups and/or individuals have published study guides and this one uses a question and answer format as a lead-in to discussion. "This book was written by members of Alcoholics Anonymous in Little Rock, Arkansas, following the example of a member in another state." Useful but not to be taken as the only approach to the Big Book (Alcoholics Anonymous) or as the only answer to a particular question or problem. Paperback. "The purpose of this book is to enable every member of the group to extract as much information as possible from each page of the text book Alcoholics Anonymous," the authors state.

642. Anonymous [Chicago Group]. Impressions of A.A. Chicago-NY?: Chicago Group of A.A.; post-1939.
Note: 3 1/2 x 6 1/2" pamphlet, 16pp.
Ten pages of commentary on alcoholism, alcoholics and Alcoholics Anonymous followed by the Twelve Steps.

643. Arnold, Emily [pseudonym]. A Craving. New York: Avon Books; 1982; 246pp.
This personal witness account details the trials of Polly during her active alcoholism, recovery attempts, and finally, sobriety through A.A.

644. "Attorney Who Saved AA Crusade Is Dead". in: Associated Press wire service. Akron, OH; Sept. 19, 1954.
This six-paragraph AP wire story reported the death of William I. Dotson. "He was 43 and apparently a hopeless alcoholic when the two founders of AA found him in Akron City Hospital, so drunk he couldn't talk," the article reported. The two AA founders were "almost ready to give up their AA work...but Dotson succeeded splendidly and never took another drink of liquor." Dotson was a native of Lexington, KY, and died at age 62 in Crile Veterans Hosp. in Cleveland. Bill D. was AA 3.

645. Badger, Edward. "Easy Does It Explores Alcoholism, Points the Way to a Cure". Birmingham, Ala. News; July 16, 1950.
This reviewer of Easy Does It by Hugh Reilly notes the book has "the endorsement of Dr. William Silkworth, physician in charge of the A.A. wing in Knickerbocker Hospital, New York.".

646. Bailey, Margaret B./Leach, Barry. Alcoholics Anonymous, Pathway to Recovery: A Study of 1,058 members of the A.A. Fellowship in New York City.: The National Council on Alcoholism, Inc.; 1965; 58pp.
This NCA booklet provides data on A.A. members' characteristics before and after membership. The sample is heavily weighted with extrememly-active and pro A.A. members.

647. BAR-Less "carries the message"; 1952-54: 32-40pp each.
Note: Apparently the journal started in 1951. 5 x 7".
This bi-monthly journal by the Indiana State Prison Group of Alcoholics Anonymous was published with "the approval of our Sponsor, Warden Alfred F. Dowd." Contents include the first anniversary of the Indiana Reformatory group, editorials, personal stories of recovery in AA, history of the prison group [in July, 1954, they celebrated 10 years], and a wide range of articles about AA both in and out of prison.

648. Barnes, Horace B. ["Barney"]. The True Life Story of an Alcoholic. Philadelphia: Dorrance & Co.; 1972; 42pp.
Personal witness. Autobiographical account of "Barney" Barnes and his life as an active alcoholic, recovery through A.A., and his work as director and counselor for Vanguard Lodge, an alcoholism treatment center, in Minneapolis, Minnesota.
Anonymity break.

649. Barry L. "Be A Double Winner". Center City, MN: Hazelden; Oct., 1985; ISBN: 0-89486-332-0.
This 13-page pamphlet discusses poly-addiction in AA and other Fellowships and emphasizes the "an addict is an addict is an addict" approach.

650. Barry L. "Historical Perspective: Homosexual Men and Women in A.A."; June, 1985.
Note: Although no formal paper is available, a tape of this lecture at the International A.A. Convention at Montreal, Canada, exists.

651. Bean, Margaret, M.D. Alcoholics Anonymous: A.A. First ed. New York: Insight Communications; Feb., 1975; 64pp.
Note: This was reprinted in Psychiatric Annals.
Bean visited over 30 AA meetings in the Greater Boston area, read AA, psychiatric, and social work literature, and interviewed AA members and psychiatrists and others who work closely with AA or with alcoholics in order to write this book. She discusses AA history, principles, recovery, expectations of psychotherapy, religion and affiliation. Her critique is balanced and clear.

652. A Beginner's Guide. Palos Park, IL: New Beginnings Pub. Co.; 1991; 80pp.
"The purpose of this text is to furnish the beginner with an overall view of Alcoholics Anonymous" the foreword states. It is not intended to replace any A.A. material. Hitting your bottom, affiliation, sponsorship, what AA is and is not, God and the Twelve Steps are discussed.

653. Berg, Steven L., Ph.D., Editor. Alcoholism and Pastoral Ministry: Readings On Recovery. First ed. Lake Orion, MI: Guest House, Inc.; 1989: over 70 references to A.A.; 282pp; ISBN: 0-9623733-0-3.
Note: pb.
Dedicated to Austin Ripley, founder of Guest House, this volume comprises 32 articles and essays all focusing on spirituality, the clergy, recovery from alcoholism, A.A. and related subjects. The 6 chapters end with Suggestions for Further Reading and are titled: AA & Historical Issues; Stories of Recovery; Spiritual Issues in Recovery; Ministry to Alcoholics; Diversity Among Alcoholics; and Alcoholic Clergy. The index lists over 70 references to AA. Berg's anthology is a resource guide for the clergy of any faith and provides an excellent overview of alcoholism and ministering to alcoholics.

654. Berg, Steven L. God as We Understand Him: An Annotated Bibliography. Chicago: Nat'l Assn. of Lesbian and Gay Alcoholism Professionals' Conference [NALGAP]; Sept. 1985.
This paper addresses the "Christian" nature of AA's spirituality and why some lesbians and gay men reject AA because of their discomfort with the Christian spiritual tradition. Reasons for this rejection are given and many examples are cited from the small press. (NALGAP 062). AA, of course, does not endorse any religion.

655. Berg, Steven L./Finnegan, Dana/McNally, Emily. The NALGAP Annotated Bibliography: Alcoholism, Substance Abuse, and Lesbians-Gay Men. Fort Wayne, IN: The National Association of Lesbian and Gay Alcoholism Professionals; 1987; cFirst; 259pp; ISBN: 0-9618753-1-3.
Note: NALGAP was founded in 1979 by Dana Finnegan & Emily NcNally. Berg met those two at the first national conference of NALGAP in Chicago in September, 1985, and their two separate efforts in this field were combined into this fine bibliography. The NALGAP Collection of Literature on Alcoholism and Homosexuality is located at The Center of Alcohol Studies Library at Rutgers University, New Jersey. The first serious attempt (and a successful one) to gather and annotate all materials on this topic. Contains 911 listings. Three excellent indexes (author/name, title, & subject) of almost 50 pages compliment the main body of the bibliography. The subject index contains over 120 references to Alcoholics Anonymous. Paperback.

656. Berg, Steven L., Ph.D. Spirituality & Addiction: A Bibliography. First ed. Wheeling, WV: The Bishop of Books; Nov., 1993; 95pp; ISBN: 1-877686-06-9.
Note: Published in a limited, numbered edition of 200 copies, signed by the author. index, 8.5 x 11" pb.
Berg has found 682 books, articles, etc. on spirituality and addiction. Much of the focus of this bibliography is on Alcoholics Anonymous. Chapter headings indicate the wide-ranging interdisciplinary nature of this work: religious attitudes & institutions, ethnic/cross cultural studies, special populations, family and psychological issues, A.A., attitudes toward Higher Power, qualities of sobriety, historical issues, literary portraits, and biographies & autobiographies.

657. Berman, Susan. "The Twelve Steps and Jewish Tradition". Center City: Hazelden; 1988.
Rabbi Berman uses her experience as an AA alcoholic to help other Jews come to terms with the AA program. The twelve steps are only mentioned in the title of the booklet. Anonymity break.

658. Berryman, John. Recovery. First ed. New York: Farrar, Straus & Giroux; 1973; 254pp; ISBN: 0-374-24817-6.
Note: Paperback.
Berryman's only novel is about "the disease of alcoholism." The author writes in a note to the book that "I don't write as a member of the American and international society, Alcoholics Anonymous, but as an author merely who has experienced certain things, witnessed things, heard things, and imagined some." The novel is roughly patterned after the Twelve Steps of A.A. and is a deep and unsparing account of an alcoholic's struggle. The foreword is written by Saul Bellow.

659. "Biblical Helps for the 'Twelve Steps". Washington, D.C.: National Episcopal Coalition on Alcohol; nd.
Selected Biblical passages are corrolated with each of AA's Twelve Steps.

660. Bienvenu, Dudley, M.D. I'm An Alcoholic; What's Your Excuse? An Alcoholic's View of Himself and His Illness. New York: Vantage Press; 1982; 103pp.
This doctor's story of his illness and rehabilitation in an alcohol-drug rehab unit is presented in three stages: denial, awareness and acceptance, and how A.A.'s Steps helped his recovery.

661. Big Book & Traditions Study Guide. First ed. Pompano Beach, FL: Seminar; 1993; 47pp.
Note: [no book title exists so the title above was suggested by the contents]. spiral bound.
This book has been used at many of South Florida's Big Book Seminars and meetings. It contains questions about alcoholics, alcoholism and recovery in A.A. and answers found in the Big Book [page numbers given]. The Twelve Traditions are also discussed in the Q & A format.

662. Bill Wilson & The Vitamin B-3 Therapy 1965-1971. Facsimile limited reprint ed. Wheeling, WV: The Bishop of Books; June, 1993; 96pp.
Note: 8.5 x 11". [for separate discussion of the three communications, refer to "Vitamin B-3..." in this chapter.]. This is a facsimile reprint in a limited edition of 200 copies of the original three "Communications" to AA's doctors written and edited by Bill W. in 1965, 1968, and 1971. The Vitamin B-3 Therapy was the last main project that occupied Bill W., the Co-Founder of AA, until his death on Jan. 24, 1971. In these communications, Bill and doctors in AA discussed and reported on their findings on the efficacy of using B-3 with alcoholics and schizophrenics. The project by Bill and the doctors was in NO way associated with AA.

663. Bill's (Wilson) Bookshelf: Studio, Stepping Stones. mimeographed copy ed. Bedford, N.Y.: (Bill & Lois Wilson); ca 1986; 4pp.
These three and one half mimeographed pages contain a list of the books on Bill Wilson's bookshelf at his home at Stepping Stones. Many of the books he referred to constantly for ideas, meditations, and intellectual and spiritual stimulation.

664. "Birds of a Feather - - Just What is Alcoholics Anonymous?". St. Louis, MO: Furlong Printing Co.; ca 1940s.
This four-page flyer gives basic information about AA, prints the Twelve Steps [with "experience" in the twelfth], and lists the 35 questions John Hopkins Hospital in Baltimore uses to determine if a person is an alcoholic or not.

665. Bishop, Charles, Jr. Alcoholism. 46 Eureka Ave., Wheeling, West Virginia 26003.: The Bishop of Books; 1984; Catalog 35; 56pp.
Note: Limited edition of 500 copies. It contains the author's own listing of the ten most important books in alcoholism literature in American history along with facsimile title pages and estimates of their cost on the rare book market. A landmark catalog, the first in American antiquarian bookselling devoted entirely to the whole range of alcoholism literature in America.
Antiquarian bookseller's catalog, 8 1/2 x 11, listing thousands of books, pamphlets, newspapers, ephemera on alcoholism, including A.A. material, for sale. Rare A.A. literature is priced.

666. Bishop, Charles, Jr./Pittman, Bill. The Annotated Bibliography of Alcoholics Anonymous 1939-1989. First Limited ed. Wheeling, WV: The Bishop of Books; Feb. 1989; 284pp; ISBN: 1-877686-00-X. LC 89-144520.
Note: Index, pb. [published in a limited, numbered edition of 1,100 copies, all signed by both authors, and sold out in 1993. The greatly-enlarged second edition was scheduled for publication in 1994.].
This was the most comprehensive bibliography of Alcoholics Anonymous literature in 1989. Over 1,400 listings included A.A. Conference-approved literature, Grapevine articles,

dissertations, articles in popular magazines and scholarly journals, books, pamphlets, and chapters in books. The book was dedicated to the late Ruth Hock Crocelius, AA's first paid employee, and Nell Wing, AA's first Archivist, both non-alcoholics. A 23-page introductory essay by Bishop discussed the spiritual and historical importance of AA literature over the first 50 years since the publication of Alcoholics Anonymous in 1939.

667. Bissel, L. "Preliminary Data on First Longitudinal Study of an AA Population". Newport, RI: American Medical Society on Alcoholism; 1981; 1p.
Some preliminary data on suicide attempts, arrests, smoking, drug use, relapse, and inpatient care are highlighted from the first longitudinal study of an AA population, 217 males and 222 females consisting of physicians, dentists, attorneys, social workers, professional women, female registered nurses, and lesbians.

668. Bissell, LeClair, M.D./Watherwax, Richard. The Cat Who Drank Too Much. Bantam, Connecticut: The Bibulophile Press; 1982; 24pp; ISBN: 0-911153-00-4.
This small booklet presents the story of an alcoholic through the medium of 20 photos with captions of a cat who progresses through its alcoholic career until, facing suicide, it makes a decision to enter through the doorways of AA at a local church and finally into a treatment center.

669. Bissell, LeClair. "The Homosexual AA Member: A Descriptive Study". Seattle: National Council on Alcoholism Conference; May 1980.
Although several sources mention this paper, it was never compiled and distributed as a formal conference paper. (NALGAP 077).

670. Bjorklund, Paul. "What is Spirituality?". Center City, MN: Hazelden; Sept., 1983; ISBN: 0-89486-182-4.
This 15-page pamphlet "is one person's interpretation of AA's Twelve Step program." Spirituality is the main topic.

671. Block, Marvin A. "Alcoholism Is a Disease". Today's Health, NCA; Sept. 1956; 34(9): pp36-39.
Note: Available as a reprint from The National Council on Alcoholism.
The chairman of the Committee on Alcoholism of the AMA's Council on Mental Health cites the help available from Alcoholics Anonymous.

672. Bloomfield, Kim. Beyond Sobriety: The Cultural Significance of Alcoholics Anonymous As A Social Movement. Berkeley, CA: Alcohol Research Group; 1988; 40pp.
Note: Unpublished copy.
This university research paper by a student discusses AA as a social movement and compares it with the Green movement. It concludes A.A. is not one of the New Social Movements and has no political, economic, or social agenda to push.

673. Blumberg, Leonard U., Ph.D. Beware the First Drink! The Washington Temperance Movement and Alcoholics Anonymous. First ed. Seattle, WA: Glen Abbey Books; 1991; 278pp; ISBN: 0-934125-22-8. LC 90-19639.
Note: Extensive notes, bibliography, index. pb.
The Washington Temperance Movement of the 1840s and Alcoholics Anonymous, founded in 1935, both helped alcoholics stop drinking. Why has A.A. succeeded while the Washingtonians failed? Blumberg's book is probably the best history of the Washingtonians. William L. Pittman contributes chapter eight on A.A.

674. Bob W. "Transition from Treatment to A.A.". Center City, MN: Hazelden; 1981.
32-page pamphlet.

675. Brian L. "Perfectionism". Center City MN: Hazelden; March, 1985; ISBN: 0-89486-259-6.
This 14-page pamphlet discusses perfectionism in AA members. Quotes from As Bill Sees It by Bill W. are included.

676. A Brief History of Alcoholics Anonymous in Alamance County, North Carolina 1942-1992. Burlington, NC: Alamance County, NC, AA; 1992.
This nine-page history of AA in Alamance County, NC, covers groups in Burlington, Graham, Eli Whitney, Elon College and Mebane.

677. Broadmoor Study Group. Twelve Steps to Recovery. Baton Rouge, LA: Broadmoor (A.A.) Study Group; nd; 22pp.
Note: pamphlet.
Probably published in the 1950-60s, the pamphlet discusses in some depth the Twelve Steps of A.A. as the road to recovery.

678. Brokenshire, Norman. This is Norman Brokenshire: An Unvarnished Self-Portrait. New York: David McKay Co., Inc.; 1954; 307pp.
Personal witness. The noted radio announcer relates the story of his battle with alcoholism and attempts at sobriety through sanitariums, the Keeley Institute cure, the Peabody Method, and final recovery through A.A.

679. Brown, Stephanie. Treating the Alcoholic: A Developmental Model of Recovery. New York: Wiley-Interscience Publication; 1985.
Brown presents a reexamination of our beliefs, values and theories about alcoholics. This book provides a comparison between the principles of A.A. and psychotherapy. Emphasizing the vital importance of a triadic therapeutic relationship , it translates the Twelve Steps of A.A. into psychological terminology.

680. Browne, Lewis. This Believing World. A Simple Account of the Great Religions of the World. Second ed. New York: The Macmillan Co.; September, 1926; c1926; 347pp.
Note: 70 illus., index.
This book reviews succinctly Christianity, Judaism, Islam, and the other great religions of mankind, present and ancient. This was one of the books Dr. Bob, Bill W., and other early AA's recommended to new Fellowship members, especially those having difficulty with finding "a God as we understand him" because of their lack of childhood membership in any religious denomination or because of their professed agnosticism, skepticism, and doubt.

681. Bufe, Charles. Alcoholics Anonymous: Cult or Cure? First ed. San Francisco, CA: See Sharp Press; 1991; 158pp; ISBN: 0-9613289-3-2.
Note: Bibliography, index, pb.
Bufe reveals several relatively-unknown facts about A.A.'s history: Bill W.'s taking LSD, its alleged roots in "religiomania," the Oxford Group's early endorsement of Hitler, etc. In two chapters, he lists 17 characteristics of cults and measures A.A. against those, concluding that A.A. is not a cult...nor a cure. This is an extremely-provocative book for Fellowship members who, we suggest, tackle it with the admonition from Bill W., responding to a early critical article about A.A., that they may be right and even if they aren't, it might bring someone to a meeting [paraphrased]. Bufe discusses similarities and differences with the Oxford Groups & A.A., the Twelve Steps and the Twelve Traditions, the effectiveness of the Fellowship and its future. The author offers "Secular Alternatives" to A.A. and the "Twelve Step Mania.".

682. Burney, Gina. Alcoholics Anonymous 1935-85. ADAMHA News Supplement. Rockville, MD: Alcohol, Drug Abuse, and Mental Health Administration of U.S. Dept. of Health & Human Services.; 1985; 8pp.
This news supplement recounts briefly A.A.'s history, includes a one page interview with Dr. Boris Tabakoff on Alcohol Research and the Self-Help Movement and an article by Will Foster on Special Groups Within A.A. The author was on the staff of the National Clearinghouse for Alcohol Information. A.A. is also congratulated on its 50th anniversary with a letter from President Ronald Reagan.

683. Burns, Elizabeth. The Late Liz. New York: Popular Library; 1957; 283pp.
"The uncensored story of a millionairre's daughter, who had too much money, and too much to drink..." the dust jacket states. She recoveredthrough A.A.

684. Burt B. "Steps to Spiritual Progress". New Brighton, MN: Frames of Mind, Inc.; 1988.
In this brief 13-page pamphlet, Burt B. gives his personal comments on the Twelve Steps and spirituality of A.A.

685. By a Member of the Staff, Div. of Alcoholism, WV Dept. of Mental Health. Alcoholics Anonymous Its Development and Capabilities. Charleston, WV: WV Dept. of Mental Health; Post-1947.
Note: 15 pages, 8 1/2 x 11".
Speech given to an annual meeting of West Virginia Summer School of Alcohol Studies. An overview of A.A., Bill W.'s begininngs in founding A.A. Last page summarizes briefly Al-Anon and Ala-Teen.

686. By a Priest Who Was One. [Father Anon, pseudonym]. "Helps for the Alcoholic". First ed. Liguori, Missouri: Liguorian Pamphlets & Books, Redemptorist Fathers; 1970; 31pp.
This pamphlet, written by an anonymous Catholic priest and A.A. member, discusses the 12 Steps, the disease concept of alcoholism, avoiding the first drink, and many of the spiritual aspects of A.A. The pamphlet is a reproduction of a talk Fr. Anon gave to an A.A. group in the Midwest.

687. Canavan, Francis, Rev., S.J. The Light of Faith. First ed. Minneapolis, MN: The International Calix Society; 1989; 91pp.
Note: pb.
Canavan, a Catholic priest and spiritual director of the Westport, Connecticut, Calix unit, gives 45 talks about spirituality, AA, and Calix. AA's Eleventh Step is especially important to Calix members. Many of these have appeared as lead editorials in the Calix Society newsletter, the Chalice, dating back to November 1983. Included are commentaries on the Twelve Steps, God as we understand Him, AA slogans, the Sermon on the Mount, powerlessness, Christianity, the Serenity Prayer, meetings, sponsorship, prayer, faith, gratitude, and numerous other topics familiar to both Calix and AA members.

688. Carol, Gail [pseudonym]. Alcoholics in Recovery. Spiritual & Cultural Revitalization. First ed. Center City, MN: Hazelden; June, 1991; 279pp; ISBN: 0-89486-730-X. LC 90-82766.
Note: [This work was first published in its unabridged form in 1989 as the author's Ph.D. thesis "Practicing Peace in Recovery with A.A." Gail Carol is the author's pen name.]
"This is a study of some of the spiritual ideas, practices and experiences of individuals who are recovering from alcoholism with the help of Alcoholics Anonymous. It is an exploration of their ways of being and seeing; of what William James describes as conversion - the religious reunifying of a discordant personality. It is a story told primarily by alcoholics in varying stages of recovery who during the initial stage of research were either (1) guests at Hazelden's Renewal Center or (2) residents of Hazelden Foundation's residential treatment program for adults.
"Two questions were considered: What evidence is there to indicate that A.A. on an organic or organizational level serves as a revitalization movement as identified by cultural anthropologist Anthony Wallace, helping members create a more satisfying culture or way of life? and... What evidence is there to suggest that the alcoholics in recovery with A.A.

involved in this study experience a transition from a relatively discordant, dualistic way of being in the world to a more harmonious, unified one?

"It ... concluded A.A. serves as a revitalization movement congruent with the universal pattern identified by Wallace, and this study's participants, as individual members of this movement, find in recovery a deepened awareness of the confluence of often opposed pairs: one aspect of the self and another, self and God or Higher Power, self and others, and self and the world as a whole.".

689. Cary, Sylvia, M.A. The Alcoholic Man. What You Can Learn from the Heroic Journeys of Recovering Alcoholics. First ed. Los Angeles, CA/Chicago, IL: Lowell House/Contemporary Books; 1990; 202pp; ISBN: 0-929923-39-1. LC 90-5441.

Note: Index, pb.

Cary interviewed 18 men with a range of 30 days to 43 years of sobriety and their stories comprise this book. All are members of A.A. Although the A.A. program, slogans, and philosophy permeates this book, the book is more about the men, "heroes." "Toward a New Kind of Hero," the first chapter, seems an idea in conflict with AA's goals of humility and unselfishness where God and others come before one's self.

690. Cecil C. Never Too Late. Minneapolis, MN: CompCare Publishers; 1989: references to AA throughout; 109pp; ISBN: 0-89638-164-1.

Note: pb.

The anonymous author recovered from alcoholism at the age of 70 and relates his personal story and experiences in A.A. He is the author of "Those Golden Years," a chapter in the Big Book of A.A., as well as articles in the A.A. Grapevine magazine.

691. Cecil C. "The Promises of Sobriety". Center City, MN: Hazelden; Jan., 1987; ISBN: 0-89486-429-7.

This 12-page pamphlet is a commentary on the twelve promises of AA found in the Big Book on pages 83-84.

692. Cecil C. Wisdom to Recover By. Study Topics for People Growing in Sobriety. First ed. Minneapolis, MN: CompCare Publishers; 1990; 135pp; ISBN: 0-89638-203-6. LC 90-1642.

Note: pb.

Although A.A. is mentioned directly only several times, the topics in this book could be heard discussed at many A.A. meetings. Classic A.A. insights blend with personal revealations in these 32 brief essays. Among the topics: honesty, acceptance, resentments, gratitude, Higher Power, slips, humility.

693. Central Bulletin; October, 1942, to present (1993); Vol. 1, No. 1, to present.
This is the earliest major AA newsletter. Published in Cleveland, Ohio, by and for AA members, it appeared monthly and continues today. Each issue is 8.5 x 11 inches, four pages. Some of the very best writing in early AA appeared in this newsletter. Usually the first page was an essay or editorial on an AA subject; for example, the series of "Editorials" on the 12 Steps beginning monthly in Dec. 1942, Vol. 1, No. 3, is classic AA writing. Wonderful articles on sponsorship, a series on the "Our Father,"gratitude, will power, and a host of other topics have appeared regularly through the years. News items and group activities and meetings usually fill up pages 2-4. Dr. Bob's death, the first Int'l AA Convention in Cleveland, ox roasts, AA bowling leagues, financial reports, meeting listings, AA ball leagues, on and on go the activities. At one time Cleveland AA had more members in the early years than Akron, Ohio, and New York City combined. Mass production of sobriety first occurred in Cleveland and the Central Bulletin reflects the close-knit fellowship there with its many AA social activities, strong emphasis on sponsorship, Twelfth-stepping and the Steps.

694. Christopher, James. How To Stay Sober. Recovery without Religion. Buffalo, NY: Prometheus Books; 1988?; 170pp; ISBN: 0-87975-438-9.
"The first book for alcoholics who have been frustrated by the 'spiritual' approach of A.A. and similar groups...for the alcoholic or addict who feels alienated by the implication that recovery is not possible without reliance on a 'Higher Power," the promotional ad states. The author identifies himself as a secular humanist and long-time sober alcoholic.

695. Chuck C. A New Pair of Glasses. First ed. Irvine, CA: New-Look Pub. Co.; May, 1984; 145pp; ISBN: ISBN 0-916733-00-9. LC 84-90798.
Note: dj.
Sober since the mid-1940s, Chuck C. gives his own interpretation and understanding of the AA program of recovery. The author, Charles A. Chamberlain (1902-1984), is anonymous in the first edition but his full name and photo is given in the 6th printing, September, 1989.

696. Clancy, Jay R. [pseudonym]. Clancy Got Well. Des Moines, Iowa: McGrevey Book Store; 1951; 163pp.
An A.A. member's interpretation of living the A.A. program since Aug. 14, 1943. He discusses the program at length, including material from his wife's point of view, AA clubs, his political career and its pitfalls, and early "good old-fashioned" AA.

697. Clarence S. "Our Charge". Lakewood, Ohio: author; 1940-50?
These six paragraphs, "Our Charge," were written by Clarenc S., Cleveland's controversial AA founder. He explains why God selected AA's above the "proud, mighty, famous, and brilliant" to carry the message of recovery to suffering alcoholics.

698. Clyde G. "My Quiet Time". Cleveland, OH: Cleveland Dist. Ofc. of Alcoholics Anonymous; ?
This 4-page pamphlet is a poem by Clyde G. about God and AA

699. "Conscious Contact: Partnership with a Higher Power". Cent City: Hazelden; 1985.
In this pamphlet, the author writes about coming to terms with his higher power. The experiences of other AA-alcoholics as well as non-alcoholics are also included.

700. Coonan, Thomas L., Rev. Eulogy of Sister M. Ignatia. Cleveland, Ohio: np; April 5, 1966.
Note: five page mimeographed copy.
Rev. Coonan's eulogy of this Catholic Sisters of Charity of Saint Augustine nun cites her unmeasurable influence in aiding the recovery of literally thousands of alcoholics. Dr. Bob, A.A. Co-founder, approached Sister Ignatia in 1935 who was then registrar of St. Thomas Hospital in Akron, Ohi In 1952, she opened a second alcoholic ward in St. Vincent Charity Hospital, Cleveland, and had it dedicated as "Rosar Hall Solarium." There alone she treated more than 10,000 alcoholics and of those, 65% were immediately restored to a happy sobriety.

701. Crewe, Charles W. "A Look at Relapse". Center City, MN: Hazelden; 1974; ISBN: 0-89486-007-0.
This 10-page pamphlet by a Hazelden therapist notes that 80 to 90% of all relapsers stopped attending AA meetings and participating in the Fellowship prior to their slip. AA is mentioned throughout.

702. Crossroads; June-July, 1954; 1(5): 56pp total.
Note: 5 x 7".
This early AA journal was published bi-monthly by the "Excelsior Group," AA, at St. Vincent de Paul Penitentiary, St. Vincent de Paul, Montreal, Quebec, Canada. This issue reports their third birthday of the AA prison group with "o hundred guests" present. Stories of recovery, How I Slippe Why I am Thankful for Today, etc., cartoons, and news items fill this issue.

703. Crowe, Cecily. The Twice-Born. First ed. New York: Random House; 1972; 181pp; ISBN: 0-394-47554-2.
The central character of this novel, Faith Farrell, slips into alcoholism in the most lady-like way and ends up physically-battered, in d.t.'s, and in a straight jacket. the end she is born again, twice-born, into A.A. and recovery.

704. Darrah, Mary C. Sister Ignatia. Angel of Alcoholics Anonymous. First & Second ed. Chicago, IL: Loyola University Press; 1992; 300pp; ISBN: 0-8294-0712-X. LC 91-40018.
Note: Photos, index, pb. A second edition of 1,000 copies in hardback was brought out.
This biography of Sister Ignatia ["Iggy"], the little Catholic non-alcoholic nun, who, with Dr. Bob, opened the first hospital ward in the world for alcoholics admitted for treatment as alcoholics, is a superlative effort, sterling in research and documentation, gold-plated with firsts, bejewelled with historical spiritualities. Darrah gives long-overdue credit to the non-alcoholic women in Akron - Anne Smith, Henrietta Seiberling, Sr. Ignatia - for their role in the formation of A.A. Darrah's revelations about the actual 5-day program Sr. Ignatia and Dr. Bob set up at St. Thomas Hospital in Akron are wonderful. And the nun's later work at Rosary Hall in Cleveland, Ohio, is also fully-explored. A foreword by John C. Ford, S.J., a section of historic photos and extensive chapter notes are bonuses. One critic, however, noted the "feminist" slant in the second half of the book. In truth, the wonderful "flower room" story, Ignatia's "tough love" approach, Catholic problems, and page after page of new history uncovered make this a "must" read for anyone interested in A.A. history.

705. Davis, Elrick R. "The New Way of Life". Cleveland, OH: Cleveland Central Committee of A.A.; 1940s.
This 28-page small pamphlet reprints the Fall, 1939, series of articles about AA by Elrick Davis in the Cleveland Plain Dealer.

706. Delenhanty, Edward J., M.D., psychiatrist. "The Therapeutic Value of the Twelve Steps of A.A.". Utah Alcoholism Foundation: Salt Lake City, Utah; after 1944 (?); 11pp.
Note: Later reprinted by Hazelden, Center City, Minnesota.
The author, a psychiatrist, discusses the 12 Steps, the Oxford Group's six steps, A.A. as group therapy, and general acceptance of A.A. treatment by the psychiatric profession, in this small pamphlet.

707. Denzin, Norman K. The Alcoholic Self. First ed. Newbury Park, California, et al.: Sage Publications, Inc.; 1987; 231pp. (Johnson, John M.; v. Vol. 18 in the Sociological Observations series); ISBN: 0-8039-2745-2.
Note: pb.
The first book in the author's triology on alcoholism. Denzin is Professor of Sociology and Humanities at the University of Illinois at Urbana-Champaign. Chap. 3 of Part I, pp 63-76, is devoted to "Alcoholics Anonymous and Alcoholism" but there are numerous references and discussions of A.A. and related topics throughout the book.

708. Denzin, Norman K. The Recovering Alcoholic. First ed. Newbury Park, CA, et al: Sage Publications, Inc.; 1987; 247pp. (Johnson, John M., general editor; v. Vol. 19 in the Sociological Observations series); ISBN: 0-8039-2747 (paperback).
Note: Part II of the book, 91-217pp, is almost entirely devoted to A.A. and the Social Worlds of Recovery. Twenty pages of bibliography contain 288 references.
The second book in a trilogy . "The recovery process is a group process, and through participation in Alcoholics Anonymous (AA) we learn how participation in the storytelling rituals and traditions of AA produces a new definition of self that flows from the group structures of the AA collective," the foreword states. Denzin presented a 27-page paper, "Slips and Relapses: Deviance and Identities within Alcoholics Anonymous," at the annual meeting of The Society for the Study of Symbolic Interaction, Aug. 31-Sept.1, 1986, New York City. That paper was drawn from this book.

709. Denzin, Norman K. "The Stories Alcoholics Tell: A Cultural Analysis". in: Midwest Sociological Society annual meeting; March 26, 1986; Des Moines, Iowa; 34pp.
"The stages of socialization that occur for the American alcoholic who becomes a member of Alcoholics Anonymous are analyzed, as are the changes in self that occur as a result of this experience. Analysis focuses on becoming a storyteller, an A.A. self, and on the self as a double structure of experience." The progress of women in AA, recovery by Blacks and Hispanics, and the Big Book stories are discussed in the light of storytelling in AA.

710. Denzin, Norman K. Treating Alcoholism. An Alcoholics Anonymous Approach. First ed. Newbury Park, CA, et al: Sage Publications, Inc.; 1987; 149pp. (Lauffer, Armand, & Garvin, Charles D.; v. Vol. 46 in Sage Human Services Guides series); ISBN: 0-8039-2907-2.
Note: pb.
The author discusses interpretive therapy, denial, treatment centers, recovery, slips and relapses, and long-term recovery. A.A.'s program of recovery and related A.A. topics are discussed throughout the book.

711. "The Devil and A.A."; Aug. 17, 1948: 18pp.
This small pamphlet published by the Chicago Area Alcoholics Anonymous Service Office is a 1948 talk by an AA member. He identifies "the source, the inspiration, the external cause of the temptations and urges that come to us in A.A." as "the Devil, the Prince of Darkness, the Father of Lies, Satan, or whatever you choose to call him." Beginners have enough trouble with a Higher Power and "now comes this butterbrain to talk about a Lower Power." The oldtimer tries to answer it all.

712. DeWitt, James, Dr. [with Hirshberg, Al]. Addict. A Doctor's Odyssey. First ed. Chicago: Cowles Book Co., Inc.; 1972; 227pp; ISBN: L.C. 79-183825.
The long journey down the path of drug addiction and alcoholism is chronicled in this personal witness book. Ending up in the gutters and bars of Dover Street, Boston, Dr. DeWitt, met his present wife, an alcoholic, and with the aid of Alcoholics Anonymous, they licked their alcoholism and his drug addiction together. Mentions A.A. throughout the book. Anonymity break.

713. Dick B. The Akron Genesis of Alcoholics Anonymous. First ed. Seattle, WA: Glen Abbey Books; 1992; 410pp; ISBN: 0-934125-31-7. LC 92-97026.
Note: Bibliography, index, pb.
Early AA in Akron, Ohio, its founding, spiritual taproots, struggles, debates, Oxford Group influences, etc. are discussed in this history of AA from 1931 to 1939. Much emphasis is laid on the Oxford Group, the Bible, and related topics. A ten-page bibliography and extensive index enhance the research. The foreword is by John F. Seiberling, former U.S. Congressman from Akron, and son of Henrietta Seiberling who introduced Bill W. to Dr. Bob, the Co-Founders of A.A.

714. Dick B. Anne Smith's Spiritual Workbook. First ed. Corte Madera, CA: Good Book Pub. Co.; 1992; 102pp; ISBN: 1-881212-00-9. LC 92-090140.
Note: Index, pb.
This book provides new information on the immense spiritual contributions that the wife of AA's Co-Founder, Dr. Bob, made to early AA's and their wives. Anne Smith never lost faith in her alcoholic husband and turned to the Oxford Group for basic Christian strength in her struggle. Her notebook in this quest is here discussed in some depth for the first time. The foreword was written by Dr. Bob's and Anne's son, "Smitty.".

715. Dick B. The Books Early AAs Read For Spiritual Growth. First ed. Seattle, WA: Glen Abbey Books; 1993; 30pp; ISBN: 0-934125-35-X.
Note: Spiral bound, 8.5 x 11".
This is probably the most comprehensive listing of what books early AAs read. Included are comments from Dr. Bob and his wife Anne; Bill and Lois W., Nell Wing, and oldtimers on the Bible, The Upper Room, Anne Smith's Spiritual Workbook, Henrietta Seiberling's books, T. Henry & Clarace Williams' Library, the Oxford Group literature, and Rev. Sam Shoemaker's books and writings. A bibliography is included.

716. Dick B. Dr. Bob's Library. First ed. Wheeling, WV: The Bishop of Books; May, 1992; 110pp; ISBN: 1-877686-04-2. LC 92-90139.

Note: Index, pb.

Dick B. discusses the 100 books Dr. Bob, Co-Founder of A.A., owned, read, and recommended to Fellowship members before the AA Big Book was published in 1939. Included are Christian classics, Daily Bible devotionals, prayer books and books by Oxford Groupers, William James, Carl Jung, etc. This book finds its roots in a quote from the AA Big Book concerning the Eleventh Step: "There are many helpful books also. Suggestions about these may be obtained from one's priest, minister, or rabbi. Be quick to see where religious people are right. Make use of what they have to offer." [p.87] The author quotes Dr. Bob to the effect that AA's got the basic ideas for the Twelve Steps from their study of the Good Book, the Bible. That idea may be open to discussion but one certainly must credit Dick B. for extensive, original research into early A.A. history. The foreword was written by Ernest Kurtz, Ph.D.

717. Dick B. New Light on Alcoholism: The A.A. Legacy from Sam Shoemaker. Kihei, Maui, Hawaii: Good Book Pub. Co.; April, 1994; ISBN: 1-881212-06-8. LC 93-77559.

Note: First Ed., 400pp, bibliography, index.

The vital contribution to AA from the famous New York Episcopal preacher is detailed here with new material from Calvary Church archives and from Oxford Group oldtimers. Forewords by Shoemaker's younger daughter, Nickie Shoemaker Haggart and by Mrs. W. Irving Harris, widow of Shoemaker's assistant minister and good friend of Bill W.

718. Dick B. The Oxford Group & Alcoholics Anonymous. First ed. Seattle, WA: Glen Abbey Books; 1992; 355pp; ISBN: 0-934125-30-9. LC 92-71255.

Note: Bibliography, index, pb.

This is "an excellent and thoroughly researched presentation of the Oxford Group's biblical principles and their influence on AA, its Big Book, and Twelve Steps," said Ernest Kurtz, Ph.D., author of Not-God: A History of Alcoholics Anonymous. Dick B. spent two years in research at libraries, archives, interviews, etc. for this book, one of four he has written about AA. All are noteworthy for their original research which has expanded our knowledge about early AA. All emphasize the "AA-Good Book [Bible] Connection." Aside from their contribution, one may point out that their emphasis on Oxford Group principles and contributions needs to be balanced by a recognition that AA left the Oxford Group early on for specific reasons: public confession of sins, opposed by Catholics; the Four Absolutes, which alcoholics found impossible to practice to "perfection"; etc.

719. Dick McK. (Sec.-Treas.). International Doctors in Alcoholics Anonymous: Objectives and History. Minneapolis, MN: I.D.A.A.; Nov. 1988; 1p.
This one page letter outlines the objectives and history of IDAA, which parallel exactly those of A.A. at large. Founded in 1949 in Clayton, N.Y., in the garage of Doctor Clarence P., this special interest group in A.A. meets annually in August and circulates a newsletter to about 2,500 members internationally.

720. "Dignity and Recovery: A Gay Catholic's Story". East Lansing, MI: Substance Abuse Task Force; 1985.
In this gay man's story, focus is placed on this recovery through A.A. He also tells how his association with Dignity helped his spiritual program.

721. a Doctor in A.A. "Alcoholism and the A.A. Program"; 1960s?: 15pp.
This small pamphlet by a doctor in AA discusses the disease of alcoholism, the "personality" of the alcoholic, recovery, God, and sobriety. It was published by the Chicago Metropolitan A.A. Group.

722. Doe, John, Fr. [pseudonym]. The Golden Book set. Firsts ed. Indianapolis, IN: The SMT Guild, Inc.; 1947-through-1967.
Note: [Fr. John Doe, a Catholic priest, was a member of A.A.].
A set of 14 booklets boxed, all with gold stiff wrappers (hence the name of the set & individual booklets), about 50pp+ each. Titles: The Golden Book of The Spiritual Side (1947); ...of Tolerance (1948) (formerly title of Charity); ...of Action (1950); ...of Sanctity (1967); ...of Attitudes (1949); ... of Decisions (1957); ... of Excuses (1952); ... of Passion (1960); ... of Living (1964); ... of Sponsorship (1953); ... of Principles (1954); ... of Sanity (1963); ... of Happiness (1951); & ... of Resentments (1955). The author, a Catholic priest and member of A.A., uses the Steps and the A.A. philosophy to discuss each topic in depth, including suggestions for solving daily problems as well as building a new life around the A.A. program.

723. Doe, John, Father [pseudonym] (a member of A.A.). Sobriety and Beyond. Indianapolis: The S.M.T. Guild; 1955; 387pp; ISBN: LC 55-9042.
Note: dj.
The author believes no alcoholic will remain sober unless he also achieves a "happiness in life" and that this state of living, this "spiritual phase of Alcoholics Anonymous" is reached "in the area "beyond sobriety." Many of the chapters were taken from this Catholic priest's earlier publication of the "Golden Book" pamphlet series. In-depth discussions of the 12 Steps and other essential A.A. subjects are addressed to alcoholics in general and A.A. in particular. "The chapter on Attitudes is MOST IMPRESSIVE..." Karl Menninger, M.D.

724. Doe, John, Father [pseudonym]. Sobriety Without End. First. Indianapolis, IN: The SMT Guild; 1957; 363pp; ISBN: LC 57-9441.
The author, a Catholic priest in A.A., discusses the entire range of the A.A. program of recovery. Topics include the Serenity Prayer, resentments, sex, Twelve Steps, slogans, spirituality, honesty, etc.

725. "The Door of A.A.". in: New Penscope; June, 1979; 2: pp15-21.
Short articles and comments by AA members of the Moundsville, WV, State Penitentiary AA Group are included in this journal.

726. "Double Winners". New York: Al-Anon Family Groups; 1977.
This 6-page pamphlet discusses membership in both Al-Anon and A.A.

727. Dove Locator to the Big Book of Alcoholics Anonymous. First ed. Jefferson City, MO: Locator Publications; August, 1987; 225pp; ISBN: LC 87-82008.
Note: pb.
This is a reference guide to the book, Alcoholics Anonymous, both the second and third editions, and each word, phrase, sentence, and topic in the first 164 pages of that book are indexed according to page, paragraph and line. This guide is two columns per page. This is not A.A. Conference-approved Literature.

728. Dove Locator to the "12 Steps and 12 Traditions". First ed. Jefferson City, MO: Locator Publications; 1990; 116pp; ISBN: LC 87-82008 (?).
Note: Softbound 8 1/2 x 11".
This is a reference guide to the book, Twelve Steps and Twelve Traditions. The index has three columns per page and every major word, phrase, sentence and topic in that book is referenced by page, paragraph and line. This is not A.A. Conference-approved Literature.

729. Dowling, Edward, S.J./Riley, Frank A. "Alcoholics Anonymous: An Interview with Edward Dowling, S.J. by Frank A. Riley". The Queen's Work, St. Louis.; 1947.
Note: 32pp.
In this pamphlet, Fr. Dowling, a Jesuit, parallels the Twelve Steps of A.A. with the Spiritual Exercises of St. Ignatius, founder of the Society of Jesus. Dr. R. V. Seliger's symptoms of drinking that may be prealcoholic or alcoholic are listed. The relation between some basic teachings of Roman Catholicism and the suggested Steps of A.A. gives importance to this pamphlet for Roman Catholic laymen. Dowling was long associated with the work of early A.A.

730. Doyle, Paul Barton/Ishee, John. In Step with God. A Scriptural Guide for Twelve Step Programs. Second ed. New York: Bantam Books, Inc.; January, 1992; c1990; 126pp; ISBN: 0-553-29292-7.
Note: The first edition was published by New Directions, Brentwood, TN, in 1990. pb.
The authors discuss each of the Twelve Steps in a chapter, complete with appropriate quotes from the Bible. They believe the steps and the Bible together can conquer any addiction.

731. "Dr. Bob's Last Talk". Niles, OH: Northeastern Ohio Area General Service Committee; 1950.
This small 4-page pamphlet commemorates Dr. Bob's last talk at the First Int'l AA Conference in Cleveland, Ohio, Sunday, July 30, 1950. The talk is reprinted along with Dr. Bob's photo and his favorite quote on humility.

732. Earle, Clifford J. "Alcohol and Christian Responsibility". Cincinnati, OH: Woman's Division of Christian Service, Board of Missions, Methodist Church; 1953.
Note: 87pp.
Alcoholics Anonymous is described in detail and church cooperation with them is strongly suggested.

733. Earle M., Dr. Physician, Heal Thyself! 35 Years of Adventures in Sobriety by an AA "Old-Timer". First ed. Minneapolis, MN: CompCare Publishers; 1989; 246pp; ISBN: 0-89638-152-8. LC 88-25691.
Note: pb.
This autobiography of a doctor with 35 years in AA is divided into four periods in his AA life: infatuation, irritability, inventiveness and insight. He discusses Bill W., the Seven Seas Club, four marriages, continent-hopping, the Ten Steps of Chemical Dependency, the Twelve Steps, old timers, and a host of other AA-related topics. His story, "Physician, Heal Thyself!" is in the Big Book.

734. Early A.A. in Baltimore. Baltimore, MD: ?; April, 1975.
Note: 5.5 x 8.5" pamphlet.
This brief 12-page first printing history of early AA in Baltimore begins June 16, 1940, and covers the early meetings and articles from The Baltimore Sun up to June 4, 1974.

735. Easy Does It. A Book of Daily 12 Step Meditations. Bill P., Editor. First ed. Seattle, WA: Glen Abbey Books-a Lakeside Recovery Press Book; 1990; 384pp; ISBN: 0-934125-12-0.
Note: pb.
These daily readings center on the slogans and philosophy of Twelve Step Fellowships. Quotes from A.A.'s Big Book, from members at meetings, and from Shakespeare, Gibran, and a host of other writers and philosophers are followed by reflections on the wisdom heard at Twelve Step meetings.

736. Ed F. God grant me the Laughter. First ed. Minneapolis, MN: CompCare Publishers; 1989; 150+ pp; ISBN: 0-89638-162-5. Note: Illus. with cartoons. pb.
This is a collection of humorous cartoons about the A.A. Twelve Step program.

737. Elbert, Joyce. Murder at AA. New York: Penguin; 1980.
This murder mystery revolves around an AA group.

738. Ellis, James H. To Hell and Back. First ed. New York: Vantage Press, Inc.; 1953; 145pp; ISBN: L.C. 53-11637.
"The story of an alcoholic" is semi-autobiographical, paralleling many events in the author's life. Ellis urges alcoholics to use the program of Alcoholics Anonymous before returning to their own church. Jimmy, the central character of the novel, joins A.A. near the end of the story and says the "whole of the program is a God-sent gift to the world. To me, it is divinely inspired." Yet Jimmy says shortly later "the ones who have stayed the longest on the program have merely formed a cult," and urges, in a letter, that "after a man has been rehabilitated, what is the common-sense thing for him to do? It is to go out into the world and live a normal life.".

739. "Enjoying the Holidays". Center City, MN: Hazelden; Oct., 1985; ISBN: 0-89486-335-5.
This 22-page pamphlet includes suggestions for staying close to AA during holidays.

740. Ernie K. 90 Meetings 90 Days. First ed. Minneapolis, MN: Johnson Institute, Inc.; 1984; 352pp; ISBN: 0-935908-26-9. Note: A Journal of Experience, Strength, and Hope. The author, a recoveredalcoholic, attended the traditional "90 meetings in 90 days" and here sets down his impressions of A.A.'s 12 Step program of recovery as he found it from the many members of A.A. at those meetings. Newcomers to A.A. are often told by their sponsors to make "90 in 90." Many of the basic ideas concerning sobriety, the 12 Steps, alcoholism as a disease, William James, God & religion, A.A. literature, honesty, humility, etc.,are discussed in depth. Not a quickie book, but rather a searching, probing volume of insights into the alcoholic's struggles and victories.
The author attended 90 A.A. meetings in 90 days to gather insights into AA's successful 12 Step program of recovery.

741. "Exploring Anonymity". New York: 39th General Service Conference-AAWS; April 23-29, 1989.
This 12-page report to the 39th G.S.C. in 1989 explores the origins and development of the anonymity idea back to 500 B.C. and up through the Washingtonians, Oxford Group, the Saturday Evening Post 1941 article, and Alcoholics Anonymous. The theme of the 39th G.S.C. was "Anonymity - Living Our Traditions.".

742. The Eye Opener. Center City: Hazelden.
Note: 380pp.
This small hardback is a long time bestseller. It contains daily meditations about AA's wisdom, Twelve Steps and Twelve Traditions.

743. Father Jack. Freeze the Disease. First ed. Detroit Lakes, MN: Lakes Publishing; circa 1960s; 93pp.
Note: Nine wonderful color drawings and photographs enchance this story. pb.
This is the autobiography of a Catholic parish priest-alcoholic who lost his pastorate and worked as a secondhand warehouseman. Happily, he joined A.A. and came back as a sober priest. The Twelve Steps are discussed.

744. Father Mac. "Fr. Mac Discusses The Twelve Steps". Milwaukee, WI: Milwaukee AA Central Office; 1984.
Fr. Mac explains each of the 12 steps of AA.

745. The Fellowship: The First 50 Years. Commemorating the Golden Anniversary of Alcoholics Anonymous.. Hearn, Edward L., Project Director. First ed. Seattle, WA: Alcoholism & Addiction Magazine; June, 1985; 96pp.
Note: Slick 8 1/2 x 11" softbound.
This privately-published special tribute to A.A. at its Int'l Convention at Montreal, Canada, includes 21 articles on aspects of A.A. and Al-Anon. Among the subjects were: alcoholism the disease, history, the Big Book, humor, the Twelve Traditions, the Co-Founders, women, anonymity, Al-Anon, GSO, and the Grapevine.

746. "Fiftieth Anniversary of A.A.'s Textbook `Alcoholics Anonymous". New York: AAWS; April 1, 1989.
This three-page press release announced the 50th anniversary celebration of AA's "Big Book." Sent to all media with over 50,000 circulation, it noted that seven millions copies of Alcoholics Anonymous have been sold in the U.S. and thousands of translations in 15 other languages have been purchased abroad.

747. Fifty Years of Freedom in the Mountain State: A History of Alcoholics Anonymous in West Virginia 1942-1992. First ed. Wheeling, WV: Alcoholics Anonymous Area 73 (WV); August, 1992; 279pp.
Note: dj.
This fine hardback history of the Fellowship in West Virginia includes historic profiles of each of the 15 districts, all the past Delegates to the General Service Conference, area assemblies and conventions, clubs, archives, redistricting, etc. It contains 2 maps, Grapevine articles, over 100 groups histories, and other illustrations. Anonymity is protected throughout.

748. "Finding Your Way: guidelines for recovery". Center City, MN: Hazelden; 1980; ISBN: 0-89486-105-0.
This 30-page pamphlet discusses briefly AA slogans, sponsorship, anonymity, medications, and "a few A.A. Terms you may have wondered about.".

749. "The Four Absolutes". Cleveland, OH: Central Bulletin Foundation, Inc.; nd.
The pamphlet describes the four absolutes and explains how they form a thread through AA's twelve steps.

750. Fowler, Richard, Dr./Hemfelt, Robert, Dr. Serenity. A Companion for Twelve Step Recovery, Complete with New Testament & Proverbs. First ed. Nashville, TN: Thomas Nelson Publishers; 1990; 80 & 558pp; ISBN: 0-8407-1542-0.
Note: pb.
This book explains each of A.A.'s Twelve Steps in the context of scriptural truths. Seven meditations for each of the 12 Steps provide Biblical commentary. The entire New Testament, Psalms, and Proverbs with over 500 highlighted verses give the reader an overview of Biblical principles of recovery. The book is addressed to alcoholics and all others suffering from some harmful addiction.

751. Gary L. "The Serenity Prayer: What Do the Words Really Mean? ". Minneapolis, MN: CompCare Publishers; 1991; ISBN: 0-89638-260-5.
The author, sober in A.A. since 1971 and a chaplain, gives his interpretation of the Serenity Prayer.

752. Gay Men of Alcoholics Anonymous: First-hand Accounts. Kus, Robert J., R.N., Ph.D., Editor. First ed. North Liberty, IA: WinterStar Press; 1990; 217pp; ISBN: 0-9625330-0-9. LC 89-052147.
Note: pb.
This is a collection of 27 life stories of gay men recovering one day at a time in Alcoholics Anonymous. It is not A.A. Conference-approved Literature.

753. Gay? Lesbian? Alcoholic? East Lansing, MI: Monday Night Gay A.A. Group; [late 1970s].
Using a question and answer format, this brochure describes how homosexuals are able to get help through A.A.

754. Gellman, Irving Peter. The Sober Alcoholic: An Organizational Analysis of Alcoholics Anonymous. First ed. New Haven: College & University Press; 1964; 206pp; ISBN: LC 63-17368.
This volume is an analysis of the social organization of A.A. The text covers three areas: 1. A.A. as a part of the vast complex of voluntary associations in the U.S. 2. The nature of deviancy and social control in an organization composed completely of social deviants. and 3. The unique characteristics of Alcoholics Anonymous. This volume is one of the first scholarly studies of the sociology of A.A.

755. Georgia A.A. Service Manual. First thru Fifth ed. Macon, GA: Georgia State Assembly Office; 1978-1991; 39pp.
Note: 5.75 x 9" blue booklet.
Georgia AA is one of perhaps two or three AA areas that has its own service manual. This volume reprints the Steps, Traditions, & Concepts as well as qualifications and duties of state officers, DCMs and GSRs, election procedures, George & Atlanta Dist. maps, and other service information on the State and Southeastern Conventions, funding, and services to be performed by the Assembly service office. There have no substantive changes since the first printing. The history section notes the first AA meeting in Georgia was in Atlanta on June 11, 1941, and the Georgia State Assembly was established in 1966.

756. Gladding, Chris F. Trudging the Road: A Work-Study Journey Through the Twelve Steps of Alcoholics Anonymous: Glad Pub.; 1991; ISBN: 0-9629091-0-6.
Note: 170pp.

757. Gleason, William F. The Liquid Cross of Skid Row. First ed. Milwaukee: The Bruce Publishing Co.; 1966; 256pp; ISBN: L.C. 66-19971.
The plight of Chicago's Skid Row alcoholics and their possible rehabilitation is the author's theme. "Besides the alcoholics who live on The Street and the successful members of Alcoholics Anonymous who try to restore them to sobriety, the main characters in the story are Tim Trohan, 40, an ex-Marine, who, eight years before, left his family and drifted to The Street; and Monsignor Ignatius McDermott, the Angel to The Street's derelicts," the dust jacket promo states.

758. "God, A.A., and Akron". Akron, OH: Interval Brotherhood Home/Akron Arid Club; 1985.
This 24-page pamphlet is "a Golden Anniversary Tribute" to AA on its 50th birthday. The pamphlet documents many of founding persons, places and events of AA in Akron. It extoles God's power in choosing Akron, Ohio, to be AA's birthplace.

759. Gorski, Terence T./Miller, Merlene. Staying Sober. A Guide for Relapse Prevention. First ed. Independence, MO: IndependencePress; 1986; 228pp; ISBN: 0-8309-0459-X.
Note: This book is an update of an earlier volume, Counseling for Relapse Prevention (1982). Gorski spent 15 years studying case histories of "end of the roaders," alcoholics who kept going back out to drink, and these two books present his CENAPS model of relapse prevention. Recommended by Father Joseph C. Martin, Cofounder, Father Martin's Ashely, Havre de Grace, Maryland, who wrote the foreword. Tackles the tough group of alcoholics who felt they were "constitutionally incapable of recovery and related to the statement in Chapter 5 of the "Big Book" that describes those unfortunates who cannot recover. Contains various references to A.A., the Twelve Steps, and other related A.A. concepts. "Relapse prevention planning does not replace AA or professional treatment, nor does it diminish the importance

of AA principles and practices. It simply adds another powerful recovery tool to the already powerful principles of AA," the authors summarize. A critic might respond that if AA is so powerful, why is necessary to add anything to it. The authors suggest that chronic relapses by alcoholics might be prevented by combining the Twelve Steps principles of AA with professional counseling and therapy.

760. "Grateful Thoughts Favorites". Fredericksburg, OH: Dan Shetler.
This 28-page pamphlet is a compilation of thoughts, quotes, and prayers about AA gratitude, anger, God, and other basic topics.

761. Griffin-Shelley, Eric. "Maintaining Sobriety Through Bibliotherapy". First ed. Center City, MN: Hazelden; February 1990; 21pp; ISBN: 0-89486-644-3.
Note: pamphlet.
The author uses The Big Book, Alcoholics Anonymous, as his prime example of successful bibliotherapy.

762. Guide to Alcoholism Treatment Research: Vol. III. Alcoholics Anonymous and Counseling. Levinson, David, Editor. New Haven, CT: HRAF Press [Human Relations Area Files, Inc.]; 1983; 546pp; ISBN: 0-87536-740-2. LC 82-105273.
The effectiveness of AA and counseling in the treatment of alcoholism are assessed. AA is used in the following ways: (1) as a treatment in and of itself; (2) as a treatment combined with other treatments such as disulfiram maintenance, outpatient counseling, or psychotherapy; and (3) as aftercare, usually following a patient's discharge from an inpatient rehabilitation program. Counseling is a major form of treatment for alcoholism, although it lacks the formal organizational structure and reputation of AA. It is estimated that counseling sessions account for over 30 per cent of all outpatient visits to the clinics sampled. It is concluded that: (1) AA is effective as aftercare; (2) Al-Anon is an effective adjunct to AA; (3) counselor training enhances counselor knowledge about alcoholism and therapeutic skills; and (4) counselor alcoholic status is unrelated to counselor effectiveness. The book is well-documented with 136 references. (NCADI abstract). Additionally, it should be pointed out that over 600 scholarly studies of AA and of counseling effectiveness are extensively documented and analyzed here. This scholarly effort is a gold mine for research.

763. "Guide to Fourth Step Inventory". Center City, MN: Hazelden; nd.
This guide to the fourth step includes sections on the seven deadly sins and the ten commandments.

764. "A Guide to Serenity". Cleveland, OH: Cleveland Dist. Ofc. of Alcoholics Anonymous; ?
This 8-page pamphlet suggests a daily moral inventory, living one day at a time, and why God chose alcoholics to carry the message to other alcoholics. The poem, "The Man in the Glass," is reprinted.

765. "A Guide to the Twelve Steps of Alcoholics Anonymous". Akron, OH: AA of Akron; 1940s (?).
Note: [Step Six is stated inocrrectly].
This 16-page small pamphlet is "intended as a simple, short and concise interpretation of the rules for sober living as compiled by the earliest members of the organization." Reprinted many times up to 1993, it still uses "experience" instead of "awakening" in Step Twelve.

766. Hall, Bill. Sister Mary Ignatia Is Dead. Cleveland, OH: Charity Hospital Group; 1966; 2pp broadside 7 x 16", both sides.
Note: Reprinted in 1990 by The Bishop of Books, Wheeling, WV, as a broadside 11 x 19" on one side only.
Sr. Ignatia died Friday, April 1, 1966. This memorial broadside sums up her life-long dedication to A.A. through the alcoholic wards she helpedto establish at St. Thomas Hospital in Akron, Ohio, and at St. Vincent Charity Hospital in Cleveland, Ohio. This non-alcoholic Catholic nun and Dr. Bob, Co-Founder, opened the first hospital ward for alcoholics in Cleveland, Ohio.

767. Hamel, Richard A. A Good First Step. First ed. Minneapolis, MN: CompCare Publishers; 1985; 91pp; ISBN: 0-89638-082-3.
"This First Step workbook is a guide to an experiential process that allows us to examine our dependencies through a structure format," the author explains. This workbook on the first of the Twelve Steps of A.A. is, of course, NOT General Service Conference Approved A.A. Literature. After page 6, the reader has the rest of the book to fill out with his experiences involving the First Step.

768. "Handles and Hodge Podge". Cleveland, OH: Cleveland Central Committee of A.A.; 1950s (?)-1993.
This 32-page small pamphlet compiled by a member of A.A. is "a stew of various thoughts to keep you from getting stewed." Contents include AA slogans, thoughts on the 12 Steps, etc.

769. "Handles For Sobriety". Cleveland, OH: Cleveland Central Committee of A.A.; 1950s (?)-1993.
This 32-page small pamphlet compiled by a member of A.A. includes slogans, tips on staying sober, comments on the Fellowship and program.

770. Hansen, P. L. Alcoholism: The Tragedy of Abundance. Minneapolis, MN: Park Printing; 1982; 86pp.
Among the author's personal observations are that spiritual values, self worth, and identity of the alcoholics are much more the key to solving their alcoholism than the physical or scientific aspects of their alcoholism and (2) that Alcoholics Anonymous has done more than any other institution to arrest the hurt and destruction in alcoholics and the affected others.

771. Harbor Area History [1941 to 1975]. Long Beach, CA: Harbor Area AArchives, CA; 1990.
Note: 8.5 x 11" orange spiral bound.
This first edition historical perspective of A.A. in the Harbor Area of Southern California on the local level with a corresponding overview of A.A. on the national level covers nearly 50 cities in the area. Contains 62pp ofexcellent history of the groups, clubs, central office, etc. John D. S., Archivist, edited this.

772. Heathmen A.A. Group; August, 1981: 38pp.
This is the journal of the Heathmen A.A. Group in the West Virginia State Penitentiary at Moundsville, WV. Personal stories of recovery by prisoners in the AA group and outside AA's are the main content.

773. Hegarty, Carol. "The Winner's Way: A Beginner's Guide to The Twelve Steps". Minneapolis, MN: CompCare Publishers; 1982; ISBN: 0-89638-175-7.
This 30-page booklet "is intended to introduce prospective [AA] members to both the mechanics and spirit of the Twelve Steps. Obviously, to be introduced to something is not to know it...".

774. "Helps for the Alcoholic". Liguori, MO: Liguorian Pamphlets and Books; 1975.
This booklet is based on an AA lead given by an anonymous priest. After giving his story, he explains the disease concept of alcoholism, the first step, spirituality in the steps, and other aspects of sobriety. [From textural evidence, we can assume that he was a resident of Guest House.].

775. Hemfelt, Robert, Dr./Fowler, Richard, Dr./Minirth, Frank, Dr./Meier, Paul, Dr. The Path to Serenity. First ed. Nashville, TN: Thomas Nelson Publishers; 1991; 345pp; ISBN: 0-8407-7691-8. LC 91-37811.
Note: dj.
"We've found our patients have had difficulty walking through the Twelve-Step process into full recovery without the involvement of a God who has a name, a face, and a history of interacting with people just like them," the four doctors state. They suggest the God of the Bible whose name is Jesus Christ in order to successfully complete the Twelve Steps. They discuss each of the Steps within this framework. Personal stories of this approach to recovery from many addictions include codependent spouses and adult children of

dysfunctional families along with those suffering from other addictions than alcohol. A.A., of course, does not endorse or oppose any religion.

776. Hickle, Bob. The Mosaic of Sobriety. First ed. Lake Mills, Iowa: Graphic Pub. Co.; 1978; 48pp.
In this booklet, Hickle writes on over 40 topics with A.A. related directly to several of them: Drunk-a-logs, Humility and Self-Esteem, I'm Glad I'm an Alcoholic, "Recovered or Recovering," the Twelve Steps, prevention, and ...in all our affairs. Indirectly the entire booklet is about A.A. and alcoholism.

777. Hickle, Bob. A Pearl of Great Price. First ed. Lake Mills, Iowa: Graphic Pub. Co., Inc.; 1976(?); 49pp.
Brief essays on the pearl of great price, sobriety, and the A.A. program, one about living, not about drinking. Many A.A. related topics.

778. Hickle, Bob. Responsible Drinking and other Myths. First ed. Lake Mills, Iowa: Graphic Pub. Co., Inc.; 1976; 40pp.
Note: Booklet.
The author has been a professional counselor of alcoholics since 1948. In this booklet he explodes some myths about alcoholics, alcoholism and professionals in the field of alcoholism. He also discusses the importance of A.A., the Big Book and other related A.A. topics.

779. Hickle, Bob. Through a Glass, Darkly. First ed. Lake Mills, Iowa: Graphic Pub. Co., Inc.; 1977; 30pp.
This counselor writes about A.A. ideas without the professional terminology of the counselor. "A non-alcoholic who seems to be able to get inside the alcoholic's head...the degree of his insight is still remarkable," said the Grapevine in June 1977 in reviewing this booklet. "Stinkin' Thinkin'" and other A.A. related topics.

780. Hill, Morris A./McMillin, Chandler Scott/Rogers, Ronald L. The Twelve Steps Revisited. First ed. Seattle, WA: Madrona Publishers; 1988; 89pp; ISBN: 0-88089-028-2. LC 88-9119.
Note: pb.
The authors discuss each of the Twelve Steps of A.A. in separate chapters. As with all outside interpretations of the Steps, this is NOTA.A. Conference-approved Literature.

781. Hirsh, Joseph. The Problem Drinker. First ed. New York: Duell, Sloan & Pearce; 1949; 211pp.
Comprehensive picture of the alcoholic in the U.S. The A.A. program is described fully.

782. A History of AA in the Harrisburg [Pa.] Area & its surrounding communities. Harrisburg, PA: Harrisburg Intergroup Service Committee; 1986 & 1989.
Note: two 5.5 x 8.5" booklets.
Initially, "A Report on the Beginning and Growth of Alcoholics Anonymous in Harrisburg and its surrounding communities" [18pp] was published in 1986 and the above title listing is the second edition 42-page booklet updating that. Harrisburg AA began in 1940 and this booklet covers group histories, District 36, Intergroup, Fellowship House, and many other historical events up through 1989.

783. The History of AA in Virginia. Early Highlights. Falls Church, VA: Virginia Area [AA] Archives Committee; 1990.
Note: 8.5 x 11" green softbound.
In celebration of the 50th anniversary of AA in Virginia, this first edition 13-page booklet was published and covers early highlights of history from the first recorded meeting of AA on June 5, 1940, in Richmond to the Northern Neck group in Warsaw in 1953.

784. A History of Alcoholics Anonymous in Oregon 1943-1983. Diana S., et al, compilers & writers. First ed. Portland, OR: The Oregon Area General Service Committee of Alcoholics Anonymous; 1983; 308pp+.
Note: pb.
This fine history of Oregon AA documents much of the early founding of groups in Portland, Mill Creek, Salem, North Coastal area, Eastern Oregon, Eugene, Hood River and Dalles, Southern, Central, and South Coastal Oregon areas, and Columbia County. Al-Anon from 1943-65 and onward, with Alateen, to 1983 are included. The Oregon General Service Area Committee and other service committees are included. A fine color cover symbol comes from the Third Annual State Conference in 1953.

785. The History of Western Pennsylvania Area 60 [AA]. Pittsburgh, PA: Western Pa. Area 60 AA Archives; 1990.
Note: 5.5 x 8.5 " blue pamphlet.
This first edition 20-page history covers Western Pennsylvania from the first AA meeting in the Hotel Henry in Pittsburgh on Dec. 13, 1940, to 1990. About 200 groups out of 900 sent in their group histories to the archives in preparation for this project.

786. Hollis, Judi, Ph.D. "When AAs go to OA". Center City, MN: Hazelden; Jan., 1986; ISBN: 0-89486-347-9.
This 19-page pamphlet discusses some AAs' resistance to taking their weight problem to Overeaters Anonymous.

787. "Homosexual Alcoholic: AA's Message of Hope to Gay Men and Women". Center City, MN: Hazelden; 1980.
This pamphlet addresses the issue of honesty as it relates to homosexuals in AA as well as answers questions about homosexual groups within AA. (NALGAP 291).

788. Hough, Henry Beetle [as told to...]. An Alcoholic to His Sons. First ed. New York: Simon & Schuster; 1954; 246pp.
The author relates the story of an anonymous alcoholic and his recovery from alcoholism in A.A. The book is dedicated to the members of the Martha's Vineyard Group of Alcoholics Anonymous whose experiences provided the author with much of the material in this personal witness book.

789. Hugh L. Finding A Sponsor. First ed. Center City, MN: Hazelden; October, 1989; 25pp.
Note: Pamphlet.
The author uses a fictitious narrative to illustrate the importance of a sponsor in A.A. and suggests criteria for choosing one.

790. Hugh L. First Meeting. First ed. Center City, MN: Hazelden; February, 1989; 22pp; ISBN: 0-89486-578-1.
Note: Pamphlet.
The author uses fictitious A.A. characters and events to describe a "typical" A.A. speaker meeting which is often the first exposure an alcoholic has to A.A.

791. Hugh L. The God Business. First ed. Center City, MN: Hazelden; February, 1989; 27pp; ISBN: 0-89486-575-7.
Note: Pamphlet.
The author uses a fictional story "intended to help A.A. newcomers understand spirituality." He discusses spirituality and religion, the concept of a Higher Power, and members' diverse beliefs.

792. Hugh L. The Meeting. First ed. Center City, MN: Hazelden; August, 1990; 212pp; ISBN: 0-89486-693-1.
Note: pb.
This fiction collection of 8 short stories focuses on the "average Step-by-Step AA group." The author says "the incidents are based on actual experiences in AA meetings." He suggests his portrayals of certain AA "characters" are proof "we are not saints." This is, of course, not A.A. Conference-approved literature.

793. Hugh L. The Slipper. First Printing ed. Center City, MN: Hazelden; October, 1989; 33pp.
Note: Pamphlet.
The author uses fictitious characters and experiences in A.A. to describe relapse, a return to drinking, a "slip." Warning signs of relapse and how to get back to AA after a slip are discussed.

794. Hunter, Willard [with assistance from M.D.B., Toledo, Ohio]. "A.A.'s Roots in the Oxford Group". First ed. New York: (A.A. Archives); 1988; 6pp.
Note: This is NOT an A.A.-Conference approved item.
Hunter, a non-alcoholic friend of A.A. from Claremont, California, was a member of the Oxford Group movement for many years. He gives his historical thoughts on Frank Buchman, founder of the Oxford Group movement, on Carl Jung's connection with A.A. through Rowland H., on Sam Shoemaker, and on what he considers the reasons why A.A. and the Oxford Group split in the late 1930s.

795. An Index of Alcoholics Anonymous Literature. Two pre-publication review copies ed. New York; 1976; 123pp & 106pp.
Note: Both 8 1/2 x 11", spiral bound and stiff folder.
This index, "Where Does It Say So," lists excerpts from the Big Book, the Twelve & Twelve, A.A. Comes of Age, and The A.A. Way of Life and indexes them by one of the four books, page and line. Although the title page states "A.A. General Service Conference approved literature," it was never approved for publication. A.A. has always resisted attempts to define spirituality into narrow textbook indexes and the like. The library also has a similar copy, Where Does It Say So? An Alphabetical Index of the Following Four Books (as above). This is dated 1976 by AAWS, Inc., New York City. Again, this copy was never published by A.A. except in a limited number of pre-publication examination or review copies. The General Service Conference of A.A. has never approved any index of A.A. literature.

796. Index to The Big Book, "Alcoholics Anonymous". Bellevue, NE: Dicobe Tapes, Inc.; nd (1980s); 112pp.
Note: booklet.
The index is in three parts: word reference & page number; subject reference & page number; and the Twelve Steps referenced to page number.

797. "International Doctors in Alcoholics Anonymous". Minneapolis, MN: I.D.A.A.; 1949-1993.
A one-page letter outlines the aims of Int'l Doctors in AA as the same as AA's aims. The first meeting of ten doctors was held in the garage of Doctor Clarence P. in Clayton, NY, in 1949. Three Canadian doctors and a psychologist were among them, thus making it international and interdisciplinary. Since 1949, an annual meeting has been held. In 1988, membership was over 2,500.

798. International Lawyers in Alcoholics Anonymous Newsletter; 1975-1993; usually 4pp each.
Founded in 1975, the International Lawyers in AA hold an annual convention. The newsletter is mailed six times a year. "The group consists of a loosely-knit conglomerate of lawyers who share the experience, strength and hope of Alcoholics Anonymous, and who have been encouraging bar associations in the U.S. and Canada to form outreach committees such as Lawyers Concerned for Lawyers.".

799. Jeff B. "The Benefits of Telling Your Story". Center City, MN: Hazelden; Jan., 1986; ISBN: 0-89486-353-3.
This 16-page pamphlet discusses the place of your story in the Twelve Steps, AA meetings, and your life. Denial, truthfulness, and sharing your story with others are discussed.

800. Jellinek, E. M. The Disease Concept of Alcoholism. First ed. New Haven, Connecticut: Hillhouse Press; 1960; 246pp; ISBN: L.C. 60-9206.
Note: 22 references to A.A. in the index. "An honest publisher would warn on the jacket of this book that temperance societies and the alcohol-beverage industry should not read it. It will not make them happy," the author wrote (from the dust jacket of the book). Jellinek is world-famous as the founder of the Yale Center of Alcohol Studies, the Yale Summer School of Alcohol Studies, the Yale Plan Clinics, the Classified Abstract Archive of the Alcohol Liteature, and the Master Bibliography of the Alcohol Literature.
One of the top ten books in history on alcoholism. Professor Jellinek herein lays the modern scientific foundation for a definition of alcoholism as a disease. From that theoritical fact plus the existence of A.A. has flowed all the modern changes in our attitudes, laws, responses, and attempts to deal with the problem of alcoholism. The Christopher D. Smithers Foundation in 1957 chose Prof. Jellinek to study the attitudes throughout the world toward the concept of alcoholism as a disease. Much of Jellinek's data came from surveys of A.A. members.

801. Joe McQ. The Steps We Took. First ed. Little Rock, AR: August House Publishers, Inc.; 1990; 179pp; ISBN: 0-87483-151-2. LC 90-641.
Note: pb. [later printings do not have the author's photo]. "A teacher of the Twelve Steps shares his experience, strength, and hope with all those recovering from addictions, all who want to recover, and all who love them," the sub title explains. The author is identified on the cover as "of the 'Big Book Study Tapes.'" The author's photo is on the back cover, a clear anonymity break (if not by the letter of the Traditions, certainly against the spirit of them). The editors characterize Joe as a "master teacher" of the 12 Steps. A.A. does not have "teachers." The content of the book is Joe's interpretation of the Twelve Steps which can be used for any addiction, not just alcoholism.

802. Johnson, Hazel Cameron. "Values of AA Members for Alcoholics Anonymous Meetings". at: Annual Meeting of The Society for the Study of Social Problems; August, 1985; Washington, DC. unpublished research paper; 20pp.
Johnson, a Univ. of California, Los Angeles, student, surveyed 8 small AA discussion groups in 1983 and concluded that past scholarly literature on AA groups has failed to focus on the variety of groups within AA. Reseachers "must also be careful not to tap only the opinions of the most vocal AA members or the 'bleeding deacons.'" She opines there "has been too much focus upon the commitment process and not

enough on what keeps people 'in AA' over the years. It is not sufficient to observe large speaker-format meetings and then to make generalizations about AA from the speaker's remarks.".

803. "Judge Claims Non-Professional Personnel Would Have Most Success With Alcoholics". in: American Law & Lawyers; April 15, 1947.
Walter J. Casey, a municipal court judge, told a WAshington Committee for Education on Alcoholism that a year-and-one-half program in which Alcoholics Anonymous members worked with the probation officer had "very definite success" with alcoholics. The AA group succeeded because "there was mutual understanding of fellow-sufferers," Casey said.

804. Keller, Mark (General Editor)/Jordy, Sarah Spock/Efron, Vera/Chen, Pei-Lan/Weinstein, Neha/Simonds, Joanne O./Beck, Anna. International Bibliography of Studies on Alcohol. Firsts ed. New Brunswick, New Jersey: Publications Div., Rutgers Center of Alcohol Studies; 1966-1968-1980; Vols. 1-2-3; 631-134-320pp; ISBN: LC 60-14437 & ISBN 911290-40-0.
This three volume bibliography lists about 200 works, journal articles, etc. concerning AA. Vols. I & II contain the References and Indexes for 1901-1950 while Vol. III contains References and Indexes for the 1951-1960 period.

805. Kellerman, Joseph L. "Reconciliation With God and Family". Center City, MN: Hazelden; 1976.
Fr. Kellerman explains how the twelve steps of A.A. help individuals reconcile themselves with God. Each step is explained to show how it is consistent with universal religious principles. Mention is made that some priests and ministers who were unable to sober up through their religions have found sobriety in A.A.

806. Ken F. Taking One's Inventory. First ed. St. Paul, MN: Ken F.; 1981; 64pp.
Note: pb.
Ken F. takes a Fourth Step inventory in A.A. humorously in this book of 64 cartoons.

807. Kessel, Joseph. The Road Back. A Report on Alcoholics Anonymous. First American ed. NY: Alfred A. Knopf; 1962; 244pp; ISBN: L.C. 61-17380.
Note: An excellent in-depth early view of A.A., based on many interivews with A.A.'s and Bill W. Early history of how A.A. began. The movie, The Days of Wine and Roses, is discussed. Translated from the French by Frances Partridge. Kessel, the noted French novelist and journalist, visited Manhattan's Bowery, A.A. meetings among prisoners at Sing Sing and among Park Avenue dwellers, observed A.A. officials, and talked with Bill W. himself, co-founder of A.A. This book is one of the earliest illuminating portraits of A.A.

808. King, Arthur. Seven Sinners. First ed. New York: Harcourt, Brace & World, Inc.; 1961; 295pp; ISBN: L.C. 61-13348.
King relates the stories of "seven sinners" who had tried the A.A. program, found it wanting eventually for various reasons, and left it. King relates how some found A.A.'s insistence on a Higher Power too difficult to accept. His 3 bibliographies at the back of the book contain many religious, philosophical, and literary titles of a broad, stimulating nature that Bill W. might have termed useful. King and Cain are still viewed by many as A.A.'s most vocal critics. The experiences of the seven sinners at A.A. meetings and discussions of A.A. concepts make up much of the book.

809. Kirkpatrick, Jean, Ph.D. W.F.S. & A.A. Quakertown, Pa.: Women for Sobriety, Inc.; 1976; 21pp.
This booklet by the Executive Director of W.F.S. outlines the similarities and the differences between W.F.S. and A.A. W.F.S. is based on Thirteen Statements of Acceptance. Their meetings do not permit smoking or coffee, two common occurances at A.A. meetings. The booklet gives a brief outline of W.F.S. structure, ideology, and practices, and ends with ads for their books and other material.

810. Klaas, Joe. The 12 Steps to Happiness. A Handbook for all Twelve Steppers. First Ballantine pb ed. New York: Ballantine Books/Hazelden Recovery Book; May, 1990; c1982; 165pp; ISBN: 0-345-36787-1.
Note: pb.
Termed a "practical handbook" for understanding and working the Twelve Step Programs for alcoholism, codependency, eating disorders and other addictions," this book discusses each of the Twelve Steps in a chapter.

811. Klaas, Joe. The 12 Traditions for All of Us. First ed. Center City, MN: Hazelden; March, 1986; 61pp; ISBN: 0-89486-357-6.
Note: pb.
The author discusses the Twelve Traditions of A.A. as they apply to the 300-plus other anonymous Twelve Step programs that have patterned themselves after A.A. The book is his own personal interpretation of A.A.'s Traditions.

812. Kominars, Sheppard B. Accepting Ourselves: The Twelve-Step Journey of Recovery from Addiction for Gay Men and Lesbians. San Francisco: Harper & Row; 1989.
Kominars, a recovered alcoholic, gives his views on each of the twelve steps.

813. Kurtz, Ernest. A.A. The Story. A Revised Edition of "Not-God: A History of Alcoholics Anonymous". First. ed. San Francisco, et al: Harper/Hazelden; 1988; 296pp; ISBN: 0-06-255457-3.
Kurtz, in this popular market version of his earlier book, Not-God, includes a new chapter that brings A.A.'s history beyond the death of Bill Wilson in 1971 and carries it forward to 1987. He "traces the roots of A.A. philosophy to such a seemingly diverse group as Carl Jung, William James, John D. Rockefeller, Jr., and Akron socialite Henrietta Seiberling, as well as the Oxford Group of Frank Buchman, a number of Irish-American Catholic priests, and fundamentalist religion. The story relates the painful writing of A.A.'s 'Big Book,' Alcoholics Anonymous, the problems caused over the years by Wilson's unofficial status as 'head' of A.A., and the fight involving the A.A. board of trustees." The book includes over 75 pages of notes and references.

814. Kurtz, Ernest. NOT-GOD. A History of Alcoholics Anonymous. First ed. Center City, MN: Hazelden Educational Services; 1979; 363pp; ISBN: 0-89486-065-8.
Note: To date the best history and interpretation of A.A. Kurtz includes much primary research on the psychiatrist Carl Jung, American philosopher William James, Akron social matron Henrietta Seiberling, John D. Rockefeller, Jr., the Oxford Group of Frank Buchman, Irish-American Catholic priests, and fundamentalist religion. index. bibliography. extensive notes for each of the eleven chapters. primary research based in part of many interviews with important persons in the history & development of A.A. Built around the theme "Not-God," ("First of all we had to quit playing God," Alcoholics Anonymous, p.62), this volume is to date the definitive intellectual history of A.A.
Authoritative account of the discovery and development from 1935 to 1971 of the program and fellowship that we know today as Alcoholics Anonymous. Kurtz was the first writer given full and complete access to the archives of the General Service Office of A.A. in New York.

815. Kurtz, Ernest. NOT-GOD. A History of Alcoholics Anonymous. Expanded [Second] ed. Center City, MN: Hazelden Educational Materials, Inc.; 1991; 436pp; ISBN: 0-89486-065-8. LC 79-88264.
Note: Bibliography, index, pb.
This expanded history of A.A. includes appendix B from Kurtz, AA: The Story, 1988, which covers the 1971-87 period; and appendix A, "Alcoholics Anonymous and 'Absolutes': 'The Spiritual' as Growth or Perfection." [The first edition history ended in 1971.].

816. Kurtz, Ernest, Ph.D. (Center for Self-Help Research, The Univ. of Michigan). "Research on Alcoholics Anonymous: The Historical Context"; 1992; Albuquerque Conference on Research on Alcoholics Anonymous; 24pp.
"Alcoholics Alcoholics has been around for going on 57 years; research on A.A. has been going on for more than 50 years. Yet we still hear mainly about how 'inconclusive' are the results of what now number many hundreds of articles, and conferences such as this one seem to verify the 'law' that Mark Keller formulated in 1972: 'The investigation of any trait in alcoholics will show that they have either more or less of it.' That seems ever truer of those alcoholics who are members of A.A.," Kurtz began. He criticizes current researchers' unscientific attitudes about AA, spirituality, and their own methods. He also finds a problem within AA itself; that is has abandoned the AA experience for "Varieties of the Alcoholics Anonymous Experience." This is an important paper for researchers who are urged to be accurate, objective, and respectful about their own methods and about their subject, A.A., and worthwhile for AA archivists and historians.

817. Kus, Robert J. "The Alcoholics Anonymous Sponsor and Gay American Men.". Budapest: 32nd Int'l Institute on the Prevention and Treatment of Alcoholism; June 1986.
Note: A similarily-titled article (unpublished) is listed in NALGAP (334) and it discusses the same material while adding how professionals may be supportive of the gay AA member. Some suggestions about how rural gay alcoholic men might be better served are provided.
The paper explores the necessity of sponsors, how sponsors are chosen, the perceived qualities and duties of the sponsor, and strategies for letting go of one's sponsor. (NALGAP 335).

818. Laundergan, J./Kammeier, M. Posttreatment Alcoholics Anonymous Attendance and Treatment Outcome. Center City, MN: Hazelden; 1978.

819. Lemert, E. W. Alcohol and Northwest Coast Indians. Berkeley, CA: Univ. of California Press; 1954.

820. "The Long Haul". Chicago: Chicago Area A.A. Service Ofc. This 20-page pamphlet finds an AA, a sober newspaperman, talking to newcomers about the Twelve Steps and his experience.

821. Louis S. ""Being Friendly with Our Friends". at: 35th Int'l A.A. Convention; July 3-5, 1970; Miami Beach, FL. Miami Beach, FL: AAWS; July, 1970; 3pp.
Note: [also reprinted in Report 54 of the North American Assn. of Alcoholism Programs].
Louis S., an AA member with 25 years sobriety, has worked in the field of alcoholism for some twenty years and here presents his experience on "How to Wear Two Hats." It can't be done is his answer. "To survive in this program, I have found it completely necessary to divorce my vocation, which

is alcoholism, from my AA," he said. Louis lists 7 suggestions "that we in the West Va. Div. of Alcoholism have found helpful in working with Alcoholics Anonymous.".

822. Louth, Cyril E. But For the Grace of God. New York: Pageant Press; 1956; 112pp.
A professional writer's experience as an active alcoholic and his recovery in A.A. are the thrust of this personal witness book.

823. Lucier, Marjorie, et al. Having Been There. The Personal Drama of Alcoholism. First ed. Luks, Allan, Editor & compiler. New York: Charles Scribner's Sons; 1979; 189pp; ISBN: 0-684-16170-2.
Note: Introduction by Ring Lardiner, Jr.
The first collection of short stories to portray all phases of the human drama of alcoholism. 18 prizewinning stories selected from over 500 entries in a national competition sponsored in part by the New York City Affiliate of the National Council on Alcoholism. Several of the short stories mention A. A. directly while many of the others utilize A.A. concepts and have underlying A.A. principles, characterizations, etc. A laudatory effort in the barely-touched rich field of fiction about alcoholism & alcoholics.

824. Luger, Arnold E., Father. Calix and the Twelve Steps. Minneapolis, MN: The Calix Society; circa 1985; 63pp.
This booklet discusses the Twelve Steps in depth for Catholic A.A. members, as well as "any others, not members of our Faith, or any others, non-alcoholics, who are concerned with the illness of alcoholism and wishto join with us in prayer..." Calix is not affiliated with A.A.

825. Lundgren, Woody. An Index to Alcoholics Anonymous. First ed. Center City, MN: Hazelden Foundation; June, 1987; 21pp; ISBN: 0-89486-475-0.
Note: "...essentially a topical index; a compilation that makes no claim to being exhaustive..." "another helpful tool in the use of the Big Book..." Lundgren was a counselor at Hazelden from 1974 until his death in 1983.
"This pamphlet has the simple purpose of identifying the passages in Alcoholics Anonymous (Big Book) which mention or explain the various attitudes, behaviors, and character defects that precede, accompany, and are the results of the disease of alcoholism.".

826. Lupton, Dilworth. "Mr. X and Alcoholics Anonymous". Cleveland, OH: Channing Press; circa 1939-40 ?
This 14-page small pamphlet by Lupton, a minister at the First Unitarian Church [Universalist-Unitarian] at Euclid at East 82nd St., Cleveland, tells the story of Mr. X, an alcoholic [Clarence S.], who was then two years sober and said his "cure is due to the efforts of a group of ex-drunks [their own term] who call themselves Alcoholics Anonymous." Lupton believed their success stemmed from "four religious principles as old as the Ten Commandments: spiritual

dependence, universality, mutual aid, and transformation." Bill W. and the Big Book are quoted.

827. Mann, Marty, Mrs./AA GSO staff member. "Alcoholism: The Problem and the Hope". in: The Catholic Hour. Washington, DC: National Council of Catholic Men; March 20 & 27, 1960; 10pp. This radio show script contains a talk by Executive Director Marty Mann on the National Council on Alcoholism and AA and a second by an anonymous GSO AA staffer on AA itself, what it is and is not.

828. "A Manual for Alcoholics Anonymous". Akron, OH: AA of Akron; 1940s (?).
This 16-page small pamphlet was written and edited by member of AA of Akron and "intended to be practical guide for new members of AA and their sponsors." Reprinted many times up to 1993, it still uses "experience" instead of "awakening" in the Twelfth Step.

829. Mark on the Gate. The History of Alcoholics Anonymous in the Tucson Area, Arizona. Tucson, AZ: The Tucson Area Intergroup Assn.; 1985.
Note: 5.25 x 8.25" yellow pb.
This 97-page first edition history begins in 1943 and ends in 1984. The first year, pioneers, the mother group divides, group rivalry, the central office, surge of growth, and present day AA are covered in 9 chapters.

830. Martin, Greg [pseudonym]. Spiritus Contra Spiritum: The Struggle of an Alcoholic Priest. Philadelphia: Westminster Press; 1977; 192 pp.
This personal witness story of a priest's ordeal with alcoholism ends with recovery in A.A.

831. Martin, Joseph C., Fr. Some Personal Comments on the Most Effective Therapy in the World: TheTwelve Steps of Alcoholics Anonymous. First ed. Aberdeen, MD: Kelly Productions, Inc.; 1984; 36pp.
This booklet presents Fr. Martin's interpretation of the Twelve Steps of AA.

832. Maupin, Robert E., M.D. "Conclusions from Fifty Years Experience in the Treatment of Alcoholics". Greensboro, NC: The Keeley Institute of North Carolina; 1949?
"We recommend to each patient leaving treatment that he become active in the work of Alcoholics Anonymous..." Dr. Maupin suggests on the last page of this 7-page pamphlet.

833. Maxwell, Milton A., Ph.D. The Alcoholics Anonymous Experience. A Close-Up View for Professionals. First ed. New York, et al: McGraw-Hill Book Co.; 1984; 175pp; ISBN: 0-07-040996-X. LC 83-16244.
Note: index.
An up-to-date portrayal is made of AA operations and dynamics, with focus on the personal participation experience of members and the dynamics of local group life. The approach is anthropological, featuring excerpts from interviews with individuals regarding their experiences before and after coming into AA. It examines the relationship between professionals and AA and illustrates how professionals may use AA as an adjunct to treatment. Maxwell was a Class A [non-alcoholic] Trustee of A.A. from 1971 to 1982 and served as Chairperson of the General Service Board of A.A. from 1978 to 1982. His book was one of the early sociological studies of A.A.

834. McCarthy, Raymond G. Facts about Alcohol. Chicago: Science Research Associates; 1951.
Note: 48pp.
This booklet is addressed to young people to help them make decisions concerning alcohol. The A.A. program is discussed.

835. McDaniel, Judith. Metamorphosis: Reflections on Recovery. Ithica, NY: Firebrand Books; 1989.
McDaniel presents a series of poems which tell the story of her addiction and recovery through AA. The book also includes an essay in which McDaniel disagrees with criticisms of AA which have appeared in the lesbian-gay press. Anonymity break.

836. McIlwain, William. A Farewell to Alcohol. First ed. New York: Random House; 1972; 143pp; ISBN: 0-394-47610-7.
A personal narrative of this newspaperman who found his marriage and job falling apart because of alcoholism, signed in at Butner, a rehab center for alcoholics in North Carolina, and has undergone recovery through the subsequent years. Although A.A. is mentioned several places in the story, it would be wrong to assume automatically that the author is a member of that society.

837. Mel B. Is There Life after Sobriety? Second ed. Jackson, MI: Author (originally articles were published by AA Grapevine); 1979; c1974; 110pp.
Note: The first edition was published by the author at Toledo, Ohio, in 1974.
Subtitled "How An AA Member Sees the Problems and Challenges of Living," this paperback (8 1/2 x 11") reprints numerous articles from the AA Grapevine over the years. A member of A.A. since 1950, Mel B. wrote his first published Grapevine article in 1955 and since then has had 40 of 45 articles submitted published by the GV. The book includes a wide range of A.A. topics from humor and sex to the God business and mental depression-unnecessary evil. All articles reprinted by permission of the AA Grapevine.

838. Mel B. "My Search for Bill Wilson". Toledo, OH: author; 1991 (?).
This 27-page talk by the author of numerous AA Grapevine articles and other books about AA discusses Bill Wilson as the Power Driving Achiever, the Fixer, the Individualist, the Enterpreneur, the Communicator, the Peacemaker and finally, Bill the Founder-Statesman.

839. Mel B. New Wine. The Spiritual Roots of the Twelve Step Miracle. First ed. Center City, MN: Hazelden; October, 1991; 193pp; ISBN: 0-89486-772-5. LC 91-73799.
Note: Index, pb.
Mel B. discusses the people and ideas that shaped early A.A. thinking about spirituality and a Higher Power. Carl Jung, Emmet Fox, Frank Buchman, Richard Peabody, Rev. Sam Shoemaker, and a host of others come alive in this excellent portrayal of the Fellowship's heart, spirituality.

840. Mel B. "The Slogans: Basic Tools for Successful Recovery". Center City, MN: Hazelden; April, 1990; ISBN: 0-89486-654-0.
This 29-page pamphlet discusses the seven great slogans of AA: First Things First, Live and Let Live, Easy Does It, Let Go and Let God, One Day at a Time, Pass It On, and Keep It Simple.

841. A Member of Alcoholics Anonymous. The Twelve Steps. Spiritual Recovery Through the Principles of A.A. Second ed. Nashville, TN: The Upper Room; 1965; 47pp.
Note: small booklet.
The author dicusses each of the Twelve Steps.

842. Members of The Hazelden Foundation. The Twelve Steps of Alcoholics Anonymous Interpreted by Members of the Hazelden Foundaiton. First ed. New York: Harper & Row/Hazelden Foundtion; 1987; 131pp; ISBN: 0-06-255444-1.
Note: Originally published as pamphlets on the individual steps in 1974, this book comes from Hazelden,in Minnesota, a pioneer rehabilitation facility for alcoholics for some 40 years. Each chapter has a different author. They are Karen Elliott (introduction), William Springborn, James G. Jensen, The Hazelden Foundation, Edward C. Sellner, James Brandon, Pat M., Mel B., and Peter Converse McDonald. Useful but, again, a warning is included to "take what fits and leave the rest.".
Short discussions that interpret each of A.A.'s Twelve Steps. Chapters on Steps one, four & eight include lists the reader may fill out.

843. Miller, J. Keith. A Hunger for Healing. The Twelve Steps as a Classic Model for Christian Spiritual Growth. First ed. New York: HarperSan Francisco, Div. of HarperCollins; 1991: AA throughout; 262pp; ISBN: 0-06-065716-2. LC 90-55295.
Note: Index, dj. [paperback version in 1992].
Miller blends Christianity with the Twelve Steps. He discusses each of A.A.'s Steps in the light of the Bible and suggests they offer a new model for Christian discipleship and spiritual maturity...even for those Christians who do not suffer from an addiction. He finds no conflict between his Christian church, the Bible, and the Steps.

844. "Ministry to Alcoholics: The Role of the Chaplain". Newport, RI: Chaplain Resource Board; nd.
Developed by the Naval Chaplains School in Newport, Rhode Island, this pamphlet focuses on the spiritual dimension of alcoholism and recovery from alcoholism. The role of AA as a treatment method is emphasized. The role of denial as a block to treatment and of the need for confrontation are explained.

845. "Misunderstanding". Cleveland, OH: Cleveland Dist. Ofc. of Alcoholics Anonymous; ?
This pamphlet has five pages of reprints of Central Bulletin [Vol. 22, Nos. 5, 7, & 8] editorials on misunderstanding, tolerance, open-mindedness, and possessiveness; anger, anxiety, criticism and envy; and arrogance, gossip, prejudice and pride.

846. Molloy, Paul. Where Did Everybody Go? First ed. New York: Warner Books, Inc.; July, 1982; 237pp; ISBN: 0-446-30375-5.
Note: Paperback. (apparently published earlier in hardback by Doubleday & Co., Garden City, NY.).
Molloy's personal witness story of his alcoholism focuses on the relapse condition of the disease. After repeated denials and treatment attempts, he finally gets it right in A.A. Along the way Molloy breaks his anonymity. He weaves into his story much about treatment centers, detox units, famous alcoholic personalities, and some solid information from such national organizations as NCA, etc.

847. Moriarty, Patrick J., Editor. Evening Prayers, Morning Promises. First ed. Seattle, WA: Glen Abbey Books; 1989; 159pp paperback; ISBN: 0-934125-14-7.
This volume is a collection of quotations, stories and life experiences. The meditations progress through the Twelve Steps of AA.

848. Morreim, Dennis C. Changed Lives. The Story of Alcoholics Anonymous. First ed. Minneapolis, MN: Augsburg Fortress; 1991; 128pp; ISBN: 0-8066-2548-1. LC 91-12673.
Note: pb.
Morreim retells the story of how A.A. was founded, grew, and spread up through the acceptance of the Twelve Traditions at the First Int'l Convention of A.A. in Cleveland, Ohio. The parable of the seeds from the Bible is used through the book as an analogy.

849. Morreim, Dennis C. The Road to Recovery: Bridges between the Bible and the Twelve Steps. First ed. Minneapolis, MN: Augsburg Fortress; 1990: (AA throughout); 142pp; ISBN: 0-8066-2456-6. LC 89-49091.
Note: pb.
"Although AA and the church are not one and the same, it is my contention that the two complement each other," Morreim says (p.131). He briefly discuss the Oxford Group Movement and the founding of A.A. in the first chapter. The remaining nine chapters discuss the Twelve Steps of A.A. and Biblical "bridges" to them.

850. Nancy T. "Reaching the Lesbian Alcoholic". in: Rutgers University Summer School of Alcohol Studies; June-July, 1978; New Brunswick, NJ. New Brunswick, NJ: Rutgers Center of Alcohol Studes; 1978; 13pp.
The author, an alcoholic lesbian and member of the "Live and Let Live" and "Lambda" gay groups of AA, describes a lack of outreach by alcoholism professionals and agencies to gay clients, especially lesbians. A 1974-5 Los Angeles, California, study documents this negative outreach and the author discusses guidelines for alcoholism counselors and agencies that will correct this.

851. Nelson, Dennis D./Noland, Jane Thomas. Young Winners' Way: A Twelve Step Guide for Teenagers. Minneapolis, MN: CompCare Publications; 1983.
The book gives an explanation of each of AA's twelve steps.

852. A New Way of Life. Alcoholics Anonymous in Mississippi Correctional Facilities. ibid.; Summer, 1986: pp1-22.
This entire issue presents the experiences of inmates and others in A.A. involved in Mississippi's prison system. Male and female inmates write of their recoveries in A.A.

853. A [New?] Way of Life. Cleveland, OH; 1940s?
The title may be just "A Way of Life." This small narrow blue pamphlet was probably written by Clarence S. The Twelve Steps and other basic information about spirituality and recovery are discussed. Many old timers carried this and used it like a portable Big Book.

854. O'Brien, Sean. Twelve Steps to Happiness: Reflections on Drinking and on Alcoholics Anonymous. New York: Exposition Press; 1965; 134pp.
The author's personal analysis of A.A. includes 12 chapters for the Steps, somewhat along the lines of A.A.'s Twelve Steps and Twelve Traditions.

855. O'Keefe, R. Sober Living Workbook. Center City, MN: Hazelden Educational Services; 1980; 240pp.
This workbook is designed to assist alcoholics in their recovery. It draws heavily on the principles of AA.

856. Only, Mark (pseudonym). High: A Farewell to the Pain of Alcoholism. First ed. Englewood Cliffs, NJ: Prentice-Hall, Inc.; 1974; 158pp; ISBN: 0-13-387332-3.
The author preserves his anonymity, a cardinal principle of A.A., in telling of his alcoholism and recovery through A.A. and its Twelve Steps.

857. Osborne, A./Rush, B., editors. Proceedings of the 2nd Annual Meeting of the Special Interest Group on Program Evaluation of the Canadian Addiction Foundation; Sept. 8-9, 1982; Regina, Canada. London, Canada: Addiction Research Foundation, Canada; 1982; 184pp.
Note: [see: McTimoney, D. C., et al, & Osborne, A. C.].
Papers presented at this conference include several on AA.

858. Our Devilish Alcoholic Personalities. By The Author of The Little Red Book.[Ed W.]. First ed. Edina, MN: Hamar Publishers; 1970; 112pp.
The author tells his own alcoholic story; lists Landmarks in A.A. History; discusses facts and misconceptions about alcohol's effects upon the alcoholic; gives new slants on old A.A. ideas; gives a sober alcoholic's version of The Our Father. "This is not an official A.A. book, but it does deal with practical application of The Twelve Steps which have brought sobriety and peace of mind to many members, including the author," he writes in the foreword.

859. Our Golden Anniversary Year 1991. The History of A.A. in the Greater Cincinnati Area, 1941 thru 1964. Cincinnati, OH: Cincinnati Area Intergroup & the Cincinnati Fellowship of A.A.; 1991.
Note: 5.5 x 8.5" yellow pamphlet.
This second edition 21-page history reprints the original 1964 pamphlet history of Cincinnati given out at Beginners Meetings and adds two newspaper articles on Cincinnati's 50th AA anniversary. The history begins in May, 1941, and continues thru 1964.

860. "Our Stories Disclose..."; 1987: 7pp.
This 8.5 x 11" pamphlet is the nuts-and-bolts story of "how a ragtag band of amateurs researched, wrote, and published a history of the Washington Area of Alcoholics Anonymous. The story of their experience is told to help others who may seek to publish their own history." This is especially helpful for archivists. Included are: background, organization, printing estimates, presales campaign, sections report, word-processing crew, rewriters, editing committee, putting it all together, copyright, and delivery at last. More information is available from three listed contacts.

861. Our Stories Disclose...A History of the Washington Area of A.A. 1941-86. First. ed.: Washington Area Assembly of A.A.; 1987; 475pp.
The history of Alcoholics Anonymous in the state of Washington by district. A gigantic, superlative effort.

862. "Out of the Fog": 16pp.
This small pamphlet published by the Chicago Area Alcoholics Anonymous Service Office has been around for quite a few years. Basically, a woman in AA shares her experiences about finding God, Step Three, and a better home life with children.

863. Pastor Paul. The 13th American. First ed. Elgin, IL: David C. Cook Pub. Co.; 1973; 190pp; ISBN: 0-912692-12-X.
Pastor Paul (anonymous), a long-time member of AA, proves that alcoholism can strike in any profession. His own personal story of recovery in A.A. and his view of an America where one of every 13 Americans will become an alcoholic are complimented by his spiritual, psychological, and historical insights into Freud, Jellinek, Tiebout, and a host of other figures in the history of alcoholism. He gives an overview of alcoholism treatments and A.A. in this paperback.

864. Patterson, Bonnie. From Hell to Here. Boston: The Christopher Publishing House; 1963; 211pp.
A female alcoholic's story from early addiction to A.A. recovery. This personal witness book is dedicated to A.A. but all names have been changed with the exception of two.

865. Paul H. Things My Sponsor Taught Me. Center City, MN: Hazelden; August 1987; ISBN: 0-89486-444-0.
The 66-page paperback is one man's interpretation of AA sponsorship, that of the so-called "hard-nosed" school. Paul H. divides all AA members into two classes, the hard-noses and the "others" who don't get well. He summarizes the hard-nosed school with the ultimate answer at the end of the book: "Shut up, don't drink, and go to meetings.".

866. Paul, Louis. Breakdown. New York: Crown Publishers; 1946; 305pp.
A novelized account of a female newspaper columnist's struggle with alcoholism and recovery in A.A.

867. "The People of the Gay Grape: A Personal Investigation". San Diego: Other Publishing Company; 1988.
The people of the gay grape are lesbian and gay alcoholics in San Diego who are members of AA. By using a participant observer technique to study AA participation of lesbian and gay men, the author who wrote this booklet provides a useful explanation of how AA works for lesbians and gay men.

868. Pfau, Ralph, Fr./Hirshberg, Al. Prodigal Shepherd. First ed. Indianapolis, IN: The SMT Guild; 1958; 252pp; ISBN: L.C. 58-9535.
Note: This book has gone through 17 printings.
This autobiography of the first Catholic priest to join A.A. details his nervous breakdowns, time in sanitariums, and eventual membership in A.A. He then devoted his life to working with alcoholics and wrote numerous pamphlets about alcoholism and A.A. under the pseudonym "Father John Doe." (See separate listing Doe). Anonymity break.

869. Phillips, Julianne. Alcoholics Anonymous: An Annotated Bibliography 1935-1972. First ed. London, Ohio: Privately Printed by author/Central Ohio Publishing Co.; 1973; 63pp; ISBN: L.C. 73-163972.
Note: This bibliography was compiled as a research paper by Phillips as partial fulfillment of Master of Library Science degree she received at Kent State University, Kent, Ohio, in December, 1972. A model of excellent annotation, despite the limited number of entries (no A.A. Grapevine articles are included, etc.), this was a good beginning. The paperback went through 3 printings as of 1979.
Included in this small paperback are literature on the history of A.A.; on A.A. programs in penal institutions and hospitals; on psychological and sociological studies of A.A. and its members; and a history and description of Al-Anon and Alateen. An appendix listed books, directories and pamphlets published by and available from A.A. World Services, New York.

870. Phillip Z. A Skeptic's Guide to The 12 Steps. First ed. Center City, MN: Hazelden; October, 1990; 241pp; ISBN: 0-89486-722-9. LC 89-82537.
Note: Index, pb.
Phillip Z., a compulsive overeater and skeptic, shares his story of coming to believe in a Power greater than himself. He discusses each of A.A. 12 Steps with "enlightenment from non-traditional Judeo-Christian concepts of God such as Buddhism, Jungian and transpersonal psychology."Phillip, a psychologist, says Step Three did "not require belief in a Supreme Being, although I did not rule out the existence of such a Being. It does indicate my belief that life will be richer and profoundly more exciting to the extent I am willing and able to tap the creative power and energy of the Self and bring the ego into its service.".

871. Pietsch, William V. The Serenity Prayer. First ed. San Francisco, CA: Harper; 1990; 116pp; ISBN: 0-06-250682-X. LC 89-46441.
Note: dj.
The unofficial "official" prayer of AA, the Serenity Prayer, is examined by Pietsch who blends psychotherapeutic knowledge with religious insight. Spiritual understanding of this classic prayer will be deepened in fresh and different ways by this book.

872. Pittman, Bill. AA The Way It Began. Seattle, WA: Glen Abbey Books; 1988; 239pp; ISBN: 0-934125-08-2.
Note: This paperback book about the early history of A.A. grew out of Pittman's early thesis work. Alcoholism Treatments in the 1890s, the "Prohibition Cure," the Oxford Group, William Griffith Wilson & Alcoholics Anonymous, and the author's conclusions are the main sections. Also useful are appendixes listing books suggested by Peabody, Nell Wing's list of books early AAs read, Sam Shoemaker books, Oxford Group books, Dr. Bob's required reading list, & additional information for AA and Al-Anon. An important volume tracing the early roots of the forces that eventually

were molded into A.A. Pittman has done a mountain of new research.

873. Pittman, Bill. Stepping Stones to Recovery. First ed. Seattle, WA: Glen Abbey Books; 1988; 282pp; ISBN: 0-934125-04-X. pb.
Note: Subtitled "Selected Spiritual Insights into Recovery drawn from the membership of Alcoholics Anonymous over the past 50 years," this book surveys the vast field of A.A. literature and collected some of the best ideas, principles and teachings into this volume. It is the best available compilation of A.A. articles, slogans and prayers published with A.A. Conference approval. Chapters include: acceptance, spirituality, meditation, serenity, fellowship, conversion, recovery, concepts, surrender, one day at a time, slogans and prayers.

874. "Pittsburgh Area Central Office Open House Week". Pittsburgh, PA: Pittsburgh AA; Sept. 11-15, 1988.
This 12-page pamphlet contains a one page brief history of the Pittsburgh Area Central Office from 1946 to 1989.

875. Polich, J. M./Armor, D. J./Braiker, H. B. The course of alcoholism four years after treatment. First ed. Santa Monica, CA: The Rand Corporation; 1980.
The Rand study concluded that it was possible for some problem drinkers and /or alcoholics to return safely to social drinking. It is mentioned in this bibliography because it prompted A.A. to issue one of its very rare public statements, decrying the report as erroneous and misleading some alcoholics into thinking they can drink again without risk. A.A. believes an alcoholic never changes his stripes and a return to "social" drinking is actually life-threatening for alcoholics.

876. "Poverello Medal". Steubenville, Ohio: The College of Steubenville; Dec. 7, 1949.
This first Poverello Medal awarded by The Franciscan College of Steubenville was presented on Dec. 7, 1949, to the Fellowship of Alcoholics Anonymous "in public recognition of the tremendous contribution the Fellowship has made to Humanity, thereby expressing in our age the Christ-like Charity which filled the life of Saint Francis of Assisi." An 8.5 x 11" certificate copy was mailed to every AA "unit" in the U.S. and Canada at the time. Sister Ignatia, Dr. Bob's partner, accepted the medal on behalf of AA.

877. Prayers for The Twelve Steps. A Spiritual Journey. Friends in Recovery/Jerry S./Pittman, Bill, compilers. First ed. San Diego, CA: Recovery Publications, Inc.; 1993; 155pp; ISBN: 0-941405-28-1. LC 93-15978.
Note: pb.
Contents include prayers and inspirational readings written and compiled by Bill Pittman and taken from The 12 Step Prayer Book [Glen Abbey Books, 1990] and prayers from the Bible with commentary by Jerry S. and Friends in Recovery.

878. Preparing for the Future. A Brief History of the Beginnings of Alcoholics Anonymous in Colorado. Denver, CO: Colorado Area Committee of A.A.; August, 1991.
Note: 5.5. x 8.5" booklet.
This first edition 41-page history includes AA's birth in Colorado in 1939, growth of groups around the state up to 1989, Colorado Area 10 GSC Delegates, and locations of the earliest groups.

879. "Presenting a Proven and Highly Successful Method of Sobering and De-Fogging Alcoholics. For use by Alcoholics Anonymous Groups.". Kansas City, KA; ca 1945.
This seven-page report explains a method of tapering off a "BABY" or new member of AA who desires help and has just come off their last drunk. The method is the "result from 4 years close study of over 1,200 alcoholics by a medical practioneer of top standing...an active member of the Kansas City AA Group...a physician who joined AA in 1941."Basically, AA Groups or sponsors are advised to administer decreasing doses of alcohol, black coffee with sugar, and salt water over a period of 30 to 60 hours to the newcomer.

880. A Program For You: A Guide to The "Big Book's" Design for Living. First ed. Center City, MN: Hazelden; April, 1991; 179pp; ISBN: 0-89486-741-5. LC 90-85763.
Note: Index, pb.
This commentary on the Big Book aims to "help people get everything out of the Big Book that we believe its author intended and to bring people back to what we think the Big Book actually does for all of us who in recovery." The anonymous authors [an A.A. group in 1973 that formed to study the Big Book] follow the Big Book through, chapter by chapter, and comment on misunderstandings, dangers of skipping chapters, etc., with accompanying annotations referenced to the Big Book [third edition] by page and line.

881. "Quit Drinking for God's Sake and for Yours". Minneapolis: The Calix Society; 1959.
This booklet offers suggestions for the alcoholic Catholic who wants to quit drinking. The need for a higher power as well as AA and Calix are stressed.

882. [R., T. W.]. The Eye Opener. 10th ed. Center City, MN: Hazelden; 1970; 365pp; ISBN: 0-89486-023-2.
Note: [one of the early "meditation" books that now flood the market].
Small volume with meditations of one page for each day of the year. Intended to be read in the morning. "Its purpose is to bring various phases of AA philosophy to the arrested alcoholic..." the preface states.

883. Rachel V. A Women Like You: Life Stories of Women Recovering from Alcoholism and Addiction. San Francisco: Harper & Row; 1985.
Rachel V. records the stories of 19 women who have sobered up in Alcoholics Anonymous. (NALGAP 832).

884. Ragge, Ken. More Revealed: A Critical Analysis of Alcoholics Anonymous & the Twelve Steps: Alert! Pub.; May, 1992; ISBN: ISBN 0-933366-0-6.
Note: 246pp, pb.

885. Randall, Thomas [pseudonym]. The Twelfth Step. First ed. New York: Charles Scribner's Sons; 1957; 568pp; ISBN: L.C. 57-11665.
Randall, a member of Alcoholics Anonymous, wrote this, his first novel, around 6 major characters, all alcoholics. The scene of the action is a hospital where they are all striving to recover from their disease. Written with wit, depth of feeling, and the strength and simplicity of the A.A. philosophy, this novel is one of a handful that truly capture the nature of alcoholism and the recovery milieu of A.A. on a personal level.

886. "Regional Forum Report from G.S.O.". New York: AAWS; 1975-93.
Nonalcoholic Past Chairperson of the AA Board and Trustee Emeritus Dr. Jack Norris first suggested the idea of regional forums as a way to close any communication gap between the "grassroots" Fellowship and the Trustees, Board, and GSO staff all located in New York. The first regional forum was held in 1975 in Atlanta, GA. Attendance is open to any A.A. member. Dr. Jack felt that contact with grassroots AA's might be lost as the Fellowship grew in numbers and the forum was designed to bring the service structure closer to the membership. The forums are staffed by Trustees, Board Members, General Service Office personnel, and Delegates. Canada and the U.S. are divided into nine regions. Four forums are held annually. The forum reports usually run 20-40 pages.

887. Reilly, Hugh [pseudonym]. Easy Does it: The Story of Mac. New York: P.J. Kenedy & Sons; 1950.
Note: First Edition, 277pp.
The story of Mac, an alcoholic, and his recovery with the help of A.A. All names in the book, including the author's, have been changed in accordance with the Traditions.

888. Research on Alcoholics Anonymous: Opportunities and Alternatives. McCrady, Barbara S./Miller, William R., editors. First ed. New Brunswick, NJ: Rutgers Center of Alcohol Studies; 1993; 430pp; ISBN: 911290-24-9. LC 92-63233.
Note: pb.
Twenty-one essays by scholars address the questions of "Should and Can AA Be Studied," "How Does Change Occur?" "Context of Change," "How Can Change be Measured?" and "How Could Studies of AA be Designed?" Among the contributors are Ernest Kurtz, Robin Room, and Frederick Glaser. This fine anthology includes discussions of research and the AA Traditions, gender, minorities, history, spirituality, etc. Each article is extensively documented and the references and footnotes will furnish archivists, researchers and professionals with a wealth of material for further study.

889. Reusing, J./Reusing, O. "WIP: A Case for Involuntary Treatment". Hagerstown, MD: Alcoholism Services, Inc.; ?; 7pp.
The authors contend jail will not serve as a deterrent to drivers convicted of driving while intoxicated who are alcoholics. They describe the Weekend Intervention Program where they feel mandated and monitored AA attendance, among other components, does facilitate recovery. The WIP is centered on the philosophy of AA as the preferred recovery program. Many AA's would object to court sentencing of alcoholics to AA meetings.

890. Richeson, Forrest. Courage to Change. np: M&M Printing; 1978.
In this book about how AA came to Minnesota, Richeson includes a chapter on "AA and Its Religious Friends.".

891. Rimer, Mary. Alcoholism: A Personal Recovery; 1985.
Rimer compares "Carl Jung's process of individualization with my recovery in the program of Alcoholics Anonymous" because she believes that they are the same journey.

892. Robe, L. B./Weisman, M. N. Abstinent Alcoholics Who Return to Drinking: Relapse & Slips. Minneapolis, MN: Johnson Institute; 1983; 52pp.
"Dry drunks," relapses, denial, and preventive measures are discussed in these two essays. Ways in which AA addresses relapse or "slips" among its members are also described.

893. Robertson, Nan. Getting Better. Inside Alcoholics Anonymous. First ed. New York: William Morrow & Co., Inc.; 1988; 298pp; ISBN: 0-688-06869-3.
This much-publicized book purporting to reveal and "demystify" the real inside story of A.A. prompted much controversy and was panned in many book reviews. Robertson broke her anonymity in A.A. and tells her own A.A. story in Chapter 10. Based on "hundreds" of interviews, the book covers A.A.'s basic history with some eye-catching revelations; e.g., that Bill W. had a mistress. Some of her charges of excessive religiosity and a publishing "empire", etc., are not new and lack substaniation.

894. Rogers, Ronald L./McMillin, Chandler Scott/Hill, Morris A. The Twelve Steps Revistied. The AA Program and the Disease of Alcoholism. First ed. Seattle: Madrona Publishers; 1988; 89pp; ISBN: 0-88089-028-2.
Note: pb.
The authors declare: "We are not trying to rewrite the Twelve Steps, nor are we trying to reinterpret the Twelve Steps. We have tried (to) relate the Twelve Steps, Step by Step, to recovery from a physiological, chronic disease process called alcoholism.".

895. Rosengren, John. Young Winners' Guide to the 'Big Book'. First ed. Minneapolis, MN: CompCare Publishers; 1990; 90pp; ISBN: 0-89638-209-5.
Note: pb.
This is a "workbook for all who are young and recovering in Twelve Step programs." Full of tests and blank lines to be filled in with the "correct" answers, this booklet and others like it give the impression that the AA spiritual program can be condensed into the narrow confines of an educational program with an implied graduation. On the other hand, much literature in this genre is relatively harmless. This booklet reports that young people won't read the Big Book because it's "too big...too old-fashioned...too much about older people." This booklet promises to bridge the generation gap between the old-Big Book and today's adolescents.

896. Rudy, David R. "Is Alcoholics Anonymous a Religion?: Meditations on Marginality". in: Society for the Scientific Study of Religion annual meeting; 1985; Savannah, GA; 20pp.
"Analogies between the structure, activities, dynamics and ideology of A.A. and those of religious organizations are apparent, but A.A. literature and A.A. members deny that A.A. is a religious organization." Rudy concludes that AA's "spiritual but not religious" statement is ambiguous and that AA is properly classified as "quasi-religious.".

897. Rudy, Norman K. Becoming Alcoholic. Alcoholics Anonymous and the Reality of Alcoholism. First ed. Carbondale and Edwardsville, IL: Southern Illinois University Press; 1986; 173pp; ISBN: 0-8093-1244-1.
Note: Also published in paperback.
Affiliation with A.A. parallels religious conversion is Rudy's thesis in this study. He asks three questions: What processes are involved in becoming alcoholic? How does the alcoholic affiliate with, and become committed to, A.A.'s belief system? What is the relationship between the world of A.A. members and that contructed by alcohologists? Rudy spent 16 months of intensive study of A.A. members in a mideastern city and the book contains numerous A.A. members' personal accounts, life-history interviews and testimonials which he used to contruct a typology of alcoholic careers. An extensive evaluation of various definitions of alcoholism is provided. The study is well-documented with 275 references cited.

898. Ryan, Elizabeth. Life Is A Lonely Place. Five Teenage Alcoholics. First ed. New York: Scholastic Book Services; 1980; 150pp; ISBN: 0-590-30056-3.
Note: pb.
The author relates the stories of five teenage alcoholics and their membership in A.A. Interspiced between the stories is basic information on alcoholism and self-administered tests to help young people find out if they are alcoholic.

899. Searcy W. Alcoholism Recovery. First & Second ed. Dallas, TX: Texas-Southwest Clinics for Alcoholism; 1989 & 1990; 160 & 128pp.
Note: 8 1/2 x 11" paperbound.
The book is sub-titled Over 43 Years of "Alcoholism Recovery" Through Discussions. These books include discussions of 32 topics about Alcoholics Anonymous: sponsorship, God, resentments, living today, the Twelve Steps, etc. Searcy W. was the sponsor in Texas of Ebby T., the alcoholic who quit drinking through the Oxford Group and religion and visited Bill W., his old friend, and told him he had quit and "got religion." Ebby later relapsed and was talked into going to Texas where Searcy sponsored him. "The True Story of Ebby T." was written by Searcy who sobered up May 10, 1946. The second edition includes "A History of Early A.A. in the Southwest.".

900. "Second Reader for Alcoholics Anonymous". Akron, OH: AA of Akron; 1940s (?).
This 16-page small pamphlet is termed a "preliminary guide to those who are entering the second phase of AA." Reprinted many times up to 1993, it attempts to answer the question: "What is there in AA for me beyond plain sobriety?".

901. "A Seed is Planted in Brooklyn and look how it flourished!". Brooklyn, NY: Brooklyn General Service Assembly; 1985.
This 8-page foldout pamphlet contains 13 historic photos and illustrations of the founding and growth of AA in the Brooklyn area. Bill W. and Ebby, Calvary Mission, and 182 Clinton St. are among the pictures used to commemorate AA's 50th anniversary. Founding dates for 17 AA groups there from 1942 to 1950 are listed.

902. Sikorsky, Igor I., Jr. AA's Godparents: Three Early Influences on Alcoholics Anonymous and Its Foundation: Carl Jung, Emmet Fox, and Jack Alexander. First ed. Minneapolis, MN: CompCare Publishers; 1990; 50pp paperback; ISBN: 0-89638-199-4.
Sikorsky, an attorney from Connecticut, proposes that Jung, Fox and Alexander were spiritual non-alcoholic godparents of AA's foundation. That thesis is weak because the influence of all three was minor on the development of A.A. ideology. The book includes the Bill Wilson-Carl Jung correspondence and the March 1, 1941 Saturday Evening Post article on AA by Jack Alexander.

903. The Silent Sponsor. First ed. Hamilton, Ontario, Canada: The Silent Sponsor; Oct., 1962; 96pp.
Note: pb.
This small yellow booklet begins with thanks "to over 300 institutional A.A. groups, many Twelve Step Houses" and many members of A.A. "who have given us the benefit of their experiences in aiding us in presenting this brochure." Each of the Twelve Steps is discussed and suggestions for further discussion are listed. The book was written by an anonymous member, "The Silent Sponsor," of the Young People's Group in Hamilton, Ontario.

904. Sipe, James W. "Youth and A.A.". Center City, MN: Hazelden; April, 1984; ISBN: 0-89486-215-4.
This 17-page pamphlet includes comments from teenage members of AA and a suggestion for alcoholic youths to participate in AA after treatment.

905. Smith, Doctor Bob. "Last Major Talk of Doctor Bob Smith. Cleveland, Ohio. 1950". Cleveland, OH: Cleveland Dist. Ofc. of Alcoholics Anonymous; ?
Note: [reprinted often].
This 19-page pamphlet reprints Dr. Bob's last major talk in which he relates the early beginnings of A.A. and comments on the early Oxford Group absolutes, the Bible, other early non-AA literature, God, humility, etc.

906. Smith, Suzanne E. "Working the Steps". Center City, MN: Hazelden; 1977; ISBN: 0-89486-036-4.
This 10-page pamphlet discusses pitfalls and honesty in working the 12 Steps.

907. Snyder, Anne. My Name is Davy. I'm an Alcoholic. First ed. New York: Signet/The New American Library, Inc.; March, 1978; 134pp; ISBN: L.C. 76-28457.
Note: The first edition in hardback was published in 1977 by Holt, Rinehart and Winston, New York.
Aimed at teenagers, this novel follows Davy into alcoholic convulsions and hallucinations and finally, with his girl friend Maxi, into A.A. and a new life.

908. Sober But Stuck. Dan F., Editor. First ed. Minneapolis, MN: CompCare Publishers; 1991: AA throughout.; 215pp; ISBN: 0-89638-246-X. LC 91-6919.
Note: pb.
Twenty-five members of AA, writing anonymously, sharing their experience in confronting and overcoming obstacles that kept them from growing in recovery. They discuss all kinds of fears, anger, unhealthy relationships, financial insecurity, compulsive sexual behavior, and low self-esteem.

909. Solbery, Dick. "Some Thoughts From An Old Timer". River Falls, WI: Kinnic Falls; 1989.
Note: This 8-page pamphlet talks about responsibility in AA. Anonymity break.

910. Solberg, R. J. "The Dry Drunk Syndrome". Center City, MN: Hazelden; 1970; ISBN: 0-89486-172-7.
Revised in July, 1983, this 12-page pamphlet has been a best-seller for many years. A dry drunk is someone in AA who has stopped drinking but still has all his character defects and past wreckage and, therefore, has not experience full sobriety.

911. Solberg, R. J. "The Dry Drunk Revisited". Center City, MN: Hazelden; July, 1980; ISBN: 0-89486-091-7.
This 10-page pamphlet discusses the dry drunk syndrome which leads to relapse. AA and the Twenty-Four Hours a Day book are at the heart of preventing a slip, the author believes.

912. Spalding, Willard B./Montague, John R. Alcohol and Human Affairs: with an Appendix on Tobacco and Narcotics. Yonkers, N.Y.: World Book Co.; 1949.
Note: 248pp.
Alcoholics Anonymous is one of four methods then used to help alcoholics. The authors describe the A.A. program in some detail.

913. Sparks, Tav. The Wide Open Door. First ed. Center City, MN: Hazelden; 1993: AA throughout; 222pp; ISBN: 0-89486-867-5.
Note: index, pb.
The author attempts to connect the Twelve Steps of A.A. to some of the world's greatest spiritual philosophies - Jungian psychology, yoga, the Tao, tribal rites of passage - opening up new avenues of thought and action about recovery from alcoholism and addiction. Subtitled "The Twelve Steps, Spiritual Tradition & the New Psychology," the book explores the historical, philosophical and spiritual roots of the steps.

914. "Spiritual Milestones in Alcoholics Anonymous". Akron, OH: AA of Akron; 1940s (?).
This 16-page small pamphlet discusses AA spirituality.

915. Spotlight on Alcoholism. Chicago Committee on Alcoholism; 1956.
Note: 62pp.
This pamphlet surveys the whole field of alcoholism for the "community in general and industry in particular." A.A. is mentioned throughout and praised in this early excellent example of adult alcohol education.

916. Spurlock, Thomas Walter. A Guided Tour of the Skidrow. A True Story By an Alcoholic with 35 Years Experience. First ed. np (West Virginia): Author; circa 1951-1955?; 58pp.
"This my story; as everyone in A.A. has their own story to tell. I belong to A.A. but I am not Anonymous. So if you need help concerning the working out of your problem of alcoholism, I will be very glad to assist you in any way I can." Spurlock tells his story in this rare booklet from his childhood, through his teenage years, and through 35 years of adult alcoholism in various West Virginia cities, Chicago, and the Bowery, and his recovery through A.A.

917. Step Four Workshop. First ed. Richmond Hill, NY: Remember When A.A. Group; 1992; 78pp.
Note: Spiral bound 8.5 x 11".
This Feb. 15, 1992, workshop on Step Four, sponsored by the Remember When A.A. Group, used the AA Big Book's foreword and first five chapters for its text with accompanying comments and explanations about it.

918. Stephanie E. "Women in A.A. Recovering Together". Center City, MN: Hazelden; Sept., 1985; ISBN: 0-89486-313-4.
This 24-page pamphlet discusses avoiding the "Thirteenth Step," sponsorship, Al-Anon, and other topics involving women in AA.

919. "The Stepping Stones Foundation". Bedford Hills, NY: The Stepping Stones Foundation; 1979.
This 4-page pamphlet gives the history of Bill and Lois W.'s home in Bedford Hills, NY, and Lois' not-for-profit incorporation of it as an historical site. Its mission is to promote, sponsor, and encourage the study of alcoholism and generally to help activities which will assist alcoholics, their families and friends, and concerned organizations in the field of alcoholism.

920. Stewart C. A Reference Guide to The Big Book of Alcoholics Anonymous. First ed. Seattle, WA: Recovery Press, Inc.; August, 1986.; 148pp; ISBN: 0-934125-01-5.
Note: This paperback contains a concordance; mottoes, slogans & terms; & a guide to changes in the Big Book.
Another useful, but not definitive, guide to the Big Book, Alcoholics Anonymous. This one identifies many historical places, events and persons referred to in the Big Book without their proper names.

921. "STINKIN' THINKIN' (Thoughts For)". Drain, OR: Bright Star Press; 1990s.
This small 64-page booklet compiled by a member of A.A. contains over "400 sayings familiar to A.A. members.".

922. Stools and Bottles. By the Author of "The Little Red Book". First ed. Minneapolis, Minnesota: Coll-Webb Co.; 1955; 159pp; ISBN: 0-89486-027-0.
Note: Hazelden, Center City, Minnesota, took over publication and distribution of this book.
"Daily Thoughts and Meditations for A.A. Members" is the subtitle of this little book, early on a very popular best-seller in the Fellowship. "Its purpose is to stimulate interest in the daily application of the A.A. program by which we arrest our alcoholism," the dedication states.The author discusses in depth the first 3 Steps and then explores even more deeply the Fourth Step with individual chapters on Resentment, Dishonesty, Criticism, Self-Pity, Intolerance, Jealousy, Anger, and Fear. The book concludes with 31 Daily Reminders and a discussion of one of A.A.'s slogans, "Live and Let Live." The book is dedicated to members of Alcoholics Anonymous. "Some years ago the author of The Little Red Book worked out a novel presentation of the first four steps of the A.A. program. Visual aids, consisting of a three-legged stool and eight empty whisky bottles, were used to portray the intangible factors of these fundamental steps. The 3 legs of the stool illustrated Steps 1-2-3. The bottles graphically depicted the character defects revealed by Step 4. Later this became known as the 'Stool and Bottle Talk.' ...now it is the 'Stools and Bottles' in this book which bears their name.

923. The Stories of the Big Book. Houston, TX: TJL Press, Inc.; Dec. 1993.
Note: 614pp.
Here are the original 66 stories of recovery from the first and second editions of Alcoholics Anonymous, the Big Book. Compiled by T. Leggett, this first printing states that "all selections originally copyright 1939, 1955, by Works Publishing, Inc., Alcoholics Anonymous Publishing, Inc., and Alcoholics Anonymous World Services, Inc., and are now in the public domain" [underlining added, editor]. The first printing was a very small press run.

924. The Story; 1966-77; 1-8: 32-48pp each.
In 1971, the A.A. Triangle Group inside the Central Prison at Raleigh, NC, celebrated its 19th AA anniversary. The AA inmates publish a quarterly journal, The Story, in which they publish their stories, poems, editorials, cartoons and experience of alcoholism and recovery in AA.

925. "The Story of Alcoholics Anonymous in San Diego County beginning 1940". Special ed. San Diego, CA: Coordinating Council of San Diego County Groups of A.A.; August, 1979; 11pp pamphlet.
This historical pamphlet traces the origin and development in A.A. in the San Diego, CA, area from 1940 to 1977.

926. Stott, L. L. "Quality Assurance Research Study AMA Discharges: Variables and Solutions". Billings, MT: Rimrock Foundation, Billings, MT; 1983 (?); 18pp.
The problem of discharges of substance abuse patients against medical advice [AMA] is a challenge to treatment facilities. This pilot study covered 25 patients discharged AMA and 171 who completed the 28-day residential treatment program. All patients were required to complete the first four of the Twelve Steps of AA.

927. Strachan, J. George. Practical Alcoholism Programming.
Strachan discusses the relationship of A.A. members to counselors and other professionals in the field of alcoholism.

928. Stromsten, A. Recovery: Stories of Alcoholism and Survival. New Brunswick, NJ: Rutgers Center of Alcohol Studies; 1982; 143pp.
A series of brief autobiographies of alcoholics, including AA's, describes their personal histories of alcoholism and their lives after recovery.

929. Swegan, W. E. From Intoxification to Emancipation. Alameda, CA: Insight; 1980; 96pp.
The author feels employee assistance programs can be the single most effective approach to the reduction of alcoholism in our society. An evaluation of some of the therapeutic benefits of AA is presented.

930. Swift, Harold A. "A.A. and Bibliotheraphy". First ed. Center City, MN: Hazelden; January, 1984; 15pp pamphlet; ISBN: 0-89486-211-1.
"Professionals generally lack understanding of therapeutic literature and the concepts of Alcoholics Anonymous," Swift writes and recommends they read The Big Book, The Twelve Steps and Twelve Traditions, and other A.A. literature.

931. "Symbol...Statement Regarding Use of Circle/Triangle". New York: AAWS; April 29, 1993.
This single sheet statement sent to all A.A. groups announced "AAWS will no longer oppose use of the circle/triangle symbol on medallions, jewelry or other items. However, AAWS will continue to oppose use of the registered trademarks `AA' and `Alcoholics Anonymous' alone, on a medallion, or in any other manner.".

932. Taintor, Eliot [pen name for Gregory Mason and Ruth Fitch Mason]. September Remember. First ed. New York: Prentice-Hall, Inc.; 1945; 322pp.
Note: [The Book Review Digest of 1945 published their real names in a review].
This excellent fictional view of A.A. and Avery Rickham's first year struggle to follow the Twelve Steps was published on the coattails of the outstanding success of The Lost Weekend the year before. One of the authors was a member of A.A. The novel is one of a handful dealing with alcoholism and A.A. to become mini-best sellers. The Chicago Sun Book Week of June 17, 1945 ran a full page ad and review on page 12.

933. Taylor, G. Aiken. A Sober Faith. Religion and Alcoholics Anonymous. First ed. New York: The Macmillan Company; 1954; 108pp.
Taylor, a minister, explores the "remarkable kinship with religion" that A.A. has. Since this is so, he asks why A.A. has succeeded where the organized church has failed? Central to Alcoholics Anonymous, Taylor says, is a belief in a God and a willingness to let that God help. He analyzes the spiritual principles of A.A., the 12 Steps, shows its parallels to religion, and shows how each can benefit from the other. The book is one of the first major attempts by a non-alcoholic to study A.A. from the standpoint of religion.

934. Ted W. The History of Western Pennsylvania A.A. Area 60. Pittsburgh, PA: A.A. Area 60; 1987; 11pp 8 1/2 x 11" mimeographed, one side only.
Archivist Ted W. outlines the history of A.A. in Pittsburgh and Western Pa. with starting dates for many A.A. groups.

935. "Teenagers and Booze: The High Without the Hassle". New York/Cleveland: New York News/Cleveland Dist. Ofc. of Alcoholics Anonymous; Feb., 1976.
This 7-page reprint from Cleveland AA of a NY newspaper article contains statistics and comments on teenage drinking in America but no information other than the address on the back about A.A.

936. Thomas, John. "A Gay Member's Eye View of Alcoholics Anonymous". Seattle: Nat'l Council of Alcoholism Annual Meeting; 1980.
Thomas adopts the concepts in "A Member's Eye View of Alcoholics Anonymous" to a gay and lesbian audience. He also discusses how AA not only helped him sober up but also helped him become comfortable with his homosexuality. He also offers the comment that "equally significant is the influence of AA on the gay world around it...Gay AA is providing one of the few role models available to the gay world that says: you can be gay without obsessive social drinking..." (NALGAP 626).

937. Thomsen, Robert. Bill W. Firsts ed. New York, Evanston, San Francisco, London/New York: Harper & Row/Popular Library; 1975 & Nov. 1979; 373pp & 349pp; ISBN: 0-06-014267-7 L.C.74-1861. (the book was also published in an abridged form by Reader's Digest Condensed Books in 1975 and in paperback by Popular Library in Nov., 1979, ISBN 0-445-04492-6.).
Note: This absorbing and deeply-moving life story of Bill Wilson (1895-1971), co-founder of Alcoholics Anonymous was the first full-length biography of him published. Thomsen based this biography on interviews with Bill's sister, Dorothy, and her husband, Dr. Leonard Strong, Jr., many of his friends and colleagues in A.A., research in the A.A. archives in NY, and more material to be found in the monthly A.A. journal, The Grapevine, and other A.A. literature and books. He also interviewed Lois Burnham Wilson, Bill's widow. This was the first biography in depth of Bill W. and as such, it achieved a remarkable degree of accuracy and insight. The author worked with Bill W. for 12 years. The book was a Reader's Digest Condensed Books selection in Spring, 1976, and was purchased to be the first film of a new production company, Talent 4. Thomsen details many of the diverse threads that Wilson synthesized into the dynamics that made A.A. the one of the most enduring 20th century fellowships.

938. Tip of the Iceberg: Slogans and Saying About Alcoholism, Drug Abuse, and Recovery. Dublin, NH: Hill Publications; 1983; 118pp.
The slogans and sayings the anonymous author has collected in the Fellowship of AA are arranged in conceptual categories with some having commentary.

939. Today's A.A. Group; March, 1975: 20pp.
This quarterly journal was published by Today's A.A. Group in the Connecticut Correctional Institution, Somers, CT. Personal stories of alcoholic prisoners, now sober, and other related A.A. news items comprise the contents.

940. Treat, Roger. The Endless Road. First ed. New York: A. S. Barnes & Co., Inc.; 1960; 301pp; ISBN: LC 60-6840.
This novel of alcoholism revolves around Jonny Baker, an alcoholic rescued from oblivion by Alcoholics Anonymous, and Peter Fletcher, a friend caught up in the labyrinth of alcoholism. One of the few fictional treatments of alcoholism that rings true, The Endless Road ranks with The Last Weekend as a stunning portrait of this disease.

941. Turner, Leslie. Carrying the Message in the Comics 1949 (or) Wash Tubs. NEA Service, Inc.: New York; April 4-May 14, 1949.
Note: Excessively scarce, however, these panels were reprinted March, 1993, in a Limited Edition of 250 copies by The Bishop of Books, Wheeling, WV.
The AA story was told in the Wash Tubs national comic strip in 35 panels that ran daily from April 4 through May 14, 1949, by cartoonist Leslie Turner. The main comic strip character, Capt. Easy, helps an alcoholic recognize his problem and get into AA and sobriety.

942. Twelfth Step Collection. Springborn, William/Jensen, James G./Sellner, Edward C., Dr./Brandon, James/Pat M./Mel B./McDonald, Peter Converse. First and Revised ed. Center City, MN: Hazelden; 1974-1983; 8-16pp each; ISBN: 0-89486-017-8, 0-89486-106-9, 0-89486-107-7, 0-89486-000-3, 0-89486-129-8,0-89486-128-X, 0-89486-135-2, 0-89486-154-9,0-89486-153-0, 0-89486-160-3, & 0-89486-167-0.
Note: All 11 pamphlets.
This "Twelfth Step Collection" of pamphlets by Hazelden attempts to interpret the Twelve Steps of A.A. Several have workbook blank pages for the newcomer to fill in. None of these pamphlets are General Service Conf. Approved A.A. Literature.

943. Twelve Steps and the Older Member. Guilford, Conn.: Older Member Press; 1964.
Note: pamphlet.
The author gives his interpretation of each of the Twelve Steps from the point of view of the older member. By "older member," he means longevity in AA and not chronological years.

944. Twelve Traditons Play. Akron, OH: The Traditions Players; 1980-90s.
This 15-page script casts 7 players in an AA group struggling with all kinds of problems and difficulties with the 12 Traditions. The humorous play has been performed for some years as part of Founders' Weekend in Akron, Ohio, each June.

945. "Twenty-Four Hours a Day The Index". Center City, MN: Hazelden; Oct., 1990.
This 16-page pamphlet is an subject index to the popular book.

946. The Vitamin B-3 Therapy: A Promising Treatment for Schizophrenia --- and its High Revelance to the Field of Alcoholism. A Communication to A.A.'s Physicians. From Bill W.. Bill W.[Wilson], Editor. First ed. NY: Bill W.; December, 1965; 28pp.
Note: "P.S. Please note that the enclosed material is not for public quotation or use. ---B.W." Original first has green cover. Photocopy of original.
The Co-Founder of AA, Bill Wilson, became interested in the beneficial qualities of massive doses of Vitamin B-3 on schizophrenics and alcoholics and gathered much research on the subject through physicians who were also A.A. members in many cases. This first communication of his on the subject covers research by doctors in Saskatchewan, Canada; Dr. Hoffer's endorsement of Niacin/Nicotinamide as Safe under All Conditions; the first mention of "Schizophenics Anonymous"; tests for, case histories of, and categories of schizophrenia; tonic properties of Vitamin B-3; bibliography; and wholesalers of niacin and nicotinamide.

947. The Vitamin B-3 Therapy: A Second Communication to A.A.'s Physicians from Bill W.. Bill W.[Wilson], Editor. Second ed. np: (Bill W.); June, 1968; 46pp.
Note: This book was edited "by Bill W." [8.5 x 11" pamphlet. reprint of 5,000 copies, but this remains a fairly-scarce pamphlet. The first printing of this pamphlet was in February, 1968, and had a yellow cover.].
The Co-founder of AA, Bill W., pursues his personal interest in the value of vitamin B-3 for schizophreniacs, alcoholics, etc. This second pamphlet contains "an account of the expansion in use of Vitamin B-3 (niacin or niacinamide) during 1966-1967 and a summary of treatment reported in the following categories: (a) Alcoholics suffering depressions, anxiety, tension, exhaustion, etc., as a result of schizo conditions, hypoglycemia, etc., (b) Schizophrenia and schizo tendencies; (c) Coronaries: recurrencies prevented; (d) Arthritis; (e) Other relevant information.
"CONFIDENTIAL: NOT FOR GENERAL PUBLICATION" Bill W. advises on the title page and elsewhere. Bill credits Drs. Abram Hoffer and Humphrey Osmond, of Sask., Canada, and Princeton, N.J., repspectively, for the pioneering work in this area of medical investigation that he detailed in his first communications two years ago. "Two years ago I mailed you a brochure concerning the Vitamin B-3 therapy - "A Promising Treatment for Schizophrenia and Its High Relevance to the Treatment of Alcoholism." Since then, Bill writes, a great expansion in the use of B-3 has happened with several thousand individuals, several hundred physicians and over 100 institutions using the B-3 therapy. Bill cites only two institutions using B-3 in the first half of 1966: Guest House, a rehabilitation facility for alcoholic priests at Lake Orion, Michigan, and the North Nassau Mental Health Center at Manhasset, L.I., N.Y. The pamphlet includes a "Model of Schizophrenics Anonymous" by Father Joseph R. (S.J.), Fordham University and members of S.A. Group. Additionally, 507 cases of alcoholism and 315 cases of schizophrenia are reported on. In chapter 11, Bill explores

the possible use of B-3 in cases involving delirium tremens (DTs), among others.

948. The Vitamin B-3 Therapy: A Third Communication to A.A.'s Physicians. Edited by Bill W.. Bill W.[Wilson], Editor. Third ed. NY: Bill W.; January, 1971; 15pp.
Note: "Confidential: Not for General Publication," the cover states. Softbound, 8.5 x 11". The third pamphlet has a white cover. None of the three Vitamin B-3 Therapy communications are A.A. approved literature.
This third and final report was edited by Bill W. in the year prior to his death. Three M.D. contributors in a preface note that 30,000 copies of the second booklet in this series had been ordered. This communication includes a report by Dr. Russell Smith on the progress of the original 500 patients plus 5,000 more alcoholics in Detroit, Michigan; Megavitamin Therapy - a Model Treatment System, a 5 year progress report on 4,000 patients by Dr. David Hawkins, including 5 illustrative case histories; and a Letter from Lois [Wilson] clarifying Bill's activities during his last years. In that letter Lois revealed that "Aldous Huxley, a great admirer of AA, introduced Bill to two psychiatrists who were researching the biochemistry of alcoholism as well as schizophrenia. Bill was convinced of the truth of their findings ... recognized this work must be kept separate and distinct from AA and wrote a letter to the AA Board so stating. As you know, Bill's last years were mainly devoted to the spread of this information among alcoholics and other ill persons. Bill's great hope was that continued research would find a means whereby those thousands of alcoholics who want to stop drinking but are too ill to grasp the AA program could be released from their bondage and enabled to join AA.".

949. Voldeng, Karl E. Recovery from Alcoholism. First ed. Chicago: The Henry Regnery Co.; 1962.
Dr. Voldeng outlines his "team approach" to treating and rehabilitating the alcoholic. His team is composed of the family and friends, the doctor, the church, employer and A.A. He recommends A.A. as the most successful method of maintaining sobriety.

950. Walker, Richmond. The 7 Points of Alcoholics Anonymous. Revised Edition of 1956 First ed. Seattle, WA: Glen Abbey Books, Inc.; 1989; 103pp; ISBN: 0-934125-16-3.
Note: pb.
This volume is the final work of Walker, author of Twenty-Four Hours a Day and sums up his knowledge on the Twelve Steps of recovery. The 7 chapters include: Admission, Fellowship, Surrender, Inventory, Restitution, Live Today and Service.

951. Walker, Richmond. For Drunks Only. One Man's Reactions to Alcoholics Anonymous. Third ed. Center City, MN: Hazelden; 1987; 46pp; ISBN: 0-89486-432-7.
Originally published in an edition of 2,000 copies in 1945, and reprinted in an edition of 6,000 copies in March, 1946, this paperback reprint is introduced by Bill Pittman. In the foreword, he notes "For Drunks Only' is Walker's personal story in following the guidelines of Chapter Five of Alcoholics Anonymous." A.A. declined to publish For Drunks Only and it would later turn down Walker's other book, Twenty-Four Hours a Day, but the two books stand apart from other literature for A.A. members by their use of Oxford Group literature and principles. A. J. Russell's For Sinners Only, which became the Bible of the Oxford Group, influenced Walker greatly, Pittman notes.
Walker divides his book into seven chapters: My Introduction to A.A.; Thinking Things Out; Spiritual Basis of A.A.; Putting A.A. to Work; Enjoying the Benefits of A.A.; & Passing on A.A. to Others.

952. [Walker, Richmond]. Twenty-Four Hours a Day. First ed. Center City, MN: Hazelden; 1956-present; 365pp; ISBN: 0-89486-012-7.
Note: This little pocket-sized gem has become one of the all-time best sellers for A.A. members. By 1977, it had gone through 26 printings and continues to sell well today. Originally offered to A.A. for publication, it was turned down. It contains one page for each day of the year with an "A.A. Thought for the Day, Meditation for the Day and Prayer for the Day.".

953. "The Walls Came Tumbling Down". A New Way of Life. Alcoholics Anonymous in Mississippi Correctional Facilities.; Summer, 1986: p15.
A one column article details the first A.A. meeting in a Canadian prison on July 8, 1950, at the British Columbia penitentiary. The rest of the 21 page journal is devoted to letters from A.A. members and reprints of A.A. approved literature.

954. Wally P. (AZ Area Archivist). "Carrying the Message: The Origin and Development of Central Office and Intergroup Associations in North America". at: Seventh Annual Central Office-Intergroup-A.A.W.S. Seminar; Sept. 18-20, 1992; Mesa, AZ. New York: AAWS; 1992; 28pp.
Note: Disclaimer from G.S.O. states that material in this presentation was thought to have come from the new unpublished AA history book but in actuality it came from "raw research data collected much earlier and which was approved by the General Service Conference for sharing with anyone who might find the data useful.".
The author found that both Bill W. and Dr. Bob were "enthusiastic supporters of Intergroup. A one room rented office set up at the Chicago Alanon Club in 1941 was A.A.'s first organized local service center, the forerunner of many Intergroup Associations we maintain in large cities today." The early Central Committees and intergroups in Cleveland,

Chicago, Akron, New York, New Jersey, Minneapolis; Charleston, WV; Edmonton, Alberta, and Toronto, Ontario, Canada; and Los Angeles are discussed. A tape of this presentation was also made but has not been released by GSO.

955. The Washington (D.C.) Group. Chapter 1. Foundations, 1939-41. First ed. Washington, D.C.: Washington Area Intergroup Association Archives Project; 1983; 80.
This booklet is a fine example of an internal area A.A. archives project, tracing the history of A.A. in the D.C. area through key early A.A. members, their letters, meetings, and articles. Four pages of footnotes document the sources, including many oral interviews tape-recorded. Five appendixes include an early D.C. chronology and the inventory of the Washington Area Intergroup Archives.

956. The Washingtonians & Alcoholics Anonymous. Three Classic Reprints Commemorating the 150th Anniversary of the 1842 Washingtonian Book. reprints ed. Wheeling, WV: The Bishop of Books; May, 1992; 123pp; ISBN: 1-877686-05-0.
Note: This was a limited edition of 250 copies. Frontis. pb.
Reprinted here for the first time in 150 years is The Foundation, Progress and Principles of the WASHINGTON TEMPERANCE SOCIETY of Baltimore, and The Influence It Has Had on the Temperance Movements in the United States by a Member of the Society [John Zug], Baltimore, Printed by John D. Toy, 1842. Also reprinted is the late sociologist Milton A. Maxwell's essay comparing the Washingtonians with A.A. and the 13-page bibliography by Leonard Blumberg from his book on the Washingtonians. Alcoholics Anonymous Co-Founder Bill W. was aware of the Washingtonians and their quick disintegration within 10 years of their founding. Bill W. said in the Grapevine the lessons he learned from their history helped in the writing and adoption of A.A.'s Twelve Traditions which were designed to protect the Unity of the Fellowship.

957. The Way Back. The Stories of Gay and Lesiban Alcoholics. Third ed. Washington, D.C.: Whitman-Walker Clinic, Inc.; 1986; 90pp.
Note: The first and second editions were published in 1981 & 1982.
A paperback collection of ten stories in which each gay person becomes willing to accept help in the form of the program of Alcoholics Anonymous. In more populated areas, gay meetings of A.A. are available and woven into the stories. (NALGAP 663).

958. "A Way of Life: Alcoholics Anonymous". Birmingham, AL: Street Printing Co.; 1945.
This 16-page small pamphlet contains "a brief outline of what an alcoholic is, what Alcoholics Anonymous is, and what AA does for the alcoholic." Compiled by the Five Points Group in Birmingham, AL, in 1945, it focuses on recovery.

959. Webb, Terry. Tree of Renewed Life. Spiritual Renewal of the Church through the Twelve-Step Program. First ed. New York: Crossroad Pub. Co.; 1992; 167pp; ISBN: 0-8245-1140-9. LC 91-35754.
Note: pb.
Webb compares A.A. to a tree and discusses its roots, trunk, branches, leaves, buds and fruit, soil and threats. She discusses the significance of "Twelve" in both A.A. and Christianity; Rev. Shoemaker, Fr. Dowling, S.J., the Oxford Group, and many other Christian topics and prayers. She does not conclude that A.A. and other Twelve-Step programs will replace Christianity or become a new religion. She advises both the committed religious and irreligious to "take one thing and leave the rest." Addressed to the religious community, the book nevertheless will be thought-provoking for Fellowship members interested in the comparisons between the Church and A.A.; in that sense, this volume echoes Shoemaker's famous article on what the Church can learn from A.A.

960. [Webster, Edward A.]. [The Little Red Book] An Interpretation of The Twelve Steps of the Alcoholics Anonymous Program. First ed. Minneapolis, MN: Coll-Webb Company; 1946; 141pp.
Note: The 1951 edition of the book incorporated the words "The Little Red Book" into the title and it has retained that affectionate title ever since. This best-selling little volume is characterized on the dust jacket as "A Suggested Outline for Reference and Study of the Working Mechanics of The Twelve Steps." The Author's Note states "the material in this little red book is an outgrowth of a series of notes originally prepared for '12-step' instruction to A.A. beginners and as a source of ideas for A.A. discussion meetings. The book is dedicated to Bill & Dr. Bob, A.A.'s Co-founders. Contents include 12 chapters, one for each Step. By 1961, the book had gone through 15 printings and it continues to sell well today. Two appendixes were added by 1950: Working with Others and We Didn't Have To...But... The first concerns sponsorship and gives a long list of questions and answers with references to pages in the book Alcoholics Anonymous; while the second appendix is a list of "voluntary Musts" with page references to the Big Book. Later, the word "Orthodox" is added to interpretation in the subtitle. Hazelden became the reprint publisher by the mid-1950s.

961. Weinberg, Jon R., Ph.D./Kosloske, Daryl, A.C.S.W. "Fourth Step Guide: Journey into Growth". Minneapolis, MN: CompCare Publications; 1977; ISBN: 0-89638-022-X.
This 46-page booklet is a workbook for AA's Fourth Step. It is NOT A.A. Conference-approved Literature.

962. Weinberg, Jon R. "An Interpretation for the Nonbeliever". Center City, MN: Hazelden; 1975.
Weinberg offers an agnostic's interpretation of each of AA's twelve steps.

963. Weisman, Maxwell N., M.D./Robe, Lucy Barry. Relapse-Slips. First ed. Minneapolis, MN: Johnson Institute, Inc.; 1983; 52pp; ISBN: 0-935908-14-5.
The second half of this paperback, pp35-52, is titled Slips, Sobriety and the A.A. Program. The first half contains many references to A.A. and related topics.

964. Weston, Drake. Guidebook for Alcoholics. New York: Exposition Press; 1964.
Weston, a recovered alcoholic, gives credit to A.A. He maintains that the work of this group does not completely solve the problem and other methods of control are often necessary. The authors presents a detailed discussion of the A.A. program and how other forms of therapy may aid A.A. members.

965. "What is A.A.?". East Moline, IL: Bright Star Press; nd.
This pamphlet reprints the Baltimore Prologue and gives "nine effective spiritual home remedies.".

966. "What is A.A.?". Center City, MN: Hazelden; 1982; ISBN: 0-89486-109-3.
This 6-page foldout pamphlet contains some basic questions and answers about AA.

967. "What is an Alcoholic...?". Newark, NJ: Intergroup of AA in New Jersey; 1950?
Six mimeographed pages discuss characteristics of alcoholics and list 35 questions used by John Hopkins Hospital to determine whether one is an alcoholic or not, along with comments on each of the questions.

968. Where Does It Say So? An Alphabetical Index of the Following Four Books: Alcoholics Anonymous, Twelve Steps and Twelve Traditions, Alcoholics Anonymous Comes Of Age, & As Bill Sees It--The A.A. Way of Life. New York City: AAWS, Inc.; 1976; 106pp.
Note: 8 1/2 x 11". wrappers.
This index of 4 A.A. books was printed in a limited number of advance or review copies (8 1/2 x 11" wrappers) but never published for the A.A. membership-at-large because it was felt it would lead to too much definitiveness, absoluteness, or certainity of truth concerning any topic in A.A. That indexing of A.A. truths would lead to a narrow-minded, perhaps perfectionist, viewpoint on many issues and seriously limit the suggested open-mindedness Bill W. and others thought a virtue in working the A.A. program.
An Index of Alcoholics Anonymous Literature, another format, probably later than 1976, in blue wrappers, 8 1/2 x 11", red plastic spiral bound, 123pp, was printed in a limited number of review copies. It was not printed for general A.A. membership for the above reasons. Apparently it has the same indexing with just updated format and typing.

969. Whitney, Elizabeth D. The Lonely Sickness. First ed. Boston: Beacon Press; 1965; 178pp; ISBN: 0-8070-27-95-2.
Note: In December, 1944, Mrs. Elizabeth Whitney founded the Boston Committee for Education on Alcoholism, the first voluntary community organization in the U.S. to specialize in the field of alcoholism.
The author uses four men and women to illustrate the ultimate isolation of the alcoholic who continues drinking. A.A. is mentioned directly or underlies much of the book. A.A. recovery & slips are discussed in this paperback.

970. "Who . . Me?". Cleveland, OH/Greensburg, PA: Cleveland Central Committee of A.A./Alcohol Education & Information Committee/Greensburg Group of A.A./Latrobe Group of A.A./Mt. Pleasant Group of A.A.; 1940s (?).
This small 4-page pamphlet lists 35 questions from the John Hopkins University Hospital guide to determine whether a patient is alcoholic or not. This is followed by 5 more questions A.A. would ask. Published by Cleveland AA and numerous reprints.

971. Williams, Lincoln. Tomorrow Will Be Sober. First American ed. New York: Harper & Brothers Publishers; 1960; ISBN: L.C. 60-12314.
Note: For abstract see "Foreign" chapter for the First Edition published in London.
This is the same as the First Edition except the American edition includes a Foreword by Harry M. Tiebout, M.D., Trustee, Alcoholics Anonymous.

972. William M. Tools for Fools for Alcoholics and Other Human Beings. Fourth ed. Plymouth, MN: Table Pub. Co.; July, 1986; c1971; 87pp.
Note: pb.
This anonymous member of AA shares his views on guilt, self pity, resentment, honesty, love, the Twelve Steps, Traditions, and treatment centers.

973. "Willingness". Chicago: Chicago Area A.A. Service Ofc.
This 12-page pamphlet is one AA member's experience and comments on a newcomer's growth in willingness.

974. Wilson, Bill. "AA's Third Tradition: Open Meeting of the 1968 General Service Conference". New York: International Advisory Council; 1968.
The document is a transcript of the portion of Bill's talk where he describes how, during year two of the Akron group, a "sex deviate" was accepted into AA.

975. [Wilson, Bill]. An address (by Bill W.) to the 11th annual meeting of the North American Association of Alcoholism Programs. Banff, Alberta, 1960.

976. [Wilson, Bill]. ALCOHOLICS ANONYMOUS The Story of How More Than One Hundred Men Have Recovered from Alcoholism. Facsimile of First Edition, First & Second ed. Akron, Ohio: CARRY THE MESSAGE, INC.; 1985 & 1989; 406 & 400pp.
This facsimile 50th Anniversary reprint of the Big Book is an exact reproduction of the original 1939 first edition except for pages 401-406, the dedication page, a preceding page which outlines the intention of this reprint, and minor changes in the publisher, date, etc. "The sole intention of this reprint:" page iii states, "For several years many of us in Alcoholics Anonymous have been concerned with the insidious gradual eroding away from our original, primary purpose of carrying the message. With the intention to reawaken and reafffirm this purpose in the hearts and minds of A.A.'s everywhere, there could be no more fitting occasion to reprint the original Big Book than the 50th Anniversary of the founding of A.A. This revised editon, a reproduction of the first printing of the Big Book is being printed with the hope that it will make possible a reawakening of and rededication to our original, primary purpose of continuous sobriety and carrying the message to the still suffering alcoholic. A portion of proceeds to Akron Area Intergroup Office, Akron, Ohio, the birthplace of Alcoholics Anonymous." Unauthorized by A.A., the publication of the Big Book by an outside source caused quite a stir in New York at GSO and throughout the Fellowship. A.A. had not keep up the copyright on the orginial edition, thus permitting this outside source to reprint the most important book in the Fellowship. A.A. issued a notice to all groups that it was not authorized or approved by A.A. And A.A. undertook an extensive revamping of all its copyright and trademark procedures in order to protect its literature and name. In 1989, Carry the Message Inc. again reprinted the book with only the original 400 pages.

977. [Wilson, Bill]. Alcoholics Anonymous: The Original Manuscript. Reprint ed. Carson City, NV: Purple Salamander Press; 1990; 76pp.
Note: 8.5 x 11" stiff cover.
This "limited edition" reprint of the original manuscript of the Big Book was published as a commemorative for the AA Int'l Convention held in Seattle, WA, July, 1990, by a private publisher.

978. [Wilson, Bill]. Alcoholics Anonymous. Croton Falls, NY: Intergroup World Services, Inc. [IWS Inc.]; 1992; ISBN: 0-9637666-0-0. LC 93-079125.
Note: 3.5 x 5.5".
This is the first abridged paperback printing of the first edition of Alcoholics Anonymous. It is not A.A. Conference-approved Literature and preceded the publication of the AAWS similiar volume. It contains the foreword, the Doctor's Opinion and the first 164 pages of the original 1939 Big Book plus Dr. Bob's Nightmare, a 3-page subject index, pp59-72 of the original 1938 manuscript, 14 pages of telephone numbers for A.A. answering services, intergroups, etc. in all the states, Canada, and numerous foreign countries, and order

forms for the book. The copyright page states "IWS is an Alcoholics Anonymous Group" but some Fellowship members would claim IWS misleads with its name, copyright, claim to AA group status, and publication of AA phone numbers; some of which, they say, violate AA Traditions.

979. Wilson, Bill. "Bill Wilson Letters to Jim B.": mimeographed copies; 1947-1965.
These 17 letters - 14 from Bill to Jim and 3 replies from Jim - are but one batch of literally hundreds, thousands, that Bill wrote. These are noteworthy since the last letter identifies Jim B. as one of the first 100 members and the one who suggested "God as you understand Him" and "the only requirement for membership is a desire to stop drinking." Jim B.'s story is in the first edition of the Big Book.

980. "The Wilson House". East Dorset, VT: The Wilson House; 1987.
This 10-page color foldout brochure gives a history of the house where Bill W. was born and its purchase and renovation by Fellowship members. Today many AA meetings are held there.

981. [Wilson, Lois]. Diary of Two Motorcycle Bums. NY?: unpublished; Dec. 1973.
Note: (Some copies were made but A.A. declined to publish this. 8 1/2 x 11". green wrappers with photo of Bill & Lois W. on motorcyle with side car and luggage. Subtitle on front cover reads "Greetings from Lois."131pp. rare.).
Lois, the wife of A.A. Co-founder Bill W., chronicles their 1925-26 motorcycling around the country so Bill could gather on-the-spot reports on companies and their factories and management for recommendations later to potential buyers of their stocks. "Although I thought Bill's stock theories were sensible," Lois writes, " I wanted to get him away from New York, with bars (saloons they were called then) on many corners, and away from his buddies, both of which I considered contributed greatly to his excessive drinking. A year in the open, which we both loved, would give me a chance to straighten him out." She sent her notes home to her Mother in letters, noting she made no references to Bill's drinking; "in fact he drank very little during the year, and the trip did us both a lot of good.".

982. Wing, Nell. Grateful To Have Been There: My 42 Years with Bill and Lois, and the Evolution of Alcoholics Anonymous. First ed. Park Ridge, IL: Parkside Pub. Corp.; 1992; 149pp; ISBN: 0-942421-44-2.
Note: pb.
For 20 years, Nell Wing, a non-alcoholic, was Bill W.'s secretary, A.A.'s first Archivist, and for 22 more years close friend and companion to Lois W., the Co-Founder of Al-Anon. Her recollections of the decades, the conventions, the early days, "Bill's Shortcoming and Character Defects," Dr. Bob, Lois W., and a rainbow of historical events and spiritualities make this book what Bill W. would have called a "ten strike." Nell gives the reader remarkable insights into the personal Bill and Lois.

983. Wing, Nell. "Stalking the Wild....Serenity Prayer". New York: Nell Wing; 1978-1981.
This 14-page effort by AA's first GSO archivist is her "unofficial" search for the origin of the Serenity Prayer which AA first used in 1941. Many different versions and authorships of the prayer are pursued by Wing in this mimeographed paper.

984. "A Word for the Problem Drinker! and Program of Prayer". Minneapolis, MN: The Calix Society; nd.
The booklet gives information on alcoholism, AA, and Calix. It ends with prayers which Calix members might use.

985. World Directory of Gay-Lesbian Groups of Alcoholics Anonymous 1986-87. New York: Int'l Advisory Council; 1986.
Note: CONFIDENTIAL.
(NALGAP 902).

986. The Young People's Group of Denver, Colorado. Day by Day. First ed. Center City, MN: Hazelden; 1974; 365pp.
Daily meditations for the year with a blank space at the bottom of the page where the reader can write in one or more character defects or spiritual topics he can work on during the day. Stresses the A.A. concept of living one day-a-time and spiritual progress. "...the product of their effort to speak directly to young alcoholics and addicts.".

987. "Young People's Groups and The International Conference of Young People in Alcoholics Anonymous: Facts, Aims, and Purposes". Indianapolis, IN: ICYPAA Advisory Council; May 25, 1985.
This four-page flyer outlines the purpose of the International Conference of Young People in AA [ICYPAA]. Founded in 1957, its purpose is to "further the principles of AA among young people." Young People's Groups in AA "try to make the newcomer understand that 20-plus years of drinking coupled with loss of family, friends, and finances are not necessary for one to be ready for sobriety." The first young people's groups appeared in 1945 in Los Angeles, CA, and Philadelphia, PA.

988. Zink, Muriel. "Blueprint for Fourth Step Inventory". First ed. Minneapolis, MN: CompCare Publications; 1977; 15pp.
The author's purpose in this small pamphlet is "to re-define the Step as presented in the Big Book of Alcoholics Anonymous, and the corresponding Twelve Traditions, and to suggest some simplified guidelines which will help you." She uses the classical list of the seven deadly sins and a chart to help. Although A.A. does not comment on outside issues like this pamphlet, some A.A. members undoubtedly would question the need to "re-define" any of the Twelve Steps.

Chapter VI = Chapters about AA in Books

989. 12 Step Prayer Book. Pittman, Bill, Compiler. First ed. Seattle, WA: Lakeside Recovery Press/Glen Abbey Books; 1990; 111pp; ISBN: 0-934125-11-2.
Note: small pb.
This is a collection of 139 favorite 12 Step prayers and inspirational readings.

990. "A.A.: Birds of a Feather". In: Madsen, William. The American Alcoholic. Springfield, IL: Charles C. Thomas; 1974.
This chapter analyzes the success of A.A. as compared to the inadequacies of the other available therapies. Unlike other therapies, A.A. is a form of folk psychotherapy relying solely on the direct evidence given by its members in shared experiences. The dynamics of A.A.'s folk psychotherapy is examined and illustrated with much case material.

991. Aaron, James E./Shafter, Albert J., Ph.D. The Police Officer and Alcoholism. First ed. Springfield, IL: Charles C. Thomas; 1963: pp 20, 26, 28, & 31.; 70pp; ISBN: LC 62-20575.
Note: Index, dj.
This two-day workshop for law enforcement officers mentions AA favorably five times. "A.A. has helped tremendously," one lecturer concluded.

992. Advani, M. T. "Alcoholics Anonymous and Group Counseling: Partners in Recovery.". in: Group Skills for Alcoholism Counselors. Washington, D.C.: GPO/ NIAAA, NCEA; 1980: pp33-37; 90pp.

993. Alasuutari, Pertti. A Cultural Theory of Alcoholism. First ed. Albany, NY: State Univ. of New York Press; 1992: About 30 references to AA.; 226pp; ISBN: 0-7914-1098-6. LC 91-22457.
Note: bibliography, index, pb.
The author discusses at some length the "A-Guild" system in Finland and compares it with AA, finding some similarities and significant differences. The cultural construction and culture-boundedness of alcoholism concepts are the main thesis and that challenges the disease concept.

994. Alcohol. Goldstein, Eleanor C., editor. First ed. Gaithersburg, MD: Social Sciences Resources Series, Inc.; 1976: 27 references to A.A.; 80 articles.
This looseleaf binder anthology contains 80 articles from newspapers, magazines, and books with Alcoholics Anonymous indexed 27 times. The project was designed for classroom and library use by grade school and high school students. Included are articles by Marty Mann, Alcoholics Anonymous members (male and female), and numerous alcoholism professionals.

995. An Alcoholic. The Life of An Alcoholic. First ed. San Jose, CA: Northern California Publishers; March 20, 1948: pp175-86; 186pp.
Note: dj.
In this anonymous autobiography, the final chapter, "Sobriety," tells the story of the author's recovery from alcoholism in AA.

996. Alcohol and Alcohol Problems: New Thinking and New Directions. Filstead, William J./Keller, Mark/Rossi, Jean J., Editors. First ed. Cambridge, MA: Ballinger Pub. Co.-J. B. Lippincott Co.; 1976: pp20, 22, 32, 35, 47, 70, 74, 89, 92-3, 150, 195, 209, & 271 (AA).; 304pp; ISBN: 0-88410-115-0. LC 76-7401.
Note: Index, dj.
Twenty-four prominent scholars and professionals in the alcohol field participated in this conference at Lutheran General Hospital, Park Ridge, Illinois, in 1973. The history, origins, social changes, concepts, biology, treatment and prevention of alcoholism were discussed. Throughout these scholarly papers, Alcoholics Anonymous is portrayed accurately in its history, ideas, and success.

997. Alcohol and Health: Report from the Sec. of HEW. Keller, Mark/Rosenberg, Shirley Sirota, Editors. First ed. New York: Charles Scribner's Sons; 1972: AA: pp 184, 194, 199, 200-02, 210-11.; 372pp; ISBN: 684-13271-0. LC 72-11115.
Note: index.
U.S. government programs, policies, and recommendations are outlined in this HEW report. It calls AA the "major influence in the past 30-odd years in gaining acceptance of the disease concept of alcoholism.".

998. Alcohol in America: Drinking Practices and Problems. Clark, Walter B./Hilton, Michael E., Editors. First ed. Albany, NY: State Univ. of New York Press; 1991: AA; pp6, 150-53, 166-78.; 380pp; ISBN: 0-7914-0696-2. LC 90-45048.
Note: bibliography, index, pb.
This book surveys changes in drinking patterns and attitudes in the last twenty years in America. AA is mentioned briefly.

999. The Alcohol Problem Visualized. Second ed. Chicago, IL: The National Forum; 1940: p94; 96pp.
This second edition lists the book, Alcoholics Anonymous, in its suggested reading. The Big Book was first published in 1939 and this early listing describes it as "the religious-social approach to cure used by the groups bearing the same same, and contains a number of case histories.".

1000. "Alcoholics Anonymous". in: Drotning, Phillip T. New Hope for Problem Drinkers. Chicago: Contemporary Books, Inc.; 1977: pp75-90.
An overview of the history and tenets of A.A. A discussion of the Fourth Step guide provided by the Lutheran General Hospital in Park Ridge, Illinois, is included.

1001. "Alcoholics Anonymous". in: Miller, M./Gorski, T./Miller, D.K. Learning to Live Again: A Guide to Recovery from Alcoholism. Independence, MO: Independence Press; 1982: pp235-255; 276pp.
"Alcoholics Anonymous is the single most effective treatment modality for alcoholism" is the first sentence in this chapter devoted to A.A. The authors emphasize the "A.A. Plus Approach," which means A.A. and professional treatment. A.A. meeting formats, sponsorship, and Traditions are also discussed.

1002. Alcoholism. Thompson, George N., Editor. First ed. Springfield, Il: Charles C. Thomas; 1956: AA: pp67-71, 454.; 548pp; ISBN: LC 55-11253.
Note: index, dj.
In chapter one, Joseph Hirsh, M.A., gives a succinct, laudatory summary of A.A. The book reviews the latest data available in 1955 and is written by 11 well-known researchers and writers. The sociology, pharmacology, neurology, pathology, physiology, and psychiatric aspects of alcoholism are discussed.

1003. Alcoholism and Related Problems. Issues for the American Public. West, Louis Jolyon, M.D., Editor. First ed. Englewood Cliffs, NJ: Prentice-Hall, Inc.; 1984: AA referenced 5 times.; 208pp; ISBN: 0-13-021478-7. LC84-13451.
Note: pb.
Public policies on alcoholism and health, law, public safety, the family, economics, and prevention are discussed. This book flowed out of The American Assembly convention April 26-29, 1984, at Arden House, Harriman, NY, of public and private officials interested in the alcoholism problem.

1004. "Alcoholism in West Virginia". Charleston, WV: Legislative Interim Committee on Alcoholism, etc.; Dec. 1, 1954.
Note: [45-page booklet].
The Twelve Steps and AA are lauded as the "most successful single method in terms of numbers of alcoholics recovered.".

1005. "Alcoholism". in: O'Doherty, E.F./McGrath, D. Desmond, editors. The Priest and Mental Health. Staten Island, NY: Society of St. Paul; 1963: 142-149.
A member of AA explains how the program works. Priests and women religious working with alcoholics is mentioned briefly.

1006. Alford, G. S. "Sedatives, Hypnotics, and Minor Tranquilizers". in: Mule, S. J., editor. Behavior in Excess: ... New York: Free Press; 1981: pp39-63; 396pp.
The pharmacology of central nervous system depressants is discussed. Alcoholics Anonymous is one of six treatment models described.

1007. Alibrandi, L. A. "The Fellowship of Alcoholics Anonymous". in: Pattison, E./Kaufman, E., editors. Encyclopedic Handbook of Alcoholism. New York: Gardner Press; 1982: pp979-986; 1230pp.
The author discusses the concept of service to others and the group therapy process employed by the AA Fellowship. A review of some of the AA literature is provided and findings from an empirical examination of AA sponsorship are summarized.

1008. Alibrandi, L. A. "The Folk Psychotherapy of Alcoholics Anonymous". in: Zimberg, Sheldon; Wallace, John; and Blume, Sheila B., Editors. Practical Approaches to Alcoholism Psychotherapy. New York: Plenum Press; 1978 & 1985.: pp239-256; 406 pp; ISBN: 0-306-40086-3.
This is a report on an empirical examination of the sponsor-protege relationship. Information obtained from intensive interviews with 6 sponsors and an analysis of A.A. literature was used to develop a list of 100 tools used in recovery. Twenty-two sponsors were asked to sort the tools into groups that they felt naturally fit together and then into groups they would use for proteges in five different time-phases of recovery. The results indicate that four distinct groups emerge from the sorting of the 100 tools. Results of the time-phase sorting demonstrate an emphasis on tools used to stay sober during early sobriety followed by a shift to tools used for self-change in the later stages of recovery. Implications of these findings for A.A.'s success and for other treatment programs are discussed.

1009. Allen, Chaney. I'm Black & I'm Sober. First ed. Minneapolis, MN: CompCare Publishers; 1978; 279pp; ISBN: 0-89638-008-4.
Note: paperback. Previously first published under the title: I'm Black and I'm Drunk in 1976.
This is the first autobiography of a Black woman alcoholic, the back cover promo states. Chaney, an Alabama minister's daughter, tells her story of fighting the disease of alcoholism and, with the help of A.A., winning. The second half of the book documents her affiliation with A.A., including her anonymity break. She became an alcoholism counselor.

1010. Allen, James. As A Man Thinketh. reprint ed. New York: Grosset & Dunlap; 1930s; 72pp.
Note: dj.
This was one of the books early A.A. members read for spiritual guidance and inspiration before the publication of Alcoholics Anonymous.

1011. Anderson, D. "A.A. and the Growing Self-Help Movement". in: Goldwig, P. A. Analysis of a World Wide Problem. Lancaster: MTP Press Limited; 1983.
Anderson describes the characteristics of self-help groups and the role of Alcoholics Anonymous as a model for their development. He discusses the origins of A.A.; the basic psychological drives of alcoholics; and why self-help is so effective for recovery from alcoholism and other chronically-disabling conditions.

1012. Anderson, Daniel J., Ph.D. Perspectives on Treatment. The Minnesota Experience. First ed. Center City, Minnesota: Hazelden; October, 1981: References to A.A. throughout text.; 57 pp; ISBN: 0-89486-133-6.
Anderson, Director of Hazelden for many years, outlines the development of the Minnesota model of treatment of alcoholism, which, at its heart, utilizes the philosophy of A.A.

1013. Anderson, Dwight. "Group Therapy and `Mr. X". in: Anderson, Dwight. The Other Side of the Bottle. New York: A.A.Wyn, Inc.; 1950: pp163-174; 258 pp.
"An especially potent combination of personal and group therapy is practiced by A.A., who base their own hope of staying sober on their readiness to help other alcoholics," Anderson begins his chapter on A.A. This is an informative review of A.A.'s Traditions and Steps, history and group therapy with references to Courtenay Baylor, Richard Peabody, The Washingtonians, and the Oxford Group.

1014. Anne W. Take What Works. First ed. Center City, MN: Hazelden; Dec. 1989: (AA throughout); 67pp; ISBN: 0-89486-636-2.
Note: pb.
Subtitled "How I Made the Most of My Recovery Program," the author discusses the Steps of AA, the "Myths of the Fellowship," and other truths she feels are commonly-accepted but in need of questioning.

1015. Anthony, Susan B., Dr. Survival Kit. Revised ed. Minneapolis, MN: CompCare Publications; 1981: pp156-68; 170pp; ISBN: 0-89638-050-5.
Originally published in 1972, Dr. Anthony provides basic information about A.A. and lauds A.A. as the beginning of the small group revolution.

1016. Antze, Paul. "Symbolic Action in Alcoholics Anonymous". in: Douglas, Mary, Editor. Constructive Drinking: Perspectives on Drink from Anthropology. Cambridge, MA, et al: Cambridge Univ. Press; 1987: Chap. 9, pp149-181.
"If we think of culture in the Geertzean sense, as a coherent web of symbols that directs human conduct, then the answer is [AA] has quite a good deal [of culture]. AA makes a fascinating case study in the power of symbols to generate new patterns of action by reconstructing the experience of persons in a standardized way. In truth AA does far more than to help the compulsive drinker shake off a troublesome

habit. It draws him into a community that globally reorders his life." Antze concludes that AA's whole outlook owes "a major debt to Christianity" while "departing sharply from those countless and mostly ill-fated attempts by Protestant evangelical groups to rescue sinners from the clutches of demon rum." He offers that evangelicals have a "God of Wrath" while AA has a "God of Mercy" who offers help in time of need. Still Antze argues "AA's teachings draw their essential logic from Protestant theology of a very traditional kind.".

1017. Appleton, Nancy, M.D. Lick the Sugar Habit. First ed. New York: Warner Books, Inc.; 1986: pp79-80; 162 pp; ISBN: 0-446-37041-X (USA paperback).
The author is critical of A.A. for providing coffee, donuts, and other sweets at its meetings. The author also points out that many alcoholics have had a sweet tooth most of their life. However, she says "A.A. is a tremendous help to alcoholics.".

1018. Apthorp, Stephen P. "Understanding and Using A.A.". in: Apthorp, Stephen P. Alcohol and Substance Abuse: A Clergy Handbook. Wilton, CT.: Barlow; 1985: pp130-137; 228 pp.
The author lists 24 questions and answers most frequently asked about A.A. by the clergy.

1019. Armor, David J./Polich, J. Michael/Stambul, Harriet B. Alcoholism and Treatment. First ed. New York, Chichester, Brisbane, Toronto.: John Wiley & Sons; 1978: pp35, 49, 118-121; 349 pp; ISBN: 0-471-02558-5.
Note: A.A. issued a rare public statement in response to the Rand Corp. report on alcoholism treatment and criticized the Rand conclusion that some alcoholics could return safely to "moderate" or "social" drinking.
This book was based on the widely-discussed Rand Corp. study which concluded, among other things, that some alcoholics could go back to moderate drinking without ill effects. The authors also concluded that most treatments have relatively uniform rates of success and that the fact of treatment is more important than the method.

1020. Ash, Mel. The ZEN of Recovery. First ed. New York: Jeremy P. Tarcher, Perigee Books, Putnam Pub. Group; 1993: AA: pp61-90, & throughout.; 243pp; ISBN: 0-87477-706-2. LC 92-14154.
Note: illus., pb.
"The Zen of Recovery, An Interpretation of the Twelve Steps," should prove provocative reading for many AA members unfamiliar with Eastern ways of meditation, especially when incorporated into the Eleventh Step. Ash presents a practical synthesis of AA's Steps and Zen's Eightfold Path.
Illustrated by the author.

1021. Aspects of Alcoholism. First ed. Philadelphia & Montreal: J. B. Lippincott Company; 1966: pp5, 50, 77; 80 pp; ISBN: L.C. 66-14706.
In the preface, Ruth Fox, M.D., Medical Director of the NCA, says that "A.A. taught us also that recovery is possible..." The book recommends A.A. as the "best known and most widely available resource" for the alcoholic.

1022. Bacon, Margaret/Jones, Mary Brush. Teen-Age Drinking. First ed. New York: Thomas Y. Crowell Co.; 1968: pp175-6; 228pp; ISBN: LC 68-13590.
The authors give a brief history of A.A. and its success with seemingly-hopeless cases.

1023. Bacon, Selden D. "Special Problems of the Adult Offender". in: Bell, M., editor. Cooperation in Crime Control. New York: National Probation Assoc.; 1945: pp230-234; 209-234pp.
This Yale University sociologist discusses AA's "great success...although only ten years old." AA, Bacon says, presents "a primary or quasi-primary group and successfully overcomes the barriers faced by the ordinary [isolated] alcoholic" whose relatives, friends, or psychiatrist are frustrated by failure with him. This early article is descriptive rather than analytical and keys on the empirical evidence of AA's success.

1024. Bacon, Selden D., Editor. Understanding Alcoholism. Philadelphia: Academy of Political and Social Science Annals; Jan. 1958; 315; 200 pp.
One of 16 articles describes A.A., including some of the factors operating against some persons joining it.

1025. Baekeland, Frederick. "Methods for the Treatment of Chronic Alcoholism". in: Gibbins, R. J., Editor. Research Advances in Alcohol and Drug Problems; Vol. 2: pp247-327.
A.A. is one of treatment methods discussed.

1026. Bahr, Howard M. Skid Row. An Introduction to Disaffiliation. First ed. NY, London, Toronto: Oxford University Press; 1973: 16 references to A.A.; 335 pp.

1027. Bailey, Willard F./Mills, Randolph. "Cumberland Heights: Use of the Alcoholics Anonymous Program in a Private Treatment Center". in: Groupe, Vincent, Ph.D., editor. Alcoholism Rehabilitation: Methods and Experiences of Private Rehabilitation Centers. First ed. New Brunswick, NJ: Rutgers Center of Alcohol Studies; 1978: Chap. 4, pp25-32; 124pp [?].
The authors discuss the incorporation of AA principles into the broad treatment plan used at Cumberland Heights near Nashville, Tennessee. Each of the Twelve Steps of AA are discussed in relation to the private treatment program at the facility.

1028. Bales, Robert F. "The therapeutic role of Alcoholics Anonymous as seen by a sociologist". in: Pittman, David J., and Snyder, Charles R., Editors. Society, Culture, and Drinking Patterns. New York & London: John Wiley & Sons, Inc.; 1962: Chap. 32, pp572-576; 616 pp; ISBN: L.C. 62-15188.

1029. Barkley, Roy. The Catholic Alcoholic. First ed. Huntington, IN: Our Sunday Visitor Pub. Div., Inc.; 1990: Chap. 8, pp132-149, etc.; 166pp; ISBN: 0-87973-445-0. LC 90-60640.
Note: pb.
This book integrates Catholic moral life into the recovery of an alcoholic. The author finds no conflict between Catholicism and A.A. Chapter 8 is devoted entirely to A.A. but the Fellowship's principles are discussed throughout the book. Social responsibility of the Catholic alcoholic, the family, treatment, the Twelve Steps, and continued recovery are discussed.

1030. Barrymore, Drew/Gold, Todd [with]. Little Girl Lost. First ed. New York: Pocket Books; February, 1990: pp 238-9, etc.; 260pp; ISBN: 0-671-68922-3.
Note: dj.
"Like everyone else, I get up at those A.A. meetings and say, `Thank you and I am very grateful about my sobriety," Drew Barrymore, star of E.T., says on the dust jacket, thereby breaking her anonymity in AA. This autobiography of the child star documents her early addiction to drugs and alcohol and her recovery.

1031. Bateson, Gregory. Steps to an Ecology of Mind. San Francisco, CA: Chandler; 1972.
Bateson, in part, identifies and explains eleven "outstanding points of the `theology' of AA.".

1032. Bauer, Jan. Alcoholism and Women. The Background and the Psychology. First ed. Toronto, Canada: Inner City Books; 1982: AA is referenced over 50 times.; 140pp. (v. Studies in Jungian psychology No. 11.); ISBN: 0-919123-10-4. Canadian 82-095091-2.
Note: index, pb.
Within the framework of Jungian psychology, Bauer explores the success of AA - for women - in terms of archetypal patterns represented by the Greek gods Apollo [structure and order], Dionysos [freedom and intoxication] and Aesklepios [the wounded healer]. She finds no conflict between AA and Jungian archetypal concepts and endorses the Fellowship. The famous Bill W.-C. G. Jung letters of January, 1961, are reprinted in Appendix 3.

1033. Bayer, Ellen/Levy, Stephen Jay. "Notes on the First Retreat for Jewish Alcoholics". in: Blaine, Allan, editor. Alcoholism and the Jewish Community. New York: Federation of Jewish Philanthropies of New York; 1980: pp333-345.
The authors describe the first retreat held for Jewish alcoholics who had recovered through AA.

1034. Beasley, Joseph D., M.D. How to Defeat Alcoholism. Nutritional Guidelines for Getting Sober. First ed. New York: Random House, Times Books; 1989: Over 40 references to AA.; 245pp; ISBN: 0-8129-1807-X.
Note: index, dj.
Dr. Beasley believes the majority of doctors continue to misdiagnose alcoholism as a psychological and mental problem and that treatment results only in short-term sobriety. He recommends a program of nutrition and vitamin and mineral supplements that heals the body. Throughout the book, AA is endorsed. "HALT" and other AA basics are discussed.

1035. Beauchamp, Dan E. "The Hidden Alcoholic". in: Beauchamp, Dan E. Beyond Alcoholism: Alcohol and Public Health Policy. Philadelphia: Temple University Press; 1980.
The hidden alcoholic, Beauchamp believes, is the central image of the alcoholism movement. To the movement, this term means that the alcoholic denies his problem and conceals himself because society stigmatizes his condition. The potency of the idea of secrecy is strikingly revealed by A.A.'s policy of anonymity, the author believes. This framework is discussed at some length in this chapter on A.A.

1036. Bell, R. Gordon, M.D. Escape from Addiction. First ed. New York et al: McGraw- Hill Book Co.; 1970: 6 references to A.A.; 201 pp; ISBN: -07-00395-7.
The author, president of The Donwood Institute, Toronto, Ontario, Canada, calls A.A.'s impact on the field of alcoholism "enormous." A.A. destroyed the climate of pessimism in the treatment of alcoholism in the 1930s and proved recovery was possible, he states. Then, secondly, A.A. fractured the stereotype of the down-and-out skid row bum as the only alcoholic. Contains a case history of Bill whose A.A. experience didn't work out and he died; however, the author still recommends, with some reservations, A.A.

1037. Bennett, A. E., M.D. "Developing Constructive Relationships between Psychiatry, General Medicine and Alcoholics Anonymous". in: Alcoholism and the Brain. New York: Stratton; 1977: pp41-63.

1038. Bennett, G./Graves, J. E./Kavanaugh, M. T./Vourakis, C. "Overview of Substance Abuse Treatment". in: Bennett, G., et al, editors. Substance Abuse: Perspectives. New York: John Wiley & Sons; 1983: pp287-312; 453pp.
A nursing perspective on community and hospital substance abuse treatment with an emphasis on Alcoholics Anonymous as the prototype self-help organization in the field.

1039. Bennett, L. A./Ames, G. M. The American Experience with Alcohol: Contrasting Cultural Perspectives. New York: Plenum Press; 1985.
A chapter is devoted to a biocultural analysis of A.A.

1040. Benson, Purnell Handy. "Functioning of the Higher Power". in: Benson, Purnell Handy. Religion in Contemporary Culture: A Study of Religion Through Social Science. New York: Harper & Brothers; 1960: pp276-329; 839 pp.
The effects of a Higher Power on personality systems are examined. "Altruistic motivation" is discussed, using examples from P.A. Sorokin, Emile Durkheim, John Dewey and C. G. Jung. A case study is thoroughly presented using Alcoholics Anonymous and concluding with the effects of Altruistic Motivation on A.A. members.

1041. Berg, Steven L., Ph.D., Editor. Alcoholism and Pastoral Ministry: Readings On Recovery. First ed. Lake Orion, MI: Guest House, Inc.; 1989: (over 70 references to AA); 282pp; ISBN: 0-9623733-0-3.
Note: pb.
Dedicated to Austin Ripley, founder of Guest House, this volume comprises 32 articles and essays all focusing on spirituality, the clergy, recovery from alcoholism, A.A. and related subjects. The 6 chapters end with Suggestions for Further Reading and are titled: AA & Historical Issues; Stories of Recovery; Spiritual Issues in Recovery; Ministry to Alcoholics; Diversity Among Alcoholics; and Alcoholic Clergy. The index lists over 70 references to AA. Berg's anthology is a resource guide for the clergy of any faith and provides an excellent overview of alcoholism and ministering to alcoholics.

1042. "A Better Kind of Music". in: The Way Back. Washington, D.C.: Whitman-Walker Clinic; 1982: pp49-56.
A lesbian musician tells of her period of active alcoholism and how she learned to stay sober in AA. (NALGAP 073).

1043. Bill W. "Alcoholics Anonymous". in: The Blue Book. New York: NCCA; 1960; XII: pp179-210; 219pp.
On April 21, 1960, Co-Founder Bill W. appeared before the Twelfth National Clergy Conference on Alcoholism [NCCA] and remembered Fr. Edward Dowling, his spiritual advisor who had just died. Bill recounts AA's beginnings, the Oxford Group, Ebby, Dr. Silkworth, etc. In the question period, Bill said "We do not wish to get in wrong with the medical profession by pronouncing alcoholism a disease entity. Hence we have always called it an illness or a malady - a far safer term for us to use.".

1044. Billy P. How to Beat the Blues. Boston, MA: The Daughter's of St. Paul; 1977.
Beginning with his own experience, Fr. Billy describes how to overcome a dry drunk.

1045. Bishop, Charles, Jr. "The First Fifty Years of Printed Progress". in: Bishop, Charles, Jr./Pittman, Bill. The Annotated Bibliography of Alcoholics Anonymous, 1939-1989. Wheeling, WV: Bishop of Books; 1989: ix-xxxi.
In a wide-ranging introductory essay to this bibliography of AA, Bishop discusses the 50 year history of the Fellowship, its spirituality, the Big Book, problems, and the philosophical and spiritual importance of the bibliography and AA in the modern world.

1046. Bishop, George. The Booze Reader. First ed. Los Angeles, CA: Sherbourne Press; 1965: pp67-69 & 4 other references to A.A.; 288 pp; ISBN: L.C. 65-26329.
The author cites two studies by Dr. D. L. Davies ("Normal Drinking in Recovered Alcohol Addicts") and Dr. Melvin L. Selzer which prove that a small percentage of true alcoholics can return to normal drinking without ill effects and contrasts these two studies with A.A.'s declaration that a return to so-called social drinking "May be all right for the next guy but it won't work for me.".

1047. Bissell, LeClair, M.D., C.A.C./Royce, James E., S.J., Ph.D. Ethics for Addiction Professionals. First ed. Center City, MN: Hazelden; October, 1987: (20+ references to AA); 70pp; ISBN: 0-89486-454-8.
Note: Index, pb.
This is a MUST reading book for all addiction professionals! It is a landmark book by two top scholars in the field of alcoholism and addictiology. Bissell and Royce describe the new profession, its boundaries, credentials, rights of patients, confidentiality, testing, evaluation of treatment success, finances, and obligations to family, colleagues, community, and other professionals. They point out the necessity of respect for A.A. Traditions and discuss A.A. Guidelines for cooperation with all in the professional community. Because so many alcoholics and addicts of all kinds are often first confronted by the treatment industry professionals and then referred to one of the Twelve Step programs, this book is strongly-suggested reading for A.A.'s who are trusted servants who cooperate with the professional field. The authors end with a sample "Code of Staff Ethics" which can be used as a starting point and with ten hypothetical case studies in ethics. Highly-recommended for both all professionals in the addictiology field as well as for members of Twelve-Step programs who cooperate with professionals.

1048. Bissell, LeClair, M.D./Haberman, Paul W. "The Professional as a Member of A.A.". in: Alcoholism in the Professions. New York: Oxford University Press; 1984: Chapter 7, pp121-137; 214 pp.
Various professions have formed special interest groups in A.A.: lawyers, doctors, etc. The authors conclude: "So long as the special group is seen as a supplement to, rather than as a substitute for, the broader A.A. experience, there seems to be a consensus that the `pluses' far outweigh the possible

hazards. Only when motivation for these groups is seen as snobbery or elitism for its own sake is there a problem.".

1049. Bittle, William E., Ph.D. "Alcoholics Anonymous and the Gay Alcoholic". in: Ziebold, Thomas O., and Mongeon, John E., Editors. Gay and Sober. Directions for Counseling and Therapy. NY-London: Harrington Park Press; 1985: pp81-88; ISBN: 0-918393-10-8.
Note: Previously published as "Alcoholism & Homosexuality," The Haworth Press, Inc., 1982, and also in the Journal of Homosexuality, Vol. 7, No.4, Summer, 1982.
Bittle proposes that a number of characteristics of A.A., as it is represented in meetings, discourage participation by gay alcoholics. These characteristics are reviewed and suggestions made for providing homosexual alcoholics with support and the tools for reasonably secure sobriety.

1050. Blane, Howard T. The Personality of the Alcoholic. Guises of Dependency. First ed. New York, Evanston, & London: Harper & Row; 1968: 6 references to A.A.; 175 pp; ISBN: L.C. 67-22523.

1051. Block, Marvin A., M.D. "Alcoholics Anonymous". in: Block, Marvin A., M.D. Alcoholism: Its Facets and Phases. New York: John Day Company; 1962: pp145-156; 320 pp.
A standard overview of A.A.'s Steps, Traditions, and history is given with 29 references to A.A. throughout the text.

1052. The Blue Book. Proceedings of the 1st through 38th Annual National Clergy Conference(s) on Alcoholism. 1948-1986. Firsts ed. Washington, DC: NCCA; 1948-1986.; from 100 to 200pp+ each.
Note: pbs.
These annual proceedings of the NCCA include many papers on Alcoholics Anonymous, spirituality, Al-Anon, the Calix Society, the Twelve Steps, Alateen, Catholicism, etc. While the majority of the NCCA membership is composed of Catholic priests, brothers and nuns, the group is open to any religious.

1053. Blum, Eva Maria/Blum, Richard H. Alcoholism: Modern Psychological Approaches to Treatment. First ed. San Francisco, CA: Jossey-Bass, Inc., Publishers; May, 1967: pp160-65; & 20+ other references to AA.; 373 pp; ISBN: SBN 87589-005-9. LC 67-13278.
The authors give basic information on A.A. but do not fully understand it as their writing is tinged with half-truths, misstatements of A.A. philosophy, etc. Still, they recommend A.A.

1054. Booth, Leo, Fr. Breaking the Chains: Understanding Religious Addiction and Religious Abuse. First ed. Long Beach, CA: Emmaus Publications; 1989: pp242-46; 269pp.
Note: pb.
Fr. Booth relates how Fundamentalist Anonymous considers the 12 Steps of A.A. to be "potentially harmful for the religious addict and the religious abused" because of the emphasis upon a Higher Power or God which would trigger a relapse. He disagrees completely, details his reasons, and recommends A.A.

1055. Borkman, T. "Where are Older Persons in Mutual Self-Help Groups?". in: Kolker, A./Ahmeds, P. I., editors. Aging. New York: Elsevier Biomedical; 1982: pp257-284.
The elderly alcoholic's participation in Alcoholics Anonymous and two other groups inspired by AA is examined.

1056. Braceland, Francis J. "Emotional Problems of Middle Life". in: Farnsworth, Dana L./Braceland, Francis J., editors. Psychiatry, The Clergy, and Pastoral Counseling. Collegeville, MN: St. John's University Press; 1969: 147-161.
Braceland writes that "sometimes the first evidence of trouble in middle age is an increasing dependence on alcohol..." Clergy are advised to refer alcoholic clients to psychiatrists or AA.

1057. Brandsma, Jeffrey M./Maultsby, Maxie C., Jr./Welsh, Richard J. Outpatient Treatment of Alcoholics. First ed. Baltimore, MD: University of Park Press; 1980.
This very detailed and technical book-length report contains the best controlled study of AA's effectiveness conducted to date.

1058. Brean, Herbert. How To Stop Drinking. First ed. New York: Henry Holt and Co.; 1958: pp149ff; 183 pp; ISBN: L.C. 58-7638.
The author recommends those who might have a drinking problem approach A.A. with an open mind and suggests they read Alcoholics Anonymous.

1059. Breese, Edward. "Love You in My Fashion". in: Luks, Allan, Editor. Having Been There. 18 Prizewinning Stories. First ed. New York: Charles Scribner's Sons; 1979: pp170-184; 189 pp; ISBN: 0-684-16170-2.
Note: Several other short stories revolve around A.A. themes.
This short story, one of 18, details a jealous husband's attempts to understand why his wife must attend A.A. meetings. One of 18 fiction winners in a national contest sponsored by the New York City Affiliate of the National Council on Alcoholism.

1060. "Brighton Hospital for Treatment of Alcoholism". Brighton, MI: Michigan Alcoholic Rehabilitation Foundation; July, 1956. Three different flyers on this facility all state "no admittance unless sponsored by a member of Alcoholics Anonymous, family physician, pastor, relative, or recognized agency." There are probably hundreds of advertising flyers like this for early treatment facilities and this example serves to point out the relationship of the AA sponsor and his new AA member to early treatment facilities. In the 1940-60s, before the Twelve Traditions were adopted in 1955 and were firmly practiced by the AA membership, the relationship between treatment facilities and the AA sponsor of a newcomer was tended more toward affiliation rather than cooperation. Many early treatment facilities were owned and run by AA members and organized as non-profit corporations or foundations.

1061. Brittle, William E., Ph.D. "Alcoholics Anonymous and the Gay Alcoholic". in: Ziebold, Thomas O./Mongeon, John E., Editors. Gay and Sober. New York-London: Harrington Park Press; 1985: pp81-88; ISBN: 0-918393-10-8.
Note: Paperback. Subtitled "Directions for Counseling and Therapy," this book was originally published in 1982 by The Haworth Press, Inc. under the title "Alcoholism & Homosexuality." It has also been published as "Journal of Homosexuality," Vol. 7, No. 4, Summer 1982.
Although the number of homosexual men and women has been estimated to be proportionately three times greater than the number of alcoholics in the general population, their participation in Alcoholics Anonymous is not consistent with this proportional representation. Brittle proposes that there are a number of characteristics of A.A. as it is represented in meetings, which discourage participation by gay people. These characteristics are reviewed, and suggestions are made for providing homosexual alcoholics with support and with the tools for reasonably secure sobriety.

1062. Brody, A. "S.O.B.E.R.: A Stress Management Program for Recovering Alcoholics". in: Altman, M./Crocker, R., editors. Social Groupwork and Alcoholism. New York: Haworth Press; 1982: pp15-24; 92pp.
This stress management program, developed by the author at St. Luke's Roosevelt Hospital Center, Smithers Alcoholism Treatment and Training Center, New York, NY, "can be integrated into the AA program, Brody asserts.

1063. Brown, S. "Partnership: AA and Psychotherapy". in: Brown, S. Treating the Alcoholic: A Developmental Model of Recovery. New York: John Wiley & Sons; 1985: Chap. 9, pp267-290; 348 pp.

1064. Buechner, Frederick. Whistling In the Dark: An ABC Theologized. New York, New York: Harper & Row; 1988.
Buechner defines AA by focusing on how AA-alcoholics help and support each other. He suggests that the Christian church could learn something from AA.

1065. Burkhalter, Pamela K., R.N. Nursing Care of the Alcoholic and Drug Abuser. New York et al: McGraw-Hill Book Co.; 1975: 8 references to A.A.; 297 pp; ISBN: 0-07-009051-3.

1066. by A Member of Alcoholics Anonymous. "I Am An Alcoholic - This Is My Story". in: D'Alonzo, C. Anthony, M.D. The Drinking Problem - and its control. First ed. Houston, Texas: Gulf Publishing Company; 1959: pp99-116; 130 pp; ISBN: L.C. 59-11570.
The life story, a "lead" in print, of an alcoholic who found his way to Alcoholics Anonymous and recovered and helped other suffering alcoholics with the A.A. program of recovery.

1067. Byer, Curtis O./Jones, Kenneth L./Shainberg, Louis. Drugs and Alcohol. First ed. New York/London/Evanston, IL: Harper & Row; 1969: pp108-09.; 132pp; ISBN: LC 69-19522.
Note: Pb, illus., index.
"The most successful approach to the problem of alcoholism today is probably Alcoholics Anonymous," the author states. Basics about A.A. are discussed briefly.

1068. C., Freddy. "How To Stay Stopped". in: Alcohol and Your Health. Toronto: Coles Publishing Co.; 1977: pp67-72; 91 pp.
The author describes how A.A. works, A.A. as the Perfect After Care Service and how the A.A. "cure" lasts.

1069. Cahalan, Don. Understanding America's Drinking Problem: How to Combat the Hazards of Alcohol. San Francisco/London: Jossey-Bass Publishers; 1988: 23 references to AA.; 234pp; ISBN: 1-55542-057-5. LC 87-45418.
Note: index, dj.
After hundreds of millions of dollars spent on treatment and education programs, the nation's alcohol problems still remain, and Cahalan accuses the alcohol merchants, the politicians, the health care industry and even well-intentioned alcohol control organizations of being "witting and unwitting co-conspirators in a gigantic shell game." A.A. is cited 23 times and Cahalan views it positively with some reservations that may be attributed to misunderstandings of what A.A. is and is not.

1070. Cain, Arthur. "Alcoholics Anonymous: Cult or Cure?". in: Cain, Arthur. The Cured Alcoholic. New Concepts in Alcoholism Treatment and Research. First ed. New York: The John Day Company; 1964: Chap. 3, pp61-76; & numerous references to AA throughout.; 252pp; ISBN: L.C. 63-10945.
Cain, recognized as the most vocal of A.A.'s critics, believed that some alcoholics could return safely to social drinking and blamed A.A. for a dogmatic attitude that wouldn't accept that "fact." He says A.A. members have "arrested" their problem of alcoholism but have not "recovered" (acquired a capability of safely drinking again, a sign of maturity) from it. He views A.A. as "fanatical and dogmatic.".

1071. Cain, Arthur. "Alcoholics Anonymous". in: Cain, Arthur. Paul King's Rebellion. First ed. New York: The John Day Company; 1967: Chap. 5, pp80-91; 187 pp; ISBN: L. C. 67-14610.
Cain, perhaps A.A.'s most vocal critic, relates the story of Paul King's membership in A.A., sobriety of four months, a slip after which he could "no longer in good conscience return to A.A." King and Cain both object to the spirituality and religion they attribute to A.A., its constant use of slogans, and what they say is A.A.'s insistence that it alone has the answer to alcoholism.

1072. Cain, Arthur H. Young People and Drinking. First ed. New York: The John Day Company; 1963: pp79-83; 94 pp; ISBN: L.C. 62-20792.
Cain provides basic information about A.A. for young people.

1073. Caldwell, Fulton J. "Alcoholics Anonymous as a Viable Treatment Resource for Black Alcoholics". in: Watts, T. S., and Wright, R., Jr., Editors. Black Alcoholism: Toward a Comprehensive Understanding. Springfield, IL: Charles C. Thomas; 1983: pp85-99; 242pp.
This excellent article adheres to AA's Traditions and finds Blacks as candidates for Fellowship membership as likely as any other ethnic group. Matter of fact, Blacks' high value on interpersonal relationships, emphasis on symbolic imagery and rhthmn, and accomodation of opposites in their logic; these all find a welcome home in AA.

1074. Carey, Macdonald. The Days of My Life. First ed. New York: St. Martin's Press; February, 1991: AA: pp 2, 76, 103, 156, 270-3, 277.; 309pp; ISBN: 0-312-05410-6. LC 90-49230.
Note: Photos, index, dj.
For 25 years Macdonald Carey was the star of NBC's Days of Our Lives, and in this autobiography, the Hollywood actor reviews his life in soap opera, Broadway, radio, TV, and film, including his alcoholism and membership in A.A., a clear-cut anonymity break with the Fellowship's Traditions.

1075. Carle, Cecil. "Alcoholics Anonymous (AA) Activities Help Overcome Drunkenness". in: Archer, Colin B., Editor. The Handbook on Alcoholism in the Bahamas. Nassau, Bahamas: Colmar/The Bahamas Council on Alcoholism; 1981: pp63-65.
A brief 3-page summary of A.A. history, the Big Book, program, etc.

1076. Cary, Sylvia. Jolted Sober. First ed. Los Angeles, CA/ Chicago, IL: Lowell House/Contemporary Books; 1989: (35 references to AA); 140pp; ISBN: 0-929923-06-5.
Subtitled "Getting to the Moment of Clarity in the Recovery from Addiction," Cary's book endorses A.A. Cary, a psychotherapist, equates her "moment of clarity" to AA's "hitting bottom," "surrender," and Dr. Tiebout's "conversion experience.".

1077. Casey, Frank. "Relationship between Religious Life and AA". in: The Blue Book. Washington, DC: NCCA; 1978; 30: pp109-141; 342pp.
Bro. Casey presents his "concept of spirituality and the concept of religious life: what community is about and what the fellowship of Alcoholics Anonymous is about." Comparisons are made between AA and Christianity. This article was part of the 30th National Clergy Conference on Alcoholism, held in New Orleans, Jan. 5-10, 1978.

1078. Casriel, Daniel, M.D. So Fair a House: The Story of Synanon. First ed. Beverly Hills, CA: Book Company of America/Prentice-Hall, Inc.; 1963: pp18-28; 206 pp; ISBN: L.C. 63-14941.
Note: Paperback.
The author relates how Chuck Dederich, founder of Synanon, attended his first A.A. meetings, his first use of LSD, and his eventual parting with A.A. as a "cult" began to form around him. At one time, Synanon seemed to be on the road to becoming the A.A. of the drug scene; however, later events saw it virtually destroyed because of corruption charges, abuses of members, and failure to "walk the talk.".

1079. Catanzaro, Ronald J., M.D., Editor. Alcoholism. The Total Treatment Approach. Third ed. Springfield, IL: Charles C. Thomas - Publisher; 1974: 35 references throughout the book.; 508pp; ISBN: 0-398-00295-9.
Note: First printing was 1968.

1080. Chafetz, M. E./Demone, H. W. Jr. "Alcoholics Anonymous". in: Dinitz, S., Editor. Deviance. New York: Oxford U. Press; 1969: pp264-272.

1081. Chafetz, Morris E., M.D./Demone, Harold W., Jr. "Alcoholics Anonymous". in: Chafetz, Morris E., M.D., and Demone, Harold W., Jr. Alcoholism and Society. First ed. New York: Oxford University Press; 1962: Chap. 9, pp146-165.; 319 pp; ISBN: L.C. 62-9823.
The authors discuss each of the 12 Steps and the 12 Traditions and other basic A.A. concepts. Their view of A.A. is somewhat critical and they question its "phenomenal growth," a supposed hostility toward other forms of therapy, the future leadership (then) of Bill W., changes in its procedures necessary for continued success, etc. Nevertheless, they laud A.A. for having made work with alcoholics "legitimate." The Oxford Group and Al-Anon are also mentioned.

1082. Chafetz, Morris E./Blane, Howard T./Hill, Marjorie J., Editors. Frontiers of Alcoholism. New York: Science House; 1970: pp 15, 173-4, 205, 247, 275.; 424 pp; ISBN: 87668-026-0.

1083. Chase, John W. "If A Man Be Mad by Harold Maine: Dipso De Profundis". New York Times Book Review; April 20, 1947.
Chase points out "there is a memorable description of the inside organization of Alcoholics Anonymous" in this story of an alcoholic's long struggle to salvation. Harold Maine is a pen name.

1084. Cheever, Susan. Home Before Dark. Second ed. Boston, MA: Houghton Mifflin Co.; 1984; 243pp; ISBN: 0-395-35297-5. LC 84-9057.
Note: Illus. with photos. dj.
This is a biographical memoir of John Cheever, the writer, by his daughter. She reveals his life-long battle with alcoholism. In his last years, Cheever became an A.A. member and didn't drink, she writes.

1085. Cheraskin, E., M.D./Ringsdorf, W. M., Jr., D.M.D. New Hope for Incurable Disease. First ed. New York: Exposition Press; October, 1971: pp67-71; 187pp; ISBN: 0-682-47387-1.
The book contains a five page letter, dated 1970, from Doctor Russell F. Smith to Bill W., Co-Founder of A.A., on massive niacin (Vitamin B3) therapy for alcoholics. The report gives data on 507 alcoholics in Michigan treated for periods of 6 to 20 months. Bill Wilson, in work outside of AA, believed in and promoted niacin therapy for alcoholics.

1086. Christopher, James. "A.A. and Beyond: Sobriety Without Superstition". in: Christopher, James. How To Stay Sober. Recovery Without Religion. Buffalo, NY: Prometheus Books; 1988: Chap. 2, & many other references to AA throughout.; 191pp; ISBN: 0-87975-457-5.
Note: Paperback. Also published in cloth, same data.
The author is very critical of the "Higher Power" that A.A. uses in the Steps and its Recovery Program. '"God as you understand Him" as a concept is difficult to swallow for secularists, humanists, and other free thinkers, according to Christopher. He terms A.A. "religious," not spiritual. His theme in the book advocates and provides guidelines for organizing "grass-roots secular sobriety groups." Christopher is the founder of Secular Sobriety Groups.

1087. Christopher, James. SOS Sobriety. First ed. Buffalo, NY: Prometheus Books; 1992: AA: Chap. 9, pp223-236, & throughout.; ISBN: 0-87975-726-4. LC 92-7772.
Note: pb.
This is another rational recovery book advertised on the cover as "more successful than AA!" [a very debatable promo] and "The Proven Alternative to 12-Steps Programs." Christopher, the founder of the Save Our Selves Movement, "lays bare the limitations of AA," critiques the "controlled drinking" concept, and emphasizes the humanist approach to recovery. Chapter nine, "Alcoholics Anonymous and the U.S. Government: Some Constitutional Issues," by James L. Monroe, Esq., discusses legal questions concerning treatment centers, courts, etc., "forcing" alcoholics to attend AA meetings, as well as other issues in the legal field involving alcoholics. Like most rational recovery books, Christopher both gives AA

credit and critizes it for its "spiritual" approach. With all these RR books, one is reminded of Bill W.'s comment on an article that criticized early AA to the effect that "they may be right," and even if they aren't, the article may just bring someone to his or her first AA meeting because of the publicity.

1088. Clapp, Charles. Drinking's Not the Problem. New York: Thomas Y. Crowell Co.; 1949: A few references to A.A.; 179 pp.
The author lists six methods alcoholics have used to gain sobriety and restore their lives, including A.A.

1089. Clapp, Charles. Drunks Are Square Pegs. First ed. New York: Island Press; 1942: pp47-51, 55; 118pp.
Clapp, an alcoholic and author of The Big Bender, states he is not an A.A. member but sends alcoholics to A.A. so they can contact someone "who has been in exactly the same spot he or she is in." A.A. members cannot themselves remain "dry" unless "they are helping someone else to get away from liquor," he writes in this early book about drunks. Clapp tells of meeting Bill Wilson in Oct. 1935 when he was in his "dry" stage.

1090. Clarke, Gerald. Capote. A Biography. First ed. New York et al: Simon and Schuster; 1988: AA, pp 495, 497, 504, 532, 537, 542.; 631pp; ISBN: 0-671-22811-0. LC 88-3144.
Note: Index, dj.
Truman Capote attended AA meetings and had several brushes with sobriety but eventually died, allegedly of an overdose of pills. This massive biography of the author of In Cold Blood and other best-selling fiction documents the progress of Truman's alcoholism through his life.

1091. Clausen, William J. "Eleventh Step". in: The Blue Book. Washington, DC: NCCA; 1983; 35: 9pp.
Note: [Conference paper].
The Eleventh Step of AA is discussed. This minister from St. Charles Borromeo Parish in Hampshire, Illinois, believes prayer and meditation is at the heart of the step and the goal is getting in touch with God. He also compares the lives of Fr. John Doe and Co-Founder Bill W.

1092. Claypool, Jane. Alcohol and You. Revised second ed. New York, et al: an Impact Book, Franklin Watts; 1988: 9 references to AA.; 128pp; ISBN: 0-531-10566-0. LC 88-10258.
Note: illus., index, dj.
Addressed to young people, this book gives teens solid information about alcoholism, drinking and driving, AA, treatment and recovery.

1093. Clinebell, Howard J., Jr. "Alcoholics Anonymous - Our Greatest Resource". in: Clinebell, Howard J., Jr. Understanding and Counseling the Alcoholic Through Religion and Psychology. First ed. Nashville & New York: Abingdon Press; 1956: Chap. 5, pp119-153; plus over 100 references to A.A. throughout text.; 336 pp; ISBN: 0-687-42801-7.
Note: Comments here based on the 1968 Revised & Enlarged Edition.
Clinebell's book has long been accepted as a classic in the field concerning ministers & related professionals counseling alcoholics. He begins his chapter on A.A.: "In all the dark history of the handling of the problem of alcoholism, the brightest ray of hope and help is Alcoholics Anonymous!" Thus, he concludes that AA is the "most effective referral resource available today and it behooves everyone concerned with helping alcoholics to be thoroughly familiar with A.A." He gives an excellent in-depth, albeit short, history of A.A. and cites nine reasons why A.A. helps alcoholics achieve active, long-term sobriety. He shows the reader how to apply the resources of Christian faith to the problems of dealing with alcoholism. He views the minister's role as including a major responsibility of referral of the alcoholic to Alcoholics Anonymous.

1094. Cobb, Thomas. Crazy Heart. First ed. New York, et al: Harper & Row; 1987; 248pp; ISBN: 0-06-015803-4. LC 87-395.
Note: dj.
The central character of Cobb's first novel, Bad Blake, is on his last leg with a bad ticker and liver. An over-the-hill country Western "picker," his bourbon-filled empty life changes when Ms. Right, her little boy, and, in time, an AA sponsor, appear.

1095. Cohen, Eugene J. "A.A. at the International Synagogue, Kennedy Airport". in: Blaine, Rabbi Allan, Editor. Alcoholism and the Jewish Community. New York: Commission on Synagogue Relations; 1980: Chap. 21, pp321-325; 363 pp.
The personal account of an understanding rabbi who helped organize the use of his synagogue for A.A. meetings.

1096. Cohen, Sidney, M.D. The Alcoholism Problems: Selected Issues. First ed. New York: The Haworth Press; 1983: 13 references to A.A.; 193 pp; ISBN: 0-86656-209-5.

1097. Colcher, Ronnie W. "Counseling the Homosexual Alcoholic". in: Ziebold, Thomas O., and Mongeon, John E., Editors. Gay and Sober. Directions for Counseling and Therapy. New York-London: Harrington Park Press; 1985: pp43-52; ISBN: 0-918393-10-8.
Note: Paperback.
The author summarizes her clinical experience with 75 homosexual alcoholics. Among eleven recommendations are several about A.A., including one that homosexuals should attend gay A.A. meetings as well as nongay ones.

1098. Collins, Marie C. "Alcoholics Anonymous". in: Collins, Marie C. Defeating Alcoholism: The Fairview Way. Philadelphia: Whitmore Pub. Co.; 1966: pp258-263; 327 pp. This Baptist minister and director of Fairview Center, an alcoholism treatment unit, reviews the use of A.A. at this center.

1099. Conley, Paul C./Sorensen, Andrew A. The Staggering Steeple. First ed. Philadelphia: A Pilgrim Press Book; 1971: pp113-117; 143 pp; ISBN: 0-8298-0195-2.
Gives basic history and information on A.A.

1100. Conrad, Barnaby. Time Is All We Have. Four Weeks at the Betty Ford Center. Paperback reprint ed. New York: Dell Pub.; Feb., 1989; 240pp; ISBN: 0-440-20245-0.
Note: First pb printing.
Conrad, an alcoholic and well-known writer, gives a personal account of his thirty days at the Betty Ford Center. A.A. is discussed throughout. Conrad breaks his anonymity in this book.

1101. Corrigan, Eileen M. Alcoholic Women in Treatment. First ed. New York/Oxford: Oxford University Press; 1980: pp1-2, 24, 147-153, 149.; 191 pp; ISBN: 0-19-502653-5.
This study - the first of its kind - documents Dr. Corrigan's examination of 150 alcoholic women entering three types of treatment facilities: hospitals, clinics, and Alcoholics Anonymous.

1102. Corwin, E.H.L./Cunningham, E. V. "Alcoholics Anonymous". In: Institutional Facilities for the Treatment of Alcoholism. New Haven: Journal of Studies on Alcohol, Inc.; 1944.
A report from The Research Council on Problems of Alcohol illustrates the use of A.A. in hospitals. New Jersey and Connecticut facilities are cited.

1103. Costales, Claire/Berry, Jo [with]. Alcoholism: The Way Back to Reality. First ed. Regal Books-G/L Publications: Glendale, CA; 1980; 157pp; ISBN: 0-8307-0742-5. LC 79-93018.
This woman shares her difficulty attending her first AA meeting and how God entered her life and saved her from alcoholism. She uses ideas from AA and Christianity and outlines her program of recovery. [Anonymity break?].

1104. Coudert, Jo. The Alcoholic in Your Life. First ed. New York: Stein and Day; 1972: pp208-214; 264 pp; ISBN: 0-8128-1459-2.
Writing for the co-alcoholic, someone in a continuing relationship with an alcoholic, the author briefly discusses A.A. and views it as a new addiction, a "replacement for drink." Criticizing the "religious" nature of some of the Steps, the "confessional character of the meetings," and other facets of A.A., the author still admits that "tiresome" A.A. is still "infinitely preferable to addiction to alcohol.".

1105. Cox, W. F. "A Spiritual Foundation". in: Golding, P., editor. Alcoholism: Analysis of a World Wide Problem. Lancaster: M & P Press Limited; 1983: Chap. 24, pp287-291.
This retired parson visited the Broadway Lodge, an alcoholism treatment centre in Weston-super-Mare weekly and was impressed with "the disciplined staff interpreting the first five steps of Alcoholics Anonymous as the road to recovery for alcoholics." As a parson, he heard the Fifth Step of many alcoholic patients. He discusses the spiritual history of AA, including the Oxford Group, psychologist C. G. Jung, William James and AA literature.

1106. Craven, H. T. "Up Off the Floor and Fighting" [book review]. Cleveland, Ohio, News; June 21, 1947.
This review of If A Man Be Mad by Harold Maine states that Maine has a good word for New York's Bellevue Hospital and "an endorsement for Alcoholics Anonymous.".

1107. Cross, Wilbur. Kids and Booze: What You Must Know to Help Them. First ed. New York: E. P. Dutton, A Sunrise Book; 1979: 16 references to AA.; 180pp; ISBN: 0-87690-355-3. LC 78-21105.
Note: index, dj.
This book gives parents and other interested parties basic information about alcoholism, intervention, AA, resources, etc.

1108. Crumbaugh, James C., Ph.D./Wood, William M., M.D./Wood, W. Chadwick, M.D. Logotherapy: New Help for Problem Drinkers. First ed. Chicago, IL: Nelson-Hall; 1980: AA: 8 references.; 159pp; ISBN: 0-88229-421-0. LC 79-18635.
Note: index, dj.
Logotherapy, originated by Dr. Viktor E. Frankl of the Univ. of Vienna Medical School, holds that the will to find meaning is man's primary source of motivation, not survival, sex, or power. The authors find no conflict between logotherapy and AA. They endorse it: "...helps more alcoholics than any other single method of treatment ... beneficial ... embodies true values...".

1109. Cunningham, John T. My Favorite Alcoholic. First ed. Norwalk, OH: Thornwood Press; 1986; 71pp.
Here is wit and wisdom about alcoholism and alcoholics distilled from 43 years of drinking coffee and eating donuts and remembered by the author. Witty jokes, graphics, slogans, quotes from Twain and Bierce, and other humor about the "program" fill this paperback. Although AA is not mentioned it's what much of this is about.

1110. Curlee-Salisbury, Joan. "Perspectives on Alcoholics Anonymous". in: Estes, Nada J./Heinemann, M. Edith, Editors. Alcoholism Development, Consequences, and Interventions. First ed. Saint Louis, MO: The C. V. Mosby Co.; 1977: Chap. 25, pp266-273, plus 10 other references to A.A.; 332 pp; ISBN: 0-8016-1529-1.
Note: large pb.
The author gives a digest of the key elements of A.A. as a therapeutic approach to alcoholism. She identifies A.A. as the leader nationally in helping alcoholics recover. Among other topics covered are beginnings, elements of the recovery program, guiding principles, and combining A.A. with other treatments.

1111. D'Alonzo, C. Anthony, M.D., Assistant Medical Director, E. I. du Pont de Nemours & Co. "Alcoholics Anonymous". in: D'Alonzo, C. Anthony, M.D. The Drinking Problem - and its Control. First ed. Houston, Texas: Gulf Publishing Co.; 1959: Chap. 8, pp 77-80 & other references to A.A.; 130 pp; ISBN: L.C. 59-11570.
"It is our intent in this chapter on A.A. to recommend that organization rather than to discuss it...and we can commend it most highly..." the author writes at the opening of this chapter. He quotes the 12 Steps, Fr. Dowling and Dr. Harry Emerson Fosdick.

1112. Damstra, D./Rhoads, J. "Recovery as a Process-Treatment and Aftercare using Alcoholics Anonymous/Narcotics Anonymous in a Medical Setting". in: Alcohol: Use and Abuse. Phoenix: Do It Now Foundation; 1979; Vol. 1: pp151-161; 200 pp.
Note: This article was published as part of the First International Action Conference on Substance Abuse, Nov. 9-13, 1977.

1113. Dardis, Tom. The Thirsty Muse: Alcohol and the American Writer. First ed. New York: Ticknor & Fields; 1989; 292pp; ISBN: 0-89919-376-5. LC 88-29394.
Note: Illus. with photos, index, dj.
Four giants of American literature, all alcoholics, Faulkner, Fitzgerald, Hemingway, and O'Neill, are studied by Dardis. He says initially alcohol served as a liberating force for them but by age 40 all had sacrificed their creativity to booze. Dardis attended over 100 A.A. meetings in California and New York and credits A.A. with much of his information and insight into the disease as it affected writers.

1114. David W. "David W.". in: Stromsten, Amy, editor. Recovery. New Brunswick, NJ: Rutgers Center of Alcohol Studies; 1982: 29-31.
David is an Episcopal priest with over 30 years sobriety. In this testimonial he discusses his addiction and recovery through AA.

1115. Day, Beth. No Hiding Place. New York: Henry Holt & Co.; 1957.
The book is the biography of Vincent Tracy, an executive whose alcoholism caused him to end up on New York's Bowery. After Tracy sobered up, he began working with alcoholics like himself, alcoholics unable to find sobriety in AA.

1116. DeJong, Alexander C. Help and Hope for the Alcoholic. Fourth ed. Wheaton, IL: Tyndale House; July, 1986; c1982: Many references to AA.; 124pp; ISBN: 0-8423-1409-3. LC 81-86092.
Note: pb.
This advice book for friends and family from a pastor who conquered alcoholism contains several sections discussing the Twelve Steps of AA in terms of Biblical quotations. DeJong opens the book by saying "as a Christian, I have come to distrust anonymity" and goes on later to reveal his membership in AA.

1117. "Depth Psychology, Morality and Alcoholism by John C. Ford, S.J." [book review]. Tablet, Brooklyn, NY; Aug. 18, 1951: p38?
This review notes that Fr. Ford adivses priests "cooperation with Alcoholics Anonymous as essential to the successful pastoral care of alcoholics.".

1118. DeWitt, William A. Drinking and What To Do About It. New York: Grosset & Dunlap; 1952: 13 references to A.A.; 186 pp.

1119. The Diagnosis and Treatment of Alcoholism. Mello, Nancy K., Ph.D./Mendelson, Jack H., M.D., Editors. First ed. New York, etc.: McGraw-Hill Co.; 1979: AA is referenced 21 times.; 405pp; ISBN: 0-07-041476-9. LC 79-4128.
Note: Index.
This anthology of 15 articles discusses diagnostic criteria, medical complications, genetics, Blacks, treatment modalities, outpatient & inpatient & pharmacotherapy treatments, behavior therapy and social setting in prevention and treatment of alcoholism.

1120. "A Discussion Guide for questions about Alcohol". New Brunswick, NJ: Rutgers Center of Alcohol Studies; 1956.
AA basics are mentioned on two pages in this 13-page pamphlet.

1121. Doniger, Simon, Ph.D., Editor. The Minister's Consultation Clinic. Pastoral Psychology in Action. First ed. Great Neck, New York: Channel Press, Inc.; 1955: pp250-256; 316 pp.
A minister asks how to counsel an alcoholic who does not want help and this book reprints 4 letters answering that query from the magazine Pastoral Psychology. One reply came from Harry Tiebout, M.D., a long-time friend of A.A.; while another was from Marty Mann, Exec. Dir. of the NCA.

1122. Dorsman, Jerry. How to Quit Drinking Without A.A. First ed. Newark, DE: New Dawn Pub. Co.; 1991: Chap. 4, pp69-75, & other AA references; 224pp; ISBN: 0-9627899-0-9. LC 90-92128.
Note: Index, pb.
"Even if you use A.A., this book can help immensely. It gives you over 100 proven techniques that A.A. doesn't offer, " the jacket states. Dorsman terms AA a "model of religious fellowship" and criticizes the insistence on belief in some God as a "must." He lists nine criticisms of AA but still endorses AA's help where it works. "A.A. insists that you call yourself an alcoholic," he states. "Why drag the guilt around by calling yourself an alcoholic long after you've quit drinking?" Subtitled "A Complete Self-Help Guide," the book's primary title seems to be more a provocative eye-catcher than an actual summary of the contents since AA occupies but one six-page chapter.

1123. Dowling, Edward, Rev. S.J. "Catholic Asceticism and the Twelve Steps". in: Pfau, et al. Alcoholism: A Source Book for the Priest. Indianapolis: NCCA; 1960: pp418-430; 685 pp.
This Jesuit priest, an early friend of AA, compares the Spiritual Exercises of St. Ignatius, Founder of the Society of Jesus (S.J.), with the Twelve Steps of A.A., and finds them compatiable. The book, Errors of Psychotherapy by Sebastian de Grazia, is discussed and Carl Jung's admission that no patient of his regained a healed new life without coming to a "religious outlook." He quotes Dr. Bob's last admonition and legacy "Don't louse it up with psychiatry." Catholics' and priests'membership in AA is approved and recommended. Dowling strongly approves of the religious and spiritual outlook in AA and rejects the psychiatric approach to the problem of alcoholism.

1124. Downing, Cynthia. TRIAD: The Evolution of Treatment for Chemical Dependency. First ed. Independence, MO: Herald House/Independence Press; 1989: pp24-29 & throughout; 59pp; ISBN: 0-8309-0543-X.
Note: pb.
Downing views chemical dependency treatment historically in three stages: Alcoholics Anonymous, the Minnesota Model, and the CENAPS Bio-psycho-social Model. Foreword by Terence T. Gorski, creator of the CENAPS Model, (Center for Applied Sciences).

1125. Drakeford, John W. "The Oxford Group and Its Most Improbable Offshoot". in: People to People Therapy. San Francisco: Harper & Row; 1978: pp25-35.
Frank Buchman, founder of the Oxford Group, and his teachings are reviewed, as well as the A.A. Co-founders' use of Oxford Group principles, the Twelve Steps and Traditions, and the use of A.A.'s Twelve Steps applied to non-alcohol problems.

1126. Drotning, Phillip T. "Alcoholics Anonymous". in: Drotning, Phillip T. New Hope for Problem Drinkers. First ed. Chicago: Contemporary Books, Inc.; 1977: Chap. 9, pp75-90; plus numerous other references to A.A. throughout text.; 144 pp; ISBN: 0-8092-8031-0.
The author strongly disagrees with A.A.'s "Once an alcoholic, always an alcoholic," and "One drink is too many and a thousand are never enough." He cites recent research that alleges that many problem drinkers can learn to control their drinking. He gives an overview of A.A. in Chapter 9, quoting extensively from A.A. literature. His book is a "compassionate look at the injury inflicted on the victims of alcohol by the insistence of AAs and many professionals that an alcoholic must want to quit drinking and be willing to give up alcohol completely before he is deserving of help." He says his proposals will not be "welcomed by ... AA.".

1127. Duff, Edward, Rev., S.J. "Alcoholics Anonymous". in: Ford, John L., Rev., S.J., editor. Alcoholism. Education for Sobriety. New York: America Press; 1950: pp20-28; 31pp.
Fr. Duff recounts Dr. Harry M. Tiebout's description of the "X factor" in Alcoholics Anonymous as "a religious component, a spiritual development, a belief in God - a conversion." Duff goes on to describe the AA "way of life" and cautions Catholic AA members on some friction points, as he sees them, between the two. For example, he still sees the necessity for Catholics to go to Confession along with taking a Fifth Step.

1128. Dunn, Jerry G. "Fellowship". in: Dunn, Jerry G. God is for the Alcoholic. First ed. Chicago: The Moody Press; 1965: pp107-126, various mentions of A.A.; 205 pp.
The author cites A.A. as an excellent example of fellowship as a means of helping an alcoholic.

1129. Dunnington, Lewis L. More Handles of Power. First ed. New York/Nashville, TN: Abingdon-Cokesbury Press; 1944: AA: Chap. X, pp 95-105.; 222pp.
Dunnington, a minister, relates how alcoholics in Duluth, Minnesota, recovered from their disease. One A.A. member, J. H., chuckled as he revealed the back room behind The N. M. Liquor Store was actually the downtown headquarters of AA.

1130. DuPont, Robert L., Jr., M.D. Getting Tough on Gateway Drugs. A Guide for the Family. First ed. Washington, D.C.: American Psychiatric Press, Inc.; 1984: 6 references to A.A. in text; 332 pp; ISBN: 0-88048-035-1.
The author recommends A.A. and discusses several Steps as extremely-helpful to young people sucked by alcohol, marijuana or cocaine into total drug dependency.

1131. Durfee, Charles H. Should You Drink... New York: The Macmillan Company; 1954: A few references to A.A.; 152 pp.
The author equates A.A. with group therapy but feels A.A. has its limitations as some alcoholics need specialized individual therapy.

1132. Earle, Clifford J. "Alcoholics Anonymous". in: Earle, Clifford J. How To Help An Alcoholic. First ed. Philadelphia: The Westminster Press; 1952: Chap. 4, pp43-50; & last chap., pp79-96.; 96 pp.
The last chapter in the book is devoted to meditations based on articles from the A.A. Grapevine. The author discusses briefly the Steps, Traditions, and meetings. He feels open A.A. meetings are an excellent means for non-alcoholics to become informed about alcoholism.

1133. East Ridge: A Laboratory for Living the Survivors Program -- The Way Out When All Other Ways Have Failed. Hankins, NY: East Ridge; nd.
East Ridge is described as "a laboratory for living the survivors program," a program based on AA's twelve steps and the four absolutes developed by the Oxford group. While living in a community setting, people learn to follow God's plan.

1134. Edwards, Griffith. "Alcoholics Anonymous". in: Edwards, Griffith. The Treatment of Drinking Problems. A Guide for the Helping Professions. First ed. New York, et al: McGraw-Hill Book Co.; 1982: Chap. 15, pp226-234; & other references to A.A.; 334 pp.
The author gives a succinct overview of A.A. and says one of the duties of a good therapist is to "signpost the way to AA...whenever appropriate.".

1135. Elkin, Michael. Families Under the Influence. Changing Alcoholic Patterns. First ed. New York & London: W. W. Norton & Co.; 1984: pp202-207 & other references to A.A.; 224 pp; ISBN: 0-393-01770-2.
"A. A. is a potent ally for both alcoholics and therapists," the author writes. He discusses his insights into confusion and insecurity as a necessary prelude to accepting some of A.A.'s "suggestions;" the avoidance of "power struggles" in the A.A. recovery program; and his reasons why "there are no A.A. counselors, only A.A. members.".

1136. Ellis, Albert, Ph.D./Velten, Emmett, Ph.D. When AA Doesn't Work for You. Rational Steps to Quitting Alcohol. First ed. Fort Lee, NJ: Barricade Books, Inc.; 1992: 11 references to AA.; 329pp; ISBN: 0-942637-53-4. LC 91-38539.
Note: index, pb.
Like many other rational recovery books, this one also rides on the coattails of AA by using AA in the title. The authors cite some AA "slogans" and sayings which probably have never been uttered at AA meetings. Nevertheless, they give AA credit where due and say rational recovery groups would never exist if many alcoholics did not perceive AA as "religious." Dr. Ellis is the founder of "rational-emotive therapy." This "self-help" book eliminates the "God part" and emphasizes the alcoholic's own power to defuse "stinking thinking," quit drinking alcohol, and deal with his own emotional problems.

1137. Englebardt, Stanley L. Kids and Alcohol, the Deadliest Drug. First ed. New York: Lothrop, Lee & Shephard Co., a div. of William Morrow & Co., Inc.; 1975: 6 references to AA.; 64pp; ISBN: 0-688-41717-5. LC 75-20327.
Note: index, dj.
Discusses favorably AA basics, especially for young people.

1138. Ernest J. Wessen and Jim Scott: A Correspondence. Klein, Frank, editor. First Limited ed. Akron, OH: Northern Ohio Bibliophilic Society; 1987; v, 26pp.
Note: [published in a limited edition of 200 copies.].
Noted Akron antiquarian bookseller Frank Klein did this biographical sketch of Jim Scott, writer, bookman, alcoholic and author of the "Traveler, Editor, Scholar" story in the first edition of Alcoholics Anonymnous. Klein was in awe of Scott when he managed a book store for his father and at eleven years old, was the first person Klein saw "totally, falling down, drunk." Scott "took my last drink in 1937" and would edit and probably help to write the Big Book. In an interview with Lionel Zwicker, another Akron bookseller, he said he and Jim spent onewhole weekend and more editing the manuscript of the first edition. "It was a total mess, punctuation, paragraphing, spelling, everything," Zwicker told Charlie Bishop, Jr., a West Virginia bookseller. Klein notes that Bill Wilson inscribed a red book first edition "To my friend Jim Scott, Who helped so much to make this book possible..." The Wessen-Scott correspondence deals mainly with books & bookscouting, etc.

1139. Estill, C. L. One Day. First ed. Charleston, WV: C. L. Estill; 1988; 32pp.
Note: pb.
This slim volume of poetry revolves around the Big Book phrase "what we were like, what happened, and what we are like now.".

1140. Ewing, John A., M.D. "Alcoholics Anonymous and Al-Anon". in: Drinking to Your Health. Reston, Virginia: Reston Publishing Co., Inc.; 1981: Chap. 32, pp176-181; numerous references throughout.; 224pp; ISBN: 0-8359-1473-9.
Note: paperback.
"My experience, like that of most doctors, is that A.A. is the single most successful treatment plan for alcoholism when an alcoholic will accept it," the author begins his chapter on A.A.

1141. Ewing, John A., M.D. "Social and Psychiatric Considerations of Drinking". in: Ewing, John A., M.D./Rouse, Beatrice A., M.Ed., Editors. Drinking: Alcohol in American Society - Issues and Current Research. Chicago, IL: Nelson-Hall; 1978: pp 105-110.; 443pp; ISBN: ISBN 0-88229-569-1.
Note: pb.
Ewing notes a study of 35 alcoholics from 1970 to 1973 who had rejected Alcoholics Anonymous and total abstinence and an attempt at controlled drinking by fourteen of that group. A follow-up study in 1975 revealed that none of the 14 had succeeded and they needed hospitalization or Antabuse.

1142. Faith. "Four". in: Swallow, Jean, Editor. Out From Under. San Francisco: Spinsters Ink; 1983: pp27-33.
Faith writes about how A.A. helped give her the tools to leave an abusive husband and, eventually, to come to terms with her sexuality. She talks about her first meeting in A.A. and eventual Twelfth Step work.

1143. Fajardo, Roque. Helping Your Alcoholic Before He or She Hits Bottom. First ed. New York: Crown Pub., Inc.; 1976: 9 references to AA.; 182pp; ISBN: 0-517-52682-4. LC76-15380.
Note: Index, dj.
The technique of "guided intervention" is expounded here by Fajardo, founder of the Samaritan Center for Alcoholics in Nashville, TN. He states it is the responsibility of the nonalcoholic spouse, parent, employer, etc., to start the process of getting the alcoholic away from the bottle and into a rehabilitation center. AA basics are discussed, although misunderstandings occur, especially in terminology and concerning cooperation with the professional community.

1144. Father A./Father X. "The Attitude of Superiors Toward the Priest in AA". in: Pfau, et al. Alcoholism: A Source Book for the Priest. Indianapolis: NCCA; 1960: pp503-509; 685 pp.
These two alcoholic Catholic priests discuss the special problems priests have with getting into AA, then addressing the problem of their alcoholism, and then carrying the message to other alcoholics, including other Catholic alcoholic priests. Both basically conclude that AA works the same whether you're a priest or a layman. And both state that their religious superiors need to know more about AA in order to help alcoholic priests get into AA.

1145. Fichter, Joseph H. "Clergy Alcoholics On and Off the AA Program". in: Fichter, Joseph H. The Rehabilitation of Clergy Alcoholics: Ardent Spirits Subdued. New York: Human Sciences Press; 1982: Chap. 7, pp113-130; & numerous references to A.A. throughout text.; 203pp.

1146. Fichter, Joseph H. "The Guest House Experience 1956-1974". in: Fichter, Joseph H. Ardent Spirits Among The Clergy. First ed. Lake Orion, MI: Guest House, Inc.; nd: pp5-8, 49, 50, 52; 52pp.
Note: This booklet was published "For Private Circulation Only from Guest House, Inc.".
In this scholarly excerpt, Fichter documents attitudes of Catholic clergy who were treated at Guest House for alcoholism and finds overwhelming support for, and participation in, A.A., by that clergy.

1147. Fingarette, Herbert. Heavy Drinking. The Myth of Alcoholism as a Disease. First ed. Berkeley/Los Angeles/ London: University of California Press; 1988: pp3, 18, 20, 31,87-91; 166pp; ISBN: 0-520-06754-1.
Note: First pb printing 1989.
Fingarette criticizes A.A. and the Jellinek disease concept of alcoholism. He calls the A.A. approach "pseudomedical" and a mild version of the old temperance abstinence method. He criticizes Jellinek for using A.A. questionnaires and the A.A. Grapevine for his empirical data. "There are no satisfactory data to justify the widespread confidence in A.A.," he writes. Fingarette is part of a minority who still criticize the disease concept of alcoholism.

1148. Fishman, Ross, Ph.D. Alcohol and Alcoholism. Second ed. New York/New Haven/Philadelphia: Chelsea House Publishers; 1986: AA: 27-8, 32, 62, 85, 88, 92-3-7.; 122pp. (The Enclyclopedia of Psychoactive Drugs); ISBN: 0-87754-762-9. LC 85-32572.
Note: Illus., index.
This volume calls AA "the first major breakthrough in the evolution of enlightened attitudes toward alcoholism." Brief discussion of AA basics.

1149. FitzGerald, Kathleen Whalen, Ph.D. Alcoholism: The Genetic Inheritance. First ed. New York, etc.: Doubleday; 1988: Chap. 11, pp196-212; numerous other references.; 248pp; ISBN: 0-385-19933-3. LC 87-9114.
Note: Index, dj.
The author suggests alcoholism be renamed "Jellinek's disease" to remove the remaining stigma and promote medical profession acceptance and treatment. Alcoholics Anonymous is discussed in chapter eleven, etc.

1150. FitzGibbon, Constantine. Drink: A Self-Help Book on Alcoholism. First U.S. ed. Garden City, NY: Doubleday & Co., Inc.; 1979: pp79, 94, 155, 161-2 (AA).; 201pp; ISBN: 0-385-14830-5. LC 78-22757.
Note: X-lib, index, dj.
This Irish-American writer, an alcoholic, documents the devastation alcoholism caused him. He also discusses a wide range of topics and their relationship to alcoholism: religion, English customs, Prohibition, psychoanalysis, depression, etc. AA and Marty Mann are discussed briefly.

1151. Fleming, Alice. Alcohol: The Delightful Poison. a history. First ed. New York: Delacorte Press; 1975: p110 (AA).; 138pp; ISBN: 0-440-01796-3. LC 74-22629.
Note: Index, X-lib., dj.
In this brief history of alcohol, Fleming credits Alcoholics Anonymous as "the most effective method that has been discovered to date for dealing with alcoholism" (page 110). He discusses the history of alcohol, its customs and language, in the Colonial, Temperance, Prohibition, and Modern eras.

1152. Follmann, Joseph F., Jr. Alcoholics and Business. Problems, Costs, Solutions. First ed. New York: AMACOM; 1976: Nine references to A.A. in text; 246 pp; ISBN: 0-8144-5410-0. The author reviews A.A. in terms of effectiveness, membership, no-cost, referrals to, and treatment in the fellowship; all in the framework of business and industry.

1153. Ford, John C., S.J. "Alcoholism and Subjective Imputability". in: Ford, John C., S.J./Kelly, Gerald, S.J., co-authors. Contemporary Moral Theology. Sixth printing ed. Cork, Ireland: The Mercier Press Ltd.; 1958; I: Chap. 13: pp277-312 (AA pp288 & 303-5).; 368pp; ISBN: LC 58-7530.
Note: Bibliography, index, dj.
In chapter 13, "Alcoholism and Subjective Imputability," Ford notes A.A. "has been more successful than any other agency. The best of all allies which the priest has in this work is Alcoholics Anonymous.".

1154. Ford, John C., S.J. Man Takes a Drink. Facts and Principles about Alcohol. First ed. New York: J. P. Kennedy & Sons; 1959: Chap. 6, pp106-109; 120 pp.
The author, a Catholic priest and recognized authority on alcoholism, characterizes A.A.'s program as in "thorough harmony with Christian theological and ascetical teaching." He cites A.A. as the main resource for the alcoholic. Its tenets are stated admission and acceptance of alcoholism and "reliance on God to achieve permanent and happy sobriety." The book is aimed at a general Catholic audience, but especially Catholic youth.

1155. Ford, John C., S.J. "Pastoral Treatment". in: Bier, William C., S.J., Editor. Problems in Addiction: Alcohol and Drug Addiction. New York: Fordham University Press; 1962; The Pastoral Psychology Series, No. 2: pp116-126; 247 pp; ISBN: L.C. 62-16224.
In this essay, this Catholic priest urges men of the cloth to refer their parishioners to A.A. and use follow-up. He praises A.A. for its "practical, psychological techniques to help the alcoholic to circumvent the compulsion to drink.".

1156. Ford, Rev. John C., S.J. "Moral Re-Armament and Alcoholics Anonymous". in: Pfau, et al. Alcoholism: A Source Book for the Priest. Indianapolis: NCCA; 1960: pp394-401; 685 pp.
Rev. Ford, Professor of Moral Theology at the Catholic University of America, discusses why AA withdrew from the Oxford Group, later called Moral Re-Armament (MRA). He states the basic reasons were the Oxford Group's four absolutes, their aggressive evangelism, the principle of "team guidance," and Catholic objections to certain elements of Buchmanism, namely open confession in front of a group. AA, Catholicism, and MRA are compared at some length along spiritual and religious lines.

1157. Forrest, G. G. "Treatment III: Alcoholics Anonymous". in: The Diagnosis and Treatment of Alcoholism. Springfield, Illinois: Charles C. Thomas - Publisher; 1975: pp110-124.

1158. Forrest, Gary G., Dr. How to Cope with a Teenage Drinker. New Alternatives and Hope for Parents and Families. First ed. New York: Atheneum; 1983: pp111-116, & others.; 174 pp; ISBN: 0-689-11346-3.
Forrest gives a brief overview of A.A. as an "self-help treatment alternative.".

1159. Forrest, Gary G., Dr. How to Live with a Problem Drinker and Survive. First paperback ed. New York: Antheneum; 1986; c1980: pp110-13.; 117pp; ISBN: 0-689-70706-1. LC85-48116.
Note: pb.
Addressed mainly to the family and friends of problem drinkers, Dr. Forrest articulates his behavorial modification techniques in simple terms. He devotes four pages to AA, calling it a "self-help" program and an "alternative to professional help.".

1160. Fort, Joel, M.D. Alcohol: Our Biggest Drug Problem. First ed. New York, etc.: McGraw-Hill Book Co.; 1973: pp131-33.; 180pp; ISBN: 0-07-021599-5. LC 72-12746.
Note: index, pb.
Dr. Fort states A.A. is among "the most important treatment approaches...self-help, semi-religious..." Its "major defect" is that "its religious philosophy, semi-anonymity, and general style are not acceptable to most alcohol abusers." Despite this brief off-target description of A.A., his book does confirm alcohol as America's most widely-used, mind-altering drug (despite all the headlines about cocaine, the drug war, etc.).

1161. Fosdick, Harry Emerson, Rev. On Being a Real Person. Fourth ed. New York/London: Harper & Brothers; 1943: pp234-5; 295pp.
Fosdick quotes a modern psychiatrist who says that "the doctrine that the will alone is the way to power is a most woe-begone theory for the relief of the morally sick." He then cites A.A. as an illustration "that what volition alone cannot do, appropriated power furnishes resource for doing.".

1162. Foster, Fred. The Up & Outer. First ed. Wheaton, IL: Tyndale House Publishers, Inc.; Sept., 1980: pp119, 136ff; 224pp; ISBN: 0-8423-7799-9, paper. LC 80-51699.
Note: pb.
This autobiography of an advertising and television executive includes his attendance at A.A. meetings. Foster attributes his recovery from alcoholism to God. A.A. is mentioned.

1163. Fowler, Richard, Dr./Hemfelt, Robert, Dr. Serenity. A Companion for Twelve Step Recovery, Complete with New Testament & Proverbs. First ed. Nashville, TN: Thomas Nelson Publishers; 1990; 80 & 558pp; ISBN: 0-8407-1542-0.
Note: pb.
This book explains each of A.A.'s Twelve Steps in the context of scriptural truths. Seven meditations for each of the 12 Steps provide Biblical commentary. The entire New Testament, Psalms, and Proverbs with over 500 highlighted verses give the reader an overview of Biblical principles of recovery compatible with the Twelve Steps. The book is addressed to

alcoholics and all others suffering from some harmful addiction.

1164. Fox, Ruth, M.D./Lyon, Peter. Alcoholism: Its Scope, Cause and Treatment. First ed. New York: Random House; 1955: pp166-194 & other references to A.A.; 208 pp; ISBN: L.C. 55-8170. The author gives a brief overview of A.A., its Twelve Steps, and meetings. She recommends the A.A. program.

1165. Fox, Ruth, M.D., Editor. Alcoholism: Behavorial Research, Therapeutic Approaches. First. New York: Springer Pub. Co., Inc.; 1967: pp24-35, 249-54, 277-83, 296-9, & 23 other references.; 340pp; ISBN: LC 66-25518.
Fox, Medical Director of the Nat'l Council on Alcoholism, assembled 30 articles from scholars on alcoholism research and therapeutic approaches. Four of the articles contain discussions of A.A. in some length.

1166. Free, James Lamb. "Alcoholics Anonymous". in: Free, James Lamb. Just One More. Concerning the Problem Drinker. First ed. New York: Coward-McCann, Inc.; 1955: Chap. 7, pp75-88; & other references to A.A. in text; 211 pp; ISBN: L.C. 55-10079.
The author, a recovered alcoholic himself, uses a fictional character, Charlie, to illustrate the A.A. program of recovery, from the first phone call asking for help and the first meeting through the Steps and Traditions and stable sobriety. The alcoholic's possible need for more than A.A. is suggested, including psychiatric and pastoral counseling and medical help. The author utilized the Richard Peabody system in his recovey and he discusses that.

1167. Fullam, Thomas [pseudonym]. Here's to Sobriety. First ed. New York: Abelard Press; 1950: pp190-99 & throughout; 208pp. The author was an A.A. member writing under a pseudonym. The next to last chapter is devoted to A.A. and the Fellowship is mentioned throughout the book.

1168. Furnas, J. C. The Life and Times of the Late Demon Rum. First ed. London: W. H. Allen; 1965: pp 88, 93, 153, & 344.; 381 pp.

1169. Garland, Robert. "Come Back, Little Sheba: An Acting Triumph for Booth, Blackmer". New York Journal & American; Feb. 1, 1950.
This laudatory review of the play by William Inge notes that Doc, the alcoholic, goes beserk and when a couple of "tough AAs arrive, they carry him off to the hospital for alcoholics which is also an asylum for the insane.".

1170. Gehring, W. Robert. RX For Addiction. Grand Rapids, MI: Zondervan Books; 1985.
Dr. Gehring tells the story of his addiction and recovery. Part of his story concerns his exposure to AA and his co-founding of Doctors Helping Doctors.

1171. Geller, A. "Alcoholics Anonymous and the Scientific Model". in: Gottheil, E., et al, Editors. Etiologic Aspects of Alcohol and Drug Abuse. Springfield, IL: Charles C. Thomas; 1983: pp306-318; 330 pp.
The AA model and the scientific model of alcoholism are described, noting how these two models were derived from different systems of thought. Some of the difficulties with the scientific model that might be encountered by a recovered alcoholic working in the field are examined, including some of the scientific findings that are in conflict with the traditional view of alcoholism. These findings concern the natural history and etiology of alcohol problems, the effects of alcohol upon the human body, and treatment outcome (i.e., abstinence versus controlled drinking). The author contends that, within the broad spectrum of alcohol abuse, there is a need to expand and modify the traditional model of alcoholism; however, the implications for treatment of this revised model are not yet clear. In particular, the criteria for selecting persons for whom abstinence would not be a preferred goal have not been established; therefore, it would be premature for treatment centers to attempt a revision of their treatment goals at the present time. It is concluded that treatment personnel with a background in AA can be helped to evaluate scientific findings in an objective manner; however, changes in treatment strategy should not be urged before there is adequate evidence to support them. 37 ref. (NCADI abstract).

1172. George, Rickey L. Counseling the Chemically Dependent: Theory and Practice. First ed. Englewood Cliffs, NJ: Prentice Hall; 1990: pp 23, 165-184, 222.; 242pp; ISBN: 0-13-181330-7. LC 89-48178.
Note: Index.
The Twelve Steps are discussed along with Traditions, Slogans, the role of the counselor and his membership in AA, spirituality, relapse, and other Fellowship topics.

1173. Gold, Ivan. Sams in a Dry Season. First paperback ed. New York, et al: Pocket Books - Washington Square Press; 1990; 244pp; ISBN: 0-671-75537-4. LC 92-16956.
Note: pb.
This novel "chronicles Jason Sam's weekend-long journey from his home in Boston to his native New York and back again - a journey that shocks him out of twenty-five years of drinking and into a shaky sobriety." The Chicago Tribune reviewed: "Alcoholics Anonymous has been done and done again, but never better than here...those who relish the wild, woolly and sometimes horrific gallows humor of AA testimony will find the best meeting ever put on the page [here].".

1174. Goodwin, D. W. "Alcoholics Anonymous". in: Goodwin, D. W. Alcoholism: The Facts. New York: Oxford University Press; 1981: Chap. 15, pp106-115; 135pp.

1175. Goodwin, D. W. "Comment on `Alcoholics Anonymous as Treatment and as Ideology". in: Ward, D. A., editor. Alcoholism: Introduction to Theory and Treatment. First ed. Dubuque, IA: Kendall-Hunt Pub. Co.; 1983: pp388-9; 557pp; ISBN: 0-8403-3824-4. LC 83-80034.
The author acknowledges AA "not only works for many alcoholics, but it is also essential for many." Goodwin's opinion is, however, that many alcoholics, including AA's, may be able "to support a lifestyle that includes controlled drinking.".

1176. Goodwin, Donald. Is Alcoholism Hereditary? First ed. New York: Oxford University Press; 1976: pp121-22, 166; 171 pp; ISBN: 0-19-502009-X.
The author calls A.A. a religion but "one of the least doctrinaire and authoritarian religions imaginable." He says the A.A. use of the term "allergy" is not valid in the medical sense.

1177. Gorski, Terence T./Miller, Merlene/Miller, David K. Learning to Live Again. A Guide for Recovery from Alcoholism. Third ed. Independence, MO: Independence Press; 1982: AA: pp235-256, etc.; 274pp; ISBN: 0-8309-0372-0.
Note: pb.
The authors outline alcoholism as a disease, recovery on the physical, psychological, social and spiritual levels, relapse prevention, AA, and spirituality. The book is used by treatment centers and others for inpatient education about alcoholism and recovery. The chapter on AA begins "Alcoholics Anonymous is the single most effective treatment modality for alcoholism." The Steps, Traditions, sponsorship, types of AA meetings, etc. are discussed.

1178. Gorski, Terence T. Passages Through Recovery. An Action Plan for Preventing Relapse. First ed. San Francisco, CA: Harper & Row/Harper-Hazelden; 1989: numerous references to AA.; 154pp; ISBN: 0-06-255487-5. LC 88-46000.
Note: index, pb.
Gorski, acknowledged relapse prevention expert, discusses each of AA's Twelve Steps as he moves through the six stages of recovery from addiction to full sobriety.

1179. Gorski, Terence T. Understanding the Twelve Steps. First ed. New York, etc.: Prentice Hall-Parkside Recovery Book; 1989; 189pp; ISBN: 0-13-934100-5. LC 89-77134.
Note: pb.
Subtitled "An Interpretation and Guide for Recovering People, " this book is based on the evidence that the best program for recovering people is the Twelve Steps of AA plus professional counseling or therapy. Gorski discusses each of the steps. His audience is addicts of all kinds, not just alcoholics. Gorski states his opinions about the steps are his own and he does not speak for A.A. or any other Twelve Step program.

1180. Gray, J. H. "Alcoholics Anonymous, A Prairie Growth Industry". in: Bacchanalia Revisited: Western Canada's Boozy Skid to Social Disaster. Saskatoon, Saskatchewan: Western Producer Prairie Books; 1982: Chap. 9, pp137-155; 206 pp.
Gray discusses the early efforts of Bill W. and Dr. Bob to establish Alcoholics Anonymous and those of Dr. E. M. Jellinek to arouse interest in alcoholism within the scientific community. He describes contributions to the understanding of alcoholism made by members of the American and Canadian Medical Associations and discusses the steady rise in alcoholism and A.A. membership in the U.S. and Canada since 1935.

1181. Greene, Karen. 12 Steps Illustrated. First ed. New York: Hyperion/A New Hope Press Book; 1991; 44pp; ISBN: 1-56282-999-8. LC 91-19150.
Note: dj.
This broad interpretation of the Twelve Steps is wonderfully-color illustrated throughout. Several pages document and praise the contribution of Frank Buchman, Oxford Group founder. The author states Buchman's ideas, "adapted and named the Twelve Steps by the founders of Alcoholics Anonymous, are the primary component of a program acclaimed as the most powerful instrument of personal transformation known to us." This is an obvious over-valuation of Buchman's contribution to A.A.

1182. Grossvogel, David I. Dear Ann Landers. First ed. Chicago/ New York: Contemporary Books, Inc.; 1987: pp15, 218, 220-22-25-31.; 278pp; ISBN: 0-8092-4675-9. LC 87-15547.
Note: Indexes, dj.
In her nationally-syndicated column, Ann Landers has long been a supporter of Alcoholics Anonymous, as well as Al-Anon and Alateen.

1183. Habas, Ralph A., Ph.D. How To Live Without Liquor. First ed. New York: Farrar, Straus & Cudahy; 1955: pp45-55; 125pp; ISBN: LC 55-0465.
Note: dj.
Chap. 5 is titled "How Alcoholics Anonymous Can Help.".

1184. Hackl, John R./Hackl, Alphons J. The Way Out of Alcoholism. First ed. Washington, D.C.: Acropolis Books Ltd.; 1984: 5 pages; 48pp; ISBN: 0-87491-761-1. LC 84-16884.
A.A. is discussed in this paperback in a section titled "How & Where to Find Help for Your Family and You." The different types of AA meetings are mentioned.

1185. Hafner, Sarah. Nice Girls Don't Drink. Stories of Recovery. First ed. New York/Westport, CT/London: Bergin & Garvey; 1992: AA throughout.; 239pp; ISBN: 0-89789-247-X. LC 91-18924.
Note: pb.
Eighteen first person stories of women who recovered from alcoholism include Marty Mann, the first woman to stay sober and recover in AA. Jean Kirkpatrick, founder of Women for Sobriety, is included. Most of the women discuss their AA membership. Anonymity is protected [Marty Mann's use of her name came before the Traditions were written and was approved by a group conscience back then].

1186. Hall, Nancy Lee. A True Story of a Drunken Mother. First ed. Plainfield, VT: Daughters, Inc.; 1974; 151pp; ISBN: 0-913789-05-7. LC 74-79918.
Note: pb.
This fictionalized autobiography is a novel about an alcoholic woman. She eventually sobers up and A.A. is mentioned in her recovery.

1187. Handbook of Hospital Based Substance Abuse Treatment. Lerner, William D./Barr, Marjorie A., Editors. First ed. New York, et al: Pergamon Press; 1990: 8 references to AA.; 218pp; ISBN: 0-08-036076-9. LC 89-16236.
Note: index, pb.

1188. Hansen, Phillip L. Alcoholism the Afflicted and the Affected. First ed. Lake Mills, Iowa: Graphic Publishing Co., Inc.; 1974: pp82-101; 103 pp.
Note: pb.
This Lutheran minister commends the A.A. program as "the best therapy for alcoholism there is, for one simple reason --- IT WORKS!" As a clergyman, he finds the door open wide concerning God, calls the 12 Steps "genius," noting that they are in the past tense and have to "be lived and experienced." Hansen finds religion and A.A. dovetailing throughout the recovered alcoholic's new life in sobriety.

1189. Hansen, Philip L. Sick and Tired of Being Sick and Tired. First ed. Minneapolis, MN: Park Printing, Inc.; 1974; 108pp; ISBN: LC 77-181-099.
Note: pb.
Hansen, a Lutheran minister, uses the Biblical theme of the prodigal son to discuss the disease of alcoholism and recovery through A.A. The Steps are discussed throughout.

1190. Harkin, Raymond F., Rt. Rev. Msgr. "Alcoholism, AA, and the Alcoholic Priest". in: Pfau, et al. Alcoholism: A Source Book for the Priest. Indianapolis: NCCA; 1960: pp484-502; 685 pp.
This Catholic priest discusses alcoholic priests, sin, conscience, shame, the Fifth and Twelfth Steps of AA, and the role of AA priests.

1191. Harris, I. "AA's Bill Wilson". in: Sam Shoemaker and the Story of Faith - at - Work. First ed. New York: Seabury Press; 1978: pp45-56; 192 pp; ISBN: 0-8164-0399-6.

1192. Harris, Sara. Skid Row U.S.A. First ed. New York: Doubleday & Co., Inc.; 1956: pp201-230; 285 pp; ISBN: L.C. 55-8401.
The author recounts A.A. efforts to help Skid Row alcoholics in the Bowery, Chicago, etc. She cites A.A. as "among the most effective of the rehabilitative efforts along Skid Row today.".

1193. Harsch, H. "The Concept of Symbiosis and the Twelve Steps of Alcoholics Anonymous". in: Golding, P., Editor. Alcoholism: A Modern Perspective. Ridgewood, NJ: George A. Bogden & Son; 1982: Chap. 8, pp87-92; 539pp.
Harsch evaluates the Twelve Steps in terms of their therapeutic ability to meet the symbiotic needs of drug dependent people. He explains the concept of symbiosis, a biological and psychological stage of development, and provides case studies to demonstrate the ways that dependent people express symbiotic needs.

1194. Hasselblad, Judith, C.R.N. Alcohol Abuse Curriculum Guide for Nurse Practioneer Faculty. First ed. Rockville, MD: NIAAA; 1984: pp112-16 & 155,; 167pp. (Health Professions Education, Curriculum Resources Series; v. 3); ISBN: DHHS Publication No. (ADM) 84-1313.
Note: Large paperbound.
Nurse Hasselblad discusses Alcoholics Anonymous' basics as one effective outpatient treatment modality and also as part of other inpatient treatment modalities. The video cassette, Alcoholics Anonymous: An Inside View, 1979, is listed as a resource film.

1195. Heather, Nick/Robertson, Ian. Controlled Drinking. First ed. London/New York: Methuen; 1981: Almost 50 references to AA.; 294pp; ISBN: 0-416-71970-8.
Note: Indexes, dj.
This book is the first comprehensive review of the literature on this controversial approach to treatment: controlled [social, moderate, etc.] drinking by alcoholics and problem drinkers. The 1976 Rand Report and its follow-up four years later, and many other origins, methods, evidence, and practices concerning controlled drinking are discussed. The authors support "controlled drinking," and cite examples of its incompatiability with AA with its goal of total abstinence.

1196. Hedlund, D. A./Liebman, M. C. "Therapeutic Community and Milieu Therapy of Personality Disorders". in: Lion, J. R., Editor. Personality Disorders: Diagnosis and Management. Second revised ed. Baltimore, MD: Williams & Wilkins; 1981: pp408-447; 592pp.
The history and development of the "therapeutic community concept" in the treatment of the mentally ill is described. The use of the therapeutic approach by Alcoholics Anonymous and the Eagleville Hospital & Rehabilitation Center to treat alcoholics is also described.

1197. Hembree, Ron. "Prisoner in a Bottle". in: Hembree, Ron. Dynamic Solutions for Tough Times. How Ordinary People Found the Way Out. First? ed. Wall, PA: Cornerstone TeleVision, Inc.; 1989: pp23-38.; 134pp.
Note: Pb.
The Twelve Steps of AA are discussed with Biblical quotations and the mission of this evangelical television Christian group.

1198. Hill, Harold, (as told to Irene Burk Harrell). How To Live Like A King's Kid. First. Plainfield, NJ: Logos, International; 1974: dedication, pp13-16; 213pp; ISBN: 0-88270-083-9.
Note: pb.
This noted industrialist dedicated his autobiography to: "my wife Ruth whom God used to get me to AA; (and to) Alcoholics Anonymous, for introducing me to God...," thus breaking his anonymity. The chapter "How To Stop Drinking" details in four short pages Hill's affiliation with A.A. and his subsequent meeting with Christ through an A.A. friend two years later.

1199. Hirsh, Joseph. "Alcoholics Anonymous". in: The Problem Drinker. New York: Duell, Sloan & Pierce; 1949: pp121-134; 211 pp.
Typical overview of A.A. with the 12 Steps and 12 Traditions reprinted.

1200. Hoffer, Abram, M.D./Osmond, Humphry. New Hope for Alcoholics. New Hyde Park, NY: University Books; 1968: about 2 dozen references to A.A. throughout text; 252pp; ISBN: LC 68-18748.
Note: Lacks index.
The authors discuss LSD therapy for alcoholics as the central theme of their book. The authors have included Alcoholics Anonymous in their program and make clear their debt to "this great movement.".

1201. Horberg, Lawrence K., Ph.D./Schlesinger, Stephen E., Ph.D. Taking Charge: How Families Can Climb Out of the Chaos of Addiction and Flourish. First ed. New York, et al: Simon & Schuster, Inc./Fireside Book; 1988: pp210-223; 283pp; ISBN: 0-671-64261-8. LC 87-28643.
The authors give a brief overview of the A.A. program of recovery, the Twelve Steps, sponsorship, meetings, literature, etc. They recommend A.A. highly as the prototype of all other "self-help" groups.

1202. Hornik, Edith Lynn. "Alcoholics Anonymous". in: Hornik, Edith Lynn. The Drinking Woman. First ed. New York: Assocation Press; 1977: Chap. 12, pp137-143; & 9 other references to A.A.; 191 pp; ISBN: 0-8096-1909-1.
The author gives a brief overview of A.A. aimed specifically at women and discusses "Women Only" groups in A.A. and related topics.

1203. Hoskins, Ray. Rational Madness: The Paradox of Addiction. First ed. Blue Ridge Summit, PA: Tab Books, Inc.; 1989: AA: 45, 84, 142, 165, 167, 195, 216, 224, & 237.; 261pp; ISBN: 0-8306-8001-2. LC 88-38256.
Hoskins attempts to expand our understanding of addiction. AA is referenced 9 times.

1204. Howard, Peter. Frank Buchman's Secret. Garden City, NY: Doubleday; 1961.
Buchman was founder of the Oxford Group out of which AA grew and from which AA borrowed many of its spiritual principles. Although this biography does not mention alcoholism, it does explain Buchman's spiritual life.

1205. Hugh L. Finding A Sponsor. First ed. Center City, MN: Hazelden; October, 1989; 25pp.
Note: Pamphlet.
The author uses a fictitious narrative to illustrate the importance of a sponsor in A.A. and suggests criteria for choosing one.

1206. Hughes, Richard/Brewin, Robert. The Tranquilizing of America. Pill Popping and the American Way of Life. First ed. New York & London: Harcourt Brace Jovanovich; 1979: 13 references to A.A.; 326pp; ISBN: 0-15-191072-3.

1207. Hutchison, Ira W. Screwtape: Letters on Alcohol. First ed. Kansas City, MO: Sheed & Ward; 1992; 120pp; ISBN: 1-55612-565-8. LC 92-18606.
Note: pb.
Screwtape, the infamous senior devil created by C. S. Lewis, is revived in this collection of 33 instructional letters from him to Rotbranch, his novice devil on earth charged with corrupting human lives by way of alcohol addiction. "Those infernal AA maggots" are mentioned by Screwtape as the chief "Enemy." This is a joyous, satirical, serious, witty, ironic, funny, and spiritually-rich book.

1208. Jack O. Dealing with Depression in 12 Step Recovery. First ed. Seattle, WA: Glen Abbey Books; 1990: pp18-19, etc.; 63pp; ISBN: 0-934125-13-9. LC 90-14047.
Note: pb.
The anonymous author, a therapist and 12 Step member, discusses the types of depression many 12 Step members experience at one time or another in their recovery. He lists practical helps as well as prayers and meditations appropriate for depressed people. Sixteen personal stories illustrate and amplify the ways to recover from depression. The pamphlet, "The A.A. Member - Medications and Other Drugs, " is quoted concerning appropriate use of prescribed drugs.

1209. Jackson, Douglas. Stumbling Block: A Study of Alcohol and Christian Responsibility. Second ed. New York, NY: Editorial Dept. of Joint Sect. of Education and Cultivation of the Board of Missions of the Methodist Church; 1960: pp60-67, 123.; 128pp paperback; ISBN: LC 60-9819.
Basic information about A.A. is given and the clergy is advised to cooperate with A.A.

1210. James, William. The Varieties of Religious Experience: A Study in Human Nature. First ed. London, England, etc.: Longmans, Green, & Co.; June, 1902; 534pp.
Bill Wilson, Co-Founder of A.A., read this book and acknowledged its contribution to his thinking concerning spirituality. A.A.'s Wilson undoubtedly was influenced to some extent by James, an American pragmatist.

1211. Jellinek, E. M., Editor. Alcohol Addiction and Chronic Alcoholism. First ed. New Haven, CT/London: Yale University Press/Humphrey Milford, Oxford University Press; 1942: pp62-65 in Chap. I.; 336pp.
Note: Subject index, two bibliographies.
This epic scholarly study of alcoholism from Yale includes "Alcohol Addiction and Its Treatment" by Karl M. Bowman and E. M. Jellinek in which they discuss Alcoholics Anonymous. They term it "religious conversion ... without preaching" and state that A.A. "maintains that only an ex-addict can effectively establish transference with an alcohol addict.".

1212. Jones, Howard. Alcoholic Addiction. A Psycho-social Approach to Abnormal Drinking. First ed. London: Tavistock; 1963: pp14-5, 31-2, 59, 119, 173-5; 209 pp.
Jones is critical of the A.A. "allergy" concept, its "religious element," and replacing one addiction with addiction to A.A.

1213. Jones, L. "The Absence of the Black Professional and Semi-Professional in the Membership of Alcoholics Anonymous". in: Moran-Sackett, Marsha, compiler. Proceedings of the Eighth Annual Meeting of ALMACA, Detroit, Michigan, October 1-5, 1979. Association of Labor-Management Administrators and Consultants on Alcoholism, Inc. Arlington, VA.: ALMACA; 1980: pp416-431; 743 pp.

1214. Kant, Fritz. "Alcoholics Anonymous and The Twelve Steps". in: The Treatment of the Alcoholic. Springfield, IL: Charles C. Thomas; 1954.
This text, written by a physician for physicians, gives an overview of alcoholism treatment and the use of the A.A. program.

1215. Karpman, Benjamin, M.D. The Hangover. A Critical Study in the Psychodynamics of Alcoholism. First ed. Springfield, IL: Charles C. Thomas - Publisher; 1957: 15 references to A.A.; 531 pp; ISBN: LC 57-10994.
Note: This contains illustrations of each of the 14 subjects studied by Wesley R. Wilken.
The author, Chief Psychotherapist at St. Elizabeths Hospital, Washington, D. C., studied 14 alcoholics, most of whom had some level of contact with A.A.

1216. Katz, Stan J., Dr./Liu, Aimee E. The Codependency Conspiracy. First ed. New York: Warner Books; May, 1992: 50 references to AA & Twelve Steps.; 233pp; ISBN: 0-446-39377-0. LC 90-50532.
Note: index, pb.
The book is subtitled "How to Break the Recovery Habit and Take Charge of Your Life." The authors challenge the codependency theory and criticize "self-help methods that can actually promote dependency" but their charaterizations of AA display a misunderstanding of what AA is and is not. "The techniques I recommend in this chapter [9] do not require an Higher Power...prayer or humility..." Obviously, this is a rational humanism approach and many Fellowship members would find this spiritually bankrupt.

1217. Keller, John E. "Alcoholics Anonymous". in: Keller, John E. Ministering to Alcoholics. First ed. Minneapolis, MN: Augsburg Publishing House; 1966: Chap.3, pp35-66; other references to AA throughout.; 158pp; ISBN: LC 66-22560.
The author, a Lutheran chaplain, spent 8 years in Minnesota counseling alcoholics and giving seminars for other pastors about alcoholism. In addition to much standard information on A.A., Keller discusses in depth the 12 Steps of Recovery in A.A., especially the Fourth & Fifth Steps. He quotes Dr. Tiebout at length. Keller's insights into A.A., Christianity, and psychiatry are aimed at clergymen and therapists who need to understand these ideas in order to help the suffering alcoholic.

1218. Keller, John E. Drinking Problem? First ed. Philadelphia, PA: Fortress Press; 1971: pp36-41; 56pp; ISBN: 0-8006-0155-6.
Note: pb.
Keller gives a brief overview of A.A. and calls it "the most available resource in terms of long term help in continuous recovery.".

1219. Keller, John E. Let Go, Let God. First ed. Minneapolis, MN: Augsburg Pub. House; 1985: A.A. mentioned often; 127pp; ISBN: 0-8066-2162-1.
Note: pb.
Keller, a Lutheran minister, attempts to integrate clinical understandings and the Gospel with the A.A. philosophy.

1220. Kellerman, Joseph L. "Alcoholism: A Merry-Go-Round Named Denial". Center City, MN: Hazelden; 1973; ISBN: 0-89486-022-4.
This 18-page pamphlet is one of the all-time pamphlet best-sellers. AA is mentioned once as the "most widespread resource for the alcoholic.".

1221. Kennedy, Raymond J. H., S.J. Steps to Sobriety. The Priest-Counselor and The Excessive Drinker. First ed. New York: Joseph H. Wagner, Inc.; 1966: pp33-42 & 63-68, etc.; 80pp.
Note: pb.
Fr. Kennedy writes about the role of the priest in counseling alcoholics and strongly suggests referral to A.A. The introduction is by John C. Ford, S.J. Two chapters in the book are devoted entirely to A.A.

1222. Kent, Leona A. "Alcoholics Anonymous Training Groups-A Suggested Group Format To Be Used By the Para-Professional". in: Staub, George E./Kent, Leona A., Editors. The Para-Professional in the Treatment of Alcoholism. Springfield, IL: Charles C. Thomas - Publisher; 1973: pp130-157.

1223. Kent, Patricia. "Alcoholics Anonymous". in: Kent, Patricia. An American Woman and Alcohol. First ed. New York, Chicago & San Francisco: Holt, Rinehart & Winston; 1967: Chap. X, pp85-92, & other references to A.A. throughout the text.; 184 pp; ISBN: L.C. 66-22203.
The author attempts to point out "what A.A. has done for thousands of other women and girls and what it can do for you." She weighs all the negative reasons for not joining A.A. and lists all the postive reasons for A.A. membership.

1224. Kessel, Neil/Walton, Henry. Alcoholism. First ed. Baltimore, MD: Penguin Books; 1965: pp139-144, 153-156, & other references to A.A. in text; 192pp.
Note: pb.
The authors provide basic information on A.A. and cite several scholarly studies of various aspects of A.A.

1225. Kinney, J./Montgomery, M. "Psychotherapy and the Member of Alcoholics Anonymous". in: Galanter, M., Editor. Currents in Alcoholism. New York: Grune & Stratton; 1979: pp79-85; 345 pp. (v. Vol. 6, Treatment and Rehabilitation and Epidemiology.).

1226. Kinsey, Nina/Kinsey, Clyde E. Nineteen Years with an Alcoholic. First ed. New York: Vantage Press, Inc.; 1954: pp157, 166ff (AA); 208pp; ISBN: LC 54-11317.
This autobiography of a woman who lived 19 years with an alcoholic husband also includes his story. A Twelfth Step call on the husband by Alcoholics Anonymous members is portrayed. In the last section of the book, Clyde Kinsey reveals he is the author of The Little Green Book, a small volume about his experience with alcoholism.

1227. Kirkpatrick, Jean, Ph.D. A Fresh Start. First ed. Dubuque, Iowa/Toronto, Canada: Kendall/Hunt Pub. Co.; 1981: references to AA throughout.; 164pp.
Note: The trials and tribulations of the early years of Women for Sobriety, Inc., are told in this tribute to a friend. Kirkpatrick includes material on her relationship with A.A. and criticism of the A.A. approach.

1228. Kirkpatrick, Jean, Ph.D. Goodbye Hangovers, Hello Life. Self-Help for Women. First ed. New York: Atheneum; 1986: references to AA thoughout.; 250pp; ISBN: 0-689-11576-8.
Note: Lacks index.
Kirkpatrick, Executive Director for Women for Sobriety, Inc., "challenges some of the premises of Alcoholics Anonymous, an organization founded by and for men that she believes fails to address the specific needs of women." She was the founder of the first national program of recovery from alcoholism exclusively for women, Women for Sobriety. Discussion of Gay A.A. and lesbians is included.

1229. Knott, D. H. "AA and Alternatives". in: Robertson, J. J., editor. 4th AMA Conference: The Impaired Physician; Oct. 30-Nov. 1, 1980; Baltimore, MD: pp79-83; 173pp.
The dichotomy between medical and nonmedical treatment approaches for alcoholism is presented. Alcoholics Anonymous is discussed as both a philosophy and a treatment strategy, and alternatives to AA are discussed.

1230. Kornblith, A. B./Karlan, S. R. "Group Approaches to Drug Treatment Programs". in: Lowinson, J./Ruiz, P., editors. Substance Abuse: Clinical Problems and Perspectives. Baltimore, MD: Williams & Wilkins; 1981: pp449-464; 885pp.
Reference is made to Alcoholics Anonymous in a discussion of the function of peer groups and the social environment in these treatment approaches.

1231. Kurtz, Ernest, Ph.D. Shame and Guilt: Characteristics of the Dependency Cycle (An Historical Perspective for Professionals. First ed. Center City, MN: Hazelden; June, 1981; 57pp. (Professional Education; v. 7); ISBN: 0-89486-132-8.
Note: pb.
Kurtz discusses how guilt and shame can be recognized, confronted, and treated in the alcoholic in A.A. Throughout this booklet, the experience and philosophy of Alcoholics Anonymous play a central role in the discussion.

1232. Kurtz, Ernest. "Spiritual Rather Than Religious': The Contribution of Alcoholics Anonymous". in: Waahlberg, Ragnar B., editor. Prevention and Control/Realities and Aspirations: Volume II. Norway: National Directorate for the Prevention of Alcohol and Drug Problems; 1989: 678-686.
The essay examines nine topics that support AA's claim that it is spiritual and not religious. These issues are explained in their historic context.

1233. Lackey, Ivan. "Who Am I?" Asks the Alcoholic. First ed. Hicksville, New York: Exposition Press; 1975: AA throughout; 224pp; ISBN: 0-682-48199-8.
This is a study based on concepts, many of them directly from A.A., a recovering alcoholic heard, heeded and now teaches.

1234. Lang, Alan R./Kidorf, Michael. "Problem Drinking: Cognitive-Behavorial Strategies for Self-Control". in: Thase, Michael E., M.D./Edelstein, Barry A., M.D./Hersen, Michel, Ph.D., Editors. Handbook of Outpatient Treatment of Adults: Nonpsychotic Mental Disorders. First ed. New York: Plenum Press; 1990: AA pp417-431; 684pp; ISBN: LC 89-23242.
Note: index.
The authors review scientific studies of the problem drinker and conclude there are no easy answers about treatment. They criticize the lack of scientific studies of AA's success and its alleged "one-size-fits-all" approach.

1235. Langone, John. Bombed, Buzzed, Smashed or Sober. First ed. Boston, MA/Toronto, Canada: Little, Brown & Co.; 1976: pp135, 138, 144-48.; 212pp; ISBN: 0-316-51424-1. LC76-8490.
Note: Index, dj.
The author gives a brief description of A.A.

1236. Langone, John/Langone, Dolores deNobrega. Women Who Drink. First ed. Reading, MA et al: Addison-Wesley Pub. Co.; 1980: pp56, 129-31, 142-4, 148-51; 186pp; ISBN: 0-201-04354-8.
Note: NALGAP 348.
One of the main points the authors make is that AA does not welcome lesbian alcoholics because many AAs find it hard to face homosexuality.

1237. Lardner, Ring, Jr. The Lardners. My Family Remembered. First ed. New York et al: Harper & Row; 1976: pp165, 195; 371 pp.
A.A. is mentioned twice in discussion of Ring Lardner, the famous playwright, though he is not identified as a member but simply as an addicted drinker.

1238. Laundergan, J. Clark. "Posttreatment Alcoholics Anonymous Attendance and Treatment Outcome". in: Easy Does It. Alcoholism Treatment Outcomes, Hazelden and the Minnesota Model. First ed. np (Center City, MN): Hazelden; March 1982: ten references to A.A.; 183 pp; ISBN: 0-89486-119-0.
The author analyzes the effect of posttreatment and A.A. participation on alcohol use outcomes and what are the socio-demographic, treatment, and follow-up characteristics of alcoholics who affiliate with A.A. in contrast to non-affiliates.

1239. Lawrence, Frederick G., M.S.SS.T. "A Clergyman's Viewpoint". in: Bier, William C., S.J., Editor. Problems in Addiction: Alcohol and Drug Addiction. New York: Fordham University Press; 1962; The Pastoral Psychology Series, No. 2: pp127-132; 247 pp; ISBN: L.C. 62-16224.
This Catholic priest, Custodian of St. Joseph's Villa in Stirling, N.J., an in-patient long-term clinic treating clergymen who are victims of alcoholism, personally views the A.A. program as "nothing more than a Christian way of life." He calls A.A. "the best therapy existing today for assisting most active alcoholics to a maintained and a happy sobriety." After a female Catholic parishioner, an alcoholic, failed to sober up despite his best efforts using the Catholic sacraments, the pledge, prayer, counseling, etc., she joined A.A. and did sober up, inviting him to an A.A. meeting in Jan. 1946. Fr. Lawrence has been attending A.A. meetings ever since out of "gratitude.".

1240. Lawson, G./Peterson, J. S./Lawson, A. "Treatment Approaches to Alcoholism". in: Alcoholism and the Family: A Guide to Treatment & Prevention. Rockville, MD; 1983: Chap. 2, pp17-29; 296pp.
The authors review several widely recognized models of alcoholism treatment, beginning with Alcoholics Anonymous. "AA is the most widespread and utilized treatment approach in the field of alcoholism," they state. [Editor's note: AA itself would not define itself as "treatment."].

1241. Lawson, Gary W./Ellis, Dan C./Rivers, P. Clayton. Essentials of Chemical Dependency Counseling. First ed. Rockville, MD: Aspen Systems Corp.; 1984: 19 references to AA.; 227pp; ISBN: 0-89443-583-3. LC 83-26573.
Note: Index.
The authors believe AA is the "second best approach ... as a surrogate family" for the alcoholic to meet his interpersonal needs. They view AA favorably, although often in a secondary role for the patient.

1242. Leach, B. "A.A.: Its Effectiveness, Nature and Availability". in: Keller, M./Majchrowicz, M., Editors. Proceedings of the 28th International Congress on Alcohol & Alcoholism. New Brunswick, New Jersey: Rutgers Center of Alcohol Studies; 1968; 1.

1243. Leach, Barry. "Does Alcoholics Anonymous Really Work?". in: Bourne, P. G./Fox, R., Editors. Alcoholism: Progress in Research and Treatment. New York: Academic Press; 1973: pp245-284.

1244. Leach, Barry/Norris, John L. "Factors in the Development of Alcoholics Anonymous (A.A.)". in: Kissin, Benjamin/Begleiter, Henri, Editors. The Biology of Alcoholism. Treatment and Rehabilitation of the Chronic Alcoholic. New York & London: Plenum Press; 1977; Vol. 5: Chap. 11, pp441-543; 631pp; ISBN: 0-306-37115-4.
In this superlative article, Leach and Norris discuss in over 100 pages the growth and size of A.A., its development and structure, and evaluations of its effectiveness. This landmark article lists some 700 major references to A.A. in books, pamphlets, dissertations, popular articles, etc. Thirteen pages are devoted to "The Literature of A.A." This was the most extensive listing of written material about A.A. to that date. The article ends with a 24-page bibliography of A.A.

1245. Leake, Chauncey D., Dr., Ph.D./Silverman, Milton, Dr., Ph.D. Alcoholic Beverages in Clinical Medicine. First ed. Cleveland: The World Publishing Company; 1966: p.124; 160 pp; ISBN: L.C. 66-16681.
The authors state "the only satisfactory treatment for chronic alcoholism is intense and long-continued psychotherapy." They rank Alcoholics Anonymous, along with the Salvation Army and others, in a group of various psychotherapeutic techniques having not more than 20 to 25% of the patients abstaining from alcohol for an appreciable period.

1246. Lee, Essie E. Alcohol - Proof of What? First ed. New York: Julian Messner; 1976: pp60, 106, 169-172, 181.; 191 pp; ISBN: 0-671-32789-5.
Young people are the target audience of this book by Dr. Lee. A brief view of A.A. is given, buttressed by case histories of anonymous A.A. members.

1247. Lender, Mark Edward. "(Biographies of) Marty Mann, William Griffith Wilson (Bill W.), Robert Holbrook Smith, M.D.(Dr. Bob), and William Duncan Silkworth, M.D.". in: Lender, Mark Edward. Dictionary of American Temperance Biography: From Temperance Reform to Alcohol Research, the 1600s to the 1980s.: Mann, pp322-323; Smith, pp455-457; Wilson, pp526-527; & Silkworth, pp446-448.
Note: Excellent reference work.
Biographies of the Co-founders of A.A., Dr. Bob & Bill W.; Mann, who founded the National Council on Alcoholism and was its first executive director; and non-alcoholic Dr. Silkworth, who worked with thousands of alcoholics who came into A.A. and wrote extensively in the field.

1248. Lender, Mark Edward/Martin, James Kirby. Drinking in America. A History. First ed. New York & London: The Free Press & Collier Macmillan; 1982: pp182-184; 222 pp; ISBN: 0-02-918530-0.
The authors give a brief look at the A.A. essentials and compare it briefly to the Washingtonians and the Reform Clubs of earlier eras.

1249. Lennon, John/Carroll, John P. "AA Retreats for Priests". in: The Blue Book. Washington, D. C.: NCCA; 1979; 31: pp100-101; 101pp.
Lennon and Carroll argue that AA retreats can be very beneficial for priests. This article was part of the Proceedings of the 31st National Clergy Conference on Alcoholism, Omaha, Nebraska, May 22-26, 1979.

1250. Leonard, Linda Schierse. Witness to The Fire. Creativity & The Veil of Addiction. First paperback ed. Boston, MA/London: Shambhala Publications, Inc.; 1990: pp46, 57, 70, 73-4, 84, 88, 119 143, 213, 225, 227-9, 241, 247-9, 255, 309, 329-330 (AA).; 390pp; ISBN: 0-87773-588-3 (pb). LC 89-42634.
Note: Index, pb.
This book "spans the realms of Jungian psychology, existential philosophy, and literary analysis to explore the relationship between addiction and creativity. By examining the lives and works of writers such as Dostoevsky, Eugene O'Neill, Jack London, and Jean Rhys, as well as the experiences of people in recovery, Linda Leonard holds out the hope that anyone bound by addiction can reclaim the power that fuels dependency for a life of joy and creativity." The author endorses A.A. philosophy.

1251. Leslie, R. R. "A Pastoral Approach to the Use of the 12 Steps". in: Golding, P., editor. Alcoholism: Analysis of a World-Wide Problem. Lancaster: MTP Press Limited; 1983: Chap. 23, pp279-285.
"As a person, theologian and pastor I have not experienced conflict between the 12 Step programme and my own theology and pastoral care concepts. If I'm going to work with alcoholics and recovering chemically dependent people, I need to have journeyed in the 12 Step programme personally and professionally.".

1252. Levin, Jerome D., Ph.D. Treatment of Alcoholism and Other Addictions. A Self-Psychology Approach. First ed. Northvale, NJ/London: Jason Aronson, Inc.; 1987: A.A. is discussed in over 100 pages.; 433pp; ISBN: 0-87668-947-0. LC 87-19563.
Note: Index, dj.
This book emphasizes "the self psychology developed by Heinz Kohut and his followers. This is a developmental view that considers alcoholism a disorder of the self - a form of self-pathology, the essential characteristic being compulsiveness. The disorder is seen in terms of ego and self-deficits stemming from failures in internalization of the functions performed by the idealized self-object. A regression to, or a fixation at, pathological narcissism results. The addict attempts to self-medicate this deficit so as not to appear dependent on others. This accounts for the dependency conflicts that are so evident in alcoholics and other addicts. What must be internalized is not alcohol but the capacity to perform the functions of alcohol. This process of replacement is the thrust of therapy." Aimed at psychotherapists and counselors who treat alcoholism, Levin advises them that A.A. "remains the best single bet for achieving and maintaining sobriety for most alcoholics." He

urges professionals to read basic A.A. literature, attend and experience A.A. open meetings and almost always make referrals to A.A. for all active alcoholics.

1253. "Liberated Woman". in: The Way Back. Washington, D.C.: The Whitman-Walker Clinic; 1982: pp65-74.
A Jewish woman tells about her period of liberation - as a lesbian and as a woman - after joining AA. (NALGAP 364).

1254. Liebelt, Robert A., Ph.D., M.D. Let's Talk About Alcoholism. First ed. Colorado Springs, CO: Platte River Press; 1989; 247pp; ISBN: 0-926719-00-9.
Note: pb.
Dr. Liebelt, Director of Ignatia Hall at St. Thomas Hospital in Akron, Ohio, has since 1982 explained to newly-admitted alcoholic patients the medical aspects of alcoholism in a wide-ranging chalk talk. He expresses his gratitude to the "many members of A.A. who visit our center regularly." AA is discussed throughout.

1255. Lindley, Doyle F./Dorris, Robert T. Am I Drinking Too Much? First ed. Malibu, CA: A. A. World Library (not affiliated with Alcoholics Anonymous); 1970: pp 111-6; 129pp.
Note: paperback 122.
The authors give a brief overview of A.A. and recommend it as the "most effective organization.".

1256. Linn, Robert, Dr. You Can Drink and Stay Healthy. First ed. New York, London, Toronto, Sydney: Franklin Watts; 1979: 4 references to A.A.; 193 pp; ISBN: L.C. 79-20887.

1257. Lovell, Harold W., M.D. "Alcoholics Anonymous". in: Lovell, Harold W., M.D. Hope and Help for the Alcoholic. New York: Doubleday; 1951: Chap. 8, pp121-145; 215 pp.
This psychiatrist gives an analysis of the A.A. program in theory and practice, the importance of Twelfth Step work, Bill W's story, and an overview of the A.A. program. "The reasons for A.A.'s success with alcoholics may be summed up in two short sentences. A.A. returns the alcoholic to a more sober - some might say a more normal - way of life. A.A. gives him a substitute for drinking.".

1258. Luks, Alan. Will America Sober Up? First ed. Boston: Beacon Press; 1983: nine references to A.A.; pp72-3, 81-3, etc.; 212 pp; ISBN: 0-8070-2154-7.

1259. Mac. A cup of butterflies & birdsongs. First ed. Minneapolis, MN: CompCare Publishers; 1976; 96pp; ISBN: LC 76-55450.
Note: pb.
This little booklet of poetry and drawings covers a wide range of A.A. related topics. A.A. is not mentioned directly but the subjects include spirituality, resentments, gratitude, humility, serenity, etc.

1260. Mack, John E. "Alcoholism, A.A., and the Governance of the Self". in: Bean, M. H./Zinberg, N. E., Editors. Dynamic Approaches to the Understanding and Treatment of Alcoholism. New York: Free Press; 1981: pp128-162; 214pp.
This extensive, exploratory essay discusses the psychosocial concept of self-governance which may affect the decision to take the initial drink of alcohol. Mack examines A.A.'s approach which he says includes psychological, biological, social and spiritual elements that comprise self-governance. This article is worthy of consideration.

1261. Mackay, Marianne. Prisms. First paperback ed. New York: Fawcett Crest-Ballatine Books; August, 1983; 341pp; ISBN: 0-449-20172-4. LC 80-42415.
Note: pb.
This novel focuses on a woman's struggle with alcoholism and ends with a Twelfth Step call. The book is dedicated "For men and women who share their experience, strength and hope." A.A. concepts, phrases, etc. are part of the story, especially at the end.

1262. MacKenzie, David/MacKenzie, Elsie/Spring, Beth [with]. Still Married, Still Sober. Hope for Your Alcoholic Marriage. First ed. Downers Grove, Il: InterVarsity Press; 1991: AA references througout.; 178pp; ISBN: 0-8308-1376-4. LC 91-21963.
Note: PB.
The MacKenzies offer solid, hard-won, first hand counsel on confronting the alcoholic, rebuilding the damaged marriage and lessening the pain for children. Their Christian conversions highlight the book. AA is discussed often; unfortunately, David breaks his anonymity, revealing his membership in AA.

1263. Madsen, William. "A.A.: Birds of a Feather". in: The American Alcoholic. The Nature-Nurture Controversy in Alcoholic Research and Therapy. Springfield, IL: Charles C. Thomas - Publisher; 1974: Chap. IX, pp154-197; & over 100 other references to AA.; 248pp; ISBN: 0-398-02726-1.
The book is dedicated to Jellinek and Bill Wilson. The author, in the above last chapter, analyzes the "success of Alcoholics Anonymous as compared to the inadequacies of the other available therapies." He calls A.A. a "form of folk psychotherapy relying solely on direct evidence given by its members in shared experiences.".

1264. Madsen, William. "Alcoholics Anonymous as a Crisis Cult". in: Marshall, M., Editor. Beliefs, Behaviors, and Alcoholic Beverages: A Cross-Cultural Survey. Ann Arbor: University of Michigan Press; 1979: pp382-388; 490 pp.

1265. Madsen, William, Ph.D. Defending the Disease of Alcoholism. From Facts to Fingarette. Second Printing ed. Akron, OH: Wilson, Brown & Co.; Oct. 1988: pp26-32; 33pp spiral-bound 8 1/2 x 11".
Madsen, a University of California Anthropology Professor, rebutes the latest attack on the medical model of alcoholism as a disease by Professor Herbert Fingarette. Madsen points out that A.A. has been and continues to be the mainstay of alcoholism treatment and not Antabuse as Fingarette falsely asserts. Madsen lists many misconceptions of A.A. from Fingarette and then sets the record straight.

1266. Malikkin, David. "My Name is Joe and I Am An Alcoholic". in: Social Disability: Alcoholism, Drug Addiction, Crime and Social Disadvantage. New York: New York University Press; 1973: pp31-39.
Joe relates his alcoholic drinking and sobriety in A.A. "In A.A. we say the best way to maintain sobriety is by helping other alcoholics. This contact with other drinkers makes you reflect on your own life. You see yourself in them, and it becomes a constant reminder that you mustn't take another drink.".

1267. Mann, Marty. "Alcoholics Anonymous". in: Mann, Marty. Marty Mann Answers Your Questions about Drinking and Alcoholism. New York: Holt, Rinehart & Winston; 1970: Chap. 13, pp95-105; 113 pp; ISBN: 03-081857-5.
Mann outlines what A.A. is and is not: meetings, sponsorship, the Twelve Steps, and other basics.

1268. Mann, Marty. New Primer on Alcoholism: How People Drink, How to Recognize Alcoholics, and What To Do About Them. New, Updated Revision ed. New York: Holt, Rinehart & Winston; 1981; 239pp.
Note: Many A.A. references.
Mann, a recovered alcoholic, was one of the first 100 members of A.A. She became the executive director of the National Council on Alcoholism and was its founder. Alcoholism is defined as a progressive disease characterized by uncontrollable drinking. No "cure" is available. The beginnings of recovery programs are outlined: Courtenay Baylor in the Emmanuel movement in Boston; Richard Peabody; and Francis Chambers; all in the early 1930s, all lay therapists. Charles Durfee's farm and its recoveries are cited. The conditioned-reflex theory was applied at the Shadel Sanitarium, Oregon, and the principles of the Oxford Group as portrayed in the book, The Big Bender. Mann then describes the formation of A.A. in 1935.
Working closely with A.A. is one of the goals of the NCA. Mann describes A.A.'s functions. One of the all-time popular best-sellers on alcoholism, Mann's contributions in the field of alcoholism are legendary.

1269. Mann, Marty. Primer on Alcoholism. First ed. New York-Toronto: Rinehart & Co., Inc.; 1950: Chap. 13, pp145-169; 216pp.
Note: Reprinted in 1958, 1978, 1981, etc.
Written to reach the widest-possible audience, the 20 millions friends, family, and employers of America's then estimated 4 million alcoholics, Mann's book is an excellent simple overview of the problem of alcoholism and its solution, part of which is Alcoholics Anonymous, Chap. 13 in the book. Mann reviews for the nonalcoholic public what A.A. is and is not, its spiritual program of recovery based on the 12 Steps, and how to reach A.A. The book was and remains one of the classic best-sellers in the literature of alcoholism. A second edition, A New Primer on Alcoholism, was enlarged by her later on. In 1944, she helped found and became the first Executive Director of the National Committee on Alcoholism.

1270. Mann, Marty. "Public Education and Alcoholics Anonymous". in: You and Alcohol. New York: Columbia Broadcasting System; Dec. 24, 1946: pp14-17; 33pp. (You and Alcohol; v. Program VI of XIV radio broadcasts.).
Note: 8.5 x 11" booklet.
Mrs. Marty Mann, Executive Director of the National Committee for Education on Alcoholism, acknowledges that role and also identifies herself as an alcoholic. "Within the closely-knit voluntary fellowship that is Alcoholics, men and women from all walks of life have found freedom together..." she said. In 1946, AA membership was 30,000, she reported. This series of CBS radio broadcasts on successive Tuesday night at 6:15 o'clock EST ran from Nov. 12, 1946, through Feb. 11, 1947.

1271. Marlin, Emily. Relationships in Recovery. Healing Strategies for Couples and Families. First ed. New York: Harper & Row; 1990: Almost 40 references to AA.; 260pp; ISBN: 0-06-096436-7. LC 89-45687.
Note: Index, pb.
This book focuses on healing relationships after sobriety. AA and Fellowship basic concepts are mentioned throughout favorably.

1272. Marshall, Shelly. Young, Sober & Free. First ed. Center City, MN: Hazelden; 1978: (AA throughout); 137pp; ISBN: 0-89486-055-0. LC 78-060061.
Note: pb.
Marshall compiled this volume of stories by fourteen young men and women who were alcoholics or drug addicts. Information and personal experiences about A.A. is contained throughout the stories.

1273. Martin, Joseph C., Fr. "First Things First: The A.A. Way". in: Martin, Joseph C., Fr. No Laughing Matter: Chalk Talks on Alcohol. First ed. San Francisco: Harper & Row; 1982: Chap. 5, pp40-48; 165 pp; ISBN: 0-06-065440-6.
The major points of A.A. recovery are covered, including the Steps and Traditions. This book is based on the author's lecture series on the treatment of alcoholism which is A.A.-oriented.

1274. Mary M. "Choices". Center City, MN: Hazelden; Nov., 1984; ISBN: 0-89486-248-0.
This 17-page pamphlet includes discussion of the first three steps of AA.

1275. Maultsby, Maxie C., Jr., M.D. A Million Dollars For Your Hangover. The Illustrated Guide for the New Self-Help Alcoholic Treatment Method. First ed. Lexington, KY: Rational Self-Help Books; 1978: pp 4-6 (AA).; 240pp; ISBN: 0-932838-00-6. LC 78-27736.
Note: Illustrated by Hank Chapman. Index, dj.
The author acknowledges his "Rational Behavior Therapy & Rational Self-Counseling" for alcoholics is indebted to the "Rational Emotive Therapy" of Albert Ellis, Ph.D. He states his self-help approach to alcoholism is necessary because professional methods and Alcoholics Anonymous treat only 15 per cent of the alcoholic population with the rest remaining unrecovered. He believes the individual does not have a problem with alcoholism but with habitual problem drinking. Practice of new mental processes is the answer, he says, and the individual himself is the primary agent in his own recovery. Those ideas conflict with A.A.'s Twelve Steps, spirituality and ideology.

1276. Maxwell, Milton A. "Alcoholics Anonymous: An Interpretation". in: Pittman, D.J./Snyder, C. R., Editors. Society, Culture and Drinking Patterns. New York: John Wiley & Sons; 1962: Chap. 33, pp577-585.
This sociologist explains the success of A.A. and also why the "A.A. recovery program has remained an unknown quantity to many, and at least something of an enigma to most." The conditions for change, the Higher Power concept, the Twelve Steps, personality changes, the A.A. group and its subculture are discussed.

1277. Maxwell, Milton A. "Alcoholics Anonymous". in: Gomberg, E. L./White, H. R./Carpenter, J. A., Editors. Alcohol, Science and Society Revisited. Ann Arbor, MI/New Brunswick, NJ: University of Michigan Press/Rutgers Center of Alcohol Studies; 1982: pp295-305; 440 pp.
Author looks at A.A. as "we enter the 1980s." Growth of A.A., factors in A.A.'s own survey, and importance of A.A.'s "Three Legacies" of Unity, Service and Recovery are discussed.

1278. Maxwell, Milton. "An Exploratory Study: Alcoholics Anonymous and Professional Relations". ?; 1964 [1972].
In section 4, Maxwell describes "AA-clergy attitudes and Relationships.".

1279. Maxwell, Milton. "Understand and Relating to Alcoholics Anonymous". in: Staub, George E./Kent, Leona M., Editors. The Para-Professional in the Treatment of Alcoholism. Springfield, IL: Charles C. Thomas - Publisher; 1973: pp106-114.

1280. Maxwell, Ruth. Breakthrough. What To Do When Alcoholism or Chemical Dependency Hits Close To Home. First ed. New York: Ballantine Books; 1986: pp 11, 172-3, 183-6, 223, 237-40.; 281 pp; ISBN: 0-345-31956-7.
Maxwell discusses the importance of the Fifth Step especially. She is critical of professionals in the field of therapy who downplay or reject A.A.'s spiritual approach to life.

1281. May, Gerald G., M.D. Addiction and Grace. 8th printing ed. San Francisco, CA: Harper & Row; 1988: pp8, 48, 90, 156, 164, 172, 178.; 200pp; ISBN: 0-06-065536-4. LC 88-45147.
Note: Index, dj.
May believes addiction is an attempt to assert complete control over our lives and is necessarily doomed. It is only with God's help, our surrendering to grace, that we come to terms with ourselves and live in harmony with the world. The nature of addiction is explored in its qualities, psychology, neurology, and theology. A.A. is referred to positively.

1282. McCann, Peter. "The Use of Alcoholics Anonymous Principles and Membership in a Residential Treatment Clinic". in: Waahlberg, Ragnar B., editor. Prevention and Control-Realities and Aspirations: Volume III. Norway: National Directorate for the Prevention of Alcohol and Drug Problems; 1989: pp92-101.
McCann argues that "Incorporating AA principles into the multi-disciplinary approach of the specialized alcoholism treatment unit ensures attention to the spiritual dimension of wholeness but also permits the individual to discover pathways he must travel to achieve this healing.".

1283. McCarthy, R. G. "The Fellowship of Alcoholics Anonymous". in: McCarthy, R. G., Editor. Alcohol Education for Classroom and Community. New York: McGraw-Hill Book Co.; 1964: pp226-234.

1284. McCarthy, Raymond G./Douglass, Edgar M. Alcohol and Social Responsibility. First ed. New York: Thomas Y. Crowell Co. & Yale Plan Clinic; December,1949: ten references to AA.; 304 pp.
Note: McCarthy was Executive Director of the Yale Plan Clinic.

1285. McCarthy, Raymond G. Drinking and Intoxication. New Haven, CT/Glencoe, IL: Yale Center of Alcohol Studies & The Free Press; 1959: 4 references to AA.; 455 pp; ISBN: L.C. 59-5289.

1286. McCormick, Patrick, C.M. Sin as Addiction. First Review ed. New York/Mahwah, NJ: Paulist Press; 1989; 200pp; ISBN: 0-8091-3064-5. LC 89-3020.
Note: pb.
"McCormick explores six models for understanding human sinfulness." In the chapter on sin as addiction, he lauds the layman's approach of Alcoholics Anonymous and the modern disease concept of alcoholism.

1287. McCormick, Robert. Facing Alcoholism. First ed. San Diego, CA: Oak Tree Publications, Inc.; 1982: references to AA throughout.; 231pp; ISBN: 0-916392-83-X.
Note: lacks index.
The author, a former NBC-TV News Correspondent, breaks his anonymity.

1288. McDougall, M. T. The Daiquiri Tree. First ed. San Diego, CA: Joseph Tabler Books; 1993; 208pp; ISBN: 0-9610330-7-X. LC 93-060799.
Note: pb.
This "Higher Power Novel" is the story of one woman's recovery through the AA program. The author is a registered nurse and has been sober for over 35 years.

1289. McElrath, Damian, Ph.D. Hazelden. A Spiritual Odyssey. First ed. Center City, MN: Hazelden; September, 1987: 40+ references to AA.; 175pp; ISBN: 0-89486-451-3.
Note: Quarto. Illustrated.
This fine history of Hazelden, the premier "Minnesota Model" of rehabilitation from alcoholism, includes much A.A. history also. Bill W., the Chicago Fellowship, Dr. Bob, the "2218" clubhouse, and other historical data about A.A. is interwoven with the story of the founding, growth, and expansion of this facility.

1290. McElrath, Damian, Ph.D. Roses of Dia Linn. A Celebration of 25 Years. First ed. Center City, MN: Hazelden; May, 1981; 18 pp; ISBN: 0-89486-134-4.
One of the first treatment facilities established for women, the farm Dia Linn opened in 1956 in Minnesota. The author relates the heart of recovery there "would always remain the simple A.A. formula: two alcoholics talking to one another over a cup of coffee." A.A. meetings, the Fifth Step, and specific problems of female alcoholics are discussed in this anniverseary booklet.

1291. McInerney, James. "Alcoholics Anonymous Members as Alcoholism Counselors". in: Staub, George E./Kent, Leona M., Editors. The Para-Professional in the Treatment of Alcoholism. Springfield, IL: Charles C. Thomas; 1973: pp91-105.

1292. McKinley, Edward H. Marching to Glory. The History of the Salvation Army in the United States, 1880-1980. First ed. San Francisco: Harper & Row, Publishers; 1980: pp177, 188; 286 pp; ISBN: 0-06-65538-0.
McKinley cites A.A. at Hofman's Cleveland SA Center in 1956 reaching a peak of 114 AA "Anniversaries," one year without a drink.

1293. McNulty, John, Rt. Rev. Msgr. "The Spiritual and Medical Aspects of Alcoholics Anonymous in New Jersey". in: Pfau, et al. Alcoholism: A Source Book for the Priest. Indianapolis: NCCA; 1960: pp431-443; 685 pp.
McNulty, President, Seton Hall University, South Orange, N.J., discusses the early history of AA in New Jersey, citing the influence of Dr. William D. Silkworth of Knickerbocker Hospital in New York where doctors and nurses from New Jersey received training in alcoholism treatment and AA methods and philosophy. He states that in New Jersey they still use the five-day pattern of Silkworth, having tried and rejected Antabuse and tranquillizers. "You walk out at the end of the fifth day. And there is an AA hanging onto your shoulder," he relates. Retreats for AA members, pastoral ultimatums for alcoholic priests, and sponsorship are also discussed.

1294. McTimoney, D. C./Campbell, E. S./Cooper, R. H. "Factors Influencing A.A. and Treatment Outcome: A Descriptive Paper". in: 2nd Annual Meeting of the Special Interest Group on Program Evaluation, Canadian Addiction Foundation; Sept. 8-9, 1982; Regina, Canada: pp68-89; 184pp.
The results of a times series evaluation of alcoholic clients treated at the Alcoholism & Drugs Dependency Commision of New Brunswick, Canada, facilities to determine whether there are differences between clients who affiliated with Alcoholics Anonymous and those who do not join AA. Clients were interviewed at baseline, 3, 6, & 12 months. It was found that: (1) at 12 months, a higher proportion (56%) of AA affiliates were married, and better than one-half reported active religious participation, compared to 16% of non-AA's; (2) a higher proportion of AA's than non-AA's reported a job was their major means of financial support; (3) at baseline, one-third of AA's reported having a job, while one-half reported having a job at 12 months; (4) drinking every day declined over time for both groups, with AA's reporting a smaller proportion of daily drinkers (10%) than did the non-AA's (21%); although drug use declined over time for both groups, a higher proportion of AA's continue to use drugs other than alcohol. In summary, this study obviously makes the point it's better to be in AA than not.

1295. a member of A.A. "I am an Alcoholic - This is My Story". in: D'Alonzo, C. Anthony. The Drinking Problem - and its Control. Houston: Gulf Pub. Co.; 1959: Appendix I, pp99-116.
This is a personal witness account by a member of A.A.

1296. "Members of Alcoholics Anonymous". in: Wholey, Dennis, Editor/Interviewer. The Courage to Change. Hope and Help for Alcoholics and Their Families. First ed. Boston: Houghton Mifflin Company; 1984: Chap. 12, pp245-283; & numerous other references.; 309pp; ISBN: 0-395-35977-5.
Wholey, the host of the PBS television series LateNight America, interviewed a who's who of alcoholics in Hollywood, politics, and many other fields, including 19 essays by members of A.A. This best-seller graphically portrays their stories of drinking, quitting and "now the happiness," much of it based on A.A.

1297. Mendelson, Jack H., M.D./Mello, Nancy K., Ph. D. Alcohol Use and Abuse in America. First ed. Boston, Toronto: Little, Brown & Co.; 1985: 11 references to A.A.; 395 pp; ISBN: 0-316-56663-2.
Contains brief history, philosophy, membership and the 12 Steps.

1298. Merrill, T. A. "Plugging TA into AA Philosophy". in: Blakeney, R. N., Editor. Current Issues in Transactional Analysis: The First International Transactional Analysis Assn. European Conference. New York: Brunner, Mazel; 1977: pp158-161; 193 pp.

1299. Meryman, Richard. Broken Promises, Mended Dreams. First ed. Boston & Toronto: Little, Brown and Company; 1984: A.A. throughout.; 351pp; ISBN: 0-316-56784-1.
The author describes the special problems of a woman alcoholic, Abby Andrews. He based much of this true book on extensive interviews with 20 women in A.A. and on attendance at A.A. meetings.

1300. Metzger, Lawrence. From Denial to Recovery. Counseling Problem Drinkers, Alcoholics and Their Families. First ed. San Francisco/London: Jossey-Bass Publishers; 1988: over 70 references to A.A.; 307 pp; ISBN: 1-55542-063-X.

1301. Meulen, Arnold J. Vander. Skid Row Life Line. The Story of the Haven of Rest Mission, Grand Rapids, Michigan. First ed. Grand Rapids, MI: Zondervan Pub. House; 1956: pp35, 82; 96pp.
Note: Illus. with photos, dj.
The author was an alcoholic, dope addict and criminal. He was saved by Christ and founded this and other missions for the skid row people. He states "what AA...jail...society...medicine couldn't do, Christ did that night.".

1302. Meyer, Lewis. Off the Sauce. First ed. Garden City, NY: Doubleday & Co., Inc.; 1967; 166 pp; ISBN: L.C. 67-12875.
Meyer, a member of A.A. for 19 years, broke his anonymity consciously to write his autobiography. "This book is my love song to Alcoholics Anonymous," he wrote and felt identifying himself as an A.A. member would help more people.

1303. Michael, John (pseudonym). Sober, Clean & Gay! First ed. Minneapolis, MN: CompCare Publishers; 1977; 19pp; ISBN: 0-89638-028-9.
Note: Pamphlet.
A.A. is a part of this sober alcoholic gay's story.

1304. Milam, James R., Ph.D. The Emergent Comprehensive Concept of Alcoholism. 8th printing, revised ed. Kirkland, WA: Alcoholism Center Associates Press, Inc.; 1977; c1970: pp54.; 70pp.
Note: Softbound 8 1/2 x 11".
This discussion of the concept of alcoholism as a disease pays tribute to "Alcoholics Anonymous, the fountainhead of the reform movement in alcoholism." He sugggests that "although AA is not a religion, one is reminded of the early Crypto-Christians nurturing their faith and transcending and surviving their oppressors by protective anonymity in caves and catacombs.".

1305. Milam, James R., Ph.D./Ketcham, Katherine. Under the Influence. A Guide to the Myths and Realities of Alcoholism. First paperback ed. Toronto, New York, et al: Bantam Books; 1983: 15 references to AA.; 237 pp; ISBN: 0-553-23788-8.
Note: The first edition was published in hardback by Madrona Publishers in October, 1981.
The authors state that "A.A. is the best program in existence for helping alcoholics to stay sober, but it is not a particularly effective vehicle for getting the alcoholic sober in the first place." That and other misconceptions and mis-interpretations of A.A. concepts are spread throughout this volume. The authors credit A.A. for much but criticize it for much more, all the while promoting their own "most important breakthrough in alcoholism since the founding of A.A. in 1935" as the front cover of the book shouts.

1306. Miller, J. P. Days of Wine and Roses. New York: Dramatists Play Service, Inc.; 1973; 52pp.
This play in three acts was adapted to the stage by J. P. Miller from his original television play. A.A. is mentioned in several scenes along with the Big Book and an AA meeting. Of course, it was also made into a major award-winning movie. A main character, Joe, gets sober in AA.

1307. Milt, Harry. "Alcoholics Anonymous". in: Milt, Harry. Basic Handbook on Alcoholism. First ed. Fair Haven, NJ: Scientific Aids Publications; 1967: pp71-74; 95 pp.
Note: Reprinted & Revised Editions published in 1969, 1972, 1976.
Milt recommends A.A. highly in Chapter 11: "There is no longer any question that Alcoholics Anonymous has been responsible for the sobriety of more alcoholics than any other method --- social, religious or medical.".

1308. "Module 14: Alcoholics Anonymous". in: Resource Manual: Chemical Dependency Intervention Course. Manitoba, Winnipeg, Canada: Alcoholism Foundation of Manitoba, Winnipeg, Canada; 1980s (?): pp271-278; 298pp.
The purpose of this module is to acquaint participants in the Chemical Dependency Intervention Course with the resources of Alcoholics Anonymous. The Twelve Steps are listed.

1309. Molloy, J. Paul. Self-Run, Self-Supported (Oxford) Houses for More Effective Recovery from Alcohol and Drug Addiction. Craft, Edwin M./Vischi, Thomas R., Editors. First ed. Washington, DC: ADAMHA; 1990; 130pp; ISBN: DHHS Pub. No. (ADM) 90-1678.
Note: Photos, large pb.
Oxford House, Inc., is a self-run, self-supporting halfway house organization for alcoholics and drug addicts. Starting up costs come from a federal-state loan and a house is rented where alcoholics and drug addicts can live and work in a sober environment. Attendance at A.A. and N.A. meetings on a regular basis is required and use of alcohol or drugs merits expulsion from the house. Oxford House residents attend an average of 6 AA or NA meetings a week and cooperate fully with those Fellowships. The first 43 pages are a technical assistance manual. Eight appendixes include a 1988 profile of Oxford House residents and the Oxford House Manual (see separate listing). Molloy lived 2 1/2 years in Oxford Houses in 1977 in the Washington, D.C., area. In 1990, there were over 150 Oxford Houses in the U.S.

1310. Monroe, Margaret E./Stewart, Jean. Alcohol Education for the Layman. A Bibliography. First ed. New Brunswick, NJ: Rutgers University Press; 1959: pp105-110; 166pp; ISBN: LC 59-7512.
The bibliography contains 15 A.A. books and pamphlets with numerous other A.A. references throughout.

1311. Mooney, Al J., M.D./Eisenberg, Arlene/Eisenberg, Howard. The Recovery Book. First ed. New York: Workman Pub.; 1992: Chaps. 6-7, pp97-143.; 597pp; ISBN: 1-56305-084-6. LC 92-50284.
Note: index, pb.
This is a "recovery dictionary" and the authors devote two chapters to AA. After outlining the Fellowship basics, they discuss "AA: The Facts and Your Feelings," an attempt to defuse "AA-phobia," the feelings, fears, and rationalizations on why you shouldn't attend AA.

1312. Moran, Megan [pseudonym]. Lost Years: Confessions of a Woman Alcoholic. First ed. Garden City, NY: Doubleday & Co., Inc.; 1985; 253pp; ISBN: ISBN 0-385-19293-2. LC 84-18850.
This female writer and editor began her alcoholic career at age 15. This autobiography, written under a pseudonym, chronicles her early family life, including an alcoholic father, drinking in college and as part of her professional life, her introduction to A.A. by a priest, and her recovery from the disease through A.A.

1313. Mowrer, O. Hobart. The New Group Therapy. First ed. Princeton, NJ, et al: Van Nostrand Insight Books; 1964: pp100-103; 262pp.
Note: pb.
Mowrer, a Psychology Research Professor at the University of Illinois, quotes an AA Grapevine article from October, 1962, by "WLG" about sharing characters defects with another person. His discussion of "How Open Should Openness Be?" in group therapy lauds the AA position.

1314. Mueller, L. Ann, M.D./Ketcham, Katherine. Recovering: How To Get and Stay Sober. First ed. Toronto, et al: Bantam Books; May, 1987: AA: Chap. 14 & 15+ other references.; 303pp; ISBN: 0-553-34303-3. LC 86-32088.
Note: Index, pb.
The Diary of Jennifer Chase [pseudonym], chap. 14, is the story of her 28-day treatment center stay and includes many comments on her introduction to AA and the 12 steps.

1315. Mullan, Hugh, M.D./Sangiuliano, Iris, Ph.D. Alcoholism: Group Psychotherapy and Rehabilitation. First ed. Springfield, IL: Charles C. Thomas, Publisher; 1966: pp5, 14-15, 22, 25-34, 57, 129-130 (AA).; 325pp; ISBN: LC 65-25743.
Note: Index.
The authors discuss group psychotherapy and rehabilitation for the alcoholic. Alcoholics Anonymous and group psychotherapy are compared and some minor misunderstandings of A.A. are evident. Nonetheless, the authors recommend to social workers that even "emergency" patients should be referred to A.A. They are entirely sympathetic to the Fellowship.

1316. Mumey, Jack. "The Fellowship Experience: AA Revisited". in: Mumey, Jack. The Joy of Being Sober. First ed. Chicago: Contemporary Books, Inc.; 1984: Chap. 11, pp111-122; plus other references to A.A. throughout text.; 214 pp; ISBN: 0-8092-5433-6.
The various types of A.A. meetings are discussed. The author hopes his guide to A.A. meeting types will help the reader to choose the A.A. meeting that best suits them.

1317. Mumey, Jack. Sitting in the Bay Window. First ed. Chicago: Contemporary Books, Inc.; 1984: 18 references to A.A.; 198 pp; ISBN: 0-8092-5418-2.
The author has written this book for parents of young alcoholics and most of the references to A.A. detail the different types of meetings available: closed, open, speaker's, step, discussion, couple groups and singles.

1318. Mumey, Jack. Young Alcoholics. A Book for Parents. Second ed. Chicago/New York: Contemporary Books, Inc.; 1984: AA: pp114-117, etc.; 198pp; ISBN: 0-8092-4852-2. LC 84-17010.
Note: Previously published under the title Sitting in the Bay Window. index, pb.
Mumey recommends AA to young people and provides basic information about the Fellowship for parents whose children are alcoholic.

1319. a Municipal Court Judge. "History of Alcoholics Anonymous". in: Pfau, et al. Alcoholism: A Source Book for the Priest. Indianapolis: NCAA; 1960: pp389-393; 685 pp.
An anonymous judge recounts his first AA meeting in 1940 at the Akron, Ohio, home of T. Henry Williams, an early non-alcoholic friend of AA. Dr. Bob and Bill W., co-founders of AA, and their early efforts from 1935 to 1940 to work with other alcoholics are discussed. The AA author concludes that AA is a "back-to-God movement, and is fundamentally Catholic throughout.".

1320. "My Name is Joe, and I Am An Alcoholic". in: Malikin, David, Editor. Social Disability. Alcoholism, Drug Addiction, Crime and Social Disadvantage. First ed. New York: New York University Press; 1973: Chap. III, pp31-39; 266 pp; ISBN: 0-8147-5361-2.
Joe anonymously relates the story of his alcoholic life and entry into A.A.

1321. Nadel, M./Petropoulos, A. W./Feroe, N. "Alcoholism Treatment Resources: Which One When?". in: Cook, et al, eds. Social Work Treatment of Alcohol Problems. New Brunswick, NJ: Rutgers Center of Alcohol Studies; 1983: pp1-15; 153pp.
Alcoholics Anonymous basics are discussed.

1322. Nelson, James Douglas, Dr. Awakening: Restoring Health Through the Spiritual Principles of Shalom, Jesus and the Twelve Step Recovery Program. First ed. Blue Ridge Summit, PA: Tab Books, Inc.; 1989; 136pp paperback; ISBN: 0-8306-9000-X.
Nelson, a minister, connects today's quest for spiritual healing to its Judeo-Christian roots and more recently to the Alcoholics Anonymous program of recovery through its Twelve Steps. A.A. and its Twelve Steps principles are discussed throughout.

1323. Nero, Jack. If Only My Wife Could Drink Like a Lady. Second ed. Minneapolis, MN: CompCare Publishers; 1982; 285pp; ISBN: 0-89638-052-1. LC 81-22166.
Note: pb.
Originally published in 1977 under the title, Drink Like a Lady, Cry Like a Man, this is the story of an alcoholic marriage. Maggie, the alcoholic, and Jack, her non-alcoholic husband, both recover through A.A. and Al-Anon, which are discussed throughout the book.

1324. Newlove, Donald. The Drunks. First ed. New York: Saturday Review Press, E. P. Dutton & Co., Inc.; 1974; 342pp; ISBN: 0-8415-0337-0. LC 74-4027.
Note: dj.
This tragicomedic novel of art and alcohol revolves around horn-playing Siamese twins Leo and Teddy who descend into alcoholism --- and recovery. The fright of split being makes for endless shadings of the disease. Newlove's gem is a sequel to an earlier novel, Leo and Theodore. AA meetings are part of the novel.

1325. Norris, J. L. "The Role of Alcoholics Anonymous in Rehabilitation". in: Groupe, V., Editor. Alcoholism Rehabilitation: Methods and Experiences of Private Rehabilitation Centers. New Brunswick, NJ: Rutgers Center of Alcohol Studies; 1978: pp121-130; 138 pp. (NIAAA-RUCAS Alcoholism Treatment Series; v. No. 3).

1326. Norris, John, M.D. "Alcoholics Anonymous". in: Whitney, Elizabeth D., Editor. World Dialogue on Alcohol and Drug Dependence. First ed. Boston: Beacon Press; 1970: pp155-172; plus 20 other references.; 400pp; ISBN: 0-8070-2776-6.
The author outlines A.A.'s history, 12 Steps and Traditions, structure, and meetings. Results of the 1968 A.A. questionairre, filled out by 11,355 members, include a higher ratio of women coming into A.A., a large number of new members under 20 years of age, a large base of members with 5 years or more of sobriety, and continued growth still depending on one member carrying the message to a newcomer.

1327. Norris, John L. "Alcoholics Anonymous and other Self-Help Groups". in: Tarter, R.E./Sugerman, A.A. Alcoholism: Interdisciplinary Approaches to an Enduring Problem. Reading, MA: Addison-Wesley Pub. Co.; 1976: pp735-776; 857pp.
Norris cites the Twelve Steps, the Twelve Traditions, the place of A.A. in recovery career, A.A. as organization, the Concepts, A.A. Committees, A.A. Literature, A.A. History, Worldwide Growth and Survey results which included frequency of attendance at meetings, sex of respondents, age, referral, and length of sobriety.

1328. North Dakota Commission on Alcoholism. The Role of Alcohol in Society: A Concise and Factual Study Guide on the Problems of Alcoholism. Bismarck, ND: North Dakota Comm. on Alcoholism.; 1957; 39 pp.
One of the seven units in this pamphlet is devoted entirely to A.A. and Al-Anon Family Groups.

1329. O'Neill, S. F./Barnes, H. N. "Alcoholics Anonymous". in: Barnes, H. N./Aronson, M. D./Delbanco, T. L., Editors. Alcoholism: A Guide for the Primary Care Physician. New York: Springer-Verlag; 1987: pp93-101; 231 pp.

1330. O'Riordan, D. "Alcoholism". in: O'Doherty, E.F./McGrath, S. Desmond, editors. The Priest and Mental Health. Staten Island, NY: Society of St. Paul; 1963: 150-154.
O'Riordan argues that "co-operation between priests, doctors, psychiatrists, and Alcoholics Anonymous in bringing back alcoholics to sobriety and normality has been most fully developed in the U.S.A." The spiritual nature of AA is explained and shown to be effective for Catholic alcoholics.

1331. O'Riordan, Sean, Rev., C.S.S.R. "Grace is Sufficient - Why Alcoholics Anonymous?". in: Pfau, et al. Alcoholism: A Source Book for the Priest. Indianapolis: NCCA; 1960: pp402-417; 685 pp.
Note: This article orginially appeared in the Jan. 1952 issue of The Furrowunder the title "Drink and Compulsion.".
The author discusses in some depth the Twelve Steps of AA from the viewpoint of a Catholic alcoholic priest. Theologically, many topics are explored: sin and neurosis, acceptance, compulsion and powerlessness, pastoral techniques, confession, God's Providence, and grace; all from the vantage point of Catholicism and spirituality. The author finds himself in agreement with AA's spirituality and principles.

1332. Ogborne, A. C./Glaser, F. B. "Evaluating Alcoholics Anonymous". in: Bratter, T. E./Forrest, G. G., Editors. Alcoholism and Substance Abuse: Strategies for Clinical Intervention. New York: Free Press; 1985: Chap. 6, pp176-192; 650 pp.

1333. Ohlms, David L., M.D. "The Disease Concept of Alcoholism". Belleville, IL: Gary Whiteaker Co.; 1983.
Note: 19pp total.
Ohlms writes "Alcoholics Anonymous people were saying that alcoholism is a primary disease. It is not itself a symptom of some other disease - and AA treated it this way. And medical science finally had to admit that AA was right! In 1956 the American Medical Assn. officially recognized alcoholism as a true disease...".

1334. Olitzky, Kerry M., Rabbi/Copans, Stuart A., M.D. Twelve Jewish Steps to Recovery. First ed. Woodstock, VT: Jewish Lights Publishing; 1991: AA throughout; 120pp; ISBN: 1-879045-09-5. LC 91-25346.
Note: Illus.,pb.
Each of the Twelve Steps are discussed in the light of the Jewish tradition. The book is subtitled "A Personal Guide to Turning from Alcoholism and other Addictions...Drugs, Food, Gambling, Sex..." One reviewer summed up: "I felt like I had visited my Jewish roots. These authors have deep knowledge of recovery as viewed by A.A." Preface by Rabbi Abraham J. Twerski, M.D., and introduction by Rabbi Sheldon Zimmerman. Illustrated by Maty Grunberg.

1335. Osborne, A. C. "Approaches to the Evaluation of Alcoholics Anonymous". in: 2nd Annual Meeting of the Special Interest Group on Program Evaluation, Canadian Addiction Foundation; Sept. 8-9, 1982; Regina, Canada. London, Canada: Addiction Research Foundation; 1982: pp60-67; 184pp.
Some challenges posed by AA to those individuals concerned with assessing its contributions to the treatment of alcohol abuse are described. Reasons why AA should be evaluated are presented.

1336. Out From Under: Sober Dykes and Our Friends. Swallow, Jean, editor. First ed. San Francisco: Spinsters Ink; 1983; 170pp+. In this collection of essays, the first book about AA and recovery in the lesbian community, Swallow brings together eight stories about lesbians in AA. Homophobia in AA, the alleged "Christian nature of AA," poems, life improvement because of AA, a song about the Third Step, a conversion experience, the role of the higher power, and dealing with anger are some of the topics covered.

1337. The Para-Professional in the Treatment of Alcoholism [A New Profession]. Staub, George E./Kent, Leona E., Editors. Second ed. Springfield, IL: Charles C. Thomas, Publisher; 1976; c1973: 4 chaps. & AA throughout.; 170pp; ISBN: 0-398-02860-5. LC 73-5518.
Note: index, dj.
The new profession of alcoholism counselor is discussed in depth. Marty Mann wrote the introduction and the book is dedicated to "Bill Wilson who started it all." Four entire chapters about A.A. include discussions of AA members as alcoholism counselors, "wearing two hats," AA "Training Groups," and understanding and relating to A.A.

1338. Patrick, G. M. "Alcoholics Anonymous - Competitive or Complementary to Occupational Consultants". in: Moran-Sackett, Marsha, compiler. Proceedings of the 8th Annual Meeting of ALMACA, Detroit, MI, October 1-5, 1979. Association of Labor-Management Administrators and Consultants on Alcoholism, Inc. Arlington, VA: ALMACA; 1980: pp33-38; 743 pp.

1339. Patrick, G. M./Jackson, J. K. "Characteristics of alcoholics in Alcoholics Anonymous". in: International Congress on Alcoholism and Drug Dependence, 34th, Calgary, Alberta, Canada, 1985. Proceedings. Lausanne: Int'l. Council on Alcohol & Addictions; 1986; Vol. 2: pp88-91; 546 pp.

1340. Peele, Stanton. Diseasing of America: Addiction Treatment Out of Control. First ed. Lexington, MA/Toronto, Canada: Lexington Books; 1989: pp24-25, 43-46, 56-58, 59-60, 73-74, 89, 90, 101, 112-113, & 190.; 321pp; ISBN: 0-669-20015-8. LC 89-31904.
Note: Index, dj.
Peele believes the modern disease concept of alcoholism and the ideology embraced by the American addiction treatment industry are emperors without clothes. He criticizes Alcoholics Anonymous as the main proponent of these alleged false ideas about alcoholism as a disease.

1341. Peele, Stanton. The Meaning of Addiction. Compulsive Experience and Its Interpretation. 13th ed. Lexington, MA/ Toronto, Canada: Lexington Books, D. C. Heath & Co.; 1990; c1985: 13 references to AA.; 203pp; ISBN: 0-669-13835-5. LC 84-54208. [hardback ISBN: 0-669-02952-1].
Note: index, pb.
Addiction, Peele argues, controversially, while real, is not a biological phenomenon. He analyzes studies of drug and cigarette addiction, alcohol, obesity and other compulsions - from running to love - and demonstrates how conventional theories fail to make sense of scientific observations. Individual, situational and cultural variations are the rule for explaining addiction, he says, disputing the empirical basis for the current disease model for alcoholism developed by Jellinek in 1946 based on 98 questionnaires from a mailing to 1,600 A.A. members. Peele is the most important scholarly critic of the disease model of alcoholism "endorsed by AA." His book provides the open-minded with provocative, scholarly reading.

1342. Peele, Stanton, Ph.D./Brodsky, Archie/Arnold, Mary [with]. The Truth About Addiction and Recovery. First ed. New York, et al: Simon & Schuster; 1991: AA: pp20-27, 29-32, 314-316, & 25 other references.; 430pp; ISBN: 0-671-66901-X. LC 90-27678.
Note: Index, dj.
Subtitled "The Life Process Program for Outgrowing Destructive Habits," Peele and his fellow authors dispute the basic assumption that addiction is a disease. They believe recovery from addictions, including alcoholism, can be attained without medical treatment or twelve-step programs, including Alcoholics Anonymous. They emphasize the self-help capability every person has. Among many objections, criticism of AA, the medical profession, and the treatment industry for describing alcoholism as a disease is included in their discussion of the problem of addiction.

1343. Peluso, Emanuel/Peluso, Lucy Silvay. Women & Drugs. Getting Hooked, Getting Clean. Second ed. Minneapolis, MN: CompCare Publishers; 1988: Nine references to AA.; 231pp; ISBN: 0-89638-144-7. LC 88-2895.
Note: index, pb.
Ten women tell their stories of addiction to alcohol and other drugs and their recoveries. Jill's story [all names were changed to insure anonymity], the first in the book, covers her alcoholism and recovery with the help of A.A. [pp 19-32].

1344. Pfau, Ralph S., Rev., M.A. "Active Participation of Alcoholic Priests in AA". in: Pfau, et al. Alcoholism: A Source Book for the Priest. Indianapolis: NCCA; 1960: pp510-546; 685 pp.
Seven priests, one layman, and Fr. Pfau discuss the role of the alcoholic priest. The early history of AA involving priest-members included a discussion of closed-priest groups in AA versus alcoholic priests' participation in general AA groups. Alcoholic priests in AA from Minnesota, Chicago, Texas, Indianapolis, and other areas of the U.S. each tell their own story of coming into AA and the history of AA in their area. This lengthy article includes discussion of the Twelfth Step by alcoholic priests in AA and other spiritual topics.

1345. Pfau, Ralph S., Rev. "Introduction. The National Clergy Conference on Alcoholism.". in: Pfau, et al. Alcoholism: A Source Book for the Priest. Indianapolis: NCCA; 1960: p1-3; 685 pp.
Fr. Pfau, Founder and Executive Secretary of the NCCA, opens the book with "By Divine Providence, I became the first priest-member of Alcoholics Anonymous back in 1943." He recounts meeting and talking with Fr. Dowling in 1948 and other early historical events in AA involving alcoholic priests.

1346. Phelps, Janice Keller, M.D./Nourse, Alan E., M.D. The Hidden Addiction And How to Get Free. First ed. Boston/ Toronto, Canada: Little, Brown & Co.; 1986: pp120-123 & other references to AA.; 250pp; ISBN: 0-316-70471-7. LC 85-6820. Note: index, pb. [also published in hardback: ISBN: 0-316-70470-9.].
All addictions are rooted in the same genetic flaw in the body, Dr. Phelps postulates. It is rooted in a concrete physiological condition which can be treated in a multi-faceted program. In the chapter on alcohol, the authors begin: "For many alcoholics, Alcoholics Anonymous provides a much stronger support system for recovery than anything else available.".

1347. Pittman, Bill/Weber, Todd. Drop the Rock. Removing Character Defects. First ed. Seattle, WA: Glen Abbey Books; 1993; 96pp; ISBN: 0-934125-27-9. LC 92-4263.
Note: pb.
Aimed at all 12-steppers, this book tackles AA's sixth and seventh Steps. Personal stories illustrate the power of these two humility steps. The seven deadly sins Bill W. lists in Twelve Steps and Twelve Traditons, character defects, are discussed.

1348. Pittman, David J./Snyder, Charles R., Editors. Society, Culture, and Drinking Patterns. New York - London: John Wiley & Sons, Inc.; 1962: 12 references about A.A. including 2 chapters (See Bales & Maxwell); 616 pp; ISBN: L.C. 62-15188.

1349. Pittman, William L. "Alcoholics Anonymous: A Successful Therapeutic Social Movement". in: Blumberg, Leonard U., Ph.D. Beware the First Drink! The Washington Temperance Movement and Alcoholics Anonymous. First ed. Seattle, WA: Glen Abbey Books; 1991: Chap. 8, 193-228.; 278pp; ISBN: 0-934125-22-8. LC 90-19639.
Note: Extensive notes, bibliography, index. pb.
Pittman compares the Washingtonian Movement of the 1840s to A.A. in the 20th century and discovers many parallels among 18 points of comparison of ideology and dynamics.

1350. Plaut, Thomas F.A., Editor. Alcohol Problems. A Report to the Nation by the Cooperative Commission on the Study of Alcoholism. First. New York: Oxford University Press; 1967: pp180-181; 200 pp.
A.A. and the National Council on Alcoholism are cited as the two primary voluntary non-governmental agencies in the field of alcoholism in the U.S.

1351. Plunkert, William J. New York City Alcoholism Study. A Report 1962. First ed. New York: The National Council on Alcoholism, Inc.; 1962: pp46-52; 77 pp.
This extensive study of alcoholism in New York City by the NCA was based in large measure on an in-depth questionairre for A.A. members. The data is eye-opening in many areas. For example, an alcoholic's close friend or spouse, rather than a doctor, minister, or other professional, first referred the alcoholic to A.A. And 148 of the 400 A.A. members responding said they had been admitted to a hospital or institution for alcoholism itself, despite policies prevalent then to the opposite. This study was an early landmark effort to study alcoholism with scientific methodology.

1352. Poley, Wayne/Lea, Gary/Vibe, Gail. Alcoholism A Treatment Manual. First ed. New York: Gardner Press, Inc.; 1979: 10 references to A.A.; 159 pp; ISBN: 0-470-26523-X.
The authors question the validity of A.A.'s success rate of 60 to 75% and estimate a "cure" rate of 30-35%.

1353. Porterfield, Kay Marie. Keeping Promises. The Challenge of a Sober Parent. Second ed. San Francisco, CA: Harper & Row-Hazelden; 1984; 145pp; ISBN: 0-06-25541-7.
Note: pb.
This practical guide for parents in recovery focuses on creating nurturing family relationships. AA is mentioned several times.

1354. Presnall, Lewis P. The Wife of the Alcoholic. Revised ed. Salt Lake City, UT: Utah Alcoholism Foundation; nd (after 1955): Chap. 2, pp14-34; 71pp.
Presnall's booklet is subtitled "A Pattern To Happiness." In chapter two, "An Interpretation of The Twelve Steps of Alcoholics Anonymous for the Non-Alcoholic," he charts that pattern so the wife of the alcoholic may understand.

1355. Preston, John. Franny The Queen of Provincetown. First ed. Boston: Alyson Publications, Inc.; May, 1985, second printing: pp57-65; ISBN: 0-932870-31-7.
Note: pb.
Chapter 7 in this gay male novel, "Franny and The Professor," concerns an alcoholic who recovers through Alcholics Anonymous.

1356. Prevention, Intervention and Treatment: Concerns and Models. First ed. Rockville, MD: U.S. Dept. of Health & Human Services & NIAAA.; 1982; Monograph 3: pp223-4, 241-2, 270, 360, 380.; 411pp; ISBN: L.C. 81-600187.
A.A.'s history, ideology, membership, and correctional institutions services are briefly discussed.

1357. Prisons, Probation, and Parole in the District of Columbia. Karrick, David B., Chairman, Committee on Prisons. First ed. Washington, DC: Board of Commissioners of District of Columbia; April, 1957: pp131a & b.; 180pp.
Note: Spiral bound, 8 1/2 x 11".
"The Committee is very impressed by the work of Alcoholics Anonymous in the District of Columbia," the report states. It cites A.A.'s start in the District in 1939 with 6 members to its present status of 38 A.A. groups with over 4,000 active members.

1358. Rachel L. "I Only Drank When I Needed It". in: One Too Many! Englewood Cliffs, NJ: A. I. M. Publishers, Inc.; 1977: pp3-5; 32pp.
Note: [This 8.5 x 11" booklet was published under the auspices of the Apinwall, PA, Police Dept.].
Rachel shares her story of the descent into alcoholism and sobriety in AA.

1359. Rachel V. Family Secrets: Life Stories of Adult Children of Alcoholics. 3rd printing ed. San Francisco, CA: Herper & Row; 1987: pp230-233.; 260pp; ISBN: 0-06-250702-8. LC 86-43017.
Note: pb. ten appendixes.
At the end of this book, the author writes of her conversations with Lois W., wife of the Co-Founder of A.A., and Bob S., Jr., son of Dr. Bob, the other Co-Founder of A.A., at the 50th A.A. Int'l Convention in Montreal, Canada, in 1985. A.A. is mentioned in many of the 15 personal stories of adult children of alcoholics.

1360. Rachel V. (pseudonym). A Woman Like You. Life Stories of Women Recovering from Alcoholism and Addiction. First ed. San Francisco et al: Harper & Row, Publishers; 1985; 223 pp; ISBN: 0-06-250701-X.
Dedicated to A.A.'s Co-Founders and their wives with a 50th Happy Birthday wish, the book recounts the stories of 19 women from all kinds of backgrounds and their stories of recovery, including many references to A.A. meetings, philosophy, etc.

1361. Rea, Frederick B. "Alcoholics Anonymous". in: Alcoholism: Its Psychology and Cure. New York: Philosophical Library; 1956: Chapter 7.
Rea states that "this programme of recovery may be divided into two sections: first, those steps that concern the conversion or turning (away) from alcoholism, the initial stage of breaking down the alcoholic addiction; second, those that concern the re-integration of personality and the rebuilding of one's life upon foundations that are able to resist the assault of the impulse to drink again.".

1362. Recent Developments in Alcoholism: Treatment and Research, Alcoholics Anonymous, the Family, Serotonin and Preference, Clinical Pharmacology. Galanter, M., editor. First ed. New York: Plenum Press; 1989; 7: 3 chapters; 371pp; ISBN: 0-306-43042-8.
This book includes three chapters on AA: Emerging Concepts, A Sociocultural History, and Some Limitations of AA.

1363. Reilly, Richard L., D.O. America's Worst Problem: Alcohol. First ed. Liguori, MO: Liguori Publications; 1974: Chap. 18, pp96-100; & other references to A.A.; 128 pp; ISBN: LC 74-84391.
Note: pb.
"It's the best to date and its track record is second to none," says this osteopath in recommending A.A.

1364. Rice, Thurman B., M.D./Harger, Rolla A., Ph.D. Effects of Alcoholic Drinks, Tobacco, Sedatives, (and) Narcotics. Evanston, IL/Elmsford, NY: Harper & Row; 1961: pp202-206; 312 pp.
This textbook gives a brief view of A.A. and a chart listing what medicine and religion say to the alcoholic followed by what A.A. says and the 12 steps.

1365. Richardson, Eudora Ramsay/Woolfolk, Josiah Pitts (pseudonym). Drink and Stay Sober. New York: Bridgehead Books; 1954: pp65-67, 104-107, 121.; 190 pp.
One of authors, a well-known novelist, claims he was cured of alcoholism, and relates several A.A. experiences along the way. The authors characterize A.A. as helpful but only scratching the surface when it comes to the entire population of alcoholics in the U.S.

1366. Richard P. "Alcoholics Anonymous". In: Tomorrow Will Be Sober. New York: Harper & Brothers; 1960.
Richard P., Founding member of the Dublin, Ireland, A.A. group, relates his drinking history and entry into A.A. Comments to text of the book by Marty Mann and Harry M. Tiebout, M.D.

1367. Richards, Thomas B. "The A.A. Halfway House and Service Center". in: Catanzaro, Ronald J., M.D., Editor. Alcholism: The Total Treatment Approach. Third ed. Springfield, IL: Charles C. Thomas; 1974: pp373-382; 508pp; ISBN: 0-398-00295-9.
Note: Originally published in 1968.

1368. Ripley, Austin. "The Guest House Concept". in: Pfau, et al. Alcoholism: A Source Book for the Priest. Indianapolis: NCCA; 1960: pp549-557; 685 pp.
Ripley, Founder of Guest House, a treatment center in Michigan for alcoholic Catholic clergy, views the alcoholic priest as a "special" case and quotes Bill W. in a letter to him written in November, 1947, as saying "that their case has special, even unique aspects, is not even debatable." Ripley sets forth three facts: (1) there is the problem of alcoholism among clergy; (2) that problem was not in the past and is not in the present (this article was written in 1949) being met intelligently or successfully - the Church has tragically failed in handling the problem; (3) there is a way of treating the problem intelligently, charitably, and successfully, which is, providing proper treatment and rehabilitative facilities. " What about Alcoholics Anonymous? " he asks. "It is...(the answer for the priest)...but unless the problems of the alcoholic priest are first recognized as being different from those of the laymen, there will be little success even here," he answers. Ripley defines the "Guest House" concept as proper treatment, care and rehabilitation of the alcoholic priest and such treatment and therapy, preparatory to AA, and as a pre-AA step, skillfully and understandingly administered on an individual basis, rather than a group basis.

1369. Roads to Recovery: A National Directory of Alcohol and Drug Addiction Treatment Centers. Moore, Jean, Editor. First ed. New York/London: Collier Books-Macmillan Pub. Co./Collier Macmillan; 1985: (AA throughout); 384pp; ISBN: 0-02-059470-4. LC 85-19538.
Note: Index, pb.
This guide to over 500 private residential treatment centers in all 50 states and the District of Columbia gives information on cost, size, insurance eligiblity, and a description of the therapeutic program, including cooperation with A.A. and other Twelve Step programs, for treatment of alcoholics and drug addicts. Also listed are centers for specific groups such as Blacks, Native Americans, priests, women only, etc.

1370. Robe, Lucy Barry. "AA and Celebrities". in: Robe, Lucy Barry. Co-Starring Famous Women and Alcohol. First ed. Minneapolis, MN: CompCare Publications; 1986: Chap.35,pp 413-420; 537 pp; ISBN: 0-89638-100-5.
The author discusses how A.A. members can help female VIPs, special A.A. groups, and when A.A. doesn't work.

1371. Robe, Lucy Barry. "Going Public". in: Robe, Lucy Barry. Co-Starring Famous Women and Alcohol. First ed. Minneapolis, MN: CompCare Publications; 1986: Chap. 36, pp421-428.; 537 pp; ISBN: 0-89638-100-5.
The author discusses A.A. anonymity, starting with Marty Mann, one of the first 100 members of A.A. and A.A. anonymity and the special problems of celebrities. She ends with the public recovery of Betty Ford, Elizabeth Taylor and Mary Tyler Moore.

1372. Robinson, D. "Alcoholics Anonymous: American Origins and the International Diffusion of a Self-Help Group". in: Edwards, G./Arif, A./Jaffe, J., Editors. Drug Use and Abuse: Cultural Perspectives. New York: St. Martin's Press; 1983: Chap. 20, pp168-175; 285 pp.
Note: This chapter is based on an earlier World Health Organization study.

1373. Robinson, David. "Help and the Helpers". in: Robinson, David. From Drinking to Alcoholism: A Sociological Commentary. New York: John Wiley & Sons; 1976.
A.A. is discussed as group treatment for alcoholics by a "shift of focus of attention from the patient-therapist, client-helper (axis) to groups of individuals who have similar or related problems.".

1374. Rodin, M. B. "Getting on the Program: A Biocultural Analysis of Alcoholics Anonymous". in: Bennett, Linda A./ Ames, Genevieve M., Editors. American Experience with Alcohol: Contrasting Cultural Perspectives. New York: Plenum Press; 1985: pp41-58; 490 pp.
An examination is made of the convergence of two aspects of recovery from alcoholism. The first is the process by which alcoholics begin to restructure their identities and reinterpret their experiences in terms of Alcoholics Anonymous ideology. The second aspect is the physiological event occurring during the early stages of sobriety, when most AA members first come to the organization. The approach is to show how the AA meeting constitutes a dramatic performance that is tailored to the biological state of alcoholics in early recovery. 31 ref. (NCADI abstract).

1375. Rogers, Ronald L./McMillin, Chandler Scott. DON'T HELP: A Positive Guide to Working with the Alcoholic. Third pb ed. New York et al: Bantam; June 1989: AA: pp10-11, 165 & 254.; 259pp; ISBN: 0-553-34716-0. LC 88-39960.
Note: The first edition was published by Education & Training Institute of Maryland, Inc., in 1984; the second by Madrona in 1988.
Five common problems with AA and how to overcome them and prevent relapse are discussed. A treatment plan for increased AA involvement is outlined on one page.

1376. Rosenberg, Shirley Sirota, Editor. Alcohol and Health, a Report from the Secretary of Health, Education and Welfare. New York: Charles Scribner's Sons; 1975 (?): 5 references totaling 7 pages; 372 pp; ISBN: 684-13271-0.
Note: pb.

1377. Ross, G. R. "Cognitive Therapy and Alcoholics Anonymous: An Integrated Approach for the Treatment and Prevention of Teenage Substance Abuse". in: Faulkinberry, R., Editor. Drugs: Problems of the 70's, Solutions for the 80's. Lafayette, LA: Endac Enterprises-Print Media; 1980: pp127-131; 440 pp.

1378. Roth, Lillian. Beyond My Worth. New York: Frederick Fell, Inc.; 1958: pp136 & following.; 317 pp; ISBN: L.C. 58-8740. Roth's book is a continuation of her "I'll Cry Tomorrow," a best seller about her alcoholic life. Here, the famous singer relates her performance before the Soledad Alcoholics Anonymous group in prison, one of only several places where A.A. is mentioned directly in the book.

1379. Roth, Lillian. I'll Cry Tomorrow. First ed. New York: Frederick Fell, Inc.; 1954: A.A. is mentioned several times.; 347 pp.
The autobiography of this famous Broadway star and her progressive descent into alcoholism was a long-time best seller. In it, Miss Roth mentions her attendance at A.A. meetings several times.

1380. Royce, James E., S.J., Ph.D. "Alcoholics Anonymous". in: Royce, James E., S.J., Ph.D. Alcohol Problems and Alcoholism: A Comprehensive Survey. First & Second Revised ed. New York/London: The Free Press-A Div. of Macmillan Pub. Co./Collier Macmillan; 1981 & 1989: Chap. 15, pp242-255, etc.; 383pp; ISBN: 0-02-927540-7. LC 81-67421. (1st Edition) 0-02-927541-5. LC 89-7782. (Second, Revised Edition, First Printing).
Note: Bibliography of 37 pages, indexes in both editions, djs.
Royce, a respected scholar and founder of the addictions studies school at Seattle University, gives a solid overview of A.A., its history, Twelve Steps and Twelve Traditions, Legacies, philosophy, etc. This book is one of the few top standard textbooks in the U.S. for alcoholism studies. Contents include the physiology of alcohol, alcoholism and addiction, prevention and intervention, and treatment and rehabilitation. A.A. is indexed over 55 times, including extensive discussion in Chapter 15 and other places.

1381. Ryan, Dale & Juanita. Recovery from Addictions. Downers Grove, IL: InterVarsity Press; 1990; ISBN: 0-8308-1155-9. This 59-page booklet from The National Assn. for Christian Recovery compares the 12 Steps of AA with Biblical quotes and Christianity.

1382. Sagarin, E. "Alcoholics: From the Twenty-First Amendment to the Twelfth Step.". in: Odd Man In: Societies of Deviants in America. Chicago: Quadrangle Books; 1969: pp32-55 (1972 pb ed.).
A.A. is examined in a social historical perspective from Increase Mather, the Washingtonians, and the Oxford Group and the way A.A., as a self-help movement, has aided deviants.

1383. "Sailor's Return". in: The Way Back. Washington, D.C.: Whitman-Walker Clinic; 1982: p41f.
The focus of this gay man's story is his many geographic cures before joining AA. (NALGAP 539).

1384. Sandmaier, Marian. The Invisible Alcoholics. Women and Alcohol Abuse in America. First ed. NY, et al: McGraw-Hill Book Co.; 1980: 14 references to A.A.; 298 pp; ISBN: 0-07-054660-6.
Includes one case history of a female American Indian alcoholic and one Black woman who both sobered up in A.A.

1385. Scanlan, Edwin L. "Questions and Answers on Alcoholics Anonymous". in: The A to Z System: A Unique New Technique for the Cure of Alcoholism. Philadelphia: Dorrance & Co.; 1976: pp68-77; 105 pp.
The author gives a brief history of A.A. and answers basic questions for the layman about A.A.

1386. Schaef, Anne Wilson. When Society Becomes an Addict. First ed. San Francisco, CA: Harper & Row; 1987: p146.; 152pp; ISBN: 0-06-254812-3. LC 86-45828.
Note: dj.
This supplementary book mentions A.A. several times, including the dry drunk concept.

1387. Schlesinger, Stephen E., Ph.D./Gillick, John J., Ph.D. Stop Drinking and Start Living. Second ed. Summit, PA: Tab Books, Inc.; 1989; c1985: AA: Chap. 4, pp77-94, etc.; 181pp; ISBN: 0-8306-3227-1. LC 88-35646.
Note: index, pb.
This basic guidebook for alcoholics and their families and friends outlines what alcoholism is and does and suggests A.A. as a solution to the problem. Chapter four is about Alcoholics Anonymous basic concepts. Al-Anon and ACOA are discussed.

1388. Schomp, Gerald. "Seeking Treatment for the Alcoholic". in: Alcohol: Its Use, Abuse and Therapy. Huntington, Indiana: Our Sunday Visitor; 1977.
Various aspects of alcoholism and its treatment are discussed including the A.A. program. Christian attitudes are emphasized, with the role of religion in recovery pinpointed.

1389. Scoppettone, Sandra. The Late Great Me. First ed. New York et al: Bantam Books; January, 1976: pp208ff.; 249 pp; ISBN: 0-553-25029-9.
Note: paperback.
This novel revolves around Geri Peters, "your everyday average girl next door: an alcoholic at seventeen," and her struggle with alcoholism and eventual entry into A.A. and sobriety.

1390. Sedlacek, Leo B., M.D. "The Alcoholics Anonymous Organization". in: Alcoholism - What Can I Do About It? Cedar Rapids, Iowa: Moershel-Trumpe Clinic; 1953: pp61-66; 91 pp.
The fundamentals of A.A. and the 12 Steps are discussed.

1391. Seeburger, Francis F. Addiction and Responsibility: An Inquiry into the Addictive Mind. First ed. Crossroad Pub. Co.: New York; 1993: 40+ AA references.; 200pp; ISBN: 0-8245-1365-7. LC 93-25168.
Note: index, dj.
Seeburger, a University of Denver philosophy professor, explores addiction and alcoholism from an existential viewpoint. AA is indexed over 40 times.

1392. Seixas, F. A. "Alcoholism". in: Mule, S. J., editor. Behavior in Excess: ... New York: Free Press; 1981: pp120-131; 396pp.
The genetic predisposition to alcoholism and characteristics of alcoholics are discussed. The success of treatment approaches, especially Alcoholics Anonymous, is described.

1393. "A Seminarians Story". in: The Way Back. Washington, DC: Whitman Walker Clinic; 1982: 21-27.
A former seminarian who recovered through AA shares his experience, strength, and hope.

1394. Seymour, Richard B./Smith, David E., M.D. Drugfree. First American ed. New York, NY/Oxford, England: Facts on File Publications; 1987: 25 references to AA.; 261 pp; ISBN: 0-8160-1363-2.

1395. Shanahan, W. J. "Recovery and Alcoholics Anonymous". in: Gody, Marshall, Editor. Alcoholism: Treatment and Recovery. St. Louis, MO: Catholic Health Assn.; 1984: pp101-116; 261 pp.
An overview is given of the issues that remain of persistent interest to both professionals and AA members on the dynamics of recovery from alcoholism through AA. The issue of what the organization is and what it proposes to be about is addressed: AA's preamble, writings from its co-founder Bill W., the 12 Steps, the five slogans of AA, and the 12 Traditions used by AA groups as guidelines are used to clarify this issue. The question of who AA is for is addressed: AA is for alcoholics, but there is debate as to how people get to AA and whether their intentions are honorable or if they are trying to avoid punishment for an offense related to drinking. The relationship between AA and the professional community and AA as a way of life for alcoholism recovery are described. (NCADI abstract).

1396. Shepherd, Ernest A. Alcoholism: A Family Guide to Understanding the Illness and What To Do About It. Concord, NH: New Hampshire State Dept. of Health; nd; 23 pp.
A brief description of A.A. is given.

1397. Sher, K./McCrady, R. "Alcoholism Treatment Research: Treatment Variables". in: Directions in Alcohol Abuse Treatment Research Conference; October, 1982; Newport, RI; 26pp.
Two treatment approaches are considered: AA and treatment based on social learning principles. Some of the similarities and differences are highlighted.

1398. Sherman, Harold. Anyone Can Stop Drinking (Even You!). First ed. New York: C. & R. Anthony, Publishers; 1950: various mentions of A.A. throughout text; 245 pp. Note: [originally titled You Can Stop Drinking, Creative Age Press].
"Every line in this book has been thoughtfully examined and approved by men and women members of the Little Rock, Arkansas, A.A. Group, and especial editorial attention has been given by K.W., T.W., and A.C.B. To these anonymous helpers, the author wishes to convey his heartfelt appreciation," the acknowledgment page states. The author's thrust is that problem drinkers have "the power within themselves to stop drinking and STAY stopped..." and this is accomplished by his technique of mastering and using "the psycho-dynamic force of their will...," a contradiction with A.A.'s Steps. The Little Rock, Ark. Gazette published a review by W. C. Meehan Nov. 19, 1950.

1399. Sherouse, D. L. "Self-Help Groups: Alcoholism Recovery". in: Professional's Handbook on Geriatric Alcoholism. Springfield, IL: Charles C. Thomas; 1983.
Sherouse provides brief historic and general information regarding A.A. He lists the Twelve Steps and Traditions and briefly discusses the relationship between A.A. and professional treatment programs. He describes the self-help groups available to gay and woman alcoholics and to family members of alcoholics.

1400. Shipp, Dr. Thomas J. "Alcoholics Anonymous". in: Shipp, Dr. Thomas J. Helping the Alcoholic and His Family. Englewood Cliffs, N.J.: Prentice-Hall, Inc.; 1963: Chap. 10, pp91-97; & 9 other references to AA.; 140 pp; ISBN: L.C. 63-9751.
This Methodist minister relates his experiences of many parishioneers who have sobered up in A.A. and show how A.A. usually works first before the church can become active in an alcoholic's life again.

1401. Shoemaker, Helen Smith. "A Rescue Mission and Alcoholics Anonymous". in: I Stand by the Door. The Life of Sam Shoemaker. First ed. New York, Evanston, and London: Harper & Row, Publishers; 1967: pp188-193; 220 pp.
The widow of Rev. Shoemaker, the Episcopal minister, tells how her husband and Bill W., Co-founder of A.A., met at the Calvary Mission at Calvary Episcopal Church in New York City. He remembered that Ebby, his old drinking buddy, had been lodged by members of the Oxford Group at Shoemaker's Calvary Mission. Drunk, Bill and a drinking Finn named Alex, reeled into the Mission and were greeted by Ebby, sober. Later at the meeting, Bill responded to the "call" and knelt among the shaking penitents. "Maybe then and there, for the very first time, I was penitent, too. Something touched me. I was hit, " Bill wrote. Later Ebby told Bill with relief that he had done all right and had "given my life to God." Bill states that "most of the principles that were afterwards embodied in the Twelve Steps of Alcoholics Anonymous" came from Sam Shoemaker.

1402. Shoemaker, Samuel M., Rev. By the Power of God, Extraordinary Living for Ordinary Men, and How to Become a Christian. New York/Grand Rapids, MI/New York: Harper/Zondervan/Harper; 1954, 1966, & 1953.
Note: All djs.
These three books by Rev. Shoemaker contain one or more minor references to A.A. and are included as background material on this Episcopal minister who helped early A.A. in its founding days in the Oxford Groups.

1403. Shoemaker, Sam. "What the Church Has To Learn From Alcoholics Anonymous". in: ...And Thy Neighbor. First ed. Waco, Texas: Word Books; 1967: Chap. 3, pp23-36; 200 pp; ISBN: L.C. 67-26935.
The Episcopalian minister, an early friend of A.A., points out 5 ideas that churches can learn from A.A. and states the "time has come for the Church to be re-awakened and re-vitalized by those insights and practices found in A.A." The pragmatic ideas he dissects are need, fellowship, true conversion, exposure to Christian experience, and direct dealing with people.

1404. Siegler, Miriam, and Osmond, Humphrey. "The Alcoholics Anonymous Model". in: Siegler, Miriam/Osmond, Humphrey. Models of Madness, Models of Medicine. First ed. New York: Macmillan Pub. Co., Inc.; 1974: pp243-266; 287 pp; ISBN: 0-02-594000-7.
In this book's acknowledgements the authors thank Bill W., A.A. Co-founder, for his help. "We were among the first to ask him how he believed A.A. worked rather than telling him why it had succeeded," the authors write. A.A. is compared to other treatment models for alcoholism.

1405. Silverstein, Alvin, Dr./Silverstein, Virginia B. Alcoholism. First ed. Philadelphia & New York: J. B. Lippincott Co.; 1975: 14 references to AA.; 128 pp; ISBN: 0 397-31648-8.

1406. Sinclair, Upton. The Cup of Fury. Great Neck, New York: Channel Press, Inc.; 1956: last chapter; 190 pp.
This noted author writes of alcoholism and the devastation it has caused among his many friends in the writing profession. A.A. is mentioned in the last chapter.

1407. Small, J. "Becoming Naturally Therapeutic". in: 1981 School of Alcohol & Addiction Studies, Anchorage, Alaska; May 4-7, 1981: pp33-50; 345pp.
The 12-Step program of AA is discussed, noting its association with psychotherapy kand the natural healing process.

1408. Smith, Scott B. Coincidences. First ed. Aptos, CA: Living Business Press; 1987; 328pp; ISBN: 0-942294-75-0. LC 87-17264.
Note: dj.
The true story of the Washington newsman, Scott Smith, reveals his alcoholism and recovery where "coincidences" of a happy nature start happening. AA's anonymity, and other Fellowship concepts, are part of the story.

1409. Sobell, Mark B./Sobell, Linda C. Behavorial Treatment of Alcohol Problems. Individualized Therapy and Controlled Drinking. New York & London: Plenum Press; 1978: 13 references to A.A.; 225 pp; ISBN: 0-306-31057-0.
"Is controlled drinking a viable treatment goal for alcoholism?" is the stated focus of the Sobells' study. The authors are critical of the A.A. concepts of "first drink, then drunk," and "once an alcoholic, always an alcoholic." They question the universal applicability of the belief that alcoholism is not reversible and trace that idea back to Jellinek's use of retrospective self-reports of alcoholics who were members of A.A.

1410. Spickard, Anderson, M.D./Thompson, Barbara R. Dying for a Drink. First ed. Dallas, TX, London, et al: Word Publishing; 1985: A.A. is indexed 24 times.; 211pp; ISBN: 0-8499-3057-X.
Note: paperback.
The authors look at A.A. from the Christian perspective and find it compatiable. They state they have "never known any alcoholic whose faith was damaged by the spiritual program of A.A." and find the contrary to be true.

1411. Spiegel, Marcia Cohn. "Alcoholism: Jewish Women Confront a Growing Problem". in: Levy, Stephen Jay/Blume, Sheila B., editors. Addictions in the Jewish Community. New York: Federation of Jewish Philanthropies of New York; 1986: 62-74.
Using case studies, Spiegel explains the issues of alcoholic, Jewish women. AA is mentioned throughout.

1412. Springborn, William/Jensen, James G./Sellner, Dr. Edward C./Brandon, James/M., Pat/B., Mel/McDonald, Peter Converse. Twelfth Step Collection. First & Revised ed. Center City, MN: Hazelden; 1974-1983; 8-32 pp each; ISBN: 0-89486-017-8, 0-89486-106-9, 0-89486-107-7, 0-89486-000-3, 0-89486-129-8,0-89486-128-X, 0-89486-135-2, 0-89486-154-9,0-89486-153-0, 0-89486-160-3, & 0-89486-167-0.
Note: All 11 pamphlets.
This "Twelfth Step Collection" of pamphlets by Hazelden attempts to interpret the Twelve Steps of A.A. Several have workbook blank pages for the newcomer to fill in.

1413. Stafford, R. "Alcoholics Anonymous and the Woman Alcoholic". in: Burtle, V., editor. Women Who Drink. Springfield, IL: Thomas; 1979: pp248-269; 274pp.
Women now comprise [in 1979] about 30% of AA. The Fellowship has long recognized the importance of women working with women and men with men, and the same-sex sponsorship is an unofficial AA tradition. The Orange County, California, Central Office Phone Service of AA received 414 "Twelfth Step Calls" from Jan to May of 1967 of which 36% were from women; during the same period of 1977, 48% of 1,559 phone calls were from women. The number of women's AA groups has been increasing.

1414. Steiner, Claude, Ph.D. Games Alcoholics Play. First pb ed. New York: Ballantine Books; Jan. 1974: pp ix, xv, 99, 136, 159, 162; 202 pp; ISBN: 0-345-32383-1.
Note: The first edition in hardback was published in 1971 by Grove Press, Inc.
"Alcoholism is neither incurable nor a disease!" is Steiner's thesis and his transactional analysis approach is in direct contradiction to most of A.A. principles and concepts. He criticizes A.A. as a "persecutor" of those alcoholics who do not believe "once an alcoholic, always an alcoholic.".

1415. Steiner, Claude M. Healing Alcoholism. First ed. New York: Grove Press, Inc.; 1979: Over 20 references to A.A.; 208pp; ISBN: 0-394-50860-2.
According to Dr. Steiner, alcoholism is not an incurable disease but a bad habit which the alcoholic can rescript. Steiner accuses A.A. of becoming a "monoply and repressive influence in the field (of alcoholism)" because of its vast success. While lauding that success, he believes A.A.'s ideology dominates the field and is "narrow-minded.".

1416. Stepping Stones to Recovery For Women. Mary B., Editor. First ed. Seattle, WA: Glen Abbey Books; 1989; 211pp; ISBN: 0-934125-15-5. LC 89-17751.
Note: pb.
The articles, poems, and slogans in this meditation anthology were written by Twelve Step women for women in recovery. AA's Twelve Steps, the Serenity Prayer, gratitude, humility, COAs, sexuality, food, anger and a host of other topics are discussed.

1417. Stepping Stones to Recovery for Men. Beal, Stephen, Editor. First ed. Seattle, WA: Glen Abbey Books; 1992; 220pp; ISBN: 0-934125-28-7. LC 92-20195.
Note: small pb.
This collection of 119 inspirational readings, prayers, and commentaries,aimed at men, covers many AA topics including the Steps, sponsorship, character defects, anger, gratitude, spirituality, relapse, Higher Power, etc.

1418. Stewart, David A. "Alcoholics Anonymous" & "Alcoholics Anonymous - A Clinical View". in: Stewart, David A. Thirst for Freedom. First ed. Center City, MN: Hazelden; 1960: AA: Part I, Chap.7, pp121-142; Part II, Chap. 7, pp316-339; etc.; 366pp.
The author covers all the basics in A.A., the Steps and Traditions, as well as commenting on A.A.'s pragmatic approach to alcoholism and recovery and its corollary rejection of the scientific or religious approach to the problem.

1419. Stewart, David A. "The Anonymous World". in: The Adventure of Sobriety: Michigan State University Press; 1976: pp54-78; 128 pp.
Discusses the A.A. Program, the Twelve Steps, the Twelve Traditions, Slogans and Prayers, etc.

1420. Strachan, J. George. Alcoholism: Treatable Illness. An honorable approach to man's alcoholism problem. First ed. Vancouver, Canada: Mitchell Press Limited; 1967: Chap. 22, pp245-269, & 100+ references to AA.; 293pp.
Note: A later revised edition was published by the Hazelden Foundation, Center City, Minnesota, in April, 1982, under title Alcoholism: Treatable Illness: An Update for the 80s (ISBN 0-89486-149-2). Another earlier edition was published in 1971 by the same press.
The author outlines the magnitude of the alcoholism problem and particularly recommends A.A. for the most effective treatment.

1421. Strachen, J. G. "The Self-Help Approach". in: Addictions: What is Their Treatment? Proceedings of a Conference on... Ottawa, Canada: Commoners' Publishing; 1981: pp102-118; 216pp.
The work done by AA, Oxford Movement, Matt Talbot Society, Self-Pledge, and alumni groups from treatment centers proves the usefulness of the self-help approach in dealing with alcoholism.

1422. Straus, Robert/Bacon, Selden D. Drinking in College. New Haven: Yale University Press; 1953: pp 17, 18, 210-211.; 221 pp.
The authors do not rate highly the efforts of A.A. on the college campus scene.

1423. Straus, Robert. Escape from Custody. A Study of Alcoholism and Institutional Dependency as Reflected in the Life Record of a Homeless Man. First ed. New York et al: Harper & Row, Publishers; 1974: Various A.A. clubs mentioned in this biography.; 388 pp; ISBN: 0-06-014149-2.
The author-professor studied the life of Frank Moore, an alcholic, (1904-1972) in great detail. Frank visited the A.A. Seamen's Club and other A.A. clubs and read the book Alcoholics Anonymous but he couldn't find his way to recovery in A.A. He died after a lifetime of roaming from jails to hospitals to skid rows, all the while drinking. The

book approaches a total portrait of an alcoholic's entire life, a stunning study in depth.

1424. Stresseman, Adele E., M.D. "A Psychiatrist's Viewpoint". in: Bier, William C., S.J., Editor. Problems in Addiction: Alcohol and Drug Addiction. New York: Fordham University Press; 1962; The Pastoral Psychology Series, No. 2: pp133-137; 247 pp; ISBN: L.C. 62-16224.
"My particular relationship to Alcoholics Anonymous is that of a psychiatrist who has seen their miracles at first hand," Stressman begins. She says psychiatrists fail because the alcoholic cannot trust them, establish "transference." And A.A. works because the alcoholic can identify with another alcoholic and then the magic of the program, A.A.'s insistence on spiritual growth can occur. She sums up: "A.A. appears theoritically sound and impressively successful...".

1425. Stuckey, R. F./Harrison, J. S. "Alcoholism Rehabilitation Center". in: Pattison, E./Kaufman, E., editors. Encyclopedica Handbook of Alcoholism. New York: Gardner Press; 1982: pp865-873; 1230pp.
In this chapter, the historical development of alcoholism rehabilitation centers, beginning with the advent of Alcoholics Anonymous, is described.

1426. Sullivan, Vincent. How To Stop Problem Drinking. New York: Frederick Fell; 1969.
Sullivan includes data here gathered by the General Service Board of A.A. in a multi-year study. His 21-day stop drinking program includes A.A. along with others surrounding the alcoholic, family, employer, etc.

1427. Teens Talk about Alcohol and Alcoholism. Dolmetsch, Paul/ Mauricette, Gail, Editors. First ed. Garden City, NY: Doubleday & Co., Inc.-A Dolphin Book; 1987: pp98-101 (AA).; 125pp; ISBN: 0-385-23084-2. LC 86-16616.
Note: pb.
Teenagers talk about alcohol, drinking, alcoholism, living with an alcoholic and getting better. Anonymity and going to your first A.A. meeting are discussed briefly.

1428. Temer, R. G./Peck, R. C./Perrine, M. W./Borok, L. S. "Study of the Relative Effectiveness of Disulfiram vs. Alcoholics Anonymous Participants in the Treatment of Drinking Driver Offenders". in: Noordzij, P. C./Roszbach, R., editors. Alcohol, Drugs, and Traffic Safety. First ed. Amsterdam: Elsevier Sciences Publishers; 1987: pp571-575; 685pp; ISBN: 0-444-80903-1.
The effectiveness of disulfiram vs. AA was tested in an outpatient treatment program with 1,914 subjects from 1981 to 1983. The program included 58 hours of group therapy, 8 of individual counselling and 20 AA meetings. Those who chose AA instead of disulfiram had a lower, but not significant, recidivism rate.

1429. Tennov, Dorothy. Psychotherapy: the hazardous cure. First ed. New York: Abelard-Schuman; 1975: pp187-88; 314pp; ISBN: 0-200-04028-6. LC 75-9856.
Note: Index, 35-page bibliography, dj.
"Psychotherapy researchers have recommended that such 'naturalistic therapeutic agents' as Alcoholics Anonymous, Psychotics Anonymous, and Weight Watchers be studied for what can be learned from them and applied to professional practices." "Since the days of Freud, it has been ackowledged that psychotherapy rarely helped the alcoholic.".

1430. Tiebout, H. M. "Psychological Factors Operating in Alcoholics Anonymous". in: Glueck, B., Editor. Current Therapies of Personality Disorders. New York: Grune & Stratton; 1946: pp145-165.

1431. Todd, Frances. Teaching About Alcohol. New York, et al: McGraw-Hill Book Co.; 1964: pp121, 130 (AA).; 230pp; ISBN: LC 63-21005.
Note: Index, pb.
This textbook for teachers gives the basic physiology of alcohol and of problem drinking and alcoholism. Teaching methods are reviewed. A.A. is briefly described in four paragraphs.

1432. Tracy, Don. What You Should Know About Alcoholism. First ed. New York: Dodd, Mead & Co.; 1975: pp133ff; 157 pp; ISBN: 0-396-06997-5.
The author recommends A.A. as the source of effective help, but not the only one. Slips and other basics are also discussed.

1433. "Treatment of Black Alcoholics". in: Brisbane, Frances Larry, Ph.D./Womble, Maxine, editors: Alcoholism Treatment Quarterly; 2(Nos.3/4).
Note: This monograph was later published separately as a paperback.
This journal monograph contains some material on "how and why Alcoholics Anonymous works for Blacks.".

1434. Trice, Harrison M. Alcoholism in America. First ed. New York, et al: McGraw-Hill Book Co.; 1966: pp14, 60, 70-72, 94, 98-101, 105-107; 152 pp; ISBN: L.C. 66-25490.
The author cites A.A.'s effectiveness but points out that many alcoholics, though exposed to A.A., do not affiliate with it. Additionally, he lays his finger on a glaring vacuum in the field of alcoholism, the evaluation and follow-up reporting on various treatment centers and programs, especially with reference to A.A. factors.

1435. Trice, Harrison M., Prof. Alcoholism in Industry: Modern Procedures. 7th printing ed. New York: The Christopher D. Smithers Foundation; 1974: pp32-33.; 77pp.
Note: Booklet.
Trice calls A.A. "the most widespread and readily available resource outside the company" in treatment of alcoholics in industry. He cautions company employee counselors, doctors, and nurses that wholesale referral to A.A. does not mean the case is managed and closed.

1436. Trice, Harrison M./Roman, Paul M. "Therapeutic Alternatives for Deviant Drinkers and Drug Users". in: Spirits and Demons At Work: Alcohol and Other Drugs on the Job. First ed. Ithaca, NY: Cornell University; Jan. 1972: 213-25; 268pp; ISBN: 0-87546-034-8 & L.C. 72-619517.
Note: paperback.
The authors term A.A. the "single most effective form of `therapy' for the chronic deviant drinker. They succinctly discuss the philosophy, organization, and practice of the Fellowship and its effectiveness on the job.

1437. Trimpey, Jack. The small book. Revised ed. New York: Delacorte Press; 1992; c1989: Chap. 2, pp 31-48, etc.; 274pp; ISBN: 0-385-30558-3. LC 91-32380.
Note: dj.
This is another rational recovery book. The "small book" title is a takeoff on AA's "Big Book." Chap. 2 is "A Discussion of the 12-Step Spiritual Healing Program of Alcoholics Anonymous." The author reviews the criticisms, not necessarily his he states, of AA and its "religious" approach. He comments on each of the 12 Steps. Basically, he believes AA "is good at what it does and to change to accomodate internal dissent would erode its fundamental principles. Moreover, The Small Book is just as partisan as `The Big Book' in persuading the reader toward its viewpoint. The philosophies of RR and AA are mutually contradictory and irreconcilable." Very true.

1438. Turnbull, Grace H. Fruit of the Vine as Seen By Many Witnesses of All Times. reprint ed. Evanston, IL: National WCTU Pub. House; 1960: pp29 & 58; 178 pp.
Note: First Edition was April, 1950.
"There is a foreshadowing of the methods of Alcoholics Anonymous in Lincoln's speech to the Washingtonian Temperance Society at Springfield, Illinois, Feb. 22, 1842, a society largely composed of drunkards who had reformed..." Turnbull is critical of A.A. later in the book: "The weak point of their ministrations is that they practice only cure, not prevention of alcoholics, who, with the present accessibility of alcohol, are being manufactured faster than they can possibly be cured." She accuses A.A. of playing "into the hands of the liquor interests...because they often convert to respectability the alcoholics who bring the trade into disrepute, but take no stand against the use of alcohol by the average drinker from whose ranks are recruited new legions of inebriates.".

1439. Twerski, A. J. "Judaism and the Twelve Steps". in: Levy, S. J., and Blume, S. B., Editors. Addictions in the Jewish Community. New York: Commission on Synagogue Relations; 1986: pp123-133; 379 pp.

1440. Twerski, Abraham J., M.D. Caution "Kindness" Can Be Dangerous to the Alcoholic. First ed. Englewood Cliffs, NJ: Prentice-Hall, Inc.; 1981: 12 references to AA.; 174pp; ISBN: 0-13-121236-2.
Note: Pb, also published in hardback.
The author, Medical Director of Gateway Rehab Center, Pittsburgh, Pa., gives a set of guidelines and resources, including A.A. primarily, that non-alcoholics can use to help a problem drinker.

1441. Twerski, Abraham J., M.D. It Happens to Doctors, Too. First ed. Center City, MN: Hazelden; April, 1982: pp79ff; 154pp; ISBN: 0-89486-157-3.
"It is my conviction that the effectiveness of Alcoholics Anonymous and N.A. so greatly surpasses other types of treatment, that it is foolish to pursue any other course of treatment except as adjunctive to A.A. or N.A.," the author states.

1442. Twerski, Abraham J., M.D. Self-Discovery in Recovery. First & Reprint ed. Center City, MN/San Francisco, CA: Hazelden/ Harper & Row, a Harper-Hazelden Book; December, 1984, & 1989: (AA discussed throughout); 120pp; ISBN: 0-89486-238-3. [first ed.] 0-06-255491-3. LC 88-45678.[reprint].
Note: pbs.
Twerski's major focus is on the development of self-esteem, which he sees as the keystone of recovery. He is "enamored" of Alcoholics Anonymous and knows of many who could benefit from the fellowship and program of A.A., "but since they don't have a drinking problem, they can't identify with the people" in A.A. Drawing on his patients' lives, he discusses the origins of low self-esteem and how the Steps of A.A. help develop a positive self-esteem. "I found (A.A.'s) basic philosophy is applicable to stress management, even when alcohol isn't involved. It should be noted that A.A. has one primary purpose, to help the suffering alcoholic; thus, it is not a program of recovery for other addictions.

1443. Ullman, Albert D. "Alcoholics Anonymous". in: Ullman, Albert D. To Know the Difference. First ed. New York: St. Martin's Press; 1960: Chap. 11, pp173-191; & 17 other references to AA.; 239 pp; ISBN: L.C.60-8770.
An excellent discussion of case histories of recovered alcoholics, especially those whose stories were told in the first edition of "Alcoholics Anonymous," is the central content of the author's chapter on A.A. The 12 Steps and other basic A.A. ideas are discussed.

1444. Understanding Alcoholism: For the Patient, the Family and the Employer. Compiled and edited by The Christopher D. Smithers Foundation, Inc. First ed. New York: Charles Scribner's Sons; 1968: foreword & 22 references; 257pp; ISBN: LC 68-17356.
Note: Index, dj.
The two-page foreword is by "W.G.W., Co-founder, Alcoholics Anonymous." A.A. is recommended throughout this early book about alcoholism.

1445. Vaillant, George E. "Paths Into Abstinence". in: Vaillant, George E. The Natural History of Alcoholism. Causes, Patterns, and Paths to Recovery. First. ed. Cambridge, MA: Harvard University Press; 1983: pp183-216; 359 pp; ISBN: 0-674-60375-3.
Dr. Vaillant discusses "The Relationship of Alcoholics Anonymous to Abstinence" by evaluating previous research in the light of his own longitudinal study of A.A. In his momumental study of more than 600 individual alcoholics over 40 years, he asserts that A.A. appears to be the most effective method of recovery, or stable abstinence. He sums up: "a great many severly alcohol-dependent Americans, regardless of their social or psychological makeup, find help for their alcoholism through Alcoholics Anonymous.".

1446. Vamos, P. "Commentary (to Self-Help Approach)". in: Addictions: What is Their Treatment? Proceeding of a Conference on... Ottawa, Canada: Commoners' Publishing; 1981; 216pp.
"The Self-Help Therapeutic Community Movement began in the 1950s when a recovering alcoholic and his drug-addicted friends were not accepted into an AA meeting in Long Beach, California. Its name was later changed to Synanon. Unlike AA, it does not consider alcoholism a disease.".

1447. Van Blair, Bruce, Rev. A Year To Remember. First ed. Seattle, WA: Glen Abbey Books; 1988; 324pp; ISBN: 0-934125-05-8. LC 87-73383.
Note: Pb.
The author has blended Christianity and the Twelve Steps in this inspirational book of 52 meditations.

1448. Van Dorn, Theodore. Drunk's Diary. First ed. New York: Philosophical Library; 1966; 116pp; ISBN: LC 66-22347.
Note: dj.
The author breaks his anonymity as a member of A.A. In this autobiography he describes his descent into alcoholism and recovery through A.A. Surrender, God, One Day At A Time, recovery, faith and other topics related to the A.A. program of recovery are discussed.

1449. Vaughan, Clark. "Alcoholics Anonymous". in: Vaughan, Clark. Addictive Drinking. The Road to Recovery for Problem Drinkers and Those Who Love Them. First ed. New York: Viking Press; 1982: pp70-97; & 100 other references to AA.; 317 pp; ISBN: 0-14-006969-0.
Note: A paperback version was published in 1984 by Penguin Books, New York.
"...A.A. offers by far the best single approach to getting well..." the author states; then outlines what a meeting is like, common misconceptions about A.A., why and how A.A. works from a stress point of view, and misguided reasons for dropping out of A.A. The author, a recovered alcoholic, pinpoints many of the excuses alcoholics use for their not-needing or dropping out of A.A.

1450. Visions of Addiction. Major Contemporary Perspectives on Addiction and Alcoholism. Peele, Stanton, Editor. 4th ed. Lexington, MA/Toronto, Canada: Lexington Books, D. C. Heath & Co.; 1990; c1988: 13 references to AA.; 244pp; ISBN: 0-669-13092-3. LC 86-45054.
Note: index.
This wide-ranging volume explores what addiction is, theories explaining it, and solutions offered by 16 acknowledged experts from many fields. The neurobehavioral, disease, genetic, classic conditioning, psychosocial, and moral views of addiction are discussed in separate chapters. Guilt and metaphors for addiction are discussed. Thisphilosophical volume references AA a dozen times, mostly with a doubting or critical mind.

1451. Vogler, Roger E./Bartz, Wayne R. The Better Way to Drink. First ed. New York: Simon & Schuster; 1982: 13 references to A.A.; 208 pp; ISBN: 0-671-44944-3.
The authors believe that not all problem drinkers are hard-core alcoholics and their "scientifically-tested program shows how most problem drinking can be moderated and controlled." They allege "the enthusiastic promotion of the `disease' approach of Alcoholics Anonymous." They are critical of A.A. as a "cut-and-dried philosophy" aimed only at "bottomed-out" end-of-the-road alcoholics.

1452. Wagner, Robin S. Sarah T. Portait of a Teen-age Alcoholic. First ed. New York: Ballantine Books; March, 1975: pp92-120; 120pp; ISBN: 0-345-34242-9.
Note: pb.
This novel of a teen-age alcoholic girl ends with her going to her first A.A. meeting and starting on the road to recovery. The book was based on the Universal Television Production written by Richard and Esther Shapiro.

1453. Wallace, John. Alcoholism: New Light on the Disease. First ed. Newport, RI: Edgehill Publications; 1985: pp54, 57, 84-5, 102-10, 112-3, 149 (AA).; 164pp; ISBN: 0-926028-08-1. LC 85-80595.
Note: Index, pb.
For several decades Wallace was dissuaded from writing yet another book about alcoholism. "For one thing, Alcoholics Anonymous had already managed the job very well without me. The book Alcoholics Anonymous and the various writings of Bill Wilson seemed to address aspects of the disease and recovery in a manner that didn't leave much room for improvement." Nevertheless, this book does present new material on alcoholism, especially about its genetics and other scientific aspects, its costs and treatment, etc. Six composite personal stories of alcoholics are included. Chapter 13 is "Alcoholics Anonymous: Myths and Realities.".

1454. Wallace, John. "Ideology, Belief, and Behavior: Alcoholics Anonymous As a Social Movement". in: Gottheil, E./Druley, K. A./Skoloda, T. E./Waxman, H. M., Editors. Etiological Aspects of Alcohol and Drug Abuse. Springfield, IL: Charles C. Thomas; 1983: Chap. 18, pp285-305; 330pp.
Wallace attempts to dispell certain misconceptions about A.A.; with particular emphasis on the myth that A.A. rejects controlled drinking for alcoholics despite empirical findings to the contrary. He evaluates this research and concludes that the evidence gathered to support controlled drinking is invalid. He also examines several sources of the misconceptions regarding A.A.

1455. Ward, Robert I. "When You Go Back To Work". Center City, MN: Hazelden; Aug., 1984; ISBN: 0-89486-235-9.
This 15-page pamphlet includes suggestions on looking to A.A. for support in the transition from treatment back to the work force.

1456. Wassmer, Arthur, Dr. Recovering Together: How to Help an Alcoholic Without Hurting Yourself. First ed. New York: St. Martin's Press; 1989; 321pp; ISBN: 0-312-03416-4. LC 07 35075.
Note: Index, dj.
This clinical psychologist recommends A.A. and it is indexed 13 times. "In the years 1935-1960, AA was the only truly effective help available to alcoholics," he states. Chapter 14 is "The Twelve Steps: The Heart of Recovery.".

1457. The Way Back. Washington, D.C.: Whitman-Walker Clinic; 1982.
This is an anthology of stories of gay and lesbian alcoholics who recovered through AA.

1458. Webb, Lance. Conquering The Seven Deadly Sins. First ed. Nashville, TN: Abingdon Press; 1955: pp181-183 (AA).; 224pp; ISBN: LC 55-6768.
Note: X-lib, index, dj.
In the chapter on Lust & Gluttony, the author unreservedly recommends the book, Alcoholics Anonymous, for "any person who wants to be truly free, not just from alcohol, but from any other slavery of self-love." He discusses A.A.'s Twelfth Step and points out that such "intimate fellowship" is lacking in many churches. (Note: the 7 Deadly Sins are discussed in A.A.'s 12 & 12 book in the Step Four chapter.).

1459. Weber, Todd. The Next Step. First pb ed. Seattle, WA: Glen Abbey Books; 1991; 140pp; ISBN: 0-934125-25-2. LC 91-32096.
Weber hopes newcomers and oldtimers in all 12-Step programs will grow in "emotional sobriety," the "13th" step, through his book. He cites Bill W.'s 1958 Grapevine article on the difficulty of achieving the emotional sobriety of the promises and peace of mind after one has worked the 12 steps. Webb summarizes the 12 Steps in Chap. 2. In the acknowledgment he thanks his homegroup, S.O.S., leaving the impression he is a member of AA. [anonymity break].

1460. Wegscheider, Sharon. "AA as a Treatment Ally". in: Wegscheider, Sharon. Another Chance. Hope and Health for the Alcoholic Family. First ed. Palo Alto, CA: Science & Behavior Books, Inc.; 1981: Chap. 16, pp205-219; & other references to A.A.; 256 pp; ISBN: 0-8314-0059-5.
The author discusses two distinct traditions that both offer an effective method of treating alcoholism: A.A. and the alcoholism treatment profession. She claims a "deep personal dedication to both" and explores and compares the common shared beliefs and differences between the two. She claims the essential point about both is the need for mutual respect and interplay between the two. She criticizes the "AA is all you need" school of thought.

1461. Weiner, Jack B. Drinking. First ed. New York: W. W. Norton & Co., Inc.; 1976: numerous mentions of A.A. throughout; 241 pp.
Note: Lacks index.
Author of The Morning After, Weiner travelled 75,000 miles and interviewed hundreds to write this book about alcoholism. His three-year wide-ranging study looks at various alcoholics: teenagers, Catholic priests, military personnel, women, doctors, and prison inmates. A.A. is woven into their fabric of recovery.

1462. Weisman, Maxwell N., M.D./Robe, Lucy Barry. Relapse-Slips. Abstinent Alcoholics Who Return to Drinking. Minneapolis, MN: Johnson Institute; 1983; 51pp+; ISBN: 0-935908-14-5.
About half this booklet concerns A.A. Twelfth Step work, compromises concerning A.A., How Many A.A. Members Slip? and other attitudes about A.A. as they concern sobriety and slips are discussed.

1463. Welch, Bob/Vecsey, George. Five O'Clock Comes Early. A Young Man's Battle with Alcoholism. First ed. New York: William Morrow & Co., Inc.; 1982: Some references to A.A.; 244 pp; ISBN: 0-688-00810-0.
Dodger pitcher Bob Welch relates his battle with alcoholism and his recovery, including attendance at A.A. meetings.

1464. White, John [pseudonym]. Ward N-1. First ed. New York: A. A. Wyn, Inc.; 1955: A.A. mentioned favorably on dust jacket.; 187pp; ISBN: LC 55-10885.
Note: dj.
"In this true account, the author tells of his five nightmarish days in the alcoholic ward of Bellevue Hospital during which he had to make up his mind whether to return to Skid Row or make the long uphill climb to self-control and responsibility," the jacket states. After leaving Bellevue, he was a member of A.A. "It helped me greatly," he said but added "the cure lies within reach of anyone with this problem. It lies deep inside all of us: Seek and Ye Shall Find.".

1465. White, Kathleen M. "Drunk Stuff". First ed. Zarephath, NJ: Pillar of Fire; 1954: pp60, 63-7.; 271pp.
Note: Illus. with photos, dj.
The author believes that A.A. should take a stand publicly against alcohol itself and "that first drink.".

1466. Whitney, Elizabeth D. Living With Alcoholism. First ed. Boston, MA: Beacon Press; 1968: (AA throughout); 149pp; ISBN: LC 68-31384.
Note: dj.
Whitney was the founder of the Greater Boston Council on Alcoholism, the first voluntary community health organization devoted to alcoholism in the U.S. She begins this book with a down-to-earth description of alcoholism and then discusses the process of treatment, entry into A.A., relapse, and maintaining sobriety. A.A. is recommended throughout the book.

1467. Wholey, Dennis. The Courage to Change. First ed. Boston, MA: Houghton, Mifflin Co.; 1984: Chap. 12, pp245-83.; 309pp; ISBN: 0-395-35977-5. LC 84-12979.
Note: dj.
Wholey, the host of the PBS television series "LateNight America," interviewed movie stars, ministers, writers, sports figures, and members of A.A. for this book. Nineteen members of A.A., appearing anonymously, are included in Chapter 12 and tell their stories.

1468. Widener, Don. Lemmon. A Biography. First ed. New York/ London: Macmillan Pub. Co., Inc./Collier Macmillan Publishers; 1975: p190; 247pp; ISBN: 0-02-628000-3. LC 75-25712.
Note: Photos, index, dj.
"In preparation for their roles [in Days of Wine and Roses], Jack Lemmon and Lee Remick spent weeks attending Alcoholics Anonymous meetings. 'I was greeted very warmly,' he said, 'which made me a little nervous. They looked like they'd been expecting me! I came away with great respect for those people and that organization.".

1469. Williams, Lincoln. Tomorrow Will Be Sober. First American ed. New York: Harper & Brothers; 1960; ISBN: LC 60-12314.
Note: For abstract, see the first edition published in London, listed in the "Foreign" chapter.
This is the same as the First Edition, published in London, except the American edition includes a Foreword by Harry M. Tiebout, M.D., Trustee, Alcoholics Anonymous.

1470. Williams, Richard L./Moffat, Gene H., Editors. Occupational Alcoholism Programs. Springfield, IL: Charles C. Thomas - Publisher; 1975: 25 references to A.A.; 282pp; ISBN: 0-398-03282-3.

1471. Williams, Roger J. Alcoholism. The Nutritional Approach. First ed. Austin, TX: University of Texas Press; 1959: 9 references to AA.; 118pp; ISBN: L.C. 58-59850.
"The author has nothing but admiration for the work of Alcoholics Anonymous," and he has dedicated the book to A.A. He gives nutritional suggestions for A.A. members "on the ragged edge" that he states will help them more easily to maintain their sobriety in "nine cases out of ten.".

1472. Willis, George W. The Bottle Fighters. First ed. New York: Random House; 1963: pp311-12, mentions AA throughout.; 312pp; ISBN: L.C. 63-9357.
Willis' novel of an alcoholic contains some mentions of A.A. clubs, meetings, etc. A note about the author of the book at the back identifies him as a member of A.A., an obvious anonymity break that is excused on the grounds that "writers can't remain anonymous...".

1473. [Wilson, Bill]. "The Fellowship of Alcoholics Anonymous". in: Alcohol, Science, and Society. New Haven: Quarterly Journal of Studies on Alcohol; 1945: pp461-463, Lecture 28.
Note: Wilson signed this article by "Bill W.".

1474. [Wilson, Bill]. "The Fellowship of Alcoholics Anonymous". in: Catanzaro, Ronald J., M.D., Editor. Alcoholism: The Total Treatment Approach. Springfield, IL: Charles C. Thomas; 1968 & 1974: pp116-124; 508 pp; ISBN: 0-398-00295-9.
Note: Wilson signed this article as "Bill W.".

1475. Wilson, Bill. (foreword to text). in: The Christopher D. Smithers Foundation, Inc., Editor. Understanding Alcoholism: For the Patient, the Family, and the Employer. First ed. New York: Charles Scribner's Sons; 1968: Foreword & 22 other references to AA.; 257 pp; ISBN: L.C. 68-17356.
Note: Wilson signed this foreword as "W. G. Wilson." In a later printing, it was signed "W.G.W.".
The Co-founder of A.A. expresses his opinion on the usefulness of this book and its openminded approach to the many facets of the alcoholism problem. Bill W. writes: "We AA's can now truly say `that in isolation we shall be limited but in cooperation with our friends, all may become possible.".

1476. Wilson, Jan R./Wilson, Judith A. Addictionary. A Primer of Recovery Terms & Concepts from Abstinence to Withdrawal. First ed. Park Ridge, IL: Simon & Schuster, a Fireside-Parkside Recovery Book; 1992: 7 references to AA.; 410pp; ISBN: 0-671-76696-1. LC 92-19070.
Note: index, pb.
AA history, Steps, Traditions, spirituality, and other basic Fellowship topics are summarized.

1477. Wilson, Richard. The Journey of the Beatitudes. First ed. Center City, MN: Hazelden; July, 1986; 49pp; ISBN: 0-89486-363-0.
Note: pb.
Wilson believes the eight Beatitudes Jesus preached in the Sermon on the Mount contain the same central message as the Twelve Steps of A.A. He compares the two sets of principles and finds them compatiable with each other.

1478. Wilson, William J. Say When. First ed. New York: Paulist Press, Emmaus Books; 1978: About dozen mentions of AA.; 112pp; ISBN: 0-8091-2074-7. LC 77-14812.
Note: pb.
Through a dozen dramatizations of alcoholics in their cups and their loved ones, this book aims at establishing a loving, emotional connection between the two. AA is recommended.

1479. Winters, Ariel. Alternatives for the Problem Drinker. A.A. is not the only way. First ed. New York/London: Drake Publishers, Inc.; 1978: Chap. 5, pp44-56 & throughout.; 160pp; ISBN: 0-84713-1701-3. LC 77-87466.
Note: index.
Winters discusses the "alcohol war" in modern times between the psychological behaviorists and the Jellinek-NCA-AA alliance. Among the topics are the Rand Report, new trends among teens and women, behavior modification, the disease concept, etc. She presents a fairly balanced criticism of AA, listing pros and cons.

1480. Wiseman, Jacqueline P. Stations of the Lost: The Treatment of Skid Row Alcoholics. Second ed. Chicago/London: Univ. of Chicago Press; 1979; c1970: AA: 45, 51, 232-33, 298.; 346pp; ISBN: 0-226-90307-9. LC 79-13632.
Note: pb.
The author states that AA "has never had much appeal for the lower-class alcoholic. Skid Row alcoholics dislike 'drunkalogs,' 'snottiness,' and 'holier-than-thou' attitudes of the reformed alcoholics or 'AA virgins,' as they call them." Early Salvation Army centers also required alcoholics to attend AA meetings. She says the vast majority of Skid Row alcoholics only attended AA meetings in order to convince someone they were drinking when, in fact, they were or soon would be.

1481. Woititz, Janet Geringer. Marriage on the Rocks: Learning to Life with Yourself and an Alcoholic. First ed. New York: Delacorte Press; 1979: 7 references to AA.; 148pp; ISBN: 0-440-05918-6.
Note: Addressed primarily to the wives of alcoholics.

1482. Woodward, Nancy Hyden. If Your Child Is Drinking... First ed. New York: G. P. Putnam's Sons; 1981: AA: pp119-124, etc.; 256pp; ISBN: 0-399-12457-8. LC 81-15420.
Note: dj.
Three out of every ten high school students may be problem drinkers and this book tackles that problem with suggestions for intervention, education, community action, etc., including a recommendation of AA, Al-Anon and Alateen. It is subtitled "what you can do to fight alcohol abuse at home, at school, and in the community.".

1483. Yablonsky, Lewis. Synanon: The Tunnel Back. First paperback ed. Baltimore, MD: Penguin Books; 1967: pp48-9, 54-5, 88, 127; 408pp.
Note: The first edition in hardback was published in 1965 by The Macmillan Company, New York, under the title "The Tunnel Back.".
"Immediately before founding Synanon, Chuck (Charles E. Dederich) had been a devotee of A.A., and although it helped him quit drinking, he found it limiting. In retrospect, it seems that any approach not 'completely' developed by Chuck himself was too binding for his roaring ego needs," Yablonsky states. " With the influx of drug addicts...a battle welled up between the addicts and some members of A.A. The break with A.A. occurred about the middle of August (1958)," Yablonsky quotes Dederich. He says the alkies didn't like the addicts particularly because of Chuck's use of LSD. "I will always be grateful to A.A. for helping me personally, (but) Synanon has nothing to do with A.A.," Dederich says.

1484. Yahraes, Herbert. "Alcoholism Is A Sickness". New York: Public Affairs Committee, Inc.; 1946.
Alcoholics Anonymous basics are discussed on pages 22-23 of this 32-page Public Affairs pamphlet 118.

1485. Yale H. The Beginners' Meetings. Center City, Minnesota: Hazelden; March, 1984; 34 pp; ISBN: 0-89486-217-0.
The stated purpose of this booklet is to present an introduction to alcoholism and the Twelve Steps suggested by A.A. for recovery. It is a printed version of four beginners' meetings held weekly among A.A. groups in Denver. Yale, an alcoholic and member of A.A., focuses the discussion entirely on the Steps.

1486. Yalom, Irvin D. The Theory and Practice of Group Psychotherapy. Third ed. New York: Basic Books; 1985; c1970: 10 references to AA.; 590pp; ISBN: 0-465-08447-8. LC 85-47566.
Note: Index.
Although this psychiatrist views AA favorably, he, like many professionals, terms it a "self-help" group, a characterization that most AA's would not use, preferring "God-help." Many professionals attempt to fit AA into psychiatric definitions which basically cannot delineate the spiritual heart of the society. Yalom discusses the rise of many 12-Step groups in some depth throughout this textbook.

1487. Youcha, Geraldine. A Dangerous Pleasure. New York: Hawthorn Books, Inc.; 1978: 18 mentions of AA.; 240pp.
Youcha writes of alcohol from the women's perspective. She calls A.A. the "most successful of the treatment approaches now available," but she questions the necessity anonymity. "But AA isn't for everyone," she says and cites "some people whose natural reticence makes it impossible for them to reveal themselves in a group.".

1488. Youcha, Geraldine. Women and Alcohol. First Revised ed. New York: Crown; 1986: pp82, 174-6, 190-1.; 242 pp; ISBN: 0-517-55978-1.
Note: The first edition was published in 1978.
Youcha, co-author of Children of Alcoholism, questions the necessity of A.A. being anonymous; labels it "middle class"; states that there are "sexual tensions" but that A.A. is a "great place to meet single men." Like most other ACOA writers, she downplays A.A.'s importance and suggests it be used in conjunction with other therapies; nonetheless, she admits "AA is generally recognized as the most successful of the treatment approaches now available.".

1489. Zimberg, S. "Alcoholics Anonymous and Al-Anon". in: Clinical Management of Alcoholism. New York: Brunner-Mazel; 1982: pp117-124; 251pp.
AA is described as one of the most successful self-help groups directed at dealing with an illness, and is the single most effective modality available for alcoholism treatment. The philosophies of AA, Al-Anon, and Alateen are briefly discussed.

1490. Zimberg, S. "Psychotherapy in the Treatment of Alcoholism". in: Pittison, E./Kaufman, E., editors. Encyclopedic Handbook of Alcoholism. New York: Gardner Press; 1982: pp999-1010; 1230pp.
The author contends many health care professionals believe the alcoholic is not motivated for treatment and could not be successfully treated even if motivated. Zimberg feels otherwise, noting that various psychotherapeutic techniques, including individual and group psychotherapy and Alcoholics Anonymous, etc., have resulted in recovery rates reported from 40 to 60%.

1491. Zimberg, Sheldon/Wallace, John/Blume, Sheila B., Editors. Practical Approaches to Alcoholism Psychotherapy. First ed. New York: Plenum Press; 1978: Over 40 references to AA.; 288pp; ISBN: 0-306-40086-3.
Note: See also: Alinbrandi, "Folk Psychotherapy of AA," a chapter in this book.

1492. Zinberg, Norman E., M.D./Fraser, Kathleen M., Ed.M. "The Role of the Social Setting in the Prevention and Treatment of Alcoholism". in: Mendelson, Jack H., M.D./Mello, Nancy K., Ph.D., Editors. The Diagnosis and Treatment of Alcoholism. First ed. New York: McGraw-Hill Book Co.; 1979: Chap. 10, pp 375-381; 405 pp; ISBN: 0-07-041476-9.
The authors discuss AA's success from the sociological point of view.

Chapter VII = Popular Magazine Articles

1493. "12th Step Back; Harry Irving at Twelfth Step House". Sign; 1951; 30(12): 32-34.
This is a pictorial essay showing Harry Irving's work with alcoholics. Irving recovered through AA [anonymity break] and founded Twelfth Step House.

1494. "A.A. A Uniquely American Phenomenon". Fortune; Feb. 1951; 43: pp99-100, 138, 141-142, 144.
This enthusiastic popular magazine article outlines the A.A. fellowship, founding, and principles. A.A. is based entirely on the reality of spiritual experience, the article states. Reprints are distributed by A.A. in English and many foreign languages.

1495. "A.A. Booklet". Weekly Unity; Dec. 7, 1940.
[?].

1496. "A.A.'s Auxiliary: Al-Anon". Time; Dec. 17, 1956: pp50-51.
Comparisons with AA are made.

1497. "A.A.'s". Bulletin [Oklahoma City, OK]; April, 1945.

1498. [AA Members]. Our Guiding Star; Spring, 1969: 28pp.
This quarterly journal was published by female inmates from the Guiding Star Group of AA at the Ohio Reformatory for Women, Maryville, Ohio. It contains articles, personal stories of recovery, poems, cartoons, etc., written by female AA inmates.

1499. "AA Groups' Dilemma: Those Other Addictions". Alcoholism: The National Magazine; 1982; 3(2): p57.
The influx of nonalcoholic drug addicts into AA meetings is a matter of growing concern to AA groups in the U.S. and Canada.

1500. "AA Means Alcoholics Anonymous". Social Action; April 15, 1950; 16(4): p27.
This small box ad states: "AA/Means/Alcoholics Anonymous/Means/Recovery for Thousands of Alcoholics/Costs Nothing/Available Everywhere/Effective/For Information Consult Your Telephone Directory.".

1501. "AA Meetings Go On The Air". Alcoholism & Addiction; June, 1988; 8(5): p10 of "Recovery" sect.
Radio station KNWZ carries an AA meeting every Sunday night at 5 o'clock for listeners in the Palm Springs and the Coachella Valley in Southern California. The meeting is taped in advance, anonymity and the other Traditions are protected, and the air time is paid by the Friday brown bag group.

1502. "AA Membership Survey". Alcoholism & Addiction; Dec. 1987; 8(2): p13.
The percentage of alcoholics who credit "rehab" or counselors for their coming to A.A. continues to increase, this article states, using data from the 1986 survey conducted by the GSO of AA.

1503. "AA Mill Creek Group". Shadows, Oregon State Penitentiary.; May, 1947.

1504. "AA on Broadway". Catholic Digest; March 28, 1945.

1505. "AA Production to Debut". Alcoholism; Oct., 1984; 5(1): p66.
This news item reveals the book, Drinking in America, A History, will be made into a documentary and include, for the first time, the beginnings of AA. The Gary Whiteaker Co., Inc., shot the scenes of Bill W. and Dr. Bob meeting to co-found the Fellowship on location in St. Louis.

1506. "AA Wants Its Trademarked Symbols Back Home!". Lifestyles of the Clean & Sober; March 1990; 1(6): pp1 & 8.
This front page article reports on AAWS's efforts to get manufacturers and retailers to stop using the circle-and-triangle symbol on products. Comments from a "spokesman" at AAWS, Wendell's which produces medallions and which stopped using that symbol with the words "Unity, Service & Recovery," AA's three legacies.

1507. Aaron Z. "Jews Can't Be Alcoholics...Can They?". Sober Times; Jan., 1993; 7(1): p10.
AA is mentioned several times in this article, including Bill Wilson: "We are only operating a spiritual kindergarten...each man's theology is his own quest.".

1508. "Addiction Self-Help Formed for Orthodox Jews". Young Israel Viewpoint; December 1981.
The article describes a special interest AA meeting formed for orthodox Jews.

1509. "Advertisement for Jack Alexander article". Newsweek; March 3, 1941.

1510. "The Al-Anon Family Group Story: A Legacy of Love". Alcoholism & Addiction; Sept.-Oct., 1985; 5(7): pp49-52.
This is part 5 of the continuing series "The Fellowship: The First 50 Years." Here, Bill Pittman discusses the founding and growth of Al-Anon and its Co-Founder, Lois W., Bill's wife. Although Al-Anon is not part of A.A., its history is intimately tied up with the Fellowship and the two cooperate but are not affiliated with each other.

1511. "Alcoholics Anonymous: Book Review". Scientific Temperance Journal; 1939; (Autumn).

1512. "Alcoholics Anonymous: Book Review". The Baptist Record; Dec. 23, 1939.

1513. "Alcoholics Anonymous: Book Review". The Baptist Leader; Jan. 1940.

1514. "Alcoholics Anonymous: Book Review". Newsweek; Feb. 19, 1940: pp56-57.
This article claims A.A. had a success rate of 25% in its first 5 years. The founding of A.A. and the Rockefeller dinner are discussed.

1515. "Alcoholics Anonymous: Book Review". Time; Feb. 19, 1940.

1516. "Alcoholics Anonymous: Book Review". The Pastor's Periscope; Aug., 1940.

1517. "Alcoholics Anonymous: Book Review". The Supreme Council, 33, Bulletin; Aug. 15, 1940.

1518. "Alcoholics Anonymous: Book Review". The Master Key; 1940-41.

1519. "Alcoholics Anonymous". The Little Chronicle of the American Grey Friars; April, 1941.

1520. "Alcoholics Anonymous". The Houghton Line; Jan., 1943.

1521. "Alcoholics Anonymous: A Little More Time". The Voice, Dayton, OH; March, 1943.

1522. "Alcoholics Anonymous". Catholic Digest; July, 1943.

1523. "Alcoholics Anonymous: Book Review". The Master Key; 1943-44.

1524. "Alcoholics Anonymous". Catholic Digest; April, 1944.

1525. "Alcoholics Anonymous". Overture [Los Angeles]; Feb., 1945.

1526. "Alcoholics Anonymous". News and Views; Sept., 1946.

1527. "Alcoholics Anonymous". Hygeia; July 1948: pp496-497+.

1528. "Alcoholics Anonymous Spurn A Trap". Christian Center; Feb. 22, 1950: p229.

1529. "Alcoholics Anonymous". Better Living [DuPont]; May-June, 1950.

1530. "Alcoholics Anonymous: Dangers of Success". Nation; March 2, 1964; 198: p212.

1531. "Alcoholics Anonymous". Health Letter; August 1978; 10: p4.
The article gives basic information about A.A.

1532. "Alcoholics Anonymous Goes to Russia". Bottom Line; 1988; 9(1): 21-23.
In part, the article explains that "to avoid offending the atheistic sensibilities of the Soviet leadership, AA literature distributed in Russia was translated from a version devised by a New York chapter for atheists and agnostics.".

1533. "Alcoholics Credit `Rehab' for AA Referrals". Alcoholism & Addiction; Dec., 1987; 8(2): p13.
The AA survey of its membership, conducted every three years, is discussed.

1534. "Alcoholics on the Air". Time; March 5, 1945: p53.
Detroit's WWJ radio station's pioneer broadcasts by A.A. members are discussed, the first such radio venture in the U.S.

1535. "Alcoholism". Consumer Report; Nov. 1960: pp614-616.
How alcoholism can be detected and community agencies' role in that are explored in this article. A.A.'s methods are discussed.

1536. Alcoholism. The National Magazine; 1980-1992; Vols. 1-12.
Note: This magazine was renamed Alcoholism & Addiction with the August, 1985, issue, and then renamed again Addiction & Recovery with the June, 1990, issue. It suspended operations several times because of financial difficulty.
This magazine contains many articles on AA. Individual article listings appear separately under title or author designations. For individual articles, the listing for the magazine title is abbreviated to simply Alcoholism. The first six issues in 1980 contained ten articles on AA including: the 45th Anniversary at St. Louis [1, pp32-33]; Kodak, early years [1, pp42-44]; Hazelden [2, pp30-32]; military [6, pp37-39]; at Family Treatment Centers [5, p5]; Indiana [2, p38]; Brookwood Lodge [6, pp34-35]; etc.

1537. "Alcoholism: New Victims, New Treatments". Time; April 22, 1974; 103: pp59-65.
Most of the new treatments mentioned owe much "to AA," the article states. In a sidebar, three of the five case histories are successful AA members.

1538. Alexander, Jack. "Alcoholics Anonymous: Freed Slaves of Drink, Now They Free Others". Saturday Evening Post; March 1, 1941: pp9-11.
This was the first major magazine article and in the year following its publication, A.A. membership soared from about 2,000 to 8,000 as a direct result of this national publicity. Alexander spent months with A.A. members, interviewing Bill W. and many others.

1539. Alexander, Jack. "Alcoholics Anonymous". Saturday Evening Post; Nov. & Dec. 1982, Feb. 1983; 254-5-7: p20+ & pp30-31+ [part I].
This is a three-part re-run of the original 1941 Alexander article.

1540. Alexander, Jack. "Drunkard's Best Friend". Saturday Evening Post; April 1, 1950: pp17-18, 74-79.
Like his first Saturday Evening Post article, this prompted a deluge of calls to A.A. and tremendous growth in membership.

1541. Almoni, Ploni. "My Name is Rabbi Almoni". JACS Journal; 1986; 3(1): 3,9.
Rabbi Almoni tells of his addiction and recovery through AA [anonymity break]. Special focus is placed on denial.

1542. Anna A. "An Alcoholic's Story". Reader's Digest (Canadian edition); Feb., 1985; 126: p79 (5).

1543. Anonymous. "An Alcoholic's Letter to His Son". Denver Post; Oct. 16, 1966.
Note: [also condensed and reprinted by Reader's Digest, Nov., 1966, issue and in a separate pamphlet reprint].
An AA member shares his story in a cautionary letter to his son, a college freshman.

1544. Anonymous. "How I Got to AA". Cosmopolitan; April, 1987; 202: p162 (3).

1545. Anonymous. "Living Sober: The 50th Anniversary of Alcoholics Anonymous". Village Voice; July 23, 1985.: pp63-74.
The founding of AA, the 12 Steps, and how agnostics and atheists can embrace the fellowship's spiritual program of recovery are discussed. Three personal witness accounts of recovery through the AA fellowship are provided.

1546. "Anonymous Ally". Time; Feb. 8, 1971: p52.
This two-column article and photo of William Griffith Wilson identifies Bill with full name and photo as the "A.A. Founder," a clear anonymity break. The article reviews briefly Bill's drinking and co-founding of AA, mentions his retirement in 1962, and notes AA now has 475,000 members in 16,000 groups in the U.S. as well as 90 foreign countries.

1547. "Anonymous Struggle for 25 Years". New York Times Magazine; June 5, 1960: p26.

1548. "The Archives of AA". Alcoholism/The National Magazine; 1985; 5(3): pp55-57.

1549. Arms, Michael. "Priest Lays to Rest 5th Step Obstacles". Chalice; 1984; 10(1): 5.
In this article, Fr. Arms "tries to show some of the obstacles [of taking step 5] and, at the same time, tries to lay to rest those obstacles.".

1550. Arnaud A. "Fifty Years with Gratitude". Alcoholism & Addiction; Sept.-Oct. 1985; 5(7): pp73-75.
This is a 3-page color pictorial essay on the 50th International Convention of A.A. in Montreal, Canada, July 4-7, 1985.

1551. "Attorney Who Saved AA Crusade Is Dead". in: Associated Press wire service. Akron, OH; Sept. 19, 1954.
This six-paragraph AP wire story reported the death of William I. Dotson. "He was 43 and apparently a hopeless alcoholic when the two founders of AA found him in Akron City Hospital, so drunk he couldn't talk," the article reported. The two AA founders were "almost ready to give up their AA work...but Dotson succeeded splendidly and never took another drink of liquor." Dotson was a native of Lexington, KY, and died at age 62 in Crile Veterans Hosp. in Cleveland. Bill D. was AA 3.

1552. Atwater, Rick. "AA and the Addiction Counselor". Alcoholism & Addiction; May/June 1987; 7(5): p45.
"AA does not need professionals. It is professionals who need AA," Atwater, a private practice addiction counselor in Illinois, begins his article. He suggests integration of therapy and the AA program by removing the "different rules we play by" and requiring patients to actively participate in AA. He also discusses the AA tradition of anonymity and the need to move away from "therapese" language. The spiritual dimension of our counseling work needs to be recognized also, he states.

1553. "Babies by Vacuum". Time; July 11, 1960; 76: p62.

1554. Bacon, S. D. "Facts about Alcoholism: Interview". U. S. News & World Report; Oct. 2, 1953: pp36-42, 104-119.
This interview with the Yale Center of Alcohol Studies Director ranges over alcoholism and disease, youth, textbooks, psychiatry, heredity, blackouts, business and industry, traffic accidents, etc. While psychiatry fails, Bacon believes AA plays "a most significant role" in treating the alcoholic.

1555. Baim, Tracy. "Being Lesbian and Alcoholic". Windy City Times; Sept. 26, 1985; 1(1): pp11+.
The article explains basic AA concepts and how they relate to lesiban alcoholics. (NALGAP 047).

1556. Baum, Gregory. "Secular Spiritualities". New Catholic World; March 1976; 219: p52.

1557. Bebe L. "The Princess and the Priest". JACS Journal; 1986; 3(2): 4-5.
Bebe focuses her testimonial on the difficulty she faced as a Jew trying to come to a God of her understanding in AA. Although she is not critical of the Christian focus of AA, she emphasizes the need for spiritual materials to be published in the Jewish tradition.

1558. Begley, Sharon. "The long road back; `after-care,' for drug and alcohol abusers.". Newsweek; May 11, 1987; 109: p66.
The article includes a smaller section on A.A.'s Twelve Steps.

1559. "Behavior: Anonymous Ally". Time; Feb. 8, 1971: p52.
This article recounts some of Bill W.'s early experiences in co-founding AA.

1560. Benton, Virginia Hall. "Women Also Turn to A.A.". The Columbia Dispatch Magazine; May 12, 1946.

1561. Berg, Steven L. "Alcoholic Priests: Are They Effective Pastors?". The Priest; August 1989: 43-45.
The article explains the type of spiritual growth a priest gets from AA and argues that a recovered alcoholic priest is an effective pastor.

1562. Berg, Steven L., Ph.D. "Spiritual Issues in Recovery from Alcoholism". Pastoral Life; Oct. 1993: pp32-37.
Berg suggests priests "would be advised to read AA's Big Book and attend a few open meetings of AA." He provides six guidelines for actions and attitudes priests should cultivate in working with alcoholics.

1563. Bergen, Teresa. "Laws on drug use are tough; AA meetings rare". Sober Times; July 1992; 6(7): p14.
Globetrotting Bergen reports on the drug scene in Indonesia and the country's two AA meetings in Bali, started by Australian Bob in Feb., 1991.

1564. Bergen, Teresa. "Travels with Teresa...Hong Kong". Sober Times; August 1992; 6(8): p16.
AA meetings in Hong Kong, the Big Book being translated into Chinese, the central office, etc., are travel-logged.

1565. Bergen, Teresa. "Travels with Teresa: Can Thai Buddhists 12-Step?". Sober Times; Dec. 1992; 6(12): p13.
Bergen discuss the lack of AA among Asians and AA meetings in Malaysia and Singapore. She mistakenly suggests Asians reject AA because of its insistence on a "Christian god.".

1566. "Big Book Hits the Big 50". Lifestyles of the Clean and Sober; Oct. 1989; 1(1): p8.
This brief article on the 50th anniversary of Alcoholics Anonymous, the "Big Book" contains basic information.

1567. "The Big Book Reviewed". Alcoholism & Addiction; May-June 1988; 8(5): p38.
The Recovery section of this magazine reprinted from 50 years ago the book reviews of "Alcoholics Anonymous" published in the Oct. 14, 1939, Journal of the American Medical Association and in the Sept. 1940Journal of Nervous Mental Disorders which were both very negative about the then new volume.

1568. Bill H. "My Name is Bill H.". Catholic Digest; December 1989; 53(2): pp1-2, 5-6, 17-18, 20, 22, 24.
Condensed from The Critic, Chicago, IL, this Catholic Irish alcoholic (CIA) tells his story of recovery in A.A.

1569. Bill M. "Straight Up". Pathways; June-July, 1992; 1(4): p62.
For this AA member, sobriety was a gift that allowed him to be fully present during his parents' final days.

1570. Bill S. "From Russia With Love". Alcoholism & Addiction & Recovery Life; Oct., 1989; 9(3-4): p32.
Twenty AA's and Al-Anon's from the U.S.A. travel to Russia with the Fellowships' message. They held a meeting in Leningrad and alcoholics there began their own meeting as a result.

1571. Bill S. "Paradise Lost - and Found". Sober Times; March, 1993; 7(3): p6.
The author was the lone recovering alcoholic on this West Indian Caribbean island who attended the first AA meeting there. The history of the island group is recounted.

1572. Bill W. "Is A.A. for Alcoholics Only?". Guideposts; Sept. 1947; 2(7): Section 2, unpaged.
Co-Founder Wilson signed this article "Bill W.".

1573. "Bill W. and the Troubled Beginnings of A.A. from Some One Who Was There". Recovery Today; May, 1992; 2(12).

1574. "Bill W.". Life; Fall, 1990; 13(12): p66.
The Co-Founder of AA, Bill W., is one of "The Life 100 Most Important Americans of the 20th Century." The two paragraphs citing him and a fellow Vermonter (Dr. Bob is not mentioned by name) are accompanied by a photo of Bill in his kitchen making coffee.

1575. The Bird Word; 1981-94.
Note: Address: The Bird Word, P.O.Box 80072, Lansing, MI 48908, USA. Suggested subscription is $4. US dollars a year. This is the quarterly newsletter of "Birds of a Feather" Int'l., a group of pilots, navigators, and other airline personnel in A.A. Usually 8 pages, 8.5 x 11". Contains stories of AA recovery, news of "nests" [groups & meetings], BOAF Int'l Convention, favorite sections from the Big Book, etc.

1576. "Birds of a Feather Flock to Annual Banquet". Alcoholism & Addiction; August, 1985; 5(6): p76.
Brief news article on May 18, 1985, banquet of Birds of a Feather AA members, pilots and other airline personnel in the Fellowship.

1577. Bishop, Charles, Jr. "The Alcoholism Collection: The Invisible Pink Elephant of Americana". AB Bookman's Weekly; Sept. 10, 1984; 74(11): pp1499, 1504, 1506, 1508.
Note: A full page ad on p1507 advertises a rare book catalogue devoted to the subject of alcoholism by Bishop. It lists rare A.A. literature for sale.
In a survey written for antiquarian booksellers, Bishop lists "Alcoholics Anonymous" as the answer that finally arrived for the problem of alcoholism in American history. The A.A. book is ranked number one of the 10 most important books in history on alcoholism.

1578. Bishop, L. K. "Alcoholics Anonymous". Young People's Standards; 1944.

1579. Blau, Melinda. "Recovery Fever". New York; Sept. 9, 1991: pp30-37.
Changes in AA meetings from discussions about "relationships, " focusing on "me," younger members, etc., reviewed. "The Woodstock generation has arrived --- and I'm glad," one older AA member commented. Other 12-step programs are compared to AA and membership in two programs is discussed.

1580. Bliss, Sonny. "I Surrender, You Surrender, He Surrenders, We Surrender...". Sober Times; Nov. 1992; 6(11): p5.
The author, a New York writer using a pseudonym, discuss William James and his book, The Varieties of Religious Experience, Bill Wilson, AA Co-Founder, and the "surrender" concept.

1581. Bob, Alcoholic. "The Guest House Experience". Wheeling, WV: The Catholic Spirit; Nov. 23, 1979.
This full page newspaper article with anonymous photo of the alcoholic Catholic priest details his alcoholism, entry into Guest House, an alcoholic rehabilitation center for clergy in Lake Orion, Michigan, and his recovery from alcoholism and re-entry into the active priesthood.

1582. Bob P. "A.A.'s start had roots in Greenwich". Greenwich, CT: Greenwich newspaper; 1985.
This article by Bob P., a Riverside resident and AAer, gives the history of Greenwich, CT, AA, which is cited as the "third oldest AA group in the world," beginning May 17, 1939 [?]. Discussed are Dr. Harry Tiebout, Marty M., and "Greenie," the first Greenwich AAer; Art S. with 46 years of sobriety; Bill W. speaking at Greenwich; and much more historical material about early AA in New York and Connecticut.

1583. Bob P. "Unforgettable Bill W.". Reader's Digest; April, 1986; 20(118): pp1-20.
Fine portrait of the Co-Founder of AA by an anonymous staff member of the General Service Office in New York.

1584. "Book Review: '90 Meetings in 90 Days' by Ernie K.". Alcoholism & Addiction; August, 1985; 5(6): p14 in "Recovery Newsletter" insert.
This book chronicles the experiences of an AA member attending 90 meetings in 90 days. "Regular AA attendance is the best safeguard against relapse.".

1585. Borracho, El. "Casting Call". Boston Magazine; Feb. 1985; 77: p104 (5).
This article is a personal narrative of alcoholism including mention of A.A.

1586. Borracho, El. "A God of one's own; the flesh was willing, but staying off the booze required a soupcon of spirit.". Boston Magazine; Nov. 1984; 76: p134 (3).

1587. Bradley, Ann M. "Keep Coming Back. The Case for a Valuation of Alcoholics Anonymous". Alcohol Health & Research World; 1988; 12(13): 192-199.
This outstanding article, well-documented with over 60 references with major studies, attempts to bridge the gap between the "solid truths" of the success of AA and the scientific methodological failure from the professional treatment community to substantiate and define those truths about the disease of alcoholism and AA's contribution to a solution for that. She points out that despite the "eloquent disputations on the science versus self-help schism," the partnership between AA and professional treatment seems to have strengthened over the years. She discusses AA as treatment adjunct, as primary intervention, as pretreatment influence, as aftercare, as multimodal treatment component, and correlates of AA affiliation and of AA participation. She concludes "Although couched in rhetoric that may provoke unease in some researchers from scientific disciplines, the AA 12-Step program nevertheless offers a model for synthesizing biomedical, psychosocial, and environmental approaches..." She recommends continuing efforts with more of an attitude of cultural anthropologists, less dissecting and more accepting of the integrity of AA's "solid truths.".

1588. Brady, William, Dr. "What Chance Has An Alcoholic?". in: Akron Beacon Journal. Akron, OH; June 20, 1949.
This columnist notes "Alcoholics Anonymous has achieved a great many complete and lasting cures.".

1589. Brennan, Eileen/Taishoff, Lee Stuckey. "No More Lost Weekends". Washingtonian; April 1981; 16: p157.

1590. Brett, Regina. "AA Pilgrims reach Mayflower". The Beacon Journal. Akron, OH; June 13, 1993; C: pp1, 5.
This newspaper article reported over 500 AA's visited the Mayflower Hotel in Akron, Ohio, this weekend. This was the hotel where Bill W. made the phone call in search of another alcoholic and where he almost went into the bar for a drink after his business venture failed. This was the first year the tenants of the hotel, now a senior citizens' residence, opened the doors so AA's could come in and see where it all started with a 10 cent phone call. AA's in Akron, the birthplace of AA, celebrate Founders' Weekend each year to recall the founding of AA June 10, 1935. Weekend AA attendance was over 6,000.

1591. Brooks, Bill. "A Spiritual Experience". Professional Counselor; 1987; 2(1): 20.
A general discussion of spirituality and the role of the higher power in AA recovery.

1592. Brophy, Beth. "I'm one drink away from a drunk.". U.S. News & World Report; Nov. 30, 1987; 103: p63.
An interview with Nan Robertson, the author of Getting Better: Inside Alcoholics Anonymous.

1593. Brown, Edgar. "So You Can't Stop Drinking? Here's How to Get a Permanent Seat on the Wagon". Chicago Herald-American; June, 1945; (six-part series).
Brown writes a fictitious profile of an alcoholic, J. Buffington Nutmeg, and his story of slips, introduction to AA, and recovery. The Twelve Steps are explored along with the Big Book, meetings, service, etc.

1594. Bucknam, Dolores. "Book Corner review: Getting Better: Inside Alcoholics Anonymous by Nan Robertson". in: Parents' Assn. To Neutralize Drug & Alcohol Abuse [PANDAA]. Annandale, VA; June, 1990; (Vol. XI, No. 2): p2.
Buckham emphasizes the personal recovery story of Nan Robertson who breaks her anonymity as a A.A. member.

1595. Bufe, Charles. "AA: Guilt and God for the Gullible". Utne Reader; Nov.-Dec. 1988: 54-55.
Although he recognizes some of the benefits in AA, Bufe is critical of AA's "cult-like atmosphere".

1596. Buhr, Thomas. "Passing the Basket...Support Groups Don't Run on Good Feelings Alone". Sober Times; June 1993; 7(6): p20.
"No dues or fees for AA membership" but Buhr reports contributions to AA intergroups and AA literature sales are declining. Competition with clubs, treatment centers, rising costs of answering services, etc., lack of understanding AA by newcomers...reasons for the financial crunch are discussed.

1597. Buhr, Thomas. "Recovery by Computer". Sober Times; Dec. 1992; 6(12): p11.
Buhr notes that Tom O. gave a presentation on computer bulletin boards at the 55th AA Int'l Convention in Seattle in 1990. AA meetings on computer bulletin boards should not replace regular meetings, sponsors, or Step work, one user noted.

1598. Burning, Martha. "AA: A Model Spiritual Organization". CoEvolution Quarterly; Summer, 1984: p74 (2).

1599. By Bill [Alcoholics Anonymous founder]. "Alcoholics Anonymous Have 50,000 Members". Vernal, Utah, Express; April 20, 1950.
Bill Wilson answers the question "Why can't A.A. principles be applied to any personal problem?" with "Yet we of A.A. cannot but feel that great things certainly await those who will earnestly try our '12 Steps' substituting their own distressing problems for that of alcohol.

1600. Cain, A. H. "Alcoholics Anonymous: Cult or Cure?". Harper's Magazine; Feb. 1963; 226: pp48-52.
Note: This article was reprinted in Discussion, April, 1963, p6.
Cain is probably the chief critic of A.A. and this is the first anti-A.A. article to appear in any mass market, popular magazine. He criticizes A.A. for being religious and anti-scientific and for having too much influence on public education about alcoholism.

1601. Cain, Arthur H. "Speaking Out: Alcoholics Can Be Cured Despite A.A.". Saturday Evening Post; Sept. 19, 1964; 237: p6.
Claiming a cure is possible, Cain criticizes A.A. for just "arresting" it. Having attended many hundreds of A.A. meetings, Cain concludes it is arrogant, dogmatic, too religious, and bigoted.

1602. Campbell, Colin. "Spirituality and the AA Movement". Priest; December 1988: 12-14.
This article is the text for a talk that Bishop Campbell delivered at the 1988 North American AA convention. He argues "that the work of the AA movement and the work of the Church are beautiful compliments to one another.".

1603. Carlson, Christina. "The Wisdom of A.A.". Alcoholism The National Magazine; Summer 1985; 5(5): p3 in Recovery section.
The author lists and discusses 16 of the most common A.A. slogans and their inherent pragmatic wisdom for the alcoholic.

1604. "Case History of an Alcoholic". Look; June 26, 1945: pp26-33.
Note: Photo-illustrated.
Produced by Paul Marcus, Editor, this fictitious story of Joe, an alcoholic, is accompanied by a dozen photographs tracing his phone call to AA for help, his hospitalization, his sponsor's help, weekly AA meetings, recovery and helping other alcoholics get into AA. Fourteen test questions from an AA pamphlet for those who have a problem with alcoholism end the article. Minnesota AA's were used in this article.

1605. Chace, Tom. "The Serenity Prayer Is Not Anonymous". Sober Times; Dec. 1992; 6(12): p21.
Chace states the Serenity Prayer was written in 1934 by Dr. Reinhold Niebuhr of Union Theological Seminary in New York City. Ruth Hock, AA's first employee and a non-alcoholic, sent the prayer out with hundreds of letters to Fellowship members around the world and it caught on.

1606. the Chalice. Calix Newsletter; 1972-93: usually 6pp per issue.
The Chalice is the official publication of the Calix Society, Minneapolis, MN, a group of mostly AA members, predominantly Catholic but open to any denomination, who try to increase their AA spirituality through the Eleventh Step in this group. Articles about AA's Steps and related topics appear often in this newsletter.

1607. Charest, Jack. "An Agnostic Works It Out". Recovery Magazine; May/June, 1984: pp14-15.
Charest, a former agnostic, reveals how he found God in one of the "classiest drunks farms in the U.S. [where they] followed the principles of Alcoholics Anonymous." Throughout the article, he breaks his annonymity.

1608. Chmel, Junalee. "Growing Up in an AA Family, Sharing Tears and Laughter". Sober Times; July 1991; 5(7): p11.
Chmel recounts the sad and glad memories of growing up with an alcoholic and then sober mom who will shortly celebrate her 14th AA birthday.

1609. Christopher, Jim. "Firewalking, Sobriety, and Magical Thinking". SOS [nat'l newsletter for Secular Organizations for Sobriety]; 1988; 1(1): 1.
Christopher is critical of "the religiosity of the typical Alcoholics Anonymous group." Secular organizations for sobriety is offered as an alternative.

1610. Clancy, Rian. "His Priestly Mission: To Heal Those Suffering from Alcoholism". The Priest; October 1981: 29-30.
Clancy tells the effect which Father Jack, an alcoholic priest who was treated at Guest House, had when he gave the Sunday sermon at Clancy's parish. Clancy tells Father Jack's story placing special emphasis on denial.

1611. Close, K. "Hope for the Alcoholic". Survey; April 1949: pp202-206.

1612. Cloud, Luther, Dr. "The National Council on Alcoholism...The First Forty Years". Alcoholism; Sept., 1984; 4(3): pp48-50.
In this and succeeding issues, articles on the NCA mention prominently Marty Mann, its first director, and the first woman in AA to maintain sobriety and publicly identify herself as an AA member [before our Traditions were written].

1613. "Cocaine Anonymous: It All Began in Hollywood". Alcoholism & Addiction; Sept.-Oct., 1986; 7(1): p21.
This news article profiles Tom Kenny, the founder of Cocaine Anonymous. "I got a number of people who I knew were tooters and free-basers in Hollywood, who got clean and sober in AA, and whose primary problem was cocaine, and that's how [CA] we got started," Kenny said.

1614. Cohen, A. B. [pseudonym]. "New Help for Jewish Addicts". Jewish Action; Winter 1982.
Cohen writes about a special interest meeting of AA formed by Orthodox Jews.

1615. Collier, G. Kirby, M.D. "Alcoholics Anonymous". The Bulletin [Rochester, NY]; April, 1945.

1616. Collins, Jean E. "Preventive Psychiatry: How To Keep a Problem From Turning Into a Problem". Glamour; May 1978; 76: p133 (3).

1617. "Compulsive Drinker. My Name is Robert. I Am an Alcoholic". Reader's Digest; Nov. 1959: pp209-210+.

1618. Conroy, Virginia. "I am the widow of an ALCOHOLIC". New York: American Medical Assn.; 1956.
This is a 16-page reprint of the original three-part article in the AMA Today's Health magazine. The author discusses her marriage to an alcoholic and her knowledge of AA.

1619. Conroy, William J. "Calix--What and Why". Columbia; April 1977: 30-33.
Conroy gives the history and purpose of the Calix Society founded in 1947 as "an association of Catholic alcoholics who are maintaining their sobriety through affiliation with and participation in the Fellowship of Alcoholics Anonymous.".

1620. [Cressey, Dr. Donald]. "Suggested as Model: Alcoholics Anonymous". Science Newsletter; June 19, 1954: p393.
This UCLA criminologist recommends A.A. as a model for other therapy groups.

1621. "A Cup of Tea". 24 Magazine; July, 1976: 15pp total.
This facsimile from the magazine was used at the First Canadian Big Book Seminar. An eleven-year member of AA offers there are three ways to work the AA program: the strong original, medium, and weak. " Gresham's Law - that bad currency drives out good - has been operative in the life of Alcoholics Anonymous. Weak AA is tending to drive out strong AA," he writes. The history of the Big Book and and its original strong message of recovery and contemporary complacency are the main themes here.

1622. Danor, Chrystel. "Astrology and Alcoholics Anonymous". World Astrology Magazine; March, 1948.

1623. Darrah, Mary. "Sister Ignatia: An Archetype for A.A.". Alcoholism & Addiction; Nov.-Dec., 1985; 6(2): p21.
Darrah retells the meeting of Dr. Bob, AA Co-Founder, and Sr. Ignatia, the non-alcoholic Catholic nun, who together set up the first alcoholic ward in any hospital in the world in Akron, Ohio, at St. Thomas Hospital in 1939. Later, Sr. Ignatia would open Rosary Hall in Cleveland, Ohio, and thousands more alcoholics would be introduced to AA sobriety and a new way of life.

1624. Dave M. "Time OFF for drinking". Guideposts Magazine; (1950s): 4 pages.
The anonymous author, a special assistant at du Pont's Wilmington, Delaware, headquarters, tells his story of recovery in A.A. and how the Fellowship has helped 400 alcoholics stop drinking at du Pont in the past 12 years. Du Pont was the first major company to pioneer a program of treatment for alcoholic employees and permit A.A. at its plants.

1625. Davenport, Walter. "Where Good Drinkers Go". Collier's; Sept. 30, 1939.

1626. Davis, Elrick B. "Alcoholics Anonymous Makes Its Stand Here [Cleveland]" [newspaper articles]. in: The Plain Dealer. Cleveland, OH; Oct. 21, 23, 24, 25, & 26 and Nov. 2 & 4, 1939: 7pp total.
Note: [the entire series has also been published as a poster].
This is one of the earliest series of newspaper articles on AA. Davis discusses the work the Cleveland AA Group is doing. The Alcoholic Foundation, Dr. Silkworth, and other historical events are discussed. The Fosdick review of the Big Book in the 1939 Religious Digest is reprinted.Davis views AA as "religious.".

1627. "Dawn of Hope" Review. Alcoholism & Addiction; May-June, 1987; 7(5): p58.
This video film about the founding of AA includes never-before-seen photos of Bill and Dr. Bob and a great film clip of the two on an old 8mm home movie camera.

1628. de Kruif, Paul. "Double-Barreled Hope for Alcoholics". Reader's Digest; October, 1950: pp130-134.
The author recounts briefly Bill W.'s spiritual experience and the beginning of AA and Dr. Bob's sponsorship of Earl, AA 13. He reports on Dr. James J. Smith whose research with alcoholics under emergency treatment at Bellevue Hospital, New York, who found that big doses of adrenal cortical extract (ACE) into DT victims. Within 24 hours their shakes, nightmares, and suicide attempts ceased. This doctors and other researchers said the ACE treatment may threaten AA because ACE "seems so much easier than the AA's search for God. "The adrenal cortex hormones clear the fog out of alcoholic brains. Mens sana in corpore sano --- a sound mind in a healthy body. This slogan of the ancient philosophers is now the joint battle cry of the hormone doctors and the AAs.".

1629. DeKruif, P. H. "How Faith Helps to Cure Alcoholism". Today's Health; April 1960; 38: p19+.
Note: The same article appeared in Reader's Digest, June, 1960, Vol.76, p172+, under the title "Mysterious Medicine of Alcoholics Anonymous.".
DeKruif discusses Bill's long depression, William James, Dr. Bob, Dr. Tiebout, Rockefeller, and other early A.A. history.

1630. DeKruif, P. H. "Mysterious Medicine of Alcoholics Anonymous". Reader's Digest; June 1960: pp172-176.
Note: (See previous listing, DeKruif, "How Faith Helps to Cure Alcoholism.").

1631. Demaris, Ovid. "First, Make Peace Inside Yourself". in: Parade Magazine. New York; March 22, 1992: pp4-6.
This profile of Nick Nolte, Hollywood actor, reveals "he hasn't had a drink in more than two years. In fact, he even attends weekly Alcoholics Anonymous meetings." Anonymity break.

1632. Dennis M. "Dreams and Adventures in Central America". Sober Times; August 1992; 6(8): p12.
Dennis recounts his meeting a Costa Rican AA with seven years sobriety whose only contact with AA was AA literature he picked up 40 miles away.

1633. Desmond, Edward W. "Out in the Open: Cover Story". Time; Nov. 30, 1987: pp82-90.
Changing attitudes and new research give new hope to alcoholics. AA is mentioned briefly.

1634. Dickey, Marilyn. "Putting Yourself Back Together". Washingtonian; April 1982; 17: p85 (8).
This article on self-help groups also discusses A.A.

1635. Dietz, Dick. "Cleveland To Be Scene of AA World Parlay". in: Akron Beacon Journal. Akron, OH; July 25, 1950: p27. This four-column newspaper article reports Alcoholics Anonymous expects 10,000 to 15,000 "rehabilitated tipplers" to attend "the largest AA meeting ever held under one roof." The Cleveland convention expects AA members from all over the U.S., Canada, Mexico, Britain, France, Holland and Scandinavia. The weekend gathering registration was $1.50.

1636. Doar, Robert. "On the Wagon". The Washington Monthly; June 1988; 20(5): pp50-53.
Book review of Nan Robertson's Getting Better: Inside Alcoholics Anonymous (Morrow, NY, 1988). Robertson's controversial book concerns her personal knowledge of A.A.'s history, teachings and structure as gathered by many interviews with A.A. members. She breaks the 11th Tradition, revealing her membership in A.A. at the level of press, commonly termed an anonymity break.

1637. Dolan, G. "Convicts Take the Cure". American Mercury; Oct. 1953: pp130-131.
The Huntsville, Texas, A.A. prison group is described. Dolan says many prisoners believe A.A. is their only insurance policy against returning to prison.

1638. Dorris, Robert. "Dr. William Silkworth: He Defined the Nature of Alcoholism Over 50 Years Ago; Helped Launch AA". Sober Times; March 1991; 5(3): pp8-9.
This profile of Dr. Silkworth includes his helping Bill Wilson, AA Co-Founder, get sober and his definition of alcoholism as a disease or allergy.

1639. Dorsman, Jerry. "You Don't Need A.A. For Successful Treatment". Addiction & Recovery; March-April, 1991; 12(2): pp75-79.
Dorsman lists 6 other programs as alternatives to AA.

1640. Doug K. "Thank God for Meetings". Newsletters Anonymous; 1987; 3: 4.
Note: Rutgers.
Doug gives guidelines for setting up gay AA meetings.

1641. Dowling, Edward, Rev. "Alcoholics Anonymous". Directors' Bulletin of the Jesuit Fathers, St. Louis, MO; March 1941.
The author was the non-alcoholic Jesuit priest who was instrumental in founding A.A. in St. Louis. Bill W. took a Fifth Step with him.

1642. Dreifus, Claudia. "Without a Drink, Who Am I?". Mademoiselle; Nov. 1983; 89: p167 (4).

1643. Duff, Edward. "Alcoholics Anonymous". America; June 10, 1950.

1644. Dunn, D. H. "Programs That Will Help You Stay On the Wagon". Business Week; Oct 26, 1981: pp193-194.

1645. DuWors, George. "New Use for an Old Tool". Alcoholism; Oct., 1983; 3(7): p45.
Without attending a single AA meeting, Hank used the Serenity Prayer to get off Antabuse and solve "some of the toughest problems I ever had" as well as stay sober.

1646. Echols, W. "Here's Hope for Alcoholics". Christian Center; Nov. 26, 1946: pp1451-1453.

1647. Edmeades, Baz. "Alcoholics Anonymous Celebrates Its 50th Year". Saturday Evening Post; July-August, 1985; 257: pp70-72, 102, 104.
The author originally became interested in the history of AA while researching the law of nonprofit corporations in Alberta, Canada. Here he reviews the founding and early history. The famous Jack Alexander 1941 article in the Post is given credit.

1648. Edwards, Griffith. "The Puzzle of A.A.". New Society; May 1964: pp10-11.
Edwards tells the story of an alcoholic, seemingly headed for an early grave, who defies the odds and his doctor's opinion and sobers up in A.A. A.A. is looked upon as a puzzling therapeutic agent with "religious" powers.

1649. Elliott, R. "My Wife Is An Alcoholic". Family Health incorporating Today's Health; August 1976: pp56-58.

1650. Ellison, J. "Help for the Alcoholic's Family: Al-Anon Family Group". Saturday Evening Post; July 2, 1955: pp17-19, 44, 48.
AA is discussed in conjunction with Al-Anon.

1651. Ellison, Jerome. "Alcoholics Anonymous: Dangers of Success". Nation; March 2, 1964: pp212-214.
This critical article charges AA's New York office has been captured by an "ultraconservative clique.".

1652. Elpenor. "A Drunkard's Progress: AA and the Sobering Strength of Myth". Harper's Magazine; October, 1986; 273(1637): pp42-48.
Note: Illus. with color.
Writing under a pseudonym, this AA member explores the spiritual, etymological, and sociological aspects of the Fellowship. This philosophical essay is serendipitious. The author's commentary on AA talking, listening and storytelling is a "ten-strike.".

1653. Englebardt, Stanley L. "When Your Child Drinks". Reader's Digest; Nov., 1986; 129: p110 (5).

1654. English, Theodore. "Alcoholics Anonymous: Plan has worked for over 700 people". Scribner's Commentator; Jan. 1941: pp58-62.

1655. Farber, L. H. "Bluegate Gospel". New Republic; May 21, 1945: p716.
Farber reviews Taintor's novel, September Remember, and A.A.'s spiritual program with a "Higher Power" at the center.

1656. Father Anonymous (pseudonym). "I Am an Alcoholic Priest". Catholic Digest; May 1987; 51(7): pp98-100.
This Catholic priest, an A.A. member, targets the fact that alcoholism is a disease, not a sin. He suggests priests who have a problem with alcohol write their Bishops confidentially about it and enter one of many programs designed to help men of the cloth who are alcoholics.

1657. "The Fellowship: The First 50 Years". Alcoholism; Jan.-Feb., 1985; 5(3): pp49-57.
In three separate articles, the founding of AA, the Archives, and statistics and milestones are discussed. This is part of an ongoing commemoration of AA's 50 years to be celebrated in Montreal, Canada, at the Int'l AA Convention.

1658. "The Fellowship: The First 50 Years. Part Two". Alcoholism; March-April, 1985; 5(4): pp45-51.
The second part of the series discusses the "Adolescent" years of AA from 1939 to 1951. A sidebar article by Trey C. on "The Message, not the Messenger" discusses Ebby T.

1659. "The Fellowship: The First 50 Years. Part Three.". Alcoholism; May-June, 1985; 5(5): pp16-27.
Part 3 of this year-long celebration of AA's 50th anniversary.

1660. Fenster, Gloria. "Bottom Line Sobriety". Alcoholism and Addiction; 1988; 8(6): 6-7.
In her letter, Fenster mentions a rabbi who argues that AA exposes many Jewish beliefs and that it is acceptable for Jews to say the Lord's Prayer at the close of meetings.

1661. Fichter, Joseph H. "Parallel Conversions: Characteristics (of) Recovered Alcoholics". Christian Century; Feb. 18, 1976; 93: pp148-150.
Note: Also reprinted in Discussion, April 21, 1976, pp397-398.

1662. Fichter, Joseph H. "Spirituality, Religiosity and Alcoholism". in: America; 1977; (May 21): [4pp]. "Priests and religious, like those in other professions, struggle to perform despite a debilitating illness. Religious practice was once seen as a curative." This article summarizes findings from questionnaires from 685 alcoholic clergy and compares religion and AA spirituality. Two quotes suffice: "If organized religion is the bastion of virtue and the bulwark against intemperance, how is it possible that alcoholism strikes some of its best people, ministers and priests, religious brothers and sisters?" and... "Ancient principles of spirituality, taught by all the churches seem to have been rediscovered and put to practice in the Twelve Steps of the A.A. Fellowship.".

1663. "Fifty Years, A Day At a Time". Time; May 20, 1985: p78.

1664. Fitzgerald, Robert, S.J. "Father Ed and AA's Bill W.". Catholic Digest; April, 1991; 55(6): pp103-106. This condenses the original article which appeared in Company, a Jesuit Magazine, Winter, 1990, issue. Fitzgerald documents the 20-year friendship between Dowling, a Jesuit priest from St. Louis, and Bill. Fr. Ed endorsed AA for American Catholics and in his Queen's Work pamphlet of 1947. Dowling was Bill's spiritual advisor for many years.

1665. Ford, J. D. "Alcoholics Anonymous Comes of Age". America; Nov. 9, 1957: pp165-166. This Catholic priest reviews the first history of A.A. in this new book. He sees no conflict between Catholicism and A.A. theologically and believes Catholics become better Catholics because of their recovery in A.A.

1666. Fosdick, Harry Emerson, Dr. "Alcoholics Anonymous: Book Review". The Christian Leader; Oct. 7, 1939. "This extraordinary book deserves the careful attention of anyone interested in the problem of alcoholism...not in the least sensational...the core of their whole procedure is religious...the book has the accent of reality and is written with unusual intelligence and still, humor and modesty mitigating what could easily have been a strident and harrowing tale," Fosdick wrote in one of the earliest first reviews of the Big Book, published in 1939.

1667. Fosdick, Harry Emerson. "Alcoholics Anonymous: Book Review". Friends Intelligencer; Nov. 18, 1939. [probably a reprint of the Oct. 7, 1939, Christian Leader book review].

1668. Fox, Vincent. "On Anonymity: Promotion Without Apology". SOS. Save Our Selves; May/June 1988; 1(2): p1.
This front page article of the National Newsletter for Secular Organizations for Sobriety discusses anonymity as practiced by AA and SOS. SOS disagrees with part of AA's Eleventh Tradition, specifically anonymity at the "top level" of press, TV, radio and the lecture circuit. "We see the traditional AA position of 'attraction rather than promotion' as tragically self-defeating," Fox says.

1669. Freddy C. "Alcohol, Who Needs Enemies?". The Plain Truth; Dec., 1976: p29.
Freddy, a well-known entertainer from Britain, tells his story of recovery from alcoholism through AA and recommends "the number of your nearest AA group is in the phone book. Dial now if you need help.".

1670. "A Funny Thing Happened on the Way to Unemployment". Sisters Today; February 1987: 349-351.
The anonymous nun tells about how having a car became an obsession with her and about how losing the car helped her better understand the AA principles of "a spiritual awakening," "acceptance," and "surrender.".

1671. Gallagher, Lee. "Putting Akron (Back) on the Map: The Akron AA Archives". Alcoholism & Addiction; Nov.-Dec., 1985; 6(2): p20.
"Akron, Ohio, the city where AA was born, seems to have disappeared in the shadow of New York City, home of GSO and the Grapevine. Gail LaCroix, the founder of the Akron Archives, wants to bring recognition to her city as the birthplace of AA, and give all members of AA an opportunity to see the historical artifacts left 50 years ago by the founders of the organization." LaCroix wants to keep the archives separate from Dr. Bob's house which is becoming a museum and historical landmark. "We feel it would violate the tradition of AA not owning property," she said. Obviously, an anonymity break.

1672. Gardner, Yvelin, Rev. "To Say She Was A Remarkable Woman...". Alcoholism; Spring, 1984; 4(3): p49.
Rev. Gardner was a close friend of Marty Mann for many years. In this profile of her, he says "she had to have courage to admit she was an alcoholic and 'beard the lions' in that male bastion that was Alcoholics Anonymous in the primitive 1930s when she entered their ranks...".

1673. Garelik, Glenn. "Moscow Beginners: Where Slava Starts Over Again". Time; April 10, 1989: pp32-34.
"At a meeting of Russia's first AA group, alcoholics learn a sort of personal perestroika, one day at a time." The group, Moscow Beginners, was started in 1987 by the Rev. J. W. Canty, an Episcopal priest from New York City. Four members discuss the group.

1674. Gastwirt, Leslie J. "A Reference Guide to the Big Book of Alcoholics Anonymous" (book review). Library Journal; June 15, 1987; 112: p59.

1675. Geiger, H. J. "Anonymous Struggle for Twenty-Five Years". New York Times Magazine; June 5, 1960: p26+.

1676. Gibbons, Boyd. "Alcohol, the Legal Drug". National Geographic; Feb., 1992; 181(2): pp2-35.
Note: Illustrated with color photographs by George Steinmetz. This wide-ranging survey of the history and customs of alcohol and treatments for alcoholism includes a brief discussion of AA on pages 29-30 & 35. This article on alcohol and alcoholism is a real departure from this influential world magazine's usual format.

1677. Gibeau, Dawn. "12-Step Programs Work for Many, Not All". National Catholic Reporter; Jan. 21, 1994: p25.
Gibeau interviews Ernest Kurtz, author of The Spirituality of Imperfection and Not-God: The History of AA. Kurtz discusses critics of AA who object to its spirituality or alleged "religiosity." Kurtz notes AA does not "need me" to defend it. "AA is not therapy...is not religion...is not 'bookstrap' philosophy. I think the main thing that's going on now is a tendency to confuse spirituality and therapy.".

1678. Glass, Carol. "The Twelve Steps and the Jewish Tradition". JACS Journal; 1985; 2(1): 6-8,12.
Rabbi Glass explains how AA's twelve steps are consistent with Jewish theology.

1679. Gonzalez, D. L. "Very Personal Computing". Newsweek; Aug. 28, 1989: p64; ISSN: 0028-9604.
This 2-page article talks about how AA and other "self-help" groups are using personal computers to give recovery advice and support.

1680. Goodall, Janis. "Consider This...". Save Our Selves; 1988; 1(3): 2.
Goodall tells of her addiction, recovery through AA [anonymity break], relapse, and recovery through SOS. The difficulty she had in accepting AA's requirement for a higher power is stressed.

1681. Goodman, James Stone. "The Knowledge of God's Will for the Price of a Phone Call". JACS Journal; 1986; 3(1): 4,12.
Rabbi Goodman, a recovered alcoholic, explains how the spirituality found in the twelve steps works in his life.

1682. Gorski, T. "Closing the Technology Gap". Alcoholism: The National Magazine; 1982; 2(5): pp49-50.
For the field of alcoholism to successfully grow in the future and also be the only hope for those who relapse and die, Gorski, a recognized alcoholism expert, believes the "solid principles and traditions of Alcoholics Anonymous must be combined with the effectiveness and efficiency of treatment technology.".

1683. Graebner, Oliver E. "Alcoholics Anonymous: Book Review". The Cresset; Sept., 1941.

1684. Graunke, D. Paul. "Alcoholism: the Road to Recovery". The Plain Truth; Dec., 1976: pp26-28.
AA basics are discussed in this article prompted in part by the May 8, 1976, press conference sponsored by the National Council on Alcoholism in Washington, D.C., where 52 prominent people announced to the world they were "recovered alcoholics.".

1685. Gray, Mildred G., Ph.D. "Medicine and the Alcoholic". Life & Health; Sept., 1938.

1686. Griffin, R. Clinton. "Secular Humanism, Religion, and Sobriety". SOS Newsletter; 1989; 2(1): 8.
Griffin argues that AA, even though it is not affiliated with any religion, is religious because its focus is on the sacred and supernatural.

1687. Gringas, Nochem. "Alcoholism and Addiction in the Jewish Community: A Progress Report". Amit Woman; February/March 1985: 18-20.
Rabbi Gringras describes the problem of alcoholism in the Jewish community, recovery through AA, how Jewish Alcoholics, Chemical Dependents, and Their Significant Others journal [JACS] can help Jews develop their spirituality in AA, and the need for Rabbis to be more involved in recovery. He makes much use of research by LeClair Bissell.

1688. Gunther, Max. "Female Alcoholism: The Drinker in the Pantry". Today's Health; June 1975; 53: p14.

1689. Hadley, H. "Hit Bottom Then Bounce". American Mercury; Oct. 1954: pp75-77.
The author discusses "hitting bottom," the A.A. concept that alcoholics must admit and accept a total defeat by alcohol before beginning recovery.

1690. Hank S. "Recovery in the Joint - It's a Daily Struggle". Sober Times; August 1992: 6(8): p4.
Hank shares his experience of being sentenced to prison for three years after he had three years of sobriety.

1691. Hardcastle, Donald H. "How I Found Freedom from Alcohol [Story of A.A.]". Signs of the Times; Aug. 13, 1946.

1692. Hart, Stan. "Second Chance: Guest House for Alcoholics". Blair & Ketchum's Country Journal; Dec. 1978; 5: pp74-83.

1693. Haverstick, J. "Big Book: Bible for Alcoholics". Saturday Review; Aug. 27, 1955: pp17-18.
The Second Edition of "Alcoholics Anonymous" is reviewed. The author also discusses the Oxford Group and the Catholic Church and their relationships with A.A. historically.

1694. Hearn, Edward L., Project Director. The Fellowship: The First 50 Years. First ed. Alcom, Inc.: Seattle, WA; 1985; 96 pp.
This slick souvenir booklet, 8 1/2 x 11", commemorating the Golden Anniversary of Alcoholics Anonymous, is a special international tribute from the Publishers of Alcoholism & Addiction Magazine. It contains 22 articles on the Disease, the Fellowship, How It Started, Grew and is Still Growing, history, humor, the Big Book, 12 Traditions, Founders, Women, the A.A. membership, Anonymity, Al-Anon, Spirituality, GSO, the Grapevine, and other A.A. topics by well-known authors and professionals in the field of alcoholism including Ernest Kurtz, Nell Wing, Jerauld D. Miller, Gloria M., Edward L. Hearn, Joseph Pursch, M.D., Stephanie Abbott, and William Pittman. Congratulatory letters from the President of the United States and other national figures are included.

1695. "Help Each Other Quit Drinking Day at a Time". Columbus, OH: Columbus Dispatch; Aug. 7, 1960.
Subtitled "Alcoholics Anonymous: 12 Steps to Usefulness," this full page newspaper article by "a prominent Ohio lawyer" gives a history and explains how AA works. Illustrated by Floyd Sanders, the article was occasioned by the 25th anniversary of AA. Twenty AA groups were active in the Columbus area at the time along with a "downtown office" and phone.

1696. "Help for Drunkards". Time; Oct. 23, 1944: pp72-75.
"Two members of AA recently shed their anonymity," this medicine column began. The two Fellowship members, Mrs. Marty Mann, executive director of the new Nat'l Committee on Education on Alcoholism, and Edward McGoldrick, head of a special New York City bureau to hold the city's estimated 12, 000 drunks, are profiled.

1697. Herman, Ellen. "The Twelve Step Program: Cure or Cover?". Utne Reader; November-December 1988: 52-53,56-57, 59-63.
Note: Rutgers.
Herman gives a critical analysis of AA and other twelve step programs. She is especially concerned that such programs take people away from political activities. The article is reprinted from Out-Look.

1698. Hernandez, Tom. "Members of SOS Abandon the AA Ship and Save Themselves". Sober Times; Feb., 1993; 7(2): p6.
Norm attended only one AA meeting and then found Secular Organizations for Sobriety [SOS] which didn't have "AA's heavy-handed reliance on an elusive 'higher power." SOS was founded in 1986 and claims 20,000 members in over 1,000 groups. "We're not competing with AA," James Christopher, SOS founder, said.

1699. Herndon, Booton. "Dr. Bob". The American Weekly; March 11, 1951.
Published by the Philadelphia Record.

1700. High & Dry; 1945-94; 1-49.
Note: Address: High & Dry, Seattle Intergroup, 1759 First Ave., S., Seattle, WA 98134-1403. Suggested subscription is $5. annually.
This monthly 12-page newsletter of the Seattle Intergroup contains AA stories, articles, history, news, etc. Intergroup finances, meetings, & services are included. Seattle AA celebrated 50 years in 1991.

1701. "High Watch Farm, An AA Tradition in Jeopardy". Alcoholism; March-April, 1985; 5(4): p60.
This news item reports "High Watch Farm in Kent, CT, the oldest alcoholic treatment facility in the country using principles of AA has closed its doors for the first time in its 45-year history. The Farm, given in trust to Bill Wilson in 1939, has been a center for detoxification and spiritual change for 20,000 alcoholics." New state laws forced the closing.

1702. Hinrichsen, J. J. "Alcoholics Anonymous". Aging; 1990; (361): p12; ISSN: 0002-0966.
This 6-page article focuses on AA which has provided more help to more people than any other treatment approach.

1703. Hoffman, Burt. "The Secret War of Father Paul". Alcoholism; Jan.-Feb., 1985; 5(3): p9 in "Recovery Newsletter" insert.
The author relates the story of Fr. Paul, pseudonym for an anonymous priest in AA.

1704. Hollobon, Joan. "World's Pioneer Self-Help Group 50 Years On". in: The Journal; Aug. 1, 1985: p5.
Hollobon praises AA on the occasion of its 50th anniversary International Convention in Montreal, Canada. She compares AA to a non-sectarian religious service. She quotes Dr. Gordon Bell, M.D., founder of the Dogwood Institute in Toronto, Canada, "whose pioneering work with alcoholics 40 years ago put him under suspicion of medical malpractice," who told a recent symposium "AA was the most significant phenomenon in the whole addictions field in this century." She notes Canada AA started in 1941 and now has approximately 70,000 members.

1705. Huffman, Jasper A. "Alcoholism: Its Cause and Cure". Christianity Today; July 17, 1961; V(21): pp5-7.
The author quotes Bill W.'s address to the NY Medical Society in May, 1944. Huffman urges churches to revive the total abstinence pledge and cites the splendid example of the Methodist Church.

1706. The Hummer Newsletter. "AA Behind Walls". Alcoholism & Addiction; Sept.-Oct. 1985: p30.
This brief one column news item outlines the first A.A. meeting behind prison walls in 1942 at San Quentin and its growth to over 1,100 programs in U.S. and Canadian prisons.

1707. Hunt, Judi. "To Russia, With AA. Visiting Soviets Learn 12 Steps to Sobriety, American-Style". Lifestyles of the Clean & Sober; May 1990; 1(8): pp14-15.
Reprinted from the Seattle, WA, P-I, April 6, 1990, this article discusses the first independent Soviet Union AA group and Russians visiting America during the AA Int'l Convention in July, 1990, in Seattle. It contains several misconceptions about AA.

1708. Hunter, A. A. "See Alcoholics Anonymous Rise, Los Angeles". Christian Center; Jan. 3, 1945: p22.

1709. Hutchison, Percy. "Alcoholics Anonymous: Book Review" "Alcoholic Experience". The New York Times; June 25, 1939.
This reviewer writes the "general thesis of Alcoholics Anonymous is more soundly based psychologically than any other treatment of the subject I have ever come upon...unlike any other book ever published.".

1710. Hyde, Lewis. "Alcohol and Poetry: John Berryman and the Booze Talking: Part 1 [of 2]". in: Addictions; 1976; 5(3): pp6-8.
Note: NCA 1026251.
Hyde explores the term "spirits" as in alcohol and "spirit" in the religious sense. Although some poets have found alcohol a spirit-helper, others have found that it kills the creative impulse as the poet becomes obsessed with alcohol. Alcoholism is defined using AA concepts.

1711. "I'm a Nurse in an Alcoholic Ward". Saturday Evening Post; Oct. 18, 1952: pp40-41, 111-116.
A nurse, formerly an active alcoholic, describes her experiences trying to help drunks at New York's Knickerbocker Hospital. She was an early member of AA.

1712. "I'm an Alcoholic Who Quit Drinking". Rotarian; Sept. 1946: pp43-45.
This personal witness relates how he recovered from alcoholism with the help of A.A.

1713. The International Student of Liquor in Life Today. [in Feb., 1953, the last 5 words were dropped from the title; later in the 1960s the words "Journal of Alcohol Studies" were added]. The International Student; October, 1939, to 1964.; (43 issues): AA articles and basics in each.
Note: 5 x 7.5" softbound.
This journal was aimed at American collegians and published in Westerville, Ohio, by The American Issue, the publishing arm of the Anti-Saloon League which spearheaded the passage of the Prohibition Amendment. AA is discussed in 43 issues during the 1939-64 period. The Big Book is advertised for sale for $3.50 in the January, 1944, issue; AA in Columbus, Ohio, is three years old in January, 1945; an anonymous panel at a college May, 1948; The Fellowship reached England in March, 1947, the Feb. 1949 issue reported; Twelve Steps to Recovery - Fully Tested by A.A.; at least a half dozen anonymous stories of recovery are published in various issues.

1714. Irwin. "Different Drummer: On Anonymity". Sober Times; Jan. 1991; 5(1): p8.
This writer believes when celebrities reveal their indebtedness to AA at the level of press "an untold number of people are inspired by their courage and honesty..." Irwin says the Eleventh Tradition was valid back when the stigma of alcoholic was prevalent, but today the public is educated and the whole matter of anonymity in the press should be an "individual" decision. Clearly, Irwin's viewpoint breaks AA's 11th Tradition.

1715. "It's Fun To Be Sober". Newsweek; Jan. 1, 1945: p74.
The founding of the A.A. Seaman's Group in New York is discussed through the story of the alcoholic seaman who sobered up and gathered other fellow drinking sailors around him to form the group.

1716. J. "AA in Israel". JACS Newsletter; 1987; 4(1): 5-6.
The author describes AA meetings he attended in Israel.

1717. J. "Bill W. and the Rabbis". JACS Journal; 1986; 3(2): 9.
J. mentions the reaction to a notice placed on the board at the Central Conference of American Rabbis announcing a hospitality suite for "Friends of Bill W.".

1718. James, William/Roth, Robert J. "William James and Alcoholics Anonymous". America; July 10, 1965; 113: p48.

1719. Jellinek, E. M./Mann, Mrs. M(arty). "What Shall We Do About Alcoholism". Vital Speeches; Feb. 1, 1947: pp252-256.

1720. Jill D. "A Tribute to a Friend of Bill". Alcoholism & Addiction; June, 1988; 8(5): p7 of "Recovery" sect.
Jill gratefully remembers old-timer Chet who died with 25 years of AA sobriety.

1721. John F. "False Gods Before Me". Alcoholism; Jan.-Feb., 1985; 5(3): pp10-11 in "Recovery Newsletter" insert.
An AA member reveals that after nine years in AA he was a failure. He said his "first" prayer one night and twenty years of atheistic "beliefs" vanished.

1722. John T. "My Journey to AA". Catholic Digest; January, 1992; 56(3): pp73-74.
This AA'er recounts his personal story of recovery and asks 10 questions of the reader who may have a problem with alcohol. He recommends an "AA meeting just around the corner" for those who answered yes to any of the questions.

1723. Johnston, Rick. "Bill W.'s Story Still Fresh in Thomsen Book". Alcoholism & Addiction; Jan.-Feb., 1986; 6(3): p60.
Robert Thomsen's biography was based in large part on his work with Bill W. for 12 years. Bill W. was originally published in 1975, was re-released in June, 1985, and continues to be in print. Johnston's review is laudatory. As biography, it fills in many gaps in Bill's personal life that were not appropriate for Pass It On.

1724. Johnston, Rick. "Book Review: Taking a Fresh Look". Alcoholism; March-April, 1985; 5(4): p10 in "Recovery Newsletter" insert.
A New Pair of Glasses by Chuck "C." is reviewed. It contains talks given by Chuck, an old-time "hard-liner" AA, at an AA retreat in 1975. The reviewer recommends his "sledgehammer" prose and spiritual uplifting.

1725. Johnston, Rick. "Book Review: Pass It On". Alcoholism; May-June, 1985; 5(5): p14 of "Recovery Newsletter" insert.
Johnston reviews Pass It On: The story of Bill Wilson and how the A.A. message reached the world. Very laudatory.

1726. Kahn, Gordon. "Morning After The Lost Weekend [film review], and AA Movie". Atlantic; 1945.

1727. Kathleen S. "The 12 Steps: De-Mystified, Revised, Reclaimed!". The Journal of Health & Recovery; Nov., 1992: pp3-4.
The author, a Jungian psychotherapist and Taoist, offers the opinion that "the 12 Steps weren't seen as `inscribed tablets given to an alcoholic Moses' by the A.A. founders." She says 12-Step fellowships, which one would assume would include AA, should update the steps with medical science, right brain techniques, and modern advances that weren't around when Bill W. wrote the 12 & 12 in the 1950s. She advises fellowships to "keep what works" from the originals and "eliminate the sexist, racist and outdated materials and outdated materials and practices which are the results of rigidity in the older fellowships.".

1728. Ken N. "I Couldn't Do It Alone". Alcoholism & Addiction; May-June, 1987; 7(5): p14 of "Recovery" sect.
From suidical thinking to AA recovery, Ken, a 20-year-old alcoholic in the Navy, shares his story.

1729. Kendall, Charles S. "Alcoholics Anonymous". The Christian Advocate; July 16, 1942.

1730. Kennedy, R.J.H. "Two New Studies of Alcoholism". America; Dec. 21, 1957: p372.

1731. The Kentuckiana News; 1990-94.
Note: Address: The Kentuckiana News, 21 Warren Court, Fort Thomas, KY 41075-2106.
This 12-page bimonthly newsletter of Kentucky AA Area 26 presents the experience, strength and hope of AA members. In addition to local AA stories, history and news, it reprints Grapevine articles and lists AA literature for sale.

1732. Kiely, Harry C. "An Instrument of Healing Grace". Sojourners; 1985; 14(7): 6.
Kiely describes the AA program giving special attention to its spiritual foundation.

1733. Kleiser, Grenville. "Twelve Steps to Freedom". Health Culture; Feb., 1944.

1734. Laign, Jeffrey. "Alcoholics Anonymous: How It Works in '89. Self-Help and Psychiatry". in: The U.S. Journal of Drug and Alcohol Dependence; May, 1989; 13(5): pp1 & 17.
Several professionals are quoted on cooperation between AA and treatment modalities.

1735. Laird. "Fear of Financial Insecurity". Newsletters Anonymous; 1987; 3: 4.
Note: Rutgers.
Laird is critical of the high prices being charged for some round-ups and other AA events.

1736. Laird B. "Of Course, I Go To Regular Meetings Too". Newsletters Anonymous; 1985; 1: p5.
Laird B. discusses the need to go to non-lesbian/gay meetings of AA as well as lesbian/gay ones. (NALGAP 852).

1737. Lake, Austen. "Heightened Hope for Alcoholics". The American Weekly [publication of The Philadelphia Record]; Oct. 27, 1940s?

1738. Lanagan, John G. "AA Doesn't Always Work". in: National Catholic Register; Aug. 16, 1987: p4.
Lanagan reveals he was a skid row alcoholic and "if I had to depend on Alcoholics Anonymous for my sobriety, I'd die on those streets, a wasted life." He criticizes AA as a "religious program of talk therapy" and the "media darling" which only reaches 1 in 36 alcoholics. Lanagan says a far superior form of treatment exists: aversion therapy, introduced in Seattle in 1935 by Dr. Charles Shadel, several months before the advent of AA. He quotes sociologist Gellman: "when an alcoholic attempts recovery in AA and fails, the burden of responsibility is shifted to the individual, and the program itself (AA) remains inviolate.".

1739. Landers, Ann. "Alcoholics Anonymous Saved Reader's Life". in: syndicated national column; July 14, 1993.
Responding to a reader who joined AA and "it saved my life," Landers writes "I started to sing the praises of AA back in 1955 when I began this column. I'm happy to say thousands of people joined AA after reading about it in this space. It's one of the things I'm most proud of.".

1740. Larry G. "A Meeting in Israel". JACS Journal; 1989; 6(i): 5-6.
Larry G., an alcoholic Jew, tells about his spiritual development in recovery. Larry was able to combine a study of Judaism with his AA program.

1741. Latimer, R. "Why Not Delinquents Anonymous?". American Mercury; March 1955: p62.

1742. Leach, Barry. "Alcoholics Anonymous". Columbia; April 1977: 17-21+.
"This article tells how AA began, how certain Catholics helped shape it, and something about its effectiveness and its impact on today's society." Stories of AA members and Catholic non-members are told and the similarity between the Twelve Steps and the Spiritual Exercises of St. Ignatious are mentioned.

1743. LeBerthon, Ted. "Twelve Steps to Sobriety". Catholic Digest; May, 1943.

1744. Lee, J.P. "How Alcoholics Anonymous Helps". Hahnemannian; 1954; 89: 207-212.
In AA, the alcoholic, among other things, begins to think about God and to learn that God loves him.

1745. Leo, John. "One Less For the Road? A New Tolerance Builds Pressure on Abusive Drinking". Time; May 20, 1985; 125: p76 (3).
This essay includes a separate related article on A.A.

1746. "Let Me Tell You About the Miraculous Redemption of a Confirmed Drunkard". True Confessions; 1946.
"Although overtly positive, this treatment was lurid in details and implication," Kurtz notes.

1747. Lewis, Jay. "Role of AA Defined: VA Settles Atheist Lawsuit". Alcoholism; Jan.-Feb., 1985; 5(3): p14.
Note: [see also: Miller, Jerauld].
The settlement of the lawsuit by John Hansen, a VA patient, and the American Atheist Addiction Recovery Groups [AAARG] against the VA and the U.S. Govt. is discussed by Lewis, editor of The Alcoholism Report. Voluntary referral to AA by VA and other government agencies was reaffirmed in the settlement.

1748. "Life Membership". Time; Feb. 24, 1947: p55.
This article summarizes the first dozen years of A.A. history and mentions William James' book, Varieties of Religious Experience, and its influence on A.A. philosophy.

1749. Lindh, Stewart. "Voices. The Blind Leading the Blind". Sober Times; April 1992; 6(4): p4.
This is the story of blind Rick whose sharing at an AA meeting about his late father keeps him from suicide.

1750. Little, Ruth A. "Mormons Face Alcoholism". Alcoholism; Jan.-Feb., 1985; 5(3): p24.
Little reports a reason "why AA has not been stressed is that Mormons who have used AA have experienced fellowship there and have tended to drift away from the Church. An organization modeled after AA has been started in Utah - (though it is not sponsored by the Mormon Church). SAVE (Substance Abuse Volunteer Efforts) incorporates many AA principles, but tailors them to the Mormon mold.".

1751. Lois B. and Susan R. "Keeping It By Giving It Away". Alcoholism & Addiction; Sept.-Oct., 1987; 8(1): p6 of "Recovery" sect.
The paradox of "keeping it by giving it away" in AA is discussed.

1752. Lord, Lewis. "Coming to Grips with Alcoholism". U.S. News and World Report; 1987; 103(22): 56-62.
The article mentions that a recovered alcoholic priest helped a practicing alcoholic. "Drunk Monks," an AA group for alcoholic clergy is also mentioned. Most of the article, however, focuses on the disease concept of alcoholism and a court case before the Supreme Court which deals with this issue.

1753. Luker, Kelly. "A.A. Runners' Group Does It One Step at a Time". Sober Times; April 1992; 6(4): p24.
The founding of the country's first AA running group, the One Step at a Time Runners, is documented.

1754. Luker, Kelly. "Alternatives to AA". Sober Times; Feb., 1993; 7(2): p7.
"As AA continues to be thrust under the microscope of public examination, its warts and blemishes offer material to fuel the discontented," Luker writes in this review of six rational recovery books offering alternatives to AA.

1755. Luker, Kelly. "Bob Smith Shares His Memories of Dad - the Co-founder of AA". Sober Times; July 1991; 5(7): pp8-10.
Dr. Robert Smith's son, Bob, fondly recalls his dad's drinking and the founding of AA with Bill Wilson. This interview contains good material about early AA.

1756. Luker, Kelly. "James Lee Burke. Crime novelist talks about his compulsion to write and his bumpy path to success.". Sober Times; Jan. 1992; (57): p8 & 10.
Dave Robicheaux, Burke's fictional cop, is the central character and an AA member in a series of crime novels. Luker interviews Burke.

1757. Luker, Kelly. "John Bradshaw: Charismatic Healer or Charlatan?". Sober Times; Feb. 1992; (60): pp16-17.
Luker interviews Bradshaw who answers various attacks on his workshops and TV work. Asked about the Eleventh Tradition, Bradshaw replied "On the one hand, I work hard to preserve that...but on the other hand, I would like to see it changed. Do [these anonymous programs] never change, grow? You get this ridigity, which is the mark of mental illness.".

1758. Luker, Kelly. "Rise of Synanon to Wealth and Power - and Its Decline in U.S. Brainchild of Charles (Chuck) Dederich". Sober Times; April 1991; 5(4): pp4-6.
Luker details Dederich's sobriety through A.A. in 1957, his frustration with AA's "religious" overtones, departure from AA, and founding of Synanon. Myths about Synanon are discussed in this article.

1759. Lynn C. "Is Anybody Up There?". Sober Times; May 1993; 7(5): p4.
Lynn discusses faith and James Trimpey, Rational Recovery founder, who provides a "no Higher Power" approach to abstaining from alcohol. She criticizes Trimpey and others who say the person of faith is not of sound mind.

1760. M. C. W. "The Last Drink". Sober Times; June 1993; 7(6): p8.
An AA member with 30 years of sobriety writes a letter to his son about how he never took his last drink because of him.

1761. Madsen, William, Ph.D. "Bill W. by Robert Thomsen" Book Review. Alcohol Health & Research World; Spring, 1976; 1(1): p26.
"This book is an insightful and sensitive biography of Bill Wilson, a man described by Aldous Huxley as 'the greatest social architect of the century.' It is a story of Bill's strengths and weaknesses, of his successes and failures," Madsen writes.

1762. Magazine Articles from 1939 [about AA]. Oklahoma: pirated edition; 1992.
The 8.5 x 11" hardback of 208 pages contains 44 popular magazine articles from 1939 to 1991 about AA, alcoholism, Al-Anon, Alateen, and related subjects. The earliest is a book review of Alcoholics Anonymous from the June 25, 1939, New York Times. Many of the articles are from The Saturday Evening Post, Reader's Digest, Time, Look, Life, and other mass market popular magazines. They "are reprinted for Alcoholics Anonymous archivists without anybody's permission." In no way is this pirated edition associated with A.A.W.S. or any Area A.A. Archives since it violates copyright laws.

1763. "Magic Medicine [AA]". The Atlantian; July, 1949.

1764. Maloney, Kenneth. "Calix International". Catholic Digest; Sept. 1975: pp12-15.
Note: Two other articles on Calix were published in the Catholic Digest in 1955 and 1964.
Calix Int'l was founded to interest alcoholic Catholics, both in and out of A.A., in total abstinence as a virtue and in deepening their sober life as Catholics and as A.A. members. The organization particularly tries to practice the Eleventh Step of AA. It is separate entirely from A.A. Founded in Minneapolis, Minnesota, in 1949, it publishes a newsletter, The Chalice.

1765. Mann, Marty. "What Shall We Do About Alcoholism?". Vital Speeches; Feb. 1947: pp253-256.
The National Committee for Education on Alcoholism and its work closely allied with A.A. is described by Mann, one of the founders of the NCEA.

1766. Manning, Anita. "50 Years of Alcoholics Anonymous". in: USA Today. New York; June 10, 1985.
This three column story in this national newspaper gives an overview of Alcoholics Anonymous through the recovery story of Bob P. He and more than a million sober alcoholics like him will mark the 50th anniversary of AA today [June 10] and plan for the Int'l AA Convention in Montreal, Canada, July 2-4, 1985.

1767. "The March of Time". Life; 1957 ?: p123.
This full page ad begins "See the New March of Time" movie. It "shows you in action the many ways in which America's fourth largest public health menace is being tackled. For example, you've often heard of 'Alcoholics Anonymous': here you see how AA works - in the dramatic story of one man's battle against alcoholism." A photo of a worried man on the telephone is the center of the ad. The movie was released by 20th Century Fox and produced by the Editors of Time and Life.

1768. Marchant, Ward. "Secular Alcoholics Want Support But No Religion". Associated Press; Oct. 7, 1990: 2 columns.
This AP writer interviews Bill Talley who founded American Atheist Addiction Recovery Groups [AAARG], later renamed Methods of Moderation and Abstinence [MOMA]. Talley criticizes AA but concedes it works for many.

1769. Markey, Morris. "Alcoholics and God". Liberty Magazine; Sept.30, 1939; 30: p6 +.
Historically, this article about AA is the second published in a major popular magazine.

1770. Marston, William Moulton. "A Miracle Cure for Drinkers". Your Life; April, 1940.

1771. Martin, Joseph C., Fr. "Getting Right With God". Alcoholism & Addiction; April 1988; 8(4): 35.
This regular columnist discusses religion versus spirituality, the churches and A.A., and the 12 Steps as the medicine for the "soul-sickness" of alcoholism.

1772. Martin, Joseph C., Fr. "Gift of Sobriety". Alcoholism; Nov.-Dec., 1984; 5(2): p4 in "Recovery Newsletter" insert.
Fr. Martin discusses Step Twelve.

1773. Martin, Joseph C., Fr. "With Love and a Blessing". Alcoholism; 1984-onward.
For years, Fr. Martin's column, "With Love and a Blessing," appeared regularly in this magazine. Almost all his columns discuss the AA program of recovery. Several of his more telling columns on AA topics are listed individually; otherwise, an issue-by-issue search is necessary.

1774. Martin, Joseph C., Fr. "With Love and a Blessing". Alcoholism; Jan.-Feb., 1985; 5(3): p3 in "Recovery Newsletter" insert.
Fr. Martin discusses the Big Book definition of alcoholism as "soul-sickness.".

1775. Martin, Paul. "Hope and Help for the Alcoholic". Christian Century; Jan. 2, 1974; 91: p16.

1776. "Marty Mann: Crusader, Reformer, Visionary". Alcoholism; Oct., 1983; 3(7): p20.
This box profile of Marty Mann states she was "the first woman to maintain sobriety in Alcoholics Anonymous." She died sober in 1980. Nominations for the Third Annual Marty Mann Award are requested.

1777. Maxwell, Milton A., Ph.D. "Helping Alcoholics Find Their Way". Alcoholism & Addiction; June, 1986; 6(5): p23.
Excerpts from "On Working with A.A.," Chap. 11 in Maxwell's The Alcoholics Anonymous Experience: A Close Up View for Professionals. Cooperation with the professional community is the topic.

1778. McAllister, J. B. "Apologies Unnecessary". Catholic World; Sept. 1947: pp515-519.
Using a case study of Joe, the author argues no apologies are necessary for the alcoholic who works the AA program for himself. The difference between self love and selfishness is explained.

1779. McElroy, C. E./O'Brien, J. A. "Alcoholism and Total Abstinence". America; Jan. 5, 1963; 108: p18.
Note: This article was reprinted in Correction, Jan. 12, 1963.
Two priests debate the total abstinence question. Christopher McElroy of the Matt Talbot Legion said A.A. is doomed because it emphasizes abstinence to the detriment of the Christian virtue of temperance; while O'Brien, a Notre Dame professor, argued for support of all programs, educational or A.A.

1780. McGoldrick, Edward. "Maybe I Can Do It Too". The Reader's Digest; Oct., 1944: pp115-118.
This article, condensed from Argosy by Helen Worden, is a brief autobiography of New York City's first alcoholic therapist, Edward McGoldrick. He reveals he is a member of AA.

1781. McIlwain, Wm. "Farewell to Alcohol". Atlantic Monthly; Jan. 1972: pp29-35.
In this personal witness story, McIlwain describes his stay at a North Carolina rehab center for alcoholics. He believes over half of his fellow alcoholic patients failed because they did not attend and join A.A.

1782. Meacham, Andrew. "Will Success Spoil AA?". The Journal; 1989; 13(5): 1,16.
In part, Meacham describes the link between AA and religion [?].

1783. "Medical Care for Alcoholics". a NYC periodical [?]; 1945 [?].
St. John's Episcopal Hospital and AA.

1784. Mel A. "Working the Steps". Alcoholism; March-April, 1985; 5(4): pp12-13 in "Recovery Newsletter" insert.
One AA's interpretation of Steps One and Twelve.

1785. member of A.A. "Turning Down a Drink Isn't Always So Easy". in: The Columbus Dispatch. Columbus, OH; Nov. 13, 1984; Alcoholism Section: p5.
An AAer shares his experiences at social and business events where the pressure to drink alcohol pops up.

1786. Michael, D. Joseph. "The Story of Calix, AA's Eleventh Step in Action". Catholic Digest; Feb. 1955: pp29-33.
The author recounts the founding in 1947 of Calix, a Catholic group of AA members who attempt to carry out the Eleventh Step of A.A. in their own Catholic faith.

1787. "A Microscopic View of Alcoholics Anonymous". The Virginia Challenge; Jan.-April, 1948: pp42-43.
Note: [This anonymous article obviously was NOT written by an AA member.].
Published by the Citizens' Temperance Foundation of Virginia, this magazine reviewed the philosophy of AA and found it lacking. "...there are infidels, agnostics and atheists among the redeemed alcoholics, it becomes very evident that all this talk about God is mere camouflage." The entire article misinterprets AA and calls it "a detriment to the Dry Cause." In a sidebar article by Robert Moorman, Jr., a "Psychological Consultant and Member of Alcoholics Anonymous, " he says "[AA's] are tolerant of moderate drinking in others, just as they try to be tolerant in all phases of life, looking on this as a personal prerogative, but ever cautioning the person of the danger involved." The reader is reminded that the AA Traditions covering anonymity had not yet been written and approved.

1788. Middlebrooks, A. E. "Urges Treatment For Alcoholics". Christian Century; Nov. 14, 1945: p1264.
The first Southern regional conference of A.A. is the author's topic. At this meeting Marty Mann advocated the establishment of free clinics for alcoholics sponsored by government.

1789. Miller, Jerauld D. "I Need Another Alcoholic...We've Got A Million of `Em". Alcoholism; May-June, 1984; 5(5): p7.
Laudatory editorial from the magazine's publisher on the 50th anniversary of AA.

1790. Miller, Jerauld D. "What God Gonna Do? Round 1: The Atheists vs. AA". Alcoholism; Jan.-Feb., 1985; 5(3): p9.
Alcoholism publisher Miller comments that "Hansen v. U.S., if carried to an illogical conclusion of hearings, appeals, and a place on the Supreme Court docket, might well have pitted the American atheist movement against God, AA, and a million recovering alcoholics. What a class action suit that might have been. Mercifully, the Colorado not-quite-landmark suit was settled out of court and allegations of 'treating a progressive, terminal disease with religion instead of accepted medical practice' were not put to the test. The claim against Fort Lyon, Colorado VA Alcohol Dependency Treatment Program was that ADTP patient John Hansen had been 'forced' to attend AA meetings and weekly classes conducted by a chaplain. The awkward settlement, agreed to by both attorneys, was to accept a so-called Professional Services Letter from the VA Central Office which restated the standing position regarding voluntary referral to AA or similar programs." Miller goes on to discuss the First Amendment, former HEW Sec. Joseph A. Califano, Jr.'s endosement of "close and continuing cooperation by all government bodies with AA," and related issues in this editorial.

1791. Miller, Judea. "Reflections on the Lord's Prayer". JACS Journal; 1987; 4(1): 9.
Rabbi Miller discusses his concern about people who encourage Jews not to say the Lord's Prayer at the end of AA, NA, and Al-Anon meetings because of its association with Christianity. He fears that such "encouragement" might keep Jews away from meetings that save Jewish lives.

1792. "A Miracle Across the Kitchen Table". The Christian Layman; March, 1943.

1793. "Misc. AA articles". The Other Fellow's Viewpoint, St. Louis, MO; 1946.

1794. Moran, E. "Drink, drink, drink...drunk". Philadelphia; Dec., 1987: p132; ISSN: 0031-7233.
The lengthy story of how one alcoholic faced up to his alcoholism through a hospital stay and AA.

1795. Mort H. "Bearing Witness". Addiction & Recovery [name changed from Alcoholism & Addiction & Recovery Life as of June, 1990, Vol. 10, No. 1 issue]; Aug., 1990; 10(2): p27.
Mort shares that "instead of trying to 'Twelfth Step' every likely candidate we came across, we carried the message by the way we conducted our lives.".

1796. Murray, Don. "The Housewife's Secret Sickness". Saturday Evening Post; Jan. 27, 1962; 235(4): pp80-83.
In this essay on the one million American women who are alcoholics, Murray quotes several anonymous female AA members. "I have attended AA meetings - once a predominantly male organization - where there were as many women as men," Murray says.

1797. "My Return from the Half-World of Alcoholism". Reader's Digest; January 1946: pp31-34.
This personal witness story reveals that an alcoholic can recover through correspondence only with other A.A. members because they talk the same language.

1798. "No Booze But Plenty of BABES!". Confidential; 1954.
An alleged "expose" of A.A., Kurtz says "A.A.'s internal response was less outrage than a philosophical `Well, we realize it isn't true, in general; but who knows? Maybe it will move some who need the program to investigate, and these - if they give it a chance - just might get what they need instead of what they want!".

1799. Nossen, Herbert Ludwig, M.D. "They Walk Again". North American Review; Summer, 1939.

1800. "Not Necessarily The Jews". JACS Journal; 1989; 6(1): 4-5.
One of the two reports in this section involves the case of John Norfolk, an atheist who claimed his constitutional rights were violated when he was forced to attend AA.

1801. O'Connell, Daniel M. "Reformed Drinkers Aid the Poor Drunks". America; Dec. 6, 1941.

1802. O'Connell, Tom. "Jewish Alcoholics Face Unique Problems". U.S. Journal of Drug and Alcohol Dependence; 1989; 13(4): 8.
O'Connell describes some of the problems Jewish alcoholics encounter in AA and how JACS is helping them address those issues.

1803. O'Connell, Tom. "Laughter is Good Medicine for Recovery". Alcoholism & Addiction; April, 1986; 6(4): pp8-10 of "Recovery" section.
The role of drinking jokes and humor in AA, ACOA and other Fellowships' meetings is detailed.

1804. O'Reilly, Jane. "Breaking the Code". Vogue; April 1988; 178: p114.
O'Reilly reviews Robertson's book "Getting Better: Inside Alcoholics Anonymous.".

1805. "Oasis Called Al-Anon". Reader's Digest; Sept. 1976: pp138-141.

1806. "One Man's Sickness". New Blackfriars; 1967; 48(568): 650-658.
This anonymous author describes his addiction and recovery through AA. His spirituality, relationship to a higher power, and Catholicism receive special attention.

1807. Oursler, Fulton. "The Law of Unselfishness". Reader's Digest; Feb., 1964 [Aug., 1946]; 84: p24-B.
Note: [condensed from Christian Herald of August, 1946].
Oursler recounts how Bill W., in a New York hospital for the fiftieth time for alcoholism, helped another alcoholic by talking with him and thereby gained an understanding of what would be Step Two.

1808. Page, Penny Booth. "Alcohol Education Materials: What Are They and Where Do You Get Them?". RQ; Summer 1980; 19: p376 (5).

1809. Paley, Karen. "Finding Their Way to AA". Alcoholism & Addiction; Oct., 1988; 9(1): p10 in "Recovery" sect.
Paley offers advice to those "bothered by someone else's drinking." The tri-annual AA survey of its membership is discussed. The author attended open AA meetings and collected 63 stories from AA members and that data matched exactly the AA survey on how alcoholics found AA.

1810. Parkhurst, Genevieve. "Laymen and Alcoholics". Harper's Magazine; Sept. 1941: pp422-429.
A.A. is a must until a chemical "cure" can be found for alcoholism, the author proposes. She recommends the grassroots A.A. or layman's approach.

1811. "Passionately Anonymous". Time; July 11, 1960: p62.

1812. Paul, Jay H., Ph.D./Stall, Ron, Ph.D./Bloomfield, Kim A., Dr.Ph.D. "Gay and Alcoholic: Epidemiologic and Clincial Issues". Alcohol Health & Research World; 1991; 15(2): pp151-160.
"Gay AA has become the largest special interest group within the Fellowship," this article reports. "As early as 1945, Bill W. expressed some concern about the difficulties gay and lesbian alcoholics were having in maintaining sobriety and participating in AA (Kus 1987). This problem no doubt was behind the formation in 1949 of the first "special interest" gay AA group in Boston; however, it foundered in the 1950s. It was not until about 1968 that another gay AA group was established on the West Coast. By 1974, 16 gay groups were known to exist in the U.S., and AA began to list gay meetings in its world directory.".

1813. Paul, Stewart, C.A.C. "The Therapeutic Mechanisms of Alcoholics Anonymous". in: The National Journal of Health & Recovery; July, 1993; 4(7): pp37-39.
This "old pro," a professional with 29 years in the field of chemical dependency and 7,000 one-to-one sessions, suggests that all professionals realize the "most effective relapse preventer has been and still is `Don't drink and go to [AA] meetings. AA has a 58 year proven track record...name me something or someone else who has!".

1814. Peale, Norman Vincent. "Twelve Tremendous Steps That Will Work for Anyone". Guideposts; April, 1989: 2-5.
Peale interprets the twelve steps from a Christian perspective and shows how they can be used for problems other than alcohol.

1815. Pendery, Mary/Madsen, William. "Alcoholism: What Can Be Done". Center Magazine; July 1976; 9: p44.

1816. "Personal Business". Business Week; April 16, 1960: pp165-166.

1817. "Personal Business: Rough Road Back from Alcoholism". Business Week; Oct. 26, 1968: pp163-164.
The article states that about half of all alcoholics can make it in A.A. and maintain sobriety.

1818. Peterson, Karen S. "Paths to Sobriety: AA and Rational Recovery interviews". in: USA Today; April 21, 1992: p4-D.
This USA Today reporter interviewed Nan Robertson, "in AA for more than 16 years" and the author of Getting Better: Inside Alcoholics Anonymous, and Jack Trimpey, founder of Rational Recovery Systems "who did not succeed with AA's recovery methods." Peterson said "AA is being challenged by other organizations with radically different philosophies and methods." Robertson breaks her A.A. anonymity. Trimpey is "turned off by the suggestion they need divine intervention to help." The article sets up Robertson as a spokesperson for A.A. which she is not; in fact, A.A. does not have any spokesperson and does not engage in public controversy because of A.A. Traditions.

1819. Phillip Z. "Psycho-Babble and the Program". Sober Times; Nov. 1991; 5(ii): p7.
The author, a psychotherapist from the San Francisco Bay area, thinks the multitude of 12-Step recovery from every imaginable addiction programs are "in fact simply self-help groups using the AA meeting format." The current rage of Inner Child work and Codependency lack the spiritual "soul work" of the original AA 12 Steps and 12 Traditions, Phillip Z. argues. "What is a profoundly spiritual approach is rapidly being lost in a sea of psychobabble and superficial thinking.".

1820. Phyllis O. "Meet My Sponsor: Beyond the Barrier of Self". Alcoholism & Addiction; May-June, 1987; 7(5): p5 of "Recovery" sect.
Phyllis shares her joy at having an AA sponsor.

1821. Pittman, Bill. "Book review: Grateful to Have Been There by Nell Wing". Sober Times; August 1992; 6(8): p22.
Pittman lauds Wing's book for her many years of service to AA as a non-alcoholic and for her revealation of how the spiritual principles of the 12 Steps have enriched her life.

1822. Pittman, Bill. "Book review: Sister Ignatia: Angel of Alcoholics Anonymous by Mary C. Darrah". Sober Times; Dec. 1992; 6(12): p22.
Pittman lauds this biography of the little Catholic nun, a non-alcoholic, who helped thousands of AA's get sober.

1823. Pittman, Bill. "Sobriety Celebrations". Alcoholism; May-June, 1985; 5(5): pp21-27.
Pittman reviews the history of AA's International Conventions starting with the 1955 Cleveland, Ohio, first and ending with the upcoming 1985 Montreal, Canada, 50th AA Int'l Convention. He also details the Big Meeting in June, 1945, in Cleveland to celebrate AA's tenth anniversary, a predecessor of the internationals.

1824. Pittman, Bill. "The Voice of AA - The AA Grapevine". Alcoholism & Addiction; August, 1985; 5(6): pp27-28.
Note: [the name of the magazine was changed this issue, "& Addiction" being added].
Pittman reviews the history of the world's most popular publication in the field of alcoholism - the AA Grapevine. From its first issue in June, 1944, to it current issue, it remains the "AA meeting in print." Famous authors, alcoholic and otherwise, cartoonists [esp. Victor E.], regular features, an FBI magazine called the Grapevine, AA members writing their personal viewpoints, all the rich history of the GV is discussed.

1825. Pittman, David J./Gorman, William/Pendery, Mary. "Alcoholism: The Moral Issue". Center Magazine; July 1976; 9: p34.

1826. Pittman, William. "The Adolescent Years. The Fellowship: The First Fifty Years". Alcoholism. The National Magazine; March-April 1985; 5(4): pp45-48.
Pittman discusses the 1939-1950 period of growth in A.A. with the publication of the Big Book, the development of the Traditions, the three legacies of Recovery, Unity and Service, the founding of the A.A. magazine The Grapevine, and the first international conference in Cleveland, Ohio, in 1950. This is the second of a six-part series.

1827. Pittman, William. "The Al-Anon Family Group Story: A Legacy of Love". Alcoholism & Addiction; Sept.-Oct. 1985; 5(7): pp49-52.
Note: The fifth of a six-part series.

1828. Pittman, William, MA, CAC. "The Doctor Who Treated Bill W.". Alcoholism & Addiction; August, 1985; 5(6): p29, 32.
This is part 4 in the series "The Fellowship: The First 50 Years." Pittman profiles Charles B. Towns, the doctor who developed the "Towns-Lambert Treatment" that Bill W. underwent at Towns Hospital in New York under the care of Dr. William Duncan Silkworth. It was here Bill W. had his "hot flash" or spiritual experience that was to lead to his sobriety and the founding of AA.

1829. Pittman, William. "For Sinners Only: The Oxford Group's `Big Book". Alcoholism & Addiction; Nov.-Dec., 1985; 6(2): pp55-56.
The Oxford Group and its literature, on which early AA's were dependent for spiritual help, are discussed. Richmond W.'s Twenty-Four Hours a Day book, offered to AA, is discussed.

1830. (Pittman, William). "The Founding of Alcoholics Anonymous". Alcoholism & Addiction; Jan./Feb. 1985; 5(3): pp49-57.
"I Need Another Alcoholic," the opening article of a six part series outlines the history of the founding of A.A., the meeting of Bill W. and Dr. Bob, the Fellowship, the Twelve Steps, the Big Book that issued from that epoch meeting and the early years. A full page is devoted to the Archives of A.A. and two pages of illustrations focus on other A.A. milestones.

1831. Pittman, William. "The Structure of the AA Fellowship". Alcoholism & Addiction; Nov.-Dec., 1985; 6(2): pp53-56.
This is the sixth and last part of the series "The Fellowship: The First 50 Years." Here Pittman reviews the development of the AA structure: the group conscience and the entire Third Legacy. The annual General Service Conference, General Service Office in New York, finances, A.A. World Services, Inc., and the Grapevine are discussed.

1832. Pittman, William L. "The Voice of A.A. - The A.A. Grapevine". Alcoholism & Addiction/ the National Magazine; August 1985; 5(6): pp27-28.
Pittman discusses the founding and growth of The A.A. Grapevine, the Fellowship's magazine and "meeting in print." This is the fourth of a six-part series, "The Fellowship: The First Fifty Years.".

1833. Pratt, Craig T., M.D. "Addiction Treatment for Health Care Professionals". Addiction & Recovery; Sept., 1990; 10(3): pp17-19, 38-41.
This survey of models of treatment for health care professionals includes AA which "focuses more on the disease as primary than many models that say they do, but don't.".

1834. Price, Larry/Gallagher, Lee/Darrah, Mary/Hearn, Ed. "A Salute to Ohio". Alcoholism & Addiction; Dec. 1985; 6(2): pp19-23.
Various authors discuss the status of A.A. in Ohio, including the birthplace of A.A., Dr. Bob's home in Akron; Sister Ignatia; and a two-page interview with Gov. Richard Celeste about alcoholism and A.A. in Ohio.

1835. "Problem Drinkers [March of Time]: a Review". Time; July 8, 1946.

1836. "Problem Drinkers". Survey; June 1947: pp180-181.

1837. Pursch, Joseph A., M.D. "Are Alcoholics Better Than Other Addicts?". Alcoholism & Addiction & Recovery Life; Nov., 1989; 9(5): p28.
Letters to Pursch complain about AA members and groups who look down on addicts and "drugs" language at meetings. Some addicts vented negative feelings by defiantly shouting out they were drug addicts at AA meetings, Pursch reported, and noted they often relapsed because of their anger. He recommends willingness to identify with the group conscience instead of remaining aloof and alone and angry.

1838. Pursch, Joseph A., M.D. "Charming Companions". Alcoholism & A ddiction; April, 1988; 8(4): p7 in "Recovery" sect.
Dr. Pursch reprints comments from Fulton Oursler in the Liberty 1940 magazine. Oursler's comment on AA people being "the most charming in the world" is remembered most.

1839. Pursch, Joseph A., M.D. "Dry Dock Revisited: What Do You Do with a Drunken Sailor?". Alcoholism; May-June, 1985; 5(5): p13.
Dr. Pursch recounts the history of AA in the U.S. Navy. Dick Jewel, the Navy Commander and AA member, and Dr. Joe Zuska, a Navy psychiatrist, are lauded for their founding the first Naval treatment center and starting AA meetings for sailors.

1840. Pursch, Joseph A., M.D. "Recovering But Not Sober". Addiction & Recovery; March-April, 1991; 11(2): p43.
Pursch discusses the "dry drunk" syndrome, what early AA's called those members who had "white-knuckle sobriety," an unhappy alcoholic who continues to refuse help and stays dry by relying on will-power.

1841. Pursch, Joseph A. "Why Alcoholics Anonymous Works". Alcoholism & Addiction; Dec., 1988; 9(2): p14 of "Recovery" sect.
Pursch disputes the myth that it is the ex-alcoholic's will power, a reflection of their "character," which stops their drinking.

1842. Pyle, Homer. "Jim and Ellie played a role in AA's birth". Free Press, Fort Myers Beach, FL; June 6, 1993.
This newspaper columnist relates how Jim Newton of Fort Myers Beach, FL, and Eleanor Forde, non-alcoholics, played a role in introducing Bud Firestone to the Oxford Group whose spiritual beliefs influenced the spiritual foundation of AA. Both AA's co-founders would meet Jim and Ellie at Oxford Group meetings in early Akron AA. Pyle quotes Dick B.'s book, The Akron Genesis of AA as his source.

1843. Reed, Susan. "Finding A.A. too male-oriented, Jean Kirkpatrick heads a Movement to Aid Women Alcoholics". People Weekly; June 29, 1987; 29: p101 (3).
A.A. is mentioned in the article, basically a biography of Jean Kirkpatrick.

1844. Reichwein, J. "Alcoholism: A Staggering Black Problem". in: National Leader; Oct. 6, 1983: pp1, 8-9, 20-22.
The National Black Alcoholism Council contends alcoholism is the number one social problem in Black America. The need for treatment of minorities by counselors who are culturally aware is pointed out. The role of AA is described.

1845. Reilly, Rick. "In a Golden State". Sports Illustrated; March 30, 1992; 76(12): pp60-69.
This profile of NBA Warriors' basketballer Chris Mullin as a recovering alcoholic includes several mentions of AA. Among the photographs is one of Mullin reading the Twenty-Four Hours a Day book. The "impression" is created that Mullin is an AA member; nearby is the Anonymity Tradition.

1846. Richard L. "One Man's Issue With Relapse". Newsletters Anonymous; 1987; 4: 4-6.
Note: Rutgers.
Richard shares his experience of having relapsed and returned to AA.

1847. Riesel, Victor. "On Job With Labor: Case of Big Elmer - Du Pont Grateful - `Curse' of Drinking". in: national syndicated newspaper column; 1950 (?).
Riesel reports that Dr. G. H. Gehrmann, du Pont Medical Director, revealed "I have spent 33 years with du Pont and for 28 years I struggled without Alcoholics Anonymous. My results were zero. For five years I have worked in conjunction with AA and we now have over 300 good members of A.A., representing 65% of the people we went to work on.".

1848. Riley, Frank A. "Alcoholics Anonymous: An Interview With Edward Dowling, S.J.": The Queen's Work; 1947.
The article describes how AA was founded, how it works, and how it relates to religion.

1849. Ritchie, Oscar W. "The Social Origin and Development of AA". ? [Kent, Ohio]; June, 1950.

1850. "The Road to Recovery". World Health; Jan., 1966: pp25-27. This special issue is devoted to alcohol. AA is mentioned several times. In an accompanying photo from the movie, "Come Back, Little Sheba," Burt Lancaster is show with "two friends from Alcoholics Anonymous." The article also states "AA are not the universal answer; some alcoholics are recalcitrant to the spiritual bases that underlie their action. But it is certain such fellowships as Alcoholics Anonymous...have been of tremendous support to patients during their treatment and invaluable help in their later reintegration into normal life.".

1851. Robe, Lucy Barry. "Gay AA Groups Help More, Lesbians Suggest". The Journal; Aug. 1, 1980: p10.
The article focuses on some of the findings of LeClair Bissell's research with lesbian AA members. (NALGAP 514).

1852. (Robert). "Compulsive Drinker". Atlantic; 1959; 204: pp41-44.
Note: The same article appeared in the Reader's Digest, Nov. 1959, Vol. 75, p209, under the title "My Name is Robert, I Am An Alcoholic...".

1853. Robertson, Nan. "The Changing World of Alcoholics Anonymous". New York Times Magazine; Feb. 21, 1988; 137: p40; ISSN: 0028-7822.
Note: Adapted from her book, "Getting Better: Inside Alcoholics Anonymous.".
Among other subjects, she discusses how more youths, Blacks, women, homosexuals, Hispanics, and alcoholics addicted to other drugs are now joining AA.

1854. Robertson, Nan. "The Intimate Enemy: Will That Friendly Drink Betray You?". Modern Maturity; Feb.-March, 1992; 35(1): pp26-28, 30, 65, & 41.
The author recommends AA. The entire issue of this magazine, "Under the Influence," is devoted to alcoholism and drug addiction. AA is also listed under "Where To Get Help." This journal is published by the American Assn. of Retired Persons.

1855. Robertson, Stewart. "Is There a Cure?". The Family Circle; Jan. 5, 1945: pp11+.
"No,' says Alcoholics Anonymous, 'There is Not' but this voluntary, nonprofit, no-dues group of ex-alcoholics has put and kept thousands on the water wagon.".

1856. Roberts, Susan/Smithwick, Patrick. "Finding God at the Bottom of the Bottle: Thousands of Baltimore Alcoholics Turn Addiction to Salvation". Baltimore Magazine; April, 1989: 37-83.
The authors describe an AA meeting in terms of its parallels to organized religion. They also describe the recovery process giving special attention to spiritual and religious issues.

1857. Rosenberg, Samuel A. "Hitting the Kneel on the Head". JACS Journal; 1986; 3(2): 7.
Rabbi Rosenberg addresses the emphasis which some AA groups place on kneeling for prayer by presenting a Hasidic parable about the proper prayer position. The parable claims that "kneeling is not only a matter of physical posture, it can be a spiritual attitude." Thus, Jews can kneel while standing up.

1858. Roth, R. J. "William James and Alcoholics Anonymous". America; July 10, 1965: pp48-50.
The author believes A.A.'s concept of God comes directly from William James' Varieties of Religious Experience which Bill W. read. This Catholic priest outlines the alcoholic's new belief in a God as he understands him as a positive change rather than a sign of weakness or defeat.

1859. Roubidoux, Gerri. "AA and the Alcoholic. New Film." [review]. Alcoholism; Sept.-Oct., 1981; 2(1): pp41-42.
This film, written and produced by Max Miller, and presented by Motivational Media & Avanti Films Production, attempts to give professionals and the general public a basic understanding of what AA is and is not. Actor John Forsythe is the moderator and explains the wide variety of AA members and meetings, anonymity, etc. Roubidoux calls the film "useful, invaluable in schools, and long overdue.".

1860. Royce, James E., S.J., Ph.D. "Let's Clean Up Our Language". Alcoholism & Addiction; July-Aug., 1986; 6(6): p48.
Royce, Seattle Univ. professor of alcohol studies, advises that we clean up our language about alcohol. He criticizes the terminology of "alcohol and drugs," "self-help," "average and normal," "disease concept," "substance abuse," and "the big book." He suggests in place "alcohol and other drugs," "disease," "chemical dependency," and "Alcoholics Anonymous" as the correct proper noun for the book. Lastly he criticizes "recovering" when the title page and throughout the AA book says "recovered.".

1861. Royce, James. "What Do You Mean Spiritual Illness?". Alcoholism: The National Magazine; 1985; 5(3): 28.
Note: [abstracted from NCADI].
Royce claims that the spiritual aspect of recovery is the most neglected part of therapy. Step 11 is stressed.

1862. Ruddick, James. "You Must Be Made Perfect". Chalice; 1987; 13(3): 5.
Ruddick gives an interpretation of step 6.

1863. Rudolf, J. S. "Books on Spirituality: The Search for a Higher Power". Sober Times; May 1993; 7(5): p6.
ST Editor Rudolf reviews six books on spirituality, including Mel Ash's The Zen of Recovery which finds AA compatiable spiritually.

1864. Rudolf, J. S. "Hazelden: From Humble Beginnings to a Top Treatment Center for Alcoholics". Sober Times; March 1991; 5(3): p5.
This brief history of Hazelden in Minnesota includes discussion of the center's cooperation with AA and "AA counselors.".

1865. Runbeck, M. L. "Letter to a Woman Alcoholic". Good Housekeeping; March 1954: pp54-55+.
The author, an alcoholic, writes of her own experiences and focuses on female alcoholics' patterns in America. She praises A.A. for women.

1866. "A Salute to Ohio". Alcoholism & Addiction; Dec., 1985; 6(2): pp19.
This is the introduction to a special issue "Salute to Ohio, Birthplace of AA.".

1867. Salyard, Wanda. "Getting the Jump on AA Jitters". Alcoholism & Addiction; April 1986; 6(4): p14 in Recovery Sect.
This alcohol/drug counselor discusses fears of newcomers going to A.A. meetings and how the sponsor-newcomer relationship brings about faith in A.A. and displaces previous anxiety.

1868. Samuelson, Jane. "The Paths to Alcoholism: The Roads to Recovory". Chicago; Sept. 1981; 30: p176 (5).

1869. Sandmaier, Marian. "Getting Better: Inside Alcoholics Anonymous" (book review). New York Times Book Review; May 1, 1988: p13.

1070. Santa, Tom, Fr. "What are '12 Step' Programs?". Dear Padre Bulletin; Feb. 2, 1992: front & back pages.
This Sunday Catholic Church bulletin gives basic infomation about AA and other 12 Step programs for Catholics.

1871. "Saved from Skid Row". Time; July 10, 1955: pp55-56.
This medicine column reports on last week's St. Louis Int'l AA Convention and the publication of the second edition of the Big Book. One of new stories, a neurosurgeon named Dr. Earl, is given as an example of a high bottom recovery.

1872. Schaeffer, James. "Interview". OMNI; Dec., 1989; 12(3): pp106-112, 128, 131-2.
Note: Photo-illustrated.
Schaeffer, an anthropologist, studies the tavern scene and the American drinker. In this interview he says "the 12-step program of AA is a blueprint for living that has helped a huge number of people recover from very serious problems with alcohol. It's a wonderful and effective fellowship.".

1873. Schmidt, J. Raymond. "Alcoholics Anonymous: Book Review". National Good Templar; April, 1940.

1874. Schneider, Jennifer P., M.D. "Teenage Recovery Means a Whole New Ball Game". Sober Times; May 1991; 5(5): pp16-17.
Introducing alcoholic teenagers to AA and the particular problems of recovering teens are discussed in this article.

1875. Schonbeck, Joan. "The Wilson House". Sober Times; August 1992; 6(8): p15.
In this travel article, the birthplace of AA Co-Founder Bill W., the Wilson house in East Dorset, VT, is portrayed as an AA hostel. The history of its rescue from disrepair into a mecca for Fellowship members is recounted.

1876. Schwartz, Milt. Lawrence Block. Interview: Author draws on his past alcoholic and recovery experiences to form characters. Sober Times; Jan. 1992; (57): pp6-7.
Schwartz interviews Block who has written nine mystery novels in which his gumshoe, Matt Scudder, is an AA member.

1877. Schwartz, Milt/Luker, Kelly. "Pasadena Couple Spent 44 Years in Forefront of the War on Alcoholism. An interview with Tom and Katherine P.". Sober Times; Jan. 1991; 5(1): pp18-19.
This extensive interview protects the anonymity of Tom P. and his wife, Katherine, a non-alcoholic, who both served on many national and California committees on alcoholism. Tom's mentor was Bill W. Tom found AA in its small downtown 7th St., Los Angeles, office in 1946. Bill & Lois W., Marty Mann, the NCA, Los Angeles community alcoholism programs, etc., are discussed.

1878. Scientific Temperance Journal. Scientific Temperance Journal; Spring, 1943, to October, 1963.; Vols. 51 thru 71: AA mentions.
Note: 5.5 x 8.5" & 5 x 7.5" softbounds.
Seventeen issues of this journal have small mentions of AA. The STJ was published in Westerville and Columbus, Ohio, and originally was part of the vast Anti-Saloon League organization which spearheaded the passage of the Prohibiton Amendment to the U.S. Constitution. These 17 issues are noteworthy in that this heir to the Prohibition movement recognized the value of AA [all mentions of AA are laudatory]. Among the authors who wrote about AA were Harry M. Tiebout, M.D., Upton Sinclair, and Harry Warner. The First Int'l Convention of AA in Cleveland, Ohio, the AA group at DuPont [the first in industry], the Twelve Steps, and AA's continuing growth are mentioned.

1879. Scott, Neil. "The AA Experience by Milton A. Maxwell, Ph.D." Book Review. Alcoholism & Addiction; July-Auig., 1986; 6(6): p58.
Scott advises the many non-alcoholic professionals working in the field of alcoholism who have never attended an AA meeting to read this book. "It is a must for anyone who works with alcoholics," Scott writes.

1880. Scott, Neil. "Cagney & Lacey: Life, Death, and Recovery". Alcoholism & Addiction; May-June, 1987; 7(5): pp18-19.
Scott reviews the CBS TV series and notes "one of the highlights of the season was an episode call "Easy Does It," which placed detectives Cagney and Lacey at a series of Alcoholics Anonymous and Al-Anon meetings." Cagney deals with the death of her alcoholic father by hitting the bottle and denial. Later she will join an AA group.

1881. Scott, Neil. "The Fingarette Fallacies". Alcoholism & Addiction; August, 1988; 8(6): pp17-19.
A&A Editor Scott refutes philosophy professor Herbert Fingarette's contention that alcoholism is not a disease. Scott also defends AA and says Fingarette misrepresents much of AA's philosophy and practices.

1882. Scott, Neil. "Growth through Sponsorship". Alcoholism & Addiction; May-June, 1987; 7(5): p4 of "Recovery" sect.
The unwritten tradition of men sponsoring men and women, women, and other aspects of sponsorship in AA and other 12 Steps programs are discussed.

1883. Scott, Neil. "The Reference Guide to the Big Book" Book Review. Alcoholism & Addiction; Sept.-Oct., 1986; 7(1): p13 of "Recovery" sect.
The Guide by Stewart C. is reviewed positively.

1884. Scott, Neil. "Stop Sending People to AA". Alcoholism & Addiction; Aug. 1988; 8(6): p3.
Note: [also reprinted in Lifestyles of the Clean & Sober, Seattle, WA, Vol. 1, 3, Jan., 1990, p9.].
The editor of this national magazine discusses court referrals, treatment center requirements that patients attend A.A. meeting, attraction vs. promotion, and similar issues in the light of the 11th & 12th Traditions.

1885. Scott, Neil. "Turning Advice into Action". Alcoholism & Addiction; Dec., 1987; 8(2): pp14-16.
This profile of newspaper columnist Ann Landers includes her advice "urging people to go to AA, Al-Anon and Alateen since the very beginning. I don't think alcoholics should go to psychiatrists or psychologists or mental health professionals. The best record for alcohol rehabilitation is Alcoholics Anonymous.".

1886. Scott, Neil. "When Sober Celebrities Speak Out". Alcoholism & Addiction; Sept.-Oct., 1986; 7(1): pp20-21.
A&A Editor Scott discusses public acknowledgment by celebrities of their addictions as therapeutic. "To some this appears to be a violation of the 11th Tradition of Alcoholics Anonymous...but wait a minute, that all-important tradition has nothing to do with acknowledging or discussing the disease of alcoholism.".

1887. "Sertoma's Honor AA Originator". in: Evening Herald. Sanford, FL; Dec. 13, 1979: p10-A.
"Clarence Henry Snyder is an alcoholic" begins this newspaper article. It goes on to identify Clarence as the "only surviving member of a group of 14 alcoholics who started Alcoholics Anonymous." It states Clarence and 13 other "dried-out drunks" started AA in Cleveland, Ohio, in May, 1939." the Winter Park Downtown Sertoma Club presented its Service to Mankind honor to Clarence. His full name and photo with the Big Book in his hands were used in the article.

1888. Sherry, Gerald E. "Sister Ignatia and the A.A.". Sign; 1956; 35(10): 9-11.
Sherry describes Sr. Ignatia's work with alcoholics and the founding of Rosary Hall. He mentions that Rosary Hall was built with the help of many AA-alcoholics and with contributions from Protestants, Catholics, and Jews.

1889. Shoemaker, Samuel M. THOSE TWELVE STEPS, As I Understand Them. ?; ?
The compilers have a mimeographed 5-page article by Shoemaker in which he comments on each of the 12 Steps.

1890. The Silent Rostrum; 1957-1989: 10pp each.
Note: 8.5 x 14".
This long-running Texas Fellowship newsletter was published in Houston, Texas, and came out irregularly, usually 6 to 12 times a year. It contained news of coming events in Texas AA and around the country, humor, reprints from the GV, etc., as well as excellent information on early Texas AA history.

1891. Simmons, Gurdon. "Alcoholics Anonymous". Read; Feb., 1944: pp47-50.
Simmons reviews the growth of AA and discuss basic ideas of the Fellowship.

1892. Skinner, B. F. "A Humanist Alternative to A.A.'s Twelve Steps: a human-centered approach to conquering alcoholism.". Humanist; July-Aug., 1987; 47: p5.

1893. "SOS Media Watch". SOS Newsletter; 1989; 2(1): 1-2.
Two articles are reprinted. The first, from the Los Angeles Times reports that the American Jewish Congress filed a brief in support of an atheist who challenged a requirement that he attend AA. The second, from the New York Times, describes the cult-like nature of addiction recovery.

1894. Stein, B. J. "Hollywood: God is nigh". Newsweek; Dec. 12, 1988: p8; ISSN: 0028-9604.
Discusses the current lack of TV and movie characters who make a decision based on religion, and suggests that strong membership in Alcoholics Anonymous may change that. Recounts the author's experiences in AA. [anonymity break?].

1895. Steve B. "General Sharing on the Steps". AA Loners-Internationalists Meeting; 1988; 13(4): 5.
Note: Rutgers.
Steve, a gay recovered alcoholic, explains how he uses letters to do twelfth step work.

1896. Stewart C. "Staying Sober Requires Brain Power". Alcoholism & Addiction; Nov.-Dec., 1986; 7(2): p14 of "Recovery" sect.
Stewart C. discusses the real intent and purpose of AA, not only not-drinking but the program of recovery through the 12 Steps.

1897. Stockton, William. "Dual Addiction: The Mounting Problem of Mixing Drugs and Alcohol". New York Times Magazine; Aug-Nov. 1978: p4 (5).

1898. Stokes, Bruce. "Taking Care of Ourselves". Environment; May 1981; 23: p42 (3).

1899. Stuttaford, Genevieve. "Getting Better: Inside Alcoholics Anonymous" (book review). Publishers Weekly; March 4, 1988; 233: p92.

1900. Swartz, Michael B. "An Unusual Encounter with AA". JACS Journal; 1987; 4(1): 8-9.
Rabbi Swartz compares the English Hebrew AA meetings he attended in Israel.

1901. Swegan, William E. "Twelve Steps Justify Temperance". Alcoholism & Addiction; July-Aug., 1987; 7(6): p6 of "Recovery" sect.
AA is mentioned as contributing to the "disease concept" of alcoholism.

1902. Talley, Bill. "AAARG!". Alcoholism; Jan.-Feb., 1985; 5(3): pp29-31.
This interview with Talley, president and founder of AAARG! (American Atheist Addiction Recovery Groups!) includes his comments on AA. Talley states he has "never considered trying to shut down AA, but it's okay to be critical. My crusade is to have an alternative. To give everyone the freedom, and also the permission...to be critical of AA. I'm not that far away from AA except for the two prayers in every meeting, and the religiosity that pervades the Big Book and just seems to overwhelm the meetings.".

1903. Ted W. "Alcoholism: A Gay Drunk's Sobering Story". Advocate; March 1981; 5: pp18-19.
Ted's article focuses on alcoholism in the gay community and recovery through AA. Special focus is given to gay groups within AA where "many of us learn for the first time that it was our drunkenness and not our homosexuality that turned people off." (quoted from AA's "The Homosexual Alcoholic") (NALGAP 660).

1904. Thierfelder, William, Dr. (Ass't Prof. English, Dowling College, Oakdale, NY). "Anonymity and Recovery in the College Classroom". in: The National Journal of Health & Recovery; Aug., 1993; 4(8): pp18-19.
This college teacher believes one's personal experiences in recovery should be shared in the classroom so that "thousands of college-aged men and women who are affected in some way by addiction...mustn't be overlooked." He states "For me, coming out about my recovery was a difficult personal choice primarily because all twelve step recovery programs have a strong statement in their traditions about being anonymous at the public level. I have been to AA anniversaries and other celebrations of recovery because of what I dared to do within the classroom forum. I took as my strength the Preamble of AA which tells me to carry the message to those still suffering.".

1905. Thurston, Joseph (as told to Lillian Pompian). "I'm a Cop Who Saves Cops". in: Family Weekly; March 12, 1967; national family magazine for newspapers: pp12-13.
Thurston, a Chicago policeman, recounts his sobriety in Alcoholics Anonymous, an anonymity break, and the founding of the Fellowship Club. That informal club helped other cops suffering from alcoholism to sober up by affiliating with other sober cops who were in A.A. The four column story is illustrated with two photos of Thurston.

1906. Tiebout, H. M. "Alcoholics Cured by Faith". Science Digest; May 1944: pp59-62.

1907. Tiemeyer, T. N. "What Yale Teaches About Alcohol". Christian Century; Sept. 29, 1948; 65(39): pp1004-1005.
Special emphasis is placed on how the pastor can cooperate with AA. The Yale School of Alcohol Studies (later Rutgers) is described. The author also discusses briefly some spiritual ideas of A.A. used at Yale.

1908. Timmins, James P. "Alcoholics Anonymous". The Sign; July, 1946.

1909. "To Lois, in Loving Memory, 1891-1988". Inside Al-Anon; Oct. 5, 1988: 4pp.
Lois Wilson died Oct. 5, 1988, and this memorial issue about Al-Anon's Co-Founder, the widow of AA Co-Founder Bill Wilson, contains reminiscences by Al-Anon Co-Founder Anne B., Henrietta S., Margaret D., Evelyn C. and Myrna H., all Al-Anons, and Nell Wing, Bill W.'s secretary. The issue includes much AA history along with Al-Anon.

1910. Tobin, Jack W., M.S. "Is A.A. 'Treatment?' You Bet". Addiction & Recovery; May-June, 1992; 12(3): p40.
Tobin quotes Fr. Martin's reference to the Twelve Steps of A.A. as "twelve steps of therapy out of the pit (of addiction.)" "His statement comes in spite of AA's Tradition to remain 'forever nonprofessional," Tobin writes. He then goes on to compare the 12 Steps to the steps in the process of therapy and finds them equal. "A rose by any other name is still a rose," he concludes. AA members would deny the premise that the Fellowship is therapy or treatment in the professional language of psychiatry, etc. AA defines itself as a "Fellowship," a "society," and "a program of recovery," among other terms.

1911. Topolnicki, Denise M. "Where To Take a Drug or Drinking Problem". Money; Jan. 1986; 15: p120 (7).

1912. Trey C. "The Message, Not The Messenger". Alcoholism. The National Magazine.; March-April 1985; 5(4): p49.
This brief article tells how Ebby T., who brought the message to Bill W. but went out to drink again, eventually died with six months of sobriety on a farm in New York on March 21, 1966.

1913. Trow, Gene. "Why Calix...Our Members Tell Us". Chalice; 1984; 10(2): 4.
Trow explains that Calix helps the Catholic, AA alcoholics work step 11.

1914. "Twelve-Step Workers Revive Spirit in Parish". Alcoholism & Addiction; April, 1988; 8(4): pp18-19.
This anonymous pastor reports how AA's Twelve Steps formed a new spiritual foundation for himself and his parish. Later, the church would become the meeting place for an AA group and 22 more Twelve Step groups.

1915. Twerski, Abraham J. "Spirituality, Prayer, the Twelve Steps, and Judaism". JACS Journal; 1986; 3(1): 6-9.
Twerski argues that the Christian nature of AA is not inherent in AA and that Jewish theologies need to develop literature for recovering Jews. He then gives a Jewish interpretation of the twelve steps.

1916. Twerski, Abraham J. "Understanding Alcoholism: A Personal Account". JACS Journal; 1984; 1(2): 6-8.
Rabbi Twerski tells how he became involved in the alcoholism field. He comments on his medical training, AA, and the rate of alcoholism in the Jewish community.

1917. "Two AA Groups Serve the Gay Community". The Illuminator; 1985; 10: 2pp.
This article announces the formation of the Lambda Group and the Sobriety Society in Fort Wayne. The Lambda Group serves homosexuals interested in AA and Al-Anon while the Sobriety Society is solely AA. The articles discusses some of the principles of AA as well as the high rate of alcoholism in the homosexual community. (NALGAP 643).

1918. "Unfair to tell Bell's AA Tie" [in]. Cleveland newspaper. Cleveland, OH; Sept. 23, 1981.
This letter to the editor criticizes the newspaper for revealing that State Rep. Thomas M. Bell "has joined Alcoholics Anonymous." Unfortunately, the letter sender included her name, M. Ronayne Kay, of Mayfield Heights, and the fact that she is "a recovering alcoholic with more than a quarter of a century sober.".

1919. Unterberger, G. "Twelve Steps for Women Alcoholics". Christian Century; Dec. 6, 1989: p1150; ISSN: 0009-5281.
This three-page article presents a revision of the 12 steps of AA based on feminist psychology.

1920. Utah School Program. "Teenagers and Alcoholism". Ladies Home Journal; April 1952: p25+.

1921. Van Dijk, Micha. "Recovery in the Promised Land". JACS Journal; 1984; 1(2): 11.
Van Dijk explains his work as director of an alcoholism treatment center in Kiryat Gat, Israel. His difficulty in beginning an AA group is discussed. The difficulty is a result of his being a non-alcoholic and that the closest meetings which could serve as a model are 2 1/2 hours away.

1922. Vonnegut, Kurt. "War Preparers Anonymous". Harpers; March, 1984; 268: p41.
Vonnegut mentions A.A.

1923. Wallace, J. K. "AA: A Modern Miracle". Overture [Los Angeles]; Feb., 1945.

1924. Walsh, Diana Chapman, Ph.D./Hingson, Ralph W., Sc.D./ Merrigan, Daniel M., Ed.D./Levenson, Suzette Morelock, M.P.H. "Treating the Employed Alcoholic: Which Interventions Work?". Alcohol Health & Research World; 1992; 16(2): pp140-148.
Part of this report suggests that an inpatient hospital treatment group of 200 employed alcoholics were able to maintain sobreity for two years at a higher rate than a group of alcoholics in AA and another group offered a choice of treatment.

1925. Walton, O. M. "Alcoholics Hold Cleveland Dinner". Christian Century; October 22, 1941; 22: p1313.

1926. Watt, Kathy. "Making It Through the Holidays Sober". Sober Times; 1989; 2(9): 1, 4.
Watt tells how using AA's twelve steps and slogans can keep people sober during the holidays.

1927. Webster, Peter. "American Indians Gain in the War on Alcoholism". Sober Times; Oct. 1992; 6(10): p10-11.
Webster discusses AA meetings for Native Americans, treatment centers, and the 12 Steps merging with the "Red Road.".

1928. Weeks, Morris T. "13 Steps to Alcoholism: Which Step Are You On?". Salute; August 1948; 3(7): pp3-7.
The author lists 13 steps toward alcoholism as an aid in pinpointing drinking patterns of those on the road to becoming an alcoholic. This magazine article was based on a survey of A.A. members by Dr. Jellinek, of the Yale Center of Alcohol Studies. Clergy, psychiatrists, and A.A. are suggested as possible avénues of recovery.

1929. "What Do You Mean, I Have a Drinking Problem?". U.S. Catholic; October 1983: 27-33.
Among the subjects covered in this interview with Fr. Joseph Martin is the spiritual foundation of the AA program.

1930. "When the Ones They Love Are Alcoholics". Good Housekeeping; Jan. 1960: pp112-113.

1931. "When You Call A.A.". Good Housekeeping; Sept. 1957: p64.

1932. Whitemore, Hank. "If I Can Come Back, So Can You". Parade; May 16, 1993: pp14-15.
This profile of John Lucas, San Antonio Spurs basketball coach, mentions that he "got therapy at the Van Nuys, California, Community Hospital and, following the principles of Alcoholics Anonymous, has stayed sober and drug free ever since.".

1933. Whitman, Howard. "Company Headache: Top-Drawer Drunks" [in]. ? ?; Aug. 7, 1959.
This article, No. 7 in a Series, included this comment from Dr. George H. Gehrmann, former medical director at duPont Co.: "I am amazed at the number of industries where they say 'Alcoholism is not a problem with us,' but as I get around in the Alcoholics Anonymous organizations in these industries, I find they have a large number of AA's they know nothing about." Cooperation between AA and Con-Edison Co., New York, duPont, and Allis-Chalmers, Milwaukee, is mentioned.

1934. "Why Alcoholics Anonymous Succeeds" [editorial]. in: Christian Science Monitor; June, 1949 (?).
A New York psychiatrist, Dr. Albert LaVerne, urged his coworkers in the medical profession to study the record and methods of A.A. in curing chronic victims of the desire for alcohol." He said "the A.A. method had produced an apparently lasting cure for over 50 per cent of 250,000 cases treated ... where both medical and psychiatric treatment had proven virtually useless." LaVerne said his research show A.A. succeeded precisely because it enabled the alcoholic to "develop and experience a newly found spiritual maturity - a source of inner strength.".

1935. Wickware, Francis Sill. "Liquor". Life; May 27, 1946; 20(21): pp66-80.
There is one line on the Fellowship in this extensive article on liquor in America: "The trend in cures is matched by expanding activity of Alcoholics Anonymous, a national organization of ex-inebriates which works on the principle that loneliness is one of the main causes of drinking and substitutes friendship and mutual encouragement for the bottle.".

1936. Wilson, C. C. "The Movies and Addiction. Film Plots Often Feature Alcoholics or Drug Addicts". Sober Times; Feb. 1992; 6(2): pp24-25.
Wilson reviews over a dozen movies, including four or five which mention AA or have characters who are AA members.

1937. Wilson, Diane. "Paris and London - A Tale of Two Cities". Sober Times; August 1992; 6(8): p12.
Travel agent Wilson details AA meetings in London and Paris.

1938. Winner, John. "Treatment or Indoctrination?". SOS Secular Organizations for Sobriety; Feb./March 1988; 1(1): p2.
Note: This is a newsletter which "will lobby for a rational, secular approach" to solving the problem of alcholism, its front page editorial states.
In this first issue of a new newsletter, the author relates his $11,000. detox and rehab treatment center stay where he felt he was force-fed A.A. as the "only game in town." After 28 days of treatment, he felt he was involved in "some kind of religious cult." He has since joined SOS as an "alternative to supernatural paths of recovery.".

1939. Yancey, Philip. "The Midnight Church". Christianity Today; Feb. 4, 1983; 27: p96 (2).
Yancey, a non-alcoholic, tells about AA meetings and beliefs. He refers to AA as a "church.".

1940. "You Can't Taper Off, AA Conclave Told; 12,000 Hear Founder Bill W.". Long Beach, CA: Long Beach newspaper; July 2, 1960.
The 25th anniversary convention of AA at Long Beach, CA, is reported. A photo of Sr. Ignatia, who spoke at the Int'l, is included.

1941. "You Gotta Have Hope". The Catholic World; 1989; 232(1390): 158-163.
This article is an interview with Dr. Robert F. Stuckey. Topics covered include family dynamics, intervention, AA, Al-Anon, and accepting a higher power in recovery.

1942. Zedaker, Lucius. "AA Yields in Argument over Symbols. Will no longer Oppose use of Logo". Sober Times; June 1993; 7(6): p10.
The April 29, 1993, letter from AA announcing they would "no longer oppose" the use of the circle-and-triangle symbol by makers and retailers of gift products, medallions, etc.

1943. Zedaker, Lucius Duvall. "Book review: Beware the First Drink! The Washington Temperance Movement and Alcoholics Anonymous by Leonard U. Blumberg with Bill Pittman". Sober Times; Nov. 1991; 5(11): p34.
The Washingtonians and AA are compared.

1944. Zedaker, Lucius. "History Buffs Gather in Minnesota to Dedicate New Archives". Sober Times; July 1993: 20.
Authors of books about AA were among those dedicating the new Pittman Archives at Hazelden in Minnesota in May, 1993. The archives contains much AA historical material.

1945. Zedaker, Lucius Duvall. "Rational Recovery Program is Designed for the Non-Spiritual". Sober Times; June 1991; 5(6): p25.
AA and Rational Recovery are compared in this article. Jack Trimpey's The Small Book [a play off the nickname of the AA text, "The Big Book"] and other rational recovery topics are discussed.

1946. Ziegler, Phillip. "Book review: The Spirituality of Imperfection by Kurtz & Ketcham". Sober Times; June 1992; 6(6): p20.
Ziegler finds a lot of AA spirituality in this new book by Ernest Kurtz and Katherine Ketcham.

1947. Zuska, Joseph J., Capt., USN Medical Corps (Ret.). "AA 12th-Steps The Armed Services". Alcoholism; Spring, 1985; 5(4): pp22-23.
Zuska recounts how Dick Jewell, a retired Navy commander with six months sobriety, convinced a Navy psychiatrist to permit the first AA meetings and inpatient treatment of alcoholics in the Navy on the U.S.S. Repose hospital ship in Long Beach, CA. From that beginning, Navy AA's grew in numbers and spread worldwide, starting new AA meetings around the world.

Chapter VIII = Scholarly Journal Articles

1948. "A.A. and the Hospital". Hospital Management; Jan. 1958; 85: p85 ff.
This editorial includes one alcoholic patient's approval of the A.A. program in hospitals.

1949. "A.A.'s Position in the Field of Alcoholism". Alcoholism Review; October, 1964; IV(1): p5.
Note: [published by The Alcoholism Foundation of British Columbia.].
This statement was issued from the General Service Office of A.A. In part, it states AA "does not engage in the fields of alcoholism research, medical or psychiatric treatment, education or propaganda in any form although members may participate in such activities as individuals. The Movement has adopted a policy of `cooperation but non-affiliation' with other organizations concerned with the problem of alcoholism." This statement is very similar to the current preamble of AA.

1950. "AA helped create research climate, says Niven". The Journal; Sept. 1, 1985; 15(9): 9.
In this news article published by Addiction Research Foundation, Toronto, Canada, Robert Niven, MD, director of the U.S. Nat'l Institute on Alcohol Abuse and Alcoholism [NIAAA], said "through developing in its members a sense of optimism, AA has brought about a lessening of the stigma formerly attached with being a researcher on alcohol." Niven spoke to the AA 50th anniversary convention in July, 1985, in Toronto. He worked in the field of alcoholism for "some" years before "a flash of insight" made him "realize I should simply accept that AA does work." The NIAAA has encouraged the integration of AA into treatment programs, he said.

1951. Abbott, M. W. "Locus of Control and Treatment Outcome in Alcoholics". in: Journal of Studies on Alcohol; 1984; 45(1): pp46-52.
Note: NCAI 13159.
This study of 106 alcoholic patients at the beginning and near the end of treatment found a locus of control that was based on the philosophy of Alcoholics Anonymous was more effective than a generalized LOC measure.

1952. Aharan, Charles. "AA and other Treatment Programs: Problems in Cooperation.". Addictions; 1970; 17(4): pp25-32.
Note: Published in Toronto, Canada.
As Director of the Lake Erie Region of the Addiction Research Foundation, Aharan discusses the requirements for successful cooperation between AA and non-AA treatment services. The author offers suggestions on how AA members may achieve more satisfaction in their recovery process.

1953. "Alcoholics Anonymous". Mount Airy Sanitarium Bulletin, Denver, CO; Aug., 1939.

1954. "Alcoholics Anonymous: Book Review". American Medical Association Journal; Oct. 14, 1939.

1955. "Alcoholics Anonymous: Book Review". Journal of Nervous and Mental Diseases; Sept., 1940.

1956. "Alcoholics Anonymous: Book Review". Mental Health Bulletin; Nov.-Dec., 1941.

1957. "Alcoholics Anonymous". Silarco Health News, Hartford, CT; Feb. 24, 1942.

1958. "Alcoholics Anonymous". W. Va. Medical Journal; Aug., 1947.

1959. "Alcoholics Anonymous". in: Medical World; March 30, 1951: p100.
This laudatory editorial begins "the medical treatment of alcoholics is generally unsatisfactory. Among psychiatric patients, the alcoholic is one of the most difficult to cure." The editorial describes the crucial stage when he must "be shown how to give it up, and the people best able to show him are fellow 'drunks' [AA's]. Without such moral support, resistance might be impossible.".

1960. "Alcoholics Anonymous in Prisons". Federal Probation; 1954: pp17-20.
The author believes A.A.'s primary goal is to develop a strong bond with the prisoner so he will join A.A. after his release. He presents data to support his thesis.

1961. "Alcoholics Anonymous as an Occupational Program Resource". Labor-Management Alcoholism Journal, NY.; 1977; 7(2): pp31-34.

1962. "Alcoholics Anonymous 1935-1985. 50 Years of Gratitude: The History of AA". Alcohol, Drug Abuse and Mental Health Administration News Supplement; 1985: pp1S-8S.
Summaries of the history of AA, alcohol research on the self-help movement, AA membership statistics, current AA activities and special groups, the AA approach as used by other organizations, the 12 Steps & 12 Traditions, a case history, and a discussion of the relationship between AA and health professionals are presented in this special ADAMNA issue dedicated to AA in honor of its 50th anniversary.

1963. "Alcoholics Anonymous Groups Getting Younger". Bottom Line; 1987; 8(2): p6.
A surprising number of young people are going to A.A., many admitting that alcohol is only part of their problem, with a variety of other drugs being involved in their cross-addiction. Since 1977, the number of young people in A.A. has nearly tripled.

1964. Alford, G. "Alcoholics Anonymous: An Empirical Outcome Study". Addictive Behaviors; 1980; 5: pp359-370.

1965. Anderson, Carl. "Guilt and Conscience". NCCA Blue Book; 1978; 30: 87-101.
Anderson, a Lutheran minister, explains how the twelve steps can be used to overcome guilt. He also mentions some of his work with alcoholics.

1966. Anderson, Dwight. "The Process of Recovery from Alcoholism". Federal Probation; 1944; 8(4): 14-19.
Anderson identifies the basic elements of AA as surrender, relaxation, and catharsis. He rejects the idea that alcoholics are attempting to escape from reality and, instead, argues that they are demanding perfection. AA's value as a recovery program is explained.

1967. Anonymous. "The Lawyer and His Health: Remarks of a Member of NYSBA Committee on Lawyer Alcoholism". The New York State Bar Journal; Jan. 1984: pp8-12.
This anonymous lawyer, a member of A.A., presented this paper first as a talk to Judges of the Ninth Judicial District, May 5, 1983. Sober since Nov. 24, 1965, he relates his experiences in A.A. on the judicial scene in the State of New York, both successes and failures. One may infer from the article that the author is a member of International Lawyers in Alcoholics Anonymous.

1968. Arnold, R. J. "AA's 12 Steps as a Guide to Ego Integrity". Journal of Contemporary Psychotherapy; 1977; 9: pp62-77.
"The therapeutic dynamics of AA, as expressed in the philosophy of the Twelve Steps, are examined. In an `Epistemology of Self,' the Twelve Steps are categorized into stages of admission, submission, restitution and construction. It is concluded that A.A.'s definition of `spiritual awakening' fits the state of `ego integrity' described by the phychologist Erik Erikson as the final healthy outcome of an individual's life cycle." [Rutgers abstract 7905175].

1969. Bacon, Seldon D., Ph.D. "A Sociologist looks at Alcoholics Anonymous". Minnesota Welfare; 1957; 10: p35-44.
"The first part is a review of the nature of the alcoholic; the second deals with the structure of Alcoholics Anonymous; and the third, the role of the social structure of A.A., is a synthesis of the two." Bacon concludes "A.A. is a social structure which provides for the re-socialization of the sick and isolated individual - a structure from which psychiatrists, penologists, teachers, ministers, social workers and sociologists, could learn a great deal.".

1970. Baer, D. J./Ordway, D. "Alcoholics Anonymous Members' Attitudes Towards Marihuana and Its Users.". Psychology Reports; 1973; 32: p950.

1971. Bales, Freed. "Types of Social Structure As Factors in 'Cures' for Alcoholic Addiction". Applied Anthropology; 1942; 1: pp1-13.
Bales compares A.A. to three European therapeutic programs and tentatively concludes that A.A.'s superior success rate is due to its unique policy of encouraging members to actively work at reforming other alcoholics. He analyzes the demographics, personality traits, and familial relations common to many alcoholics and explains how A.A. involvement satisfies conflicting needs that develop in alcoholics during childhood interactions with family members.

1972. Bales, Robert Freed. "Social Therapy for a Social Disorder - Compulsive Drinking". Journal of Social Issues; Dec., 1945: pp1-9.
The author postulates that alcoholics are social outcasts and A.A.'s only qualification for membership, "a desire to stop drinking" which is the problem, permits the alcoholic to re-enter society. A.A. works because its open door policy for membership accepts anyone with a drinking problem. Use of this Third Tradition principle in other areas was the "re-education" topic of this article and this issue of the journal.

1973. Bales, Robert Freed, Ph.D. (Assistant Sociologist, Yale Plan Clinic, Hartford, Conn.). "The Therapeutic Role of Alcoholics Anonymous as Seen by a Sociologist". QJSA; 1944; 5: pp267-278.
Bales discusses the specific role that A.A. plays in helping alcoholics achieve sobriety. He discusses A.A. at a structural level and explains how the group solidarity is maintained in the absence of rigid organization features. He also describes the psychological state of the compulsive drinker and the advantages and limitations of A.A. in treating alcoholic personalities.

1974. Barbara O'B./Phil M./John V. "Alcoholics Are People". NCCA Blue Book; 1973; 25: 68-83.
Three members of AA tell their story of addiction and recovery.

1975. Basel, Joseph. "After-Care". NCCA Blue Book; 1976; 28: 132-133.
Fr. Basel describes his aftercare program. He mentions doing twelve step work with other priests and brothers.

1976. Bassin, A. "Proverbs, Slogans and Folk Sayings in the Therapeutic Community: A Neglected Therapeutic Tool.". Journal of Psychoactive Drugs; 1984; 16(1): pp51-56.
Bassin lists some of the favorite slogans and proverbs used by a number of drug therapy communities and Alcoholics Anonymous. He discusses the therapeutic value of slogans as promoting group cohesiveness and defining behavior codes.

1977. Bassin, A. "Psychology in Action: Red, White and Blue Poker Chips; an AA Behavior Modification Technique.". American Psychologist; 1975; 30: pp695-696.

1978. Bateson, Gregory. "The Cybernetics of 'Self:' A Theory of Alcoholism". in: <u>Psychiatry</u>; Feb., 1971; 34: pp1-18.
"The 'logic' of alcoholic addiction has puzzled psychiatrists no less than the 'logic' of the strenuous spiritual regime whereby the organization Alcoholics Anonymous is able to counteract the addiction. In this essay it is suggested: (1) That an entirely new epistemology must come out of cybernetics and systems theory, involving a new understanding of mind, self, human relationship, and power; (2) that the addicted alcoholic is operating, when sober, in terms of an epistemology which is conventional in Occidental culture but which is not acceptable to systems theory; (3) that surrender to alcoholic intoxication provides a partial and subjective short cut to a more correct state of mind; and (4) that the theology of A.A. coincides closely with an epistemology of cybernetics.".

1979. Bean, M. "A.A. and Religion". <u>Psychiatric Annals, NY</u>; 1975; 5(3): pp36-37, 40, 42.
This article discusses some of the major aspects of organized religion that are used by A.A. Many meetings resemble conventional religious services, with prayers, confessions, a collection, and readings from the A.A. "Bible." The role that these religious elements play in facilitating recovery is discussed.

1980. Bean, M. "Alcoholics Anonymous Principles and Methods". <u>Psychiatric Annals, NY</u>; 1975; 5(2/3): pp7-13, 17, 21.
Bean's analysis is based on visits to 30 or 40 A.A. meetings in the Boston area, A.A. literature, and interviews with members and medical professionals involved with A.A. She discusses A.A.'s development as a mutual support group, lists the Twelve Steps, and discusses them in psychotherapeutic terms, as part of a semi-religious conversion process. The experiences of A.A. newcomers, the role of Twelfth Step workers, and the pattern of women's drinking is described. The meetings, their language, and duties of speakers are also discussed.

1981. Bean, M. "Alcoholics Anonymous: Etiology and Treatment". <u>Psychiatric Annals, NY</u>; 1975; 5(2): pp22-25, 28-30, 32.
Bean proposes three stages of drinking wherein the desire to drink has different determinants at each stage. Drinking is anlayzed as a learned habit that is reinforced by four specific compenents. The success of past and present treatment programs in changing this learned behavior is discussed. Recovery among treated and untreated alcoholics is compared. Particular attention is paid to the merits and limitations of psychoanalysis as a treatment method.

1982. Bean, M. "Alcoholics Anonymous: Psychodynamics of Recovery". Psychiatric Annals, NY; 1975; 5(2): pp35, 38-39, 43-44, 46-47, 51-54.
Active drinkers utilize a number of immature defense mechanisms to justify and protect their drinking habit. This article describes the shift to more mature defenses that takes place during recovery and how A.A. facilitates this shift. It also discusses the superiority of the A.A. treatment method over treatment by nonalcoholic professionals.

1983. Bean, M. "Alcoholics Anonymous: Expectations of Psychotherapy". Psychiatric Annals, NY; 1975; 5(2): pp57-61.
Psychotherapists and other alcohol professionals regard a patient's return to drinking as a complete erasure of all progress made during the course of the therapy. The therapist views the drinking as a personal attack and both patient and therapist feel guilty because of their perceived failures. In A.A., a return to drinking is a slip that confirms the power of alcohol over A.A. members while simultaneously stressing the need for their continued membership. Slipping is not seen as a threat to the value of A.A. or to the effectiveness of its members in helping each other. These two perceptions of drinking and their role in the treatment method are discussed.

1984. Bean, M. "Alcoholics Anonymous: Problems in Affiliation". Psychiatric Annals, NY; 1975; 5(3): pp20-21, 25, 28-29, 33.
This articles describes the psychological and sociological characteristics of alcoholics who successfully affiliate with A.A. Certain demographics of A.A. members, such as age, gender, and martial status, are discussed. Possible explanations for the skewed membership are considered. Particular emphasis is placed on the difficulties that alcoholic adolescents experience in the affiliation process.

1985. Bean, M. "Alcoholics Anonymous: A Critique of A.A.". Psychiatric Annals, NY; 1975; 5(3): pp7-11, 14-16, 19.
This critique considers the drawbacks of A.A.'s insistence that members forsake all interests and commitments outside of A.A.; that they regard all past and present experiences in terms of their relationship to alcohol; and that they surrender a life-long dependency to A.A. by permanently identifying themselves as alcoholics in varying stages of recovery. The rigidity of the A.A. method and its simplification of life to the conquest of alcohol is discussed in terms of its limiting effects on the personal growth of members.

1986. Bean, M. "Alcoholics Anonymous: Two Careers in A.A.". Psychiatric Annals, NY; 1975; 5(3): pp43-44, 50-51.
Fictional profiles of two A.A. members are presented to highlight the different ways A.A. is used and experienced by different members. The profiles are fictitious, but all of the experiences were described by the author in speakers' stories or in individual conversation with A.A. members.

1987. Bean, M. "Alcoholics Anonymous. Appendix: Descriptions of A.A.". Psychiatric Annals; 1975; 5(3): pp52-53, 56-57.

1988. Bebbington, P. E. "The Efficacy of Alcoholics Anonymous: the Elusiveness of Hard Data". British Journal of Psychiatry; 1976; 128: pp572-580.

1989. Beckman, L., Ph.D. "An Attributional Analysis of Alcoholics Anonymous". QJSA; 1980; 41(7): pp714-725.
Beckman provides an attributional analysis of A.A.'s success. According to her, A.A. works because it absolves alcoholics of personal guilt by teaching them that they are not responsbile for having a disease, but only for their recovery. Attributing their drinking problems to an external disease is a crucial element in the recovery process. The types of people most likely to succeed in A.A. and ideas for further research in attribution theory and alcoholism are discussed.

1990. Berenson, D. "Alcoholics Anonymous: From Surrender to Transformation". Family Therapy Networker; 1987; 11(4): pp25-31.
Note: Journal published by U. of California, Div. of Family Practice and Community Medicine, San Francisco.
The history of A.A. is presented and the author traces its origins back to Carl Jung. The Twelve Steps as the core of the AA program are discussed and their affinity with the Serenity Prayer. AA's distinction between religion and spirituality is emphasized.

1991. Berger, Fred, M.D. "Alcoholism Rehabilitation: A Supportive Approach". in: Hospital & Community Psychiatry; Nov. 1983; 34(11): pp1040-1043.
The author presents several possible components of an alcoholism treatment program in which recovery is defined as total abstinence with improved life functioning. The components include individual psychotherapy, group psychotherapy, Alcoholics Anonymous, family therapy, behavior modification, and medications.

1992. Berstein, M., and Molloy, D. "Putting Alcoholics Anonymous To Work in Business and Industry". ALMACAN; 1985; 15(6): pp8-10.
A case study is presented of how two organizations with employee assistance programs (EAPs) relate to AA. The first organization, the GTE Corporate EAP, utilizes AA as its most important tool in handling alcoholic employees. The other, the National Maritime Union Pension & Welfare Plan Alcoholism Program, has AA as a pervasive influence throughout all its activity. (NCADI abstract).

1993. Bill C. "The Growth and Effectiveness of Alcoholics Anonymous in a Southwestern City, 1945-1962.". QJSA; 1965; 26: pp279-284.
This is a case study of the membership of Alcoholics Anonymous located in a Southwestern city. The data reflect the growth of A.A. from its formation in this city in 1945 to its condition at the time of the study in 1963. Percentages are used to express growth of membership and success in maintaining abstinence. The author is a member of A.A. in the city under study.

1994. "Bill W.". in: Alcoholism Review. Vancouver, B.C., Canada: The Alcoholism Foundation of British Columbia.; Feb.-April, 1971; 10(2): pp1-3; 12pp.
Note: This article is reprinted from "Friday Letter," published by the NCA, Jan. 1970, Special Edition.
This is a two page memorial article on Bill W. and A.A. and has a full page photograph of Bill Wilson with Dr. E. M. Jellinek taken in 1960.

1995. Bissell, D./Paton, A./Ritson, Bruce. "Help: Referral". in: British Medical Journal; Feb. 13, 1982; 284: pp495-497.
Alcoholics Anonymous is listed as one of the basic resources general practioneers in Britain can use for patients with an alcohol problem.

1996. Bittle, William E., Ph.D. "Alcoholics Anonymous and the Gay Alcoholic". Journal of Homosexuality; 1982; 7(4): pp81-88.
The prevalence of alcohol abuse among homosexuals is not consistent with their low participation in Alcoholics Anonymous. This article discusses some of the characteristics of A.A. meetings that may discourage gay involvement. It suggests ways to improve the quality and level of gay participation in A.A. (See also NALGAP 078).

1997. "Blacks and AA". in: Alcoholism Treatment Quarterly; 1985; (Winter).
"The historical relationship between Black alcoholics and the Fellowship of Alcoholics Anonymous is reviewed by Henry L. Hudson, director of the Staff Counseling Unit at Montefiore Medical Center, Bronx, New York. How and Why Alcoholics Anonymous Works for Blacks is a detailed analysis of the growth and development of local AA groups in a Black urban community from 1947 to 1984 and the strength and effectiveness of AA as a treatment resource in the Black community. Survey data indicate that the AA program of recovery will work effectively for Black alcoholics regardless of socio-economic status or class. Finally, a hypothesis of cultural affinity is offered as a probably explanation of the cross-cultural success of the AA Fellowship with Black alcoholics.".

1998. Blissenbach, Louise. "The Final Word is--Love". School Sisters of Notre Dame Studies in Spirituality; Fall 1985: 1-10.
Blissenbach gives an overview of alcoholism and co-dependency; specifically as it relates to the religious community of the School Sisters of Notre Dame. Basic concepts are explained and treatment action is suggested. Of special interest is the Catholic influenced re-writing of the Twelve Steps of AA that close the article.

1999. Blumberg, Leonard. "The Ideology of a Therapeutic Social Movement: Alcoholics Anonymous". QJSA; 1977; 38(11): pp2122-2143.
Blumberg traces the medical, psychological, and religious origins of A.A. The contribution of Dr. William D. Silkworth to the concept of alcoholism as an allergy is considered and other proponents of the disease concept are discussed. The activities of pre-A.A. missionaries and the significance of religious conversions are discussed and their influence on A.A.'s development is examined. Comparisons between A.A. and the nineteenth century Washingtonian Movement are also made.

2000. Bonacker, Ralph D., Rev. "Alcoholism and Alcoholics Anonymous Viewed Symptomatologically". Mental Hygeine; Oct. 1958; 42(4): pp562-566.
Bonacker defines alcoholism as a symptom of a deeper psychological disturbance. He describes three primary psychological needs common to the alcoholics he has interviewed and explains how A.A. substitutes for alcohol in filling these needs.

2001. Booth, F. L. "Alcoholism and the Fourth and Fifth Steps of Alcoholics Anonymous". Journal of Psychoactive Drugs; 1987; 19: pp269-274.

2002. Boscarino, J. "Factors related to 'stable' and 'unstable' affiliation with AA". Internat'l Journal of the Addictions; 1980; 15: pp839-848.

2003. Boscarino, Joseph, Ph.D. "A.A. Ideology among Alcohol Treatment Directors". in: British Journal of Addiction; 1980; 75: pp65-71.
Mail-return questionairres were used to test the hypothesis that Alcohol Treatment Center Directors who scored high on measures of A.A. treatment ideology would evaluate A.A. favorably, come from centers which offer more A.A. activities, and recommend A.A. for a broader range of problem drinkers. The hypothesis was supported by the questionairre responses, which indicated that directors who favorably evaluated A.A. felt it more suitable for all types of problem drinkers than did those whose evaluation was less favorable.

2004. Braceland, F. J. "Alcoholism, Varied Approaches to Treatment". in: Psychiatric Annals; 1982; 12(4): pp372-3. Note: NCAI 3182.
This brief history of alcohol use and alcoholism treatment from the 1920s to the present includes a brief discussion of AA's birth.

2005. Bridgman, L. P. "Success of Alcoholics Anonymous: Locus of Control and God's General Revelation". Journal of Psychobiology and Theology; 1987; 15(2): pp124-131.
"The success of the A.A. program for non-Christian members is a source of cognitive dissonance for Christians. Where does the power to change come from for these individuals, since AA does not emphasize a personal relationship with Christ? This article proposes that the research data demonstrates that it is the alcoholic's change from an internal to an external locus of control (LOC) regarding his/her drinking behaviors which accounts for the success of the AA program. A dual LOC theory, one LOC for drinking behaviors and one LOC for life events in general, is proposed to explain some of the conflicting data in the research. (36 references cited)" Abstract supplied from NCADI.

2006. "A Brother Tells His Story". NCCA Blue Book; 1974; 26: 152-156.
This anonymous brother tells the story of his addiction and recovery. Uniquely, he was the first brother admitted to Guest House.

2007. Brown, Paul. "The Problem Drinker and the Jail". QJSA; Sept. 1955; 16: pp474-483.
Brown, Warden of the Westchester County, NY, Penitentiary for over 25 years, believes alcoholism stems from a stunted growth in the individual in his adolescence. He values A.A. because it unearths emotions that stimulate personality growth.

2008. Brown, Reginald. "An Aftercare Program for Alcoholics". Crime & Delinquency; Jan. 1963; 9: pp77-83.
The author outlines an A.A. program for prisoners after their release.

2009. Brundage, V. "Gregory Bateson, Alcoholics Anonymous, and Stoicism". Psychiatry; 1985; 48(1): pp40-51.
Gregory Bateson's theory of alcoholism is analyzed from the viewpoint that it does not parallel the principles of AA as closely as he claimed and that the philosophical tradition of Stoicism reconciles the differences. In 1971, Bateson put forward an "entirely new epistemology," or view of the world, that he described as cybernetic. He claimed that his cybernetic epistemology "coincides closely" with the epistemology of AA, which he said had the "only outstanding record of success" in the treatment of alcoholism. However, Bateson's discussion of AA dealt with only four of the Twelve Steps of AA's program. Although the epistemology of cybernetics and AA agree in some respects, they contradict each other in many others. Common ground is found in the

ancient philosophical tradition of Stoicism. In it, the contradictions between the two are sources for an ethics and psychology of great power. Stoicism offers the cybernetic epistemologist a solid base for theory. It offers the clinician who deals with chemical dependency practical insights into the processes of recovery. 19 references. (NCADI abstract).

2010. Buck D. "Cooperate with AA". NCCA Blue Book; 1971; 23: 25-32.
Buck accepts the idea that "the first person to get an inquiry about alcoholism is a member of the clergy." He argues that the best referral the clergy can give the alcoholic is to AA or a member of AA.

2011. Burd, Joseph G., M.D. "The Doctors and Alcoholics Anonymous". Journal of the Tennessee Medical Assn.; July, 1978; 71: p537.
This doctor suggests the A.M.A. give one hour credit to doctors for attending an A.A. meeting in order to see how "the Serenity Prayer can do a better job than Thorzaine." Cooperation between the medical profession and the Fellowship is urged.

2012. Burns, John. "Recovery Through A Program of Twelve Steps". NCCA Blue Book; 1973; 25: 107-117.
While explaining the spirituality in AA, the author uses examples from his own addiction and recovery.

2013. Burt, Daniel W. "A Behaviorist Looks at AA". Addictions; 1975; 22(3): pp56-69.
Note: Published by Addiction Research Foundation of Ontario, Toronto, Canada.
"Behaviorists' skepticism of AA seems largely due to reservations about `medical modelism;' AA workers are concerned about creeping `controlled drinkingism.' Both camps lack a thorough understanding of the others' approach and these fears seem to be grossly inflated upon closer inspection. Many of the methods of each are similar or compatible and there are some areas where cross pollination may prove fruitful," Burt concludes. This article attempts to bring these "uneasy bedfellows" together. Burt says recent publicity about "controlled drinking" and the behaviorists is not characteristic, citing a review of the literature revealing the great majority of studies done had total abstinence as the goal.

2014. Burton, Genevieve. "The Alcoholic and His Community Search for Help.". American Journal of Public Health; July 1960; 50: pp980-988.
The author's research on marriage conflicts and drinking suggests that alcoholism is both a disease and a social problem. Therefore, he concludes, a multi-pronged approach to controlling it must include many agencies, along with A.A.

2015. Byrne, Marcella. "Resocialization of the Chronic Alcoholic". American Journal of Nursing; Jan. 1968; 68: pp99-100.
The program for resocialization of the chronic alcoholics at the Mayview Hospital's Dr. Samuel Shoemaker Pavilion, Bridgeville, Pa., is outlined. Nurse Byrne states "the Fellowship of A.A. is at the present time the most effective way of obtaining and maintaining comfortable sobriety for the greatest number of alcoholics. AA groups from the surrounding Pittsburgh area conduct five meetings a week at the unit." Since the program began in 1963, 35% of the patients have maintained sobriety.

2016. Canavan, David I., M.D. "Impaired Physicians Program: Support Groups". in: Journal of the Medical Society of New Jersey; Nov., 1983; 80(11): pp953-4.
Dr. Canavan, Medical Director, Impaired Physicians Program, Lawrenceville, NJ, briefly discusses the founding and the principles of AA.

2017. Carroll, J. L./Fuller, G. B. "The Self and Ideal-Self Concept of the Alcoholic as Influenced by Length of Sobriety and/or Participation in Alcoholics Anonymous". Journal of Clinical Psychology; 1969; 25: p363.

2018. Carroll, John P. "1979 NCCA Convention - Convention Special Session on Pastoral Concerns". NCCA Blue Book; 1979; 31: 52-56.
Carroll offers advice to priests who are asked to hear a fifth step.

2019. Cary, Lorin Lee. "Book review: AA: The Way It Began by Bill Pittman". Social History of Alcohol Review; Fall 1989; (20): pp16-18.
Cary concludes Pittman's book is "uneven.".

2020. Cash, T. F./Briddell, D. W./Gillen, B./MacKinnon, C. "When Alcoholics Are Not Anonymous: Socioperceptual Effects of Labeling and Drinking Pattern". Journal of Studies on Alcohol; 1984; 45(3): pp272-275.
The influence of being perceived as an alcoholic by one's peer group and the relevance of an interpersonal stigma to alcohol-related problems and treatment were examined. College students, composed of 40 men and 40 women listened to a tape recorded bogus interview in which a male interviewee reported either a normal or excessive drinking pattern after either being labeled or not being labeled an alcoholic by the experimenter. Subjects then related their reactions to the interviewee on several dimensions. Relative to the normal drinker, the excessive drinker was more likely to be judged by both sexes as deviant, an alcoholic, not in control of his drinking, poorly adjusted, psychologically ineffective, unlikely to improve, in need of professional help, and responsible for his behavior. He was even more strongly rejected as a potential friend and co-worker. It was suggested that the label of alcoholic, which is integral to many treatment programs, would be contratherapeutic if it

fostered the interpersonal alienation known to be functionally related to maladaptive alcohol consumption. (NCADI abstract).

2021. Chambers, F. T., Jr. "Analysis and Comparison of Three Treatment Measures for Alcoholism: Antabuse, The Alcoholics Anonymous Approach, and Psychotherapy.". British Journal of Addiction; 1953; 50(1): pp29-41.
Chambers discusses the advantages and disadvantages of three distinct alcohol treatment methods. Special emphasis is placed on the ideological differences between the A.A. and psychotherapeutic approaches. Chambers, a psychotherapist, stresses the goal of psychotherapy as solving not only the alcohol problem, but also the personality problems that lead a person to drink excessively.

2022. Chandler, Jane/Hensman, Celia, M.A./Edwards, Griffith, M.A. "Determinants of What Happens to Alcoholics.". QJSA; 1971; 32: pp349-363.
This study examines some of the factors that influence the varying experiences of alcoholics. Over 300 males were surveyed to determine how social class, neurotic personality traits, and age at the onset of the problem drinking affect the occurrence of complications in the life of an alcoholic. Complications include job loss, maritial break-up, imprisonment, and physiological dependency on alcohol. Of the sample, 246 were male members of A.A. in London.

2023. Clagett, Arthur F., M.A. "Primary Essentials for Organizing and Administering a Successful Institutional A.A. Program". Mental Hygiene; July 1962; 46(3): pp438-447.
This paper reports on the organization and administration of an A.A. group of inmates at Louisiana State Penitentiary. If the alcoholic inmate is given an opportunity to learn the A.A. program and thereby is motivated to affiliate with an "outside" A.A. group following their release from prison, their chances for staying out of future trouble will be significantly enhanced.

2024. Clancy, J. "The Use of Intellectual Processes in Group Psychotherapy with Alcoholics". QJSA; 1962; 23: pp432-441.
Clancy describes the techniques of psychotherapy adopted by a group of 23 alcoholics united in the mutual goal of abstinence. Most members were either unattracted to the A.A. program or had failed to respond to it. Many were also unsuccessful with individual psychotherapy. The series of therapeutic techniques used by the group is discussed and compared to the A.A. method. The personality changes that affect an alcoholic's success with A.A. are also discussed.

2025. Clark, H. W. "On Professional Therapists and Alcoholics Anonymous". Journal of Psychoactive Drugs; 1987; 19: pp233-242.

2026. Clausen, William J. "Homity--June 17, 1986". NCCA Blue Book; 1986; 38: 125-127.
Clausen comments on Fr. Ralph Pfau, an alcoholic priest who recovered through AA and founded the NCCA.

2027. Clausen, William J. "Keynote Address: Sharing Our Story...Lights the Way". NCCA Blue Book; 1985; 37: 4.
Clausen tells the story of NCCA giving special attention to the historical attitudes toward alcoholic priests.

2028. Cohen, Felix, M.D. "Alcoholics Anonymous Principles and the Treatment of Emotional Illness". Mental Hygiene; 1964; 48: pp621-626.
Cohen examines the usefulness of Alcoholics Anonymous' Twelve Steps in the treatment of personality disorders not associated with alcoholism. His hypothesis is based on the observation of 50 A.A. members, who, in addition to achieving sobriety, demonstrated a number of mental health benefits as a result of participating in the program.

2029. Cohen, Felix, M.D. "Personality Changes among members of Alcoholics Anonymous". Mental Hygiene; 1962; 46: pp427-437.
This is a study of personality changes observed in A.A. members. Cohen tests the hypothesis that A.A.'s who have a strong emotional dependence on a Higher Power have a correspondingly low dependence on other people and an increased sense of inner well-being. Thirty-one A.A. members who achieved sobriety were interviewed and ranked according to these three factors. The figures indicate a high correlation between the dependent variable, increased dependence on a Higher Power, and the two independent variables used to measure personality change. Cohen provides excerpts from interviews to demonstrate how he numerically ranked the information gathered from the interviews.

2030. Collins, G. B./Barth, J./Zrimec, G. L. "Recruiting and Retaining Alcoholics Anonymous Volunteers in a Hospital Alcoholism Program". Hospital Community Psychiatry; 1981; 32: pp130-132.

2031. Collins, G. B./Barth, J. "Using the Resources of AA in Treating Alcoholics in a General Hospital". Hospital Community Psychiatry; 1979; 30: pp480-482.

2032. Colvin, M. "Counseling Approach to Outpatient Benzodiazepine Detoxification". in: Journal of Psychoactive Drugs; 1983; 15(1-2): pp105-108.
Note: NCAI 8134.
In California, at the Haight-Ashbury Free Medical Clinic, patients who have an alcoholic history and are using Alcoholics Anonymous to stay dry are encouraged to maintain maximum program participation throughout the detoxification. Many of these clients feel that they initially got the courage to detoxify from the AA support meetings.

2033. Conley, Robert. "Ministry to the Separated and Divorced". NCCA Blue Book; 1985; 37: 9.
Conley argues that alcoholism is generally the root cause of problems which lead to separation or divorce. He advises pastoral ministers how to counsel in such a situation and recommends AA and Al-Anon be included as part of recovery.

2034. Conran, Peter. "The Mental Effects of Alcoholism". NCCA Blue Book; 1973; 25: 25-32.
Conran first explains how alcoholism adversely affects the mental development of the alcoholic. He then shows how AA helps the alcoholic grow.

2035. Constant, George A. "Alcoholism and the Church". Guild of Catholic Psychiatrists Bulletin; 1966; 13(3): 141-146.
Constant emphasizes that Catholics, like the Jews, need to "emphasize and re-emphasize the scientific truths about drinking" and to put into action these truths. The importance of AA is stressed.

2036. Cooper, Stewart E., Ph.D. "Survey of Studies on Alcoholism". in: The International Journal of the Addictions; 1983; 18(7): pp971-985; ISSN: 0020-773X/83/1807-0971.
The author, in the section on A.A., says it "is the most popular and influential force in the treatment areas, but primarily due to its emphasis on anonymity, the empirical evidence to support it is limited.".

2037. Corrington, J. E., Jr. "Spirituality and Recovery: Relationships between Levels of Spirituality, Contenment and Stress during Recovery from Alcoholism in AA". in: Alcoholism Treatment Quarterly; 1989; 6(3-4): pp151-165; ISSN: 0734-7324.
The results of this study found that independent of the amount of time a person had in AA there was a direct correlation between his level of spirituality and his level of contenment in life. Also, continued attendance at AA reduced stress.

2038. Cort, John C. "Views of Homosexuality". New Oxford Review; 1988; 55(6): 26-30.
Note: Rutgers.
In this review of James P. Hanigan's Homosexuality and John F. Harvey's The Homosexual Person, Cort remembers that Harvey founded Courage. Courage, designed to change homosexuals, "makes generous use of the wisdom of AA [Alcoholics Anonymous], the father of all other spiritual support groups.".

2039. Coulter, Mary. "Comment on Community Attitudes". NCCA Blue Book; 1976; 28: 110-112.
Sr. Coulter, a nun, describes her experience of living in a religious community after she completed treatment.

2040. Cozart, R. "Release Preparation of the Prisoner". Federal Probation; 1952; 14: pp13-16.
The author proposes that A.A. programs in prisons not be limited and that prison staff be prohibited from attending A.A. meetings.

2041. Crotty, Francis J. "Fourth and Fifth Steps: Part II". NCCA Blue Book; 1978; 30: 273-277.
Note: [see Cunningham for Part 1].
In analyzing steps 4 and 5 from a Catholic perspective, Bro. Crotty explains the need for taking these steps. He also argues it is more important to know why behavior took place than to know that it took place.

2042. Crotty, Francis. "NCCA After Twenty-Five Years". NCCA Blue Book; 1973; 25: 4-11.
In this brief history of the NCCA, Bro. Crotty gives special attention to the life of Fr. Pfau who was the first alcoholic priest to sober up in AA and who founded the NCCA.

2043. Crotty, Francis. "The Retreat Facilitator". NCCA Blue Book; 1985; 37: 14.
Bro. Crotty gives guidelines for individuals facilitating AA or Al-Anon retreats.

2044. Crotty, Francis. "Time for Decision". NCCA Blue Book; 1976; 28: 144-148.
Brother Crotty discusses denial and conversion.

2045. Cunningham, John P. "Fourth and Fifth Steps: Part 1". NCCA Blue Book; 1978; 30: 268-272.
Note: [see Crotty for Part 2].
Cunningham argues that "clergy and religious are in a particularly good position to accept the fourth and fifth steps from the people in the [AA] program." He explains the procedure he follows in doing steps 4 and 5 with an individual.

2046. Cunningham, John P. "Problem Drinking in the Priesthood". NCCA Blue Book; 1967; 19: 72-92.
In describing ways to help the alcoholic priest, Cunningham explains why such traditional cures such as making a retreat don't work. He concludes that the program of AA coupled with support from the Bishop and other priests is most helpful.

2047. Cunningham, John. "Retreats for Alcoholics, Alanon, Alateen". NCCA Blue Book; 1972; 24: 81-91.
Fr. Cunningham answers questions about how he conducts retreats for members of AA, Al-Anon, and Alateen.

2048. Curlee, Joan, Ph.D. "Combined Use of Alcoholics Anonymous and Outpatient Psychotherapy". Bulletin of the Menninger Clinic; 1971; 35: pp368-371.
Note: An NCA reprint was also published.
Similar in content to "How a Therapist Can Use A.A.".

2049. Curlee, Joan, Ph.D. "How a Therapist Can Use Alcoholics Anonymous". Annals of the New York Academy of Sciences; 1974; (233): pp137-143.
Curlee relates "one major barrier to the effective treatment of alcoholics has been the tendency on the part of some traditional therapists [psychiatrists & other professionals] to feel that alcoholism is merely a symptom of an underlying problem or personality defect, and that if this defect were remedied, the drinking would take care of itself. Similarily...prescribing tranquilizers or antidepressants ...have been doomed to failure. ...blocking the avoidance behavior, the drinking itself... it is exactly at this point that Alcoholics Anonymous can be most useful." At Indianapolis Veterans Adm. Hospital, Curlee notes "we strongly recommend A.A. participation" along with four weeks of inpatient treatment and a year of counselor or group therapy. She urges all professionals to utilize and recommend AA more.

2050. Daley, Dennis C. "Relapse Prevention with Substance Abusers: Clinical Issues and Myths". in: Social Work; March-April, 1987: pp138-142.
This article discusses relapse reasons, including AA's self-fulfilling prohecy of "one drink, one drunk.".

2051. Darrah, M. "Sister Ignatia: The Pioneering Years in Akron". Employee Assistance Quarterly; 1985; 1(1): pp51-61.

2052. Davis, C. Nelson, Dr. "Alcoholics Anonymous". Archives of Neurology and Psychiatry; 1947; 57: pp516-18.
"I have observed the work of Alcoholics Anonymous for the past six years. 'How does it work?' I do not know," this psychiatrist states, but "it is doing worth while work." Dr. Davis makes six observations about AA and concludes the disease concept, AA clubhouses, and 41 AA members who have remained "dry since the first year or two" are strong indications of its value. AA closed meetings are not far removed from the direct application of psychotherapy, he states.

2053. Davis, D. I. "Alcoholics Anonymous and Family Therapy". Journal of Marital & Family Therapy; 1980; 6(1): pp65-73.

2054. Deevers, Martin. "Alcoholism: Challenge to Medicine". in: Medical Economics; 1944; 22: pp61-64.
"The medical profession has not claimed any large-scale success comparable with that reported by AA," the author writes. "The whole problem [of alcoholism] is a 'natural' for psychiatry. But look at the figures: only 3,000 psychiatrists in the country, and already the A.A.'s have 12, 000 members. That's something to think about - if you're trying to guess who's going to make the best showing in the next ten years.".

2055. Degooyer, G./Spiegel, D. "A Clarification of AA's Official Position on Drugs and on the Medical Profession". Hospital Community Psychiatry; 1978; 29: p134.

2056. Delehanty, Edward J. "Motivation in the Alcoholic". Diseases of the Nervous System; July 1956; 27: pp224-227. The author states that the success of A.A. has caused many psychiatrists to re-evaluate their methods of treating alcoholics. Delehanty is chairman of the Colorado Commission on Alcoholism.

2057. Delehanty, Edward J. "Treatment of Alcoholism with Help from Alcoholics Anonymous". Modern Treatment; May 1966; 3: pp537-541.
The author calls A.A. the doctor's best friend in helping the alcoholic. He lauds A.A.'s success and easy availability.

2058. Diller, Otto J. "The Priest and the Alcoholic". The Bulletin of the Guild of Catholic Psychiatrists; 1966; 13(1): 29-37.
This case study is used to demonstrate how the faith of Catholic alcoholics give them "greater reason and ability to live Alcoholics Anonymous program and keep sobriety.".

2059. Ditman, Keith/Crawford, George/Forby, Edward/Moskowitz, Herbert/MacAndrew, Craig. "A Controlled Experiment on the Use of Court Probation for Drunk Arrests". in: American Journal of Psychiatry; Aug., 1967: pp64-67.
This is a report on one of only two experiments on the effectiveness of AA in this area.

2060. Doar, Robert. "Getting Better: Inside Alcoholics Anonymous". Washington Monthly; June 1988; 20: p50 (4).
Note: Book review.

2061. "Doctors in Alcoholics Anonymous". QJSA; Dec. 1962; 23: p686.
The International Doctors in A.A. meeting in Moline, Illinois, is discussed.

2062. Dodes, L. M. "Psychology of Combining Dynamic Psychotherapy and Alcoholics Anonymous". in: Bulletin of the Menninger Clinic; 1988; 52(4): pp283-293; ISSN: 0025-9284.
This study found AA and psychotherapy can be combined in an effective treatment plan, although it requires a technical change in which idealizing and mirroring transference are assigned to AA by the patient rather than to the therapist.

2063. Doe, John, Fr. [pseudonym]. "A Factual Case". Alcoholism: A Source Book for the Priest. Indianapolis: National Clergy Conference on Alcoholism [NCCA]; 1960: 671-676.
Fr. Doe gives a brief account of his recovery form alcoholism and how he became involved in working in the alcohol field.

2064. "Dominican Preacher Spreads Message of Love". Guest House; 1985; 16(1): 1,4-5.
This story of Valerian LaFrance, an alcoholic priest who recovered at Guest House, mentions that he is a traveling preacher who attends AA meetings in each of the cities he visits.

2065. Donnelly, Phillip. "The Experience of Spiritual Recovery". NCCA Blue Book; 1974; 36: 180-192.
In this article, Donnelly addresses the religious nature of AA. Focus is on gratitude and the role of a higher power in the alcoholics life.

2066. Donohoe, Hugh. "A Bishop's Concern with Problems in the Priesthood". NCCA Blue Book; 1968; 20: 18-27.
As part of his recommendations as to how to better educate priests on alcoholism, Bishop Donohoe suggests teams of AA priests give talks at seminaries.

2067. Donovan, M. E. "Sociological Analysis of Commitment Generation in Alcoholics Anonymous". British Journal of Addiction; 1984; 79(4): pp411-418.
A conceptual framework of commitment generation in voluntary organizations formulated by Rosabeth Moss Kanter is utilized to provide a sociological explanation for the success of AA in the treatment of alcohol abuse. AA is demonstrated as being systematically organized around the process of sacrifice, investment, renunciation, communion, mortification, and transcendence. How these processes function to generate and sustain a strong commitment to sobriety is examined. These powerful mechanisms are shown to subject to social control those aspects of collective life that have implications for commitment, including individual identity, interpersonal intimacy, work, group contact, recruitment, sanctions, ideology, and extra-group ties. (NCADI abstract).

2068. DuWors, G. "His Majesty, the Baby". in: Alcohol Health and Research World; 1984; 8(2): 43pp.
Note: NCAI 14095.
"According to Harry Tiebout, a psychoanalyst who worked with treatment failures and Alcoholics Anonymous 'conversions,' within the drinker's unconscious mind dwells an infant who still feels entitled to all the privileges of infancy, i.e., the attitude of 'His Majesty, the Baby.' This attitude is reflected in a child wanting candy and an alcoholic wanting a drink, regardless of the consequences. Tiebout failed as an analyst until he studied and understood the AA conversion experience as it actually happened, and was only then able to treat patients; especially those not yet 'ready' for AA. His intervention approach had two functions: to stop the infantile ego of alcoholics and to help them accept 'messages from reality.".

2069. "Easy Does It!". Federal Probation; March, 1948.
Written anonymously.

2070. Eckhardt, W. "Alcoholic Values and Alcoholics Anonymous". QJSA; 1967; 28: pp277-288.
In this study, 12 case histories in Alcoholics Anonymous (the book) underwent value analysis to determine the presence of egocentric and other ethical values in pre-alcoholic, alcoholic, and recovering alcoholic personalities. Statements that expressed concern primarily with personal satisfaction and success were scored as egocentric values while the expression of concern for others was scored as an ethical value. Egocentric values were found to be significantly higher during pre-alcoholic and alcoholic time periods, where ethical values prevailed. A discussion of societal attitudes toward drinking that facilitate alcoholism is also included.

2071. Edwards, G./Hensman, C./Hawker, A./Williamson, V. "Alcoholics Anonymous: The Anatomy of a Self-Help Group". Social Psychiatry; 1967; 1: p195.

2072. Edwards, G/Hensman, C./Hawker, A./Williamson, V. "Who goes to Alcoholics Anonymous?". Lancet; 1966; 2: pp382-384.

2073. Elder, Thomas C. "Alcoholism and its Onset in a Population of Admitted Alcoholics (An AA Study)". in: British Journal of Addiction; 1973; 68: pp291-294.
The chronological measure of the onset of alcoholism was studied in A.A. groups in Fort Wayne and North Webster, Indiana, and Defiance and Bryan, Ohio, and included only sober alcoholics who were active in the AA Fellowship. Time was divided into the social drinking period, prodromal, alcoholic drinking, and sober time. While the onset of alcoholism in males was definite, it was indefinite in females. Those who quit drinking early had three times the years of sobriety as late quitters.

2074. Ellis, A./Marlatt, G. A./Twerski, A. J. "Alcoholics Anonymous: Third Edition". Employee Assistance Quarterly; 1985; 1(1): pp93-100.
Three professionals in the field of addictive behaviors review "Alcoholics Anonymous," better known as the "Big Book." Albert Ellis, Ph.D., discusses why AA is probably doing more harm than good by advocating a "Higher Power." Alan Marlatt, Ph.D., addresses the question of whether a reliance on a "Higher Power" is incompatible with the learning of self-management skills. And Abraham Twerski, M.D., clarifies the purpose of the "Big Book." (NCADI abstract).

2075. Ellis, Albert, Dr./Schoenfeld, Eugene, Dr. "Divine Intervention and the Treatment of Chemical Dependency". in: Journal of Substance Abuse; 1990; (2): pp459-468 & 489-494.
This is an analysis of AA's Twelve Steps.

2076. Emrick, Chad D. "Alcoholics Anonymous: Affiliation Processes and Effectiveness as Treatment". DATA, Brown Univ. Digest of Addition Theory & Application; April 1988; 7(2): pp66-69.
This brief article analyzes published studies about characteristics of AA's members and AA's treatment effectiveness. It concludes that all alcoholics can be considered candidates for AA.

2077. Eric W., M.D. "Replies to Dr. Zinberg". in: Alcoholism Clinical Experimental Research; 1977; 1: pp276-277.
This anonymous doctor in AA criticizes Dr. Zinberg's article, "Alcoholics Anonymous and the Treatment and Prevention of Alcoholism" for his emphasis on AA as a "strictly structured, compulsory program" rather than its "suggestions" approach, and his implication that AA is only for "hard-core alcoholics.".

2078. Erickson, L./Stout, J. K./Williams, J. M. "Comparison of the Importance of Alcoholics Anonymous and Outpatient Counseling to Maintenance of Sobriety Among Alcohol Abusers". Psychological Reports; 1986; 58(3): pp803-806.
Note: Alcoholics' self-reported rating of the importance of AA to maintenance of sobriety was assessed. Thirty-six individuals, 24 men and 12 women, ranging in age from 19 to 61 years, who were enrolled in the alcoholism rehabilitation program in the State of New York, volunteered to participate in the study. They drank 5 to 15 drinks a day during a one month period immediately prior to becoming sober and their drinking histories ranged from 2 to 11 years. AA was rated significantly higher in importance to maintenance of sobriety by participants with above median days (160 days) of sobriety than those with below median days of sobriety or than outpatient counseling by those with below or above median days of sobriety. A significant, positive correlation of 0.79 between attendance at AA and days of sobriety was found. It is suggested, however, that more direct evaluation of the role of AA in promoting sobriety is needed before firm conclusions can be drawn. The authors cite 18 references. (NCADI abstract). The study was conducted under the auspices of The University of Scranton, Dept. of Human Resources, Scranton, Pa.

2079. Ewing, John A., M.D. "Biologic and Psychotherapeutic Vectors in Alcoholism". in: Current Psychiatry [?]; May 22, 1982: pp135-144.
"Unfortunately, the [traditional] psychiatric model seeks 'the underlying causes' of emotional disorders [and alcoholism]," Ewing begins. His approach offers a biopsychosocial model. He concludes that "the AA referral represents the most useful single step for the alcoholic patient.".

2080. Ewing, John A. "Some Recent Attempts to Inculcate Controlled Drinking in Patients Resistant to Alcoholics Anonymous". Annals of the New York Academy of Sciences; April 1974; 233: pp147-154.

2081. "Experts Guide Jamaicans". Guest House; 1976; 7(2): 2.
This brief article describes a task force sent to Jamaica to educate people on alcoholism, AA, and Al-Anon.

2082. F., J. I. "Alcoholism - an Occupational Disease of Seamen. Approaches to a Solution of the Problem in the Port of New York.". QJSA; 1947; 8: pp498-505.

2083. Fantana, A.F./Dowds, B.N./Bethel, M.H. "A.A. and Group Therapy for Alcoholics: An Application of the World Hypothesis Scale". QJSA; 1976; 37(5): pp675-682.
This report discusses the different assumptions embodied in group therapy and A.A. treatment approaches and tests the hypothesis that "formistic" thinkers do well in A.A. but not in group therapy and that the opposite is true of "mechanistic" thinkers. Levels of formistic and mechanistic thinking were determined by evaluating the responses of 47 male A.A. members and hospitalized alcoholics to the World Hypotheses Scale, which is described in the report. Levels of contextual and organistic thinking were also assessed. The findings support the hypothesis that formistic thinking is positively related to A.A. participation but do not support the hypothesized relationship between mechanistic thinking and participation in the treatment programs.

2084. Father Bob. "Gay, Alcoholic Priest". NALGAP News; 1988; 10(1): 5-6.
Fr. Bob, a gay priest, tells the story of his addiction to alcohol and his recovery through AA.

2085. Father Joe. "A Priest's Story". NCCA Blue Book; 1975; 27: 131-137.
In telling his story of addiction and recovery through AA, Fr. Joe gives special attention to steps 4 and 6.

2086. Father Paul. "A Priest". NCCA Blue Book; 1969; 21: 3-10.
Fr. Paul, an alcoholic priest who recovered at Guest House, gives special attention to his conversion experience.

2087. Favazza, Armando R., M.D. "Alcoholism". in: American Family Physician; 1983; 27(2): pp274-278.
AA is discussed briefly. "The physician should insist that his patients make an attempt to participate in a compatible AA group," Favazza writes.

2088. Fisher, Dorrice, M.Ed./Weiner, Harvey, D.S.W. "Sobriety is Not Enough: A New Pattern in Referral and Treatment". in: Journal of Psychoactive Drugs; Oct.-Dec., 1981; 13(4): pp385-87.
The authors note a new pattern of clients with two to nine years of sobriety requesting mental health services. The ten AA clients all shared a "high degree of sexual preoccupation and difficulty." Severe emotional problems after sobriety for the group are discussed in eleven shared characteristics.

2089. Fletcher, A. N. "Alcoholics Anonymous". Trained Nurse; 1944; 112: p194.

2090. Flores, Philip. "Alcoholics Anonymous: A Phenomenological and Existential Perspective". Alcoholism Treatment Quarterly; 1988; 5(1): 73-94.
Flores compares AA to existential philosophy and to phenomenology. Emphasis is placed on the issues of shame, suffering, and narcissism. In his discussion of suffering, Flores notes the similarities between Victor Frankl's understanding of suffering in a concentration camp with how AA alcoholics understand suffering.

2091. Fontana, Alan F./Dowds, Barbara Noel/Bethel, Maxine Harris. "A.A. and Group Therapy for Alcoholics: An Application of the World Hypotheses Scale". in: QJSA; 1974; 37(5): pp675-682.
"The results of a study suggest that alcoholics with a preference for formistic thinking [as defined by Pepper's World Hypotheses] are more likely to benefit from participation in Alcoholics Anonymous than from group therapy. Of all the professional analyses of A.A., few have recognized that the central premise of the A.A. approach is the identification and labeling of the problem of alcoholism with the active avoidance of pursuing its causes. Most professional discussions...identify the exploration of underlying conflicts as a major feature.".

2092. Foster, Lloyd/Mann, Marty/Rice, Otis R. "Alcoholism". Pastoral Psychology; 1958; 9(48): 21-24.
A transcript of a discussion that followed one of the "Someone You Know" radio installments in the Autumn of 1949. These installments were sponsored by the Protestant Radio Commission. A brief synopsis of the story is given prior to the panel discussion. Emphasis is placed on the idea that a pastor need not handle the drunk alone and that referrals to AA are important.

2093. Freedman, Mark. "Being Naturally High Much Better". Advocate; April 1974: p43.
Freedman is critical of A.A.'s insistence on total abstinence because this viewpoint, which is not universally true for all problem drinkers, has alienated thousands of alcoholics who might otherwise have been helped. Gay and lesbian issues are emphasized.

2094. Fry, L. J. "Social Thought, Social Movements, and Alcoholism: Some Implications of AA's Linkages with Other Entities". Journal of Drug Issues; 1985; 15: pp135-146.

2095. Fuqua, D./Gade, E./Hurlburt, G. "Personality Differences between Alcoholics Anonymous Members and Non-Members". Journal of Studies on Alcohol; 1984; 45(2): pp170-171.
Personality differences between AA members and nonmember alcoholics were examined. The Eysenck Personality Questionnaire was administered to 91 AA's and 91 non-member alcoholics. EPQ tests for toughmindedness, emotionality, extroversion, and lies were used. Results indicated that AA members were psychologically more healthy than non-members. It is questioned whether AA members' mental health is improved as a result of their membership or whether AA

attracts individuals with these personality traits. (NCADI abstract).

2096. Furman, J. C. "The Alcoholics Anonymous Organization in the United States of America". International Congress on Alcoholism; 1949; 23: p209.

2097. Galanter, M./Talbott, D./Gallegos, K./Rubenstone, E. "Combined Alcoholics Anonymous and Professional Care for Addicted Physicians". in: American Journal of Psychiatry; 1990; 147(1): pp64-68.
The authors studied 100 impaired physicians who were successfully treated in a program combining professionally-directed phychotherapeutic treatment and peer-led self-help [AA]. An average of 33 months after admission, all reported being abstinent and rated AA more important to their recovery than professionally directed modalities.

2098. Gallant, Donald M., M.D. "Assessing the Efficacy of A.A.". in: Alcoholism: Clinical & Experimental Research; Winter, 1983; 7(1): pp100-101; ISSN: 0145-6008/83/0701-0100.
Dr. Gallant comments on an article by Glaser and Osborne, "Does A.A. Really Work?" Gallant notes "while the authors agree with the assertion that A.A. works, they point out that an extensive review of the literature leads to the conclusion that the efficacy has not yet been proved." To get this proof, they recommend various new types of studies.

2099. Garrett, H. E. "Sober is Fun: Looking at the Recovery Process". in: Florida Bar Journal; 1983; 57(1): pp40-41.
Note: NCAI 5370.
The basic steps to recovery from alcoholism are discussed.

2100. Gartner, A. J./Riesaman, F. "Self-Help and Mental Health". in: Hospital and Community Psychiatry; 1982; 33(8): pp631-5.
Note: NCAI 2584.
The authors define the meaning of self-help in such groups, including AA.

2101. "Gay AAs No Longer Anonymous". Advocate; July 17, 1974: p16.
This article reports the decision of the delegates of the annual A.A. World Services Conference in New York to list lesbian/gay AA groups in the upcoming edition of the AA world directory, a landmark decision in A.A. history.

2102. "Gay Honesty Needs a Gay Ear". Advocate; February 24, 1973; 13.
Gay A.A. groups have begun to form across the country, in part because communication blocks impede the recovery of some gay alcoholics in regular A.A., the article begins. It relates that many gay alcoholics cannot be fully honest at regular A.A. meetings and expresses the hope that eventually Gay A.A. groups will be recognized and listed in the A.A. world directory. (See also NALGAP 226).

2103. Geary, J. R. "Alcoholics Anonymous: An Effective Form of Behavior Therapy". Paper read at The First Annual Meeting of the Association for the Advancement of Behavioral Therapies, Washington, D.C., Sept. 2, 1967.; Sept. 2, 1967: 20pp.
Note: mimeographed.

2104. George, O. "Alcoholics Anonymous". Journal of the American Medical Assn.; 1976; 236: pp1505-1506.

2105. Giannetti, Vincent J., Ph.D. "Alcoholics Anonymous and the Recovering Alcoholic: An Exploration Study". American Journal of Drug and Alcohol Abuse; 1981; 8(3): pp363-370.
This article reports on the impact of A.A. membership upon the recovering alcoholic in treatment. Giannetti hypothesizes that A.A. members in treatment demonstrate less existential anxiety, less alienation, a more internal locus of control, and greater expectations regarding the outcome of treatment. Standarized scales were used to measure these variables. Results confirm the hypothesis regarding all of the variables except alienation. Length of A.A. membership was positively correlated to less existential anxiety and a greater sense of internal locus of control and there was a consistent relationship between high existential anxiety and high alienation to severity of the drinking problem.

2106. Glaser, F. B./Ogborne, A.C. "Does A.A. Really Work?". British Journal of Addiction; 1982; 77: pp123-129.
Glaser and Ogborne discuss different aspects of the word 'work' and how A.A. may or may not work on a number of levels. They propose experimental research methods to measure the efficacy of A.A. and to determine the types of people who are most likely to benefit from it. A review of the pros and cons of various research designs is included.

2107. Glaser, Frederick B., M.D. "The Origins of the Drug-Free Therapeutic Community". in: British Journal of Addiction; 1981: pp13-23; ISSN: 0007-0890/81/0110013.
Glaser attempts to trace the roots of therapeutic communities from Synanon to Alcoholics Anonymous to the Oxford Group, then back to the Protestant Reformation to primitive Christianity as embodied in the Dead Sea Scrolls. He concludes today's measured acceptance of AA and similar Twelve Step fellowships is a reminder of the strength of a two millenia old tradition with strong religious roots.

2108. Glatt, M. M., M.D. "Treatment of Alcohol Dependence: Long-Term Treatment of the Psychological Effects". in: British Medical Bulletin; 1982; 38: pp106-108.
"...though AA groups are rather repressive and inspirational in character...they are found all over Great Britain and can be very valuable allies to doctors who want help for their alcoholic patients.".

2109. Golden, Therese. "Time for Decision". NCCA Blue Book; 1976; 28: 140-143.
Sr. Golden describes her work with alcoholic nuns.

2110. Gorski, P. W. "Evaluation of the Auxiliary Function of AA Clubs in the Treatment of Alcoholism". Probl. Alkzmu, Warsaw; 1979; 26(5): pp7-8.

2111. Grau, Al. "Rational Emotive Therapy". NCCA Blue Book; 1980; 32: 1-10.
Fr. Grau uses his own Guest House experience to show how Rational Emotive Therapy works for the alcoholic.

2112. Gregory, Jack. "Benefits of the Therapy for the Alcoholic Priest in His Efforts Toward Recovery". NCCA Blue Book; 1970; 22: 93-113.
Gregory explains the benefits that psychotherapy has for the recovering alcoholic priest. But he stresses that the bulk of therapy needs to be AA.

2113. Greil, A. L./Rudy, D. R. "Taking the Pledge: The Commitment Process in Alcoholics Anonymous". Sociological Focus; 1987; 20(1): pp45-59.
Revision of a paper presented at the Annual Meeting of the Eastern Sociological Society, New York, NY, March 1980. An investment model of the process of commitment to an organization is developed. The commitment process can be described as a funnel wherein commitment demands are gradually escalated as people invest more and more of their resources in the line of action sponsored by the organization. The utility of this model is illustrated through an analysis, based on observational data, of the commitment process as it occurs in A.A. The work, documented with 27 references, was undertaken at Morehead State University, Dept. of Social Work, Morehead, KY. (NCADI abstract).

2114. Griffith, Gavin. "Principles of Recovery: Stepping Into Freedom". NCCA Blue Book; 1977; 29: 61-77.
Griffith emphasizes the importance of taking the twelve steps in order. He also claims that the best way to learn about alcoholism is to apprentice yourself to someone in AA or Al-Anon.

2115. Groves, David H. "Charasmatic Leadership in Alcoholics Anonymous". QJSA; 1972; 33: pp684-691.
A four year case study of the role of the chairperson of a Chicago A.A. group. Qualities of charasmatic leadership and its effect on the group in the years following the leader's departure are discussed.

2116. Grutchfield, L. "AA as a Learning Tool". Employee Assistance Program Digest; 1986; 6(3): pp37-43.

2117. Haertzen, C. A., et al. "Nonsignificance of Membership in Alcoholics Anonymous in Hospitalized Alcoholics". Journal of Clinical Psychology; Jan. 1968; 24: pp99-103.
"Members and nonmembers of A.A. in a hospital setting were compared on the Addiction Research Center Inventory and Inventory of Habits and Attitudes; both instruments measure subjective experiences associated with alcohol use, alcohol withdrawal, environmental pressures to use alcohol, etc. The study shows that A.A. membership was not, in this instance, significant in determining individual differences in responses. The article includes a detailed analysis of samples used and the results." (Phillips bibliography citation).

2118. Hal S. "Alcoholism: A Treatable Disease". NCCA Blue Book; 1968; 20: 28-45.
As part of his story, Hal, a medical doctor, tells how an Episcopal priest got him involved in AA.

2119. Hampton, Peter J. "But for the Grace of God". Medical Record; Sept. 1945; 158: pp551-554.
Hampton includes a brief history of A.A. and calls Bill W. "Mr. Brown.".

2120. Hanfmann, E. "The Life History of an Ex-Alcoholic". QJSA; 1951; 14: pp468-485.

2121. Heersema, Philip H., M.D. "Present Role of 'Alcoholics Anonymous' in the Treatment of Chronic Alcoholism.". Minnesota Medicine; March 1942; 25: pp204-205.
Dr. Heersema reports the cases of two former patients he treated unsuccessfully for chronic alcoholism. He praises Alcoholics Anonymous for the progress made by the two men since joining. He describes the advantages A.A. has over the medical profession in the treatment of alcoholism and proposes a mutually beneficial relationship between the two organizations.

2122. Henningan, L. P. "Alcoholics Anonymous: Something of Value". Maryland State Medical Journal; 1980; 29(10): pp65-68.

2123. Henry, S./Robinson, D. "Talking Out of Alcoholism: Results from a Survey of Alcoholics Anonymous in England and Wales". Journal of the Royal College of General Practioneers; 1978; 28: pp414-419.
Note: [published in England].
Only 1.8% of 171 AA members surveyed said they had never spoken at an AA meeting. Over 80% had told their own story and there was some relationship between dropping out and not telling your own story. A majority (69%) found "drunkalogues," negativism, and irrelevant personal problems "not helpful" in other peoples' stories. The importance of "talking out" was revealed in 45% of those who had told their stories had never stopped going to meetings versus 29% who had not told their story.

2124. Henry, S./Robinson, D. "Understanding Alcoholics Anonymous: Results from a Survey in England and Wales". Lancet; 1978; 1: pp372-375.
Note: [medical journal published in Great Britain].
A questionnaire completed by 171 randomly-selected AA members in England and Wales in 1976 showed that, besides attending meetings, most routinely read AA literature, held office, twelfth-stepped, and sponsored newcomers. New friends in AA replaced, rather than augmented, old friends from the drinking days.

2125. Herrington, Roland E., M.D./Benzer, David G., D.O./ Jacobson, George R., Ph.D./Hawkins, Michael K., Ph.D. "Treating Substance-Use Disorders among Physicians". in: JAMA; April 23/30, 1982; 247(16): pp2253-2257.
Of 40 participants in a two-year program for rehabilitating alcohol- and other-drug-dependent physicians, 7 dropped out and of the remaining 33, 31 have returned to full practice and 22 have experienced no relapse. "The importance of AA participation is suggested by preliminary data... which showed a marked decline in hospital admissions, suicide attempts, and arrests, as well as a relapse rate of less than 15% after at least one year in the fellowship." Psychotherapists are urged to cooperate with the AA and NA fellowships.

2126. "History's Most Powerful Prayers". Guest House; 1980; 11(3): 5,4.
The article focuses on the significance of the Lord's Prayer and the Serenity Prayer/prayers used at AA meetings.

2127. Hoffman, Norman G./Harrison, Patricia Ann/Belille, Carol A. "Alcoholics Anonymous after Treatment: Attendance and Abstinence". International Journal of the Addictions; 1983; 18(3): pp311-318.
Follow-up data on 900 inpatients at eight hospital-based chemical dependency treatment centers in Minnesota demonstrates a high correlation between total abstinence 6 months after discharge and weekly attendance at A.A. during that period. Almost three-fourths (73%) of the regular attendees remained chemically-free, compared with one-third of the non-attendees. These results suggest that A.A. is an appropriate and beneficial aftercare for the majority of treatment inpatients.

2128. Holleran, Paula R./Novak, Alyce H. "Support Choices and Abstinence in Gay-Lesbian and Heterosexual Alcoholics". Alcoholism Treatment Quarterly; 1989; 6(2): 71-83.
Holleran and Novak studied the therapeutic choices made by lesbian-gay and heterosexual alcoholics entering recovery. The authors specifically investigated affiliation with Employee Assistance Programs, AA, private therapy, and religion.

2129. Holmes, Robert M. "Alcoholics Anonymous as Group Logo-Therapy". Pastoral Psychology; March 1970; 21: pp30-36.
Holmes compares A.A. and Victor Frankl's logotherapy and finds them compatiable.

2130. Hudson, Henry L. "How and Why Alcoholics Anonymous Works for Blacks". Alcoholism Treatment Quarterly: Treatment of Black Alcoholics; 1985-86; 2(3/4 [Fall/Winter]): pp11-30.
The historical relationship between Black alcoholics and the fellowship of AA is reviewed. A detailed analysis of the growth and development of local AA groups in a Black urban community from 1947 to 1984 and the strength and effectiveness of AA as a treatment resource in the Black community are discussed. Survey data indicate that the AA program of recovery will work effectively for Black alcoholics regardless of socio-economic status or class. Finally, a hypothesis of cultural affinity is offered as a probable explanation of the cross-cultural success of the AA fellowship with Black alcoholics. 21 ref. (NCADI abstract).

2131. "I am Clancy. I am an Alcoholic". Guest House; 1987; 18(1): 1-2.
In this story of a Catholic priest's addiction and recovery at Guest House, overcoming denial in AA is stressed.

2132. "I Think You Guys Mean It". Federal Probation; 1947; 9.
The first prison A.A. group at San Quentin from 1942 through 1947 is discussed with emphasis on setting up the group, sponsors, outside help, etc.

2133. Ignatia, Sister Mary. "The Care of Alcoholics: St. Thomas Hospital and A.A. Started a Movement Which Swept the Country.". Hospital Progress; Oct. 1951; 32: pp293-296.
This Catholic nun describes how she and Dr. Bob developed the first alcoholic ward in Akron, Ohio, in the 1930s, treating thousands upon thousands of alcoholics over the years. The five-day plan developed there is outlined along with other guidelines for cooperation between A.A. and hospitals.

2134. Irvine, Janice. "Secrets of Fear, Shame and Love: Children of Alcoholic Parents". Gay Community News; 1984; 12(5): pp8-9.
Although Irvine's focus is on children of alcoholics, she includes a lengthy critique of A.A.'s "religious" nature and the disease concept of alcoholism.

2135. Jackson, J. K./Connor, R. "Attitudes of the Parents of Alcoholics, Moderate Drinkers, and Non-Drinkers Toward Drinking". QJSA; 1953; 14: pp596-613.
This study investigates the attitudes of the parents of diagnosed alcoholics, moderate drinkers and non-drinkers toward drinking. The findings indicate that alcoholics come from families where both parents drink or do not share the same attitude towards drinking more often than do moderate drinkers and non-drinkers. Data on parental attitudes was gathered from hospitalized alcoholics, A.A. members, inmates from a rehabilitation farm and from moderate drinkers and

non-drinkers who support the Washington Temperance Association.

2136. Jackson, J. K./Patrick, G. M. [Conference paper & address. (A.A. survey)]. "Conference paper & address" at: Alcohol, Drugs and Tobacco: An International Perspective. Past, Present, Future. Proceedings of the 34th International Congress on Alcoholism and Drug Dependence.; Aug. 4-10, 1985; Calgary, Alberta, Canada. P. O. Box 140, Ch-1001, Lausanne, Switzerland: ICAA; 1985; Vol. II: pp88-91; 546 pp. Characteristics and trends of interest to AA members as determined by surveys conducted by the General Service Office of AA are examined. Membership in AA grew at an average rate slightly over 8 per cent per year from 1968 to 1983. In 1968, women were 22 per cent of the sample; by 1983 they constituted 30 per cent of the AA membership. Young people membership (under 31 years of age) rose from 7 per cent to 18 per cent in the same period. One characteristic that remained stable was the macro-dynamics of the recovery process - the length of time, on average, spent by members in various stages of recovery.

2137. Jackson, J. K./Connor, R. "The Skid Road Alcoholic". QJSA; 1953; 14: pp468-486.
This paper addresses the manner in which Skid Row culture perpetuates alcoholism and stifles rehabilitation. The different social groups that comprise the Skid Road population are defined and the role of the group in serving the needs of its members is discussed. The success of A.A. in rehabilitating the Skid Road alcoholic is also discussed. Data for this analysis was gathered from interviews with hospitalized alcoholics and A.A. members who had spent time on the Seattle, Washington, Skid Road.

2138. James, J. F. "Symptoms of Alcoholism in Women: A Preliminary Survey of A.A. Members". Journal of Studies on Alcohol; 1975; 36: pp1564-1569.

2139. James, R. Joseph. "The Catholic Remedy--Spirituality and the Twelve Steps". NCCA Blue Book; 1987; 39: 31-38.
Fr. James describes the spirituality in AA from a Catholic perspective.

2140. Janes, Jodith. "Getting Better: Inside Alcoholics Anonyous". Library Journal; May 1, 1988; 113: p83.
Note: Book review.

2141. Jellinek, E. M., Ph.D. "Phases in the Drinking History of Alcoholics: Analysis of a Survey Conducted by the Official Organ of Alcoholics Anonymous". QJSA; June 1946; 7: pp1-88.
Jellinek outlines the drinking phase of alcoholism itself in this landmark analysis of the data from a questionnaire used by A.A. and reported in the A.A. Grapevine.

2142. Jensen, Sven E. "A Treatment Program for Alcoholics in a Mental Hospital". QJSA; June 1962; 23: pp315-320.
The author reports a Canadian mental hospital study of male alcoholics. Various methods of treatment were used, including A.A., and a later study showed that abstinence was highest among those in the A.A. and LSD treatment methods.

2143. Jilek-Aall, L. "Psychological Aspects of Drinking Among Coast Solish Indians". Canadian Psychiatric Association Journal; 1974; 19: 4+.
Jilek-Aall argues that AA groups which are modified to incorporate Native Canadian cultural traditions hold great promise. [cited in Joan Baker's "Alcoholism and the American Indian."].

2144. Jindra, Neil J., M.A./Forslund, Morris A., Ph.D. "Alcoholics Anonymouos in a Western U.S. City". Journal of Studies on Alcohol; 1978; 45(2): pp170-171.
This article describes two A.A. groups and includes data on the relationship between attendance during a 4-month period and abstinence at 6-month and 30-month follow-up studies." After extensive data, the authors conclude that "success" in A.A. cannot be measured with scientific numbers as the norm. ""Success in AA is measured in terms of individuals and it is a phenomenon of the present. A basic precept of AA is to try to stay abstinent just 24 hours at a time. Regrets for yesterdays are unproductive; tomorrow has not yet arrived-think about it when it gets here." Observed were all 105 meetings of the groups.

2145. Jones, Robert Kenneth. "Sectarian Characteristics of Alcoholics Anonymous". in: Sociology; May, 1970; 4(2): pp181-195.
"From available information on the development of A.A. an appreciable level of religious commitment among members might be expected, but a study of AA groups in Merseyside did not find this." This article attempts to compare AA with religious sects, finding both similarities and differences.

2146. Jones, Thomas T., M.D. "Medical Horizons Concerning Alcoholism". Memphis & Mid-South Medical Journal; May, 1963: 8pp.
Note: [reprinted & distributed by the Nat'l Council on Alcoholism, Inc., New York, 1963].
Jones says there are three great powers for cure of alcoholism: treatment, fellowship, and faith. He advises doctors to "suggest, not command," AA to their patients who may have a problem with alcohol. He endorses AA wholeheartedly.

2147. Kathleen B./Danny K./Fr. Joseph V. "Three Victims of Alcoholism Tell Their Stories". NCCA Blue Book; 1972; 24: 14-33.
The three individuals who share their stories are alcoholics who recovered through AA. In her story, Kathleen mentions how she had sought help from a parish priest and the spiritual awakening she had in AA. Danny is a former seminarian. Fr. Joseph is a graduate of Guest House.

2148. Kawe, M. G. "Recovered Physician: Experiences of the British Doctors' Group, Hazards in Recovery, Issue, Intervention and Other Roles". in: British Journal of Alcohol and Alcoholism; 1982; 17(4): pp155-157.
Note: NCAI 4411.
The author contends the British Doctors' Group has been an important factor in the recovery of alcoholic physicians in the United Kingdom since its founding in 1973. The Group's cooperation with Alcoholics Anonymous is described.

2149. Kelleher, Jim. "Alcoholism and Sexuality". NCCA Blue Book; 1986; 38: 43-61.
Kelleher describes social issues which affect lesbians and gay men then relates those issues to treatment for alcoholism. AA receives special focus.

2150. Kellerman, Joseph L. "AA - A Family Affair". Addictions; 1974; 21(1): pp19-33.

2151. Kenny, Mary Alice. "The After-care Program". NCCA Blue Book; 1979; 31: 59-62.
Sister Kenny describes the aftercare program at Mercy Center in Aurora, Illinois. She explains that this program involves attendance in AA or Al-Anon.

2152. Kerins, Joseph L. "Spirituality in Recovery". NCCA Blue Book; 1984; 36: 5.
Fr. Kerins claims that Catholics have a rich spiritual tradition they can bring to their AA recovery. He also discusses Ernest Kurtz's Not God and a model of "Our Holy Grandmother the Church" which had been offered by Fr. Jim Dunning.

2153. King, B. L./Bissell, L-C./O'Brien, P. "Alcoholics Anonymous, Alcoholism Counseling, and Social Work Treatment". Health Social Week; 1979; 4(4): pp181-198.
Note: [published in New York].

2154. Kinnell, H. G./Glatt, M. M. "Alcoholics Anonymous". Lancet; 1; (pp714).
Note: [published in Great Britain].

2155. Klores, Stanley. "From Human Alienation to Personal Integration". NCCA Blue Book; 1986; 38: 13-34.
Klores gives an overview of his dissertation, "From Human Alienation to Personal Integration: A Study of Alcoholics Anonymous from the Perspective of Spirituality." He writes that "at its deepest level, the dissertation is concerned with the physical, psychological and spiritual realization of integrated, divine-human, personal existence in the complimentory dimensions of both individualism and community.".

2156. Kolb, D./Coben, P./Heckman, N. "Patterns of drinking and AA attendance following alcohol rehabilitation.". Military Medicine; 1981; 146: pp200-204.

2157. Krupka, L. F./Blume, E. S. "Alcoholics Anonymous in a Therapeutic Community". Journal of Drug Education; 1980; 10(2): pp145-151.

2158. Kurtz, Ernie. "An Addition Syllabus: How to Educate About the Disease". NCCA Blue Book; 1987; 39: 21-30.
Kurtz argues that in educating about the physical, emotional, and spiritual aspects of alcoholism, the education must focus not only on the progress of the disease, but also on the process of recovery. Emphasis is placed on how AA offers spiritual recovery because it acknowledges that it doesn't have all the answers.

2159. Kurtz, Ernie. "Origins of AA Spirituality". NCCA Blue Book; 1986; 38: 35-42.
Kurtz describes how AA alcoholics grow in spirituality.

2160. Kurtz, Ernest/Kurtz, Linda Farris. "The Social Thought of Alcoholics". Journal of Drug Issues; Winter, 1985: pp 119-134.
Note: This article explores the historic development of social thought regarding alcoholism. It discusses the origins of and the differences between the social thought adopted by Alcoholics Anonymous and that accepted by modern professionals. The results of empirical research that clarifies these ideological differences are provided and buttressed with 108 references.

2161. Kurtz, Ernest. "Why A.A. Works: The Intellectual Significance of Alcoholics Anonymous". Journal of Studies on Alcohol; 1982; 43(1): pp38-80.
"Because of the nature of its origins and sources, the parallels between its insight and existential philosophy, and the influence of its ideas on other social phenomena, Alcoholics Anonymous deserves recognition as a movement of unique intellectual significance." Deserving of attention by AA archivists and historians, this article is well-documented with 125 references.

2162. Kurtz, L. F. "Linking Treatment Centers with Alcoholics Anonymous". Social Work in Health Care; 1984; 9(3): pp85-94. Note: (see next entry.).
Professional coordination with AA was studied by surveying directors of state-operated treatment centers and AA members. Questionnaires were mailed to 42 center directors and 100 AA members in the same communities; staff of 3 of the centers and 11 AA members were interviewed. Good relationships with AA were reported by 36 center while 6 centers refrained from cooperating with AA. (NCADI absract).

2163. Kurtz, Linda Farris. "Cooperation and Rivalry Between Helping Professionals and Members of AA". Health Social Week; 1985; 10(2): pp104-112.
"Because AA is an important resource for recovering alcoholics, most treatment centers want to work cooperatively with it. To identify factors that enchance this cooperation, the author survey AA members and professionals in the same communities and obtained a profile of their interactions, ideological similarities, and linking activities." A mail survey and interviews focused on three treatment centers and 31 AA's from 19 communities and found various levels of cooperation.

2164. Kurtz, Linda Farris. "Ideological Differences Between Professionals and A.A. Members". Alcoholism Treatment Quarterly; Summer, 1984; 1(2): pp73-85.
Note: (see preceding entry.).
This report examines the ideologies of professionals and A.A. members and tests the hypothesis that ideological differences influence the level of cooperation between the two groups. Krutz gathered data by means of a mail questionairre that is included in the report and follow-up interviews with some of the respondents. The findings indicate that the two groups differ ideologically and that these differences influence cooperation between them.

2165. Kus, Robert J. "Bibliotherapy and Gay American Men of Alcoholics Anonymous". Journal of Gay and Lesbian Psychotherapy; 1989; 1(2): 73-86.
Kus describes how gay men use reading as part of AA recovery. He explains the types of books which are read and gives specific titles which gay men have found especially helpful.

2166. Kus, Robert J. "Gays and Their Higher Power". National Association of Lesbian and Gay Alcoholism Professional's Conference: ; September 1985; Chicago, IL.
Kus explains how gay American men in AA communicate with their higher power and how their higher power communicates with them.

2167. Kus, Robert J. "A Holistic Health Assessment Model for Doing the A.A Fourth Step". 35th International Congress on Alcoholism and Drug Dependence; July 31 - August 6, 1988; Oslow, Norway.
Kus reports on the limitations and advantages of the WinterStar Fourth Step Guide, a guide designed around the needs of gay men in AA.

2168. Kus, Robert J. "Working the Program': The Alcoholics Anonymous Experience and Gay American Men". Holistic Nursing Practices; 1988; 2(4): 62-74.
Using a sample of 30 gay men, Kus describes what it means for them to work the AA program.

2169. Latimer, Ruth. "The Social Worker and the A.A. Program in a State Hospital". Journal of Psychiatric Social Work; 1953; 22: pp175-180.
"What happens to the patient in a state hospital when he `gets' the AA program? What personality modifications, changes in thinking, feeling, acting? What is the social worker's role in this?" Latimer and Florence Startsman, Longview State Hospital, Cincinnati, social workers, answer these questions in this article. "There is nothing unique in the AA group working with state hospital patients; what was new was the integration of the activities of the AA man and the social worker," Latimer writes. Cooperation with AA is stressed and lauded. AA principles are discussed.

2170. Lawrence, Frederick G. "Thirty Years Rehabilitating the Priest". in: Alcoholism: A Source Book for the Priest. Indianapolis: National Clergy Conference on Alcoholism [NCCA]; 1960: 604-630.
Fr. Lawrence reports on the Missionary Servants of the Most Holy Trinity who work with alcoholic priests. AA and communion wine are given special mention. (The text was written in 1956.).

2171. Leach, Barry, M.A./Norris, John L., M.D./Dancey, Travis, M.D./Bissell, LeClair, M.D. "Dimensions of Alcoholics Anonymous: 1935-1965". Int'l. Journal of Addiction; Dec., 1969; 4(4): p507-541.
The 30-year history of A.A., resulting in 12,040 groups holding 15,991 weekly meetings, its 347 social clubs, its 356 service committees, and over 13 million distributed communications, is "worthy of continuing and intensive scientific and professional attention," the authors conclude.

2172. Lee, John Park. "Alcoholics Anonymous as a Community Resource". Social Work; Oct. 1960; 5: pp20-26.
Note: Also an NCA reprint.
The author outlines A.A. and suggests avenues of cooperation social workers can pursue with A.A.

2173. LeVann, L.J. "A Clinical Survey of Alcoholics". Canadian Medical Association Journal; 1953; 69(6): 584-588.
LeVann concludes that because primary alcoholics tend not to accept a "father figure," "the Oedipal Conflict [in alcoholics] must be resolved and a father figure firmly incorporated into the superego" if recovery is to take place. Jews and Chinese which have a strong figure in the biological father tend to have low rates of alcoholism and AA provides such a figure in the six steps that deal with God.

2174. Levinson, Harry. "Alcoholism in Industry". Menninger Quarterly; 1957; 11(3-A, Special Issue): 20pp.
Note: Describes current developments in the field, including programs structured primarily around Alcoholics Anonymous, with examples at du Pont and Eastman Kodak which are operated through the medical departments of the firms.

2175. Lindt, Hendrik. "The Rescue Fantasy in Group Treatment of Alcoholics". International Journal of Group Psychotherapy; Jan. 1959; 9: pp43-52.
The author discusses sponsorship and proposes the alcoholic can be "rescued" in a fantasy by his sponsor. He further suggests that sobriety will only be maintained as long as the sponsorship relationship endures.

2176. Little, George A. "The God Concept in Alcoholics Anonymous". in: Religion in Life; 1948; 18(1): pp25-33.
The author terms AA "a spiritual movement, a faith cure for alcoholism. Surrender to a Higher Power is not difficult for alcoholics because for years they have surrendered to a lower power." Little explains how denominational differences can be "so completely submerged" and how will power in AA becomes God's Will. This is a wise religious article. "In time it is found that the A.A. program of recovery is founded upon universal spiritual experience.".

2177. Littman, G. "Alcoholism, Illness, and Social Pathology Among American Indians in Transition". American Journal of Public Health; 1970; 60: 1769-1787.
Littman notes that AA spirituality may conflict with Indian religious values. He also explains that when the AA program is modified on the reservations (e.g. by permitting the whole family to attend closed AA meetings), a greater degree of success is achieved. [cited in Joan Baker's "Alcoholism and the American Indian."].

2178. Lloyd, G. "I Am an Alcoholic". British Medical Journal; 1982; 285 [6344]: pp785-6.
Note: NACLI record no. 3570.
"The author, a physician, provides a personal account of how he was first introduced to alcohol and became an alcoholic, and how he sought help for his problem. Through the help of Alcoholics Anonymous, a psychiatrist, and a group of uncompromising alcoholic fellow patients, he was able to maintain sobriety for eleven years. However, a single glass of wine triggered his alcoholism, with an occasional drink becoming a daily habit, causing the disruption of his

professional and personal life. Upon reestablishing contacts with this triad of AA, a psychiatrist, and a group of fellow alcoholic patients, he was able to regain his sobriety.".

2179. Lofland, John F./Lejeune, Robert A. "Initial Interaction of Newcomers in Alcoholics Anonymous: A Field Experiment in Class Symbols and Socialization.". Social Problems; 1960; 8(2): pp102-111.
This paper reports the results of a field experiment that tested the following hypothesis: initial social interaction between A.A. members and newcomers is greater if they display similar social class presentations and lower if the newcomer appears to be a different social class than the members. The authors describe their experimental design and offer an explanation as to why their hypothesis was not supported by the research.

2180. Lois W. "Vignettes From the Past: Bill & Thomas Edison". in: The Parkside Magazine; Winter/Spring 1990; II(2): p 27.
Lois relates how Bill W., Co-Founder of A.A., applied for the job with Thomas Edison in 1918. A week later he took a job as an insurance investigator. Two weeks later The Edison Co. called to offer him a job. Lois wonders what their life would have been like had Bill accepted.

2181. Lovern, Thomas/Sedlar, Dan/Lawrence, Fred. "Retreats for AA, Alanon, and Alateen". NCCA Blue Book; 1971; 23: 71-79.
"This panel was designed to present guidelines on how to structure retreats for members of AA, Al-Anon, and Alateen.".

2182. Luger, Arnold, Rev. "Don't Copy A.A. Meetings Calix Units Are Told". The Chalice; May-June, 1985; 11(3): p1.
The Spiritual Director of Calix International, Fr. Luger, in this front page article in the Calix Newsletter, Minneapolis, Minnesota, cautions Calix units that they are not A.A. and should not structure their meetings around the vocabulary of the Twelve Steps. The Catholic priest states that Bill Wilson, when asked about the founding of Calix, replied that the choice of the name "Calix" itself for the Apostolate was proof that "our purpose was to be entirely separate from A.A." Calix is a society of Catholics and others who also are members of A.A. Their aim is the "spiritual progress of each person involved in our society" and "to help all alcoholics to achieve, maintain, and nourish sober and serene lives." Calix focuses on the 11th Step.

2183. Luger, Arnold. "Special Session on Calix". NCCA Blue Book; 1981; 33: 7.
Luger explains the history and purpose of Calix. He emphasizes that Calix in no way conflicts with AA. The first five steps are explained.

2184. Machell, David F. "Alcoholics Anonymous: A Wonderful Medication with Some Possible Side Effects". Convention of the American Psychological Assn.; August, 1986; Washington, D.C. Danbury, CT 06810: David F. Machell, Dept. of Justice & Law Administration, Western Connecticut Univerity; 8 pp. Note: Reprints available from the author.
The author terms AA an effective self-help modality, necessary in the treatment of many alcoholics. Its primary goal is abstinence and AA seems initially to tolerate an unhealthiness psychologically in order to achieve that goal of abstinence first. The author believes many psychotherapists short ciruit that process by moving quickly to help the alcoholic work on himself psychologically, displacing the primary goal of first abstinence. Psychotherapists should learn to understand the curative process of AA and must learn how to elaborate on the aspects of tolerated unhealthiness as necessary side effects of a wonderful medication, the author states.

2185. Machover, S./Puzzo, F. S./Plumeau, F. E. "Values in Alcoholics". QJSA; 1962; 23: pp267-273.
This study tests the hypothesis that (1) the distribution, within the individual, of "value energy" is more uneven in the alcoholic, whether actively drinking or not, than within the nonalcoholic and (2) the remitted Alcoholics Anonymous member has a greater investment in social and religious values than the unremitted A.A. member. The results of testing the values of 23 abstaining A.A. members, 23 who failed to sustain sobriety, and 23 normal drinkers support the first hypothesis but not the second. The researchers suggest that the second hypothesis was rejected because grouping the data from each category of subjects masked the individual variations in value scores.

2186. Makela, Klaus, Ph.D. "International Comparisons of Alcoholics Anonymous". in: Alcohol Health & Research World; Feb. 1993; 17(3): pp228-234; ISSN: 0090-838X.
The author of this NIAAA journal article compares the demographics of AA in eight countries. The rapid rise of AA in Latin America is noted with over one-third of the two million world membership of the Fellowship now in South America. Makela discusses various interpretations of spirituality, the establishment mode of AA in various countries, and AA's cooperation with professional treatment. He concludes AA has adapted to many cultures. "It is important to make a clear distinction between AA as a mutual-aid movement and professional treatments that are based on the 12 steps of AA. In the United States, it has become increasingly difficult to draw this distinction because of the interpenetration of AA and the treatment system," he ends.

2187. Makela, Klaus. "Social and Cultural Preconditions of Alcoholics Anonymous (AA) and Factors Associated with the Strength of AA". in: British Journal of Addiction; 1991 [1989?]; 86: pp1405-13.

2188. Mangam, Eugene K. "Scope of the Problem". NCCA Blue Book; 1972; 24: 7-12.
Mangam describes the scope of the alcohol problem from his perspective as a judge. He cites cases of people who have recovered through AA and also of some who died as a result of their addictions.

2189. Mann, Marty. "Alcoholics Anonymous: A New Partner for Hospitals". Modern Hospital; Jan. 1946; 66: pp77-78.
Mrs. Mann proposes that A.A. can help hospitals far more than other methods of dealing with alcoholics.

2190. Mann, Marty. "The Pastor's Resources in Dealing with Alcoholics". Pastoral Psychology; 1951; 2(13): 11-19.
Mann writes that "the purpose of this article [is] to explain the working of Alcoholics Anonymous as a method of recovery." In doing so, she not only explains the spiritual role of the program, but also the relationship of a non-alcoholic pastor to the local AA group. Questions which pastors might have about AA are anticipated and answered.

2191. Marcoux, Thomas. "Recovery of Alcoholic Priests: Part II". NCCA Blue Book; 1977; 29: 99-102.
Fr. Marcoux discusses steps 6, 7, 11 and 12.

2192. Martin, Joseph C. "What is Alcoholism". NCCA Blue Book; 1971; 23: 3-16.
In this essay, Fr. Martin comments on the effects of alcoholism on the body, the causes and consequences of alcoholism, and recovery through AA.

2193. Martin, Kiernan. "Problems of Sobriety". NCCA Blue Book; 1984; 36: 12.
Msgr. Martin focuses his comments around the issues of AA attendance, anonymity, and community concerns.

2194. Mary. "A Woman Who is Alcoholic". NCCA Blue Book; 1980; 32: 11-14.
In her story of addiction and recovery through AA, Mary mentions that she sought help from a priest. Step 3 is emphasized in her talk.

2195. Mascarenhas, E./Hanrahan, F. R./Plucinsky, J. J. "Rosary Hall: An AA-Oriented Hospital Alcoholic Care Unit". Ohio State Medical Journal; 1970; 66: p812.

2196. Master, L. "Jewish Experiences of Alcoholics Anonymous". in: Smith College Studies in Social Work; 1989; 59(2): pp183-199.
Note: [partial work on M.S.W., Smith College].
All 18 of the Jewish alcoholics in AA studied here reported positive experiences with AA and would advise a Jewish alcoholic to attend AA.

2197. Maxwell, Milton A. "Contemporary Utilization of Professional Help by Alcoholics Anonymous Members". Annals of the New York Academy of Sciences; 1976; 273: pp436-441.

2198. Maxwell, Milton A. "Interpersonal Factors in the Genesis and Treatment of Alcoholism". Social Forces; 1951; 29(4): 443-448.
The article records the personality changes recorded by 150 AA-alcoholics. Maxwell concludes that "These findings are held to support the growing consensus that alcohol addiction is a sociogenic personality disorder, and that a permanent 'arresting' of alcohol addiction requires personality changes...".

2199. Maxwell-Lyte, P. "Employee Assistance in Britain". in: EAP Digest; 1983; 3(3): pp38-39.
Note: NCAI 9786.
This news article reported "those [employee assistance] programs incorporating the philosphy of Alcoholics Anonymous have the most successful recovery rates." Findings from a survey of one in four attendees of the 1,440 AA groups registered in England, Scotland and WAles as of March 1981 indicate that (1) total AA membership in Great Britain is estimated at 27,000 with the average size group having 17 members; (2) 51% of AA members received some form of treatment or counseling before joining AA with 63% of those stating outside help directed them to AA; and (3) compared to the U.S., Belgium, Brazil, Finland, France, New Zealand and Canada, Great Britain had the second smallest proportion of young members and the highest proportion of women, unemployed persons, and members with less than two years of sobriety.

2200. McCarthy, John B. "Rosary Hall--Model of Treatment". NCCA Blue Book; 1970; 22: 67-78.
McCarthy describes the treatment program at Rosary Hall. In part he mentions the work of its founder, Sr. Ignatia.

2201. McClellan, K. "Golden Anniversary of Alcoholics Anonymous". Employee Assistance Quarterly; 1985; 1(1): pp3-5.
The beginning of AA is discussed and the meeting of Bill Wilson and Dr. Robert Smith in Akron, Ohio, is described. AA is saluted on its 50th anniversary.

2202. McDonagh, Andrew J./Pisani, Vincent D. "Alcoholism: A Response to Stress in Ministry". Chicago Studies; 1979; 18(1): 69-86.
The article describes the disease of alcoholism. It also describes a specific attempt by the Archdiocese of Chicago to help alcoholic priests.

2203. McDonald, Andrew J. "The Bishop Speaks". NCCA Blue Book; 1977; 29: 187-192.
Bishop McDonald begins by telling about how he learned of the seriousness of alcoholism through his years in the seminary to the present. He then compares each of AA's twelve steps to experiences in his own life.

2204. McElroen, Lawrence J., B.S./Faltico, Gary J., Ph.D. "Reality Therapy and Alcoholics Anonymous: A Comparison of Two Approaches to Behavior Change". Corrections Social Psychiatry; 1977; 23: pp79-82.
The authors compare the Twelve Steps of AA with the "Reality Therapy" of Viktor Frankl. "The chief difference between the normal drinker and the abnormal one is that the first drinks in moderation socially, in order to make reality more pleasurable while the second drinks in order to escape from reality." [Ray, 1972]. The authors find great similiarities between AA and RT.

2205. McInerney, J. "The Use of Alcoholics Anonymous in a General Hospital Alcoholism Treatment Program". Medical Ecology & Clinical Research, Park Ridge, IL.; 1970; 3(1): p21-26.
Note: This article is also in: Goby, M.J., & Keller, J.E., Editors, Perspectives on the Treatment of Alcoholism, Park Ridge, Illinois, Lutheran General Hospital, Inc., 1978. pp102-111.

2206. McKinney, George F., Rev. "Alcoholics Anonymous at New York's Wallkill Prison". Prison World; 1946; 8(2): pp20 & 31.
The Catholic prison chaplain relates the first AA meeting at Wallkill was on April 20, 1945. He concludes this first year report with a staff evaluation of "marked progress" and "success" with an encouragement to continue to expand the AA group.

2207. McLatchi, B. H./Lomp, K. G. E. "Alcoholics Anonymous Affiliation and Treatment Outcome among a Clinical Sample of Problem Drinkers". in: American Journal of Drug and Alcohol Abuse; 1988; 14(3): pp309-324; ISSN: 0095-2990.
No major findings resulted in this study of 173 consecutive problem drinker admissions to a residential treatment program. It is suggested monitoring AA attendance may be useful indices of outcome and planning aftercare.

2208. McMahan, H. G., M.D. "The Psychotherapeutic Approach of Chronic Alcoholism in Conjunction with the Alcoholics Anonymous Program". Illinois Psychiatric Journal; 1942; 2: pp15-20.
This is a preliminary report on a cooperative psychothereapeutic program between A.A. and the Manteno State Hospital designed to prepare alcoholics for successful A.A. involvement upon their hospital release. Participants were male patients admitted for alcoholism who volunteered to attend individual and group psychotherapy sessions led by a psychiatrist and group sessions led by A.A. members. All three treatments were based on A.A.'s Twelve Steps and encouraged patients to make personality changes needed for sobriety. The results are discussed and possible reasons for failure are considered.

2209. McNamee, Lee/Ryan, John. "Post-Treatment Stress and Relapse". NCCA Blue Book; 1977; 29: 180-186.
AA is recommended as a way to prevent relapse.

2210. Medvene, Louis J. "An Organizational Theory of Self-Help Groups". in: Social Policy; Winter, 1985; 15(3): pp35-37. "Both AA and Recovery, Inc., are used to illustrate the concept" of the infrastructure of helping roles.

2211. Mehl, Duane. "Facing Loss of Control". Military Chaplains' Review; Winter 1977: 51-63.
Mehl, a recovered alcoholic minister, explains the process by which alcoholics lose control. He uses his own experience as a model. He gives special attention to the futility of controlled drinking and the "God steps." Specific suggestions are offered for working with alcoholics on these steps.

2212. Mendenhall, Warner D., Ph.D. "NOT-GOD: A History of Alcoholics Anonymous by Ernest Kurtz. Book Review". in: Alcoholism Treatment Quarterly; Spring, 1984; 1(1): pp143-149; ISSN: 0734-7324.
Mendenhall's review of Kurtz's book is laudatory.

2213. Metcalfe, Grant E., M.D. "Alcoholics Anonymous". Journal of Indiana Medical Assn.; Dec. 1944; 37: pp684-686.
Note: Presented at a meeting of the St. Joseph County Medical Society at South Bend, Indiana, on Jan. 25, 1944.
Metcalfe describes the role of Alcoholics Anonymous in treating alcoholism and the cooperative efforts of A.A. and the medical profession. He provides the results of several medical attempts to treat alcoholics with the help of A.A. He speculates that A.A.'s success is due to the program's emphasis on religion and its group approach to a shared illness.

2214. Miller, P. M. "Behavior Modification and Alcoholics Anonymous: An Unlikely Combination". Behavior Therapy; 1978; 9: pp300-301.

2215. Miller, R. "Some Questions for the 'Grateful,' Adult Children of Dr. Bob". Employee Assistance Quarterly; 1985; 1(1): pp41-49.

2216. Minogue, S. J. "Alcoholics Anonymous". The Medical Journal of Australia; May 1948; 35: pp586-587.
Minogue reviews the founding of A.A. in America and discusses the difficulties of establishing the movement in Australia. He describes the mentality of many alcoholics, the principles of A.A., and the manner in which the group successfully attracts alcoholics and supports them through their recovery. He encourages fellow psychiatrists to explore treatment methods that appeal more to emotions than to intellect.

2217. "More Women and Young People Are Joining AA". Medical World News; 1978; 19(21): p81.

2218. Mowrer, O. Hobart. "Alcoholics Anonymous and the 'Third' Reformation". in: Religion in Life; 1965; 34(Summer): pp383-397.
Mowrer, past president of the American Psychological Assn., discusses the "scandal of separation" in 20th century Christianity and "ecumenicity." Two evangelical & semi-ecumenical movements, world communism and world science, threaten Christianity, "but I conjecture that the quiet example and subtle challenge of Alcoholics Anonymous in some ways has been even more significant." He criticizes Freud's approach and believes "alcoholism and other forms of personality disorder arise because of fraudulence, not wrong faith." Confession and AA's Fifth Step are compared; conversion, integrity, wholeness, and honesty are discussed. Summarizing: "I like to think of Christianity itself as the First Reformation...the Protestant Reformation of the 16th century was the Second Reformation...can it be we are now well into the Third Reformation, spearheaded by a lowly organization known as Alcoholics Anonymous which does not even call itself 'religious?" Mowrer speculates that AA and similar 12-Step groups may be the real church, "the very Christ incognito." This is a fine interpretative article from the author of The Crisis in Psychiatry and Religion.

2219. Mulry, J. T. "Chemical Dependency: A Unified Illness". in: American Family Physician; 1984; 29(3): pp285-290.
Note: NCAI 13763.
Alcoholics Anonymous is mentioned as facilitating ongoing recovery from chemical dependency. [many AA's would substitute alcoholism for chemical dependency.].

2220. Murdock, Paul J. "Alcoholism: A Practical Approach". Homiletic and Pastoral Review; April, 1981: 26-32,48-51.
Using a fictitious case study, Fr. Murdock explains how a priest might help an alcoholic. Familiarity with AA--especially its spirituality--is stressed.

2221. Murphy, Mary Martha, Ph.D. "Values Stressed by Two Social Class Levels at Meetings of Alcoholics Anonymous". QJSA; 1953; 14: pp576-585.
This investigation analyzes and compares the values stressed by middle and lower class speakers at closed A.A. meetings of a state hospital and at open meetings of suburban groups. The findings indicate that middle and lower class speakers are equally represented at A.A. meetings and the same values are stressed by members of both social classes. Middle and lower class patients tended to select the same group of speakers as preferred. Their selections were evenly divided between the middle and lower class speakers.

2222. Musholt, Dan Martin. "Three Crises in the Psychotherapy of a Recovering Alcoholic". Alcoholism Treatment Quarterly; 1988; 5(1): 95-104.
Musholt uses a case study of an alcoholic to show various crises which come up in therapy. A portion of the article describes AA's spiritual dimension.

2223. Nace, Robert K. "Alcoholics Anonymous Speaks to the Church". Journal of Clinical Pastoral Work; 1949; 2: pp124-132.
Note: Nace discusses parallels between the A.A. movement and Christianity. He analyzes the Fellowship, the Twelve Steps, and Twelfth Step Work in relation to the practices of Christianity and concludes that A.A.'s success confirms the validity of the central teaching of the Church. He also suggests that the church incorporate certain A.A. practices that clergymen frequently neglect.

2224. Norris, J. L. "Bridging the Gap between Active Treatment and Normal AA Involement". in: Alcohol Health & Research World; 1982; 6(4): pp6-9.
Note: NCAI 2379.
Dr. Norris discusses the role and responsibility of treatment professionals in the alcoholic's transition from active treatment to AA membership.

2225. Norris, John L. "What AA Can Offer Professional Schools and What It Cannot". Annals of the New York Academy of Sciences; 1971; 178: pp61-65.

2226. Nunan, Thomas R., Lt. "A Note on the Handling of Alcoholics in a Navy Camp". QJSA; Dec. 1944; 5: pp426-429.
This Naval officer outlines the use of A.A. for Navy personnel at Camp Peary, Va.

2227. Nystrom, Francis [pseudonym]. "The Plastic Chalice". NCCA Blue Book; 1970; 22: 145-158.
Nystrom, an alcoholic who recovered through AA, begins her article by presenting the case of an alcoholic priest and an alcoholic woman. In both cases she asks what type of response might other priests have. She then provides basic knowledge of alcoholism and concludes with some stories that demonstrate how AA works.

2228. O'Connell, Tom. "New Inhibitionists' ignore history lessons". U.S. Journal of Drug & Alcohol Dependencies; Jan., 1985; 19(1): pp1 & 18.
O'Connell reports on an address at North Conway Institute in Boston by Mark Keller, one of the world's leading scholars on alcoholism. Keller said those promoting the "New Temperance Movement" are "The New Academic Inhibitionists," a throwback to Prohibition. "Repressive laws during more than 4,000 years have never succeeded in suppressing drinking problems but religion has worked," Keller said. Shortly after Prohibition ended, Alcoholics Anonymous was formed, with its distinctive "religious" tone and spirit.

2229. O'Connor, Tom. "Through the Blessed Gateway Called Guest House". Guest House Newsletter; 1981; 12(2): 1,5.
Fr. O'Connor of Guest House emphasizes his pastoral ministry with AA-alcoholics.

2230. O'Leary, D. E./Haddock, D. L. "Alcohol Use Patterns and Alcoholics Anonymous Affiliation as Predictors of Alcoholism Treatment Outcome". Research Communications on Substance Abuse; 1980; 1: pp197-209.

2231. O'Leary, M./Calsyn, D./Haddock, D./Freeman, C. "Differential alcohol use patterns and personality traits among three Alcoholics Anonymous attendance level groups: Further considerations of the affiliation profile.". Journal of Drug & Alcohol Dependance; 1980; 5(2): pp135-144.

2232. Obitz, F. W./Wood, J. D./Cantergiani, N. "Alcoholics' Perceptions of Group Therapy and Alcoholics Anonymous". British Journal of Addictions; 1977; 72: pp321-324. A group of 64 similar alcoholics rated their perceptions of AA and group therapy on 30 variables. AA was more preferred than group therapy. It was viewed as more tolerant and sympathetic.

2233. Ogborne, Alan C., Ph.D./Glaser, Frederick B., M.D. "Characteristics of Affiliates of Alcoholics Anonymous: A Review of the Literature.". Journal of Studies on Alcohol; 1981; 42(7): pp661-675. "Certain demographic, social, personality, and perceptual characteristics, as well as a drinking history characterized by binge drinking, dependence on alcohol and loss-of-control drinking, appear to be associated with affiliation with Alcoholics Anonymous." The study concludes "the empirical evidence reviewed supports clinical impressions and deductions from physchological theory, and suggests that problem drinkers who affiliate with A.A. are in many significant ways different from those who do not.".

2234. Olsen, Ron. "The 12 Steps of Alcoholics Anonymous: One Man's Story". in: The Journal. Toronto, Canada; Oct.-Nov., 1991; (Vol. 20, No. 7): p12. As part of its 40th anniversary, the Alberta Alcohol & Drug Abuse Commission ran a writing contest for staff on any subject in the addictions field and this is the winner. Olsen tells the story of Jim, a young, angry, Japanese alcoholic in America right after WWII who got sober in AA and now has a new wonderful life with 37 years of sobriety.

2235. Orrick, Judson H. "A Conspiracy of Silence". in: The Florida Bar Journal; Jan. 1983; 57(1): pp13-18. Orrick, Assistant Editor of the FBJ, finds practicing law a stressful occupation with an estimated 10 to 15% of all lawyers having alcohol problems. He surveys the current scene with half the nation's state bars and 21% of local bars having alcoholic assistance programs in place for alcoholic lawyers. "Certainly the most widely recognized and, perhaps, most successful support organization for the sober alcoholic is Alcoholics Anonymous.".

2236. Osborne, Alan C./Bornet, Andrew. "Abstinence and Abusive Drinking Among Affiliates of Alcoholics Anonymous: Are These the Only Alternatives?". in: Addictive Behaviors; 1982; 7: pp199-202; ISSN: 0306-4603/82/020199-04.
The authors took Rand report data and new information from a follow-up study of halfway house residents and showed that regular AA members who drank reported more physical and other negative consequences than drinkers who attended AA less often.

2237. Paddock, Richard. "Alcoholism and the Clergyman". NCCA Blue Book; 1971; 23: 110-117.
Paddock explains some difficulties priests have in identifying their alcoholism. He argues "the best recognized approach to arresting this disease is the program of Alcoholics Anonymous." The Guest House experience is mentioned.

2238. Page, Penny Booth. "Book review: Pass It On: The Story of Bill Wilson and How the A.A. Message Reached the World". Social History of Alcohol Review; Fall 1985; (12): p28.
Page calls this AAWS volume "more comprehensive than Thomsen's effort but Kurtz remains the clear authority on Wilson's and A.A.'s intellectual roots. Still, valuable...".

2239. "Panel of People who Work with Alcoholics". NCCA Blue Book; 1968; 20: 64-83.
Representatives of various facilities who work with alcoholic priests describe their programs. Most stress involvement with AA.

2240. Paster, S. "The Treatment of Chronic Alcoholism". Memphis Medical Journal; 1948; 23: 88-91.
AA is described with special focus on the issue of spiritual awakening and "acceptance of a personal, benign, protective power.".

2241. Peele, S. "Research Issues in Assessing Addiction Treatment Efficacy: How Cost Effective are Alcoholics Anonymous and Private Treatment Centers?". in: Drug and Alcohol Dependence; 1990; 25(2): pp179-182; ISSN: 0376-8716.
AA as a program in private treatment centers is characterized as not "effective." Peele recommends private treatment centers should participate in actual clinical-trials "if an effective alcoholism treatment system is to be developed in the U.S.

2242. "A Personal Look at AIDS and Recovery". NALGAP News; 1987; 8(4): 2,5.
This anonymous gay man reflects on how AIDS has affected his AA program. Special emphasis is placed on how he thanks God for permitting him to enjoy the day. Sponsorship, medication for pain, and resentments are emphasized.

2243. Petrunik, M. G. "Seeing the Light: A Study of Conversion to Alcoholics Anonymous". Journal of Volun. Action Res.; 1972; 1: pp30-38.

2244. "Philadelphia Alcoholics Anonymous". Philadelphia Medicine; Feb. 12, 1942.

2245. Phillips, S. "Gay AA's Multiply". Advocate; 9 June 1971: p12.

2246. Pope, Benjamin. "Attitudes Toward Group Therapy in a Psychatric Clinic for Alcoholics". QJSA; June 1956; 17: pp233-254.
The author compares group therapy among alcoholics in a clinic to A.A. in terms of a total value system.

2247. Povish, Kenneth. "45 Years for Sobriety". Guest House; 1982; 13(2): 3.
Bishop Povish explains that AA works well for Catholic alcoholics.

2248. R.C.A. "In Memoriam: Father Ralph Sylvester Pfau, 1904-1967". NCCA Blue Book; 1967; 19: xii-xvi.
This memorial article describes the life of Fr. Ralph Pfau, founder of the NCCA.

2249. Ramsey, E. "From Guilt Through Shame to AA: A Self-Reconcilation Process". Alcoholism Treatment Quarterly; 1987; 4(2): pp87-107; ISSN: 0734-7324.
"The community of AA provides a safe and caring environment in which the shamed/addictive person can begin to heal. AA avoids judgments, labelling, and shaming a person by requiring a person to be only himself, a principle which is reinforced by 8 of the 12 Traditions. The 12 Steps of AA are an outline for the reconciliation of the self.".

2250. Rather, B. C./Sherman, M. F. "Relationship between Alcohol Expectancies and Length of Abstinence among Alcoholics Anonymous Members". in: Addictive Behaviors; 1989; 14(5): pp531-536; ISSN: 0306-4603.
Note: [based on Master's thesis by Rather under direction of Sherman at Loyola College, Maryland].
This study of 114 AA members with extended abstinence found dramatic reductions in alcohol expectancy scales [future drinking potential].

2251. Read, E. M. "Alcoholic, the Probation Officer, and AA". in: Professional Counselor; 1988; 3(2): pp38, 40, 42-43.
Education of the probation officer about AA and suggestions on how he or she may introduce their charges to the Fellowship are the main thrust of this article.

2252. Richards, Thomas B. "Minister and the Bum". Pastoral Psychology; 1955; 6(54): 9-15.
Richards gives special emphasis to alcoholism among men on skid row as well as AA as a treatment program.

2253. Richey, Terry/Gannon, Thomas/Carroll, Jack. "Meetings! Meetings! Meetings! Relapse in Continuing Treatment". NCCA Blue Book; 1977; 29: 103-111.
Richey, Gannon, and Carroll each tell why attending AA meetings helps prevent relapse.

2254. Richie, Oscar W. "A Sociohistorical Survey of Alcoholics Anonymous". Quarterly Journal of Studies on Alcohol; 1948; 9(1): 119-156.
In one section of his survey, Richie explains the spiritual factor in AA.

2255. Rienhoff, O. "The Composition of Alcoholics Anonymous in the Federal Republic of Germany". Deutsch. Medical, Wschr.; 1979; 104: pp81-84.
A questionnaire survey of 1,190 AA members in Germany showed membership increases about 30% yearly and will probably reach 23,000 in 1980. The median age of respondents was 40.

2256. Ripley, Herbert S., M.D./Jackson, Joan K., Ph.D. "Therapeutic Factors in Alcoholics Anonymous". American Journal of Psychiatry; 1959; 116: pp44-50.
The concept of A.A. and the treatment methods it employs are discussed, with emphasis on the different forms of group therapy it offers. A.A. techniques are examined in light of their similarity to techniques used in individual and group psychotherapy. The program's exclusive committment to the solitary goal of sobriety is also examined.

2257. Ritchie, Oscar W., M.A. "A Sociohistorical Survey of Alcoholics Anonymous". QJSA; 1948; 9: pp119-156.
Note: This survey discusses the social origin of Alcoholics Anonymous, with emphasis on the activities of Bill W., Dr. Rob, and the earliest members of the movement. A.A.'s ideology is discussed as an outgrowth of certain principles of other movements. The concept of alcoholism as a disease, the spiritual factor of the program and the value of Twelfth Step work are presented through various personal accounts. A.A.'s organizational structure is analyzed in terms of membership requirements, financial issues and mechanisms for the exercise of authority.

2258. Robinson, David. "The Growth of Alcoholics Anonymous". Alcohol & Alcoholism (printed in Great Britain); 1983; 18(2): pp167-172.
Robinson traces the growth of Alcoholics Anonymous from its earliest days in Akron, Ohio, to its present position of international acclaim. He identifies characteristics of A.A.'s self-help method that are more acceptable in some cultures than in others and argues for a more systematic approach to the study of A.A. as a worldwide organization.

2259. Rohan, William P. "A Followup Study of Hospitalized Problem Drinkers". Diseases of the Nervous System; April 1970; 31: pp259-265.
A.A. membership during hospitalization aided later recovery, this study showed.

2260. Room, Robin (Medical Research Institute of San Francisco, Alcohol Research Group, Berkeley, CA). "Alcoholism and Alcoholics Anonymous in U.S. films, 1945-1962: The party ends for the 'wet generations.". International Group for Comparative Alcohol Studies conference.; Sept. 24-28, 1985; Helsinki, Finland. Berkeley, CA: Alcohol Research Group, Institute of Epidemiology and Behavioral Medicine, Medical Research Institute of San Francisco, 1816 Scenic Ave., Berkeley, CA 94709; 1985; 23pp.
Note: [this article is also available in Journal of Studies on Alcohol, Rutgers, NJ, Vol. 50, 4, July, 1989, pp368-383.].
"Between 1945 and 1962, at least 27 Hollywood movies were made in which one or more major characters were portrayed as alcoholics. The films of the period were influenced by efforts to secure humane treatment for the alcoholic. The historical background of these films is examined in terms of: The portrayed social position of film alcoholics; alcoholism portrayed as a generational problem and Alcoholics Anonymous (AA) as a generational solution; incorporation of 12-Step work, AA philosophy, and AA-oriented recovery from alcoholism into films; the divergent models of motivation for drinking and of treatment options; attitudes regarding alcohol and cultural assumptions regarding drunkenness; emphasis on moral, spiritual, or physical deterioration due to alcohol; film resolutions; gender roles; and critical reviews of the films at the time of their release. It is contended that the efflorescence of alcoholism films of that period was in large part a generational phenomenon, reflecting the life experiences of the middle class youth generations of the 1920 and 1930s." (NCADI abstract).

2261. Room, Robin. "Alcoholism and Alcoholics Anonymous in U.S. Films, 1945-1962: The Party Ends for the 'Wet Generations.". in: Journal of Studies on Alcohol; July, 1989; 50(4): pp368-383.
"At least 34 Hollywood films were made between The Lost Weekend(1945) and Days of Wine and Roses(1962) with an alcoholic as a major character: six depicted an Alcoholics Anonymous-like self-help organization." The vast majority had willpower and mutual help as paths to recovery, with professional treatment and AA's spirituality rarely shown. "For women alcoholics [17 of 39 depicted, an overrepresentation by gender of the 5.5 to 1 ratio in America], drinking went with sexuality, but for men it replaced it. 'Creative' occupations were hugely overrepresented, reflecting the 'wet generations' of the time. AA was founded and peopled by members of these same cohorts as a generational solution to their eventual life-problems." Room's study is highly-recommended for anyone interested in alcoholism in the movies and his insights into AA characters in the films are on target.

2262. Rosen, A. "Psychotherapy and Alcoholics Anonymous: Can They Be Coordinated?". Bulletin of the Menninger Clinic; 1981; 45(3): pp229-246.

2263. Rosenman, Stanley, Ph.D. "Pacts, Possessions, and the Alcoholic". The American Imago; Fall 1955; 12(3): pp241-274. The distinctive aspects of alcoholism as compared with other mental illnesses are pointed out. Rosenman views alcoholism psychoanalytically as an underlying fantasy in the individual. A.A. and its spiritual or religious implications are discussed in that framework in a four page section of the article.

2264. Ross, Jack L. "Alcoholics Anonymous: A Neglected Adjunct to Hospital Treatment". Kansas Medical Society Journal; Jan. 1965; 66: pp23-27.

2265. Royce, James E. "Alcohol and Other Drugs in Spiritual Formation". Studies in Formative Spirituality; 1987; 6(2): 211-222.
Fr. Royce writes about the problem of addiction among priests and nuns and how addiction adversely affects religious development. The role of AA in helping to promote spirituality in recovery is emphasized.

2266. Royce, James. "Sin or Solace? Religious Views on Alcohol and Alcoholism". Journal of Drug Issues; 1985; 15(1): 51-62. Fr. Royce includes brief sections on Biblical attitudes toward alcohol use, and the spirituality in AA. He mentions that "Clergymen are learning to look upon Alcoholics Anonymous as complimentary rather than competitive to formal religion, and to use Al-Anon as a spiritual resource in their family counseling.".

2267. Rudy, David R. "Slipping and Sobriety: the Functions of Drinking in Alcoholics Anonymous". QJSA; 1980; 41(7): pp 727-731.
Note: This report describes slipping as a vital mechanism in the maintenance of Alcoholics Anonymous. When a members slips (has a drink of alcohol) group solidarity is enhanced and the boundaries of behavior for all group members are reaffirmed and strengthened.

2268. Rudy, David R./Greil, Arthur L. "Taking the Pledge: The Commitment Process in Alcoholics Anonymous". Sociological Focus; Jan., 1987; 20(1): pp45-59.
The authors develop an investment model and its utility is illustrated through an analysis, based on observational data, of the commitment process in A.A. in a Mideastern city.

2269. Ryan, John. "What to Say to an Alcoholic". NCCA Blue Book; 1974; 26: 31-36.
Ryan explains not only what to say when confronting an alcoholic about their drinking, but also about what not to say. When AA is discussed, he emphasizes that the individual must wipe out the alcoholic's misconceptions of the program.

2270. Sadler, P. O. "The 'Crisis Cult' as a Voluntary Association: An Interactional Approach to Alcoholics Anonymous". Human Organization; 1977; 36: pp207-210.

2271. Sampson, James. "Importance of the Spiritual Condition". NCCA Blue Book; 1984; 36: 7.
Sampson gives a detailed explanation of how members of the clergy can effectively minister to the alcoholic who has just entered treatment. He tells how to do a spiritual evaluation of the alcoholic and how to help the alcoholic grow spiritually.

2272. Sapir, J. V. "The A.A. Story in Connecticut". Connecticut Review of Alcoholism; 1957; 8: p25.

2273. Saunders, Edward J., M.S.W. "Homosexual Recovering Alcoholics". in: Alcohol Health & Research World; Winter, 1983-84: pp18-22.
In his disussion, Saunders recommends "greater availability of gay AA or Al-Anon groups" among his conclusions. Alcoholism treatment professionals should not try "to cure" homosexuals of their homosexuality, he found from his study of 29 cases.

2274. Schaefer, Susan/Evans, Sue. "Women, Sexuality, and the Process of Recovery". Journal of Chemical Dependency Treatment; 1987; 1(1): 91-120.
Schaefer and Evans claim that an integral part of the recovery process for women "is to reclaim the spiritual aspects of themselves." While AA helps, "additional methods are needed due to the highly personal and complex nature of women's spirituality." Spirituality and sexuality are compared.

2275. Schwartzman, J. "Alcoholics Anonymous and the Family: A Systemic Perspective". American Journal of Drug & Alcohol Abuse; 1985; 11(1/2.): pp69-89.
A cybernetic paradigm for understanding addictive drinking by those individuals defined as alcoholics is utilized. Their behavior is anomalous because it is so self-destructive and concurrently often produces a dysphoria that exacerbates the experiential state that is said to be its cause. A cybernetic perspective is illustrated by a description of two social systems: alcoholics and their families, and as members of AA. For some alcoholics, alcoholism can be perceived as the "solution" to the paradoxical psychosocial context within which they find themselves, to which their addictive drinking is an adaptive response, and AA a better "solution." 54 references.

2276. Seiberling, Henrietta/Seiberling, John F. "Origins of Alcoholics Anonymous". Employee Assistance Quarterly; 1985; 1(1): pp33-39.
U.S. Congressman John F. Seiberling provides a May, 1972, transcript of a conversation with his mother, Henrietta Seiberling, recollecting the origins of Alcoholics Anonymous. The first meeting in 1935 of Bill Wilson and Dr. Robert Smith, Co-Founders of AA, is described.

2277. Seiden, Richard. "The Use of Alcoholics Anonymous Members in Research on Alcoholism.". QJSA; Sept. 1960; 21: pp506-509. The author concludes that A.A. members should not be used in research projects on alcoholism because they are not typical or representative of the total alcoholic population. He based his conclusion on differences in psychological factors and other performance data.

2278. Seixas, F. A. "Alcoholism Treatment: A Descriptive Guide". in: Psychiatric Annals; 1982; 12(4): pp375-6, 381-5. Note: NCAI 3183. Included in this history of alcoholism treatment is an examination of the beginning of AA. Because hospitals would not admit alcoholics, some AA members took them home to care for them and this practice, the author points out, eventually grew into acute and intermediate care resources.

2279. Seixas, F. A./Washburn, S./Eisen, S. V. "Alcoholism, Alcoholics Anonymous Attendance, and Outcome in a Prison System". in: American Journal of Drug and Alcohol Abuse; 1988; 14(4): pp515-524; ISSN: 0095-2990. The hypothesis that greater AA attendance would predict followup outcome was not confirmed in this study of 102 subjects measured for alcoholism at a miniumum security prison.

2280. Sell, J. T. "An Experience with Alcoholics Anonymous". Federal Probation; 1946; 10(4): p42.

2281. Selzer, Melvin. "On Involuntary Hospitalization for Alcoholics: Suggestions for an Inpatient Treatment Program.". QJSA; Dec. 1958; 19: pp660-667. The author includes A.A. as part of his proposed treatment program.

2282. Sessions, Percy M. "Ego Religion and Superego Religion in Alcoholics". Quarterly Journal of Studies on Alcohol; 1957; 18(1): 121-125. Superego religion is authoritarian and emphasizes the unworthiness of the individual. Ego religion respects authority but "transfers a substantial measure of responsibility to the individual reason and conscience." It emphasizes personal relationship with God. Alcoholism recovery is discussed both in terms of superego religion and ego religion--the religion of AA. [Editor's note: AA is NOT a religion].

2283. Shanahan, W. J. "Fifty Years of Alcoholics Anonymous: Celebrate the Traditions Too". Employee Assistance Quarterly; 1985-86; 1(2): pp83-99. The 12 Traditions of AA are discussed, along with their history. The relevance of the Traditions for contemporary alcoholism professionals is also covered. 4 ref.

2284. Shanahan, William/Powderly, James J. "Needs -- Reluctance -- Resistance". NCCA Blue Book; 1979; 31: 98-99.
The authors "explore and share thoughts, ideas, etc.," concerning priests in AA. They also "discuss possible incentives or reasons to encourage -- even cajole, greater involvement and participation in AA.".

2285. Sheeren, Mary, M.H.S. "The Relationship between Relapse and Involvement in Alcoholics Anonymous". Journal of Studies on Alcohol; 1988; 49(1): pp104-106.
Fifty-nine AA members responded to a questionnaire assessing the occurrence of relapse and its correlation to their level of involement in AA. Those who did not slip were found to have a high level of involvement in the Fellowship compared to those who slipped. The most significant factor in preventing relapse was a sponsor and reaching out to other AA members for help.

2286. Silkworth, William D., M.D. "A Highly Successful Approach to the Alcoholic Problem". Medical Record; Aug. 6, 1941; 154: pp105-107.
Dr. Silkworth praises the A.A. program. Bill W.'s doctor, he quotes other doctors and professionals who approve of A.A.

2287. Silkworth, William D., M.D. "A New Approach to Psychotherapy in Chronic Alcoholism". The Journal-Lancet; July, 1939; 59(7): pp312-314.
Note: [journal published in Minneapolis].
This is the first article on AA published in a medical journal!

2288. Simon, Howard. "The Jewish Community and the Use of Alcohol". NCCA Blue Book; 1971; 23: 105-109.
Rabbi Simon explains that Jews think alcohol, like all things, should be used in moderation. He emphasizes that Rabbis need to work to dispel the myth that there are no Jewish alcoholics. He also mentions his own work in helping to establish Shalom AA group, a group that is predominately Jewish.

2289. Sisson, Robert W., Ph.D./Mallams, John H., Ph.D. "The Use of Systematic Encouragement and Community Access Procedures to Increase Attendance at Alcoholics Anonymous and Al-Anon Meetings". American Journal of Drug and Alcohol Abuse, N.Y.; 1981; 8: pp371-376.

2290. Skulska, W. "Under the AA Aegis: A New Club and a New Orientation". Problm. Alkzmu, Warsaw; 1979; 26(1): pp17-18.
A new Alcoholics Anonymous-type club called "Syrena" opened in Drewnice, Poland. It cooperated with the local psychiatric hospital. Members were encouraged to share their experiences about alcoholism while drinking yogurt cocktails.

2291. Slagle, A. L./Weibel-Orlando, J. "Indian Shaker Church and Alcoholics Anonymous: Revitalistic Curing Cults". Human Organization; 1986; 45(4): pp310-319.
Note: This was originally published as a 47-page memeographed copy by the Neuropsychiatric Institute, University of California, Los Angeles, California, in 1985.
Chronic misuse of alcohol is a major health problem among American Indians. Growing frustration with the limited success of conventional alcoholism treatment programs to either initiate or maintain sobriety among Indian clients prompted the study of indigenous treatment of alcohol abuse. How the Indian Shaker Church functions as a culture-based alcoholism intervention is discussed. Common socio-structural features of the Indian Shaker Church and AA are considered as well as those culture-specific features which appear to account for the Shakers' particular success in supporting sobriety among American Indians. The authors, at the University of California at Berkeley Native American Studies Program, document their article with 58 references.

2292. Small, J. "AA Volunteers Provide Support to Inpatients". in: Alcohol Health & Research World; 1982; 6(3): pp34-35.
Note: NCAI 956.
The use of volunteers from AA to staff the Cleveland, Ohio, Metropolitan General Hospital's "Friendship Room" and to assist inpatients in the hospital's alcohol rehabilitation center is described.

2293. Small, J. "Holistic Recovery from Alcoholism: Psychosynthesis Parallels the Twelve Steps...and Goes Beyond". in: Focus on Alcohol and Drug Issues; 1983; 6(1): pp12-13.
Note: NCAI 5464.
Small compares the four stages of holistic psychosynthesis [acceptance, attunement, alignment, and application] to the Twelve Steps of A.A. but places more emphasis on understanding who the "self" is.

2294. Small, J./Johnson, M. "Perspectives: An AH&RW Interview feature". in: Alcohol Health & Research World; 1982; 6(4): pp24-25.
Note: NCAI 2378.
A staff member of the GSO of AA is one of three interviewed on the interface between treatment programs and 12 Steps groups, including AA.

2295. Smith, D. I. "Evaluation of a Residential AA Program". International Journal of Addiction; 1986; 21: pp33-49.

2296. Smith, Percy L., M.D. "Alcoholics Anonymous". Psychiatric Quarterly; 1941; 15: pp 554-562.
Smith describes the personality traits of alcoholics and the A. A. approach to their recovery. He emphasizes the role that the newcomer must take to facilitate his own sobriety. He also discusses a Rockland State Hospital program for alcoholics wherein interested patients attend weekly A.A. meetings in the community and conduct weekly meetings at the hospital. Results indicate that readjustment to community life upon release from the hospital was good for program participants.

2297. Smith, Russell. "Alcohol and Spiritual Collapse". NCCA Blue Book; 1976; 28: 74-90.
Smith explains how AA's twelve steps help the alcoholic move closer to God.

2298. Smith, Russell F. "Meeting the Special Challenges of Alcoholism in Clergy and Religious". NCCA Blue Book; 1974; 26: 21-30.
Smith describes the specialized problems of alcoholic clergy, the treatment team concept of treatment, and the AA program as treatment aftercare.

2299. Sproxton, Judith. "Alcoholics Anonymous". The Tablet; Aug. 2, 1980; 2?: pp746-747.
Sproxton explains what happens after the alcoholic calls A.A. A general description of why A.A. works is given.

2300. Sr. Florence. "Recovery". NCCA Blue Book; 1974; 26: 144-152.
Sr. Florence, an alcoholic nun who recovered in AA, argues that "staying sober has to be learned." AA is described as a tremendous way to facilitate this process.

2301. Starr, B. L. "Let's Be Thankful for Alcoholics Anonymous". Labor-Management Alcoholism Journal; 1982; 12: pp96-97.

2302. Staver, S. "Impaired MD's Ragged Road to Recovery". in: American Medical News; Feb. 26, 1982: pp7 & 18.
Note: NCAI 3869.
An alcoholic physician describes how he became an alcoholic and his recovery problems. AA is discussed briefly.

2303. Steinberg, J. "The Role of AA in Treatment and Recovery of Impaired Professionals". Maryland Medical Journal; 1987; 36: pp241-244.

2304. Steiner, Lee R. "Alcoholics Anonymous: Book Review". The News-Letter of The American Assn. of Psychiatric Social Workers; 1940; (Autumn).

2305. Stephens, T.A./Varney, E.D./Winegar, N. "Alcoholics Anonymous and the Alcoholic Defense Structure". Social Casework: The Journal of Contemporary Social Work; 1987; 68(4): pp223-228.
Alcoholics Anonymous is the oldest, largest, and perhaps most successful self-help group. However, many social work practitioneers do not effectively utilize AA because they do not understand how it relates with therapeutic interventions. The ways in which AA compliments therapy are discussed. (NCADI abstract).

2306. Stewart, David A. "The Dynamics of Fellowship as Illustrated in Alcoholics Anonymous.". QJSA; June 1955; 16: pp251-262.
The author believes the dynamics of the group can best be studied through A.A. because it lacks the dominance of a leader. A.A.'s higher power is also discussed at length.

2307. Sullivan, Paul V. "The Spiritual Effects of Alcoholism". NCCA Blue Book; 1973; 25: 32-36.
Sullivan argues that "the person involved in the throes of alcoholism is in every sense alone. He isolates himself from God even though he may still believe in God." He focuses on the healing power of AA.

2308. Sutro, L. D. "Alcoholics Anonymous in a Mexican peasant-Indian Village". in: Human Organization; 1989; 48(2): pp180-186.
Note: [an earlier verion of this paper was presented at the 8th annual Texas Tech Alcoholism Confrc., El Paso, TX, 1984]. This study of an AA Group in Santa Ana, Mexico, found no crosscultural deterents to the validity of AA measured against the writings of George Vaillant [the attributes of AA].

2309. Tate, J. Bennett, M.Div. "Aftercare: Protecting Your Investment". in: EAP Digest; Jan.-Feb., 1984: pp24-26.
Tate, Employee Health Assistance Mgr. with Kaiser Aluminum & Chemical Corp., Oakland, CA, states "the best aftercare treatment plan...is involvement in Alcoholics Anonymous." The role of the industrial counselor in this work is discussed.

2310. "Ten Tips from Alcoholics Anonymous for Family Doctors". in: Medical Times, Manhasset, NY; June 1975; 103(6): pp74-76.
Written by a "writer-member of AA," this article suggests doctors begin with "if you think your patient is an alcoholic, tell him." Physicians also are advised to go to an AA meeting themselves, get to know some AA members for referrals, and 7 other helpful suggestions.

2311. "This Is AA. Medicine Looks at Alcoholics Anonymous.". Challenge; July-Sept., 1961; 3(3): pp21-3, 32.
Note: Special Issue devoted to "The Female Alcoholic.".
This article from the quarterly published by the Alabama Commission on Alcoholism was prepared by the General Service Office of A.A., New York. It recalls the contributions of Drs. Silkworth, Tiebout, and others in the early development of A.A. as well as its Co-Founder, Dr. Robert H. Smith, of Akron, Ohio.

2312. Thompson, Bill. "Understanding Treatment of Alcoholism". Guest House; 1985; 16(2): 4-5.
Thompson explains the disease process of alcoholism and how an alcoholic moves to sobriety. He then describes the need for AA as part of recovery and the role Guest House plays in the recovery of priests and brothers.

2313. Thompson, Charles E., Ph.D./Kolb, William P., M.D. "Group Psychotherapy in Assocation with Alcoholics Anonymous". American Journal of Psychiatry; July, 1953; 110(1).
Note: Presented before the Mid-Continent Psychiatric Association, Kansas City, 1952, and the American Psychological Assocation, Washington, D.C., 1952.
Thompson and Kolb report on the activities of an A.A. chapter established in the Veterans Administration Hospital in Arkansas. The group is patient-run and all meetings are attended by a therapist who introduces elements of group psychotherapy. Excerpts of the minutes taken by patient-secretaries at meetings during the course of the year are provided.

2314. Thompson, David. "Anonymity and Alcoholics Anonymous". Journal of the American Medical Assn.; 1983; 249: p3019.

2315. Thompson, Howard W. "Alcoholism -- After Treatment Then What?". Confidential Information Bulletin; 1986; 1(4): 1-4.
Thompson describes the after care program at Guest House. The role of AA is stressed.

2316. Thompson, Hugh S. "An Experience of a Non-alcoholic in Alcoholics Anonymous Leadership.". QJSA; June 1952; 13: pp271-295.
The author helped to establish and lead an A.A. group, even though he was not an alcoholic. He believes sponsorship in A.A. demands certain leadership qualities and not just an alcoholic history.

2317. Thoreson, R. W./Nathan, P. E./Skorina, J. K./Kilburg, R. R. "Alcoholic Psychologist: Issues, Problems, and Implications for the Profession". in: Professional Psychology: Research & Practice; 1983; 14(5): pp670-684.
Note: NCAI 12177.
Alcoholism constitutes a special dilemna for psychologists who hold a strong belief in the powers of the mind and its capacity to comprehend and alter behavior. Currents efforts, modeled after the principles of A.A. in combination with professional treatment, are examined.

2318. Thoreson, R. W. "Professional-executive, Work Obsession and Implications for Employee Assistance Programs": Univ. of Missouri-Columbia EAP; August, 1981; 10pp.
Note: NCAI 13313.
Observations of professional, executive patients at an alcohol treatment facility, whose program draws heavily upon the basic tenets of A.A., as well as from the best current medical, neuropsychological, and family approaches, are described. Implications for higher education EAP's are discussed.

2319. Thorner, Isidor. "Ascetic Protestantism and Alcoholism". Psychiatry; 1953; 16(2): 167-176.
Thorner examines the evidence which suggests that there is a relationship between alcoholism and religious denominations before considering tendencies within those groups which might cause believers to respond to strain by overusing alcohol. Judaism, as well as AA, is also discussed.

2320. Thune, Carl E. "Alcoholism, and the Archetypical Past: A Phenomenological Perspective on Alcoholics Anonymous". QJSA; 1977; 38: pp75-88.
"The stereotype A.A. member's life story becomes a model of his past and a model for reanalysis and re-creation of his life.".

2321. Thurstin, A. H./Alfano, A. M./Nerviano, V. J. "Efficacy of AA Attendance for Aftercare of Inpatient Alcoholics: Some Follow-Up Data". in: Int'l Journal of the Addictions; 1987; 22(11): pp1083-1090; ISSN: 0020-773X.
This study of 145 inpatient alcoholics at 6, 12, and 18 months at the Tuscaloosa, Alabama Veterans Adm. Medical Center revealed higher percentages of abstinence for AA attenders but only at 18 months. Those who attended AA for the entire 18 months achieved a 50% abstinence rate.

2322. Thurstin, A. H./Alfano, A. M./Sherer, M. "Pretreatment MMPI Profiles of A.A. Members and Nonmembers". Journal of Studies on Alcohol; 1986; 47: pp468-471.

2323. Tiebout, Harry M., M.D. "Alcoholics Anonymous: An Experiment of Nature". QJSA; March 1961; 22: pp52-68.
An early friend of A.A., Dr. Tiebout discusses four needs essential to the A.A. program of recovery: hitting bottom, surrender, humility, and deflation of the ego. He was the first psychiatrist to boost A.A. and use A.A. principles in his own practice.

2324. Tiebout, Harry M., M.D. "Therapeutic Mechanisms of Alcoholics Anonymous.". American Journal of Psychiatry; Jan. 1944; 100: pp468-473.
Dr. Tiebout, a psychiatrist and early ally of A.A., discusses Bill W.'s spiritual awakening. He stresses the religious or spiritual essence of A.A. as the reason why vast personality changes in depth can take place and cites one of his female patients who underwent that change in A.A.

2325. Tournier, Robert E. "Alcoholics Anonymous as Treatment and Ideology". Journal of Studies on Alcohol; 1979; 40(3): pp230-239.
"Summary: proposed that AA's continued domination of the alcoholism treatment field has fettered innovation, precluded early intervention and limited treatment strategies." Sociologist Tournier concludes "I am not suggesting that we abandon A.A. or in any way reduce its role in the treatment and aggressive aftercare of addictive alcoholism vital to long-term recovery. I am only proposing we become aware of the implications of generalizing the A.A. philosophy to all intervention and that we evaluate on their own merits alternative and innovative strategies for dealing with the extremely complex range of problems too often lumped under the rubric of `alcoholism.".

2326. Trice, Harrison M., Ph.D. "The Affiliation Motive and Readiness To Join Alcoholics Anonymous". QJSA; June,1959; 20: pp313-320.
This "present investigation attempts to explore further the extent to which those alcoholics who easily accept A.A. have a stronger emotional need to establish and maintain positive, affective relationships than alcoholics who find it difficult to affiliate." The chief difference between two groups of 37 AA affiliates and 37 non-affiliates was that the affiliates had higher-status job backgrounds.

2327. Trice, Harrison M. "Alcoholics Anonymous". Annals of the American Academy of Political and Social Sciences; Jan. 1958; 315: pp108-116.

2328. Trice, Harrison M./Sonnenstuhl, W. J. "Contributions of AA to Employee Assistance Programs". Employee Assistance Quarterly; 1985; 1(1): pp7-33.

2329. Trice, Harrison M./Roman, Paul Michael. "Delabeling, Relabeling and Alcoholics Anonymous". Social Problems; Spring 1970; 17(4): pp538-546.
Trice and Roman discuss the success of A.A. in delabeling socially stigmatized alcoholics and redefining them with labels that are socially acceptable. They discuss the elements of alcoholism that facilitate acceptance of alcoholics when their deviant behavior has ceased and contrast this with the difficulty of removing the social stigma attached to former narcotic addicts and mental patients.

2330. Trice, Harrison M. "The `Outsider's' Role in Field Study.". Sociology & Social Research; Oct. 1956; 41: pp27-32.
The role of the researcher or the outsider is discussed along with differences between alcoholics who join A.A. and those who are unable to do so.

2331. Trice, Harrison M./Wahl, J. Richard, Ph.D. "A Rank Order Analysis of the Symptoms of Alcoholism". QJSA; 1958; 19: pp636-648.
A Wisconsin study of 252 alcoholic males compared their ranking of 13 symptoms of alcoholism in order of occurrence to the ranking obtained in an earlier Grapevine study. The researchers indicate that the ranking of symptoms in the earlier study masked significant clustering of individual symptoms. Their analysis concludes that rather than a steady progression from symptom to symptom, alcoholism is a process of transition from one cluster of symptoms that occur together to another cluster. The lists of symptoms and data gathered from both studies is provided.

2332. Trice, Harrison M. "Social Factors in Association with A.A.". Journal of Criminal Law, Criminology & Police Science; Dec. 1957; 48: pp378-386.
The author provides basic principles governing membership in groups, especially in A.A.

2333. Trice, Harrison M./Roman, Paul Michael. "Sociopsychological Predictors of Affiliation with Alcoholics Anonymous. A Longitudinal Study of `Treatment Success.". Social Psychiatry; Jan. 1970; 5(1): pp51-59.
This study of almost 400 alcoholics reports that psysical and/or psychological factors are more important than social factors as predictors of probable membership in A.A.

2334. Trice, Harrison M., Ph.D. "A Study of the Process of Affiliation with Alcoholics Anonymous.". QJSA; March 1957; 18: pp39-54.
The author studied extensively the process of joining A.A. and suggests that group therapy before A.A. could remove some of the prejudices and misunderstandings about A.A. that cut off some from joining.

2335. Trudeau, David L., M.D. "Substance Abuse: How Physicians Recover". in: Journal of the Kansas Medical Society; 1981; 82(11): pp495-6, 527 30.
Trudeau discuss briefly Dr. Bob, the Co-Founder of AA, Harry M. Tiebout, psychiatrist and early AA friend, and the AA Fellowship. Physicians in Kansas participate in AA and NA, he states, with 120 weekly AA meetings in Wichita alone. Basic information about International Doctors in AA is given.

2336. Turner, Sandra. "Community Residential Treatment of Skid Row Alcoholics". in: Health & Social Work; Nov., 1979; 4(4): pp165-180; ISSN: 0360-7283/79/0404-0163.
Turner, MSW, Outreach Chief, St. Vincent's Hospital, New York, postulated that homeless "skid row" alcoholics are often too disintegrated to go to AA or any other treatment program on their own. The author describes the Keller Program in the Keller Hotel on Barrow St. in Greenwich Village, New York City, where an AA meeting was begun in December, 1975, in the hotel lobby aimed at the thousands of homeless and "skid row" alcoholics living in the area. Over the next eight months, the meeting grew to thirty members

most of whom rented a single room at the hotel. The Keller outreach program of St. Vincent's Hospital there found homeless alcoholics were able to join the AA group and stay sober.

2337. Upton, Charles H. "Alcoholics Anonymous". Federal Probation; 1944; 8(3): p29.
Upton, Chief U. S. Probation Officer, San Francisco, recommends A.A. to correctional officers and social workers for the rehabilitation of prisoners. Case study, the story of Bill W., the founding of A.A., and the principles and growth of AA are presented.

2338. Vaillant, G. E./Clark, W./Cyrus, C./Milofsky, E.S./ Kopp, J./Wulsin, V. W./Mosielnicki, N. P. "Prospective Study of Alcoholism Treatment: Eight-year Follow-up". in: American Journal of Medicine; 1983; 75(3): pp455-463.
Note: NACI 14368.
One hundred patients admitted for alcohol withdrawal were followed for eight years. At the end, 25% had been abstinent for 3 years or more and 29% had died. Attendance at Alcoholics Anonymous meetings made a significant contribution to sustained abstinence.

2339. Valle, Stephen K., Sc.D. "A Model for Alcoholism Treatment in General Hospitals". in: Maryland State Medical Journal; March 1980: pp77-79.
Alcoholics Anonymous meetings are one component in this model. Valle says attendance "should be encouraged.".

2340. Van Suetendael, Peter. "The Alcoholic Patient - His Needs as Met by Alcoholics Anonymous and the Caseworker.". Military Medicine; Dec. 1959; 74: pp851-855.
The author compares the concepts and language of A.A. and the caseworker.

2341. "Veteran Counselor Tells How Guest House Works". Guest House; 1981; 12(1): 2,4.
The focus of this article is how Guest House is a bridge between a life of alcoholism and regular attendance at AA.

2342. "Veterans Administration (VA) Told...". Alcoholism Report; 1984; 12(24): 4-5.
The article is about the Veterans Administration's decision not to require attendance at AA for individuals in treatment at VA facilities because of the "religious" nature of AA.

2343. Voegtlin, Walter L./Lemere, Frederick. "The Treatment of Alcohol Addiction: A Review of the Literature". Quarterly Journal of Studies on Alcohol; 1942; 2: 717-803.
The authors conclude a section on religious methods of therapy by saying that "Religious appeal is apparently successful in from 30-70 per cent of cases so treated. This approach is best exemplified by 'Alcoholics Anonymous'."
[Editor's note: AA is not a religion].

2344. Voord, G.A.V. "Michigan Doctors Recovering in Alcoholics Anonymous". Michigan Medicine; 1987; 86(8): p531.
On October 31, 1987, Michigan Doctors in Alcoholics Anonymous celebrated 20 years of mutual sobriety and affiliation with the International Doctors in A.A. The history of the group is briefly described.

2345. W. W. [Wilson, Bill]. "Alcoholics Anonymous in a Postwar Emergency". QJSA; Sept. 1945; 4: pp239-242.
Note: The article was written by "W. W.".
The co-founder of A.A. reviews the situation following World War II and potential for more drinking in the U.S. He concludes that A.A. is capable of rapid growth and handling all suffering alcoholics who accept its help.

2346. "The Walls Came Tumbling Down". A New Way of Life. Alcoholics Anonymous in Mississippi Correctional Facilities.; Summer, 1986: p15.
A one column article details the first A.A. meeting in a Canadian prison on July 8, 1950, at the British Columbia penitentiary. The rest of the 21 page journal is devoted to letters from A.A. members and reprints of A.A. approved literature.

2347. Walther, Lillian/Sears, Mary/Curran, Jean. "The Woman Alcoholic". NCCA Blue Book; 1970; 22: 79-92.
This panel was designed to help the conference participants to better understand AA and alcoholism in women.

2348. Warren C. "Thirty-One Years in Cleveland AA". NCCA Blue Book; 1970; 22: 132-144.
Warren tells of his addiction to alcohol and recovery through AA.

2349. Warsh, Cheryl Drasnick. "Book review: Not-God: A History of Alcoholics Anonymous by Ernest Kurtz". Social History of Alcohol Review; Fall 1989; (20): pp19-20.
Warsh calls Kurtz's book the "best history of AA and [his] analysis of the organization's philosophy remains unmatched.".

2350. a West Virginia lawyer. "One Man's Story". West Virginia State Bar Journal; Winter-Spring, 1983; 3(1): pp 11, 41.
A West Virginia lawyer tells his story of alcoholism and recovery in A.A. in the article, published in Charleston, West Va.

2351. "What AA Meetings Taught a Non-AA Counselor". Alcohol Health & Resource World; 1979; 3(3): pp15-17.
The personal insights and professional advantages gained by an alcoholism educator in attending A.A. meetings are described.

2352. "What is Alcoholics Anonymous?". Philadelphia Medicine; Feb. 5, 1942.

2353. Whitefield, C. L. "Outpatient Management of the Alcoholic Patient". in: Psychiatric Annals; 1982; 12(4): pp447-451, 455-6, 458.
Note: NCAI 3191.
The author contends alcoholism is a primary dysfunction and should not be treated as a symptom of an underlying psychotic disorder. AA is one of seven alternative provisions outlined in treatment.

2354. Whitley, Oliver R. "Life with Alcoholics Anonymous: The Methodist Class Meeting as a Paradigm". Journal of Studies on Alcohol; 1977; 38: pp831-848.
"A.A. meetings are found to be similar in structure and methods to Methodist class meetings.".

2355. Wilding, Donald J. "Alcoholics Anonymous in Melbourne, Australia. Observations of a welfare worker.". QJSA; 1949; 9: pp609-613.
A social worker describes the A.A. techniques adopted by a welfare organization in Australia to promote the rehabilitation of alcoholic welfare recipients.

2356. Wilkey, W. W. "Influence of Alcoholics Anonymous on Alcoholism Treatment". Employee Assistance Quarterly; 1986; 1(4): pp1-17.
Note: Presented at the Commemoration of the Golden Anniversary of Alcoholics Anonymous, Akron, Ohio, June 13, 1985.
The relationship of AA to modern alcoholism treatment is the theme of this article/address. In the early years of AA, hospitalization was an absolute requirement for attending an AA meeting, the author states. Basic changes began about 1955 with some acceptance of AA by the medical community, many states developed alcoholism programs, alcoholism was recognized as a disease, and patients with alcoholism could be hospitalized. Rest farms and drying-out places run by AA generally were not successful, but treatment centers influenced by AA began to develop and were the principal places of recovery in the U.S. for many years. Most of today's treatment programs are a blend of the mental health approach, the psychiatric approach and the disease concept approach. The number of treatment centers today has increased because of favorable legislative action, expansion of insurance coverage, and a change in American attitudes toward alcoholism. The author outlines some of the future trends he sees in the treatment field. It is noted that the percentage of people who come to AA as a result of counseling or rehabilitation increased significantly between 1977 and 1983 from 19 to 31 per cent. The need for cooperation between AA and treatment facilities is suggested and the author concludes that treatment professionals have the responsibility of assuring an appropriate blend of AA and treatment toward the common goal of helping the alcoholic to stop drinking.

2357. Williams, J. M./Stout, J. K./Erickson, L. "Comparison of the Importance of Alcoholics Anonymous and Outpatient Counseling to Maintenance of Sobriety among Alcohol Abusers". Psychological Reports; 1986; 58: pp803-806.

2358. [Wilson, Bill]. "Alcoholics Anonymous". New York State Journal of Medicine; July 1950: pp1708-1710.
Note: The article was written by "W. G. W.".
Co-founder Bill W. discusses the Twelve Steps, "the Big Book," and the history and growth of A.A. Dr. Harry Tiebout and Marvin A. Block also participated in this panel discussion.

2359. [Wilson, Bill]. "The Society of Alcoholics Anonymous". American Journal of Psychiatry; Nov. 1949; 56: pp370-375.
Note: The article was written by "William W.".
Bill gives a brief history of A.A. and his own story. The Oxford Group and the role of psychiatrists in helping recovering alcoholics are discussed.

2360. Wilson, Bill/Jung, C. G. "Spiritus contra Spiritum". in: Paraqbola. New York: Society for the Study of Myth and Tradition, Inc.; May, 1987; 12(2): pp68-71; 128pp.
This famous exchange of letters between Bill Wilson and Carl Jung was first published in the A.A. Grapevine, Jan. 1963, 19 (8), pp2-7 (see 1012). This issue of Parabola was devoted to addiction.

2361. Wilson, William G.*. "Basic Concepts of Alcoholics Anonymous". N.Y. State Journal of Medicine; Aug. 15, 1944; 44(16): p1805-1810.
"* One of the originators of Alcoholics Anonymous." [The Twelve Traditions were not yet written and adopted by A.A.].

2362. "Women, blacks, and homosexuals charge AA with bias". The Journal; Sept. 1, 1985; 15(9): 9.
Note: Published by Addiction Research Foundation, Toronto, Canada.
At a seminar on minorities at the 50th anniversary AA convention in Toronto, Canada, a black sociologist charged AA "should stop living in a color-blind world." A black homosexual agreed: "We have a meeting here for homosexuals and for women, but we have no meeting for blacks." John L. from Georgia, however, cited the historical developments which resulted in AA's Third Tradition: "the only requirement for membership is a desire to stop drinking.".

2363. Woolverton, John F. "Evangelical Protestantism and Alcoholism 1933-1962: Episcopalian Samuel Shoemaker, The Oxford Group and Alcoholics Anonymous". in: Historical Magazine; circa 1982: pp53-65.
This is an excellent summary of Rev. Samuel Shoemaker's important role in the coming together of low church, Episcopalian evangelicalism, the Oxford Group of Frank N. D. Buchman, and Alcoholics Anonymous. Woolverton traces their mutual roots to Protestant evangelicalism and sidesteps several religious and political interpretations of them as dangerous.

2364. Wrich, J. T. "AA and the EAP Movement". Employee Assistance Quarterly; 1986; 1(3): pp83-89.

2365. X [pseudonym]. "Alcoholics Anonymous". Kansas Medical Society Journal; 1954; 55: p451.

2366. Yasko, R. G. "Alcoholics Anonymous: The Utilization of Social Experience in the Classroom". in: Health Education; 1988; 19(1): pp48-49; ISSN: 0097-0050.
This article urges educators to have students attend open AA meetings to provide them with an preventative awareness of what becoming an alcoholic is like.

2367. Young, Ray. "A Visit with Lois W.". in: The Parkside Magazine; Winter 1989 & Winter/Spring 1990; II(1 & 2): 27.
This is a two part interview with Lois, widow of A.A. Co-Founder Bill Wilson.

2368. Zimberg, Sheldon. "Sociopsychiatric Perspectives on Jewish Alcohol Abuse: Implications for the Prevention of Alcoholism". American Journal of Drug and Alcohol Abuse; 1977; 4: 571-579.
Zimberg argues that the rate of alcoholism in the Jewish community increases as Jews lose their Jewish identity. Because of the stigma attached to Jewish alcoholics, treatment is difficult. However, he argues that opening the doors of synagogues to AA meetings might lessen the stigma.

2369. Zimmerman, Robert. "Some Countries Are Slow To Embrace AA". The U.S. Journal of Drug and Alcohol Dependence; July, 1988; 12(7): p15.
A.A.'s growth problems in West Germany, Sweden, and Israel are discussed in this account of the 14th annual Alcohol Epidemiology Symposium held at the University of California in Berkeley.

2370. Zinberg, Norman E., M.D. "Alcoholics Anonymous and the Treatment and Prevention of Alcoholism". Alcoholism: Clinical and Experimental Research; 1977; 1(1): pp91-102.
This Harvard psychiatrist believes AA "principles are aim with remarkable subtlety at the treatment of the hard-core alcoholic [but] may well be equivocal or antagonistic to avenues of prevention." Zinberg states "many psychiatrists and other professionals...by suggesting an interest in the 'motives' for drinking give leave for the drinking to continue." This is an excellent article, displaying in-depth understanding and explanation of AA principles as well as cautionary professional insights into what AA cannot do: prevent alcoholism, etc. "This failure of organized medicine and psychiatry to deal with alcoholism, plus the relative success of A.A.," should not lead to a "confrontation" between the two, he cautions.

2371. Zon, Kate. "Roseburg has a Gay A.A. Group". RFD; 1983; 35: p47.
The author writes about the gay A.A. meeting in Roseburg, how it developed, declined, and experienced a rebirth.

2372. Zuska, J. J. "AA 12th-Steps the Armed Services". Alcoholism/The National Magazine; 1985; 5(4): pp22-23.

Chapter IX = Scholarly Dissertations

2373. Albers, Robert Herbert. The Theological and Psychological Dynamics of Transformation in the Recovery From the Disease of Alcoholism: School of Theology at Claremont; 1982; 452pp. UMI Order AAD82-21501.
This Ph.D. dissertation concluded in part that the Recovery approach of Alcoholics Anonymous provides a solid psycho-social-theological foundation and framework for the pastor to work with the family system. Material for the study was drawn from the literature of AA and Al-Anon, the Lutheran Church, and two units of clinical pastoral education. (for more information, See Theology, Page 1198 in Vol. 43/03-A of Dissertation Abstracts Int'l.).

2374. Alibrandi, Lucinda Ann. The Recovery Process in Alcoholics Anonymous: The Sponsor as Folk Therapist.: Univ. of California, Irvine.; 1977.
Note: Ph.D. dissertation, 95pp.
(See Psychology, Clinical, Page 4436 in Vol. 38/09-B of Dissertation Abstracts Int'l.)(UMI Order AAD78-02422).

2375. Anderson, Jack Glenn. Communication Skills Training with Alcoholics for Increased Performance of Recovery Steps in Alcoholics Anonymous.: Fuller Theological Seminary, School of Psychology; 1987; 152pp.
Note: Unpublished Ph.D. dissertation.
This study's objectives were (1) to train inpatient alcoholics in communication skills using a visual feedback device and (2) to determine if this training would improve their ability to understand Steps 4 and 5 (the "moral inventory") of the 12 Steps of A.A. Forty-one male patients were assigned to one of three treatment groups: communication skills training, discussion of A.A. stpes, and no treatment control. Eight hours of training focused on the issues of self-disclosure, character traits in relationship to drinking, and taking responsibility for personal actions. Structure video-taped interviews were rated and indicated that the trained subjects improved significantly on 3 of 6 dimensions of communication. This skills training may increase the likelihood of alcoholics' affiliation with A.A. (See Psychology, Clinical Page 3671 in Vol. 48/12-B of Dissertation Abstracts Int'l.) (UMI No. 88-01944).

2376. Archibald, Norman Gregory. College Administrator and Student Perceptions Relative to Probable Effectiveness of Alcohol Education Programs (Drinking).: Texas Tech Univ.; 1985; 139pp. UMI Order AAD85-28572.
Note: Ed.D. dissertation.
Both college presidents and their student affairs officers and students from private,, church-related colleges and universities in Texas perceived student chapters of Alcoholics Anonymous groups as the most effective of seven college alcohol education programs in this study. (for more information, See Education, Administration, Page 2862 in Vol. 46/10-A of Dissertation Abstracts Int'l.).

2377. Bennett, E. G. Stress, Social Integration, and Self-Concept: A Study of Young Alcoholics in Recovery: Univ. of Texas, Austin; 1983. Dissertation Abstracts Int'l 44 (04): 1059-B-1060-B.
Among other findings, this study of 45 young alcoholics, 18 to 30 years old, found AA was the most common source of social support.

2378. Berg, Steven Lorain. AA, Spiritual Issues, and the Treatment of Lesbian and Gay Alcoholics: Michigan State Univ.; 1989; 220pp. Order AAD89-23831. [see Vol. 50/07-A of Dissertation Abstracts Int'l, p2121].
Note: Ph.D. dissertation.
"Although AA claims it is spiritual and not-religious, this distinction is blurred because it is a spiritual program based on religious tenets. Lesbians and gay men victimized by church sanctioned hate and persecution are likely to reject the AA program because of its religious elements." This study then identifies the religious elements and reviews the lesbian/gay press for four objections to the Christian tradition. It then traces the American trends toward perfectionism and individualism from the 18th century to the publication of Alcoholics Anonymous in 1939. Berg says AA works for Christians, non-Christians and those with no formal tradition. He suggests seven strategies to help lesbians and gay men to integrate AA into their lives.

2379. Bloomfield, Kim. Beyond Sobriety: The Cultural Significance of Alcoholics Anonymous As A Social Movement. Berkeley, CA: Alcohol Research Group; 1988; 40pp.
Note: Unpublished Xerox copy.
This university research paper by a student discusses AA as a social movement and compares it with the Green movement. It concludes A.A. is not one of the New Social Movements and has no political, economic, or social agenda to push.

2380. Bloomfield, Kim Audrey. Community in Recovery: A Study of Social Support, Spirituality, and Voluntarism among Gay and Lesbian Members of Alcoholics Anonymous: Univ. of California at Berkeley; 1990; 289pp. Order AAD91-03619. [see Vol. 51/09-B of Dissertation Abstracts Int'l, p4298].
Note: Dr.P.H. dissertation.
At the annual gay and lesbian AA conference, 645 participants were surveyed for this doctoral study. It found social support and social network size increased significantly during the first year of AA membership. Four areas of spirituality were used: New Age, Church, anti-religious, and the AA Program. Church and program spiritualities increased while New Age declined with length of AA membership. Those most involved in voluntarism tended to have lower rates of AA involvement.

2381. Blum, Steven B. Changes in Alcoholics' Self-Esteem in Relationship to Perceptions of Drinking and Sober Roles During Treatment.: Univ. of Nebraska at Lincoln; 1980; 108pp. UMI Order AAD81-09978.
Note: Ph.D. dissertation.
The Alcoholics Anonymous philosophy of the necessity of "hitting bottom" before recovery can be initiated is consistent with one of the findings in this research. (for more information, See Psychology, Clinical, Page 4252 in Vol. 41/11-B of Dissertation Abstracts Int'l.).

2382. Boggs, J. P. Locus of Control, Self-Concept, and Demographic Variables as Factors in the Attrition of Alcoholics from AA-Oriented Treatment Programs: Mississippi State Univ.; 1983; 90pp.
Note: Ph.D. dissertation.
(UMI No. AAD84-13930).

2383. Bohince, E./Orensteen A. An Evaluation of the Services and Program of the Minneapolis Chapter of Alcoholics Anonymous.: Univ. of Minnesota; 1950; 80pp.
Note: Unpublished Master's thesis.

2384. Boscarino, Joseph. Alcohol Career Patterns in Alcoholics Anonymous: A Systemic Approach to Alcoholic Defined Behavior.: New York Univ.; 1977.
Note: Ph.D. dissertation, 283pp.
(See Sociology, Public and Social Welfare, Page 6353 in Vol. 38/10-A of Dissertation Abstracts Int'l.)(UMI Order AAD78-03065).

2385. Bridgman, Laird Patrick. Locus-of-Control, Drinking-Related Locus-of-Control, Exposure to Alcoholics Anonymous, Length of Sobriety, and Severity of Alcoholism: A Study of Relationships (Sobriety, California): Rosemead School of Psychology, Biola Univ.; 1990; 75pp. Order AAD91-12954. [see Vol. 52/01-B of Dissertation Abstracts Int'l, p557].
Note: Psy.D. dissertation.
Eighty male and female subjects from various inpatient and outpatient sources, and A.A. meetings in the Los Angeles area participated in this study. The findings are discussed in the light of previous research and from the perspective of the A.A. program.

2386. Brook, Rupert Ramsay. Personality Correlates Associated with Differential Success of Affiliation with Alcoholics Anonymous: Univ. of Colorado at Boulder; 1962.
Note: Ph.D. dissertation, 124pp.
(See Psychology, Clinical, Page 1778 in Vol. 23/05 of Dissertation Abstracts Int'l.)(UMI OrderAAD62-06263).

2387. Browne, Marilyn Anne. The Relationship of Anxiety to Social Drinkers and Members of Alcoholics Anonymous.: U.S. Int'l Univ.; 1976.
Note: Ph.D. dissertation, 107pp.
(See Psychology, Physiological, Page 5851 in Vol. 36/11-B of Dissertation Abstracts Int'l.)(UMI No.AAD76-10584.).

2388. Brush, Stuart Camp. Ministering to the Afflicted through Combining the Spiritual Resources of the Church and Alcoholics Anonymous: The Hartford Seminary; 1988; 171pp. Order AAD89-13091. [see Vol. 50/06-A of Dissertation Abstracts Int'l, p1693].
Note: D.Min. dissertation.
As a clergy alcoholic, the author seeks to open the doors of understanding to the 900 fellowship meetings in "our Church halls, rooms and basements" in Connecticut. He suggests "we as Churches and A.A. as a 'rehabilitating agency' [quotes supplied: AA would reject such a definition] can become more effective through combining their spiritual resources.".

2389. Bucka, John R. Partners in Ministry: How the Church and A.A. Meet the Needs of Recovering Alcoholics (Alcoholics Anonymous): Princeton Theological Seminary; 1991; 173pp. Order AAD91-33837. [see Vol. 52/06-A of Dissertation Abstracts Int'l, p2177].
Note: D.Min. dissertation.
How can the church minister more effectively to its recovering alcoholic members in conjunction with Alcoholics Anonymous? A task force of nine AA members, four of whom were also church members, produced a changed perspective about the value of Law-Gospel theology and programmatic efforts to minister to shame based people. Cooperation between the church and AA, the value of the A.A. community, the value of the sacraments, and church education about AA were supported.

2390. Burke, Kathleen. When Words Aren't Enough ... A Study of the Use of Art Therapy in Treatment of Chemically Dependent Adolescents With Special Focus upon the Spiritual Dimension (Addiction, Alcoholism, Drug Abuse, Healing & Art, Intervention).: Union for Experimenting Colleges/U. Without Walls & Union Grad Sch.; 1985; 360pp. UMI Order AAD05-23669.
Note: Ph.D. dissertation.
Burke's study supports the use of art therapy with alcoholic adolescents as part of the creative process of recovery. The 12 Steps of AA and its "Higher Power" are part of the teenagers' spiritual process. One hundred original illustrations by the teens are a significant nonverbal part of the study. Art therapy can harmonize with the principles of AA, she concludes. (for more information, See Education, Art, Page 2166 in Vol 46/08-A of Dissertation Abstracts Int'l.).

2391. Burkette, Tyrone L. Spiritual Renewal in the Midst of Crisis: An Alcoholics Anonymous Twelve Steps Approach.: United Theological Seminary of the Twin Cities; 1983.
Note: Unpublished D. Min. dissertation.

2392. Burrows, Charles. A Model for Pastoral Ministry to Alcoholics [Dissertation]: Pittsburgh Theological Seminary; 1984.
Burrows outlines a model of ministry where a chaplain assists hospitalized patients work step 3, step 4, and step 5 which are the "spiritual heart" of the AA program. The minister and the group work proved to be acceptable and redemptive for alcoholic patients.

2393. Cain, Arthur H. Philosophical Psychology of the Socially Estranged Alcoholic [Dissertation]: Columbia University; 1960.
Cain presents a recovery program including physical training, educative counseling, reading, social reorganization, vocational guidance, aesthetic training, religious investigation, and social participation. To qualify for the program, the patient must have tried some form of recognized therapy, AA, or pastoral counseling without success.

2394. Cannold, Stuart A. An Investigation of Alcoholics Anonymous and Its Impact on Americans Under Thirty-Six.: U.S. Int'l Univ.; 1980.
Note: Ed.D. dissertation, 216pp.
This study concluded that AA has a positive effect on alcoholics who regularly attend AA meetings and that the AA 12-Step program introduces a stabilizing factor in the life of the alcoholic. (for more information, See Education, Administration, Page 4223 in Vol. 41/10-A of Dissertation Abstracts Int'l.) (UMI No.AAD81-07092).

2395. Chaiken, Marcia Rosenblum. Alcoholics Anonymous: A Sociological Study: Univ. of California, Los Angeles; 1979.
Note: Ph.D. dissertation, 390pp.
(See Sociology, General, Page 2276 in Vol. 40/04-A of Dissertation Abstracts Int'l.)(UMI No.AAD79-21379).

2396. Chrouser, Kelley Renee. A Critical Analysis of the Discourse and Reconstructed Stories Shared by Recovering Female Alcoholics in Alcoholics Anonymous: Univ. of Nebraska at Lincoln; 1990; 387pp. Order AAD91-18448. [see Vol. 52/02-A of Dissertation Abstracts Int'l, p343].
Note: Ph.D. dissertation.
Polarities of male/female understandings and separation/participation are examined. The concept of linguistic split is assumed. The author suggests women in recovery construct stories of dominance, abuse, separation, and power by subverting the dominant linguistic system. Chrouser states "the dominant language system excludes women. Furthermore, the absence of a language of touch may be sentencing men to silence their needs to talk about pain as well. Conclusions demonstrate the need to privilege and empower the voice of female recovery and to revise treatment modalities." [the abstract leads one to note the obvious feminist agenda.].

2397. Click, Nancy Elder. Comparison of Work Values and Self-Actualization for Recovering Members of Alcoholics Anonymous.: California State Univ. at Long Beach; 1986; 203pp. Order AAD13-28050.
Note: Unpublished master's thesis.
(See Business Administration, General Page 341 in Vol. 24/04 of Masters Abstracts.).

2398. Cooper, Calvin Crump. Descriptive Variables Related to the Continued Sobriety of Former Alcohol Abusers.: George Peabody College for Teachers; 1981; 82pp. UMI OrderAAD82-08443.
Note: Ed.D. dissertation.
While alcoholism is a major problem in the U.S. and treatment programs are available, continued sobriety of the graduates of these programs is negligible. This study's findings from subjects at a VA Medical Center in Murfreesboro, Tennessee, indicate that alcohol treatment programs should continue to indoctrinate patients in Alcoholics Anonymous work, should encourage the use of Antabuse, should help the alcoholic plan meaningful employment and free time activity, and strive to involve the patient's family in the treatment process. (for more information, See Education, Guidance and Counseling, Page 4721 in Vol. 42/11-A of Dissertation Abstracts Int'l.).

2399. Covey, Kenneth Eugene. Predicting Alcoholism Treatment Drop-Out: A Study of Toxicity, the Minnesota Multiphasic Personality Inventory, and Resultant Methodological Issues.: Univ. of Akron; 1982; 152pp. UMI Order AAD82-04139.
Note: Ph.D. dissertation.
The drop-out problem in alcoholism treatment is studied here. Among 18 hypotheses examined were affiliation with AA and drop-out from AA. It was found demographic data had significant predicative value for potential drop-out from AA. (for more information, See Psychology, Clinical, Page 3819 in Vol. 42/09-B of Dissertation Abstracts Int'l.).

2400. Crawford, Robin Clinton. Accompanying People Through the First Three Steps of Alcoholics Anonymous [Process Theology]: School of Theology at Claremont; 1990; 241pp. Order AAD90-34144. [see Vol. 51/07 A of Dissertation Abstracts Int'l, p2408].
Note: Ph.D. dissertation.
This study aims in part to describe the first three steps of AA and patterns of pastoral intervention, including "storytelling theology." Object relations theory, research methodology in using the "semantic differential" tool, theories of "co-dependence" as denial, pastoral conversations with recovering patients, and process theology are other major parts of this dissertation.

2401. Daniels, Lois Anne. Drinking Patterns Among Women: A Sociological Study: Washington Univ.; 1980; 164pp. UMI Order AAD80-18725.
Note: Ph.D. dissertation.
"Also of interest in the study are the differences between the halfway house portion of the sample and those drawn from the general population of Alcoholics Anonymous women in the metropolitan area. Fewer differences than expected were found between the halfway house (and indigent) women and the A.A. women." (for more information, See Sociology, Public and Social Welfare, Page 1236 in Vol. 41/03-A of Dissertation Abstracts Int'l.).

2402. Dawson, Harry Loren. The Initial Psychological Processes of Recovery in Alcoholics Anonymous.: U.S. Int'l Univ.; 1978; 59pp. UMI Order AAD86-19053.
Note: Ph.D. dissertation.
"The problem of the study was to analyze and describe the psychological processes of the early stages of recovery through which the newly recovering person passes in Alcoholics Anonymous and to create a means by which these processes may be compared to the goals of a hospital treatment program. The importance of the study derived from the lack of goal orienting data available to those directing such programs. "The Solution. All data were secured from official Alcoholics Anonymous literature by an examination of each of the psychological processes describing what is occurring in the newly recovering person. "Results. Analysis revealed six distinguishable psychological processes which were arranged in schematic form and applied in vivo to a hospital treatment program." (Psychology, Clinical, Page 2156 in Vol. 47/05-B of Dissertation Abstracts Int'l.).

2403. Desmond, Thomas Clark. A Descriptive Study of Method of Referral as a Predictor of Treatment Outcome Among Alcoholic Patients.: Boston Univ. School of Education; 1980; 134pp. UMI Order AAD80-24089.
Note: Ed.D. dissertation.
Active participation in Alcoholics Anonymous was one of six treatment objectives identified and changes described in this study. Among the six major findings were (1) over 80% of patients legally coerced into treatment continue to drink after treatment and not attend AA meetings; (2) AA not only receives referrals, it also refers alcoholics to treatment centers; and (3) although only 52% of the self-referred alcoholics were totally abstinent during the previous 12 month, over 80% of them were participating actively in AA. (for more information, See Education, Page 1907 in Vol. 41/05-A of Dissertation Abstracts Int'l.).

2404. Dinitz, Simon. The Role of Alcoholics Anonymous as a Therapeutic Agent: U. of Wisconsin; 1949.
Note: Unpublished master's thesis.

2405. Dunlap, Naomi Gibson. Alcoholism in Women: Some Antecedents and Correlates of Remission in Middle Class Members of Alcoholics Anonymous.: Univ. of Texas at Austin; 1961.
Note: Ph.D. dissertation, 188pp.
(See Education, Psychology, Page 1904 in Vol. 22/06 of Dissertation Abstracts Int'l.)(UMI Order AAD64-04688).

2406. Fappiano, Eugene Rydin. The Alcoholic Priest and Alcoholics Anonymous: A Study of Stigma and the Management of Spoiled Identity.: New School for Social Research; 1984; 223pp. UMI AAD84-14833.
Note: Ph.D. dissertation.
Alcoholics Anonymous has a positive image in alcoholism treatment, yet some professional or occupational groups, such as clergy, have difficulty in accepting participation in AA as beneficial for them. The "Twelve Steps" as a sect-like phenomenon, and the Catholic priesthood as a distinct subculture may be mutually-exclusive groups, presenting an obstacle to successful participation of clergy in AA programs. However, the alcoholic priest may negotiate these obstacles while affiliating with AA, the central focus of this study. (See Sociology, General, Page 1211 in Vol. 45/04-A of Dissertation Abstracts Int'l.).

2407. Fletcher, Bettye Ward. Sociocultural Correlates of Normative Drinking Behavior and Utilization of Treatment Resources: A Study of 113 Black Female Mississippians.: Univ. of Alabama; 1987; 150pp. UMI AAD87-20699.
Note: D.S. dissertation.
The final area of analysis in this study focused on the utilization of treatment resources by black females. The data revealed that if confronted with an alcohol-related problem, respondents would turn to, in descending order, their physician, Alcoholics Anonymous, siblings, parents, mental health center, friends or minister. (for a fuller description of this study, see Social Work, Page 2453 in Vol.48/09-A of Dissertation Abstracts Int'l).

2408. Foley, Charles Patrick. An Understanding: Alcoholism and the Family for General Ministry [Dissertation]: Andover Newton Theological School; 1982.
The dissertation is primarily based on the Rev. Foley's experience in working with alcoholics. Of special interest is the concluding chapter of this dissertation which gives a theological interpretation of working with alcoholics and their families as well as AA.

2409. Ford, Leigh Arden. A Bormannean Fantasy Theme Analysis of "The Big Book" of Alcoholics Anonymous (Rhetorical Vision, Substance Abuse).: Western Michigan Univ.; 1985; 97pp. Order AAD13-27295.
Note: Unpublished master's thesis.
(See Speech Communication, Page 175 in Vol. 24/03 of Masters Abstracts).

2410. Fortin, Mary Lynch. Symptom Progression of Alcohol Addiction in Females and Correlates of Loss of Control Over Drinking.: Univ. of San Francisco; 1981; 159pp. UMI Order AAD81-21623.
Note: Ed.D. dissertation.
The sample for this study consisted of 78 recovering female alcoholics who were members of Alcoholics Anonymous in the San Francisco Bay Area. (for more information, See Education, Guidance and Counseling, Page 1488 in Vol. 42/04-A of Dissertation Abstracts Int'l.).

2411. Frank, Wanda Frances. Length of Sobriety and Affiliative Attributes of Recovering Alcoholic Women (Aspects, Treatment, Socialization): Columbia Univ. Teachers College; 111pp.
Note: Ed.D. dissertation.
This study explored the relationship between length of sobriety and affiliative tendency, sensitivity to rejection and dependency among 58 alcoholic women in the recovery process in A.A. Short and long term sobriety differences, reactions of "loners," and one-to-one (sponsor) versus group interaction in AA were some of the major areas investigated. (For more information, See Health Sciences, Nursing; Sociology, Public and Social Welfare, Page 4183 in Vol. 46-12-B of Dissertation Abstracts Int'l.).

2412. Frigo, Daniel Callistus. Relapse in Alcoholism Treatment: Supportive Families and Posttreatment Therapy.: Washington Univ.; 1982; 119pp. UMI AAD83-10928.
Note: Ph.D. dissertation.
Findings in this study indicate that aftercare attendance significantly decreased the probability of relapse after treatment. Another conclusion was that continuous drinkers are more likely to benefit from attending AA meetings than binge drinkers. (for more information, See Social Work, Page 4044 in Vol. 43/12-A of Dissertation Abstracts Int'l).

2413. Gaskin, Wanda Reed. Symbolic Representations of the AA Twelve Steps Produced in Art Psychotherapy: A Descriptive Study (Addictive Disorder): Texas Woman's Univ.; 1991; 141pp. Order AAD92-03079. [see Vol.52/08-B of Dissertation Abstracts Int'l, p4116].
Note: Ph.D. dissertation.
Thirty addictive disorder patients in an AA Twelve Step treatment program submitted 79 art pieces from from one art piece per patient was selected. Thirteen works representing Step One and 17 representing Steps 2 through 12 were selected. Step one (powelessness) art used the color black and abstract style most often while yellow and pictorial representations were used in the other group (acceptance of a Higher Power). The study concluded art psychotherapy is a useful tool for patients to express their level of accomplishment in the Twelve Steps.

2414. Gellman, Irving Peter. Alcoholics Anonymous: An Autonomous Organization of Social Deviants.: New York Univ.; 1962.
Note: Ph.D. dissertation, 227pp.
(See Sociology, General, Page 3954 in Vol. 27/11-A of Dissertation Abstracts Int'l.) (UMI AAD67-04816).

2415. Giannetti, Vincent J. The Effect of Personal Religious Orientation and Alcoholics Anonymous Membership Upon Alienation, Locus of Control and Expectancies in Therapy Among Male Alcoholics in Treatment.: Univ. of Pittsburgh; 1979.
Note: Ph.D. dissertation, 139pp.
"The purpose of this study was to examine the relationship of selected aspects of religiosity and Alcoholics Anonymous affiliation to social-psychological variables which bear some relationship to alcoholism etiology and treatment. The association of specific dimensions of religious attitudes and Alcoholics Anonymous membership with variables related to the successful outcome of alcoholism treatment offered limited evidence for the therapeutic benefits of religious approaches to alcoholism such as Alcoholics Anonymous." (for more information, See Social Work, Page 806 in Vol. 41-02-A of Dissertation Abstracts Int'l.)(UMI Order AAD80-18279).

2416. Goldenthal, Lyn M. Personality Characteristics of Alcoholics in a Religious Treatment Program.: Univ. of Windsor (Canada); 1981. [not available from UMI].
Note: Ph.D. dissertation.
"Alcoholics Anonymous is a spiritually-based alcoholism treatment program and, as such, its members should differ from other alcoholics (who are either receiving a secular form of treatment or who are untreated), and from non-alcoholics. (A questionnaire of demographic information and several personality scales was given to 49 AA members, 11 alcoholics not affiliated with AA, and 45 non-alcoholics. Many significant differences were revealed between the groups.)" (for more information, See Psychology, Social, Page 1231 in Vol. 42/03-B of Dissertation Abstracts Int'l.).

2417. Gottlich, James Howard. Gender Role Affiliation of Certain Male AA Members in North Central Texas (Alcoholics Anonymous): Univ. of Texas at Arlington; 1987; 57pp. UMI AAD13-31909.
Note: M.S. dissertation.
This study endeavored to determine if personality attributes of the male alcoholic could be identified. Past researchers' work was studied. The author surveyed several Alcoholics Anonymous clubs in the counties of Tarrant and Dallas, Texas. (For a fuller description, see Social Work, Page 204 in Vol. 26/02 of Masters Abstracts).

2418. Greven, Gary L. Effects of a Rational-Emotive Therapy Program on the Irrational Beliefs of Inpatient Alcoholics (Locus-of-Control): Indiana State Univ.; 1985; 136pp. UMI AAD86-08965.
Note: Ph.D. dissertation.
This study, as part of its sample, utilized 30 volunteers from the Alcoholics Anonymous group at Marion, Indiana, Veterans Administration Medical Center. (for more information, See Page 787 in Vol. 47/02-B of Dissertation Abstracts Int'l.).

2419. Habberfield, Tedd R. Alcohol Use Expectancies: Their Relationship with Participation in Treatment, Participation in AA, and Treatment Outcome: State Univ. of New York at Buffalo; 1990; 215pp. Order AAD90-22160. [see Vol. 51/06-B of Dissertation Abstracts Int'l, p3131].
Note: Ph.D. dissertation.
Fifty-two hospital detoxification unit patients, with a follow-up study of 43, were studied. This study indicates researchers cannot rely on a priori assumptions about the desirability of alcohol effects.

2420. Harrell, Charles Travers. Counseling the Abstaining Alcoholic: Univ. of Massachusetts; 1981; 390pp. UMI AAD82-01339.
Note: Ed.D. dissertation.
Considerable attention and critique is given to the program of Alcoholics Anonymous in this study. (for more information, See Psychology, General, Page 3400 in Vol. 42/08-B of Dissertation Abstracts Int'l.).

2421. Harrington, Keith A. Spiritual Resources to Chemically Dependent Adolescents (Recovery, Alcoholics Anonymous): Drew Univ.; 1991; 167pp. Order AAD92-13391. [see Vol. 53/04-A of Dissertation Abstracts Int'l, p1179].
Note: D.Min. dissertation.
The spiritual growth of 48 adoloscents in a residential chemical dependency treatment facility at Conifer Park, Scotia, NY, was studied. The author states his view of addiction as anything which alienates a person from his/her spiritual self. Harrington discusses his own spiritual addiction to alcohol and overeating, biblical sources on the use of alcohol, Fr. Joseph Martin's work, and the first three steps of the twelve step program which are used in the pilot project with the adolescents.

2422. Heil, Richard A., Jr. A Comparative Analysis of Therapeutic Factors in Self-Help Groups (Alcoholics Anonymous, Overeaters Anonymous): Univ. of Pittsburgh; 1992; 171pp. Order AAD92-26528. [see Vol. 53/08-B of Dissertation Abstracts Int'l, p4373].
Note: Ph.D. dissertation.
"The therapeutic factors of group cohesiveness, instillation of hope, and universality were perceived to be the most helpful for these groups. The need for professionals to respect and support self-help groups was underscored." The

sample of 80 included 20 each from AA, Alon-Anon, OA, and Parent-to-Parent.

2423. Heise, Robin Glenn. Spirituality and Contented Sobriety: A Model (Alcoholics Anonymous): Memphis State Univ.; 1991; 100pp. Order AAD92-00113. [see Vol. 52/10-A of Dissertation Abstracts Int'l, p3529].
Note: Ed.D. dissertation.
A proposed model of contented sobriety was tested using questionnaires filled out by volunteers from AA groups in Shelby County, Tenn. While the model was not supported, "results indicated spirituality was not significantly related to contented sobriety." Major differences between men and women in terms of AA attendance, life-satsifaction, spirituality, and contented sobriety were noted.

2424. Helmle, Karen Eleanor. Organizational Acceptance of Individual Differences As Perceived By Persons Affiliated with Two Twelve-Step Recovery Programs (Alcoholism).: Univ. of Wisconsin at Madison; 1984; 166pp. UMI AAD84-14239.
Note: Ph.D. dissertation.
Alcoholics Anonymous and Al-Anon were studied to determine how they accomodate individuals differences among members and what pertinence this might have for educational administration. (for more information, See Page 1254 in Vol. 45/05-A of Dissertation Abstracts Int'l.).

2425. Herban, Nancy Lynn. An Inquiry Into the Meaning and Significance of Sobriety As Described By Recovering Alcoholics.: Univ. of Alabama in Birmingham; 1986; 97pp. UMI AAD87-09352.
Note: D.S.N. dissertation.
This study of 20 AA members (half male and half female) with a minimum of one year's sobriety revealed that sobriety constitutes a role change of greater magnitude than may have been thought previously. (For further details, see Health Sciences, Nursing, Page 89 in Vol. 48/01-B of Dissertation Abstracts Int'l.).

2426. Hettinger, Bettsy Hewitt. An Investigation Into the Modification of Locus-of-Control in Outpatient Alcoholics and Its Relationship to Preference for Alcoholics Anonymous.: The College of William and Mary; 1976; 163pp. UMI AAD77-04986.
Note: Unpublished Ed.D. dissertation.
(See Education, Guidance and Counseling, Page 5606 in Vol. 37/09-A of Disseratation Abstracts Int'l).

2427. Hoggson, Robert L. Alcoholics Anonymous, A Study in Solidarity.: Fordham Univ.; 1952; 215pp.
Note: Ph.D. dissertation.
(See Sociology, General, in Vol. W1952.).

2428. Hudson, Henry L. The History of Blacks and Alcoholics Anonymous. Graduate Center, CUNY,New York: unpublished doctorial dissertation; 1978.

2429. Jackson, Margery Leithliter. Actualization of Alcoholics Anonymous Members.: U.S. Int'l Univ.; 1980.
Note: Ph.D. dissertation, 135pp.
"The problem of the study was to assess whether persons who have been abstinent active members of Alcoholics Anonymous score better on measures of self-actualization than do people from selected other groups. Results. (1) The recovered A.A. sample group made significantly more positive scores in measures of self-actualization than the A.A. newcomers and the religious abstainers. (2) Comparison of the A.A. sample with published results from the POI Handbook disclosed that this group made more positive scores than the scores for the general public, a group of clinically selected self-actualizers and an advanced therapy group. (the A.A. sample group was comprised of AA members with three through eight years of sobriety)." (for more information, See Psychology, General, Page 1091 in Vol. 41/03-B of Dissertation Abstracts Int'l.)(UMI No.AAD 80-19033.).

2430. Jahnke, Vernon John. Extending Recovery into the Life of the Church (Twelve Step Programs): School of Theology at Claremont; 1991; 101pp. Order AAD91-35032. [see Vol. 52/06-A of Dissertation Abstracts Int'l, p2093].
Note: D.Min. dissertation.
While churches have housed Twelve Step meetings and pastors have couseled recovering people, Jahnke believes the Christian community has made little effort toward helping recovering people explore recovery within the church community itself. Hinderances to this are the absolute nature of some traditional church doctrines and an atmosphere of denial of dependency problems in some faith communities.

2431. James, Bart M. Study of the Personal and Social Adjustment Characteristics of Members of Alcoholics Anonymous.: Kent State University, Ohio; 1950.
Note: unpublished master's thesis.

2432. Johnson, Hazel Cameron. Alcoholics Anonymous in the 1980s: Variations on a Theme.: Univ. of California at Los Angeles; 1987; 717pp. UMI AAD87-21038.
Note: Ph.D. dissertation.
"Previous research on Alcoholics Anonymous has claimed that members and groups are much alike and that the movement is characterized by rigidity and dogmatism. Members of AA groups do have characteristics in common. So do the the groups, or "meetings," which they attend. However, both members and groups also exhibit variation and, in addition, are subject to change over time. Variation and change occur because of the need to adapt to new conditions in the external environment but they also result from problems which arise during member interactions. These may be due to similarities or to differences. Despite tensions among members, troubles in AA group do not appear to harm the movement. This study explores similarities and differences among members and groups. It examines the variety of form a meeting may take. It then goes on to observe what may happen when "trouble" arises in

an AA meeting.
Because AA is based on autonomous cells, egalitarian standards, and fosters networking among members and groups, tensions in meetings can actually be productive, as norms and values which are considered valuable will be reinforced; new norms will be adopted if they are felt to be useful; members will spread ideas from group to group if they switch affiliations; and new cells are formed when intragroup solutions fail. This study is based on four years of participant observation of over three dozen group of AA. Surveys of members, formal and informal interviews, and historical methods were also employed in doing this research." (Sociology, General, Page 1890 in Vol. 48/07-A of Dissertation Abstracts Int'l).

2433. Kahler, Joseph Keith. <u>The Role of Alcohol Expectancies and Quality of AA Participation in Recovery from Alcoholism</u>: Univ. of Texas at Austin; 1987; 148pp. UMI AAD87-17449.
Note: Ph.D. dissertation.
"The relationship of alcohol-related expectancies with the continuous abstinence and quality of participation in A.A. by persons having completed private inpatient and outpatient chemical dependency programs was investigated. Fifty-two subjects whose primary or secondary drug of choice was alcohol and had postdischarge periods ranging from 11 to 23 months, indicated their beliefs about the consequences of alcohol consumption through the Alcohol Expectancy Questionnaire (AEQ). Subjects responded regarding their progress in the 12 Steps of AA, AA sponsorship, AA meeting attendance, and their perceived relationship with a 'Higher Power.
"Multivariate analysis of variance supported previous findings with more restricted samples that limited expectancies of alcohol were associated with continuous abstinence. Multiple regression analysis revealed that predictor variables of having an AA sponsor, number of AA meetings attended weekly, AEQ scores, and whether the subject is sponsoring someone in AA accounted for a statistically significant 19.9% of the criterion of continuous abstinence since the time of discharge from treatment.
"Significant negative linear relationships were found between completing AA's 9th Step and positive expectancies of alcohol in general, as well as in the areas of sexual performance and experience, social assertiveness and relaxation. Analysis of variance yielded a significant difference between subjects who had complete an AA 4th Step and those who had not in terms of number of consecutive days abstinent up to the time of contact for the study. Furthermore, analysis of variance revealed significant differences on the same measure of treatment success between persons who had progressed no further than AA's first three Steps, and those who had completed Step 9."(Education, Psychology, Page 1152 in Vol. 48/05-A of Dissertation Abstracts).

2434. Kay, Richard Steven. Alcoholism Relapse Among Alcoholics Anonymous Participants: U.S. Int'l Univ.; 1985; 107pp. UMI AAD86-17918.
Note: Ph.D. dissertation.
The Problem. Recent research has revealed that the relapse rates among alcoholics are high and that the factors and circumstances associated with relapse have not been clearly defined. Moreover, little has been done to compare the relapse rates of self-help alcoholics with those of alcoholics who have received various types of alcoholism treatment.
Method. The study utilized a comparative survey design in which a sample of 223 subjects were administered the Alcoholic Profile Questionnaire designed to elicit information related to the key variables under study. In addition, 12 subjects falling in discrete categories were interviewed. All subjects were A.A. participants with no more than one year of sobriety.
The study revealed: (1) Subjects receiving treatment in individual psychotherapy, counseling, or in-patient detoxification did not report relapse rates significantly different from those by subjects who did not report receiving treatment outside of A.A.; (2) A.A. members attending A.A. meetings at the time of relapse reported lower relapse rates than A.A.'s not attending meetings at the times of relapse; (3) Subjects who reported high levels of previous consumption were found to report lower relapse rates than subjects who reported low levels of prior consumption; (4) Reported frequency of attendance at religious services did not have a significant affect on relapse. Of 4 variables tested, reported ethanol consumption and A.A. attendance were the best variables under study in predicting relapse rates, whereas, exposure to treatment and attendance at religious services added little to the regression equation. (Psychology, General, Page 2141 in Vol. 47/05-B of Dissertation Abstracts Int'l).

2435. Kleist, Jeffrey. Network Resource Utilization Patterns of Members of Alcoholics Anonymous: Univ. of Akron; 1990; 233pp. Order AAD90-26905. [see Vol. 51/05-A of Dissertation Abstracts Int'l. p1781].
Note: Ph.D. dissertation.
This study assessed how AA members utilized the total range of their network resources. Data came from 228 AA's in five cities in three midwestern states.

2436. Knippel, Charles Taylor. Samuel M. Shoemaker's Theological Influence on William G. Wilson's Twelve Step Spiritual Program of Recovery (Alcoholics Anonymous): St. Louis Univ.; 1987; 357pp. UMI AAD87-15077.
Note: Ph.D. dissertation.
"William Griffith Wilson (1895-1971), a co-founder of Alcoholics Anonymous, formulated and interpreted the Twelve Step Spiritual Program of Recovery currently used by Alcoholics Anonymous and approximately 18 other American self-help groups. This dissertation explores the theological influence of Samuel Moor Shoemaker, Jr. (1893-1963), an

Episcopal clergyman, on Wilson's formulation and interpretations. "William Wilson gained his sobriety in 1934 through his association with the Oxford Group Movement, of which Shoemaker was the American leader from the mid-1920s until 1941. From Shoemaker, Wilson learned much about Christian theology as Shoemaker espoused it from his particular Episcopalian and Oxford Group perspectives. Of special significance, he adapted Shoemaker's inclusivistic approach in order to help alcoholics of all faiths and no faith at all.
"This study demonstrates that Wilson's entire program of recovery is basically rooted in Shoemaker's applied theology. Very much of what Shoemaker taught about Christian conversion is what Wilson taught in order to bring about recovery from alcoholism. Like Shoemaker, Wilson affirmed the importance of an experimental and experiental approach to God; that human beings are powerless to change their lives; that God is able and willing to help people; that self-surrender to God as the Higher Power, however He might be conceived, is necessary for receiving help; and that God comes with help to those who use their freedom of will to approach Him. Wilson followed Shoemaker in valuing confession, restitution, the power of prayer and meditation, and the importance and necessity of fellowship and witnessing about one's own experience to others. A final chapter examines and evaluates from a traditional Christian perspective Wilson's ideological and inclusivistic approaches in working with alcoholics within a pluralistic setting. In addition to providing a summary statement and several observations, the conclusion offers suggestions to traditional Christians for relating to the Twelve Step Program and for enhancing the life and mission of the Church." (Theology, Page 957 in Vol. 48/04-A of Dissertation Abstracts Int'l).

2437. Kovach, Judith Ann. The Relationship Between Treatment Failures of Alcoholic Women and Incestuous Histories with Possible Implications for Post Traumatic Stress Disorder Symptomatology.: Wayne State Univ.; 1983; 100pp. UMI AAD83-15604.
Note: Ph.D. dissertation.
One hundred-seventeen women members of Alcoholics Anonymous comprised the sample and almost 30 per cent of them experienced childhood incest. Forty per cent of that group experienced post traumatic stress disorder and were more depressed and anxiety-controlled during recovery. Women with incest histories developed drinking problems at an earlier age. (for more information, See Education, Psychology, Page 710 in Vol. 44/03-A of Dissertation Abstracts Int'l.).

2438. Kurtz, Ernest. Not-God: A History of Alcoholics Anonymous: Harvard Univ.; 1978.
Note: Ph.D. dissertation.
Published in hardback by Hazelden Educational Services, Center City, Minnesota, 1979. (See separate listing in "Books about AA" chapter of this book.) (See History, United States, in Vol. X1978).

2439. Kurtz, Linda Farris. Cooperation between Alcoholics Anonymous members and Alcoholism Treatment Centers in Georgia.: Univ. of Georgia, Athens; 1983.
Note: D.P.A. dissertation, 249 pages.
Literature describing the relationships between mutual-aid groups and professionals has indicated that tensions exist between these two forms of human assistance, with preliminary fieldwork and observation confirming the conflictual nature of such relationships. A study was conducted to examine relationships between professionals and AA members, by surveying the state alcoholism treatment centers and AA members in 42 communities in Georgia. It was found that (1) AAs have relatively low respect for professionals, although the reverse was not found; (2) both AAs and professionals experience a degree of dependence on each other; (3) those programs that cooperate well, interact frequently; (4) linking activities that were most effective included attending one another's meetings or programs, having AA members work in centers as volunteers or as staff; and (5) professionals and AAs had different ideologies, with differences increasing between them when comparisons were controlled for outcome on the dependent variable, cooperation. (See Political Science, Public Administration, Page 573 in Vol. 44/02-A of Dissertation Abstracts Int'l.)(UMI Order No.AAD83-14732).

2440. Lahey, W. W. A Comparison of Social and Personal Factors Identified with Selected Members of Alcoholics Anonymous: Univ. of Southern California; 1950.
Note: M.A. thesis.

2441. Leavitt, Stewart Bruce. Social Uses and Communication of Myth in a Rescue Organization: Alcoholics Anonymous.: Northwestern Univ.; 1974.
Note: Ph.D. dissertation, 264pp.
(See Speech Communication, Page 6841 in Vol. 35/10-A of Dissertation Abstracts Int'l.)(UMI OrderAAD75-07943).

2442. Lehman, Carol Vogel. The Alcoholic Bottom: Problem Recognition and Help Seeking by Alcoholics: Univ. of Michigan; 1984; 239pp. UMI AAD84-22277.
Note: Ph.D. dissertation.
This study used a cross-section sample of 150 recovering alcoholics who are AA members in metropolitan Detroit. One finding was professionals need to understand the therapeutic dynamics of AA. (see Education, Guidance and Counseling, Page 1992 in Vol. 45/07-A of Dissertation Abstracts Int'l.).

2443. Levin, Jerome David. A Study of Social Role Conflict in Chronic Alcoholic Men Affiliated with Alcoholics Anonymous: New York Univ.; 1981.
Note: Ph.D. dissertation, 225pp.
The study hypothesized that there is a positive relationship between length of sobriety in AA and normative role structuring and that alcoholics entering AA are more deviant in social role structuring than non-alcoholic peers. These two ideas were supported by findings. (for more information, See Psychology, Social, Page 4970 in Vol. 42/12-B of Dissertation Abstracts Int'l.)(UMI Order AAD82-10924).

2444. Lull, David Carner. Alcoholics Anonymous Attendance, Aftercare, and Outcome: A Secondary Analysis of Two Years Posthospitalization Data: Univ. of Minnesota; 1988; 220pp. Order AAD88-23548. [see Vol. 49/08-A of Dissertation Abstracts Int'l, p2393].
Note: Ph.D. dissertation.
This study of two years posthospitalization data from 2,950 subjects enrolled in an outcome registry found AA attendance was important in determining sobriety, not aftercare treatment. For four follow-up intervals, AA attendance was the most important factor in both sobriety and regression.

2445. Lusero, Gilberto Telesforo. Alcoholics Anonymous in a Chicano Community: An Analysis of Affiliation and Transferability.: Brandeis Univ. The Florence Heller Graduate School for Advance Studies in Social Welfare.; 1977; 269pp. UMI AAD77-25045.
Note: Ph.D. dissertation.
(See Social Work, Page 3732 in Vol. 38/06-A of Dissertation Abstracts Int'l.).

2446. Machell, David Francis. Belongingness - The Critical Variable in the Residential Treatment of Alcoholism: Fordham Univ.; 1984; 140pp. UMI AAD84-09262.
Note: Ed.D. dissertation.
This study tried to test the effectiveness of programs which stress "fellowship" (the AA concept) or a sense of belongingness as a means for successful treatment of alcoholics in a residential setting. One of the three major questions explored was: In a halfway house setting, is the highly structured program (A.A. halfway house treatment precedent) a significant factor in increasing client perceived belongingness. The study concluded there was no significant relationship between the program structure and belongingness level. (see Page 86 in Vol. 45/01-A of Dissertation Abstracts Int'l.).

2447. Maracle, Marilyn Frances. Beyond Abstinence: A Study of Recovery among Women in Alcoholics Anonymous: Washington Univ.; 1989; 286pp. Order AAD89-24400. [see Vol. 50/07-A of Dissertation Abstracts Int'l, p2257].
Note: Ph.D. dissertation.
This study finds that women first identify AA meanings found or given in AA and then create personal meanings. Understanding recovery as an on-going, long-term experience focused also on spiritual growth. Four different affiliation patterns for women were identified along with their influence on relapse.

2448. Maroney, Stephanie Manning. Post Rehabilitation Center Follow-Up Alcoholics: Factors Correlated with Abstinence (Recovery, AA, Sobriety).: Bryn Mawr College; 1986; 151pp. UMI AAD86-17657.
Note: Ph.D. dissertation.
"Clinical and theortical literature on alcoholism and the recovery from alcoholism do not clarify many issues. This study explore one method utilized in recovery, abstinence. A sample of 35 men and women between the ages of 20 and 51 was studied from the time they completed a 28 day program in either 1 or 2 alcoholism rehabilitation centers. The sample was measured at the time of release and at 90 days using the Beck Depression Inventory, a Semantic Differential, a questionnaire and structured interview. A comparison was made between those able to abstain from alcohol (20) and those who resumed drinking (15). Results indicated a correlation between affiliation with A.A. and abstinence at 90 days, a period critical in recovery. There was also a correlation between low levels of depression, high levels of self esteem and abstinence." (Psychology, Clinical, Page 2174 in Vol. 47/05-B of Dissertation Abstracts Int'l.).

2449. Marques, Clarissa Colell. Behavior Control Self-Help Groups: Members' Attitudes Regarding Health Care Professionals: Univ. of Arizona; 1983; 275pp. UMI AAD84-01249.
Note: Ph.D. dissertation.
How members of AA and three other groups patterned after AA feel about health care professionals was the subject of this study. Among the 110 volunteers completing the questionnaire from the four groups, there was strong criticism of the professional community, strong support for the group's decision (excepting Parents Anonymous) to "remain forever nonprofessional," and AA and NA were firmly against professional involvement of professionals in group activities. (for more information, See Page 3202 in Vol. 44/10-B of Dissertation Abstracts Int'l.).

2450. Marrus, Francine Elizabeth. A Way Back to Life: Descriptions and Discoveries about the Role of Communication in the Enculturation Performance of Alcoholics Anonymous: Ohio Univ.; 1989; 402pp. Order AAD90-11335. [see Vol. 51/03-A of Dissertation Abstracts Int'l, p680].
Note: Ph.D. dissertation.
The role of communication in AA is explored in this study of 30 AA meetings and interviews with 60 AA members. Meetings, stories, myths, metaphors, "quickies," rituals, ceremonies, the Steps and Traditions, AA literature, sponsors, and newcomers [the main focus] are discussed in this framework.

2451. Mastrich, James L., Jr. Influences on the Successful Treatment of Alcoholics Referred Through Employee Assistance Programs (Triggering Incident, Alcoholics Anonymous): Rutgers, The State Univ. of New Jersey, New Brunswick; 1985; 151pp. UMI AAD85-24231.
Note: Ed.D. dissertation.
Attendance at AA meetings was one of the factors in client success in this study of 310 alcoholic employees in ten companies where they participated in employee assistance programs involving alcoholism treatment. (see Psychology, Industrial, Page 3251 in Vol. 46/09-B of Dissertation Abstracts Int'l).

2452. Mathias, Rudolph E. S. An Experimental Investigation of the Personality Structure of Chronic Alcoholic, Alcoholics Anonymous, Neurotic, and Normal Groups.: State Univ. of New York at Buffalo; 1955.
Note: Ph. D. dissertation. 128pp.
(See Psychology, Clinical, Page 156 in Vol. 16/01 of Dissertation Abstracts Int'l.) (UMI Order AAD-00-13748).

2453. Maxwell, Milton A. B. Social Factors in the Alcoholics Anonymous Program: Univ. of Texas at Austin; 1949.
Note: Ph.D. dissertation, 209 pages. [not available from UMI].
(See Sociology, General, in Vol. W1949, of Dissertation Abstracts Int'l.).

2454. McAfee, Raymond Mack. Male and Female Abstainers Attending Alcoholics Anonymous: Their Adjustments in Personality Structure, Cognitive Orientation, and Interpersonal Relationships.: Univ. of Houston, TX; 1980.
Note: Ed.D. dissertation, 231pp.
Fifty-seven males and 53 females participated in this study with 34 males and 28 females members of A.A. only while the remainder had treatment from both A.A. and a professional person. The main finding of this study was that significant adjustments in the personality structure of both male and female abstainers are predicted by abstinence intervals. (for a more-detailed summary, See Education, Psychology, Page 2020 in Vol. 41/05-A of Dissertation Abstracts Int'l.) (UMI No.AAD80-27013).

2455. McAfee, Wallace T. Alcoholics Anonymous: an Evaluation Study: Univ. of Chicago.; 1952.
Note: Ph.D. dissertation, 222 pages.
(See Sociology, General, in Vol. W1953.) (not available from UMI).

2456. McBride, James Lebron. The Association between Participation in Alcoholics Anonymous, Abstinence Patterns, Family Member Attendance of Al-Anon, Family Stress, and Family Functioning: The Florida State Univ.; 1988; 146pp. Order AAD88-14424. [see Vol. 49/06-A of Dissertation Abstracts Int'l, p1588].
Note: Ph.D. dissertation.
This study of 50 AA members in eight cities in Florida and Georgia found positive values for lengthy Al-Anon attendance and lower intra-family stress for both the AA and Al-Anon spouses; a positive coorelation between length of time in Al-Anon and the number of month for an AA's abstinence; resulting in better communication, problem solving, and general family functioning. AA attendance and length of abstinence helped maintain sobriety.

2457. McDowell, Lowell Burdette. Personality Changes in Members of Alcoholics Anonymous as a Function of Their Membership: California State Univ. at Long Beach; 1977.
Note: UMI AAD13-10270.
M.A. thesis, 54pp.
(See Psychology, Experimental, Page 240 in Vol. 15/04 of Masters Abstracts.).

2458. McEwen, S. B. Tools of Recovery in Alcoholics Anonymous and their Relationship to Inpatient Treatment, Length of Sobriety, and Gender: Univ. of New Mexico; 1989; 120pp. contact author.
Note: sociology thesis.
Over 300 persons from 14 cities completed a questionnaire on 100 tools of recovery in AA. One hundred seventy-seven had 28 days or more of inpatient treatment. Among the findings: as the "Surrender" score decreased, sobriety increased.

2459. McNally, Emily B. Lesbian Recovering Alcoholics in Alcoholics Anonymous: A Qualitative Study of Identity Transformation: New York Univ.; 1989; 294pp. Order AAD90-04305. [see Vol. 50/09-B of Dissertation Abstracts Int'l, p4227].
Note: Ph.D. dissertation.
Eight women who identified themselves as lesbian recovering alcoholics in AA were studied in terms of the process of transforming their stigmatized identity. Eight profiles and five themes emerged. The author offers a model of lesbian recovering alcoholic identity transformation.

2460. Meyer, William Torvald. The Application of Role Theory in an Investigation of Affiliation with Alcoholics Anonymous.: Western Michigan Univ.; 1967.
Note: M.A. thesis, 54pp.
Order AAD13-01356. (See Sociology, General, Page 106 in Vol. 06/03 of Masters Abstracts.).

2461. Minkowsky, Alan. Attitudinal Bias and Logical Performance in Alcohol Abusing and Recovering Groups: California School of Professional Psychology, San Diego; 1982; 126pp. UMI AAD82-21787.
Note: Ph.D. dissertation.
Three groups, AA members, alcohol abusers and control subjects, were tested with syllogisms biased toward the tested group to determine if problems concerned with the use of alcohol would result in systematic errors in reasoning. Results question the validity of the use of the syllogism as a research tool in this area. (see Psychology, General, Page 1239 in Vol. 43/04-B in Dissertation Abstracts Int'l.).

2462. Moore, James Frederick. Psychological Mindedness in Alcoholics in Treatment: Individual Differences in Relation to Involvement in Alcoholics Anonymous, Level of Ego Development, and Five Other Variables: Harvard Univ.; 1983; 271pp. UMI Order AAD83-20184.
Note: Ed.D. dissertation.
Most treatment programs, and AA, encourage alcoholics to control thought processes found to be detrimental to sobriety. This study revealed individual differences in the degree to which such self-management is seen by the alcoholic to be important to recovery. This understanding was termed psychological mindedness. Twenty male alcoholics in a Veterans Adm. 31-day residential treatment program voluntarily completed a semi-structured interview sometime between their 13th and 31st day in treatment. This interview was scored to rate degree and type of pyschological mindedness. A significant positive relationship was found between degree of psychological mindedness and AA involvement. No significant relationship was found between psychological mindedness and IQ or ego development. A negative relationship was found between psychological mindedness and level of education. Overall, psychological mindedness does not seem to reflect a stable underlying personality trait, but may result from learning experiences, especially in AA. (See Psychology, Clinical, Page 1600 in Vol. 44/05-B of Dissertation Abstracts Int'l.).

2463. Morreim, Dennis C. A Theological-Biblical Perspective of The Twelve Steps of Alcoholics Anonymous for Implementation in Ministry: Luther Northwestern Theological Seminary; 1984.
Note: D.Min. dissertation.

2464. Murphy, Mary Martha. Social Class Differences in Responsiveness to the Program of Alcoholics Anonymous.: Univ. of Chicago; 1952.
Note: Ph.D. dissertation, 334 pages.
The author found no difference in values of AA members from the middle and lower social classes. (See Sociology, General, in Vol. W1952.).

2465. Nagel, George, Jr. Identity Reconstruction: Communication and Storytelling in Alcoholics Anonymous: Univ. of Utah; 1988; 158pp. Order AAD88-12793. [see Vol. 49/05-A of Dissertation Abstracts Int'l, p998].
Note: Ph.D. dissertation.
The author attended AA meetings as both participant and researcher to develop his thesis that AA language and storytelling alter the alcoholic's identity and they reconstruct "new selves out of old" by speaking of "what it was like, what happened, and what it is like now.".

2466. Nelson, Gail Carol. Practicing Peace in Recovery with A.A.: Univ. of Minnesota; 1989; 403pp. Order AAD90-05246. [see Vol. 51/01-A of Dissertation Abstracts Int'l, p202].
Note: Ph.D. dissertation.
This study of the spiritual ideas, practices and experiences of 12 AA members who were treated at Hazelden is supplemented by a questionnaire answered by 88 recovering alcoholics. It explores in prose, poetry and pictographs William James' conversion experience, the religious reunifying of a discordant personality. It concludes AA serves as a revitalization movement congruent with the universal pattern identified by anthropologist Anthony Wallace.

2467. Nelson, James Douglas, Rev. Stepping Stones to Recovery: A Comparison of the Healing Practices of Jesus Christ, Carl Jung and The Twelve Steps of A.A. Colgate Rochester: St. Bernard's Institute; 1984; 167pp.
The dissertation demonstrates the parallel principles of Jesus, Jung & AA and provides a model for teaching them in a seminary setting.

2468. O'Connor, Kathleen Anne Ballinger. Alcoholics Anonymous' Tools for Sobriety: An Examination of the Therapeutic Mechanisms of Various Stages of Sobriety: Univ. of Cincinnati; 1987; 191pp. UMI AAD87-22065.
Note: Ed.D. dissertation.
"The focus of the present study was the relationship among length of sobriety, sex, and utilization of the tools of recovery of Alcoholics Anonymous by members of the program. An index of how the recovery tools are applied was obtained by having 189 members of AA rate each of the 100 tools in terms of usefulness to their sobriety on a multiple choicequestionnaire. Hypotheses were based on two assumptions: (a) AA members would vary in their use of the recovery tools due to different lengths of sobriety, and (b) male and female members of AA would differ in their use of the recovery tools due to differences in the seriousness of the implications of alcoholism for women.

Frequency counts were used to establish the frequency with which respondents applied the 100 tools of AA to their sobriety. A factor analysis indicated no statistically significant differences in utilization of the tools as a function of length of sobriety. There was a significant difference in the application of the tools according to sex, with female members of AA endorsing tools to avoid drinking more than men. The results were discussed in terms of the stigma of alcoholism, implications for treatment, and directions for future research." (Psychology, Clinical Page 2105 in Vol. 48/07-B of Dissertation Abstracts Int'l.).

2469. O'Neill-Barber, Kathleen Marie. Female Adolescent Alcoholics Aged 16-21: A Descriptive Study (Alcoholics Anonymous): Boston Univ.; 1984; 204pp. UMI AAD84-16675. Note: Ed.D. dissertation.
Research on adolescent alcoholism and alcoholism among females has been limited. This study revealed the prevention of alcoholism in female adolescents is not a feminine or adolescent issue but a humanistic issue. In every case, one significant person suggested Alcoholics Anonymous as a possible source of help, which, indeed turned out to be the case after they attended several meetings and established AA relationships of nurturing. (for more information, See Psychology, Social, Page 1322 in Vol. 45/04-B of Dissertation Abstracts Int'l.).

2470. Obinali, Menaja C. U. Factors Which Characterized Alcoholics Who Successfully Completed A Residential Treatment Program.: Univ. of Tennessee; 1985; 98pp. UMI AAD86-00046. Note: Ph.D. dissertation.
Attendance at AA meetings was one of the major components in this study. One of the conclusions was that patients should be encouraged to attend "especially AA meetings since these can be a strong support after discharge." (see Psychology, Clinical, Page 4042 in Vol.46/11-B of Dissertation Abstract Int'l.).

2471. Pasquella, Mary J. Alcoholics Anonymous Members: Personality Characteristics as Related to Motivational Style, Utilization of the Twelve Steps and Value Change: Howard Univ., Washington, D.C.; 1986; 121pp. UMI AAD87-03300. Note: Ph.D. dissertation.
"The purpose of this study was to systematically describe Alcoholics Anonymous members' Jungian personality types, drinking history, motivation for drinking, social value development and adherence to the Twelve Steps of AA. The sample consisted of 405 A.A. members. Among five instruments utilized was the Twelve Step Questionnaire, a self-report instrument developed for this study measured the utilization of the AA Twelve Steps.
"Data indicated that the alcoholics' Jungian type distribution was similar to general population norms with a slight exaggeration of introversion and feeling percentages. A shy motivational pattern for drinking was predicted by introversion and feeling especially in females. Looking at utilization of the 12 Steps - introversion, intuition and

perceiving were associated with difficulty working the steps whereas extraversion, sensing, and feeling were associated with benefitting from working the steps. Steps 1, 2, and 3 were used universally and other steps were less used. Women were more likely than men to use Step 5 which requires admitting wrongs. Social value change that occurred as a function of utilizing the AA program was found to be differentially associated with extraversion for men and women; male extraverts developed more social values while female extraverts developed more personal values the longer in AA. Shy motivated drinking and drug use (particularly by women) predicted severity of alcoholism. Drug using alcoholics were more likely to be feeling-perceiving types and drug free alcoholics were more likely to be predominantly thinking-judging types. Data focusing on slipping indicated that men slipped more than women and that introverts were more likely to slip. (Psychology, Clinical, Page 4310 in Vol. 47/10-B of Dissertation Abstracts Int'l.).

2472. Pittman, William L. Alcoholics Anonymous and the Neo-Alcoholism Movement 1939-1945: The Mobilization of a Social Movement: Univ. of Massachusetts at Boston; 1985.
Note: M.A. thesis.
This deals with the organizations and individuals that helped the growth of A.A. in the early 1940s.

2473. Pittman, William L. Alternative Explanations for the Beginnings of Alcoholics Anonymous 1934-1939: Univ. of Minnesota.; Feb. 1983.
Note: Summa cum laude thesis, 276pp.
Pittman explores the historical debt A.A. owes to the Oxford Group; reviews the life of William Griffith Wilson up to 1939; and includes 6 appendixes of books suggested in Peabody's book, Nell Wing's books early A.A.'s read, Sam Shoemaker and Harold Begbie books, written by Oxford Group members, critical of Oxford Group volumes, and Dr. Bob's "Required Reading List." Pittman's conclusions are controversial at times but his historical explorations are always provocative. "There appears to be many other sources that influenced Bill Wilson than those that have been previously reported," Pittman summarizes. "...to dispel the 'absoluteness' of the 'Big Book,' ...to credit sources not acknowledged by that organization (A.A.)," and his characterization of "Sam Shoemaker (as) the pivotal and most influential individual in the founding, formation, and publication of Alcoholics Anonymous are but three of his aims. His digging into the past for the unpublished truth about the "precursors" of Alcoholics Anonymous is laudatory. (This thesis was revised and published later as AA The Way It Began. See separate listing in "Books about AA" chapter.).

2474. Przybilla, Carla M. The Ongoing Development and Formalizing of a Pastoral Care Program for Chemically-Dependent Men and Women Religious: The Catholic Univ. of America; 1984; 233pp. UMI AAD84-10891.
Note: D.Min. dissertation.
The findings of this research pinpoint the Steps of A.A. as the single most important factor for helping an alcoholic religious toward a spiritual rebirth or reintegration. (see Sociology, Public and Social Welfare, Page 967 in Vol 45/03-A of Dissertation Abstracts Int'l.).

2475. Reinert, Duane F. Effects of Participation in Alcohol Self-Help Groups on Surrender and Narcissism among Adult Males (Men, Alcoholics Anonymous, Rational Recovery): Loyola College in Maryland; 1992; 149pp. Order AAD92-30879. [see Vol. 53/07-B of Dissertation Abstracts Int'l, p3827].
Note: Ph.D. dissertation.
Forty-five AA members and ten in Rational Recovery participated in this study, with the AA's divided into "High" and "Low" groups. It was hypothesized that those who participated more actively in AA (the High AA group) would decline in narcissism, compared to the other two groups. The "Surrender" instrument, designed by the researcher for this project, was able to discriminate between the three groups. "As predicted, the High AA group scored higher on surrender than did the other groups. The results appear to be consistent with AA's philosophy which advocates surrender to a Higher Power...".

2476. Ritchie, Oscar W. A Sociological Analysis of Alcoholics Anonymous.: Kent State Univ., Ohio; 1947.
Note: M.A. thesis.

2477. Rusen, Judith. Changes in Self-Esteem and Spirituality after Participation in an Alcoholics Anonymous-Based Inpatient Substance Abuse Treatment Program: California Institute of Integral Studies; 1990; 80pp. Order AAD91-20017. [see Vol. 52/02-B of Dissertation Abstracts Int'l, p1081].
Note: Ph.D. dissertation.
Thirty-two alcohol and/or drug-dependent inpatients were tested at the beginning and end of their 28-day treatment program which emphasized AA principles, meetings and materials. Self-esteem and spirituality increased significantly in consequence of enforced abstinence and AA's emphasis on spiritual potential.

2478. Rudy, David Robert. Becoming Alcoholic: Accounts of Alcoholics Anonymous Members.: Syracuse Univ.; 1977.
Note: Ph.D. dissertation, 288pp.
(See Sociology, Public and Social Welfare, Page 5084 in Vol. 38/08-A of Dissertation Abstracts Int'l.)(UMI OrderAAD77-30756).

2479. Saquet-Shire, Jeannette Labeebee. Time in the House: A Study of Alcoholic Women in Halfway House Recovery: Northeastern Univ.; 1981; 301pp. UMI AAD82-05050.
Note: Ph.D. dissertation.
The socialization process, the dynamics of the treatment process, and shared perspectives of staff and residents are studied at Sobriety House, located in Massachusetts, a halfway house with a recovery program based on the Alcoholics Anonymous program. (see Sociology, Public and Social Welfare, Page 4173 in Vol. 42/09-A of Dissertation Abstracts Int'l.).

2480. Sarowitz, Myrna. Social Interest in Alcoholics Who are Members of Alcoholics Anonymous; 1992; 122pp. Order AAD93-13035. [see Vol. 54/01-B of Dissertation Abstracts Int'l, p478].
Note: Psy.D. dissertation.
"The problem under investigation in this study was the relationship between social interest and the length of time in AA. The subjects were 71 members of AA in Chicago and the Southern Suburbs and 28 members of the Rotary Club in Homewood, Illinois. It concluded that AA contains principles which can help to develop social interest.".

2481. Schaef, Anne Wilson. When a Society Hits Bottom: The American Culture as Addict.: Union for Experimenting Colleges-Univ. Without Walls and Union Grad. Sch.; 1986; 224pp. UMI AAD87-19626.
Note: Ph.D. dissertation.
Schaef's study postulates that American society is sick just as an individual addict is. It concludes that both the individual and the society can recover by a process of "naming," which is the admission of the functioning in the addictive process, by methods epitomized by AA and its Twelve Steps of Recovery, and by shifting to a spiritually-oriented system. (For futher information, see Psychology, Clinical, Page 4313 in Vol. 47/10-B of Dissertation Abstracts Int'l.).

2482. Schnall, Sandra Joy. An Interpersonal Approach to Alcoholism: The Transformation of Self Through Alcoholics Anonymous.: Univ. of Massachusetts; 1980.
Note: Ph.D. dissertation, 292 pages.
The author presents a theory of how the Self is bestowed, maintained and transformed through interpersonal experiences and focused on the transformation process. Twenty A.A. members were interviewed. "A significant finding is that a new spiritual Self can exist independently of and alongside the former alcoholic Self." (for more information, See Psychology, Clinical, Page 3197 in Vol. 41/08-B of Dissertation Abstracts Int'l.)(UMI OrderAAD81-01393).

2483. Schrenk, Linda. Psychotheraptists' Attitudes Toward Alcoholics and Their Treatment: Toward Development of a Treatment Model (AA, Alcoholics Anonymous).: California School of Professional Psychology, San Diego; 1986; 358pp.
Note: Ph.D. disseration.
This study investigated (1) psychotheraptists' attitudes toward alcoholics and alcoholism treatment; (2) the impact of alcoholism training on those attitudes; (3) the impact of an explanation of AA's 12 Steps to recovery in familiar psychological terms on attitudes toward AA. (for more information, See Psychology, Clinical, Page 389 in Vol. 47/01-B of Dissertation Abstracts Int'l.).

2484. Schrenzel, Jeff. Developmental Gains Associated with Long-Term Membership in Alcoholics Anonymous (Internalization): Smith College School for Social Work; 1990; 160pp. Order AAD90-23466. [see Voo. 51/05-A of Dissertation Abstracts Int'l, p1777].
Note: Ph.D. dissertation.
This study of 40 AA members, half with 6 mo. to one year sobriety and half with 4 to 7 years, found no evidence to support the thesis that long-term sobriety is internalized and psychic structure is thereby acquired.

2485. Scott, Kamakaokalani Penny. Social Interest Among Three Groups of Women (Life Task, Incarceration, Twelve-Step, Adlerian): The Union Institute; 1992; 100pp. Order AAD93-06020. [see Vol. 53/10-B of Dissertation Abstracts Int'l, p5462].
Note: Ph.D. dissertation.
Among the 100 in this sample, 47 were in AA, Al-Anon, and CoDependents Anonymous. Social interest, a fundamental concept in Adlerian psychology, was found to be significantly lower in women in twelve steps groups than the other two groups.

2486. Seiden, Richard H. An Experimental Test of the Assumption That Members of Alcoholics Anonymous Are Representative Alcoholics: Univ. of Denver; 1955.
Note: M.A. thesis.

2487. Sellner, Edward Cletus. The Event of Self-Revelation in the Reconciliation Process: A Pastoral Theological Comparison of A.A.'s Fifth Step and the Sacrament of Penance: Univ. of Notre Dame; 1981; 261pp. Order AAD81-09119. [a short version of this was published by Hazelden in 1981 as "Christian Ministry and the Fifth Step.".
Note: Ph.D. dissertation.
"This study is a pastoral theological comparison of two types of confessional encounters: Alcoholics Anonymous' Fifth Step and the Roman (Catholic) Church's sacrament of penance (i.e., the 1973 revised first rite)." The focus of this study is on the actual experiences of four alcoholics who took the Fifth Step and four Roman Catholic parishioners who participated in the revised rites of the sacrament. "Based on the dialogue between their life-stories and specific psychologists and theologians, conclusions are reached and pastoral proposals

made primarily concerned with the Church's ministry in the entire reconciliation process and the event of the first rite. What is ultimately advocated is the selection and training of gifted lay people as spiritual guides-confessors who would be recognized as valid ministers in parishes of the first rite itself." (an insightful study, see Theology, Page 4744 in Vol. 41/11-A of Dissertation Abstracts Int'l.).

2488. Silcott, Ernie June. The Correspondence between Alcoholics Anonymous and the Adaptive Capacities of Its Members.: Smith College School for Social Work; 1971.
Note: D.S.W. dissertation, 159pp.
(See Social Work, Page 5348 in Vol. 32/09-A of Dissertation Abstracts Int'l.)(UMI OrderAAD72-08406).

2489. Smith, Annette R. Alcoholics Anonymous: A Social World Perspective. First ed. San Diego, CA: Univ. of California, San Diego; 1991; 139pp.
Note: Ph.D. dissertation.
AA as a social world is the subject of study here. "Success in AA is dependent on integration into the social world," Smith postulates. And this integration leads to the "AA conversion, a transformation of self-identity in which the alcoholic accepts at the deepest level of being that he or she is an alcoholic and that recovery depends on the acceptance of AA values and practice of AA principles." She explores the social construction of group dependency in AA, the AA conversion, and the typology of AA members.

2490. Smith, Linda Mieth. A Qualitative Comparison of the Processes of Self-Actualization and Recovery (Alcoholics Anonymous): Univ. of Northern Colorado; 1992; 230pp. Order AAD92-35595. [see Vol. 53/07-B of Dissertation Abstracts Int'l, p3757].
Note: Psy.D. dissertation.
Three AA and three Al-Anon members with six months or less of participation, one to three, and five or more years shared their family backgrounds, addiction histories, and recoveries. "Results indicated the processes of recovery and self-actualization are related and the psychological growth in recovery can be explained from the perspective of self-actualization.".

2491. Sommer, Susan M. A Way of Life: Long-Term Recovery in Alcoholics Anonymous (Sobriety): Massachusetts School of Professional Psychology; 1992; 178pp. Order AAD91-36722. [see Vol. 53/07-B of Dissertation Abstracts Int'l, p3795].
Note: Psy.D. dissertation.
This study asked 12 recovering alcoholics in AA with four-through-seven years of sobriety what were the most important things they had learned in sobriety and how they solved problems in their lives today. They answered much work remains to be done in recovery from alcoholism and there is a difference between the quality of early, current and future sobriety.

2492. Stewart, Susan. The Rhetoric of Alcoholics Anonymous: Univ. of Pittsburgh; 1990; 317pp. Order AAD90-28452. [see Vol. 51/05-A of Dissertation Abstracts Int'l, p1443].
Note: Ph.D. dissertation.
"The central hypothesis of this study is that the process by which AA 'treats' the 'disease' of alcoholism is purely rhetorical, and can be understood, in the terms of Kenneth Burke, as a transformation of motives. AA 'treats' the meaning of alcoholism to the alcoholic rather than any specific disease-as-entity." Burke's work was based on AA books and hundreds of interviews and AA meetings. "The agency of recovery, AA, is always subordinate to the purpose; that is, the form of AA itself is derived from the spiritual principles which AA asserts are the core of recovery from alcoholism. The form of the oral rhetoric derives from the myth which serves as its representative anecdote. Members share their 'experience, strength, and hope,' that is, their own spiritual journeys, with other members as the chief way of carrying the message of recovery. Taken together, the oral and written rhetoric recommend that to recover the alcoholic must replace the attitudes and actions of hierarchic society with those based on community." [judging from the abstract, this is a "ten-strike." CB, Jr.].

2493. Swan, Margie Louise. Mediational Styles Associated with Differential Success of Affiliation with Alcoholics Anonymous: U.S. Int'l Univ.; 1990; 104pp. Order AAD90-26919. [see Vol. 51/07-B of Dissertation Abstracts Int'l, p3583].
Note: Ph.D. dissertation.
Four mediational styles were examined: Random and Concrete Abstract, and Abstract and Concrete Sequential. Sixty AA members [30 each in successful and unsuccessful affiliation groups] in Irvine, Glendale and Van Nuys, Calfornia, were studied. [apparently a spelling or typographical error: "meditational" instead of "mediational"].

2494. Talan, Beverly Steinman. Power and Control: Predictors for the Alcoholic Woman's Choice and Effectiveness of Treatment: Univ. of Detroit; 1981; 138pp. UMI AAD82-15996.
Note: Ph.D. dissertation.
This study of 115 subjects from Alcoholics Anonymous and Women for Sobriety investigated internal and external LOC on reaction to treatment, length of treatment, and treatment outcome. (see Psychology, Clinical, Page 1630 in Vol. 43/05-B in Dissertation Abstracts Int'l.).

2495. Taylor, Mary Catherine. Alcoholics Anonymous: How It Works. Recovery Processes in a Self-Help Group.: Univ. of California, San Francisco.; 1977.
Note: Ph.D. dissertation, 213pp.
(See Sociology, General, Page 7532 in Vol. 39/12-A of Dissertation Abstracts Int'l.)(UMI No.AAD79-13241.).

2496. Thiele, William Edward, Jr. A Critical Analysis of the Relationship Between the Spiritual Attitudes Implicit in Representative Writings on Contemplative Spirituality and Those Found in the A.A. Twelve Steps: New Orleans Baptist Theological Seminary; 1992; 203pp. Order AAD-93-11814. [see Vol. 53/12-A of Dissertations Abstracts Int'l, p4267.].
Note: Ph.D. dissertation.
Thiele suveys contemplative spiritual attitudes of communion, awareness, willingness, honesty, humility, simplicity, and dependence as evidenced in metaphors of the divine-human relationship. He repeats the process for spiritual attitudes in AA's Twelve Steps including spirutual awakening, awareness, contact, willingness, honesty, confession, humility and dependence. He compares the two and includes a synthesis with applications for addiction recovery and spiritual growth.

2497. Trevino, Alberto Javier. The Feminine Ethic of Alcoholics Anonymous: A Study in the Sociology of Organizations: Boston College; 1990; 283pp. Order AAD91-01699. [see Vol. 51/08-A of Dissertation Abstracts Int'l, p2881].
Note: Ph.D. dissertation.
Trevino's central thesis is that AA, as an organization, is consonant with women's ways of knowing and doing and women find social satisfaction in AA because its organizational structure makes it conducive and accesible to them. The "AA feminine ethic" is revealed in interviews with 12 women AA members.

2498. Trice, Harrison Miller. A Study of the Process of Affiliation with Alcoholics Anonymous.: Univ. of Wisconsin at Madison.; 1955.
Note: Ph.D. dissertation, 252 pages.
(See Sociology, Public and Social Welfare, Page 594 in Vol. 16/03 of Dissertation Abstracts Int'l.) (OrderAAD-00-14782).

2499. Volk, Roger Malcolm. A Comparison of Selected Values of Social Work with Alcoholics Anonymous: Virginia Commonwealth Univ.; 1989; 197pp. Order AAD90-01907. [see Vol. 50/08-A of Dissertation Abstracts Int'l, p2653].
Note: Ph.D. dissertation.
Two central social work values of self-determination and self-realization are not espoused by AA literature nor by AA members surveyed here, this study of 278 members of the Va. Chap. of the Nat'l Assn. of Social Workers and of 182 AA members in the Norfolk, VA, area, concluded.

2500. Vourakis, Christine Helen. The Process of Recovery for Women in Alcoholics Anonymous: Seeking Groups "Like Me": Univ. of California at San Francisco; 1989; 252pp. Order AAD89-17924. [see Vol. 50/08-B of Dissertation Abstracts Int'l, p3393].
Note: D.N.S. dissertation.
The preferences of 31 female AA members with at least 1.5 years of sobriety for all-women's versus mixed-sex AA groups were studied. The main conclusion was that women seeks AA groups "like me.".

2501. Webber, Peter Howard. <u>The Meaning of "Spiritual" in Contemporary Counseling: A Study Based on the Work of Martin Buber and the Twelve Steps of Alcoholics Anonymous</u>: Univ. of Montana; 1990; 107pp. Order AAD90-29106. [see Vol. 51-06-A of Dissertation Abstracts Int'l, p1913].
Note: ED.D. dissertation.
"This study examines the writings and thought of Martin Buber in order to arrive at an understanding of `spiritual' recovery. Buber's <u>I and Thou</u> and his investigation of the Hasidim are key works here. The Twelve Steps of AA encourage a building of authentic relationships by gently preparing the individual at each step for an increase in the quality of relationship, first with an idea, then a person, then with the Higher Power, before starting the cycle over with an encounter with the unrecovered self in `the alcoholic who still suffers.' It is precisely this `coming into relationship' that would seem to constitute the essence of the `spiritual' as it applies to counseling. This stands in contrast to views of the spiritual as being either an amorphous or a deeply egotistical experience.".

2502. White, Byron E. <u>An Alcoholism Study Testing: Drinking Behavior, Social Adjustment and Alcoholics Anonymous Effectiveness</u>: The Fielding Institute; 1983; 119pp. Order AAD89-02401. [see Vol. 50/02-A of Dissertation Abstracts Int'l, p739].
Note: Ph.D. dissertation.
Testing the effectiveness of AA and of abstinence, forty-two clients were surveyed at four 3-month intervals after treatment. "This study's findings do not support the popular image of AA's effectiveness. However, the one-year time period of this study may be a limitation materially affecting the study's results.".

2503. White, Stephen Thomas. <u>The Disease Concept of Alcoholism: Correlates of Alcoholics Anonymous Membership (Substance Abuse)</u>: University of Maine; 1991; 194pp. Order AAD92-18016. [see Vol.53/04-A of Dissertation Abstracts Int'l, p1063].
Note: Ed.D. dissertation.
White says "considerable data" exists which demonstates the "relative ineffectiveness" of the "disease concept of alcoholism." A "Social Learning Model" is an alternative and assumes "effective treatment with substance abusers is attainable only if individuals attribute responsibility for their successes to themselves." Of 400 distributed surveys, 158 were completed and returned by AA members who were mostly single, older males and one-time rehabilitation facility patients. Eighty per cent ascribed to the disease concept of alcoholism. White concluded the "more involved AA members tended to have an external locus-of-control with lower self-efficacy, self-esteem, and social satisfaction than those who were less-involved in AA.".

2504. Wilkerson, Albert Ernest, Jr. A History of the Concept of Alcoholism as a Disease: Univ. of Pennsylvania; 1966; 330pp. UMI Order AAD67-00188.
Note: Doctorate in Social Work dissertation.
Wilkerson traces the historical development of the concept of alcoholism as a disease from the Physicians' Temperance Movement in the late 1790s to modern conceptions such as A.A. Chapter 6 contains material about A.A. His bibliography on the subject totals 17 pages.

2505. Williams, Florence. Psychological, Demographic and Supportive System Variables Associated with Recovery of Hospitalized Alcoholics: U.S. Int'l Univ.; 1978; 104pp. AAD85-08428.
Note: Ph.D. dissertation.
This study tried to determine factors which might forecast successful abstinence for patients one year after discharge from a hosptial alcoholism treatment format. Attendance at the weekly hospital 10-week follow-up program, affiliation with AA, the level of AA's 12 Steps completed, and affiliation with an AA sponsor - all were significant predicators of success or failure. The findings imply treatment should focus on helping the patient engage in AA meetings, the Steps and finding an AA sponsor. (for more information, See Psychology, Clinical, Page 668 in Vol. 46/02-B of Dissertation Abstracts Int'l.).

2506. Williams, Lola Janet. A Comparative Study of Self-Actualization of Female Alcoholics in Alcoholics Anonymous.: U.S. Int'l Univ.; 1980.
Note: Ph. D. dissertation, 122pp.
(See Psychology, General, Page 337 in Vol. 41/01-B of Dissertation Abstracts Int'l.)(UMI No.AAD80-16283.).

2507. Wilson, Larry Creighton. Personal and Social Functioning Levels of Recovering Alcoholics: A Cross-Sectional Analysis: Univ. of Nebraska-Lincoln; 1986; 120pp. UMI AAD86-29541.
Note: Ph.D. dissertation.
This study tried to determine if persons with more education and longer periods of sobriety are better adjusted personally and socially than persons with less education and short-term sobriety. Three hundred AA members across the state of Nebraska participated in the study which concluded in part that only minimal support for the hypothesis that people with higher levels of education are better adjusted socially. (For a more detailed abstract, see Page 3884 in Vol. 47/10-A of Dissertation Abstracts Int'l.).

2508. Wolcott, Nancy Dunn. Alchemy and Alcoholism Based on the Psychology of C. G. Jung: The Stages of Alchemy and the Steps of Alcoholics Anonymous As a Therapeutic Model.: The Union for Experimenting Colleges & Universities; 1978.
Note: Ph.D. dissertation, 375pp.
(See Psychology, General, Page 6105 in Vol. 39/12-B of Dissertation Abstracts Int'l.)(UMI AAD79-09902).

2509. Wood, Paul. The Selection of Members of Alcoholics Anonymous: Kent State Univ., Ohio; 1969.
Note: M.A. thesis.

2510. Wootton, Paul Richard. A Study of the Minnesota Multiphasic Personality Inventory Profiles of Alcoholics Anonymous Members: Univ. of Southern California; 1990; ? Order from: Micrographics Dept., Doheny Library, Univ. SC, Los Angeles, CA 90089-0182.
Note: Ph.D. dissertation.
"This study was concerned with the relationship between the personality characteristics, as measured by the MMPI, of a sample of 93 AA members with at least one year of sobriety from four AA meetings in Los Angeles, and the aspect of the AA 'treatment' [quotes supplied] program they reported as most helpful." The study concluded the sample AA's are different from inpatient alcoholics who are not AA members.

2511. Zismer, Daniel Kevin. A Value-Expectancy Explanation of the Psychological Conversion in Alcohol Treatment.: Univ. of Minnesota; 1982; 172pp.
Note: Ph.D. dissertation.
This study sought to apply and test a version of Rotters' Social Learning Theory to measure and explain the psychological conversion process in adult alcohol rehabilitation programs using an Alcoholics Anonymous philosophy of treatment. (for more information, See Psychology, Clinical, Page 335 in Vol. 44/01-B of Dissertation Abstracts Int'l.).

Chapter X = Foreign Publications

2512. 12th World Service Meeting 1992 Final Report. New York: AAWS; April, 1993.
Note: CONFIDENTIAL: for AA members only since it contains full names of AA's in service. 8.5 x 11".
This 56-page booklet on the 12th WSM held in New York City, Oct. 25-29,1992, includes chapters on individual country reports, finances, the Twelve Concepts for World Service and past and future visions of the WSMs. With the theme, "Service - Everyone's Privilege," much of the conference focused on the Twelve Concepts for World Service, their spirituality, development from Tradition Two, Workshop report-backs and a WSM evaluation questionnaire. Thirty-nine delegates from 25 countries attended this conference.

2513. "29th National Convention of Alcoholics Anonymous Australia". Gold Coast, Queensland, Australia: A.A. Australia; April 8-12, 1993.
This 16-page program contains the preamble, Steps, Traditions, Concepts, Serenity Prayer and events. A brief history notes the first correspondence from Australia to GSO, NY, was in 1942; and the first national A.A. Convention was held in Melbourne, Victoria, in 1959.

2514. AA in El Salvador; 1988-1993.
Note: Address is AA in El Salvador, 29 Calle Pte. No. 517, Apartado Posal (06) 132, San Salvador, El Salvador, Central America, and the subscription rate is $15. per year.
This quarterly GV format magazine, usually 40 pages, is written in Spanish and includes the usual mix of local and GV reprints.

2515. AA-Informationen; Jan. 1963 to 1993; (monthly).
Note: Address is AA-Informationen, Postfach 45-02-07, 8000 Munchen 46, Germany, and subscription rate is 3,500 German Marks per year.
This monthly 18-page journal published by AA in Munich, Germany, contains the Steps, Traditions, and the full range of stories, news, and articles on AA recovery, unity, and service. Victor E. cartoons and fine photos of historic German scenes enhance its 8.5 x 11.5" attractive format.

2516. Akron-1935; 1971-1993; 130.
Note: Address is Akron-135, Aparatado 170, 33400 Aviles, Asturias, Espana, and the subscription rate is $15. a per for 6 issues and the newsletter.
Published since Jan., 1971, and written in Spanish, this magazine is bi-monthly and usually 36 pages long. Also mailed with each issue is the newsletter "Compartiendo." It contains the usual mix of local stories, cartoons, Victor E., GV reprints, etc.

2517. Alcoholic.
Note: Address is Moscow Intergroup Office, P. O. Box 33, Russia 129128 Moscow, Commonwealth of Independent States. Written in Russian.

2518. "Alcoholicos Anominos". El Nuevo Mexicano; March 9, 1944.

2519. Alcoholics Anonymous. Dutch Big Book. First ed. Belguim: Nederlandstalige AA in Belgie; 1965; 177pp.
Note: dj.
"Anonieme Alkoholisten" is the Dutch translation of the Big Book with the first 164 pages of the basic text of A.A. and Dr. Bob's Story and A.A. Number Three, plus two other chapters.

2520. Alcoholics Anonymous. Icelandic Big Book. First ed. Reykjavik, Iceland; 1976; 289pp.
Note: dj. This translation was in its fourth printing in 1988.
This Icelandic translation of the Big Book includes the first 164 pages of the basic text of A.A., Dr. Bob's and other stories, and the Twelve Traditions. The book has a bright red dust jacket with the letters "AA" in white and black.

2521. Alcoholics Anonymous. Portuguese Big Book. First ed. Sao Paulo, SP - Brazil; 1976; 183pp; ISBN: LC 55-14751.
Note: pb.
"Alcoolicos Anonimos" is the Portuguese translation of the Big Book and includes the first 164 pages of the basic text of A.A., Dr. Bob's Story, and the 6 appendixes.

2522. "Alcoholics Anonymous & the Social Worker". Melbourne, Australia; March 25, 1976; 69pp.
Note: NACI 806.
The role Alcoholics Anonymous can play in rehabilitation and how social workers can cooperate with A.A. is discussed.

2523. Alcoholics Anonymous. Afrikaans Big Book. First Afrikaans ed. South Africa; 1980; 352pp; ISBN: 0-620-05245-7.
Note: dj.
"Alkoholiste Anoniem" is the Afrikaans translation of the Big Book with 14 stories and the appendixes.

2524. Alcoholics Anonymous. Italian Big Book. First ed. Rome, Italy: Alcolisti Anonimi; 1980; 310pp.
Note: pb. The Italian translation was in its fourth printing in 1988.
"Alcolisti Anonimi" includes the first 164 pages of the basic text of A.A., Dr. Bob's Story and 14 other stories, The Twelve Traditions, the Spiritual Experience, and other appendixes.

2525. Alcoholics Anonymous. Finnish Big Book. First ed. Helsinki, Finland: Suomen AA-Kustannus R. Y.; 1981; 574pp; ISBN: 951-9015-62-0.
Note: dj.
The first Finnish translation of the third editon of the Big Book.

2526. Alcoholics Anonymous. Norwegian Big Book. First ed. Oslo, Norway; 1981; 354pp; ISBN: 82-990885-1-8.
Note: dj.
"Anonyme Alkoholikere," the Norwegian translation of the Big Book, contains the first 164 pages of the basic text of A.A., Dr. Bob's Story, stories from all three editions, and the 6 appendixes.

2527. Alcoholics Anonymous. German Big Book. First German ed. Munich, Germany: Anonyme Alkoholiker deutscher Sprache; 1983; 434pp.
Note: dj.
"Anonyme Alkoholiker" is the German translation of the Big Book with the first 164 pages of the basic text of A.A., Dr. Bob's Story, and A.A. Number Three along with 23 personal stories of German members of A.A. who have recovered and the original appendixes.

2528. Alcoholics Anonymous. Netherlands Big Book. First ed. Amsterdam, Netherlands: Stichting Werkgroepen A.A. Nederland, Hameland Pers; 1983; 350pp; ISBN: 90-7981-220-7.
Note: dj.
This translations contains the first 164 pages of the basic text of A.A., the Big Book, Dr. Bob's and other stories, and eight appendixes.

2529. Alcoholics Anonymous. Spanish Big Book. First ed.; 1986; 174pp.
Note: pb. The Spanish translation is also available in hardback [$5].
"Alcoholicos Anonimos," the Spanish translation of the Big Book, includes the first 164 pages of the basic text of A.A., Dr. Bob's Story, and the 6 appendixes.

2530. Alcoholics Anonymous. Korean Big Book. First ed.; 1986; 286pp; ISBN: Korean 0-916856-00-3.
Note: dj.
This Korean translation of the Big Book was approved and permission grated to Korean National Intergroup, July 28, 1985. The text includes the first 164 pages of the Big Book, Dr. Bob and other stories, and appendixes.

2531. Alcoholics Anonymous. Australian Big Book. First Australian ed. Beaconsfield, New South Wales, Australia: General Service Board of A.A. Australia by permission of AAWS.; 1986; 575pp; ISBN: 0-916856-00-3.
Note: dj.
This first Australian edition of the Big Book is a reprint of the third edition, 21st printing. In 1991, the book was in its fourth printing.

2532. Alcoholics Anonymous. Swedish Big Book. First Swedish ed. Finland: AA-FORLAGET, Stockholm, Sweden; 1988 [?]; 258pp; ISBN: 91-970935-0-5.
Note: dj.
This Swedish translation of the Big Book includes the first 164 pages of the basic text of A.A., Dr. Bob's and AA No. 3's Stories, and the Twelve Traditions.

2533. Alcoholics Anonymous. French Big Book. First French ed. Montreal, Canada: AA du Quebec; 1989; 347pp; ISBN: 2-920203-077-X.
Note: dj.
"Les Alcooliques Anonymes" is the French translation of the third edition of the Big Book.

2534. Alcoholics Anonymous. Polish Big Book. First Polish ed. Wroclaw, Poland; 1989; 163pp.
Note: pb.
The Polish translation of the Big Book includes the basic text of AA with Dr. Bob's Story and 18 pages of groups in Poland listed in the back.

2535. Alcoholics Anonymous. Czech Big Book. First Czech ed.; 1989; 186pp.
Note: pb.
The Czech translation of the Big Book includes the first 164 pages of the basic text of A.A.

2536. Alcoholics Anonymous. Russian Big Book. First ed. [printed in the Federal Republic of Germany]; 1989; 184pp; ISBN: 0-916856-25-9.
Note: pb.
This Russian translation includes the first 164 pages of the Big Book, the Twelve Traditions and the Twelve Concepts.

2537. Alcoholics Anonymous. Arabic Big Book. First Arabic ed.: AAWS; 1990; 128pp; ISBN: 0-916856-34-8.
Note: pb. A second printing was done in 1992.

2538. Alcoholics Anonymous. Hungarian Big Book. First Hungarian ed.; 1990; 146pp.
Note: pb.
The Hungarian translation of the Big Book includes the first 164 pages of the basic text of A.A. and Dr. Bob's Story.

2539. Alcoholics Anonymous. Vietnamese Big Book. First Vietnamese ed.; 1991; 240pp; ISBN: 0-916856-44-5.
Note: pb.
The first Vietnamese translation of the Big Book includes the first 164 pages of the basic text of A.A., Dr. Bob's Story, and the appendixes.

2540. Alcoholics Anonymous. Turkish Big Book. First Turkish ed. New York: AAWS; 1991; 162pp; ISBN: 0-916816-364.
Note: pb. A second printing came out in 1992.
The Turkish translation of the Big Book includes the basic text of A.A., Dr. Bob's Story, and appendixes from the Big Book.

2541. Alcoholics Anonymous. Swahili Big Book. First Swahili ed. New York: AAWS; 1993; 590pp; ISBN: 0-916856-47-X.
Note: pb.
The Swahili translation of the Big Book is the Third Edition, containing all the stories selected from the first, second, and third editions.

2542. Alcoholics Anonymous. Chinese Big Book; 1994.

2543. Alcoholics Anonymous. Persian Big Book; 1994.

2544. Alcoholics Anonymous. Thai Big Book; 1994.

2545. Alcoholics Anonymous. Japanese Big Book; 566pp.
Note: dj.

2546. Alcoholics Anonymous. Danish Big Book.

2547. Alcoholics Anonymous. Lithuanian Big Book.

2548. Alcoholics Anonymous. Flemish Big Book.

2549. "Alcoholism in the United States". La Revue de L'Alcoolisme; 1975; 21(1): pp xiii-xv.
Note: NACLI record no. 4603.
In addition to a broad overview of the alcoholism problem in the U.S., basic information on Alcoholics Anonymous is provided.

2550. Antenna; 1991-1992.
This quarterly, written in English, was the National Magazine of A.A. Australia. The spring, 1991, issue was 40 pages. It replaced The Reviver, a suspended publication. It included local stories and GV reprints. December 1992 was the last issue due to lack of support.

2551. "[articles]". in: Newsletter. Lausanne, Switzerland; Oct. 31, 1981: 8pp.
Note: NACI 142.
This newsletter contains a report on the activities of the European organizations of A.A., Al-Anon, and Alateen.

2552. Avesani, O. "Alcoholics Anonymous: An Analysis". Lav. Neuropsichiat.; 1978; 62(1-2): pp133-39.
"Gli Anonymous Alcoholics: Nota Critica" [Italian].

2553. Bircher, Ralph, M.D. "A.A.' - Alcoholics Anonymous or the Alliance of 'nameless drinkers". Wendepunkt, Zurich; 1946; 23: pp214-220.
Note: QJSA abstract no. 4791.
This is a early description of AA in a journal in Switzerland. It cites the Big Book. "A physician who recently became acquainted with an A.A. group in America is astonished at their sincerity and insight. 50% are claimed to be cured immediately; another 25% after a few relapses. A.A. has only 1 aim: to help alcoholics. Only the 'former' drinker can help the alcoholic. Parallelism between psychiatric and religious teaching is stressed. The difference is that the psychiatrist teaches the alcoholic to rely on himself, the religious leader to rely on God. The new A.A. member is left free to choose between these two ways. Experience has shown that those who choose the 2nd are almost invariably helped, while those who do not freely follow the 12 steps usually relapse. The 12 Steps are cited. Many who do not wish to follow the steps nevertheless eventually revert to them unconsciously, for they experience an inner change after being with the group. Many A.A.'s cannot follow the church, but have developed a personal God who helps them. They experience true conversions. The founders of A.A. learned through experience that psychiatry and religion meet in their field.".

2554. Blackburn, Raymond. I Am An Alcoholic. London: Allan Wingate; 1959; 218pp.
Brief mention of A.A., confusion of cure, mentions Antabuse, personal story of drinking.

2555. Boks 205; 1992-93.
Note: To receive 12 monthly issues wire $54. to The Den Norske Bank in Oslo, Account 5033.05-12587. Address of the magazine is Postboks 205 Sentrum, 0 103 Oslo 1, Norway.
Written in Norwegian in the standard GV format, it is 16 pages and includes stories of experience by local AA's and intergroup news.

2556. Box 334; 1993.
Note: Address is Box 334, Postboks 334, DK-1503 Kobenhavn, Denmark, and the subscription rate is $27. per year.
Published 6 times a year in Danish, the traditional GV format is usually 30 pages with a mix of local stories and U.S. GV reprints.

2557. Box 916; 1992-93.
Note: Address is Box 916, % Tachibana Bldg., 9th floor, 2-23-3 Ikebukuro Toshima-Ku, Tokyo 171, Japan, and the subscription rate is $36 a year for 12 issues.
Written in Japanese, Box 916 follows the standard GV format with local stories, GV reprints, maps to meeting places and phones, etc.

2558. Bristol Fashion; 1967-May, 1993; (1-298).
Note: 8.5 x 11".
This monthly journal "for alcoholics, their families and friends," is published in Clifton, Bristol, England, usually 4 pages per issue. The masthead slogan is "Alcoholics Anonymous has never been tried and found wanting - it has been found difficult and left untried." Contents include AA anniversaries [anonymity protected], news events about the Fellowship, and articles, stories, and humor about AA recovery. It was founded by the late Travers C.

2559. British Journal of Addiction.
Note: [many citations from this journal and other foreign journals may be found in the "Journals" chapter].

2560. Bullentinen AA; 1993.
Note: Address is Bullentinen AA, Box 16387, 103 27 Stockholm, Sweden, and the subscription rate is $40. per year.
Published bi-monthly in Swedish, it is usually 28 to 40 pages with all articles written by local AA's in Sweden. An annual meeting directory is mailed to subscribers.

2561. Ceruti, C. "Recovery of the Alcoholic". in: Minerva Medica; 1982; 73(21): pp1463-68.
Note: [Italian journal] NCAI 8114.
The Steps, tenets, and beliefs of Alcoholics Anonymous are reviewed and guidelines for successful involvement in the program are presented.

2562. Charles, Vernon. Goodbye to Bacchus: An Alcoholic Actor's Escape from Hell. Arthur James Limited: Eversham, England; 1953; 186pp.
"The book is a narration of both success and failure dealing with alcoholism as a disease by an actor, who, with the aid of Alcoholics Anonymous, accepted the challenge of alcohol and won," the dust jacket states.

2563. Compartimiento; 1992-93.
Note: Address is Compartimiento, 11 Avenida "A" 7-62 Zona 2, Apartado Postal 1736, Guatemala, Guatemala, Central America.
Written in Spanish, it follows the standard GV format.

2564. De Boei; 1993; 36.
Note: Address is De Boei, Donauweg 4 Postbus 1594, Amsterdam 1000-BN, Netherlands.
Published bi-monthly in Dutch, this journal includes AA, Al-Anon, and Alateen in 32 pages, all written by local Fellowship members. It follows the pocket-size GV format and prints the Steps, Traditions, cartoons, and other standard GV features.

2565. Devoto, A./Giannoni, G. "A Contribution to the Meaning of Alcoholics Anonymous". Alcoholism, Zagreb; 1977; 13: pp114-7.
"Contributo Alla Interpretazione Degli Alcoolisti Anonimi" [Italian].

2566. Dimension; 1992-93.
Note: Address is Dimension, Independenica No. 101 Desp. 14, Apartado Postal 546, C. P. 06000 Mexico, D. F.
Written in Spanish.

2567. El Mensaje; 1972-1993.
Note: Address is El Mensaje, Apartado Aereo 3070, Medellin, Columbia, South America, and the subscription rate is $4. US per issue or 10 issues for $36. US Funds. Mailed in unmarked brown paper bound in waxed red string.
Founded in Dec., 1972, this quarterly GV is usually 36 pages in Spanish. It follows the U.S. GV format with stories by Columbia AA's.

2568. "European Service Meetings": GSO of Argentina; May, 1993.
This ten-page paper gives the history of the European Service Meetings from the first in 1981 in Frankfurt, Germany, to the sixth in 1991, also in Frankfurt. Delegates from A.A.'s general service conferences in European countries attend and share their service experience in order to better carry the message of AA in Europe.

2569. Fosdick, Harry Emerson. "Alcoholics Anonymous: Book Review". La Nueva Democracia; April, 1940.
Spanish magazine.

2570. Gallimberti, L./Orlandini, D./Cibin, M./Ricci, G. P. "Experiences in Collaboration Between an Alcoholism Service and an Alcoholics Anonymous Group". in: Bollettino Farmacodipendenze e Alcoolismo; 1981; 4(4-6): pp616-624.
Note: NACI 8326.
In a cooperative rehabilitation effort, patients at the Venice, Italy, Alcoholism Service are transported to local A.A. meetings.

2571. Gemeinsam; August, 1992, to 1993.
Note: Address is Gemeinsam, Stenbergstrasse 9, 8052 Graz, Austria, and the subscription rate is 3,500 German Marks per year.
Published 6 times a year in German, the mimeographed format is 8 x 11.75" and usually 20 to 24 pages. It includes artwork, photos, literature lists of both AA and Al-Anon and news.

2572. Halmstraid; 1986-1993.
Note: Address is Halmstraid, Tjarnargata 20, 101 Reykjavik, Iceland, and the subscription rate is 1200 Icelandic Kroners per year.
This standard GV format magazine is published 4 times a year in Icelandic. The title translates to "the last straw." A slick front cover photo and the standard mix of local and GV reprints are included.

2573. "Ibero-American Service Meetings". New York: GSO of Argentina; May, 1993.
This 12-page paper traces the history of Latin American Service Meetings from the first in 1979 in Bogota, Colombia, to the most recent seventh in 1991 in Buenos Aires, Argentina. Delegates from many Latin American countries attend these biannual sessions to share their service experiences particular to their countries and cooperate in carrying the message.

2574. Insieme in AA; 1982-1993.
Note: Address is Insieme in AA, Via Di Torre Rossa, Scala B Int. 18, 00165 Roma, Italy, and five sample issues cost $5.
Started in Jan., 1982, this standard GV format magazine is published 6 times a year in color and in Italian. All the stories are by Italian AA's and it's usually 48 pages.

2575. Irgendwo AA; 1992-1993; (monthly).
Note: Address is Irgendwo AA, Postfach 150, ch-4018 Basel, Switzerland, and the subscription rate is 40 Swiss Francs or about $40. U.S. Funds per year.
This German Fellowship magazine prints the Steps, Traditions, and Responsibility Creed in each 24-page monthly issue along with stories of AA recovery, news, and articles on the full range of Fellowship topics.

2576. Jilek-Aall, L. "Acculturation, Alcoholism and Indian-style Alcoholics Anonymous". in: Journal of Studies on Alcohol; 1981; Supplement(9): pp143-158.
Note: NCAI 8267.
"The roles of Alcoholics Anonymous and church organizations in helping Coast Salish Indians with alcohol problems are described; emphasis is on how, based on the Indians' own initiative, the incorporation of Indian culture into AA has helped develop a successful anti-alcoholism program. It is contended that only when the Indian people can regain their cultural identity and self-respect will they have the inner strength necessary to fight alcoholism." The author is with the Univ. of British Columbia, Dept. of Psychiatry, Vancouver, Canada.

2577. Johnson, N. "Sobriety Clubs a Japanese Version of Self-Help for Alcoholics". Alcohol Health & Research World; 1982; 6(4): p29.
Note: NACLI record no. 2383.
"The development and activities of self-help groups or `sobriety clubs' in Japan are described, specifically, the All Nisson Sobriety Assn. [ANSA]." AA is mentioned.

2578. Kulisiewicz, T. "Aims and Prospects of the AA Movement in Poland". Probl. Alkzmu, Warsaw; 1978; 25(8-9): pp19-20.
"Cele I Perspektwy Ruchu AA W Polsce" [Polish].

2579. Lehmann, A. "Information Week: Publicity with the Help of Addiction Patients". in: Suchtsefahren; 1981; 27(4): pp230-233.
Note: NCAI 239.
Alcoholics Anonymous participated, with three other organizations, in the "Drug Information Week" in Bensheine, West Germany.

2580. Living Sober. Polish translation: AAWS; 1986.
Note: 170pp. pb.
[see American edition for abstract].

2581. Mainstay; 1951-93; 1-42.
Note: Address is Mainstay, P. O. Box 6458, Wellington, New Zealand, and the subscription rate is $30. New Zealand dollars per year.
This English language monthly magazine of the New Zealand General Service Conference of Alcoholics Anonymous is usually 24 pages and contains Grapevine reprints, AA stories of recovery, news, humor, cartoons, and the full range of topics about AA recovery, service and unity. It is published in Wellington, New Zealand. The Steps, Traditions, and Preamble are printed in each issue. A "News & Views" section publishes information items about books and other material which may be "contrary to AA philosophy.".

2582. Makela, K. "Way-of-Life Perspective and Research on Treatment". in: Alkoholipolitiikka; 1983; 48(5): pp250-255.
Note: NACI 11534 [Finnish journal].
Similarities between cognitive behavioral therapy and Alcoholics Anonymous are discussed. Cognitive behavioral therapy, like AA, is "only mildly interested in the causes of drunkenness and only advises the alcoholic on ways to stay sober," the article states.

2583. Meeting; 1992-93.
Note: Address is Meeting, 1399 Budapest, Postafiok 701-439, Hungary.
Written in Hungarian, it follows the standard GV format.

2584. Opracowal, Wybral I. Jestem Alkoholikiem: SWIADECTWA AA. W Drodze: Poznan; 1986.
A book of stories written by Polish alcoholics who have recovered through AA. The text is in Polish.

2585. Partage; 1977-1993.
Note: Address is Partage, 11 Rue Du Boulet, B-1000 Brussels, Belguim and the subscription rate is $20. a year.
The standard GV 48-page pocket size format magazine is published 6 times a year in French. Local French AA's articles are used along with GV reprints and sections called "My Experience," "Point of View," "A.A. Around the World," and a crossword puzzle.

2586. Pat. I Walk No More in Darkness. First & Second ed. 27 Upper Sherrard St., Dublin 1, Ireland: Pioneer Magazine, Pioneer Total Abstinence Assn. of the Sacred Heart.; April, June, July-August, & September, 1969; (4 issues).
Note: This was reprinted by Alcohol Affairs, Inc., Baton Rouge, LA, USA, in 1977 (?) in a 36 page booklet.
Pat was an A.A. member and Pioneer Total Abstinence Assn. member. He tells his story of alcoholism and recovery in A.A. As of 1976, he had 39 years sober.

2587. Poikolainen, K. "Alcoholism: A Social Construct". in: Journal of Drug Issues; 1982; 12(4): pp361-367.
Note: NACI 4049.
This Finnish university author discusses the development of the disease concept and model of alcoholism, including Alcoholics Anonymous andacceptance of that approach.

2588. Puente, Silva, F.G. "Center of Assistance for the Alcoholic and His Family: Sociodemographic aspects and profiles of the client population". in: Salud Mental; 1982; 5(2): pp60-65.
Note: NACI 13777 [Spanish article].
Religion, the family, and Alcoholics Anonymous fulfilled essential functions in the therapy and rehabilitation of the alcoholic patient, this study found.

2589. Pumpkinvine; 1993.
Note: Address is Pumkinvine, Basdeo House, 81-82 Main Road, Trinidad, West Indies.
Published in English.

2590. Rajmund. "Meaning of the AA Program's 12 Steps". Probl. Alkzmu, Warsaw; 1977; 24(3): pp17-19.
"Jak Rozumiem--I Co Mi Daje 12 Stopni AA" [Polish].

2591. Regmaker. The Journal of AA in South Africa; 1966-93; 1-28; ISSN: 0034-3471.
Note: Address is The Regmaker, P. O. Box 23005, Joubert Park 2044, Johannesburg, South Africa, and the subscription rate is 12 Rand or $5. in U.S. Funds.
The Regmaker is the Journal of Alcoholics Anonymous in South Africa. Published monthly since July, 1966, it is published by the General Service Committee, Johannesburg, and is usually 32 pages. The Steps, Traditions, and Preamble are in each issue along with a quote on the back cover from "AA Archie." It contains Grapevine reprints, stories of AA recovery, news, humor, and articles on the full range of AA topics of recovery, unity, and service. Written in English. "Regmaker" means "right maker," which is a term for the first drink of the day to "make it right.".

2592. the Reviver; 1942-91; 1-41(12 issues annually).
Note: Address is The Reviver, P. O. Box 56, Croydon NSW 2132, Australia.
The Reviver was the New South Wales, Australia, version of the Grapevine. Published for almost 40 years in monthly issues, it usually ran 32 to 48 pages and contained stories of AA recovery, service articles, AA literature and tapes order forms, directory of AA meetings, humor, and other AA news. The Steps, Traditions, Preamble, AA Declaration, and Serenity Prayer were printed in each issue. Grapevine articles were reprinted. It was published by Alcoholics Anonymous Central Service Office, Croydon, NSW, Australia.

2593. Rienhoff, O. "The Composition of Alcoholics Anonymous in the Federal Republic of Germany". Dtsch. Med. Wschr.; 1979; 104: pp81-84.
"Die Zusammensetzung Der Anonymen Alkoholiker in Der Bunderrepublik Deutschland" [German]. A questionnaire survey of 1,190 members [most of them weekly attenders] of A.A. in the German Federal Republic showed the membership increases by about 30% yearly and will probably reach 23,000 in 1980 [there are 1.2 to 1.8 million alcoholics in the GFR]. The median age was 40 [mean, 41]; 34% were women.

2594. The Road Back; 1949-1993.
Note: Address is The Road Back, A.A. G.S.O., 109 South Circular Road, Dublin 8, Ireland, and the subscription rate is $10. per year foreign rate.
First published in April, 1949, (300 copies), this bi-monthly is usually 20 pages in English with local articles and GV reprints.

2595. Robinson, David. Talking Out of Alcoholism: The self-help process of Alcoholics Anonymous. London: Croom Helm Ltd.; 1979.
This book deals with the history, growth, organization and finance of A.A. and with questions about affiliation, membership and meetings. Robinson, sociologist from the University of London, writes of the self-help process of A.A., through which members come together, share their experience, cope with their problem and through involvement in the Fellowship, build new relationships, find new friends, and help each other to talk themselves out of their alcoholism.

2596. The Roundabout; 1985-1993.
Note: Address is The Roundabout, Baltic Chambers, 50 Wellington Street, Glasgow G2 6HJ, Scotland, and the subscription rate is $35. a year for 12 monthly issues mailed to the U.S.
Written in English, this monthly publication is usually 24 pages in the standard pocket size GV format. All articles are by AA's in Scotland, but it reprints articles from all AA literature, books, and the U.S. GV.

2597. Ruch AA-Zdroj; 1985-1993.
Note: Address is Ruch AA-Zdroj, Sekretariat Witold Kosiacki AA, Ul. Maleckiego 11, Poznan 60-70-6 Poland, and the subscription is $10. U.S. Funds a year.
Written in Polish, the magazine is 16 pages in a large 8.25 x 11.25" format. Stories are by both local AA and Al-Anon members.

2598. Rusterholz, Alfred. "A.A. -- Alcoholics Anonymous". Gesundh. u. Wohlfahrt, Zurich; 1946; 26: pp626-630.
Note: QJSA abstract no. 4640.
"A.A. is described from W.W.'s paper, 'The Fellowship of A.A.' Comment: the mentality of the American alcoholic is very different from that of the Swiss. Swiss alcoholic would never go to a doctor and ask to be sobered up. From the point of view of promoting abstinence, the A.A. movement does not do much: 15,000 abstinents as compared to 100,000 members of Washingtonian movement in 1840-43; the latter started with a few alcoholics too. A.A. members do not pay dues, but who financed the book 'Alcoholics Anonymous?' There are perhaps connections between American alcohol capital and AA. And how can one believe that an American employer will let an employee leave his work at any time to go and help another alcoholic? Great skepticism expressed with respect to A.A. Many movements have grown and then declined when based on the personality of 1 man who leads them. In Jellinek's A.A. questionnaire, 1 question appears again and again: was there prohibition when the subject begins to drink, and was any of the family a prohibitionist? It seems that American alcoholics, after hitting bottom, begin to see the light; Swiss ones also see, but not deep enough. It is also very strange that A.A.'s seem to get along without a 'Heilkur.' One aspect that the Swiss movements have in common with A.A.: the cured alcoholic must be in the movement against alcoholism.".

2599. S. S. His Own Enemy: The Story of An Alcoholic. Auckland: New Zealand: Blackwood & Janet Paul; 1965; 200pp.
"The story of an alcoholic and his wife and family as they go through the hell and the darkness of the problem - the grappling with and acceptance of his condition as a disease - and the ever-strengthening grip on the recovery programme of A.A.".

2600. Share; 1972-1993.
Note: Address is Share, P. O. Box 1, Stonebow House, Stonebow York YO1 - 2NJ, England, and the subscription rate is $36. per year.
Written in English and usually 26 pages, this standard pocket size GV format magazine began in October, 1972, when the newsletter was retitled "Share." Stories are local, intergroup news is shared along with new AA meetings and a section of slogans and sayings called "shareisms.".

2601. Shaw, S. "What is Problem Drinking?". in: Plant, M. A., Editor. Drinking and Problem Drinking. First ed. London, England: Junction Books; 1982: pp1-22; 226pp; ISBN: NACLI record no. 3576.
"The author discusses how Bill Wilson and Dr. Bob got together to form Alcoholics Anonymous and discusses the relationship between AA, Prohibition, and the temperance movement.".

2602. Silva, Puente, F.G. "Center of Assistance for the Alcoholic and his Family: Sociodemographic aspects and profiles of the client". Salud Mental; 1982; 5(2): pp60-65.
Note: NACLI Record No. 13777.
This Center's study in Mexico City found most alcoholics surveyed were working age men for whom religion, family and Alcoholics Anonymous played important roles in their rehabilitation. The article is in Spanish.

2603. Skulska, W. "Is There Any AA Club Activity At All?". Probl. Alkzmu, Warsaw; 1979; 26(9): pp9-10.
"Dzialalnosc Klubow AA, Czy Jest O Czym Mowicc?" [Polish].

2604. Skulska, W. "Under the AA Aegis: A New Club and a New Orientation". Probl. Alkzmu, Warsaw; 1979; 26(11): pp17-18.
"Spod Znaku AA: Nowy Klub, Nowa Propozycja" [Polish]. A new AA-type club called "Syrena" has been opened in Drewnice, Poland. It aims to cooperate with the local psychiatric hospital. The members are encouraged to share their experiences with alcohol, while drinking yogurt cocktails.

2605. Skulska, W. "The Urgent Need of AA Clubs for Service and Coordinating Improvements". Probl. Alkzmu, Warsaw; 1978; 25(10): pp17-18.
"Kluby AA Przed Wazna Decyzja" [Polish].

2606. Sondheimer, G. "Alcoholism Therapy". in: Zur Therapie des Alkoholismus; 1982; 39(8): pp594-601.
Note: NACI 6331 [German journal].
Sondheimer, of the Winterthur Canton Hospital, Psychiatric Polyclinic, Winterthur, Switzerland, suggests cooperation between the physician, the social worker, and organizations of former alcoholics, including AA.

2607. Spanish AA Pamphlets. New York: AAWS; current.
Over 40 pamphlets published by AAWS and the Grapevine have been translated into Spanish.

2608. "Survey of Alcoholics Anonymous in Great Britain: 1981". London, England: General Service Board of A.A. [Great Britain]; 1982; 22pp; CODEN: NACI 7078.
Note: [This survey form was also used in other countries. This 1981 survey of the AA membership in Great Britain was answered by 2,071 AA members. Information included sex, age, occupation, and length of sobriety of the members, their reasons for joining AA, the length of time of membership in AA, the frequency of AA attendance, and the amount [if any] of prior treatment or counseling.

2609. <u>This is Alcoholics Anonymous Australia</u>. First ed. Sydney, NSW, Australia: GSO, AA, Australia; 1980 [?]; 64pp.
This yellow booklet contains 47 short articles on AA and Australian AA. It was printed to fill a need for an Australian AA with an identity of its own and has early Australian history articles, the Steps, the Traditions, and other service and recovery stories.

2610. <u>Thoughts for the Month</u>. Clifton, Bristol, England: Bristol Fashion; October, 1992.
Note: pamphlet.
This 6 x 8" pamphlet of 16pp contains one paragraph quotes from A.A. literature and past issues of <u>Bristol Fashion</u> about recovery, service, gratitude and a host of other favorite Fellowship topics. It is dedicated to Travers C., the founder of the AA-oriented magazine.

2611. Turull Torres, F. "Sociocultural Aspects in the Demand for Attention in an Alcoholism Service in Mexico City: The Center of Assistance for the Alcoholic and His Family". in: <u>Salud Mental</u>; 1982; 5(2): pp66-73.
Note: NACI 13779.
Findings of this study indicated the center was not as affective as it could have been because it had failed to coordinate its efforts with other services, especially Alcoholics Anonymous, which fulfills a secondary and tertiary role for alcoholics.

2612. <u>The Twelfth Step</u>; 1978-1993.
Note: Address is The Twelfth Step, P. O. Box 16958, Byculla, Bombay-400 027, India, and the subscription rate is $10. per year.
Written in English, it is published 6 times a year. It is usually 20 pages and has the usual mix of local and GV reprints.

2613. <u>Twelve Steps and Twelve Traditions</u>. <u>Polish translation</u>: AAWS; 1987.
Note: 154pp. pb.
[see American edition for abstract].

2614. La Vigne AA; 1964-1993; 1-29(6 issues annually).
Note: Bibliotheque nationale D-715499. Address is La Vigne, 187 Rue Jules-Verne, Montreal, Quebec H2R - 1M6, Canada, and subscriptions are accepted in Canadian Dollars only at $12. per year.
This is the Canadian "Grapevine" in French. Published by AA in Montreal, Quebec, Canada, six times a year, it is usually 48 pages and contains [all in French] stories of AA recovery, news, humor, service announcements, reprints from the Grapevine, illus., the Steps, Traditions, Preamble, and Responsibility statement.

2615. La VIGNE AA. 1965-85. First French ed. Montreal, Quebec, Canada: La Vigne AA; July, 1985; 192pp.
Note: illus., pb.
This souvenir edition in French published for the International Covention of A.A. held in Montreal, Canada, July, 1985, celebrates AA's 50th year and also the 20th year of the French Grapevine. It contains numberous past GV articles, history, many past articles, cartoons, Bill W. writings, etc.

2616. Vivencia; 1983-1993; ISSN: 103-3549.
Note: Address is Vivencia, Caixa Postal 1217, Fortaleza Cearr, 60001-970, Brasil, and the subscription rate is $10. per year.
This quarterly GV is a pocket size magazine in Portuguese which includes photos, articles by non AA doctors, Victor E., cartoons, and articles by Brasilian AA's. A meeting directory is in the back.

2617. Whitingten, R. E./Paterson, D. B./Meaton, R. G./Wolfenden, K. R. "Alcoholism: A Country Hospital's Approach to this Community Problem". in: First Pan-Pacific Conference on Drugs and Alcohol; Feb. 26-March 5, 1980; Canberra, Australia: pp428-430; 473pp.
The Manning River District Hospital's alcohol policy in Tarce, Australia, is described. The withdrawal program there uses Alcoholics Anonymous members instead of drug therapy.

2618. Williams, Lincoln. Tomorrow Will Be Sober. First ed. London: Cassell; 1960; 207pp.
Note: bibliography, index, dj. [an American edition was also published in 1960.].
E. Lincoln Williams, a British psychiatrist, studied alcoholism programs in Seattle, Milwaukee, and Chicago, and. upon his return to England, helped to establish A.A. there. This book combines the scientific and A.A. developments in the post-Prohibition era and recognizes both the disease concept of alcoholism and A.A.'s recovery program from it. The book concludes with "Alcoholics Anonymous" by Richard P., Founder Member of the Dublin, Ireland, A.A. group and "The Spiritual Approach" by the Rev. F. B. Rea, Principal of Epworth Theological College, Salisbury, Southern Rhodesia.

2619. "World Service Meetings: A History". New York: GSO; 1993. Note: [see also "European Service Meetings" and "Ibero-American Service Meetings"] 8.5 x 11" paper revised May, 1993.
This 58-page GSO staff paper documents the history of AA World Service Meetings first held Oct. 9-11, 1969, in New York City, and held every two years since, excepting the second in 1972, in various major cities around the world. Representatives at the 12th WSM in New York included 39 delegates from 24 countries. The 1st WSM in 1969 was attended by 27 delegates from 16 countries. "The primary purpose of WSMs is to carry the A.A. message of recovery to alcoholics who still suffer, wherever in the world they may be, whatever language they speak.".

2620. Young, J. W., Rev. "The Cure of the Alcoholic". Lombard News; Summer, 1954; 3(2): p10.
Rev. Young, Gen. Sec., Council of the Methodist Church in Ireland, says "as a minister of religion I can appreciate and heartily approve of the methods used by Alcoholics Anonymous in its splendid work. The Belfast group [of AA] in particular is exercising a very fine influence...".

Chapter XI = Audio Tapes & Records

2621. 1st International A.A. Convention, Cleveland, Ohio, 1950; July 1950.
Three major tapes are available from this first Int'l AA Convention: Dr. Bob's last major talk before his death, the "Big Meeting" with Bill, and Bill W. speaking on the Twelve Traditions.

2622. 2nd International A.A. Convention, St. Louis, Missouri, 1955; July 1-5, 1955.
Nineteen tapes are available from the 2nd Int'l AA Convention. Included are Bill Wilson, Ebby T., Chuck C., John D., Fr. Ed Dowling, Dr. Harry Tiebout, Rev. Sam Shoemaker, Bernard Smith, and Lois Wilson. Don B., Jack H., Hugh T., and Neely D. are on 8 different tapes.

2623. 3rd International A.A. Convention, Long Beach, California, 1960. Long Beach, CA; July 2-3, 1960.
Seventeen tapes are available from the 3rd Int'l AA Convention. Among them are Sister Ignatia, Msgr. John Daugherty, Rev. Sam Shoemaker, Walter O'K., Marty Mann, Bill Wilson, and Col. Edward B. Towns, the son of the founder of Towns Hospital. Panels and workshops on medicine, prisons, the Twelve Steps, spirituality, and hospitals were held.

2624. 4th International A.A. Convention, Toronto, Canada, 1965. Toronto, Canada; July 2-3, 1965.
Eighteen tapes are available from the 4th Int'l AA Convention in Toronto. Along with Bill and Lois Wilson, the speakers included Dr. Jack Norris, Chuck C., Gene, Bernard Smith, Marty Mann, and others. AA and the Clergy, the Twelve Traditions, and AA's history were discussed among a wide range of topics.

2625. 5th International A.A. Convention, Miami, Florida, 1970. Miami, FL; July 3-5, 1970.
Thirteen tapes are available from the 5th Int'l Convention. Those sharing included Bill Wilson; Dr. Paul O. of Redmond, WA; Charles D. of Detroit, MI; Chuck C.; and others. This international would be the last time Co-Founder Bill W. would speak publicly before his death in 1971.

2626. 6th International A.A. Convention, Denver, Colorado, 1975. Denver, CO; July 4-6, 1975.
Almost 100 tapes from the 6th Int'l are available. In addition to numerous Alkathons, panels and workshops were held on: Loners, the AA Grapevine, AA and Clergy, Armed Forces, Court Programs, Intergroups & Central Offices, Young People, Industry, Hospitals, Cooperation with Alcoholism, Medical and Rehabilitation Professionals, Alcoholism Agencies, Prisons, Public Information, the Native American, the Big Book and the Media. As is AA tradition at the Int'ls, the big Spiritual Meeting was held on Sunday morning. Alkathons were sponsored by the Southeastern and other Regions and areas of AA.

2627. 7th International A.A. Convention, New Orleans, Louisiana, 1980. New Orleans, LA; July 4-6, 1980.
Well over 150 tapes are available from the 7th Int'l. Many states, areas, and Canadian provinces sponsored their own meetings. In addition to many panels and workshops similar in topic to prior internationals, there were meetings on Joy in Recovery, Resentments, Twelve Concepts, Oldtimers, Archives, Newsletters & Bulletins, Sponsorship, Anonymity, Telephone Answering Service, the 12 Promises, Doctors in AA, Principles before Personalities, Women in AA, and a combined AA-Al-Anon meeting. Marty Mann and Lois Wilson were two of the remaining original pioneers on the program.

2628. 8th International A.A. Convention, Montreal, Canada, 1985. Montreal, Canada; July 5-7, 1985.
About 200 tapes are available from the 8th AA Int'l. Celebrating its 50th anniversary, this Int'l revealed the worldwide spread of the Fellowship: Spanish tapes, Loners & Internationalists, AA Around the World, How AA Began in Latin American, Canada & USA, Europe. Not listed in previous internationals, new topics for workshops and panels included Alateen, Rule 62, Gays, Self-Supporting, AA in the year 2001, Birds of a Feather [airline personnel], AA & Minorities, Slogans, Meeting for the Hearing Impaired, AA & Native People, Lawyers in AA, Emotional Involvement, and Why 90 Meetings in 90 Days? to name but a sampling. Meetings were devoted to specific topics based on a line from the Big Book or a quality in sobriety: the Spiritual Life is not a Theory, Faith in Action, Letting Go of Old Ideas, God Comes to Most Men Gradually, We Treat Sex Like Any Other Problem, Gratitude: the Language of the Heart, etc. Focusing on history, meetings, workshops and panels were devoted to Archives, Oldtimers in AA, Golden Oldies, What Happened to the Oldtimers, and 50 Years with Gratitude [the Int'l's theme].

2629. 9th International A.A. Convention, Seattle, Washington, 1990. Seattle, WA; July 1990.
Almost 250 tapes of the 9th Int'l are available. With the theme,"55 Years - One Day at a Time," the Int'l was truly international. Almost 50,000 AAs from over 100 countries attended. Meetings were translated into many languages: Unidad Y Servicio, Reunionen Espanol, Les 12 Etapes, Comites Institucionales, Les 12 Traditions, Wie A.A. in Deutchland, 12 Tradizioni, 12 Passi, Estructuras de Servicio, Die Drei Zwoelfen: Schritte, Traditionen, Reunion Francais, 55 Jahre in Denkbarkeit, A.A. Meetings in Japanese, 55 Ans-Un Jour a la Foi, and Oficinas de Servicios. Historical perspectives focused on AA Around the World, Black Men & Women, AA in Western Europe, Latin America, Africa, Asia, Australia, Italy, Germany, France, etc. Signed language and hearing impaired meetings were available. Among the new panels and workshops were the Home Group, Cooperation with other 12-Step Programs, Carrying the Message through the Media, and the Group Conscience.

2630. A.A. Comes of Age. NY: AAWS.
These eight tapes in a binder are a reading of the book A.A. Comes of Age and are accompanied by a 12-page booklet of photographs depicting A.A. history.

2631. A.A. on Trial. Annaheim, CA; October 1969.
Four members of the legal profession discuss AA and the law profession.

2632. AA Finances - Self Supporting. Fargo, ND; Sept. 12, 1987.
A discussion of Traditions Six and Seven at the West Central Regional Conference in Fargo, North Dakota.

2633. Al S. Memories of AA Beginnings; March 27, 1977.
This New Yorker discusses AA early years.

2634. Alcoholics Anonymous. Detroit, MI; Nov. 1946.
This is a 20 minute tape of a radio program on station WWJ in Detroit.

2635. Alcoholics Anonymous [The Big Book]. NY: AAWS.
This set of seven tapes in a binder is a reading of the first eleven chapters and first two stories in the Big Book.

2636. Anna C. Her Story. Monroe, LA; March 14-15, 1969.
Anna, the first AA lady in Akron, Ohio, shares her story.

2637. Archives. Lincoln, NE; Oct. 25, 1981.
At the 38th AA anniversary at Lincoln, Nebraska.

2638. Archives. Seattle, WA; July 1990.
Two tapes from the 9th Int'l AA Convention at Seattle in 1990.

2639. Archives at 48th Southeastern Regional Conference. Charleston, WV; August 12-15, 1992.
This two-tape set features the only panel in AA history of four authors of books about AA. They were Mel B., author of New Wine: The Spiritual Roots of AA, and of numerous Grapevine articles; Bill Pittman, author of AA The Way It Began; Mary Darrah, author of Sister Ignatia: Angel of Alcoholics Anonymous; and Mitchell Klein, author of the forthcoming book Clarence Snyder and the Early Days of AA in Cleveland, Ohio. The only AA member was Mel B. of Toledo, Ohio. They participated in the SE Regional Confrc. which was also the 40th West Virginia Area Convention celebrating 50 years of AA in the Mountain State.

2640. Archives Interview; 1983.
An Old Timers panel at the Loners International AA Conference.

2641. Archives Workshop. New Orleans, LA; July 1980.
At the 7th Int'l AA Convention, New Orleans.

2642. Archives Workshop. Montreal, Canada; July 5, 1985.
At the 8th Int'l AA Convention.

2643. Attitudes. New York: A.A. Grapevine.

2644. Austin R. His Story. Ruidosa, NM; May 15, 1954.
Austin shares his story at the Tri State AA Conference at Ruidosa, New Mexico. He was also influential in the early history of treatment centers in Minnesota and surrounding area. Austin was from Colfax, Wisconsin.

2645. Back to Basics. New York: A.A. Grapevine.
These two tapes stress the importance of having a home group, anonymity, sponsorship, and other fundamental AA principles.

2646. Barry L. Traditions. North Carolina; 1968.
Barry, from New York City, discusses the 12 Traditions.

2647. Bauer, W. W., Dr. Biloxi, MS; Aug. 24, 1956.
One of AA's early non-alcoholic friends in the medial profession talks at the 12th Southeastern Regional Conference in Biloxi, Mississippi. Dr. Bauer was from Chicago, Illinois.

2648. "Bill" and "Dr. Bob". The Big Meeting. Cleveland, Ohio; July 28-30, 1950.
Note: [other early AA talks were recorded on old reel-to-reel tapes and 78 & 33rpm records].
Rockhill Recording of New York City recorded the First International Conference of AA at Cleveland, Ohio, July 28-30, 1950, on a set of two large long-playing 33rmp records. Sets are rare.

2649. Bill B. His Story. Shreveport, LA; Nov. 4, 1989.
Bill, from New York City, shares his story. He is the author of the movie "My Name is Bill W.".

2650. Bill D. San Francisco; 1946.
AA 3 shares his story. Bill D. was from Canton, Ohio.

2651. Bill G. "There's Nothing Wrong With Me!"; 1954.
Bill G.'s story, "There's Nothing the Matter With Me!" is in the second edition of the Big Book. Bill was from Mutley, New Jersey.

2652. Bill Wilson/Dr. Bob. 1st Int'l Convention at Cleveland, Ohio. Cleveland; 1950.
The AA Co-Founders share at the 1st Int'l Convention.

2653. Bill Wilson. 1st Oklahoma Conference. Oklahoma City, OK; May 1951.
2 tapes.

2654. Bill Wilson. AA & Medicine. Long Beach, CA; July 2, 1960.
Note: [2 tapes].
Bill W. and others at the 3rd Int'l Convention in Long Beach, California, in 1960 discuss the medical aspects of alcoholism and AA's attitudes about them.

2655. Bill Wilson. AA Book. Atlanta, GA; July 14, 1951.
Bill talks about the Big Book.

2656. Bill Wilson/others. AA in Prison. Long Beach, CA; July 1960.
At the 3rd Int'l Convention in Long Beach, California, in 1960, Bill & others recall how AA reached into prisons to help the suffering alcoholic.

2657. Bill Wilson. Adolphus Hotel interview. Dallas, TX; 1951.
Two tapes.

2658. Bill Wilson. Al-Anon World Service Conference. New York; April 1961.

2659. Bill Wilson. Annual Bill W. Dinner, New York City. New York: 1951-1970.
Note: [14 tapes].
Bill spoke at the New York Intergroup annual Bill W. Dinner [usually held in October or November] in 1950-52, 1954-55, Nov. 9, 1957, Nov. 17, 1958 [2 tapes], 1963, 1965-through-1970. Among the topics were: Bill's Last Drunk, Gratitude, How AA Got Started [often called "The Bed Time Story"], the First Recovery Story [Bill's own], "on Varieties of Religious Experience," etc. Lois, his wife, often shared the podium with Bill at these annual affairs and one year Rev. Samuel Shoemaker shared the microphone with Bill.

2660. Bill Wilson. Big Book Meeting. Cleveland, OH; 1950.

2661. Bill Wilson. Bill's Last Talk. Miami, FL; July 5, 1970.
Bill shares at the 5th Int'l Convention held in Miami, Florida. This was his last public talk before his death.

2662. Bill Wilson/J. T. Des Moines, Iowa. Iowa; 1948.

2663. Bill Wilson. The First Recovery Story; 1955.
Bill's own story on 20th anniversary of sobriety.

2664. Bill Wilson. Founders Day. Akron, OH; 1954, etc.
Bill spoke at the annual Founders Day weekend in Akron, Ohio, the birthplace of AA, in 1954-through-1960 & 1965. The annual celebration is held on the nearest weekend to June 10, AA's founding date. Among his topics over the years were: How AA Got Started, Communication, History of the Big Book [to Al-Anons], etc. Sharing some of these talks are Lois W., Tom P., etc.

2665. Bill Wilson/Jim S./Fr. Ed D./Sam S. God as We Understand Him. St. Louis, MO; July 3, 1955.
Bill & Jim S. & two clergymen share their experience about God as AA understands Him. The four were on the program of the 2nd Int'l Convention in St. Louis, Missouri, in 1955.

2666. Bill Wilson. His Last Meeting. Miami, FL; July, 1971.
recording of Bill W.'s last AA meeting before his death.

2667. Bill Wilson. History of the Big Book. Fort Worth, TX; June 13, 1954.
Bill recalls the writing of the Big Book.

2668. Bill Wilson. How AA Got Started. Akron; 1954.
Bill relates our historical beginnings at Founders Day in Akron.

2669. Bill Wilson. How AA Started. Toronto, Canada; July 1965.
Bill recalls our founding years at the 4th Int'l Convention in Toronto, Canada, in 1965.

2670. Bill Wilson. How the Big Book Was Put Together. Fort Worth, TX; June 12, 1954.
Bill recalls the writing of the Big Book.

2671. Bill Wilson/Cliff W. How We Learned to Recover. St. Louis, MO; July 1955.
Bill and Cliff W. discuss recovery at the 2nd Int'l Convention in St. Louis, Missouri, in July, 1955.

2672. Bill Wilson/Lucky S. How We Learned to Stay Together. St. Louis, MO; July 1955.
Bill and Lucky S. talk about unity at the 2nd Int'l Convention in St. Louis, Missouri, in July, 1955.

2673. Bill Wilson/Lois Wilson/Bernard S. How We Learned to Serve. St. Louis, MO; July 4, 1955.
The trio shared their experiences about the Third Legacy of Service at the 2nd Int'l Convention in St. Louis, Missouri, in 1955.

2674. Bill Wilson. How We Learned to Serve. St. Simons Island, GA; March 1964.
Bill talks about service, AA's Third Legacy.

2675. Bill Wilson. International Doctors in A.A. Indianapolis, IN; 1966.

2676. Bill Wilson/Lois Wilson/Ebby T./Sister Ignatia. One Man's Story. Long Beach, CA; 1960.
Bill tells his story at the 3rd Int'l Convention at Long Beach, California, in 1960.

2677. Bill Wilson. Our Responsibility to AA's Future. Toronto, Canada; July 3, 1965.
Bill talks at the 4th Int'l at Toronto, Canada.

2678. Bill Wilson. Sponsorship. San Francisco, CA; March 20, 1951.

2679. Bill Wilson. A Talk by Bill; April 1947.
Old reel-to-reel tape. This short talk is also available on modern cassette.

2680. Bill Wilson. Third Legacy. Fort Worth, TX; 1954.

2681. Bill Wilson. Three Legacies at 1st General Service Conference. New York; April 1951.
Bill talks about Recovery, Unity and Service at the 1st Gen. Service Confrc.

2682. Bill Wilson. Three Legacies. NY: AAWS.
Co-Founder Bill W.'s talk on Recovery, Unity and Service.

2683. Bill Wilson. Traditions. Cleveland, OH; 1950.
Bill and 6 Oldtimers discuss the Traditions at the 1st International Convention in Cleveland, Ohio, in 1950.

2684. Bill Wilson. Workshop. New York City; Oct. 10, 1970.
Note: [2 tapes].

2685. Bill Wilson. Yale School of Alcohol Studies. New Haven, CT; 1943.
Seven members of AA attended the famous Summer School of Alcohol Studies at Yale and Bill W. was one of the lecturers in the early 1940s.

2686. Bill Discusses the Twelve Traditions. NY: AAWS.
This tape cassette of Co-Founder Bill W. is the soundtrack from the AA film of the same title.

2687. Bill Wilson Memorial. Bristol, England; 1971.
Many memorial services were held around the world following Bill's death.

2688. Blue Bonnets Convention. Dumfries, Scotland; Oct. 5, 1975.
Various AA speakers.

2689. Bob B. Third Legacy. Eden Prairie, MN; Dec. 19, 1986.
Bob, from St. Paul, Minnesota, discusses the 12 Concepts.

2690. Bob Smith [friend]. Dr. Bob's Son. Montana; October 1989.
Dr. Bob's son shares his memories of growing up in Akron, Ohio, with his father, the Co-Founder of AA. Bob is from Nacona, Texas.

2691. Bud P., Dr. AA and Treatment in Minnesota. Cleveland, OH; August 1984.
Bud's address to the Int'l Doctors in AA in Cleveland focuses on the history of AA and treatment facilities in Minnesota.

2692. Captain Jack. Akron, Ohio; June 1985.
Capt. Jack was the founder of Internationalists in A.A. and he tells his recovery story at this 3rd annual Loners' Int'l Conference. The Seaman's Club in New York City was a Fellowship club for many seamen in AA, loners since they spent many months at sea without contact with another AA member. He read an article about AA in Reader's Digestduring World War II in the South Pacific. He went to his first AA meeting, the only one in Boston in 1945 or 1946. Fifteen months sober, he slipped and it took him about eight more months to get the program. He was 34 years sober when this was recorded in Akron, Ohio, in 1985. [30 minutes].

2693. Cecil C. ["Teet"]. "Those Golden Years". Los Angeles, CA; Dec. 1983.
Cecil's story, "Those Golden Years," is in the second edition of the Big Book. From Los Angeles, Cecil talked at the Valley Club, Los Angeles, meeting.

2694. Character Defects. New York: A.A. Grapevine.
Past GV articles on this tape focus on coping with anger, resentment, fear and other problems in sobriety.

2695. Charles B. His Story. San Louis, Obispo, CA; April 26, 1976.
Note: [in another tape, August 15, 1980, he discusses some early AA history.].
Charles was AA 6.

2696. Charles J. His Story. Vicksburg, MS; June 22-24, 1962.
The author of The Lost Weekend shares at the Mississippi State AA Conference. He was from New York City.

2697. Charles L. "The Arkansas Traveler". Chenier Lake, LA; Feb. 1959.
His story is in the Big Book.

2698. Chico C. Service Manual Seminar. Memphis, TN; July 1984.
Chico was from West Palm Beach, Florida.

2699. Chuck C. His Early Days. Birmingham, AL; 1954.
Note: [7 tapes].
Chuck, from Laguna Beach, California, shares at the Birmingham AA Convention. "In All Our Affairs," a set of 6 tapes of a retreat given by him to 64 men at Palm Mesa, CA, in January, 1975, eventually became the book A New Pair of Glasses. Chuck C. died in 1984.

2700. Chuck L. History of AA; Jan. 1963.
At the Southwest Regional Conference, Chuck, from Oklahoma City, shares AA history.

2701. Clarence S. History of A.A. & How It Works. Phoenix, AZ; July 10-11, 1982.
Note: [4 tapes].
Clarence S. of Cleveland, Ohio, and Casselberry, Florida, discusses AA history and"How It Works" in these two sets of two tapes. Clarence made major contributions to AA in Cleveland in the early years, including sponsorship, the use of the initials "A.A.", the first intergroup and newsletter, etc.

2702. Clarence S. The Twelve Steps. Las Vegas, NV; 1973.
Clarence discusses the 12 Steps in these two tapes. His story, "The Home Brewmeister," is in the first edition of the Big Book. Clarence founded Cleveland AA.

2703. Classics. New York: A.A. Grapevine.
These three tapes contain a selection of articles from the annual "Classic" Grapevine issues.

2704. Cliff W. History of AA in California. CA; 1975.
Note: [Cliff's earliest tape is 1953].
Cliff and Mort J. were the founding members of AA in Los Angeles.

2705. Conor F. Such is the Warp and Woof of AA Everywhere; 1973.
Archival talks by Conor F. of Philadelphia, the AAer who carried the message and started the first group in Europe; Richard P. and Jimmy R. of Dublin who were his first pigeons; together with talks given by the Bristol Akron Group in 1973 by Aidan of Cork and Sackville of Dublin.

2706. Curtis M. How an AA District Works. Bellevue, NE; April 30, 1988.
Curtis of New York City discusses service in the AA district structure.

2707. Dan A. AA and Finding the Way; 1977.
The Hazelden director shares.

2708. David A. History of Service Work. Little Rock, AR; Jan. 1987.

2709. David A. History of AA. Scottsdale, AZ; April 23, 1988.
David, from Dallas, Texas, discusses AA history, service, Traditions, and the Big Book at the North Scottsdale Fellowship Club in this set of four tapes.

2710. Dewey S. His Story. Sacramento, CA ?; July 29, 1967.
Dewey was from Samato, California, and was one of the first 100 in AA.

2711. Dick & Peggy M. AA Love and Relationships; July 1986.
This AA couple from Bellevue, Nebraska, discuss the "13th Step" and its dangers and the new AA way of life involving love, sex, relationships, and related topics.

2712. Dick M. Sponsorship. Ft. Collins, CO; March 1984.
How to Choose a Sponsor, How to be a Sponsor, and How to be Sponsored are dicussed by Dick, from Bellevue, Nebraska, in this set of three tapes.

2713. Dick M. The Washingtonians. Nebraska; March 24, 1986.
Dick leads a workshop on the Washingtonians, the 1840s society of sober alcoholics. The Washingtonians did not last long and AA learned valuable lessons from their demise which helped AA formulate the Traditions and protect its unity and thereby, its very existence.

2714. Doctors and A.A. Charleston, WV; Nov. 1982.
Five doctors share in this workshop at the 38th Southeastern Regional Conference in Charleston, West Virginia.

2715. Doe, Fr. John. Golden Books. Indianapolis, IN.
Set of 15 tapes of the "Golden Books" written by Fr. John Doe, pseudonym for the first Catholic priest to join AA. A wide range of spiritual topics about the AA program.

2716. Don B. Structure of General Service. Rochester, MN; Jan. 11, 1985.
Don is from Bloomington, Minnesota.

2717. Don M. Archives Interview. Omaha, NE; Feb. 27, 1981.
Don is from Kansas City, Missouri.

2718. Don P. AA Goes to Russia. Nashville, TN; July 1989.
Don, from Aurora, Colorado, shares his experiences in Russia.

2719. Dottie S. St. Francis of Assisi Prayer. Eugene, OR; 1970s.
Dottie from North Hollywood, California, discusses the St. Francis of Assisi prayer, well-known among early AAs.

2720. Dr. Bob. Cleveland, Ohio; 1950.
Note: [see also "Voices of Our Co-Founders" under "Bill Wilson."].
Robert Smith, M.D., the Fellowship's Co-Founder, speaks at the 1st Int'l Convention of AA in Cleveland, Ohio.

2721. Dr. Bob. Detroit, Michigan; 1948.
Co-Founder Dr. Bob Smith shares his story.

2722. Dr. Bob. History of AA. New York; 1950.
Co-Founder Dr. Bob recalls the Fellowship's beginnings.

2723. Dr. Bob. Meeting Bill W.; 1949.
The Co-Founder recalls his meeting Bill W. and AA's beginnings.

2724. Duffy, Warden Clinton P. Angelo Prison Anniversary. ?; ?
The warden of San Quention participates in the silver anniversary of the AA Group at Angelo Prison. As Warden at San Quentin, Duffy approved the founding there of the first AA group in any prison.

2725. Earle M. His Story. New York City; October 1958.
This psychiatrist and surgeon from San Francisco shares his story at the Central AA Group in NYC. His story, "Physician, Heal Thyself!"is in the second edition of the Big Book. In 1989, with 35 years of sobriety, he recorded his memories of early AA in the book Physician, Heal Thyself!

2726. Ebby T. His Story. Ft. Worth, TX; 1954.
Ebby was Bill Wilson's first sponsor and carried the first message to him.Ebby is Bill's friend on page 9 of the Big Book.

2727. Ebby T. His Story. Shreveport, LA; 1956.
He carried the first message to Bill W. Ebby's only full length talk on tape was given at Memphis, TN, on September 14, 1958.

2728. Ebby T. & Searcy W. Tri-State Conference: Iowa, Illinois, & Wisconsin; 1960.
Ebby T. carried the message to Bill W. Ebby would later slip and was sent to Texas by train where Searcy W. sponsored him. Here the two recount their experiences in and out of sobriety in those early years.

2729. Ed H. History of AA in Texas. Blairstown, NJ; 1969.
Ed, from Austin, Texas, relates Texas AA History at the Alena Lodge Anniversary in New Jersey.

2730. Ed W. Stools & Bottles. Chicago, IL; May 1965.
Sober since Dec. 13, 1941, Ed W., of Minneapolis, MN, gives his famous "Stools & Bottles" presentation graphically depicting the first Four Steps of the AA program. His book, Stools & Bottles, was popular with early AAs.

2731. Elizabeth W. Her Story. North Carolina; August 21-23, 1958.
This Boston, MA, woman shares her story at the North Carolina State Conference. She founded the first community-based alcoholism education committee in the U.S. in Boston.

2732. Ernie G. His Story. ?; ?
Ernie was one of the first 100 AAs. His story in the first edition of the Big Book is "The Seven Month Slip.".

2733. Esther A. Her Story. Lubbock, TX; May 1953.
This is the story of the first AA lady in Texas. Esther was from Dallas.

2734. Ethel M. Her Story. Parkersburg, WV; 1961.
The first AA lady in Ohio shares. Her story, "From Farm to City," is in the first edition of the Big Book. Ethel was from Akron and Barberton, Ohio.

2735. The Founding of A.A. in West Virginia. St. Albans, WV; Oct. 24, 1979.
These two tapes were recorded at the home of the late Delegate Bill B. of St. Albans, WV. Participating were early WV AA members Bill B., Charlie C., Harold R., Buzz R., and others who discussed the founding and first two years of AA in the Mountain State.

2736. Fran P. Her Story. Colorado Springs, CO; Sept. 7-9, 1990.
Fran started AA in Romania.

2737. Frank L. 25 Years of AA in the South; 1965.
Frank, from Alexandria, Virginia, recounts early AA in the South.

2738. Frank M. History of AA. Scranton, PA; 1981?
The GSO Archivist talks about AA's history and the archives in New York.

2739. Frank M. History of AA. New Orleans, LA; Sept. 1, 1989.
Frank, the AA Archivist from GSO, New York, shares the Fellowship's history.

2740. Garry Peek. History of "The Week That Was" Group. Manhattan, KS; April 1988.
Garry, from Wamego, Kansas, recounts TWTW group history.

2741. Gay.
Some tapers' catalogs devote an entire section to tapes of Gays in AA. While this may seem to lend an air of uniqueness or difference to homosexuals or lesbians in AA, one is reminded of AA's Third Tradition: The only requirement for AA membership is a desire to stop drinking.

2742. Gert B. God Isn't Dead; 1957.
Gert, from Houston, Texas, shares her experiences concerning God.

2743. Gert B. Her Story. Amarillo, TX; October 1958.
The author of The Late Liz shares her story of recovery at the Top-O-Texas AA Roundup. Gert was from Palm Springs & Medisto, California.

2744. Grapevine tapes.
Note: = LIST THEM IN THIS CHAPTER =.

2745. Harold H. His Story. Florida; 1958.
This member of the U.S. Congress shares his recovery story. He was the author of the act setting up the National Institute of Alcohol Abuse & Alcoholism in 1971. In another talk, he gave a history of the National Council on Alcoholism. He was from Des Moines, Iowa.

2746. Harold W. The Big Book. TX; August 1971.
Harold, from Midland, Texas, discusses the first eleven chapters in the Big Book.

2747. Harry G. Phone Call with Bill Wilson; 1952.
Harry was from Tyler, Texas.

2748. History of A.A. in Augusta, Georgia. Decatur & Augusta, GA; August 1979 & June 1988.
Twelve oldtimers at the home of Neely D. in Decatur in 1979 and 6 oldtimers at the Augusta meeting in 1988 discuss the history of AA locally.

2749. History of AA. Amarillo, TX; March 11-13, 1988.
At the Oldtimers Reunion.

2750. History of AA in North Grand Rapids, Minnesota; Nov. 10, 1984.

2751. History of Area 40, Kalispell, Montana; April 26, 1991.

2752. History of GSO. Long Beach, CA; July 1960.
The beginnings and workings of the General Service Office in New York are discussed at the 3rd AA Int'l Convention at Long Beach, California.

2753. Hock, Ruth. Discussion of the Big Book. Glendale, CA; March 12, 1982.
Ruth Hock was AA's first paid employee and Bill W.'s first secretary. She retyped the Big Book in many drafts and had an intimate knowledge of the first years of AA and the Big Book.

2754. How A.A. Got Started in England. England; 1969.
Sackville, Jimmy, Connor F., Richard P. and others recount the beginnings of AA in England.

2755. How AA Started in Ireland. Dublin, Ireland; 1969.
Conor F., Jimmy, and Richard P. remember the founding of AA in Ireland.

2756. ICYPAA.
Numerous tapes are available for International Conference[s] of Young People in AA.

2757. Indian Alcothon. Phoenix, AZ; Oct. 24-25, 1987.
Six Native Americans = Emmett W., Sharon A., Eleanor G., Betty S., Cecil R., and Randy A., all from Phoenix = share their recovery stories.

2758. Jackie J. History of AA in Abilene, Texas. Abilene, TX; April 30, 1988.
At the Abilene 42nd AA Anniversary celebration.

2759. Jellinek, Morton, Dr. untitled; Oct. 29, 1957.
Early AAs cooperated with Jellinek at Yale University. Jellinek, of course, formulated the disease concept of alcoholism. Those early AAs were his "guinea pigs.".

2760. JERMAC Recordings distributed by A.A. World Services, Inc. Atlanta, GA: JERMAC Recordings; 1950s.
Note: [16 stories on 11 tapes].
We have a series of eleven modern audiocassettes which have been re-recorded from seven old 1950s reel-to-reel recordings produced by JERMAC Recordings of Atlanta, Georgia. JERMAC is a contraction of the late Jerry Mac......, a doctor and member of Int'l Doctors in A.A. These old recordings were "Distributed by: A.A. World Services at the old New York 17, New York" address. The sixteen stories on the tapes include two by Bill Wilson: The First Recovery Story [1954] and How We Learned to Serve [July 1955]; In the Middle Einstein [Allan A.]; An A.A. Priest Tells His Story; An Executive Tells His Story [Allan B.]; Give No Quarter - Seek No Quarter [Nancy]; Her Attitude of Mind Changed; A Doctor, A Surgeon, A Learned Man; He Recognized Others Problems, But Not His Own [psychiatrist]; Some Words of Wisdom from an Author; An Alcoholic, A Chemist, and a Clergyman [Johnny Van D.]; Listen to a Psychiatrist; This Housewife and Mother Drank Only at Home [Midge]; An A.A. quintet of women [2 tapes]; Our Way to Recovery [John Park L.]; & As Others See Us [non-A.A. friends Judge Emmett McNoggmanee, Rev. Kenneth S. Brown & Dr. John Norris]. The flyers from AAWS advertising the tapes state "the opinions expressed in these talks are those of the

speakers and not necessarily the opinions of the A.A. Fellowship as a whole.".

2761. Jim L. "My Wife and I". Huntsville, AL; Nov. 1960.
Jim's story, "My Wife and I," is in the original first edition of the Big Book. Jim was from Washington, D.C.

2762. Jimmy B. Early Story of AA in New York. Sacramento, CA; June 15, 1957.
Jimmy was one of the first 100 in AA.

2763. Jimmy B. His Story. Amarillo, TX; October 1952.
Jimmy, an AA from California, was one of the first 100 in AA. On this tape from the Top-O-Texas AA Roundup, he shares his recovery. His story was not included in the first edition of the Big Book at his own request but it is in the third edition under the title "The Vicious Cycle.".

2764. Jimmy B. How the [Big] Book Was Written. Winslow, AZ; 1955.
Jimmy, from San Diego, California, and Bill W. corresponded often in the early years of AA. Jimmy was responsible for "God as we understand Him." Here, Jimmy shares his intimate knowledge of the writing of the Big Book.

2765. Joe L. [Wino Joe]. History of AA. ?; 1970-80s.
Joe discusses AA history in this set of three tapes.

2766. Joe McQ./Charlie P. The Big Book Comes Alive. Lawton, OK; 1977.
For many years the Joe & Charlie Big Book Study Seminars have been very popular around the AA world. This set of four tapes was one of the earliest; later seminars over weekends would be expanded to 8 tapes.

2767. John B. History of AA in Kansas City, Missouri; May 15, 1975.
John was from Kansas City.

2768. John C. Archives Interview. Bellevue, NE; Jan. 24, 1981.
Note: Two tapes.
John is from Brownwood, Texas.

2769. John P. "The Professor and the Paradox". Akron, OH; June 1979.
His story is in the second edition of the Big Book under the above title. John was from Kent, Ohio.

2770. Joseph M., Fr. His Story. Florissant, MO; Nov. 22, 1974.
This Catholic priest tells his story of recovery. He is well known in professional and AA circles for his video "Chalk Talk.".

2771. Kurtz, Ernest, Ph.D. History of A.A. Willingway ?; April 12, 1985.
A friend of AA, this professional historian and author of Not-God: The History of AA, discusses the Fellowship's history. A two-tape set is also available of readings from that book by him.

2772. Lefty H. Yale University; July 13, 1954.

2773. Lynn C. His Story. Columbia, SC; Aug. 20, 1961.
Lynn shares his story at the South Carolina State AA Confrc. Lynn was from Center City, Minnesota.

2774. Lynn C. Twelve Steps. MN?; 1971.
12 tapes.

2775. Mac L. History of AA in Palestine, Texas. Palestine, TX; May 1990.

2776. Maintaining Spirituality. New York: A.A. Grapevine.
How we grow in the AA way of life and spirituality.

2777. Mann, Marty. 7th Int'l AA Convention. New Orleans, LA; July 2, 1980.
Marty M., one of the first 100 in the Fellowship, remembers her beginning in AA and the early history. She was the first lady AA member in New York.

2778. Mann, Marty. Her Story. New York City; Dec. 1, 1952.
This New York City woman was one of the first 100 in AA and here shares her story of recovery at the Tudor AA Group in NYC.

2779. Marty Mann. San Francisco, CA; 1946.
Marty was one of the first 100 and the first woman in AA to maintain sobriety. She used her full name after discussing this with fellow AA's [this was before the Traditions were written]. She founded the National Council on Alcoholism.

2780. Maxwell, Milton. World Service Conference; 1967.
Dr. Maxwell was one of the first sociologists to endorse AA. In his writings, he compared AA and the Washingtonians. A non-alcoholic, he was one of AA's trusted servants.

2781. Mel B. My Search for Bill Wilson. Toledo, OH; 1980s.
Mel, author of numerous Grapevine articles and a book about AA's spiritual roots, recounts his long investigation into the personality, actions and facets of AA Co-Founder Bill Wilson.

2782. Morris B. Story in the Big Book. Madison, TN; Feb. 22, 1990.
Morris is from Lumberton, North Carolina.

2783. <u>NBC Radio Catholic Hour - Recovery Unlimited</u>. New York; 1960.
Jane F., Tom P., and Marty M. share the AA message on this early radio program.

2784. Noel B., Fr. <u>Spirituality vs. Religion</u>. Saint Simons Island, GA; May 7, 1988.
Fr. B., from Atlanta, Georgia, discusses the important differences between spirituality in AA and religion.

2785. Norris, Dr. Jack. <u>4th Interntional A.A. Convention</u>. Toronto, Canada; July 1965.
General Service Board Chairman John L. Norris shares his memories of AA. The non-alcoholic servant from Rochester, NY, was affectionately called "Dr. Jack" by AAs.

2786. <u>Not for Newcomers Only</u>. New York: A.A. Grapevine.
These two tapes suggest AA tools for newcomers and using the principles to deal with everyday problems.

2787. <u>Old Timers in AA before 1950</u>. Bedford Hills, NY; Oct. 2, 1982.
This set of two tapes includes comments from many of the remaining old timers in AA [before 1950] who gathered at the home of Bill & Lois W. in Bedford Hills, NY, in 1982. Lois Wilson is also on the tape.

2788. <u>Oldtimers, Longtimers, Golden Oldies, & Pioneers meetings</u>.
There are literally hundreds of meetings, panels, and workshops by AA oldtimers where the history of AA is discussed and early experiences of recovery are shared. These "oldtimer" tapes are excellent primary source material for AA archivists, researchers, and Fellowship members.

2789. <u>Our Experience Has Taught Us [Traditions]</u>. New York: A.A. Grapevine.
How the Twelve Traditions came about.

2790. <u>Pathways to Spirituality</u>. New York: A.A. Grapevine.
How we come to believe in God, spirituality, etc.

2791. Paul K. <u>The Four Absolutes</u>. St. Louis, MO; Dec. 6, 1985.
Pual, from Manchester, Missouri, discusses the Four Absolutes of the Oxford Group where AA first got started. He still views the absolutes as valauble "spiritual tools." The absolutes were used before the 12 Steps were written.

2792. Paul O. <u>Big Book Anniversary</u>; Sept. 30, 1989.
Dr. Paul's story, "Doctor, Alcoholic, Addict," is in the second edition of the Big Book. Here he shares his story and discusses Big Book history on the 50th anniversary of the publication of the first edition.

2793. Paul W. <u>AA History</u>. Houston, TX; 1961.

2794. Practice These Principles [Traditions]. New York: A.A. Grapevine.
How the Twelve Traditions work in AA groups and in the lives of Fellowship members.

2795. Public Service Announcements. New York: AAWS.
Note: [available in English, Spanish, and French].
Four public information announcements of thirty seconds each. GSO offers these in the AA catalog as a means of carrying the message to the suffering alcoholic over radio and television. They focus on how to get in touch with AA if you think you may have a drinking problem.

2796. Recovery Revisited: The History of Alcoholism. Bellevue, Ne; Oct. 15, 1988.
Most of this four-tape set on the history of alcoholism focuses on the period 1935-1990s. Dr. Jung, the Traditions and a wealth of AA historical events are discussed.

2797. Richard P. The Best of Bristol. Bristol, England; Sept. 1971.
Richard P. shares his story and some AA history at the First European Convention in England. There was also a memorial service held in Bristol Cathedral for the late Co-Founder Bill W.

2798. Roger G. Archives Interview. Omaha, NE; March 24, 1985.

2799. Rosary Hall Dedication. Cleveland, OH; Dec. 1957.
Note: [2 tapes].
Tom O'B and O'Grady share at the dedication of Rosary Hall in Cleveland. Rosary Hall was the second hospital where Sister Ignatia helped so many thousands of alcoholics get their start in recovery in AA.

2800. Russell H. How AA Got Started in Little Rock, Arkansas. Little Rock, AR; June 25, 1983.

2801. Ruth B. Her Story. Nashville, TN; April 1949.
Ruth, from Washington, D.C., shares her story.

2802. Sackville. His Roots Grasped a New Soil. Bristol, England: Bristol Fashion.
The whole of this 90 minute tape is devoted to articles, talks, broadcasts and personal letters attributed to Sackville, of Dublin, Ireland, narrated here by Travers C.

2803. Searcy W. His Story. Big Spring, TX; Oct. 25-26, 1952.
Searcy W., of Dallas, Texas, shares his story. Seacy sponsored Ebby T.

2804. Shoemaker, Sam, Rev. History of AA. Charlotte, NC; June 17, 1962.
Episcopal minister Shoemaker from New York City was an Oxford Grouper and spiritual advisor to Bill W. He was one of the early non-alcoholic friends of the Fellowship who aided AA's development of the 12 Steps.

2805. Shoemaker, Sam, Rev. What the Church Has to Learn from AA. Charlotte, NC; Feb. 16, 1958.
AA's friend, Rev. Shoemaker, discusses what organized religion could learn from AA.

2806. Sister Ignatia/Bill Wilson. How AA Got Started in Akron Hospital. Long Beach, CA; July 1960.
At the 3rd Int'l Convention in Long Beach, California, in 1960, Sister Ignatia recalls how St. Thomas Hospital became the first hospital in the world to admit alcoholics and how AA grew there. Bill W. recalls the founding of AA.

2807. Smith, Bernard. Paradoxes of AA. St. Louis, MO; July 3, 1955.
The non-alcoholic Chairman of the Board of Trustees of The Alcoholic Foundation talked at the 2nd Int'l AA Convention at St. Louis about the paradoxes of AA.

2808. Sonidos de Sobriedad. New York: A.A. Grapevine.
This tape has selected articles in Spanish on a variety of AA topics.

2809. Les Sons de la Sobriete. New York: A.A. Grapevine.
This tape contains articles in French on a variety of AA topics.

2810. Southeastern Regional Conference. Charleston, WV, etc.; 1944-92.
The oldest regional conference in AA comprises eleven states in the Southeastern U.S. and held its 48th gathering in 1992 in Charleston, WV. Hundreds of tapes of speakers and workshops are available for this and many other regional conferences, forums, area conventions, jamborees, round-ups, and other AA gatherings.

2811. Southwest Archives Conference. Phoenix, AZ: Smile God Loves You Tapes/Golden Age Groups of AZ; Feb. 12, 1994.
The three-tape album includes talks by Nell Wing, AA's first Archivist and Bill Wilson's secretary; Sue Windows, Dr. Bob's daughter; and Mary D., author of Sister Ignatia: Angel of Alcoholics Anonymous. Additionally, Oldtimers from Arizona and around the country shared their stories on two more tapes from this huge, successful archives gathering. Nell Wing was unable to catch her plane out of New York City because of a winter blizzard shutting down the airport but shared in a telephone hookup.

2812. Sponsorship. New York: A.A. Grapevine.
These two tapes have articles by AAs who have made a solid start because of sponsorship, and whose lives have been enriched by sponsoring others.

2813. Sue Windows [friend]. Dr. Bob's Daughter. Dublin, GA; July 1988.
Dr. Bob's daughter shares her memories of growing up in Akron, Ohio, with her father, the Co-Founder of AA. Sue still lives in Akron.

2814. Sybil C. Her Story. Louisville, KY; Aug. 8, 1974.
The first lady AA in California shares her story.

2815. Terry R., Fr. The Serenity Prayer. The Bahamas; May 10, 1989.
AA's most popular prayer is explored.

2816. "Thirst Without End". New York: Cavalcade of America; April 29, 1948.
Note: Available only from the Hagley Museum and Libary, P.O. Box 3630, Wilmington, DE 19807.
This is a copy of the radio show on the regular Cavalcade of America sponsored by DuPont. This episode [477], "Thirst Without End," starred James Cagney as an alcoholic, Bob Corbin, who may have been involved in a hit-and-run car accident while in a blackout. His wife calls AA and Corbin finds sobriety in AA for himself and his family. [30 minutes].

2817. Tiebout, Harry, Dr. Anonymity, the Ego Reducer. St. Louis, MO; July 5, 1955.
Dr. Tiebout, a non-alcoholic, was the first psychiatrist to recognize and use AA principles. At the 2nd Int'l AA Convention in St. Louis he spoke about the value of anonymity in the Fellowship.

2818. Tom B. Prayer & Meditation. ?; 1963.
Tom discusses the 11th Step and prayer and meditation.

2819. Tom P. About God. Cincinnati, OH; 1960.
Tom, from Chappaqua, New York, talks about God and spirituality in AA.

2820. Towns, Col. Edward B. Towns Hospital. Long Beach, CA; July 3, 1960.
At this 3rd International A.A. Convention in Long Beach, CA, the son of the founder of Towns Hospital in New York shared his memories of his father, Charles B. Towns. Bill Wilson was admitted to this drying-out medical center on Central Park West four times in 1933-34.

2821. Travers C. 20 Years of Bristol Fashion. England; 1989.
The editor of the English AA newsletter, Bristol Fashion, shares memories of its founding and progress over the years.

2822. Twelve Steps and Twelve Traditions. NY: AAWS.
These five tapes in a binder are a reading of the book Twelve Steps and Twelve Traditions.

2823. Twelve Steps, Traditions, Concepts.
Hundreds of workshops, panels, seminars, and speakers tapes are available on the steps, traditions, and concepts.

2824. Twenty-Four Hours a Day. Center City, MN: Hazelden; 1956-1994.
This 6-tape set is a reading of the book.

2825. Voices of Our Co-Founders. NY: AAWS.
Five excerpts from different talks by Dr. Bob & Bill W. are on this 28-minute tape cassette.

2826. Voices of the Big Book.
This two-volume set of 12 tapes includes the voices of early AA's who are in the Big Book. Recorded are Bill W., Dr. Bob, Bill D., Jim B., Clarence S., John P., Dr. Earl M., Dr. Paul O., Morris B., Bill G. Wynn L., and Bob P.

2827. Wallace Tom G. His Story. Columbia, TN; 1940.
Wallace, from Nashville, Tennessee, tells his recovery story from the early days of AA.

2828. Wally P. AA: The Greatest Spiritual Movement of the 20th Century. Black Canyon City, AZ; Nov. 29, 1992.
At the Sunday Breakfast AA Meeting in Black Canyon City, AZ Archivist Wally of Tucson, Arizona, reviews AA history and discusses its spiritual importance for alcoholics and the rest of the world. Wally quotes Rev. Norman Vincent Peale, Aldous Huxley, and other spiritual leaders, and cites the growth of other anonymous programs.

2829. Wally P. Arizona AA History. Tucson, AZ; Oct. 2, 1993.
At the Arizona Area AA Convention in Tucson, Archivist Wally P. reviews the history of the Fellowship in Arizona.

2830. Warren C. His Story. Canton, OH; 1964.
Warren was from Cleveland, Ohio, and was the 12th man in AA.

2831. Wilson B. Short Lead. ?; 1940.
One of the earliest AA leads on tape.

2832. Wing, Nell. History of AA; 1977.
Introduced by Lois W., Nell, Bill's secretary and AA's first archivist, shares her personal memories of AA's history while on the "Emerald Seas" ship during the Ocean Roundup II, a Fellowship "cruise without booze.".

2833. Women in AA.
This set of four tapes includes Marty Mann, Margaret C., Eve M. and Marge R.

2834. Wynn L. "Freedom from Bondage". CA; Oct. 1972.
This lady from Oxnard, California, shares her recovery story, "Freedom from Bondage" in the third edition of the Big Book.

Chapter XII = Television, Films & Videos

2835. 8 Million Ways to Die [TV movie]; 1986.
Jeff Bridges is an alcohlic cop and Rosanna Arquette is a high-priced hooker in Hal Ashby's grim crime thriller. AA is mentioned.

2836. A.A. - Rap With Us. AAWS. New York: AAWS; 1992; 15 min. VHS.
Note: Also available in closed captioned for the hearing impaired.
This features four anonymous young A.A. members. Rap music and lyrics bridge these four young people's stories of alcoholic despair and A.A. recovery.

2837. AA and the Alcoholic. Motivational Media. Studio City, CA: Motivational Media; 1990; ?
This video is narrated by actor John Forsythe. It is a basic introduction to AA and alcoholism and answers some of the myths about both.

2838. Alcoholics Anonymous - An Inside View. AAWS. New York: AAWS; 1979; 28 min. VHS.
This video depicts alcoholics, recovering in A.A., going about their daily lives, attending a variety of A.A. meetings and other gatherings. Anonymity is carefully protected. It emphasizes the idea that AA is a way of life: any time two members get together there is an AA meeting. [recommended in Hasselblad, Alcohol Abuse Curriculum Guide for Nurse Practioneer Faculty, p155].

2839. Alcoholics Anonymous: GSO Today, Circles of Love & Service, [and] Markings of the Journey. Unitel Video. New York: AAWS; 1987; approx. 10-15 minutes each. VHS.
Three short films on the General Service Office of AA in New York, on Service in AA, and on the history of the Fellowship.

2840. Alcoholics Anonymous [The BIG BOOK] in American Sign Language. New York: AAWS; 1992; 9 hours & 53 minutes total. Five 1/2" VHS video cassettes.
This boxed set of 5 video cassettes presents the Big Book in American Sign Language.

2841. Bill Discusses the Twelve Traditions. AAWS. New York: AAWS; 1969; 60 min. VHS. also in Spanish 16mm film.
Note: For A.A. internal use only!
Bill W. tells how the principles safeguarding A.A. unity developed.

2842. Bill's Own Story. AAWS. New York: AAWS; 1965; 60 min. VHS. Also in Spanish 16mm film.
Note: For A.A. internal use only!
Co-Founder Bill W. tells of his drinking and recovery.

2843. Cagney & Lacey [TV crime drama series]; May 11, 1987; 60 min.
This crime drama series stars Sharon Gless as Christine Cagney and Tyne Daly as Lacey. In this part two of the season finale, Cagney hastens her steps down the same alcoholic path taken by her late father. In other episodes, Cagney and Lacey go undercover at AA meetings.

2844. Can You Stop People from Drinking?. NOVA: NOVA; Dec. 22, 1992; 60 min.
In this television special, physician David Musto studies efforts to combat alcoholism in the U.S. and the former U.S.S.R. The segments about AA in Russia include anonymity breaks.

2845. Come Back Little Sheba. Hal B. Wallis; Daniel Mann. U.S.: Paramount; 1952; 99 min. black & white.
The screenplay was written by Ketti Frings from the play by William Inge. Shirley Booth, who won an Oscar as a slatternly middle-aged housewife, is paired with Burt Lancaster, her alcoholic husband in this movie. AA action revolves around the husband.

2846. Come Fill the Cup. Henry Blanke; Gordon Douglas. U.S.: Warner; 1951; 113 min. black & white.
The motivation for drinking here closely matches AA's thinking; namely, the deep, dark 'why' you drink is really not that important in recovery. Fired, the hardbitten newsman Lew Marsh [James Cagney] replies to his boss's angry question, "Why do you swill all that talent right down the drain?" with "a lush can always find a reason if he's thirsty." Later, Lew explains the spiritual this way: "There's only one thing pulls a drunk up short - that's the sound of angel feathers - a peek into the void. We run away from life but we run away from death, too." Robin Room notes "Lew's path to recovery follows a classic AA model: drunks helping drunks," apparently the first 12th Step in movies. Written by Ivan Goff from the novel of the same title by Harlan Ware. Gig Young, playing the newspaper owner's alcoholic son, was nominated for an Academy Award for his performance.

2847. Dawn of Hope: The Founding of Alcoholics Anonymous, An Historical Perspective. Jack Gieck. Akron, OH: Cinemark, Inc.; 1987; 30 minutes VHS.
Note: Video cassette case autographed by Jack Gieck.
This film depicts the founding of A.A. in Akron, Ohio, in 1935, including the first meeting of Bill and Dr. Bob. Dr. Bob's children, Sue and Smitty, and Henrietta Seiberling's son, former U.S. Congressman John F. Seiberling, comment on the early years. AA's Twelve Steps are discussed. Produced by Jack Gieck in cooperation with Akron's Tri-County Employee Assistance Program, it was funded in part by grants from Firestone, Goodyear, Ohio Bell, GenCorp., Ohio Edison, Akron's St. Thomas Hospital and the L. Frank and Angela Wilson Trust Fund of the Akron Community Foundation.

2848. Days of Wine and Roses. Martin Manulis; Blake Edwards. Burbank, CA: Warner Bros., Inc.; 1962; 118 minutes Warner Home Video VHS.
Based on the teleplay by J. P. Miller, this movie was nominated for five Oscars including two for co-stars Jack Lemmon and Lee Remick, and the Henry Mancini-Johnny Mercer title song which won an Oscar. San Francisco public-relations hotshot Joe Clay [Lemmon] is a social drinker who never stops socializing. His pretty wife [Remick] Kirsten starts drinking to keep him company. The good times turn bad because of the bottle and Joe eventually has to leave his wife who refuses to stop drinking. Joe stays sober through A.A. meetings. Jack Klugman plays Joe's A.A. sponsor in the film. Critically, Days of Wine and Roses ranks with The Lost Weekend as the best two movies ever made about alcoholism.

2849. Francesca Baby. Burbank, CA: Walt Disney Educational Media; 1976.
This 46-minute color film shows a mother's excessive drinking as the cause of social and emotional problems for her daughters. The mother eventually goes to Alcoholics Anonymous. Based on a book of the same title, it is especially good for teenage children of alcoholics and recommends Alateen as helpful in resolving their problems. (see Hasselblad, Alcohol Abuse Curriculum Guide for Nurse, p153.).

2850. Hope: Alcoholics Anonymous. AAWS. New York: AAWS; 1990; 15 min. VHS.
A young man, on his way to his first A.A. anniversary, reviews his drinking days and his first year of sobriety. He explains what A.A. is and what it is not, A.A.'s primary purpose, sponsorship, the home group, the Steps and Traditions, and other basic principles of the A.A. program.

2851. How Long the Night. TV, Radio & Film Commission of the Methodist Church: General Board of Temperance of the Methodist Chruch; 1958; 30 min. 16 mm film.
A wife's attempts to help her alcoholic husband includes A.A. meetings.

2852. Hunger for Healing [12-part TV series]. Trinity Episcopal Church, New York City: VISN TV network; 1992; 30 min.
Author and counselor J. Keith Miller explores the Twelve Steps [of AA] and applies them to "all who feel a need for spiritual or emotional healing." The twelve-part series aired on VISN [Vision Interfaith Satellite Network] television.

2853. I Am an Alcoholic. McGraw-Hill Book Co.: McGraw-Hill Book Co.; 1957-8 ?; 19 min. 16mm film.
This short film tells how members of A.A. bring a man back to his rightful place in society and discusses the origin and development of the Fellowship.

2854. I'll Cry Tomorrow. Lawrence Weingarten; Daniel Mann. U.S.: MGM; 1955; 119 min. black & white.
Susan Hayward, Jo Van Fleet, Eddie Albert and Richard Conte star in this screenplay written by Helen Deutsch and Jay Richard Kennedy from the book of same title by Lilian Roth, the Broadway and Hollywood star who tells her true story of alcoholism and recovery. Hayward received an Academy Award nomination for her performance. "One solution to the problem of how to fit twelfth-step work into the plot was to have it be the vehicle of boy-meets-girl, as in I'll Cry Tomorrow. In the real world of AA, it is clear that such cross-gender 'thirteenth-stepping' was discouraged as potentially disruptive" [Room, JSA, July, 1989, p370].

2855. It Sure Beats Sitting in a Cell. AAWS. New York: AAWS; 1987; 17 min. VHS.
Filmed inside correctional facilities in the U.S. and Canada, this film tells the story of four young A.A.s who were in prison as a result of drinking, yet today are sober in A.A.

2856. John Larroquette [TV comedy series]: NBC; 1993-94; 30 min.
This TV comedy series' main character is a member of AA and Fellowship talk, characters, humor are prominent.

2857. Life of the Party: The Story of Beatrice; 1992; 105 minutes.
This made-for-TV movie documents the story of Beatrice who sobered up in AA and went on to found the first halfway house for alcoholic women in Los Angeles, CA. It starred Carol Burnett and Lloyd Bridges.

2858. The Lost Weekend. Charles Brackett; Billy Wilder. Universal City Studios, Inc., CA: Paramount Pictures; 1945; 102 min. 1990 MCA Home Video VHS.; ISBN: 1-55880-651-2.
This movie was the "Best Picture of 1945" and remains as gripping today as then. The screenplay by Charles Brackett and Billy Wilder was chosen as the best screenplay of the year; Ray Milland was Best Actor; and Billy Wilder, Best Director. Adapted from the best-selling novel by Charles Jackson, the story of a would-be writer's dissatisfaction with his life leads him on a self-destructive three-day binge. The movie lacks any of the spirituality AA offers as a solution to alcoholism.

2859. Marcus, Larry. "One Day At A Time" (The Alcoholics Anonymous Story). Revised television script ed. "revised in cooperation with A.A. Founder (Bill Wilson) and officials". Culver City, CA: Four Star Films, Inc.; Sept. 9, 1955; 46pp. Note: 8.5 x 11" photocopy of script.
The television script was first aired Nov. 15, 1955, at 9:30 pm EST on The Cavalcade Theater sponsored by DuPont on the national CBS (?) network. The TV GUIDE listing for it states: "James Daly stars in 'One Day At A Time.' In this true-life drama, Daly portrays a successful businessman whose career was destroyed by his addiction to alcohol. With the help of a physician friend similarly addicted, the businessman started the group that became Alcoholics

Anonymous. (Film)" The cast included: Bill (Wilson)...James Daly; Dr. Bob...James Bell; Dr. Silkworth...John Litel; Ann (Dr. Bob's wife)...Eve March; Lois (Bill's wife)...Barbara Eiler; and Harry...James Best. The listing appeared in the TV GUIDE for the week of Nov. 12-18, 1955, on pages A-52-53.

2860. Markings on the Journey. AAWS. New York: AAWS; 1981; 35 min. filmstrip [filmstrip projector & cassette player needed]. Also available in VHS.
Note: For A.A. internal use only!
This color film depicts 45 years of A.A. history, using rare material from the A.A. Archives.

2861. My Name is Bill W. First ed. New York: Learning Enrichment, Inc., New York; April, 1989; 4pp. May be reproduced for educational purposes.
This ABC-TV Community Relations Viewer's Guide for the television production of My Name is Bill W. discusses the founding of A.A., pre-viewing activities, and synopsis. It lists 6 discussion topics for after the TV program. The TV movie was aired nationally April 30, 1989, as a Hallmark Hall of Fame presentation written by William Borchert.

2862. My Name Is Bill W. [TV movie]. Hallmark Hall of Fame: ABC Sunday Night Movie; April 30, 1989; 120 min.
Directed by Daniel Petrie, the story of the founding of AA starred James Woods as Bill W.; James Garner as Dr. Bob; JoBeth Williams as Lois; Gary Sinise as Ebby; Fritz Weaver as Dr. Burnham; Ray Reinhardt as Dr. Silkworth; George Coe as Frank Shaw; Robert Harper as Dr. Partlin; and Rick Warner as Bill Dotson.

2863. Problem Drinkers. March of Time: March of Time; 1957-8 ?; 19 min. 16mm film.
An alcoholic's downfall and rehabilitation through the work of A.A., the Research Council on Problems of Alcohol and the Yale School of Alcoholic Studies is this film's subject. It attempts to have alcoholism recognized as a disease.

2864. Something To Live For. George Stevens; George Stevens. U.S.: Paramount; 1952; 89 min black & white.
"Mr. & Mrs. Anonymous" was the tentative title for this movie but was changed to "Something To Live For" on the advice of several consultants who were AA members. Ray Milland, Joan Fontaine, Teresa Wright, Richard Derr and Douglas Dick star in this screenplay written by Dwight Taylor. "A commerical artist member of Alcoholics Anonymous falls for a dipsomaniac actress but refuses to break up his marriage. Glossy romantic melodrama with some style but no depth; the casting makes it seem like a sequel to The Lost Weekend." [Halliwell, 4th Ed., p757]. The alcoholic actress is saved by the artist AAer.

2865. To Your Health. Halas & Batechelor for World Health Org.: Center for Mass Communication, Columbia Univ. Press; 1956; 10 min. 16mm film.
Professionals and Alcoholics Anonymous are the two methods of recovery this color animated cartoon depicts.

2866. Twelve Steps. . .the Video. Rogers, Gerald T., writer, producer, director. Skokie, IL: Gerald T. Rogers Productions, Inc.; 1986; 35 min. video cassette. VHS or BETA; also 3/4" and 16mm film.
Described as "the first video interpretation of the 12 principles practiced by Alcoholics Anonymous and other programs," Rogers states that "a visual protrayal, while no substitute for belonging to a support group, can be a valuable introduction" to the 12 Steps.

2867. Understanding Heart. Lewislor Enterprises; 1957; 29 min. 16mm film.
The programs of both Alcoholics Anonymous and Al-Anon are protrayed through women. One wife gains sobriety through AA. A spinoff from the Loretta Young Show, a television series.

2868. The Voice in the Mirror. Gordon Kay; Harry Keller. U.S.: Cinemascope/Universal-International Pictures; 1958; 102 min. black & white.
Note: written by Larry Marcus.
Jim, the alcoholic [Richard Egan], his longsuffering wife Ellen [Julie London], fellow alcoholic Bill [Arthur O'Connell], twelfth-stepping, relapse, and finally an 10 year anniversary sobriety dinner: all the ingredients of a typical AA story are here in this film. Robin Room says this movie "faithfully reflects the contemporaneous view of the world of AA" and is perhaps the "closest and most detailed AA worldview. The film closes with an AA-like meeting, complete with the Serenity Prayer on the wall." And "the unflinching presentation of the explicitly spiritual dimension of AA is rare." [Room, JSA, July, 1989, pp368-383].

2869. Welcome to Akron, Birthplace of Alcoholics Anonymous. Bill's Tapes. Akron, OH: Bill's Tapes, Chattanooga, TN; 1992; 60 min. VHS.
This is a historic tour of the main places in Akron, Ohio, where Alcoholics Anonymous was founded in June, 1935. Visited are Dr. Bob's grave, his home, the King School, the Seiberling home, etc.

2870. Young People and A.A.. AAWS. New York: AAWS; 1988; 28 min. VHS.
Note: Also available in U-Matic and in Spanish and in 1/2" VHS close-captioned in English for the hearing impaired.
In this film, four young A.A. members describe what it was like drinking, what happened to bring them to A.A., and what their lives are like sober today. In keeping with A.A. tradition, the identity of the A.A. members is protected.

Chapter XIII = AA Ephemera !

2871. "1st Canadian National A.A. Convention" [poster]. Halifax, Nova Scotia, Canada: Convention '88 Assn.; Aug. 18-21-1988; 17 x 11".
This poster proclaims: "Le Chemin a la Sobriete Mene a Halifax...The Road to Sobriety Leads to Halifax. 1 re. Convention Nationale/Canadienne D'A.A./Halifax N.S./1st. Canadian National/A.A. Convention/Halifax N.S./Aug.18-21, 1988." In red, white, blue and gray colors. At bottom right is the Maple Leaf, symbol of Canada, with the circle and triangle and three Legacies inside.

2872. <u>1st Canadian National A.A. Convention</u>; August 18-21, 1988; Halifax, Nova Scotia, Canada; 4 page flyer.
This registration and housing form for the First Canadian National A.A. Convention in Halifax's World Trade & Convention Centre and the Metro Centre outlines the AA meetings, workshops, etc., in English and French and signed meetings for the Deaf. Estimated attendance was 7,000.

2873. "35th A.A. Anniversary International Convention". Miami Beach, FL: AAWS; 1970.
The July 3-5, 1970, program lists all the events and meetings. There is also a two-page advance program with tips on clothing, housing, new books, entertainment, use of cameras and tape recorders at the convention, etc.

2874. "40th International A.A. Convention, Denver, Colorado, July 4-6, 1975, Program". Denver: AAWS; 1975.
This 8-page program includes all A.A. and Al-Anon and Alateen events.

2875. "45th Anniversary International AA Convention in New Orleans, LA, July 3-6, 1980, Program: The Joy of Living". New Orleans: AAWS; 1980.
This 8-page program lists all the A.A. and Al-Anon and Alateen events, souvenirs, etc.

2876. <u>Badges, Name Tags, Ribbons</u>.
Many AA gatherings require badges or name tags to be worn as proof of registration. They are also often used to identify hosts who can answer questions and provide information to the visitor. Some examples: "A.A. 58th Anniversary, Founders' Day, 1993, June 11, 12, 13, Akron, Ohio, Alcoholics Anonymous 1935-1993" is a red 9" ribbon usually attached to a Founders' Day name tag. The ribbon and name tag verify the wearer has paid the registration fee for the event. A badge with "I Visited Ignatia Hall" is a nice memento of Akron, Ohio. Collections of such badges, ribbons, and name tags make colorful archives' displays as well as document the history of a Fellowship event.

2877. "Bill W. Anniversary Dinner". New York: NY Intergroup Assn.; 1969-1993.
This 4-page program for the annual Bill W. Anniversary Dinner in New York at the Grand Ballroom of the Hilton Hotel includes the candlelight meeting and Bill W., introduction of Delegates to the First World Service Meeting, the menu, and other information. The annual Bill W. dinner has been a New York tradition for many years, this program noting Bill's 35th year of sobriety in 1969.

2878. Bookplate: 50th Anniversary Int'l AA Convention. Montreal, Canada: AAWS; July, 1985.
This 3x4" bookplate had a maple leaf with "50" inside it and the words "For the Library of .... from the 50th Anniversary International AA Convention Montreal, Quebec July 4-7, 1985." The momento has a peal-off adhesive back so you can affix it to a book.

2879. "Canada's 50th AAniversary". Toronto, Canada: A.A. Canada; July 2-4, 1993.
This form for Canada's 50th AAniversary celebration in Toronto contains information for registration, hotel rooms, airline flights, and American Express Travel Offices. The Metro Convention Centre and 5 hotels were reserved for the July 2-4 event which drew over 6,000 AA, Al-Anon and Alateen members.

2880. Catalogs: Conference-Approved Literature & Other Service Material. New York: AAWS; 1939-1994.
AA has since the early 1940-50s mailed out regularly to all AA groups' GSR's in the U.S. and Canada catalogs of its A.A. Conference-approved Literature & other material. The current catalog is 14 pages and lists books, booklets, pamphlets, posters, radio and TV announcements, other audiovisual material, handbooks for various service committees, foreign language translations [notably Spanish], literature packages, and a host of other material approved by the General Service Conference. Of course, the best seller has been the Big Book. The earliest literature order form was the 1939 postcard advertising the book Alcoholics Anonymous [see separate listing for postcard under "Works Publishing Co." in this chapter]. These catalogs provide a continuous record of AA's progress in carrying the message through printed and audiovisual materials.

2881. Come to AA's 50th Birthday Party: AAWS; 1985.
This 17 x 22" poster announces the "International Convention, Montreal [Canada] July 4-7, 1985. 50 Years with Gratitude." In blue, yellow and white, it's a fine framing piece. Posters from the international conventions and a raft of other AA gatherings make colorful displays for AA Archivists.

2882. Envelopes & letterheads. New York: AAWS; 1940-94.
Envelopes and letterheads from the early days of The Alcoholic Foundation to the present AAWS make a fascinating display for AA archivists. In the 1940s and 1950s it was "P.O. Box 459, Grand Central Annex, New York 17, N.Y." A letterhead from "The Alcoholic Foundation" in 1943 is subtitled "National Headquarters - Alcoholics Anonymous." An "A.A. Grapevine" letterhead from 1953 lists its address as "P.O. Box 85, Knickerbocker Station, New York 2, N.Y.".

2883. "First International Conference of Alcoholics Anonymous on the occasion of its Fifteenth Anniversary". Cleveland: Pioneer Groups of Akron & Cleveland; 1950.
Speakers in this 4-page program for the 1st Int'l July 28-30, 1950, included Lois W., Warden Clinton Duffy, Dr. Meyer Texon of the Knickerbocker Hospital in New York City, Louis Seltzer, Cleveland Press Editor, and, of course, Dr. Bob and Bill.

2884. Flyers.
Note: Usually one page, flyers advertise to the Fellowship coming AA events, conventions, anniversary dinners, service assemblies, and group, district, area and national gatherings of all kinds. Often, they contain valuable information on the history of the event. For example, the flyer on the 1972 Southeastern Regional Conference in Charleston, West Virginia, notes that the first SE Regional was held five years before the first International Conference of AA. And the flyer lists all the cities where the SE Regionals were held from 1945 through 1971. It also notes the SE Regional is the first regional, the "granddaddy of all AA Conferences." Flyers, then, are a treasure house of history for AA Archivists.

2885. "Founders Day Herald & Celebration Program". Akron, OH: Founders Day Committee; 1935-1993.
This one-page flyer and accompanying six-page foldout small pamphlet list all the AA events held annually for 56 years on the nearest weekend to AA's birthday, June 10, in Akron, Ohio. In recent years, the Fellowship has taken over the Akron University campus and crowds in the 1990s reached 5, 000-6,000 AAs from around the world.

2886. "International A.A. Convention, Long Beach, CA, 1960" [newspaper articles]. in: Independent-Press-Telegram. Long Beach, CA; Jan. 25 & Nov. 15, 1959; Feb. 15, March 30, May 19, June 19 & 30, July 1, 2 [6], 3 [2], & 4, all 1960.
Coverage of the Int'l A.A. Convention at Long Beach, CA, in 1960 began more than one year earlier in this newspaper. Among the coverage were articles on Bill W.'s and AA's 25th anniversary sober, 4,000 advance registrations, mystery guests, Long Beach won over San Francisco as the site in a coin toss, message from President Eisenhower, anonymity Tradition, Sister Ignatia, Col. Edward B. Towns of Towns Hospital in New York City, Al-Anon, AFL-CIO official William J. Smith, Bill W., A.M.A. official Dr. W. W. Bauer, Rt. Rev.

Msgr. John J. Dougherty of South Orange, NJ, and Rev. Samuel M. Shoemaker of Pittsburgh, PA.

2887. Letterhead: W. G. W. New York: Bill W.; 1950-70.
This was Bill Wilson's personal stationary. The top of the 8.5x11" sheet had "W. G. W. - Box 459 Grand Central Station - New York, N. Y. 10017.".

2888. Meeting Cards.
These list AA meetings in any area and usually include the name of the group, day and time of meeting, address, kind of meeting. Early meeting cards often listed phone numbers and group "secretaries [early GSRs]" names. Early ones often printed various versions of the Preamble, Steps, Serenity Prayer, and sometimes questions to help the newcomer decide if he were an alcoholic. They are valuable in establishing when groups, clubs, and intergroups/central offices began, where they moved to through the years, names of early members, etc.

2889. Photos: International AA Conventions.
As momentoes of the last four AA Int'l conventions, AAWS authorized the publication of a long 24" panoramic color photograph of the Big Spiritual Meeting. All four photos protect the anonymity of individual members.

2890. Program 20th Anniversary Convention of Alcoholics Anonymous.
Note: Programs for AA events document the who, what, when, and where of the Fellowship's history. They provide historical information not available from any other source sometimes and are valuable in writing area histories. One fine example of a program is the "20th Anniversary Convention of Alcoholics Anonymous, Kiel Auditorium, St. Louis, Missouri, July 1-2-3, 1955." This 10.5 x 4.5" two-tone blue program is a six page fold-up that lists all the convention data for the three days and brief biographies of the ten non-A.A. speakers.

2891. Sacred Heart medal. Akron, OH; 1940s or earlier.
This was the first AA medallion, Ernest Kurtz notes. This large Catholic medal of the Sacred Heart of Jesus was given by Sr. Ignatia to AAs who were leaving St. Thomas Hospital in Akron and going back out into the real world where alcohol and the possibility of slipping existed. Sr. Ignatia would give the dry AA newcomer the medal with the instruction that if he were going to drink, he had to return the medal to her first. The 2.5" x 1.5" oval medal reads on one side "Cease! The Heart of Jesus is with me!" with an illustration of the heart surrounded by thorns with fire and the crucifix at the top and drops of blood at bottom. "Thy Kingdom Come!" is at the bottom. On the reverse is an illustration of Jesus pointing to his sacred heart. The inscription at the top is "Apostleship of Prayer in League with the Sacred Heart." This religious medal, thus, was the ancestor of all the anniversary medallions, sobriety poker chips, and such that are common at AA meetings today.

2892. "Sister M. Ignatia, C.S.A.". Akron, OH: The Sister Ignatia Institute, et al; Jan. 15, 1989.
This folded wallet card celebrates the centennial of Sr. Ignatia's birth. Her photo is on the front; the Institute, St. Vincent Charity Hospital, St. Thomas Medical Center, and the Interval Brotherhood Home Alcohol Rehabilitation Center are on the back; inside are the 12 Steps and 12 Traditions of A.A. Under her name is the legend "Once in Every Hundred Years." This nonalcoholic Catholic nun was, of course, Dr. Bob's partner in founding the first alcoholic ward in any hospital in the world in Akron, Ohio, at St. Thomas Hospital.

2893. Sobriety Calendar. Wheeling, WV: The Bishop of Books; 1990-1994.
Note: [46 Eureka Ave., Wheeling, WV 26003].
Compiled annually for the past five years by Charles Bishop, Jr., this wall calendar is 11x17" open and 28 pages. Each month has a historic photo or illustration from the history of AA or alcoholism in America and one of the Twelve Steps and a favorite Fellowship prayer. Each day of the year has an historic event from AA history, a Fellowship slogan, humorous one-liner, or quote from the Big Book. The 1990 printing was 1,000 and subsequent annual printings of 5,000 to 6,000 have all sold out each year.

2894. Ticket stubs.
Ticket stubs to AA events are valuable records of the who, what, when, and where of the Fellowship history. One example: "Appreciation Dinner Given in Honor of Dr. 'Bob' Smith of Akron, Ohio, one of the founders of the A.A. Movement, Lake Shore Hotel, 12506 Edgewater Drive, [Cleveland], Sunday, October 5, 1941. 1:30 P.M. This dinner was suggested by the Parma Group. $1.35 per plate. Cuyahoga County Central Committee." That data documents the existence of the Parma Group, the Central Committee, etc., in 1941, the use of full names within the Fellowship, etc.

2895. "Works Publishing Co. [postcard]". New York: The Alcoholic Foundation; 1939.
Note: 7 x 5.5".
This rare double postcard was mailed to thousands of doctors on the East Coast and asked them to buy the book Alcoholics Anonymous for $3.50. The order form was a tear-off return postcard. The back advertised the "We The People" Columbia Network radio program for April 25th, 1939, entitled "How Many Alcoholics Return from Institutions Cured?" the story of one "alcoholic released from an insane asylum, and pronounced incurable, found over 100 men who had discovered a method of recovery proven successful over a period of five years. Fully described in the new sensational book, 'Alcoholics Anonymous,' with personal stories.".

Chapter XIV = Works in Progress

2896. Alcoholics Anonymous Study Edition. Croton Falls, NY: IWS Inc.; March 1994; ISBN: 0-9637666-1-9. LC 93-080377.
This volume with its maroon leather covers is composed of 570 pages of the original first edition's first 164 pages plus "Doctor Bob's Nightmare" with each page with an opposite lined page for notes and study. After that is 26-page index, followed by a facsimile of Clarence Snyder's copy of the multilith Big Book.

2897. The Cleveland Central Bulletin. Wheeling, WV: The Bishop of Books; 1994.
Note: pb. 200pp.
This will be an anthology of early Cleveland Central Bulletins, some of the best early writing in AA.

2898. Courage to Change: The Amazing Power of the Twelve Steps: Baker Book House; 1994; ISBN: 0-8007-5439-5.
Note: pb, 224pp.
Compiled and edited by Bill Pittman and Dick B., this promises to be another good book about Rev. Samuel Shoemaker, the Episcopal minister from Calvary Church in New York City, who helped AA in its formative years. Oxford Group ideology, the Twelve Steps, and other early contributions are discussed.

2899. Dick B. New Light on Alcoholism: The A.A. Legacy from Sam Shoemaker. Corte Madera, CA: Good Book Pub. Co.; March 1994; ISBN: 1-881212-06-8. LC 93-77559.
Note: pb.
The life of Shoemaker is explored in the light of what he taught from the Bible and the Oxford Group, the First Century Christian Fellowship, to which early Alcoholics Anonymous members belonged.

2900. Dick B. Quite Time, The Morning Watch, Daily Meditations: Good Book Pub. Co.; 1994; ISBN: 1-881212-07-6. LC 93-77569.
Note: Illus., 192pp.

2901. Fitzgerald, Robert, S.J. The Soul of Sponsorship: The Friendship of Fr. Ed Dowling and Bill W. Center City, MN: Hazelden; Nov. 1994.
Note: pb, 112pp.

2902. History Lights the Way. New York: A.A. Grapevine; June, 1994.
This tape is devoted to AA history.

2903. History of Alcoholics Anonymous 1935-1990s [working title]. New York: AAWS; 1995-6?
Note: 400pp+.
This history of AA, as yet untitled, has been worked on for years by several authors. The General Service Conference of A.A. has postponed any action on it for two years. It may be published in the near future, depending, of course, on the General Service Conference, AA's group conscience. It will, if published, be A.A. Conference-Approved Literature. Originally, it was projected to cover AA history from 1955 to the present, the era not covered in Alcoholics Anonymous Comes of Age: A Brief History of A.A., but was expanded to include more historical information on the 1935-55 era.

2904. A History of Alcoholics Anonymous in Ireland.
work in progress: contact Billy at 13 Oakleaf Place, Knockmay, Portlaoise, Co. Laois, Ireland.

2905. Merton M. Black Sheep. New Jersey: 1994-5?
The story of Hank P. who wrote the chapter "To Employers" in the first edition of the Big Book. Much material on New Jersey AA is also projected for this volume.

2906. Mitch K. How It Worked: The Story of Clarence Snyder & Early Cleveland A.A.; 1994-5?
Note: 450pp.
Foreword by Ernest Kurtz, Ph.D.

2907. Wally P. A History of AA Intergroups and Central Offices. Wheeling, WV: The Bishop of Books; fall, 1994.
Note: 200p.
This book will document the founding and growth of the first Fellowship intergroups and central offices around the U.S.

2908. What We Were Like. New York: A.A. Grapevine; June 1994.
This will be a tape of the experiences of oldtimers in AA.

RESOURCES (non-AA)

[the following have extensive archives or libraries, computer databases, catalogs, or journals of information on the history of alcoholism and AA that Fellowship members & archivists, researchers, and other professionals may find helpful.] [you may also consult the ads in the back of this book for free catalogs, etc.]

Addiction Research Foundation
33 Russell St.
Toronto, Ontario, Canada M5S - 2S1
[416] 595-6100

The Bishop of Books
46 Eureka Ave.
Wheeling, WV 26003
[304] 242-2937

Nat'l Clergy Conference on Alcoholism
1200 Varnum St., N. E.
Washington, DC 20017
[202] 832-3811

Pittman Archives at Hazelden
P.O. Box 433
Center City, MN 55012
[800] 257-7800

Rutgers Center of Alcohol Studies
P. O. Box 969 = Library
Piscataway, NJ 08854
[201] 932-2190

Stepping Stones
P. O. Box 452
Bedford Hills, NY 10507
[914] 232-4822

University Microfilms International, 300 Zeeb Road, P.O. Box 1346, Ann Arbor, MI 48106 [orders:dissertation copies or scholarly journal articles 1-800-521-3042]

INTERNATIONAL A.A. CONVENTIONS

1945		Cleveland, Ohio*
1950	1st	Cleveland, Ohio
1955	2nd	St. Louis, Missouri
1960	3rd	Long Beach, California
1965	4th	Toronto, Canada
1970	5th	Miami Beach, Florida
1975	6th	Denver, Colorado
1980	7th	New Orleans, Louisiana
1985	8th	Montreal, Canada
1990	9th	Seattle, Washington
1995	10th	San Diego, California
2000	11th	St. Paul-Minneapolis, Minnesota

* The 1945 Cleveland convention of over one thousand AA's could be considered the first unofficial "international" based on attendance.

The GENERAL SERVICE CONFERENCE of A.A. has met since 1951 every April in New York City.

RESOURCES = ALCOHOLICS ANONYMOUS

Alcoholics Anonymous Archives
General Service Office
P. O. Box 459 = Grand Central Station
New York, NY 10163
[212] 870-3400

A.A. Grapevine
Grand Central Station
P.O. Box 1980
New York, NY 10163
[212] 870-3400

Afrikaans
General Service Office
P. O. Box 23005
Joubert Park
2044 Johannesburg
Transvaal, South Africa

Dutch
Anonieme Alcoholisten Nederland
Postbus 1594
1000 BN Amsterdam, Netherlands

French
La Service des publications
francaises des AA du Quebec
230, Henri-Bourassa Est, bureau 100
Montreal (Quebec), Canada H3L-1B8

Icelandic
Landspjonustunefnd
Aasamtakanna A Islandi
Postholf 1149
121 Reykjavik, Iceland

Japanese
A.A. Japan Service Office
c/o Tachibana Bldg., 9th Floor
2-23-3 Ikebukuro, Toshima-ku
Tokyo 171, Japan

Norwegian
A.A. Servicekontor
Postboks 205, Sentrum 0103
Oslo 1, Norway

Portuguese
Centro de Distribucao de Literatura
A.A. Para O Brasil (CLAAB)
Rua Itaipu 31, CEP 04052
CX, Postal (01051) 3180
Bairro Mirandopolis,
Sao Paulo, Brasil

Danish
Anonyme Alkoholikere
Postbox 334
DK - 1503 Kobenhavn V
Denmark

Finnish
A.A. Toimisto
PL 137, SF - 00521
Helinski, Finland

Flemish
Algemeen Dienstbureau (ADB)
Grote Steenweg 149
B 2600 Antwerp, Belgium

German
Anonyme Alkoholiker
Gemeinsames Dienstburo
Postfach 46 02 27
D 8000 Munchen 46, Germany

Italian
Servizi Generali Italiani
Alcolisti Anonimi
Via di Torre Rossa 35
Scala B Int. 1B
00165 Rome, Italy

Korean
Korean National Intergroup
C. P. O. Box 1167
Seoul, Korea 100

Polish
Secretariat Sluzby Krajowej AA
ul. Maleckiego 11
60-706 Poznan, Poland

Swedish
Centralkommitten for AA I Sverige
Box 16387
S 10327 Stockholm 16, Sweden

I N D E X

The Twelve Steps of Alcoholics Anonymous

The First Legacy of Recovery

1. We admitted we were powerless over alcohol - that our lives had become unmanageable.

2. Came to believe that a Power greater than ourselves could restore us to sanity.

3. Made a decision to turn our will and our lives over to the care of God as we understood Him.

4. Made a searching and fearless moral inventory of ourselves.

5. Admitted to God, to ourselves, and to another human being the exact nature of our wrongs.

6. Were entirely ready to have God remove all these defects of character.

7. Humbly asked Him to remove our shortcomings.

8. Made a list of all persons we had harmed, and became willing to make amends to them all.

9. Made direct amends to such people wherever possible, except when to do so would injure them or others.

10. Continued to take personal inventory and when we were wrong promptly admitted it.

11. Sought through prayer and meditation to improve our conscious contact with God as we understood Him, praying only for knowledge of His will for us and the power to carry that out.

12. Having had a spiritual awakening as the result of these Steps, we tried to carry this message to alcoholics, and to practice these principles in all our affairs.

The Twelve Traditions of Alcoholics Anonymous

The Second Legacy of Unity

1. Our common welfare should come first; personal recovery depends upon AA unity.

2. For our group purpose there is but one ultimate authority - a loving God as He may express Himself in our group conscience. Our leaders are but trusted servants; they do not govern.

3. The only requirement for AA membership is a desire to stop drinking.

4. Each group should be autonomous except in matters affecting other groups or AA as a whole.

5. Each group has but one primary purpose - to carry its message to the alcoholic who still suffers.

6. An AA group ought never endorse, finance, or lend the AA name to any related facility or outside enterprise, lest problems of money, property, and prestige divert us from our primary purpose.

7. Every AA group ought to be fully self-supporting, declining outside contributions.

8. Alcoholics Anonymous should remain forever nonprofessional, but our service centers may employ special workers.

9. AA, as such, ought never be organized; but we may create service boards or committees directly responsible to those they serve.

10. Alcoholics Anonymous has no opinion on outside issues; hence the AA name ought never be drawn into public controversy.

11. Our public relations policy is based on attraction rather than promotion; we need always maintain personal anonymity at the level of press, radio, and films.

12. Anonymity is the spiritual foundation of all our Traditions, ever reminding us to place principles before personalities.

I am responsbile. When anyone, anywhere reaches out for help,
I want the hand of AA always to be there. And for that:
I am responsible.

The Twelve Concepts of Alcoholics Anonymous for World Service

The Third Legacy of Service

Concept I. The final responsibility and the ultimate authority for A.A. world services should always reside in the collective conscience of our whole Fellowship.

Concept II. When, in 1955, the A.A. groups confirmed the permanent charter for their General Service Conference, they thereby delegated to the Conference complete authority for the active maintenance of our world services and thereby made the Conference - excepting for any change in the Twelve Traditions or in Article 12 of the Conference Charter - the actual voice and the effective conscience for our whole Society.

Concept III. As a traditional means of creating and maintaining a clearly defined working relation between the groups, the Conference, the A.A. General Service Board and its several service corporations, staffs, committees and executives, and of thus insuring their effective leadership, it is here suggested that we endow each of these elements of world service with a traditional "Right of Decision."

Concept IV. Throughout our Conference structure, we ought to maintain at all responsible levels a traditional "Right of Participation," taking care that each classification or group of our world servants shall be allowed a voting representation in reasonable proportion to the responsibility that each must discharge.

Concept V. Throughout our world service structure, a traditional "Right of Appeal" ought to prevail, thus assuring us that minority opinion will be heard and that petitions for the redress of personal grievances will be carefully considered.

Concept VI. On behalf of A.A. as a whole, our General Service Conference has the principal responsibility for the maintenance of our world services, and it traditionally has the final decision respecting large matters of general policy and finance. But the Conference also recognizes that the chief initiative and the active responsibility in most of these matters should be exercised primarily by the Trustee members of the Conference when they act among themselves as the General Service Board of Alcoholics Anonymous.

Concept VII. The Conference recognizes that the Charter and the Bylaws of the General Service Board are legal instruments: that the Trustees are thereby fully empowered to manage and conduct all of the world service affairs of Alcoholics Anonymous. It is further understood that the Conference Charter itself is not a legal document: that it relies instead upon the force of tradition and the power of the A.A. purse for its final effectiveness.

Concept VIII. The Trustees of the General Service Board act in two primary capacities: (a) With respect to the larger matters of over-all policy and finance, they are the principal planners and administrators. They and their primary committees directly manage these affairs. (b) But with respect to our separately incorporated and constantly active services, the relation of the Trustees is mainly that of full stock ownership and of custodial oversight which they exercise through their ability to elect all directors of these entities.

Concept IX. Good service leaders, together with sound and appropriate methods of choosing them, are at all levels indispensable for our future functioning and safety. The primary world service leadership once exercised by the founders of A.A. must necessarily be assumed by the Trustees of the General Service Board of Alcoholics Anonymous.

Concept X. Every service responsibility should be matched by an equal service authority - the scope of such authority to be always well defined whether by tradition, by resolution, by specific job description or by appropriate charters and bylaws.

Concept XI. While the Trustees hold final responsibility for A.A.'s world service administration, they should always have the assistance of the best possible standing committees, corporate service directors, executives, staffs and consultants. Therefore the composition of these underlying committees and service boards, the personal qualifications of their members, the manner of their induction into service, the systems of their rotation, the way in which they are related to each other, the special rights and duties of our executives, staffs and consultants, together with a proper basis for the financial compensation of these special workers, will always be matters for serious care and concern.

Concept XII. General Warranties of the Conference: in all its proceedings, the General Service Conference shall observe the spirit of A.A. Tradition, taking great care that the conference never becomes the seat of perilous wealth or power; that sufficient operating funds, plus an ample reserve, be its prudent financial principle; that none of the Conference Members shall ever be placed in a position of unqualified authority over any of the others: that all important decisions be reached by discussion vote and whenever possible, by substantial unanimity; that no Conference action ever be personnally punitive or an incitement to public controversy; that though the Conference may act for the service of Alcoholics Anonymous, it shall never perform any acts of government; and that, like the Society of Alcoholics Anonymous which it serves, the Conference itself will always remain democratic in thought and action.

THE STUDY EDITION
(actual pages are larger)

EACH PAGE OF THE BASIC TEXT HAS A FACING JOURNAL PAGE

60 HOW IT WORKS

60:0 12. Having had a spiritual awakening as the result of these steps, we tried to carry this message to alcoholics, and to practice these principles in all our affairs.

60:1 Many of us exclaimed, "What an order! I can't go through with it." Do not be discouraged. No one among us has been able to maintain anything like perfect adherence to these principles. We are not saints. The point is, that we are willing to grow along spiritual lines. The principles we have set down are guides to progress. We claim spiritual progress rather

60:2 than spiritual perfection.

Our description of the alcoholic, the chapter to the agnostic, and our personal adventures before and after make clear three pertinent ideas:

(a) That we were alcoholic and could not manage our own lives.

(b) That probably no human power could have relieved our alcoholism.

60:3 (c) That God could and would if He were sought.

Being convinced, *we were at Step Three*, which is that we decided to turn our will and our life over to God as we understood Him. Just what do we mean

60:4 by that, and just what do we do?

The first requirement is that we be convinced that any life run on self-will can hardly be a success. On that basis we are almost always in collision with something or somebody, even though our motives are good. Most people try to live by self-propulsion. Each person is like an actor who wants to run the whole show; is forever trying to arrange the lights, the

[1] In the first edition, this read: "Having had a spiritual experience."

[2] In the first edition, this read: "That God could and would if sought."

60

THE ENTIRE ORIGINAL MANUSCRIPT INCLUDING THE STORIES

Page 26.

Chapter Five

HOW IT WORKS

Rarely have we seen a person fail who has thoroughly followed our directions. Those who do not recover are people who cannot or will not completely give themselves to this simple program, usually men and women who are constitutionally incapable of being honest with themselves. There are such unfortunates. They are not at fault; they seem to have been born that way. They are naturally incapable of grasping and developing a way of life which demands rigorous honesty. Their chances are less than average. There are those, too, who suffer from grave emotional and mental disorders, but many of them do recover if they have the capacity to be honest.

Our stories disclose in a general way what we used to be like, what happened, and what we are like now. If you have decided you want what we have and are willing to go to any length to get it -- then you are ready to follow directions.

At some of these you may balk. You may think you can find an easier, softer way. We doubt if you can. With all the earnestness at our command, we beg of you to be fearless and thorough from the very start. Some of us have tried to hold on to our old ideas and the result was nil until we let go absolutely.

Remember that you are dealing with alcohol -- cunning, baffling, powerful! Without help it is too much for you. But there is One who has all power -- That One is God. You must find Him now!

Half measures will avail you nothing. You stand at the turning point. Throw yourself under His protection and care with complete abandon.

Now we think you can take it! Here are the steps we took, which are suggested as your Program of Recovery:

1. Admitted we were powerless over alcohol -- that our lives had become unmanageable.

2. Came to believe that a Power greater than ourselves could restore us to sanity.

3. Made a decision to turn our will and our lives over to the care and direction of God as we understood Him.

4. Made a searching and fearless moral inventory of ourselves.

5. Admitted to God, to ourselves, and to another human being the exact nature of our wrongs.

6. Were entirely willing that God remove all these defects of character.

7. Humbly, on our knees, asked Him to remove our shortcomings -- holding nothing back.

8. Made a list of all persons we had harmed, and became willing to make complete amends to them all.

9. Made direct amends to such people wherever po[...] jure them or others.

WHO WE ARE

THE IWS INDEX

* Topic is discussed but not directly mentioned on this page.

8000 REFERENCES 200 DEFINITIONS

STATEMENT OF PURPOSE

IWS is an A.A. group dedicated to our program's Fifth Tradition. Our primary purpose is to carry the message to the still-suffering alcoholic.

We feel the best way to do this is through the distribution and study of the unadulterated message of A.A. as contained in our basic texts.

We hold The Traditions dear and want to emphasize that we are a group "inside" A.A. rather than an "outside enterprise." We are an A.A. group staying sober by helping as many alcoholics as we can.

Our group is entirely nonprofessional. Nobody is making money at IWS and we are certainly not organized. However, in order to adhere to The Sixth Tradition, our service arm, IWS Inc., is incorporated. This is to ensure that the material is kept separate from the spiritual.

Tens of thousands of copies of the first 164 pages (along with lists of local telephone numbers to call A.A.) have been donated to hospitals, shelters, detox units and other places where the price of a Big Book is a hardship.

All proceeds are used to help the still-suffering alcoholic.

The IWS Group

NATIONAL CATHOLIC COUNCIL ON ALCOHOLISM
and Related Drug Problems

210 NOEL ROAD
BROAD CHANNEL, N.Y. 11691-1091

The National Catholic Council on Alcoholism and Related Drug Problems, an affiliate of the National conference of Catholic Bishops and the National Catholic Conference, is committed to assisting its members in a greater awareness and acceptance of alcoholism, other chemical addictions and prevention issues.

A primary goal of its mission is:

TO PROMOTE appropriate treatment for all clergy, religious and lay employees of the Roman Catholic Church in the United States.

TO EDUCATE members of the Church about alcoholism and related drug problems. This will be accomplished through an annual conference, and upon request, regional and diocesan workshops, educational programs in Catholic schools and parishes, institutions of higher learning, houses of formation and seminaries.

TO COOPERATE with other organizations which have aims and purposes similar to those of the N.C.C.A.

You are cordially invited to associate with this 45 year old organization by sending a check or money order, payable to N.C.C.A., for $35 (annual individual membership) to the above address. You will receive periodic newsletters and an annual Blue Book containing the proceedings of the annual symposium.

BELIEVING

Dick B. Presents:

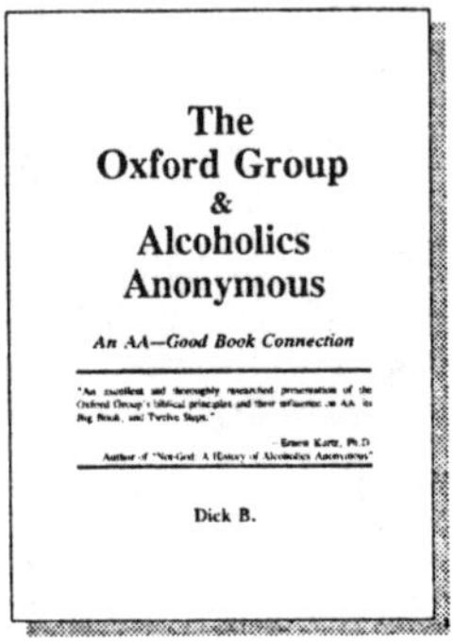

Please mail the Order Form below, with your check or money order, to: Dick B. 2747 South Kihei Road, #D-110, Kihei, HI 96753. If you have questions, phone: 1-808-874-4876. Please make check payable to: **"Dick B."**

ORDER FORM

	#		
Please send:	____	Dr. Bob's Library @ $10.00 ea.	$________
	____	The Akron Genesis of Alcoholics Anonymous @ $16.00 ea.	$________
	____	The Oxford Group & Alcoholics Anonymous @ $14.95 ea.	$________
	____	New Light on alcoholism (Sam Shoemaker) @ $18.00 ea.	$________
	____	Books Early AAs Read For Spiritual Growth @ $8.00 ea.	$________
	____	Anne Smith's Spiritual Work Book @ $13.50 ea.	$________

Shipping and Handling
Add 9% of retail price (minimum $2.90)

Shipping and Handling $________

Sales Tax (Cal.) $________

Total Enclosed $________

Name: ____

Address: ____

City ____________________ State: ________ Zip: ______ Telephone: ______________

The Rutgers Summer Schools in Alcohol and Drug Studies

Advanced School of Alcohol and Drug Studies
(First week in June)

A one-week program for professionals working in the alcohol and drug fields. Advanced-level courses, state-of-the-art updates and reviews of current research will enhance knowledge and skills in selected areas of interests. Rutgers University grants 4.0 Continuing Education Units for the Advanced School, equivalent to **40** contact hours toward certification/recertification in most states.

Summer School of Alcohol and Drug Studies
(Last two weeks in June)

The Summer School of Alcohol and Drug Studies, an internationally renowned school, is known for its tradition of excellence in teaching and a dynamic student body. The school is an intensive, two-week program of specialized courses relating to alcohol and other drug issues taught by leaders in the alcohol and drug field. Rutgers University grants 8.0 Continuing Education Units equivalent to **80** contact hours toward certification/recertification in most states.

New Jersey Summer School of Alcohol and Drug Studies
(Third week in July)

The one-week New Jersey Summer School offers basic knowledge and training courses, as well as advanced courses, for both lay and professional persons whose work bring them into contact with problems related to alcohol and other drugs. Lectures and special interest seminars are also part of the program. The school is approved for 4.0 Continuing Education Units or **40** contact hours toward certification/ recertification in most states.

These summer programs are held on the College Avenue Campus of Rutgers University in New Brunswick, New Jersey, with convenient access via car, bus and train to New York City and Philadelphia.

For information and catalogs contact:
Education and Training Division, Center of Alcohol Studies,
Rutgers University, New Brunswick, NJ 08903.
Telephone: (908) 932-04317.

The Pittman Archives at Hazelden

A research + publishing center on the last 200 years of Alcoholism in America.

Hazelden Staff Library
P.O. Box 11
Center City, MN 55012